D0832399

The Black Community

The
Black
Community

DIVERSITY AND UNITY
THIRD EDITION

JAMES E. BLACKWELL

Professor Emeritus
University of Massachusetts at Boston

HarperCollins*Publishers*

Sponsoring Editor: Alan McClare
Project Editor: Ellen MacElree
Design Supervisor: Jaye Zimet
Cover Design: Circa 86, Inc.
Production: Linda Murray
Compositor: ComCom, A Division of Haddon Craftsmen, Inc.
Printer and Binder: R. R. Donnelley & Sons Company
Cover Printer: New England Book Components, Inc.

UWEC McIntyre Library

APR 1 2 2005

DISCARDED

The Black Community: Diversity and Unity, Third Edition

Copyright © 1991 by HarperCollins Publishers Inc.

All rights reserved. Printed in the United States of America. No part of this book may be
used or reproduced in any manner whatsoever without written permission, except in the
case of brief quotations embodied in critical articles and reviews. For information
address HarperCollins Publishers Inc., 10 East 53rd Street, New York, NY 10022.

Library of Congress Cataloging-in-Publication Data

Blackwell, James Edward, 1925–
   The Black community : diversity and unity / James E. Blackwell.—
3rd ed.
      p.   cm.
   Includes bibliographical references and index.
   ISBN 0-06-040737-9
   1. Afro-Americans—Social conditions.   2. Afro-Americans—Economic
conditions.   3. United States—Race relations.   I. Title.
E184.86.B53   1991
305.896'073—dc20   90-19594
                                                          CIP

91 92 93 94 9 8 7 6 5 4 3 2 1

E
185
.86
.B55
1991

0013732397

To Myrt

Contents

List of Tables and Figures

TABLE

Preface

This book examines the institutional structure and status of black Americans as a subordinate or minority group within American society. Its major theme is that the black community in the United States was originally formed in response to white oppression, racism, and repression. State-sanctioned racial oppression and separation helped create a highly diversified but interrelated people who united into relatively cohesive structures for their own survival and to recapture some elements of a distant social past. As a result, blacks created, evolved, and strengthened an institutional fabric and community under untoward conditions.

Even though blacks continue to coalesce in response to manifestations of racism against them, diversity or hetereogeneity is a major feature of black American life today. Diversity characterizes every aspect of daily living among black Americans—family structure, educational attainment, residential patterns, social class structure, political ideologies and behavior, life chances, access to decent health care, and equality before the law. However, there is also a sense of community and shared fate developed throughout the history of black experiences in the United States which is maintained because of the continuing subordinate status of blacks in a country that has yet to rid itself of racial prejudice and discrimination.

The third edition of this book describes and analyzes myriad societal and structural changes within the past five years that have contributed to the current status of the black community and to patterns of race relations in American society today. As demonstrated in two previous editions, "to be black in America" contrasts profound individual achievements and group gains with the economic, educational, and political deprivation of a growing underclass. Both situations are social products of an enormously complex society that continues to base life chances on such factors as race, color, and class.

Significant events within American society, as well as within the black community itself, are forcing an unprecedented examination of the institutional fabric of the black community by blacks themselves. As stressed in this third edition, racism and discrimination are persistent realities in contemporary American life. The so-called "resurgence of racism," manifested in the escalating number of hate crimes attributed to newly formed white supremacy groups such as Skinheads and White Aryan Resistance (WAR) and to racially motivated college campus groups, is a stark reminder of a problem that affects the totality of American society.

Issues that black leaders once either avoided or discussed furtively in closed circles are more publicly recognized as conditions in urgent need of amelioration. Examples treated in this third edition include the rapid spread of Acquired Immune Deficiency Syndrome (AIDS) in certain sectors of the black community; the interrelationships between economic and social conditions and drugs, gang warfare, and the devastating death toll among young black males; teenage pregnancy and the social responsibilities of the black unwed father. Comparisons among blacks, whites, and Hispanics are made not only with respect to the above issues but on a number of structural factors that affect life chances.

New chapters are devoted to (1) The Church and Religion in the Black Community, (2) The Health of Black Americans, and (3) Blacks and the Criminal Justice System. Remaining chapters have been thoroughly updated to reflect societal changes, especially those impacting on the black community since 1984. Representative of these changes are the emergence of Rev. Jesse Jackson as a major political force; the social policy implications of recent U. S. Supreme Court decisions on efforts of blacks, other minorities, and women to achieve equality of opportunity; the role of the government in housing, specifically, the scandals involving the Department of Housing and Urban Development (HUD), which helped to create a major housing crisis that affects large segments of the black community, other minorities, as well as poor white Americans; and, finally, the crisis of savings and loans institutions, and the impact of their failure on a growing economic recession on black capitalism. Power theory has been added as still another useful paradigm by which the historical and current position of the black community may be examined. The salience of Afrocentricity in the black community is given special treatment.

This edition draws upon a plethora of empirical investigations by social and behavioral scientists, public health officials, and social critics and commentators to update the data base for augmenting our understanding of the complexities of the black community.

In the preparation of the third edition, I am indebted to an array of people who have assisted me in a number of ways: Wornie Reed, Doris Y. Wilkinson, and Robert Hill offered continuing insights into my work. I express sincere appreciation to Anne Foxx and research assistants, past and present, who performed invaluable services: James Venable, Zaki A. Sakin, William Straqualursi and Karen Dapremont Foster. Gratitude is also expressed to staff at HarperCollins for the special attention given to this book.

I would also like to thank the following reviewers for their helpful criticism:

Sheryl Brisset Chapman	University of Maryland
Gerald Foster	Hampton University
Seymour Leventman	Boston College
Clyde C. Perry	Marshall University
James F. Scott	Howard University
Debra B. Stallworth	Hampton University
Maurice C. Taylor	Hampton University
Clovis L. White	Oberlin College

Above all, I am profoundly grateful to Myrt, my wife, whose sensible insights, humanness, unwavering commitment to social justice, and constructive criticisms sustained me throughout this project.

James E. Blackwell

The Black Community

Chapter
1

Introduction: To Be Black in America

*T*o understand fully the meaning of being a black American we must assess the impact of representative institutional structures on members of the black community. This assessment describes the formidable role of prejudice in patterning systems of denials to black people as manifested in institutionalized racism—both de jure and de facto. Historical evidence shows that there has been a significant qualitative change in the categorical treatment of blacks when compared to treatment patterns a few years ago. This does not mean, however, that blacks are no longer subjected to categorical treatment as a low-status group, which would be a gross misrepresentation. It would be equally misleading to deny the progress, albeit limited, that blacks have made toward achieving equality and full participation as citizens. The apparent disjunction between these two perspectives lies in the ever-widening gap between white gains and the inaccessibility of societally shared values to the black population.

Four brief examples, elaborated in subsequent chapters, will help illuminate this point. First, public school segregation, mandated in its de jure form by the 1896 *Plessy* v. *Ferguson* decision, was overturned in the case of *Brown* v. *Board of Education of Topeka, Kansas,* in 1954. In its de facto form housing patterns seemed to have been the major culprit in perpetuating a dual educational system outside the South. But the promise of equal education envisioned in 1954 is unfulfilled. *While many school districts are desegregated, numerous schools within these districts are more segregated now than they were in 1954.*

Second, in the economic sphere a number of executive orders and equal-opportunity mechanisms were issued in the United States during and after World War II; they were designed to eradicate income dispari-

1

ties between the two major racial groups. Although some income-equalizing devices have led to significant income gains for blacks, they have not successfully closed the gaps in income distribution between black and white Americans. In fact, blacks continue to lose ground in efforts to attain equality of income opportunity, which, if earned, could be transformed into other economic, health, and educational benefits.[1] Blacks, moreover, are invariably the most seriously affected by economic recessions.

Third, the rise of blacks as a major political force poses other dilemmas. This emergence occurred through the enactment of enabling legislation, such as the voting rights bills of the 1960s, and a reduction of violence against those blacks who sought participation in the political process. The emergence of blacks as mayors of 19 of America's largest cities heightened participation by blacks in the political process. Given the existence of a national/federal administration for almost all of the 1980s that was perceived as hostile to the aspirations of black Americans and the steady shift of financial resources away from cities, it became increasingly difficult for black leaders to devise strategies that were appropriate responses to the aspirations of the black populace and met the needs of others within those communities as well. Further, despite a massive increase in voter registration among blacks during the 1970s and 1980s, only once in that period did the votes of black Americans result in the election of a presidential candidate to whom they had given 90 percent or more of their votes. Even in 1990, blacks represent only a fraction of the membership in the U. S. House of Representatives and have no members of their race in the U. S. Senate.

Housing provides a fourth illustration of the hiatus between white gains and the inaccessibility of shared values for black Americans. Since 1917 various Supreme Court decisions have attempted to curb housing discrimination. In some instances these decisions, along with limited enforcement by state, local, and federal governments, have led to neighborhood desegregation. But in all parts of the nation, neighborhoods are becoming increasingly segregated and it is often extremely difficult, if not impossible, for blacks to obtain mortgages for houses they wish to purchase in a predominantly white area. "White flight" from the city has occurred so rapidly that the inner cities are almost all black. Only 6.1 percent of the nation's black population live in the suburbs, while those residing in the largest cities have a black suburban population that ranges from 4.7 (Dallas) to 21 percent (Memphis) of the total population.[2] The phenomenon of territorial segregation has enormous implications for institutional segregation and discrimination (for instance, all-black schools in the cities and all-white schools in the suburbs).

The patterns of denial found in institutional segregation and discrimination also imply patterns of denial in day-to-day living. Consequently, to be black in America now is an extension of what it meant to be black a century or so ago. It means a struggle for equality of opportunity, appropriate rewards, and access to the shared values of the nation whether in housing, jobs, income, voting rights, political offices, good medical care and health services, schools, and protection from crime. It also means a struggle against the painful reality that rising expectations are relatively unfulfilled and that the future of a disproportionate number of black children is threatened by the ravages of poverty and deprivation. To be black in the 1990s is qualitatively different from being black in the 1890s. Theoretically, laws are ideally color blind; but, actually, their implementation is not. Blacks today confront different historical experiences and sociopolitical forces than their forbears of a century ago. Unlike them, blacks today have the benefits of voluminous scientific research about personality, the nature of self, and the roles individuals play in complex social systems. They know that other black people have won their freedom from white domination and established independent nation-states that suggest other alternatives to the traditional goals of assimilation within the American society. To be black today is to exist in a society of immense intragroup contradictions with respect to access to highly prized values and scarce rewards.

To be black in America today is to have come to terms with notions of black identity and yet still be somewhat divided as to what precise values and dimensions of culture are peculiarly and distinctively black. It means increasing recognition among black Americans themselves of factors that differentiate various members of the black community from each other as well as from the dominant group.

To be black is to acknowledge the principle that unity without uniformity is acceptable within the community of black people. Yet, it is also confronting the often bitter reality that the majority of white Americans feel that blacks are given preferential treatment in terms of access to jobs, or that blacks are "getting too much too soon" and given an unfair and undeserving advantage in the labor force. It means dealing with such attitudes despite the contrary evidence.

To be black means demanding covenants from white firms doing business in the black community by which such firms agree to return some of the resources they extract from blacks to blacks in terms of jobs and financial support for black institutions. It may also mean believing that racism is no longer the dominant contributing factor to untoward conditions of black Americans. Just as it may mean greater movement of some of the black well-to-do toward helping less fortunate blacks, it may also mean accelerated distancing between some of those who perceive of themselves as "having made it" in a white world and those blacks who are even more deeply mired in abject poverty than they were before the social upheavals of the 1950s, 1960s, and early 1970s.

To be black in the United States in the 1990s is a realization by blacks, whites, and members of other minority groups that the black community is indeed a complex heterogeneous entity whose strength and vitality emanate from its diversity. To be black in the 1990s means all these things and much more. It means being men and women of integrity, personal accomplishments, commitments to the goals of a democratic and free society, and persons who continue to make significant contributions to the totality of American culture.

Being black in the 1990s means being:

1. Thurgood Marshall, an Associate Justice of the U. S. Supreme Court.
2. Dr. Louis Sullivan, a member of the President's cabinet.
3. Judges in all types of courts in almost all sections of the nation.
4. President of the Ford Foundation, mayors of 19 of America's largest cities, and an astronaut in America's space shuttle program.
5. Service, past and present, as President of the Planned Parenthood Association; president of the Children's Defense Fund; president of the American Express Consumer Card Group, USA; and CEO of TIAA/CREF.
6. Benjamin Carson, M. D., a gifted 36-year-old neurosurgeon, who has performed delicate brain operations, including an operation on a hydrocephalic baby while in its mother's womb, and was a member of a 1987 team of physicians at the John Hopkins University Medical School who successfully separated Siamese twins joined at the skull.
7. Barbara Harris, the first woman ordained as a Bishop in the Episcopal Church and James A. Forbes, Jr., the first black to be named Senior Pastor of the world-famed Riverside Church in New York City.
8. Don Jackson, a police officer in Long Beach, California, who waged a major struggle against racism in the police force.
9. Educators past and present such as Mary McCleod Bethune, Benjamin E. Mays, Kenneth Clark, and David Satcher.
10. Attorney Ronald Brown, who, in 1988 was elected Chairman of the Democratic National Committee and became the first black to hold such a post.
11. Distinguished musicians, actors, actresses, choreographers and artists such as: Paul Robeson, Marian Anderson, Leontyne Price, Alvin Ailey, the Dance Theatre of Harlem, The Negro Ensemble Company, James Earl Jones, Ruby Dee, Oscar Davis, Sidney Poitier, Denzel Washington, Cicely Tyson, Claudia McNeill, Quincy Jones, Winton Marsailes, Dionne Warwick, and Spike Lee, filmmaker.
12. Entertainer/philanthropists such as Bill Cosby, star of one of the most successful programs in the 50-year history of television; Whitney Houston and Michael Jackson, two of the most successful performers and recording artists in the music video field, Oprah Winfrey and Lionel Ritchie who have also contributed millions of dollars to historically black colleges and universities.
13. Successful business people such as Reginald E. Lewis, Chairman

and Chief Executive Officer (CEO) of TLC Beatrice International Holdings Inc. whose sales exceed the $100 billion mark, Barry Gordy, founder of MoTown Enterprises, Earl Graves, founder and publisher of *Black Enterprise Magazine,* and John H. Johnson, founder, publisher, and CEO of the Johnson Publishing Company (publishers of *Ebony* and *Jet* magazines).

14. William "Bill" White who, in being named in 1989 President of the National Baseball League, became the first black to head a major league professional organization.

15. Olympic medalists such as: Jesse Owens, Ralph Metcalf Harrison Dillard, Rafer Johnson, Wilma Rudolph, Carl Lewis, Ralph Boston, Florence Griffith Joyner, Jackie Joyner Kersee, and many others.

16. Debbie Thomas, the first black singles champion in figure skating in the United States, and also winner of the World's Figure Skating Championship as well as winner of the Bronze medal in the 1988 Olympics.

17. Stars in professional tennis: Althea Gibson, Arthur Ashe, and Zena Garrison.

18. Stars in professional basketball: Bill Russell, Wilt Chamberlain, Oscar Robertson, Elgin Baylor, Lenny Wilkins, K. C. Jones, "Magic" Johnson, Julius Erving, Michael "Air" Jordan, Kareem Abdul Jabbar, and Dominic Wilkins.

19. Stars in professional baseball: Henry "Hank" Aaron, the world's greatest home run producer; Willie Mays, Frank Robinson, Reggie Jackson, Bob Gibson, Vida Blue, Ernie Banks, Dwight Gooden, Tomy Gwynne, Dave Stewart, Darryl Strawberry, and Eric Davis.

20. Stars in professional football and other sports: Doug Williams, Warren Moon, Randall Cunningham (three successful quarter-backs in the National Football League); Jerry Rice, Hershel Walker; the immortal Joe Louis; "Sugar Ray Robinson, called by many, "pound-for-pound, the best boxer of all times," and Michael Tyson in boxing.

21. Oprah Winfrey, owner of the highest rated syndicated television talk show in history.

22. Rev. Martin Luther King, Jr., civil rights leader and Nobel Peace Prize winner and Malcolm X, champion of racial justice, who was also assassinated during the turbulent sixties.

23. The Rev. Jesse Jackson, president of the Rainbow Coalition, and candidate for President of the United States in 1984 and 1988, and Rep. William Gray, Majority Whip of the U.S. House of Representatives.

24. Miss America and Miss. U.S.A.: a recognition of beauty and talent.

Hence, to be black means for many an uncontestable commitment to free enterprise and the Protestant work ethic not indistinguishable from those who share such beliefs among the white ruling class. For others, perhaps a greater emphasis is devoted to social justice and group survival. How did these conditions come about? What factors account for the emergence of a black community as distinguished from any other American community? What theoretical models are useful for sociological interpretations of this community? What are the characteristics of the people who comprise this segment of the American population? The answers to these and other questions appear in subsequent sections in this chapter. We turn now to the theoretical issues.

A SEARCH FOR A RELEVANT THEORY

The absence of theoretical models developed solely by black scholars for analysis of what is labeled as the authentic black experience in America is a vexing problem for ideologists of "blackness." The latter question the validity of most existing theoretical constructs because the white middle-class social scientists who designed them unavoidably based them on the white middle-class norm. According to this view, the norms of white America should not be equated with the norms of black America. There are wide divergencies and startling contrasts in the normative structures of white middle-class America and those of the black community; in fact, the majority of black people cannot be labeled middle class. This position, however, may be more political than scientific.

On a political level this claim achieves its greatest relevance, since as outsiders blacks are able to provide a perspective on the same phenomena different from interpretations made by white outsiders.[3]* It is this possibility of rectifying incorrect interpretations of the past that gives this view its greatest acceptability. On a more scientific level, however, such views encounter serious problems.[4] The utility of a theory, for example, does not lie totally and exclusively in such considerations as those posited by ideologists of blackness. Even if theories were dichotomized into black theories and white theories, similarities of functions would be inevitable. The search for a relevant theory would continue. The functions of sociological theory would not be dissimilar, black or white. Sociological theory explicates, defines, and provides generalizations about observable social phenomena as they exist—it does not prescribe what social behavior ought to be. The most advanced theories are based upon objective knowledge rather than upon social philosophy. They are, in effect, verified generalizations gained from repeated observations of social phenomena. Without verification generalizations might merely be speculative thought.

---

*In the insider-outsider controversy, advocates of the insider doctrine maintain that members of a given racial or ethnic group, who are usually "outsiders" to the dominant group, are more uniquely qualified to provide meaning to their experiences than are individuals who are not members of that group. On the other hand, outsiders claim that, by not being members of such groups, they are able to bring intellectual objectivity to the analysis of the experiences of less favored and often oppressed groups.

Sociological questions are raised both in terms of their theoretical relevance and as guidelines for ascertaining solutions to specific problems. In the latter instance the concern is an expression of a social value while in the former it focuses on the explanation of the regularities or patterns of social behavior as well as on the discontinuities or deviations from prescribed social norms. Some problems defy analysis by a single-theory formulation because it may be too narrow in scope to account for the complexities of the problem being studied. No single theoretical model can adequately or appropriately explain the structural and organizational entities of this complex and diverse phenomenon. No single theory can fully explain the authentic black experience in America. Again the point should be stressed that there is no single authentic black experience in America except that which developed as a consequence of ubiquitous white racism, color consciousness, and the institutional manifestations of prejudice, segregation, and persistent race-based discrimination. Because of variations in manifestations of racism and color consciousness, multiple black experiences occurred, each one as authentic as the other. The common denominator for all of them, however, is the coalescence of racism and color. Such experiences are deeply rooted in slavery since it was during that period that the structure of white dominance was established and solidified in American society. An examination of black experiences during slavery facilitates our understanding of why it is necessary to draw upon multiple paradigms in the development of a black sociological perspective. Used together, the paradigms that follow the discussion of slavery permit a juxtaposition of black and white interpretations of the same behavioral patterns when appropriate.

Slavery

As Jessie Bernard contends, slavery provided a model of integration predicated upon separation.[5] Blacks were in America physically but were only tacitly a part of the country. The policies of separation extended to all institutional forms, and because of them blacks were relegated to a position of inferiority within the social structure. The result of this situation was the institutionalization of white dominance and black subordination. The institutionalization was achieved through legislation and aided substantially by the inhumane treatment of black people.

The first step in the process was to provide a rationale for treating black people differently, and it came with the statutory recognition of slavery by Virginia in 1661. Virginia's bold step established a precedent for subsequent legislation enacted in most other colonies. Legalizing slavery was followed by interpretations of slaves not as human beings but as prized property. This definition justified behavior among slaveowners and their surrogates that ranged from maltreatment (such as extreme brutality, physical assaults, sexual exploitation, imposed roles as studs, and slave transfers that severed family units), on the one hand, to manifestations of concern for the welfare and protection of slaves, humane treatment of subordinated individuals, and generalized love on the other. The efficacy of these options varied immensely from colony to colony and from plantation to plantation. Just as alternatives relative to the disposition and treatment of slaves varied, so did conceptualizations of slaves throughout the nation.

Despite divergent views of slaves and slavery, a common denominator remained—the perception of slaves as property. Chattels were used quite effectively to bolster the economic structure of the period. Similarly, they were also the foundation for the development of a society based upon white domination over a relatively defenseless black populace. Having rationalized the interrelationship between the economic necessity of slavery and the promotion of white superiority, the white power structure had to devise a method of maintaining that relationship. Black codes were invented for that purpose—the maintenance of white superordination and the protection of private property.

The Black Codes

Containment, conformity, and subjugation reached their zenith perhaps in the articulation of the inhumane *code noir,* or the black codes, which spread with alarming speed throughout the colonies, especially those of the South. These codes underscore the magnitude of control that white colonists had over even the most mundane aspects of the lives of enslaved black people. Codes limited their movement on and off plantations and required written authorization from a master for off-plantation travel. The penalty for rape and murder was death by hanging and masters were then given financial compensation by the colony (as in Virginia, Maryland, and New Jersey) for this economic loss. Mutilation was the penalty for crimes of robbery and burglary as well as for generally petty offenses. Often the severing of an ear or the nailing of a slave's ear to a pillory post was accompanied by branding, floggings, and lacerations. Throughout the colonies, North and South, the major capital offenses were murder, rape (of white women), arson, escape from a plantation, robbery, and burglary.[6] Other laws forbade marriage without the master's permission[7] and denied blacks the privilege of engaging in any form of trade at all or to be in possession of any type of weapon without a permit.[8]

Some codes, as in Georgia, forbade teaching slaves reading and writing. Obviously, this law was often violated. Others forbade slaves the right to own and acquire property. In general, too, a child took the status of his mother so as to guarantee enslavement of children fathered by white men with black slave women. Planters rationalized these laws on the grounds that black people were barbaric, uncivilized, and in need of humanizing influences that only contact with Christian colonists could provide. Thus it was to the slave's benefit to be enslaved, brutalized, and dehumanized in the process. Kenneth Stampp argues that the slave codes were designed to socialize the slave into accepting a rigid discipline invoked by the white slave master, to render the slave completely dependent upon the owner, to force slaves into unequivocal submission, and to induce them to adopt the master's standard of acceptable behavior.[9]

Codes were initially significant first steps. However, the undeniable consequence of the codes was the establishment of a pattern of superordination and enforced subordination buttressed by a prevailing mentality that permitted its occurrence. By reassuring white superordination through legal sanctions, the codes were instrumental in creating a sociopsychological state among most white Americans that is indelible and that has had far-reaching implications—that is, the belief in the inherent inferiority of the black race and the natural superiority of white people. In time, many blacks internalized this view. It remains among a significant number of whites today both as a deeply entrenched sense of group position and as an acceptance of notions of biological superiority—it is one explanation for the failure of many desegregation programs and other programs originated to eradicate segregation along with discrimination. This is maximum racism in its most expressive form.[10]

House Slaves and Field Slaves: Social Stratification

It is the contention of many historians that slavery rescued a dying economy in many parts of the American colonies.[11] Assuming that there is merit in this claim, we can further observe that the economic structure of the plantation, which is treated extensively by Ulrich Phillips and Kenneth Stampp,[12] evolved a complex division of labor among blacks that has profound implications for their lives today.

During slavery (1661–1865) the most important status distinctions stemmed from the occupational stratification of blacks as either house slaves (for instance, serving as maids, butlers, cooks, nursemaids, coachmen, laundry workers, and companions) or as field slaves (performing nonhousehold roles on the plantation such as that of a field hand). The distinction between house slaves and field slaves was paramount. The former were accorded a higher status than the latter. Not unexpectedly, they attempted to safeguard their high-status positions as much as possible. Thus some informed about other slaves; some attempted to delimit their contacts with field hands unless such contacts maximized their advantages with the masters. Urban blacks, including slaves, worked as skilled artisans, as bricklayers, carpenters, machine operators, mechanics, cotton-press operators, and cabinetmakers. The allocation of slave roles depended upon variables such as the size of the plantation, sex, the type of crops produced, and the work season.

House slaves had a much greater exposure to the dominant culture, greater opportunities to learn its customs, values, and life styles and to share, even though in a subordinate position, in its culture. Field hands, however, were more likely to retain their African heritage. We should keep in mind that the plantation structure crystallized the division between master and slave and bifurcated the slave social system. In each system institutions arose to meet certain socially defined needs. The differences among the institutions within these basic stratification subsystems were a function of the intensity of cultural homogenization or isolation between slaves and masters. The differences were greater among field slaves. As ethnolinguistic units among slaves were destroyed through the trade and transfers, the alternative available to slaves was to learn the culture of the master. This became both functional and necessary for survival. Where ethnolinguistic units remained relatively intact, institutional differences between the superordinates and subordinates were maximum. In both cases there occurred unique adaptations to the American experience that formed the framework for the development of parallel institutions and a form of pluralism. If it is a fundamental and incontestable truth that field hands, the true pariahs of the system, were more likely to retain their original culture, one must look to them for survivals of the African past. Similarly, is it also likely that some of these same cultural survivals in contemporary times are more probably located among the field hands of the rural South and the socially isolated of the urban ghetto?

It is this distinction between house slaves and field slaves that is so critical in the development of parallel institutions, in the assimilation of some slaves into the culture of the whites (acculturation), and in the argument for African cultural-survivals among North American slaves.

African Survivals

The debates between E. Franklin Frazier and Melville Herskovits of more than a quarter of a century ago framed the issues of African survivals. The debates involved much more than a discussion of the prevalence of African survivals, and indeed concerned the emergence from them of a distinctive black culture in America. Their ideas seem to have an uninterrupted continuance in the arguments advanced today by scholars like Andrew Billingsley[13] and Robert Blauner,[14] on the one hand, and Nathan Glazer and Daniel P. Moynihan[15] and Irving Kristol,[16] on the other. Like Herskovits, Billingsley and Blauner take the position that in spite of the harshness of slavery and its deliberate efforts to dispossess blacks of their cultural past, a black culture has survived in America.

Much of what has survived originated in an African past. Survivals include family patterns and attitudes, songs, dance, religious practices, superstitions, ways of walking, verbal expressions, orientations toward recreation and pleasure, epicurean traditions, sex-related role expectations, music, given names for children, and traditional foods. Thus Blauner and others[17] advance the notion that an authentic black culture survived slavery and is to be found today largely in the urban ghettos of black America. That culture has its roots in the parallel institutions that evolved and crystallized social relationships among the members of the black community.

Frazier claims that Herskovits and his followers overstate the case for African survivals and a black culture.[18] He maintains that the black American's African past was gradually "sloughed off" as a consequence of his experiences in America. Glazer and Moynihan and, to some degree, Kristol extend this theoretical position in their claim that blacks are peculiarly and distinctly American, knowing no culture other than the American culture. The disagreement between Frazier and Herskovits is not so much over kind as degree. The issue is not whether there are any African survivals at all in the United States, but rather the degree to which these survivals persist and whether they persist in sufficient strength to influence current or contemporary patterns of black behavior. We will return to this argument at various points in subsequent chapters.*

It should now be easier to understand how the convergence of prejudice and mandates for segregation within the social structure fostered the development of parallel structures and cultural cohesion. As blacks were excluded and prevented from participation in institutions of the larger society, they developed their own institutional forms. This process was gradually abetted by the promulgation of numerous laws, beginning with black codes and continuing through the implementation of Jim Crow legislation at the turn of the twentieth century. These legal constraints, coupled with intimidation and violence, either threatened or actually visited upon black people by white Americans, created a boundary system that separated the races and gave rise to parallel structures. The more extreme the barriers were between the races, the greater the tendency for blacks to establish their own institutional forms, and to create an identifiable black community in the United States.

BLACKS AS A MINORITY GROUP

The single most important consequence of the involuntary immigration of Africans to the United States was the creation of a pattern of dominance and subordination based upon race. Blacks became a minority or a subordinate group to a dominant and more powerful white population. Minority status may be based upon such factors as race, ethnicity, tribal identification and membership, religion, and language. This status permits the dominant group to subject subordinated people to unequal treatment and to use their own prejudices and beliefs in their inherent superiority over others as a rationalization for segregation, discrimination, violence, and oppression. Inasmuch as minorities are generally distinguishable from dominant groups by virtue of physical and cultural characteristics or "marks," as Wirth called them,[19] their position in the social structure is

---

*This debate continues in the 1990s particularly in discussions of Afrocentricity (see Chapter 13).

ascribed rather than achieved. That identification and categorization as a subordinated or minority group will result in severe restrictions of the life chances of members of these groups and all but exclude them from society's opportunity structure. In such instances, minority group members will not have the same opportunity as dominant group members for education, occupational attainment and income, access to health services, participation in the political structure, free movement from one area to another, the same quality of housing, nor to engage in the same types of recreational pursuits. Dominant groups will often establish rigorous barriers against exogamy or marriage outside one's racial, ethnic, or religious group as an attempt to control sexual relations between dominant and subordinate group members as well as a means of creating social boundaries between such groups.

Even when individual members of minority groups achieve high status within the parameters or normative guidelines established by the dominant group, many will still experience some form of dominant group prejudice and discrimination. No matter how comfortable such individuals may become in their associations with members of the dominant group and with their high status attainment, consciously or subconsciously, they are aware of birth ascription and of the probability that the status resulting from that ascription may be employed against them by persons who resent their success and possible superordinate rank over such persons. In any event, the options of responses to their subordinated status open to minorities range from acceptance, accommodation, assimilation, pluralism, and separation to aggression and rejection.

PARALLEL STRUCTURES AND PLURALISM

Minorities in America, it is typically assumed, will eventually assimilate into mainstream American society. According to this view, assimilation is tantamount to incorporation into the American system; in essence, the incorporated group loses its identity and becomes similar to the group that engulfed it. This theoretical framework, endorsed by most liberal American sociologists, has persistently guided studies in race and ethnic relations. It is grounded in the liberal conviction that there are unlimited opportunities for all who are willing to do so to enter into the mainstream of American society regardless of their cultural origins. The major flaw in this theory of incorporation, however, is that it was addressed largely to northern and western European immigrants rather than to *all* minorities. Even in their case, this belief did not anticipate the unfulfilled aspirations of European ethnics evidenced in the resurgence of a new ethnicity following the Civil Rights Movement and highly publicized achievements by black Americans. Hence, its application to non-European immigrants is a recent phenomenon; even now, the question is still debated as to whether or not blacks are "assimilable" in American society. Metzger calls attention to Reuter's influential pioneer study of racial problems in America, which makes it clear that many early American sociologists did not view blacks as assimilable.[20] This is especially the case when we observe that assimilation is synonymous with equality or equal access to the shared values within the opportunity structure. There is, however, a significant caveat: Opportunity means also a mandate to discard one's ethnicity.[21] We should note that it is somewhat easier to discard one's ethnicity or characteristics associated with nationality or various cultural patterns than it is to discard one's race. However, much evidence exists showing that the latter does occur in the United States through the phenomenon of "passing"—that is, voluntarily relinquishing one's assigned racial identity to become a member of another race by virtue of possessing biological features common to the new race. Members of subordinate groups usually use passing to achieve access to shared values and better opportunities.[22] Other questions such as desirability of absorption of minority groups into the dominant culture or the possibility of assimilation as a manifestation of the democratic ethos as opposed to a form of containment of black minorities will be elaborated in succeeding chapters.

One of the more salient consequences of patterned discrimination and enforced segregation of black people in the United States has been the creation of dual but parallel structures presently giving way to pluralism within the black community. Pluralism in this case means the development of institutions (e.g., separate educational institutions and businesses, churches, banks catering specifically to blacks) that are similar to those found in the larger society but were fostered by forces in the larger society in such a manner as to give rise to a black community. The institutions and, consequently, the community emerged from racial separation as well as from the exclusionary policies of the dominant group. Slavery, for example, was accompanied by racism. Racism in turn helped to legitimate discrimination and enforced segregation, which were instrumental in establishing boundary-maintenance systems. These systems then prevented the incorporation of blacks into the larger social system. In time blacks were forced to evolve institutional arrangements necessary to meet functional needs common to any other human group. Thus black people, being denied entry as equals into the mainstream social system, created their own institutional forms in religion, marriage and the family, education, government, economics, recreation, and so forth.

THE DEVELOPMENT OF PLURALISM

In time, parallel institutions became the foundation for pluralism. Immediately, it should be apparent, as Richard A. Schermerhorn argues, that there are different types of pluralism. He identifies four prevalent usages of the term pluralism: (1) as an ideological designation called normative pluralism, which refers to doctrinal beliefs ascribed to a minority group whose members wish to preserve their way of life despite its sharp differences from the dominant group patterns; (2) as a political designation called political pluralism, which refers to "the multiplicity of interest groups and associations" that exert pressure on the decision-making process as well as on the implementation of decisions through organizations such as political parties or lobbies and through a skillful use of mass media; (3) as a cultural designation, also called cultural pluralism, in which the cultural differences of a group set it apart from other groups, dominant or minority—these differences may be perceived in terms of language, religion, nationality, kinship forms, tribal affiliation, and other normative patterns that may heighten their distinctions—race may also become a potent variable in defining stratification patterns and express itself in the norm of cultural pluralism; and (4) as a structural designation, also called social pluralism, which refers to the presence of parallel institutional forms within a particular group that differ structurally from those of other groups existing in the same society. The differences in (4) are magnified when the factors of race and language are significant in the society. Schermerhorn also speaks of this type as institutional pluralism and admits its similarity to Milton Gordon's structural pluralism.[23]

Irving Rinder speaks of accommodative pluralism, which is characteristic of moderately deprived minorities that are able to retain much of their true or original cultures while conforming to the economic structure of the host country (as in the case of Jews).[24] Both accommodated pluralism and Schermerhorn's normative pluralism are new ways of expressing what Louis Wirth identified as a pluralistic minority based upon "the goal toward which the minority and the dominant group are striving."[25] It is in normative, cultural, and structural pluralism that the arguments for pluralism find expression today. In the black community the stress is upon cultural pluralism, although its advocates seem to use the term to include those attributes identified by Schermerhorn as pertaining to all three designations: normative, structural, and cultural. Structural pluralism is more apparent in terms of the diverse institutional forms that emerged throughout the black experience in America. Cultural nationalists would also claim that an identifiable black culture evolved through the medium of distinct black institutional structures. Thus there is, in their view, a black way of life that is to be distinguished from white culture. Like all other cultures, it is learned through a socialization process, undergirded by a system of norms and values that guides conduct and is transmitted both formally and informally. This is precisely the claim of advocates of a black sociology or a black psychology. But claims of pluralism are not new in American sociology. The term was popularized as it applied to American Jews in the works of its chief proponent, Horace M. Kallen, and of others including Isaac B. Berkson, Louis Adamic, and, more recently, Stewart and Mildred Cole and S. N. Eisenstadt and others. However, there is a fact of profound importance here. Although the black community (broadly defined) originated as a defense against white racism, it soon took on a special dynamism or character of its own, so that today even though its institutions may parallel those of the larger society, they possess their own uniqueness and intrinsic values.

On a theoretical level, then, the concept of pluralism can be employed for understanding the black community as a separate structure and distinctive cultural unit within the total American society.

INTERNAL COLONIALISM

A second theoretical perspective that can serve as a framework for understanding the black community and the experiences of black people in America is the internal colonialism model. The chief advocate of this perspective among sociologists is Blauner, whose provocative essay "Internal Colonialism and Ghetto Revolt" created considerable theoretical controversy among American sociologists.[26] The following discussion is based upon Blauner's theoretical formulation.

The central theme of internal colonialism is that black-white relations in the United States are essentially those of colonizer and colonized. The primary emphasis in this model is on domestic colonialization as a process or as an experience instead of the classical or traditional perspective of colonialization as a system. In theoretical terms it is an attempt to bring conceptual clarity to race relations theory by converging missing links from such frameworks as "caste and racism, ethnicity, culture, and economic exploitation" theory into an all-encompassing theme.[27]

Exploitation and control are essential elements in both traditional or classical colonialism and in internal or domestic colonialism. The colonizers seize and maintain control over all resources and over the land on which colonizers and colonized alike settle. Legitimated authority and power over the political processes are maintained through the establishment of formal mechanisms, which the colonizers also control. In the traditional sense, however, the colonizers are generally outsiders and numerical minorities who use superior technological power, skill, and know-how as instruments for subordinating the indigenous majority people, who by definition are technologically, if not culturally, inferior. Thus colonialism is quite similar to what Stanley Lieberson has termed migrant superordination.[28] In either case, racism is one of the more observable consequences.

Blauner asserts that colonialization involves an interplay of four variables or components: (1) the point of entry of the racial group (how it entered the dominant society); (2) acculturation, with culture loss by the colonized group; (3) administrative control of the affairs of the colonized group by the colonizing power; and (4) manifestations of racism. Therefore, internal colonialism is typified by situations in which a colonized group involuntarily enters the dominant society as, for example, through slavery; the destruction of its original culture through a systematic mechanism of denial; the control and manipulation of the internal affairs of the colonized group by forces external to its community (e.g., control and manipulation of all institutions except perhaps the church); and the articulation of a racist structure in which notions of the superordinate group's alleged biological superiority rationalize oppression and subordination of the colonized. This process is often achieved through the institutionalization of legal structures evidenced in de jure segregation and discrimination.[29]

As applied to the black community, the internal colonialism model takes on a special meaning. Most American blacks have as ancestors former slaves who had little choice about being uprooted from their original homes for entry into a society as a subject people. Options available to European immigrants, as, for example, payment for their labor, were not available to them. One could argue that unfair labor practices and the relatively low position of blacks in the labor market today still attest to the limited options available to black laborers. Similarly, just as slave masters isolated slaves and denied them their culture with the resultant development of parallel institutions within the black community, new black cultural structures are maintained in part as a consequence of continued structural isolation and separation. Further, just as an external white power structure manipulated and managed the lives of preemancipation blacks, so today an external white structure manipulates and manages many facets of daily life among black people. The powerlessness of blacks in urban ghettos and rural farm areas all over the United States reduces them to a state of dependency. This condition is reflected in occupations and income, general economic state, politics, education, health care, and police protection—all controlled largely by people outside the black community. Decision-making power on issues of primary importance to them is beyond their pale. The limited opportunities for escape from the wall of the ghetto coupled with powerlessness in the several dimensions just cited typify a protracted state of domestic colonialization. Kenneth Clark in *Youth in the Ghetto*, Richard Schermerhorn in *Comparative Ethnic Relations*, and others also share this view.

Using the evidence of cities like Gary and Cleveland as the situation appeared in the late 1960s and early 1970s, James E. Blackwell and Marie Haug questioned the then widely held belief that the gaining control of the mayoralty by blacks automatically results in significant social and political rewards for the black masses.[30] They argued that the election of a black mayor does not necessarily lead to meaningful changes in the day-to-day living conditions. Political victories do not ipso facto result in economic, educational, medical, or housing payoffs for blacks. Indeed, white ruling elites who control institutionalized economic and social power may continue to dictate various aspects of decision-making that influence the life opportunities of blacks. However, with the election of a much larger number of black mayors in key cities with more solid constituencies and who understand fully the uses of political power in ways that influence the shape of quid pro quos, coupled with imaginative implementation of legis-lative mandates, many blacks did in fact benefit substantially in the 1970s and 1980s from the election of black mayors. For instance, black mayors used their appointive powers to enlarge the participation of blacks in city hall, to extract contracts from firms doing business with the city (which guaranteed greater use of black manpower), and to extend the delivery of social and economic services to the black community to a degree never implemented by their white predecessors. In other cities and towns, the advantages are not as crystallized and may only have a symbolic value. In Gary, Atlanta, and Birmingham, for example, the black political leader-ship strengthened its position and broadened its services to the city resi-dents.

Nevertheless, the internal colonialization model is of value in provid-ing insight into power conflict theory especially when the focus shifts to the continuing struggle faced by blacks to redistribute power and eco-nomic resources in ways that elevate "colonized" blacks, especially in urban ghettos, to a new status. This model is limited, however, in not being applicable to the situation of some white ethnics and in its inadequate treatment of the important variable of mobility among some blacks.

SYSTEMS THEORY AND THE BLACK COMMUNITY

A third theoretical framework within which to study the sociology of the black community is that of systems analysis. Systems theoreticians, like Talcott Parsons, who advocate the notion of societies in a state of equilib-rium, usually follow an organic model traceable to the pioneer works of Herbert Spencer. Those who oppose the organic model of equilibrium, such as George Homans, owe much of their theoretical formulations to the works of Valfredo Pareto. However, Parsons' views seem to have enjoyed wide popularity and greater influence on sociological thought in the United States.

In general, systems theory begins with the notion that societies can be viewed as a system in which the whole has predominance over all of its parts. Societies are viewed as "going concerns," dynamic as it were, but their survival or maintenance is dependent upon meeting important needs or functional imperatives. These functional imperatives are a neces-sary precondition of survival. A basic requirement for meeting these needs is the articulation of certain structures or uniformities of action that recur as particular situations demand. These structures are specified in the form of social organization as social institutions, such as the family, reli-gion, education, economy, and government, called for by the society. However, societal needs dictate the organization of these structures into a system of interrelated activities that are, in turn, mutually supportive. This property of interdependence creates order and cohesion within the system.

As long as they are of functional utility for maintaining the whole system, the components of the concept of order may include legitimized institutional patterns, deviance, conflict, and even subcultural forms. Boundary-maintenance devices are established to assure the maintenance of order and societal equilibrium. Such devices, that is, formal and informal socialization, structures for social control, and "mechanisms of defense," possess some degree of constancy or continuity about them. Thus societal units are interlocked in a network of mutually shared expectations, normative structures, sentiments, and value constructs.[31] The social system is, therefore, a configuration or a network of interrelated parts organized into a whole. These parts include values, norms, sentiments, roles, statuses, patterned behaviors, and institutions. In general, these components are expected to exist in a homeostatic relationship, but this is not always the case, since perfect equilibrium is never attained. Systems are always subject to stresses and strains. Deviance and conflict occur, but the ability of the system to survive as a whole rests on its success in handling those internal and external factors that create consensus and unity.

The black community can be perceived as a social system. Within the community value consensus and congruence exist; a significant segment of its constituents share norms, sentiments, and expectations. Structures are developed to meet defined needs and are hierarchically arranged according to their ability to respond to certain needs. Thus roles and statuses emerge in relation to societal expectations and differential rewards that are assigned. Even though diversity exists within the community, its members are held together by adherence to commonly shared values and goals.

POWER-CONFLICT THEORY

Relationships between blacks and whites in the United States may also be viewed from the perspectives of power differentials between the two groups, the conflict that results when subordinated blacks attempt to gain greater measures of power, and the long history of dominant group exploitation of people assigned a minority status. While the black community as a structural entity may be examined as a social system, the people who constitute it are in a constant struggle to alter power relations between themselves and the dominant white population. It is only through transformation or fundamental changes in how power is distributed that blacks can improve their status and overall life chances in American society.

Yet it is precisely that effort to improve the collective status of the black population that accelerates tension and conflict between blacks and whites who believe that the gains of blacks are to the detriment of white status and privilege. Changing power relations becomes inordinately difficult when contending groups are so unequal in economic, political, and educational resources and when they are competing for extremely scarce rewards. In social systems characterized by the dominance of one group over another and in which members of that dominant group are convinced that membership in such groups ipso facto entitles them to priorities in power, privilege, resources, and rewards, not only is a caste-like structure created but a system of prejudice emerges as justification for that arrangement. Prejudice often leads to the exploitation of its victims. Exploitation is manifested in institutional discrimination such as, again, in structural inequality (e.g., denial of access to fair housing, jobs, equitable incomes, promotions, quality schooling). Exploitation also has physical and emotional consequences. It may lead to widespread abuse of power by gatekeepers of established social boundaries such as law enforcement officers whose actions against minority groups help to maintain dominant group power. Hate groups may also become a major instrument for preventing or deterring minority groups from pursuing their individual or collective effort to restructure power relations. In such instances, minority groups become obvious victims of prejudice, hatred, and discrimination.[32] Exhibitions of hatred and exploitation are further evidence of efforts of members of a dominant group to protect vested interests and control access, distribution or allocation of scarce rewards, and values.[33]

It is evident from the foregoing discussion that *power* refers to the ability to monopolize economic, political, educational, and social resources within a given community or a society and to control the decision-making processes that determine the distribution of such resources among members of that society. Hence, whenever a society is characterized by the coexistence of dominant and subordinate groups, power is regarded as a monopoly vested among dominant group members. In turn, they zealously guard and protect it against subordinates who understand that their own status can only be altered through changes in power relations.

In sum, each of these theoretical schemes has much to offer in providing frameworks for the analysis of the black community, the nature of its present condition in relation to the larger social structure, and the dynamics of its organization. We see these frameworks not as totally independent constructs but as mutually reinforcing ones, providing understanding and linkage where a hiatus exists in the study of race relations today. They help provide better insights into the nature of the collective responses that black Americans have made in the past and continue to make to the conditions of subjugation, discrimination, prejudice, and institutionalized racism. These collective responses are typified by individual reactions to external conditions imposed upon the black community as a whole as well as to the internal state of affairs within the community itself. Responses crisscross a number of different boundaries. For example, such responses may be related to educational, economic, and familial variables found in the black social system or they may be a function of the administrative power exercised on that system from without. The interplay of these forces is of incontestable importance in terms of impact on the behavioral patterns within and among the members of the black community.

THE BLACK COMMUNITY TODAY

In this work the black community is viewed as a social system engaged in a number of interrelated activities. These activities are organized around structures called social institutions, which function to meet specific needs and which parallel those institutions existing in the larger society. In many respects the community exists only in a colonized state, since much of what occurs in it is controlled and manipulated by a power structure that is external to the community itself. The manipulation from the outside is only partial, however, since a structure prevails within the black community itself. Nevertheless, the power exercised by the leadership there is at best relative, for it is neither fully autonomous nor fully a creation of the rank-and-file community member. Whatever the case, black people in America, in spite of the admitted diversity, find themselves in what Thomas C. Shelling aptly describes as "the same boat together."[34]

Even though the community itself may be a socially constructed system, its members may be, indeed, subjected to a state of domestic or internal colonialism and, without question, wage a never-ending struggle to transform power relations in their quest for equality and first-class citizenship.

Components of Community

There are, of course, varied perceptions of the concept "community." The term embraces such factors as territoriality or spatial distribution, and human aggregates distributed within certain ecological boundaries who share common experiences, value systems, and social institutions. Community also connotes power distribution; it means how the members are organized at both formal and informal levels or in a social class structure; it also refers to associational character and friendship cliques.[35] Conceptually, community is not characterized by unidimensionality. It is multifaceted. It can be used in both an ecological sense (territoriality and propinquity) or in sociopsychological terms. In the latter sense we are speaking of the role of shared values in creating a sense of identity with a particular group that may or may not live within the same geographic boundary. People are brought together in community because they happen to share common interests and values. They have accepted sets of definitions of situations, life experiences, or other conditions that give them a uniqueness apart from others whose views, values, and experiences are dissimilar. Shared values, in the formation of a community, may supersede geographic boundaries; they may cross over social class and color lines. A community, therefore, may be considered as a "combination of social units and systems which perform the major social functions having locality reference."[36]

Functions of a Community

Roland Warren identifies five major functions of a community that have locality relevance. These are: (1) *production-distribution-consumption,* which concerns the availability of goods and services essential to daily living in the immediate locality (and includes all social institutions found in the community); (2) *socialization,* which refers to the transmission of basic values and behavioral patterns to the individual members of the system; (3) *social control,* which is the structural arrangement for influencing members toward behavioral conformity; (4) *social participation,* which refers to those structures that facilitate incorporation into the community by virtue of opportunities for participation in its life; and (5) *mutual support,* which describes the process of care and exchanges for help among the members of a group, especially in times of stress. Mutual support may be performed by socializing agents, family members, religious bodies, informal associations, friendship cliques, and so forth.[37]

This definition subsumes a number of important elements of community and permits the elaboration of other issues. For example, a constellation of such variables as resource availability and utilization, leadership structure, power distribution, community control, and access to shared value may be examined. We will call upon these variables in appraising various structures within the black community throughout this book. The reader is reminded, however, that members of a community develop positive sentiments or feelings toward one another. These emerge from the interests they share as well as from the commonality of their experiences with an external, hostile environment. Just as sentiments may serve as the source of normative integration, they also show the diversity among a community's members. This diversity is particularly noticeable when sentiments are transformed into values, as, for example, the value of integration versus the value of separation, which threatened to polarize the black community during the late 1960s (see Chapter 13).

DEMOGRAPHIC CHARACTERISTICS

This section introduces a variety of characteristics and distinguishing features of the American black population today. When appropriate, historical comparisons will be drawn for illustrative purposes. Special attention is given to such characteristics as size of population, migration patterns, distribution of the population, fertility and mortality, and the age-sex structure. Subsequent chapters of the book will treat most of these characteristics in somewhat greater detail. The discussion that follows is drawn largely from an analysis of U.S. census data, which has the most reliable national statistics on population characteristics available.

Size

The more than 30 million blacks or African-Americans in the United States constitute 12.1 percent of a national population of 250,000,000. Between 1940 and 1988, the black population more than doubled. However, the percent black of the U. S. total rose from 9.8 to 12.1 during that period. As reflected in Table 1.1, the black population increased by 17.5 percent over the ten-year period from 1970 to 1980 while the national increase was by only 11 percent. According to Leo Estrada, 60 percent of the national increase during the 1970s was due solely to immigration. Since

Table 1.1   POPULATION GROWTH OF AFRICAN-AMERICANS IN SELECTED YEARS, 1790–1988*

Year	Total U. S. population	Total African-American	Percentage African-American
1790	3,929,214	757,000	19.3
1800	5,308,483	1,002,000	18.9
1820	9,638,453	1,772,000	18.4
1840	17,069,453	2,874,000	16.8
1860	31,443,321	4,521,000	14.1
1880	50,155,783	6,753,000	13.1
1900	75,944,575	9,185,000	11.6
1920	105,710,620	10,890,000	9.9
1940	131,669,275	13,454,000	9.8
1960	179,323,175	18,872,000	10.5
1966	195,000,000[a]	21,220,000	11.0
1967	197,000,000[a]	21,600,000	11.0
1968	198,900,000[a]	21,900,000	11.0
1970	203,200,000[a]	22,600,000	11.0
1980	226,504,825	26,488,218	11.7
1985	238,740,000	28,887,000	12.0
1988	246,000,000[a]	30,000,000[b]	12.1

*In March 1990, the U. S. Bureau of the Census estimated a total U. S. population of 250,000,000. Assuming that the percent black of the total population remained constant at 12.1 percent, then it is estimated that the 1990 population of black Americans is 30.25 million.

[a]Figures are rounded off.

[b]Estimated population data.

Source: U. S. Department of Commerce, Social and Economics Administration, Bureau of the Census, Current Population Reports; Historical Statistics of the United States, Bureau of the Census, Department of Commerce, 1960; Statistical Abstracts, 1973, 1983, 1988, Bureau of the Census, Department of Commerce.

so few blacks or African-Americans immigrated to the United States, and because their fertility rates continue to exceed those of whites, it may be concluded that increases experienced in the black American population during that period were due primarily to natural growth.

Although the black American population constitutes approximately 12 percent of the national total, it is considerably larger than the total population of many nations. For instance, it is larger than the total population of Canada and of all but two nations on the continent of Africa (1) Nigeria (77 million); and (2) Ethiopia (32 million).

Table 1.1 illustrates the number of fluctuations in population size since 1790. These fluctuations also illustrate how the black population is increasing but at a decreasing rate. Changes in population size may be explained by a number of factors that need not be elaborated here but may be listed as: (1) termination of the slave trade; (2) the end of slavery; (3) a continuing decline in infant mortality and adult mortality rates; (4) changes in the birth rate among women of childbearing ages; and (5) the relatively small proportion of foreign born among the white, Hispanic, and other population groups in the United States. In fact, the continuing influx of white immigrant groups, coupled with that of persons of Hispanic and/or Asian origin, and the reduced birth rate of native born blacks, may ultimately reduce the proportion of blacks in the total U.S. population. Further, although the absolute number of black Americans has more than tripled since 1820, the proportion of blacks declined significantly since that year.

Distribution and Nativity

For several centuries the black population was concentrated in the rural South, where agriculture was its principal occupational pursuit. As recently as 1900, almost 90 percent of the black population still remained in the southern states. However, commencing with the 1915 exodus, when more than 225,000 blacks outmigrated, the rest of the nation witnessed a continuous, if not always dramatic, influx of blacks until the mid-1970s. Another period of massive outmigration from the South was during the 1940–1950 decade. This redistribution of blacks was due in a large measure to wartime mobilization associated with World War II.[38] By 1970 the South accounted for 53 percent of the total black population. Due to a greater inmigration than outmigration of blacks in the South during the 1970s, the southern black population remained at 53 percent of the total U. S. population in 1980. By 1988, the distribution of blacks within the United States remained relatively unchanged. For example, of the 30,155,000 blacks in the United States, 15,925,000 or 52.8 percent reside in the South; 5,862,000 or 19.4 percent are in the Midwest; 5,565,000 or 18.4 percent live in the Northeast, and 2,812,000 or 9.3 percent are located in the West (Table 1.2). The attraction of the South as a place of residence for blacks in the 1990s may be attributed to its changing racial climate, improved economic opportunities and working conditions for

Table 1.2 WHITE AND BLACK POPULATION PROJECTIONS, BY STATE: 1988 TO 2000

Region, division, and state	White Number (1,000) 1988	1989	1990	2000	White Percent of total population 1990	2000	Black Number (1,000) 1988	1989	1990	2000	Black Percent of total population 1990	2000
United States	207,326	208,808	210,247	221,144	84.1	82.6	30,165	30,597	31,026	35,006	12.4	13.1
Region:												
Northeast	43,634	43,672	43,714	43,880	86.4	84.7	5,565	5,635	5,705	6,363	11.3	12.3
Midwest	52,696	52,709	52,705	51,687	88.2	86.7	5,862	5,929	5,995	6,542	10.0	11.0
South	67,761	68,556	69,343	76,252	79.5	78.7	15,925	16,153	16,379	18,546	18.8	19.1
West	43,234	43,871	44,486	49,326	85.1	83.0	2,812	2,880	2,947	3,555	5.6	6.0
Northeast	12,131	12,197	12,263	12,769	93.8	92.7	584	594	605	702	4.6	5.1
ME	1,179	1,188	1,197	1,252	98.7	98.5	4	4	4	4	.3	.5
NH	1,070	1,096	1,122	1,300	98.2	97.5	7	7	7	10	.6	.8
VT	546	550	555	580	98.7	98.2	2	2	2	3	.4	.5
MA	5,470	5,475	5,482	5,595	93.2	91.9	275	280	284	327	4.8	5.4
RI	933	939	943	974	94.1	92.9	37	37	38	45	3.8	4.3
CT	2,933	2,948	2,964	3,069	90.4	89.1	259	264	269	313	8.2	9.1
Middle Atlantic	31,504	31,475	31,451	31,110	83.9	81.8	4,982	5,040	5,100	5,661	13.6	14.9
NY	14,418	14,375	14,338	14,062	80.7	78.2	2,791	2,824	2,858	3,180	16.1	17.7
NJ	6,455	6,492	6,531	6,855	82.7	80.2	1,089	1,111	1,134	1,349	14.4	15.8
PA	10,631	10,608	10,582	10,193	89.5	88.6	1,101	1,105	1,108	1,131	9.4	9.8
East North-Central	36,272	36,267	36,247	35,261	86.2	84.5	4,997	5,056	5,113	5,584	12.2	13.4
OH	9,516	9,510	9,501	9,225	88.0	86.8	1,166	1,177	1,188	1,274	11.0	12.0
IN	5,024	5,027	5,028	4,922	90.6	89.5	458	463	469	513	8.4	9.3
IL	9,469	9,456	9,443	9,173	81.3	79.2	1,832	1,851	1,869	2,029	16.1	17.5
MI	7,760	7,770	7,774	7,543	83.7	81.5	1,319	1,337	1,355	1,497	14.6	16.2
WI	4,503	4,502	4,501	4,417	93.6	92.3	222	227	231	273	4.8	5.7

Table 1.2 (*Continued*)

Region, division, and state	White						Black					
	Number (1,000)				Percent of total population		Number (1,000)				Percent of total population	
	1988	1989	1990	2000	1990	2000	1988	1989	1990	2000	1990	2000
West North-Central	16,424	16,442	16,457	16,405	92.9	91.9	865	874	882	958	5.0	5.4
MN	4,096	4,117	4,138	4,250	95.7	94.7	64	66	67	77	1.6	1.7
IA	2,727	2,704	2,681	2,462	97.2	96.6	50	51	52	58	1.9	2.3
MO	4,527	4,551	4,573	4,705	88.1	87.4	549	554	559	600	10.8	11.2
ND	636	631	627	592	95.0	94.0	3	3	3	4	.5	.6
SD	644	643	642	635	90.7	89.0	2	2	2	2	.3	.3
NE	1,516	1,513	1,510	1,470	95.1	94.5	53	54	54	58	3.4	3.7
KS	2,278	2,283	2,286	2,292	91.7	90.6	142	144	145	158	5.8	6.2
South Atlantic	32,814	33,332	33,842	38,277	77.4	76.6	8,850	9,007	9,164	10,673	21.0	21.3
DE	519	524	528	561	79.4	76.5	120	123	126	155	18.9	21.1
MD	3,291	3,322	3,352	3,597	70.9	68.2	1,176	1,205	1,233	1,469	26.1	27.9
DC	183	184	184	193	30.0	30.5	426	423	421	430	68.6	67.8
VA	4,707	4,775	4,840	5,346	78.6	77.7	1,136	1,154	1,171	1,332	19.0	19.4
WV	1,820	1,806	1,792	1,664	96.5	96.6	57	55	54	45	2.9	2.6
NC	4,937	5,005	5,071	5,653	75.8	75.5	1,445	1,463	1,480	1,641	22.1	21.9
SC	2,392	2,421	2,451	2,694	69.1	69.0	1,043	1,055	1,067	1,170	30.1	30.0
GA	4,604	4,704	4,803	5,698	72.1	71.6	1,716	1,752	1,789	2,151	26.9	27.0
FL	10,360	10,591	10,820	12,870	84.4	83.5	1,732	1,778	1,823	2,279	14.2	14.8
Eastern Southern-Central	12,235	12,301	12,364	12,782	79.3	78.5	3,070	3,096	3,122	3,354	20.0	20.6
KY	3,441	3,443	3,444	3,414	92.0	91.5	276	278	280	294	7.5	7.9
TN	4,066	4,097	4,127	4,331	83.0	82.2	792	801	810	887	16.3	16.8
AL	3,032	3,054	3,076	3,225	73.6	73.1	1,055	1,063	1,071	1,136	25.6	25.8
MS	1,695	1,706	1,717	1,812	63.6	63.0	946	954	962	1,037	35.6	36.1

TABLE 1.2 WHITE AND BLACK POPULATION PROJECTIONS, BY STATE: 1988 TO 2000 (Continued)

Region, division, and state	White Number (1,000) 1988	1989	1990	2000	White Percent of total population 1990	2000	Black Number (1,000) 1988	1989	1990	2000	Black Percent of total population 1990	2000
West Southern-Central	22,713	22,924	23,137	25,192	82.8	82.2	4,006	4,049	4,093	4,520	14.6	14.8
AR	1,989	2,000	2,011	2,093	82.9	82.8	384	385	387	398	15.9	15.7
LA	3,080	3,073	3,065	2,978	67.9	65.9	1,362	1,371	1,380	1,452	30.6	32.1
OK	2,803	2,795	2,789	2,810	84.9	83.2	222	222	223	231	6.8	6.8
TX	14,841	15,056	15,272	17,311	86.2	85.7	2,037	2,071	2,104	2,439	11.9	12.1
Mountain	12,462	12,672	12,876	14,572	92.0	90.9	340	348	356	432	2.5	2.7
MT	758	755	752	734	93.4	92.5	2	2	2	2	.2	.2
ID	982	986	989	1,013	97.3	96.7	4	4	4	6	.4	.5
WY	487	485	483	467	96.3	95.4	4	4	4	4	.8	.8
CO	3,138	3,174	3,211	3,535	93.5	92.7	128	130	133	156	3.9	4.1
NM	1,371	1,404	1,436	1,711	88.0	87.0	27	28	29	34	1.7	1.7
AZ	3,184	3,278	3,369	4,108	89.8	89.0	94	98	99	123	2.7	2.7
UT	1,643	1,667	1,692	1,879	95.2	94.4	12	12	12	13	.7	.7
NV	899	922	944	1,125	87.8	86.3	69	72	74	94	6.9	7.2
Pacific	30,772	31,199	31,609	34,754	82.6	80.1	2,473	2,532	2,591	3,123	6.8	7.2
WA	4,178	4,216	4,251	4,488	91.3	89.9	113	113	114	116	2.4	2.3
OR	2,584	2,596	2,607	2,674	94.3	92.9	43	44	44	50	1.6	1.7
CA	23,206	23,570	23,920	26,641	82.1	79.5	2,278	2,335	2,392	2,909	8.2	8.7
AK	431	439	447	519	77.5	75.6	19	19	20	23	3.4	3.4
HI	372	379	385	432	33.7	32.1	20	21	21	24	1.8	1.8

Source: U.S. Bureau of the Census, Current Population Reports, series P-25, forthcoming report.

blacks, a change of "pace of life" easily distinguished from the hectic and impersonal characteristics attributed to other parts of the nation, a desire to be closer to other family members, and a warmer social climate. It is also viewed as a refuge from the problems of urban life in the large cities of the West, Northeast, and Midwest.

The exodus of the black population from the South, which began in 1915, marked a turning point in the geographical distribution of black Americans. This movement signaled something greater than merely the shift of the population from one region to another. Although the shift proved to have profound consequences for structural changes in the black community, it also resulted in fundamental changes in the rural-urban distribution of the black population. Thus, the 1980 U. S. census showed that 81.1 percent of black Americans live in metropolitan areas of the United States and by 1988, it was estimated that 82.0 percent of all blacks live in metropolitan communities. (By contrast, 77 percent of whites live in metropolitan areas.) In becoming a metropolitan population, blacks, either by choice or because of the inability to find suitable housing elsewhere, have tended to concentrate in the inner cities (57 percent, nationally) in every region of the country. As a general rule, the larger the metropolitan area, the greater the proportion of black people residing in the central cities. Simultaneously, the white population has become increasingly suburbanized by moving away from all parts of the city. As a result, an ecological pattern of succession has already occurred as blacks replaced whites in many cities, and the metropolitan areas have become, as aptly described by Reynolds Farley, "chocolate cities and vanilla suburbs."[39]

In terms of their total population, the largest concentrations of blacks are found in the following cities: (1) New York City (1,784,124), (2) Chicago (1,197,000), (3) Detroit (738,939), (4) Philadelphia (638,878), (5) Los Angeles (505,208), (6) Washington, D. C. (448,229), (7) Houston (440,257), (8) Baltimore (431,151), (9) New Orleans (308,136), (10) Memphis (307,702), and (11) Atlanta (282,912).[40]

Relative to the proportion of blacks in the total population of a given city, as of 1988 the black population comprised 50 percent or more of the total population in the following cities: (1) Gary (70.8), (2) Washington, D. C. (70.3), (3) Atlanta (66.6), (4) Detroit (63.1), (5) Newark (58.2), (6) Birmingham (55.6), (7) New Orleans (55.3), (8) Baltimore (54.8), and Richmond (51.3). In 1990 each of these cities had a black mayor.[41]

In addition, the black population has now reached 40 percent or more of the following large cities with a population in excess of 100,000: Chicago; Cleveland; Durham, North Carolina; Flint, Michigan; Jackson, Mississippi; Oakland, California; Philadelphia, Pa.; Portsmouth, Virginia; St. Louis; Savannah, Georgia; Shreveport, Louisiana; and Winston-Salem, North Carolina. However, between 1970 and 1980, among these cities, three actually lost significant percentages of blacks from the total population. In St. Louis, the loss of black residents totaled 18.8 percent; in Cleveland, it was by 12.7 percent, and by 16.6 percent in Washington, D.C. The loss of blacks from the urban population may be attributed to the suburbanization of blacks into nearby communities, to the relocation of blacks to other cities, and to a decrease in the movement of blacks from rural areas into these communities.[42]

Suburbanization

During the 1970s the suburbanization of the black population occurred at an unprecedented rate. In that decade black suburbanization increased by 49.4 percent in contrast to a gain of 17.3 percent in the white suburban population. At the beginning of the 1970s, blacks comprised 4.8 percent of the residents in suburban communities. In the preceding decade, 1960–1970, some 800,000 blacks moved into the suburbs. However, by 1980, even with the movement of 1.8 million blacks into suburbs, blacks constituted only 6.1 percent of the suburban population in the United States. In the "exurban" fringes beyond the immediate city suburbs, the proportion of blacks declined from 9.2 percent of the population in 1970 to 6.1 percent in 1980. These changes occurred as the percentage of blacks in central cities actually declined from 58.2 percent in 1970 to 55.7 percent in 1980. However, the proportion of blacks as components of the total central city population increased from 20.6 percent in 1970 to 23.4 percent in 1980.[43] Hence, there is significant evidence to support the contention that central cities are becoming "blacker" while suburban and exurban communities are becoming "whiter." It should be noted that residential resegregation also occurs in the suburbanization of the black population. That is, blacks tend to move into suburban communities that already have a substantial black population and in close proximity to other blacks in many of these situations (see also Chapter 7).

The unabated trend toward the metropolitanization and urbanization of the black population has escalated the redistribution of the black population who are almost entirely native born. About 99 percent of all black people in the United States are native born. Only the American Indian population can make a similar claim (see also the discussion of housing patterns in Chapter 7).

Why did blacks emigrate from the South, and what have been some of the consequences for them? Mass movements of people from place to place are frequently explained by a combination of "push-and-pull" forces. In the case of the black population, the major pull factors prior to the post-1954 civil rights era were the lure of improved living and working conditions, the possibility of better incomes, and a life relatively free from the increasing difficulties and problems embodied in the Jim Crow social system of the South. The major push factor was, concomitantly, the oppressive, pernicious, and demoralizing life as second-class citizens in a quasi-caste social system that persisted like a "cake of custom" in the South. Unfortunately, the freedom sought was seldom gained and was, at best, only a relative phenomenon.

A push factor of major significance in the redistribution of blacks was, of course, the mechanization of agriculture. Not only did mechanization contribute to the great exodus of Southern blacks, it is of special importance in explaining the impoverished conditions of many rural Southern blacks today. In 1930, approximately two-thirds of American blacks were still engaged in agricultural pursuits. At that time, there was still a need for black farm labor to support an essentially retrogressive and traditional method of farming. Mechanization brought with it tractors, harvesters, and other large-scale farm equipment as a basis for commercial farming. Black farmhands or laborers were one of its notable casualties. Thus, by 1980, according to the U.S. Department of Commerce, less than 9 percent of black male workers were classified as farm workers. Nevertheless, some 222,000 blacks still reside in rural areas, many of them jobless. In many ways, they are the true pariahs, the "lumpen-proletariats" of the American social and economic system. They lag behind others in educational attainment and other marketable skills so that when they do migrate to the city, they often become dependent upon public welfare for survival. Black rural residents comprise a large share of the subemployed, unemployed, and the total number of persons living below the poverty line, often earning no more than wages considerably below the minimum wage whenever they are fortunate enough to find work. Hence, their abject poverty, their abysmally inadequate housing, and their unimaginably poor nutrition. Their subservient economic condition is, in part, maintained by the inability of black small-scale farmers to obtain sufficient financial leverage through loans or assistance from the United States Department of Agriculture (USDA) to enable them to cope with increasing agricultural mechanization. In order to make ends meet, thousands of rural southern blacks have become peripatetic migrant workers, following opportunities for seasonal employment in the harvesting of fruit, vegetables, and sugar cane. Because they are rootless and often exploited, it becomes increasingly difficult for these black victims of mechanized agriculture to survive.

Most southern black transplants to the North and West did not initially (and do not now) find living as easy as they previously envisioned; they have found somewhat more subtle prejudice and discrimination, nonetheless demeaning, when compared to that experienced in the South. Specifically, rural southern blacks were lured—by promises of a better life by friends, relatives, and labor agents—from the share-cropping system and tenant farms of the South only to become the modern new industrialized laborers and semiskilled operators in the factories of Detroit and Chicago, or the menial workers in the manufacturing industries of Philadelphia and Newark, or in the garment industry of New York, or in the steel mills of Pittsburgh and Cleveland. And black women discarded the role of "mammy" to white Southerners only to become exploited household servants of the established rich and the ever-widening white middle classes of the urban North and West. Undoubtedly, disillusionment as a result of white racism and discrimination encountered within the the marketplace in the North, coupled with the devastating job losses experienced by blacks during the recessions of the 1970s, the depression-level unemployment among blacks in the 1980s, and fear of urban violence spurred the reversal of the outmigration of blacks from the South and accelerated the new trend of black outmigration from the North and West.

Fertility and Life Expectancy

When speaking of fertility rates, we are referring to the *total fertility rate,* which is defined by the Bureau of Census as "the number of births that 1,000 women would have in their life time if, at each year of age, they experienced the birth rates occurring in the specified calendar year."[44] On the other hand, *the intrinsic rate of natural increase* refers to the "rate that would eventually prevail if a population were to experience, at each year of age, the birth rates and death rates occurring in the specified year and if those rates remained unchanged over a long period of time."[45] As evident in Table 1.3, blacks and whites differ sharply in total fertility and intrinsic rate of natural increase.

The total fertility rate of blacks and other races has been substantially higher than that of the white population for at least a half century. Since 1965, however, the decline in total fertility rate among the white population has been far more precipitous than is evident in the black population. While the natural population increase due to births is 14.6/1,000 for whites, it is 20.9/1,000 for blacks.[46] The intrinsic rate of natural increase in the white population has been negative in every year since 1971. By contrast, the intrinsic rate of natural increase for blacks and other races has been positive. However, that rate declined between 1972 and 1987 but not as drastically as that of the white population (Table 1.3).

These data support the notion that the black population is increasing but at a decreasing rate. The facts that the black population is younger and that the number of black mothers is increasing suggest a number of problems related to mother-child care, prenatal health care, the ability to afford proper diets during pregnancy and after parturition, and differentials in the quality of facilities and access to postnatal treatment available to white and black women in the United States.

As will be elaborated in Chapter 11, even with all the advances in health technology and overall improvements in health care in the United States, blacks still cannot expect to live as long as whites.

Age-Sex Structure

The black population is essentially young. On the average, whites tend to be about six years older than blacks. Their respective median ages are 33.1 for whites and 27.3 for blacks. The youth of the black population is reflected in the comparative proportion of blacks and whites within the various age cohorts or groupings (Table 1.4). For instance, 9.4 percent of blacks, compared to 6.8 percent of whites, are under the age of five. More

Table 1.3 TOTAL FERTILITY RATE AND INTRINSIC RATE OF NATURAL INCREASE: 1940 TO 1986

Annual average and year	Total fertility rate			Intrinsic rate of natural increase		
	Total	White	Black and other	Total	White	Black and other
1940–1944	2,523	2,460	3,010	4.6	3.9	9.8
1945–1949	2,985	2,916	3,485	11.7	10.9	17.2
1950–1954	3,337	3,221	4,185	16.8	15.4	25.7
1955–1959	3,690	3,549	4,716	21.1	19.5	30.7
1960–1964	3,449	3,326	4,326	18.6	17.1	27.7
1965–1969	2,622	2,512	3,362	8.2	6.4	18.6
1970–1974	2,094	1,997	2,680	-.7	-2.5	9.1
1975–1979	1,774	1,685	2,270	-6.6	-8.5	3.0
1980–1984	1,819	1,731	2,262	-5.4	-7.3	3.0
1985–1986	1,839	1,748	2,272	-4.9	-6.7	3.2
1965	2,913	2,783	3,808	12.1	10.3	23.1
1966	2,721	2,603	3,532	9.7	7.9	20.4
1967	2,558	2,447	3,299	7.4	5.6	18.2
1968	2,464	2,366	3,108	5.9	4.2	16.0
1969	2,456	2,360	3,061	5.7	4.1	15.4
1970	2,480	2,385	3,067	6.0	4.5	14.4

Year	Total fertility rate			Intrinsic rate of natural increase		
	Total	White	Black and other	Total	White	Black and other
1971	2,267	2,161	2,920	2.6	.8	12.6
1972	2,010	1,907	2,628	-2.0	-3.9	8.6
1973	1,879	1,783	2,444	-4.5	-6.5	5.7
1974	1,835	1,749	2,339	-5.4	-7.2	4.0
1975	1,774	1,686	2,276	-6.7	-8.6	3.0
1976	1,738	1,652	2,223	-7.4	-9.3	2.1
1977	1,790	1,703	2,278	-6.2	-8.1	3.2
1978	1,760	1,668	2,264	-6.8	-8.8	2.9
1979	1,808	1,715	2,310	-5.7	-7.7	3.8
1980	1,840	1,749	2,323	-5.1	-7.0	4.0
1981	1,815	1,726	2,275	-5.5	-7.4	3.3
1982	2,829	1,742	2,264	-5.2	-7.0	3.0
1983	1,803	1,718	2,225	-5.7	-7.5	2.5
1984	1,806	1,719	2,224	-5.6	-7.4	2.4
1985	1,842	1,754	2,263	-4.8	-6.6	3.1
1986	1,836	1,741	2,281	-4.9	-6.8	3.3

Source: Statistical Abstracts of the United States, 1989. Washington, D.C.: U.S. Department of Commerce, Bureau of the Census.

Table 1.4   AGE AND SEX OF PERSONS, BY REGION AND RACE: MARCH 1988,
1985, AND 1980
(Numbers in thousands)

Age and sex	1988		1985		1980	
	Black	White	Black	White	Black	White
United States						
Age						
Total persons	29,333	203,869	28,151	199,117	26,033	191,905
Percent	100.0	100.0	100.0	100.0	100.0	100.0
Under 5 years	9.4	7.3	9.6	7.3	9.4	6.9
Under 18 years	33.4	25.1	33.9	25.6	36.1	27.3
18 years and over	66.6	74.9	66.1	74.4	63.9	72.7
18 to 24 years	12.3	10.6	13.4	11.7	14.3	12.9
65 years and over	8.1	12.6	7.9	12.2	7.8	11.4
Median age	27.3	33.1	26.4	32.2	24.8	30.8
Males per 100 females	87.8	95.7	87.6	95.1	87.3	95.0
South						
Age						
Total persons	16,403	64,813	14,937	63,148	13,599	59,597
Percent	100.0	100.0	100.0	100.0	100.0	100.0
Under 5 years	9.4	6.8	10.0	7.1	9.8	6.7
Under 18 years	34.2	24.7	34.3	24.9	36.7	27.3
18 years and over	65.8	75.3	65.7	75.1	63.3	72.7
18 to 24 years	12.6	10.4	13.3	11.5	14.4	12.3
65 years and over	8.4	12.8	8.8	12.6	8.9	11.7
Median age	26.8	33.6	26.3	32.7	24.5	31.3
Males per 100 females	85.7	95.8	87.4	95.0	86.8	96.5
North and West						
Age						
Total	12,931	139,056	13,214	135,969	12,435	132,307
Percent	100.0	100.0	100.0	100.0	100.0	100.0
Under 5 years	9.4	7.5	9.2	7.4	9.0	7.0
Under 18 years	32.3	25.3	33.4	25.9	35.4	27.3
18 years and over	67.7	74.7	66.6	74.1	64.6	72.7
18 to 24 years	12.0	10.6	13.7	11.7	14.1	13.2
65 years and over	7.8	12.5	7.0	12.0	6.7	11.3
Median age	28.0	32.8	26.6	32.0	25.2	30.6
Males per 100 females	90.6	95.6	87.8	95.1	87.8	94.3

Source: U.S. Bureau of the Census, The Black Population in the United States (Current Population Reports,
Series P-20, No. 442, November 1989).

than a third (34.2 percent) of blacks are under the age of 18, compared
to one-fourth (24.7 percent) of all whites in this category. While almost
two-thirds of all blacks, in contrast to three-fourths of all whites, are 18
years and older. Significantly, and undoubtedly reflecting differences in
life expectancy rates, the 65 and older age cohort is increasing much more
rapidly for whites than for blacks. In 1980, for instance, 11.7 percent of
the white population was age 65 and older, By 1988, that proportion had

increased to 12.8. By contrast, the 65 and older cohort in the black population dropped from 8.9 percent in 1980 to 8.4 percent in 1988. Age differences between the races are subsequently manifested in the racial composition of schools, participation in the labor force, availability of men as marital partners, and the distribution of such benefits as social security.

Blacks and whites also differ with respect to sex ratio. As shown in Table 1.4, there are significantly more white males (95.7) per 100 females than there are black males (87.8) per 100 black females in the population. As will be shown in Chapter 11, these differences not only reflect sex ratio disparities at birth but the lower life expectancy of black men compared to that of white men. Regional differences in the proportion of males per 100 females are not significant for whites. However, an examination of Table 1.4 shows that there are about five fewer black males (85.7) per 100 black females in the South than is the case in the North and West (90.6). Again, the larger number of women than men has certain important implications for family life, marriage, labor force participation, and other features that will become more apparent in subsequent chapters.

NOTES

1. See *The Social and Economic Status of the Black Population in the United States, 1971,* U. S. Department of Commerce, Bureau of the Census (July 1972), pp. 29–30, and Bureau of the Census, *The Black Population in the United States, 1985* (Current Population Reports, Series P-20, No. 442, November 1989).
2. Harry A. Ploski and James Williams, *The Negro Almanac: A Reference Work on the Afro-American* (New York: John Wiley & Sons, 1983), p. 460.
3. For a discussion of the insider-outsider controversy see Robert K. Merton, "Insiders and Outsiders: A Chapter in the Sociology of Knowledge," *American Journal of Sociology* 78 (July 1972): 9–47.
4. I am indebted to Professor Walter Wallace for ideas concerning the dichotomization of perspectives on the insider-outsider controversy.
5. Jessie Bernard, *American Community Behavior* (New York: Holt, Rinehart and Winston, 1949), p. 226.
6. For a discussion of the life and condition of blacks during slavery, see John Hope Franklin, *From Slavery to Freedom* (New York: Alfred A. Knopf, 1952), pp. 77–78; A. Leon Higginbotham, Jr., *In the Matter of Color: Race and the Legal Process* (New York: Oxford University Press, 1978); and Mary F. Berry and John W. Blassingame, *Long Memory: The Black Experience in America* (New York: Oxford University Press, 1982).
7. Franklin, *op. cit.*
8. *Ibid.,* pp. 340–345.
9. Kenneth Stampp, *The Peculiar Institution* (New York: Alfred A. Knopf, 1956).
10. Richard A. Schermerhorn, *Comparative Ethnic Relations: A Framework for Theory and Research* (New York: Random House, 1970), p. 148.
11. This viewpoint is explored in considerable detail in Stanley Elkins, *Slavery* (Chicago: University of Chicago Press, 1959).

12. Cf. Ulrich B. Philips, *Life and Labor in the Old South* (Boston: Little, Brown, 1929), pp. 194–217 and Stampp, *op. cit.*
13. Andrew Billingsley, *Black Families in White America* (Englewood Cliffs, N. J.: Prentice-Hall, 1968), Chap. 1.
14. Robert Blauner, "Black Culture: Myth or Reality," in Norman Whitten and John Swed (eds.), *Afro-American Anthropology* (New York: Doubleday, 1970), Chap. 19.
15. Nathan Glazer and Daniel P. Moynihan, *Beyond The Melting Pot* (Cambridge, Mass.: The M. I. T. Press, 1963), p. 51.
16. Irving Kristol, "The Negro Today Is the Immigrant of Yesterday," *New York Times Sunday Magazine*, September 11, 1966, p. 50.
17. Blauner, *op. cit.*
18. Cf. arguments advanced by E. Franklin Frazier in both *The Negro in the United States* (New York: Macmillan, 1949) and *The Negro Family in the United States* (Chicago: The University of Chicago Press, 1939).
19. Louis Wirth, "The Problems of Minority Groups," in Ralph Linton (ed.), *The Science of Man in the World Crisis* (New York: Columbia University Press, 1945), pp. 347–372.
20. Paul L. Metzger, "American Sociology and Black Assimilation: Conflicting Perspectives," *American Journal of Sociology* 76 (January 1971): 632.
21. *Ibid.*, p. 628.
22. James Y. Conyers, "Negro Passing: To Pass or Not to Pass," *Phylon* 24(1963), 215–224.
23. Schermerhorn, *op. cit*, p. 122.
24. Irwin Rinder, "Minority Orientations: An Approach to Intergroup Relations Theory," *Phylon* 26 (Spring 1965): 5–17.
25. Wirth, *op. cit.*
26. Robert Blauner, "Internal Colonialism and Ghetto Revolt," *Social Problems* 16 (Spring 1969): 393–408.
27. *Ibid.*, p. 394.
28. Stanley Lieberson, "A Societal Theory of Race and Ethnic Relations," *American Sociological Review* 26 (December 1961): 902–910.
29. Blauner, *op. cit.*
30. James E. Blackwell and Marie Haug, "Relations Between Black Bosses and Black Workers," *The Black Scholar* 4 (January 1973): 36–43.
31. Cf. Talcott Parsons, *The Social System* (New York: The Free Press, 1951) and Walter Buckley, *Sociology and Modern Systems Theory* (Englewood Cliffs, N. J.: Prentice-Hall, 1967).
32. Richard T. Schaefer, *Racial and Ethnic Groups* (2nd ed) (Boston: Little, Brown and Company, 1984), Chap. 1.
33. *Ibid.*
34. Thomas C. Shelling, *The Strategy of Conflict* (Cambridge, Mass.: Harvard University Press, 1960), pp. 11–12.
35. Bernard, *op. cit.* pp. 3–10.
36. Ploski and Williams, *op. cit.*
37. Roland Warren, *The Community in America* (Chicago: University of Chicago Press, 1972), p. 9.
38. *Ibid.*
39. Reynolds Farley, "Chocolate City, Vanilla Suburbs: Will the Trend Toward Racially Separate Communities Continue?" *Social Science Research* 7 (December 1978): 319–344.

40. Bureau of The Census, *Statistical Abstracts of the United States, 1989* (Washington, D. C.: U. S. Government Printing Office, 1989), pp. 33–35.
41. *Ibid.*
42. Ploski and Williams, *op. cit.*, p. 467.
43. *Ibid.*
44. *Statistical Abstracts*, p. 64.
45. *Ibid.*
46. *Ibid.*, p. 9.

Chapter
2

Employment, Poverty, and Welfare

*T*he progress of the black community toward incorporation and assimilation, cultural pluralism, or toward the construction of a separate but viable system is affected by such factors as income, occupational distribution, unemployment, persistent poverty, and the position taken by the federal government with respect to the goals that blacks articulate. Throughout the history of black people in America, these factors have contravened progress, exacerbated problems, and combined to create disillusionment, despair, and alienation among significant segments of black communities. Income inequities, menial occupational distribution, and poverty provide extremely potent weapons for heightening group diversity and intensifying or solidifying class boundaries.

Without question, many segments of the black community experienced major economic progress in the period between the enactment of the Civil Rights Act of 1964, which was followed by the promulgation of presidential executive orders that ushered in Affirmative Action policies and guidelines, and in 1980 when Ronald Reagan was elected president of the United States. It is largely because of this progress that several persons have claimed in recent years that race is no longer a significant determinant of the overall life chances of black Americans.[1] While that position seems to be embraced by black neoconservatives and whites who wish to shift the focus of race relations from the emotionally laden race variable to a less contentious class variable, it is soundly rejected by many others in American society. Persons in this camp insist that, despite social and economic gains experienced by blacks between 1950 and 1990, and irrespective of the reduction of public manifestations of virulent racism, structural inequities, and discrimination, the persistence of racism in American life is still evident.[2]

There are also those social scientists who essentially argue for what Paul Blumberg calls a *class convergence theory.* In this view, the post-World War II expansion of job opportunities enabled affluence to become a more generalized characteristic of American society. In effect, this economic improvement broadened those educational opportunities and reduced distinctions in life styles that previously differentiated social classes. As a result, since World War II, the United States has experienced a minimization of class differentiation or a convergence of the classes.[3] The opposing view is taken by persons identified by Blumberg as *class stability theorists.* This group acknowledges post-World War II economic improvements in American society. However, it is their view that these improvements in living standards did not eliminate or even reduce class differentiations because those persons in the upper-social strata have continued to maintain their distance between themselves and those at the bottom social strata. They still have more goods, services, and better life chances than persons at the bottom.[4]

Theory aside, an objective reality is that, irrespective of race, during the early 1980s unemployment was higher than it had been at any time since 1941 when the nation was moving out of the Great Depression. In subsequent sections of this chapter, the fact that black Americans actually experienced Great-Depression joblessness, destitution, and continue to be victimized by inordinate unemployment levels will be discussed. This chapter also devotes attention to the consequences of unemployment, including hunger and homelessness, as well as employment and occupational distribution, income maldistribution, poverty, welfare, and the impact of Reaganism on the black community.

Hunger is pervasive in all parts of the nation, especially in those regions hardest hit by the recession of 1981–1982. While the Reagan Administration consistently denied the severity of the problems of hunger and homelessness in the United States, evidence will show that, measured by normative American standards and privileges of the dominant white population, hunger and homelessness are, indeed, major social problems. In several metropolitan areas, homeless American citizens are forced to construct makeshift accommodations from cardboard boxes, either for sleeping or protection from the unkindness of winter weather. Presidential commissions claim to be unable to document the extent of hunger in the United States. However, ordinary visits to the numerous soup kitchens that sprang up throughout the nation during the early 1980s and which remain in the 1990s provide compelling evidence of intolerable numbers of hungry, malnourished individuals and a higher-than-the-national-average rate of infant mortality among blacks.

The 1980s recorded home foreclosures, bankruptcies, and business failures in epidemic proportions throughout America. Consequently, much more so for blacks than whites, social and economic conditions deteriorated and many of the gains achieved during the civil rights period were decimated by the onslaught of Reagan's New Federalism. Nevertheless, during the latter part of the 1980s, as the nation began to experience six years of unprecedented economic expansion and a major economic recovery from the devastation of the early 1980s, some blacks did prosper. However, the black community continues to suffer from a disproportionate share of the underclass—the lumpen-proletariat of American society.

EMPLOYMENT AND OCCUPATIONAL DISTRIBUTION

Historically, blacks have constituted a major proportion of the work force at the lower echelons of the occupational scale. Their experiences in the labor market illustrate what Sethard Fisher calls a process of halt, progress, and retardation.[5] Prior to emancipation a class of black artisans, including masons, carpenters, plumbers, painters, repairmen, and machinists, could be found largely in the urban areas. Following emancipation, there was an increase in educational opportunities, and even though a disproportionate number of blacks were still employed in agricultural and domestic work, a select few turned to the professions of teaching and preaching. This trend persisted for several decades after the Civil War. Three factors can be cited to explain this situation: (1) the destruction of the artisan class of blacks, which came about as a result of the influx of 9 million members of white ethnic groups from Europe who were given jobs, especially in the North, that normally would have gone to blacks; (2) the displacement of blacks by white artisans during the post-Reconstruction period, aided considerably by the failure to enforce post-Reconstruction civil rights legislation, and by the enactment of Jim Crow legislation; and (3) the rise of the sharecropping and tenancy system, which was buttressed by a system of legalized peonage in the South.

The sharecropping system permitted white planters to exploit black farmers. The latter agreed to live and work on land owned by white planters with the understanding that the profits gained would be equally divided after expenses were deducted. The general practice was for white planters, who always kept the books, to subtract so much from the sale of crops that black tenant farmers ended up owing them for the privilege of working from sunrise to sundown on their land. Blacks could never get ahead and found themselves struggling under a new form of slavery. Moreover, the constraints and structure of southern laws prevented blacks from moving from a given farm until all their debts had been paid to white landowners. Thus black farmers were cheated, exploited, and reduced to peonage.[6] The conditions found in agriculture were equally applicable in other occupations in many parts of the South. Consequently, the black worker was denied access to money, technology, and jobs that would assure advancement and secure incomes.

With the aid of the Freedman's Bureau, the support of the federal government during the Reconstruction period, and the individual initiative of enterprising blacks, thousands of blacks were able to accumulate millions of acres in landholdings in various parts of the nation, particularly in the South.[7] Over the years, a great deal of landholdings, which included a large portion of rich farm land, was lost by blacks, especially in the American South. This loss of black-owned land can be attributed mainly to the following seven reasons: (1) lack of legal and technical advice that results, among other things, in foreclosures for nonpayment of taxes and expropriations by dishonest land merchants; (2) voluntary and involuntary sales; (3) "insufficient capital to maintain the farm land"; (4) unequal access to agricultural loans that would enable blacks to hold on to farm land; (5) undue pressure from well-financed, white agribusinessmen that persuade blacks to relinquish their holdings; (6) the persistence of discrimination in the implementation of land policies; and (7) absentee ownership. Brooks reports that about 1.6 million nonsouthern blacks own land in the rural South today. Many of these persons opt to sell rather than attempt to maintain holdings from a distance.[8] As a result of these factors, it is estimated that blacks are losing 500,000 acres of farm land each year. Two million acres of land were lost by blacks during the period from 1969 to 1978. That loss was equivalent to 57 percent of the active farm land owned by blacks. In a 1983 study of trends in land ownership, Brooks reported that in 1969, blacks owned 6.2 million acres in 133,000 operating farms. In 1978 that was reduced to 4.2 million acres and 57,000 farms. As a result of these situations, blacks' interest in farming as an occupation has decreased dramatically since World War II.[9]

Since World War I the trend for black Americans has been toward broader representation in the occupational structure rather than agricultural pursuits. This can be attributed to such factors as: (1) a greater need for black laborers following the curtailment of the immigration of certain white ethnic nationalities by virtue of the immigration laws of 1917, 1921, and 1924;* (2) pressure from professional and predominantly black civil rights groups such as the National Association for the Advancement of Colored People (NAACP), the National Urban League (NUL), and (as it operated during the 1950s and 1960s) the Congress of Racial Equality (CORE); (3) direct action in the form of pickets, boycotts, "don't buy where you can't work" campaigns, and lobbying; (4) pressure tactics such as sit-ins and stand-ins; (5) the issuing of executive orders; (6) the enactment of fair employment practices, laws, and civil rights legislation outlawing discrimination in hiring practices; and (7) federal and local enforcement of Affirmative Action policies (Affirmative Action programs generally call for either the hiring of or an expressed commitment toward the eventual hiring of a number of minorities equal to their percentage in the population of the particular locale).† Without this set of factors, it does not seem even probable that the employment and occupational gains made by black Americans up to the 1980s would have occurred.

---

*The debate over the role that immigration plays in the employment of black Americans once again became a matter of serious debate during the 1970s and into the 1980s with the arrival of increasing number of Asians, Cubans, and Haitians. This issue is discussed in greater detail in another section of this chapter.

†Affirmative Action is discussed in greater detail in a subsequent section in this chapter.

Striking differences and disparities still persist between the races with respect to employment opportunities and occupational distribution. As shown in Table 2.1, a significantly larger proportion of white Americans as opposed to black Americans continue to be employed in the higher salaried, more prestigious white-collar jobs. Between 1970 and 1981, the proportion of all Americans employed in white-collar jobs rose from 48.3 percent in 1970 to 49.8 percent in 1975, and then to 52.7 percent in 1981. The total percent of male workers, regardless of race, rose from 41.0 to 42.9 percent in all white-collar jobs. Among women, regardless of race, the rise in white-collar employment was from 60.5 to 65.9 percent between 1970 and 1981. One of the apparent explanations for the larger share of white-collar employees among women than among men is the preponderance of women relegated to lower-paying clerical positions in which more than one-third were employed in 1981.

With specific reference to black/white differences in white-collar employment, Table 2.1 also shows that whites are more likely to be employed in those positions than are blacks. For instance, in 1975, more than half (51.7 percent) of all white persons had white-collar jobs. By contrast, less than one-third (30.9 percent) of all blacks were employed in such positions. Moreover, whites were significantly more likely to hold employment in professional and technical positions that blacks. As shown in Table 2.1, in 1975, 15.5 percent of whites held professional and technical positions compared to 9.4 percent for blacks. In 1981, although blacks also had gained in their representation in professional and technical positions, they still lagged behind whites by a difference between 11.6 percent for blacks and 16.7 percent for whites holding such positions.

The absolute number of blue-collar workers for both races increased between 1975 and 1981. However, the actual percentage of workers holding such positions declined in that period. In 1975, for example, almost one-third (32.4 percent) of all white workers were employed in blue-collar jobs. By 1981, this percentage was reduced to 30.7 and the absolute number had climbed from 24,794,000 in 1970 to 27,191,000 in 1981. By contrast, the absolute number of blue-collar workers among blacks rose from 3,097,000 in 1975 to 3,414,000 in 1981. Yet, the actual percentage that these numbers represented of the total number of blacks employed in blue-collar jobs fell from 39.2 in 1975 to 36.5 percent in 1981 (see Table 2.1).

In 1981, blacks were about twice as likely to be employed as nonfarm laborers as whites and almost twice as likely as whites to be employed as farm workers although farm work represented a fraction of the total number of workers among both blacks and whites. However, a great racial disparity is shown in Table 2.1 in terms of employment as service workers.

About one-fourth of all blacks were employed in service jobs in 1981 compared to one-eighth of all white workers. Although disparities of this magnitude may reflect educational differences between the races or the relatively higher proportion of younger blacks, and differences in the numbers of black and white women in the labor force, at least part of this difference may be explained by continuing patterns of discrimination in hiring practices as well as the relative inability of blacks to move into higher level blue- and white-collar jobs.

The absolute number of whites employed as craft and kindred workers seemed to have peaked in 1979 whereas the number of blacks in that area of employment appeared to have peaked in 1980. Both groups experienced a decline in their absolute numbers of craft and kindred workers since then. This downturn in employment within this category may have been a consequence of the overall decline in the economy, especially in the building or construction trades, as well as the lingering difficulties experienced by blacks in gaining access to jobs in the building industries. Less than one-tenth of blacks held jobs as craft and kindred workers in 1981 compared to about one-seventh of all white workers.

The dominance of white men and women in the upper echelon, higher-status, better remunerated professional occupations continued into 1989 (Table 2.2). More than one-fourth (27.4 percent) of all white persons, compared to only 15.7 percent of all blacks, were employed in managerial and professional positions. Whereas little differentiation could be made between the proportion of white men and women holding such positions, black women were significantly more likely than black men to occupy such jobs. Almost one-third (31.1 percent) of all white persons in 1989 were employed in technical, sales, and administrative occupations. By contrast, slightly more than one-fourth of all blacks held these positions. Women, irrespective of race, were more than twice as likely as men to occupy technical, sales, and administrative roles. However, black women are about twice as likely as white women, more than twice as likely as white men, and about three times more likely as black men to hold sales and administrative roles.

While one in eight (11.9 percent in 1989) whites held service occupations, almost one in four blacks filled such positions in the labor market. Black men and women occupied the bottom levels of the occupational scale. This fact is manifested in their overrepresentation in positions categorized as operators, fabricators, laborers, and farmers (Table 2.2).

Despite existing racial disparities in the distribution of jobs, Bernard Anderson points out that between 1984 and 1988, as economic expansion was in full swing, the rate of growth for blacks in sales occupations was almost three times the rate of growth for all sales workers. He also maintains that the rate of growth among black managers and professionals was twice that of all workers in these categories.[10] Nevertheless, underrepresentation of blacks in upper echelon jobs and their inordinate concentration in lower tier positions remain a significant attribute of their labor market participation in the 1990s.

The underrepresentation of blacks in the professions is particularly dramatic in such fields as medicine, dentistry, law, optometry, pharmacy, engineering, and in college and university teaching positions. In

Table 2.1   OCCUPATION OF EMPLOYED WORKERS BY SEX AND RACE: 1960–1981[a]

Occupation group, sex, and race	Total employed (× 1000)						Percentage distribution		
	1960	1970	1975	1979	1980	1981	1970	1975	1981
Total	65,778	78,678	85,846	98,824	99,303	100,397	100.0	100.0	100.0
White-collar workers	28,522	38,024	42,788	50,334	51,882	52,949	48.3	49.8	52.7
Professional and technical	7,469	11,149	12,934	15,378	15,968	16,420	14.2	15.1	16.4
Teachers, except college	1,620	2,645	3,049	3,166	3,209	3,197	3.4	3.6	3.2
Managers and administrators	7,067	8,295	9,006	10,719	11,138	11,540	10.5	10.5	11.5
Salesworkers	4,224	4,857	5,528	6,284	6,303	6,425	6.2	6.4	6.4
Retail trade	2,487	2,959	3,087	3,276	3,225	3,262	3.8	3.6	3.2
Clerical workers	9,762	13,723	15,321	17,953	18,473	18,564	17.4	17.8	18.5
Blue-collar workers	24,057	27,807	28,303	32,669	31,452	31,261	35.3	33.0	31.1
Craft and kindred workers	8,554	10,164	11,107	13,119	12,787	12,662	12.9	12.9	12.6
Operatives, except transport	{11,950	13,916}	9,751	11,111	10,565	10,540	{17.7	11.4	10.5
Transport equipment operatives			3,252	3,671	3,531	3,476		3.8	3.5
Nonfarm laborers	3,553	3,728	4,192	4,768	4,567	4,583	4.7	4.9	4.6
Service workers	8,023	9,719	11,798	13,084	13,228	13,438	12.4	13.7	13.4
Farm workers	5,176	3,127	2,955	2,737	2,741	2,749	4.0	3.4	2.7
Male	43,904	48,990	51,857	57,607	57,186	57,397	100.0	100.0	100.0
White-collar workers	16,423	20,067	21,405	23,786	24,260	24,608	41.0	41.3	42.9
Professional and technical	4,766	6,847	7,592	8,727	8,904	9,100	14.0	14.6	15.9
Teachers, except college	456	892	895	925	936	940	1.8	1.7	1.6
Managers and administrators	5,968	6,972	7,241	8,071	8,219	8,372	14.2	14.0	14.6
Salesworkers	2,544	2,765	3,175	3,451	3,450	3,509	5.6	6.1	6.1
Retail trade	1,006	1,125	1,156	1,222	1,185	1,191	2.3	2.2	2.1
Clerical workers	3,145	3,483	3,398	3,537	3,687	3,626	7.1	6.6	6.3

Table 2.1 (Continued)

Occupation group, sex, and race	Total employed (× 1000)						Percentage distribution		
	1960	1970	1975	1979	1980	1981	1970	1975	1981
Blue-collar workers	20,420	23,033	23,498	26,646	25,642	25,433	47.0	45.3	44.3
Craft and kindred workers	8,332	9,832	10,599	12,367	12,018	11,859	20.1	20.4	20.7
Operatives, except transport	8,617	9,610	6,003	6,678	6,334	6,350	19.6	11.6	11.1
Transport equipment operatives			3,067	3,372	3,248	3,167		5.9	5.5
Nonfarm laborers	3,471	3,591	3,829	4,229	4,040	4,056	7.3	7.4	7.1
Service workers	2,844	3,288	4,461	4,931	5,036	5,097	6.7	8.6	8.9
Farm workers	4,219	2,602	2,492	2,245	2,250	2,260	5.3	4.8	3.9
Female	21,874	29,688	33,989	41,217	42,117	43,000	100.0	100.0	100.0
White-collar workers	12,099	17,957	21,382	26,549	27,621	28,341	60.5	62.9	65.9
Professional and technical	2,703	4,302	5,341	6,651	7,063	7,319	14.5	15.7	17.0
Teachers, except college	1,164	1,753	2,154	2,241	2,273	2,257	5.9	6.3	5.2
Managers and administrators	1,099	1,323	1,764	2,649	2,920	3,168	4.5	5.2	7.4
Salesworkers	1,680	2,092	2,353	2,833	2,853	2,916	7.0	6.9	6.8
Retail trade	1,481	1,834	1,931	2,055	2,040	2,072	6.3	5.7	4.8
Clerical workers	6,617	10,240	11,923	14,416	14,787	14,938	34.5	35.1	34.7
Blue-collar workers	3,637	4,774	4,805	6,022	5,810	5,828	16.1	14.1	13.6
Craft and kindred workers	222	332	509	752	769	802	1.1	1.5	1.9
Operatives, except transport	3,333	4,305	3,748	4,433	4,231	4,190	14.5	11.0	9.7
Transport equipment operatives			185	399	283	309		.5	.7
Nonfarm laborers	82	136	363	538	528	527	.5	1.1	1.2
Service workers	5,179	6,432	7,339	8,154	8,193	8,342	21.7	21.6	19.4
Farm workers	957	525	463	492	492	490	1.8	1.4	1.3

Table 2.1   OCCUPATION OF EMPLOYED WORKERS BY SEX AND RACE: 1960–1981ᵃ (Continued)

Occupation group, sex, and race	Total employed (× 1000)						Percentage distribution		
	1960	1970	1975	1979	1980	1981	1970	1975	1981
White	58,850	70,216	76,411	87,259	87,715	88,709	100.0	100.0	100.0
White-collar workers	27,409	35,659	39,507	45,876	47,267	48,147	50.8	51.7	54.3
Professional and technical	7,138	10,379	11,823	13,912	14,444	14,794	14.8	15.5	16.7
Teachers, except college	1,503	2,393	2,759	2,841	2,885	2,875	3.4	3.6	3.2
Managers and administrators	6,889	7,996	8,578	10,094	10,512	10,867	11.4	11.2	12.3
Salesworkers	4,123	4,677	5,272	5,957	5,963	6,075	6.7	6.9	6.9
Retail trade	2,421	2,852	3,027	3,071	3,005	3,037	4.1	4.0	3.4
Clerical workers	9,259	12,607	13,835	15,913	16,350	16,410	10.0	18.1	18.5
Blue-collar workers	21,277	24,241	24,794	28,462	27,327	27,191	34.5	32.4	30.7
Craft and kindred workers	8,139	9,471	10,279	12,038	11,683	11,590	13.5	13.5	13.1
Operatives, except transport	10,536 }	11,909 }	8,336 }	9,374	8,884	8,836	17.0 }	10.9 }	10.0
Transport equipment operatives			2,792	3,131	2,984	2,938		3.7	3.3
Nonfarm workers	2,602	2,861	3,387	3,918	3,776	3,826	4.1	4.4	4.3
Service workers	5,827	7,518	9,398	10,439	10,593	10,814	10.7	12.3	12.2
Farm workers	4,335	2,798	2,712	2,481	2,527	2,558	4.0	3.5	2.9

Table 2.1 (Continued)

Occupation group, sex, and race	Total employed (× 1000)						Percentage distribution		
	1960	1970	1975	1979	1980	1981	1970	1975	1981
Black	(NA)	(NA)	7,894	9,359	9,313	9,355	(NA)	100.0	100.0
White-collar workers	(NA)	(NA)	2,440	3,296	3,409	3,539	(NA)	30.9	37.8
Professional and technical	(NA)	(NA)	740	985	1,016	1,085	(NA)	9.4	11.6
Teachers, except college	(NA)	(NA)	263	287	287	281	(NA)	3.3	3.0
Managers and administrators	(NA)	(NA)	290	429	418	459	(NA)	3.7	4.9
Salesworkers	(NA)	(NA)	184	232	252	251	(NA)	2.3	2.7
Retail trade	(NA)	(NA)	138	143	165	165	(NA)	1.7	1.8
Clerical workers	(NA)	(NA)	1,224	1,651	1,724	1,744	(NA)	15.5	18.6
Blue-collar workers	(NA)	(NA)	3,097	3,584	3,471	3,414	(NA)	39.2	36.5
Craft and kindred workers	(NA)	(NA)	701	889	904	865	(NA)	8.9	9.2
Operatives except transport	(NA)	(NA)	1,247	1,446	1,368	1,395	(NA)	15.8	14.9
Transport equipment operatives	(NA)	(NA)	427	493	507	498	(NA)	5.4	5.3
Nonfarm laborers	(NA)	(NA)	722	757	691	656	(NA)	9.1	7.0
Service workers	(NA)	(NA)	2,149	2,277	2,271	2,266	(NA)	27.2	24.2
Farm workers	(NA)	(NA)	210	200	162	136	(NA)	2.7	1.5

NA: Not available.

[a]Civilians 16 years old and over. Annual averages of monthly figures. Beginning 1975, not strictly comparable with prior years due to reclassification of occupations. White-collar managers and administrators exclude persons on farms. See Historical Statistics, Colonial Times to 1970, series D182–232, for related but not comparable data.

Source: U.S. Bureau of Labor Statistics, Employment and Earnings, unpublished data.

Table 2.2 EMPLOYED CIVILIANS BY OCCUPATION, RACE, AND SEX
(Percent Distribution)

Occupation and race	Total		Men		Women	
	Apr. 1988	Apr. 1989	Apr. 1988	Apr. 1989	Apr. 1988	Apr. 1989
Total, 16 years and over (thousands)	113,905	116,347	62,719	63,664	51,186	52,683
Percent	100.0	100.0	100.0	100.0	100.0	100.0
Managerial and professional specialty	25.7	26.3	25.7	26.4	25.6	26.2
Executive, administrative, and managerial	12.4	12.7	13.7	14.0	10.9	11.1
Professional specialty	13.2	13.6	12.0	12.4	14.7	15.0
Technical, sales, and administrative support	31.1	30.8	19.9	19.5	44.7	44.5
Technicians and related support	3.1	3.1	2.8	2.8	3.3	3.4
Sales occupations	12.0	11.9	11.3	11.0	12.7	13.0
Administrative support, including clerical	16.1	15.8	5.8	5.7	28.7	28.2
Service occupations	13.3	13.1	9.5	9.6	17.8	17.2
Private household	.7	.7	.1	.1	1.5	1.5
Protective service	1.6	1.6	2.6	2.6	.4	.5
Service, except private household and protective	10.9	10.7	6.9	7.0	15.8	15.2
Precision production, craft, and repair	11.9	11.7	19.7	19.6	2.3	2.1
Operators, fabricators, and laborers	15.1	15.4	20.5	20.6	8.5	9.1
Machine operators, assemblers, and inspectors	6.9	7.1	7.5	7.5	6.1	6.6
Transportation and material moving occupations	4.1	4.1	6.7	6.7	.9	1.0
Handlers, equipment cleaners, helpers, and laborers	4.1	4.2	6.3	6.3	1.5	1.6
Farming, forestry, and fishing	3.0	2.8	4.6	4.4	1.1	1.0

Table 2.2 (Continued)

White

Occupation and race	Total Apr. 1988	Total Apr. 1989	Men Apr. 1988	Men Apr. 1989	Women Apr. 1988	Women Apr. 1989
Total, 16 years and over (thousands)	99,141	100,941	55,119	55,926	44,021	45,015
Percent	100.0	100.0	100.0	100.0	100.0	100.0
Managerial and professional specialty	26.7	27.4	26.8	27.6	26.7	27.2
Executive, administrative, and managerial	13.1	13.5	14.4	14.9	11.5	11.7
Professional specialty	13.7	14.0	12.4	12.7	15.2	15.5
Technical, sales, and administrative support	31.5	31.1	20.1	19.6	45.7	45.4
Technicians and related support	3.0	3.0	2.9	2.9	3.2	3.2
Sales occupations	12.5	12.4	11.9	11.5	13.3	13.6
Administrative support, including clerical	16.0	15.6	5.4	5.2	29.2	28.5
Service occupations	12.0	11.9	8.4	8.7	16.5	15.9
Private household	.6	.6	.1	.1	1.3	1.2
Protective service	1.5	1.6	2.4	2.4	.4	.5
Service, except private household and protective	9.9	9.8	6.0	6.2	14.8	14.2
Precision production, craft, and repair	12.3	12.1	20.4	20.2	2.3	2.0
Operators, fabricators, and laborers	14.3	14.5	19.5	19.4	7.7	8.4
Machine operators, assemblers, and inspectors	6.5	6.7	7.2	7.2	5.5	6.0
Transportation and material moving occupations	3.9	4.0	6.4	6.4	.8	.9
Handlers, equipment cleaners, helpers, and laborers	3.9	3.9	5.9	5.8	1.4	1.5
Farming, forestry, and fishing	3.1	3.0	4.7	4.6	1.1	1.1

Table 2.2 EMPLOYED CIVILIANS BY OCCUPATION, RACE, AND SEX (Continued)

Black

Occupation and race	Total		Men		Women	
	Apr. 1988	Apr. 1989	Apr. 1988	Apr. 1989	Apr. 1988	Apr. 1989
Total, 16 years and over (thousands)	11,394	11,699	5,758	5,775	5,636	5,924
Percent	100.0	100.0	100.0	100.0	100.0	100.0
Managerial and professional specialty	15.5	15.7	13.8	13.0	17.2	18.3
Executive, administrative, and managerial	6.5	6.6	6.6	6.1	6.4	7.0
Professional specialty	9.0	9.1	7.2	6.8	10.8	11.3
Technical, sales, and administrative support	27.3	27.8	16.8	16.5	38.1	38.8
Technicians and related support	2.8	2.9	1.9	2.0	3.7	3.8
Sales occupations	7.2	7.0	5.9	5.4	8.4	8.6
Administrative support, including clerical	17.3	17.9	8.9	9.1	26.0	26.5
Service occupations	23.5	22.4	19.0	17.9	28.1	26.9
Private household	1.7	2.0	.1	.1	3.3	3.8
Protective service	2.8	2.7	4.6	4.7	1.1	.7
Service, except private household and protective	19.0	17.8	14.3	13.1	23.7	22.3
Precision production, craft, and repair	9.0	9.2	15.4	16.2	2.5	2.5
Operators, fabricators, and laborers	22.6	23.1	31.4	33.5	13.6	13.1
Machine operators, assemblers, and inspectors	10.3	10.6	9.8	11.5	10.8	9.7
Transportation and material moving occupations	5.9	5.8	10.5	10.3	1.2	1.4
Handlers, equipment cleaners, helpers, and laborers	6.4	6.8	11.0	11.6	1.6	2.0
Farming, forestry, and fishing	2.1	1.7	3.7	3.0	.5	.4

Source: U.S. Bureau of Labor Statistics, Unpublished data, 1989.

Mainstreaming Outsiders: The Production of Black Professionals, Blackwell provided data that showed that blacks composed only 2.0 percent of all physicians, 2.3 percent of all dentists, 2.1 percent of the engineers, 2.6 of the lawyers, 1.0 percent of the optometrists, and about 1.0 percent of all persons holding faculty positions in predominantly white colleges and universities.[11]

In fact, within all occupational categories, underrepresentation and concentration of black Americans in specific types of jobs are the general rule. As depicted in Table 2.3, one is less likely to find a black architect (3.1%), natural scientist (2.9%), college or university teacher (3.9%) or a librarian, archivist, curator (6.1%) than to find a black employed as a typist (16%), mail and messenger clerks (26.1%), cleaners and personal servants (36%), or a short-order cook (20.7%).

As Bonacich points out,[12] in her characterizations of a dual or split labor market in the United States, racial stratification in the marketplace is widespread. Again, whites dominate the upper-tier, higher paying and more rewarding jobs while blacks are generally concentrated in the lower-paying positions. White persons are the primary gatekeepers and decision-makers who establish criteria for admission to the upper tier, determine the proportion of selectees for such positions so rigidly or with bias as to restrict the selection of blacks to upper-tier positions. Whites also decide when and under what conditions blacks and other minorities, as well as white women not in power, will be elevated to that tier or when they may be prevented from upward mobility out of the lower tier and promotion within either occupational level.

As in any situation characterized by dominance and subordination, dominant group decision-makers can and do exercise inordinate power in the marketplace. It is this persistence of white power to manipulate and control economic activities and the overwhelming desire to protect and safeguard selfish economic interests, often at the expense of blacks and other racial minorities, that helps explain a major impediment to the economic empowerment of black Americans and, in turn, accounts for the overrepresentation of blacks in lower-tier jobs. Protecting vested economic interests is a dominant force in day-to-day operations of the marketplace; it is, indeed, pervasive in areas discussed in the following sections.

MASS MEDIA EMPLOYMENT

Racial stratification is also a major characteristic in the mass media. During the Civil Rights Movement of the 1960s, blacks insisted upon receiving wider opportunities for employment in this industry. They won a few skirmishes and a larger number of blacks were employed. In some areas, gains in employment opportunities for blacks were significant and continue to expand. In others, especially since the mid-1970s, there has been a steady and systematic erosion of those gains.[13]

Table 2.3 EMPLOYED PERSONS, BY SEX, RACE, AND OCCUPATION: 1985

[For civilian noninstitutional population 16 years old and over. Annual average of monthly figures. Based on Current Population Survey; see text, section 1 and Appendix III. Persons of Hispanic origin may be of any race]

Occupation	Total employed (1,000)	Percent of total		
		Female	Black	Hispanic origin
Total	107,150	44.1	9.8	6.2
Managerial and professional specialty	25,851	42.7	5.9	3.3
Executive, administrative, and managerial[a]	12,221	35.6	5.3	3.5
Officials and administrators, public	462	40.7	8.7	3.3
Financial managers	394	35.7	3.1	3.1
Personnel and labor relations managers	110	44.5	5.6	3.3
Purchasing managers	99	24.4	4.0	2.7
Managers, marketing, advertising and public relations	419	23.8	3.9	2.5
Administrators, education and related fields	480	48.2	9.4	2.6
Managers, medicine and health	106	59.2	8.1	4.6
Managers, properties and real estate	342	41.0	5.1	5.9
Management-related occupations	3,318	45.7	6.5	4.0
Accountants and auditors	1,263	44.1	5.9	4.2
Professional specialty[a]	13,630	49.1	6.3	3.0
Architects	130	11.3	3.1	4.6
Engineers[a]	1,683	6.7	2.6	2.6
Electrical and electronic	544	8.3	3.4	2.0
Mechanical	272	3.7	2.2	2.1
Mathematical and computer scientists	571	31.1	5.6	2.8
Computer systems analysts, scientists	359	28.0	5.5	3.1
Natural scientists	376	20.8	2.9	2.4
Health diagnosing occupations[a]	728	14.8	3.2	3.1
Physicians	492	17.2	3.7	3.9
Dentists	131	6.5	2.6	2.1
Health assessment and treating occupations[a]	2,006	85.6	7.0	2.4
Registered nurses	1,447	95.1	6.8	2.1
Therapists	257	76.2	7.2	4.2
Teachers, college and university	643	35.2	3.9	3.0
Teachers, except college and university[a]	3,523	73.0	9.2	3.1
Prekindergarten and kindergarten	329	96.8	11.9	5.4

Table 2.3 (*Continued*)

Occupation	Total employed (1,000)	Percent of total		
		Female	Black	Hispanic origin
Elementary school	1,360	84.0	11.1	2.7
Secondary school	1,175	54.0	7.6	3.2
Counselors, educational and vocational	177	55.9	11.7	5.8
Librarians, archivists, and curators	215	84.7	6.1	2.6
Librarians	201	87.0	6.6	2.8
Social scientists and urban planners	286	42.6	5.2	3.1
Psychologists	150	50.4	6.6	3.4
Social, recreation, and religious workers	873	45.6	12.6	4.7
Social workers	438	66.7	17.6	5.6
Lawyers and judges	671	18.2	3.3	2.3
Writers, artists, entertainers, and athletes	1,725	44.5	4.7	3.3
Technical, sales, and administrative support	33,231	64.7	8.4	5.0
Technicians and related support	3,255	47.2	8.9	4.0
Health technologists and technicians	1,115	83.4	13.6	4.1
Licensed practical nurses	402	96.9	19.6	4.5
Engineering and related technologists and technicians	904	18.1	6.4	4.9
Electrical and electronic technicians	304	13.1	9.1	5.0
Science technicians	211	33.3	8.1	3.8
Technicians, except health, engineering, and science	1,026	36.4	6.2	3.2
Computer programmers	534	34.3	6.4	2.5
Sales occupations	12,667	48.1	5.5	4.4
Supervisors and proprietors	3,316	31.2	3.8	4.0
Sales representatives, finance and business services[a]	2,099	41.0	3.4	2.7
Insurance sales	541	27.7	4.7	2.7
Real estate sales	659	51.6	2.3	2.7
Securities and financial services sales	266	24.6	2.2	1.2
Sales representatives, commodities, except retail	1,509	17.5	2.3	3.1
Sales workers, retail and personal services	5,682	68.5	8.2	5.6
Cashiers	2,174	83.1	12.1	6.4
Sales-related occupations	63	63.7	2.1	3.1

Table 2.3 EMPLOYED PERSONS, BY SEX, RACE, AND OCCUPATION: 1985
(*Continued*)

Occupation	Total employed (1,000)	Percent of total		
		Female	Black	Hispanic origin
Administrative support, including clerical	17,309	80.2	10.4	5.6
Supervisors	712	53.4	12.3	4.5
Computer equipment operators	779	66.4	13.5	5.9
Computer operators	774	66.5	13.5	5.9
Secretaries, stenographers, and typists[a]	5,002	97.7	8.2	4.5
Secretaries	4,059	96.4	6.5	4.3
Typists	880	95.6	16.0	5.8
Information clerks	1,257	90.1	8.4	6.4
Receptionists	679	97.6	6.7	6.2
Records processing occupations, except financial	842	81.1	14.1	7.0
File clerks	290	81.0	17.4	8.5
Financial records processing	2,503	90.3	5.5	4.2
Bookkeepers, accounting, and auditing clerks	2,037	91.5	4.7	4.1
Duplicating, mail and other office machine operators	65	69.4	11.7	8.9
Communications equipment operators	223	88.0	17.7	5.4
Telephone operators	215	88.8	17.9	5.5
Mail and message distributing occupations	805	33.9	19.8	5.4
Postal clerks, except mail carriers	258	41.4	26.1	5.0
Material recording, scheduling, and distributing clerks	1,669	39.9	11.6	7.1
Adjusters and investigators	723	71.8	11.2	6.6
Miscellaneous administrative support[a]	2,728	85.1	12.9	6.8
General office clerks	694	80.1	12.0	6.7
Bank tellers	484	93.0	6.0	6.6
Data entry keyers	353	90.7	19.5	7.6
Teachers aides	379	93.6	17.8	11.1
Service occupations	14,441	60.6	17.5	8.1
Private household[a]	1,006	96.2	28.9	9.8
Child care workers	399	96.9	8.9	4.3
Cleaners and servants	550	95.8	42.3	13.3
Protective service[a]	1,718	13.2	15.1	5.8
Firefighting and fire prevention	209	1.4	5.9	3.7
Police and detectives	652	10.1	13.5	6.1
Guards	722	20.9	20.2	6.6

Table 2.3 (*Continued*)

Occupation	Total employed (1,000)	Percent of total		
		Female	Black	Hispanic origin
Service except private household and protective	11,718	64.4	16.8	8.3
Food preparation and service occupations[a]	5,094	62.5	12.0	8.3
Bartenders	324	47.9	4.9	3.8
Waiters and waitresses	1,367	84.0	4.7	5.5
Cooks, except short order	1,553	51.3	18.4	9.1
Short-order cooks	103	36.5	20.7	4.4
Food counter, fountain, and related occupations	333	79.5	10.0	4.9
Kitchen workers, food preparation	134	74.3	18.0	9.9
Waiters' and waitresses' assistants	350	40.1	12.2	15.2
Health service occupations	1,760	89.9	24.5	5.6
Dental assistants	168	99.0	3.6	7.2
Health aides, except nursing	350	85.6	17.8	7.1
Nursing aides, orderlies, and attendants	1,242	89.9	29.2	4.9
Cleaning and building service occupations[a]	2,815	40.2	25.0	11.1
Maids and housemen	563	83.5	30.8	12.7
Janitors and cleaners	2,049	29.4	24.0	10.9
Personal service occupations[a]	2,049	80.9	11.0	6.8
Barbers	91	15.5	12.9	7.2
Hairdressers and cosmetologists	707	89.9	8.2	7.0
Attendants, amusement and recreation facilities	125	39.9	9.3	4.9
Public transportation attendants	65	78.8	13.2	4.8
Welfare service aides	82	92.6	23.3	13.4
Child care workers, except private household	738	96.1	10.6	5.9
Precision production, craft, and repair	13,340	8.4	7.1	7.4
Mechanics and repairers	4,475	3.4	6.9	6.6
Mechanics and repairers, except supervisors[a]	4,209	3.1	6.9	6.8
Vehicle and mobile equipment mechanics and repairers	1,850	.8	6.2	7.8
Automobile and motorcycle mechanics	906	.7	7.5	8.3
Electrical and electronic equipment repairers	701	8.1	8.3	6.5
Telephone installers and repairers	229	12.8	9.1	6.5

Occupation	Total employed (1,000)	Percent of total		
		Female	Black	Hispanic origin
Construction trades	4,745	2.0	6.7	6.9
Construction trades, except supervisors	4,143	2.1	7.2	7.2
Carpenters	1,259	1.2	4.8	6.4
Extractive occupations	194	1.1	2.6	9.2
Precision production occupations	3,926	22.3	8.1	8.9
Operators, fabricators, and laborers	16,816	25.4	14.7	10.0
Machine operators, assemblers, and inspectors[a]	7,840	40.3	14.3	11.7
Textile, apparel, and furnishings machine operators[a]	1,336	79.8	19.2	15.7
Textile sewing machine operators	760	90.8	14.9	19.9
Pressing machine operators	142	68.6	29.3	15.2
Fabricators, assemblers, and hand working occupations	1,833	30.8	13.0	11.0
Production inspectors, testers, samplers, and weighers	815	51.2	12.5	8.1
Transportation and material moving occupations	4,535	8.3	13.7	7.0
Motor vehicle operators	3,303	10.2	14.1	6.9
Trucks, heavy and light	1,838	2.1	12.9	5.9
Transportation occupations, except motor vehicles	208	2.0	5.8	3.1
Material moving equipment operators	1,024	3.2	13.8	8.0
Industrial truck and tractor operators	398	3.1	20.9	10.2
Handlers, equipment cleaners, helpers, and laborers[a]	4,441	16.7	16.3	10.2
Freight, stock, and material handlers	1,594	16.0	17.0	7.5
Laborers, except construction	1,066	18.0	16.3	10.6
Farming, forestry, and fishing	3,470	15.9	7.8	9.4
Farm operators and managers	1,359	13.9	1.4	1.1
Other agricultural and related occupations	1,948	18.3	11.9	15.6
Farm workers	993	23.3	11.6	17.1
Forestry and logging occupations	101	3.9	17.9	1.8
Fishers, hunters, and trappers	61	5.0	1.1	9.5

[a]Includes other occupations, not shown separately.

Source: U.S. Bureau of Labor Statistics, *Employment and Earnings,* January 1986.

In the film and television industry, this pattern of gains and erosions is particularly noticeable. This assertion has validity despite the notable successes of such talk-show hosts, actors, and industry giants as Bill Cosby, Oprah Winfrey, Bryant Gumbel, Ed Bradley, Eddie Murphy, Denzel Washington, and the continuing but sometimes grudgingly given recognition of other highly competent and versatile blacks in film, including Lou Gossett, Jr., and Danny Glover.

With respect to blacks in the film industry, several important employment patterns have been observed. In 1981, of the 240 movies released, only twelve blacks were seen in leading roles. Of 299 films studied in a survey by the Black Motion Picture and TV Producers Association and released between 1979 and 1981, blacks were hired for less than 3 percent of all speaking roles.[14] According to data released by the Screen Actors Guild (SAG), blacks were awarded about 6 percent of the speaking roles. The major drawback of SAG's statistics is that no distinction is made between "split second comments" and major speaking roles. All are treated equally in their numerical account of racial and ethnic data.[15]

Allegations of racism and discrimination in the film industry are widespread. Such allegations include racism and discrimination in employment as actors and actresses, writers, producers, directors, and photographers for major productions; access to influential agents and studio personnel; as well as in other areas of the industry. This problem is so endemic in the industry that Eddie Murphy, a motion picture box-office superstar of the 1980s, verbalized his abhorrence of racism in Hollywood during the 1988 Oscar Awards Ceremony. Even though SAG and other industry-affiliated organizations have also acknowledged the underrepresentation of blacks, few improvements resulted. For example, in 1988, less than 1 percent of all films produced by the Hollywood industry were directed by blacks. There were no blacks in executive positions sufficiently powerful as to "put a movie on the screen," and only two producers at ABC and NBC were black and CBS had no black producers.[16]

Blacks are not well represented among writers and producers nor among the craftsmen in the industry. It is virtually impossible for blacks to obtain jobs controlled by the International Association of Theatrical and State Employees. This union has been accused of nepotism in the allocation of jobs and of relying heavily on its so-called "experience roster" for hiring. Since most blacks are excluded from the experience roster, they cannot hope to be employed as electricians and carpenters, for example, until the roster is exhausted.[17] Joy Horowitz's March 1989 article on this subject in *Premier Magazine* spoke to "the arrogance of Hollywood's kingpins," who refuse to grant interviews on the subject of racism in the industry's employment practices and who seem committed to the maintenance of their power, exclusivity, and dominance in the industry.[18] A May 1989 study, prepared for the *Hollywood Writers' Report,* by William and Denise Bielby[19] for the Writers' Guild of America (WGA), showed that blacks, Asians, Hispanics, Native Americans, and Eskimos accounted for a paltry 2 percent of WGA's active membership. White males constituted 80 percent of WGA membership. Of the 6,211 members, only 101 were black, 43 Hispanics, 24 Asians, 13 Native Americans, and 4 Eskimos.[20] The Bielby data showed that at the time of their study the most progressive studio for the hiring of minorities was Columbia while the worst records were assigned to MTM Productions and Disney Productions. It was because of its dismal record in the hiring of blacks that the National Association for the Advancement Colored People threatened to boycott and picket Disney Productions.

One consequence of racism and discrimination in hiring is a significant disparity in financial rewards among those who are successful in employment. The Bielbys reported that minorities earn only 63 cents for each dollar earned by white males. The emotional trauma resulting from the discrimination also takes a heavy toll on its victims. Many blacks have reported bouts with prolonged depression, anxiety, insecurity, and low self-esteem. This situation is encountered even among many who have established credentials by virtue of successful projects that were not followed with the kinds of job offers and opportunities received by young white males.[21]

The experiences of blacks in the television industry is quite complex. Bozell, Inc. reported in 1989 that blacks watch 44 percent more television than whites.[22] The average weekly viewing of television was 74.1 hours and 51.4 hours for blacks and whites, respectively. Given the fact that blacks make up at least 28 percent of the viewing audience, which translates into billions of dollars annually for the industry,[23] one might expect that that industry would be more open to equal employment opportunities across racial and ethnic lines. Quite the contrary; blacks are underrepresented in all aspects of the television industry, from actors to broadcasters to ownership of television and radio stations.

The underrepresentation of blacks in electronic and print media (television/radio broadcasting and newspaper personnel) is not only a serious issue concerning employment opportunities, but it also has significant implications for the power of the media in determining the public's perception of blacks in the labor force and general population. If blacks are not prominent in upper-tier, influential policy-making roles that determine coverage and what shall or shall not be aired or published, opportunities for distortion of reality and selective perception by viewers are fostered. Although some improvements in the hiring of blacks in this industry occurred since the 1968 Kerner Commission warned of two worlds in the United States, one distinctly black and the other distinctly white and separate, that progress gives little cause for a sanguine state of mind. Noah W. Griffin reported in 1989 that minorities account for 16.2 percent of all full-time broadcast employees in the United States. Minorities also account for 14.4 percent of full-time employees in the upper-four categories of officials and managers, professionals, technicians, and sales workers. However, minorities constitute 21.3 percent of the national labor force; therefore, parity has not been attained by minorities in the broadcast industry.[24]

Disaggregation of the four top job categories by race reveals just how enormously underutilized blacks are in this industry. Black females and black males represent only 2.4 percent and 2.8 percent, respectively, of all persons holding positions as managers and officials. In the category of professionals, 4.8 percent are black males and 3.4 percent are black females. The double bind of racism and sexism often encountered by black females may be evident also in the fact that black females compose 2.7 percent of persons employed as technicians while, in contrast, black males constitute 8.7 percent of all persons in this category. Blacks represent only about 2.5 percent of all persons employed in media sales but minorities as a group constitute 40 percent of the lowest tier—laborers—in this industry.[25] In the last decade of the twentieth century, blacks remain unlikely to hold positions in the broadcast industry as news directors since black men represent only 0.3 percent of the total number of news directors. Neither are they likely to be found as daily network anchors. Only the late Max Robinson, from ABC News, and Bernard Shaw of CNN have ever held such positions for major networks. Charlene Hunter Gault is a frequent anchor for the "McNeil-Lehrer News Hour." Few blacks have ever served as weekend anchor for the major networks. Recently, perhaps the most notable examples of blacks in this role were Carol Simpson who often anchored the ABC network Saturday Evening News and Cassandra Clayton who occasionally substituted for Maria Shriver on NBC Saturday Evening News. In addition, a growing number of blacks now serve as correspondents or reporters for national network news. Among these are Jacqueline Adams of CBS-Radio and Ron Allen of CBS News, and Noah Nelson of NBC News.

In the 1960s, the overwhelming majority of the 1,760 newspapers in the United States would not hire blacks. Undoubtedly, in response to the escalating demands of blacks and other minorities for broader opportunities in this field, some of those barriers have fallen since that time. However, in 1989, an American Society of Newspaper Editors' Survey indicated that racial minorities constituted only 7.5 percent of the 56,000 newsroom employees and that more than half (54%) of those newsrooms are all white. Three-fifths of the nation's newspapers do not employ even one journalist who can be classified as a racial minority.[26] Hatchett[27] reports that the staffs of top ten newspapers such as *The Washington Post*, the *New York Times*, and the *Baltimore Sun*, range from 10 to 15 percent minority. Their success is attributed to such factors as their elite status, higher salaries, major resources, and challenging reporting environment. However, he cautions that that success has to be measured in light of the fact that these papers are located in cities in which the black and Hispanic population ranges from 50 to 70 percent of total city population. Therefore, it is not unreasonable to expect such newspapers to employ a much greater proportion of blacks and Hispanics on their staffs.

As suggested earlier, the paucity of blacks in decision-making roles such as that occupied by Robert Maynard, publisher of the *Oakland Tribune,* or as editors, has implications for perceptions of blacks by the American public. This fact is of special importance with respect to the way newspapers and broadcasters treat or depict blacks in the world of work. As will be detailed in a subsequent section, although blacks are overrepresented among the poor in America, the majority of poor Americans are white. This fact is rarely mentioned by the media and that failure often leaves the impression that public policies designed to alleviate the untoward problems of the poor are primarily, if not exclusively, for blacks and other minorities. Welfare mothers, more often than not, are depicted as black or Hispanic even when there is ample evidence to show that the majority of welfare (translated "AFDC mothers") in the United States are white women. The poor interested in obtaining jobs are depicted as white while the poor queuing up for hand-outs are vividly portrayed as black. These shots on the evening news further distort reality and reinforce race-specific stereotypes.

The complexity of the employment profile in the mass media industry is further evident by the interest shown by several decision-makers, leaders of major media organizations and in the corporate structure, to take aggressive steps designed to make this industry more representative of the nation's population. Caucuses and national/regional organizations of black journalists and broadcasters have consistently raised the level of consciousness about this issue. Consequently, some news organizations, led, perhaps, by the Gannett group, are becoming more successful in their efforts to expand equal employment opportunity.

Network programs in which blacks play a leading or prominent role remained among the top attractions throughout the latter half of the 1980s. These include "The Bill Cosby Show," "A Different World," "227," "In the Heat of the Night," and "Amen." Despite attacks against Bryant Gumbel for candid remarks he made about some members of his staff at the request of management, his *Today Show* remained the highest rated morning program in its category in 1989. However, the *Today Show* lost its top rating in 1990. Oprah Winfrey in 1989 won a third consecutive Emmy for the best talk show in her category. Black celebrities obtained lucrative television commercial contracts. Perhaps the most ubiquitous of these are Michael Jordan, Bill Cosby, "Magic" Johnson, Bo Jackson and Ray Charles. Their commercials are responsible for the sales of millions of dollars in products ranging from Coke, Pepsi-Cola, "Air Jordan" Nikes, Hanes underwear, Jell-O pudding to Kentucky Fried Chicken and Disney World. However, many persons whose personal achievements would, under most circumstances, have led to major opportunities to advertise in commercials, were neglected. For example, Jerry Rice, a wide receiver for the San Francisco 49er professional football team won the Most Valuable Player Award for his performance in the 1989 Super Bowl but was literally snubbed for endorsements. The most prominent endorsements received by quarterback Doug Williams of the Washington Redskins and the 1988 MVP of the Super Bowl seemed to have come from black-owned *Ebony* magazine, not from television or radio commercials. Relatively few black female celebrities have been successful in obtaining opportunities in the endorsement enterprise. Among those black females observed in the late 1980s were Lena Horne, Evelyn Ashford, and Jacqueline Joyner-Kersee. However, none approximated the incomparable successes of either Bill Cosby or Michael Jordan. The failure of black female athletes to receive lucrative endorsements compared to the inordinate success of untried white females is evident in the experiences of Zena Garrison, who ranks fifth in the world as a tennis player, and Jennifer Capriati, who only turned professional in 1990. Garrison, who is black, never had a major endorsement until 1990 while Capriati, who is a white teenager, received multimillion dollar endorsements as she turned professional and was unranked.

BLACKS IN SPORTS

Since the historic appearance of Jackie Robinson as a professional baseball player for the old Brooklyn Dodgers in 1946, black Americans have become a fixture in the most visible team sports in the United States. Their presence as the majority on some collegiate basketball teams and their starring roles on some collegiate football teams, as well as in professional basketball, football, and baseball, have created the impression that the athletic route is a guaranteed path to economic success. This is an illusion at best. Only 8 percent of all athletes who play collegiate basketball and football are drafted each year for professional teams. Only 2 percent of these athletes actually sign a professional contract, and then their average career lasts from approximately three to five years in professional basketball and professional football, respectively.[28]

Nevertheless, blacks play a prominent role on the field in professional sports. In baseball, several blacks have reached the $2 to $3 million per year salary club. These include Dwight Gooden (New York Mets); Jim Rice (Boston Red Sox); Ozzie Smith (St. Louis Cardinals); Eddie Murray (L. A. Dodgers); Rickey Henderson (Oakland Athletics); Willie Wilson (Kansas City Royals); Tim Raines (Montreal Expos); Andre Dawson (Chicago Cubs); and Kirby Puckett (Minnesota Twins).[29] Superstars in basketball, such as Michael Jordan, "Magic" Johnson, Moses Malone, Isaiah Thomas, and Kareem Abdul Jabarr, whose retirement in 1989 was chronicled on television throughout the season—all among the highest scoring players in that sport—call attention to the visibility of blacks in the profession.

The casual viewer of sports television or spectators at various games may be greatly impressed by the visibility of blacks in basketball, football, and baseball. In fact, 75 percent of the players in the National Basketball Association (NBA) are black; 54 percent of the players in the National Football League (NFL) are black, and about 17.9 percent of baseball players are American-born blacks.[30] As mentioned earlier, several black athletes, such as Magic Johnson, Bo Jackson, Dominique Wilkins, and Michael Jordan earn millions each year over and above their salaries as athletes from endorsements of products ranging from orange juice to sneakers to soft drinks to men's underwear.

For those who have fought for expanded opportunities for blacks in sports, such as a chance to perform at the so-called "thinking" positions in football, significant achievements were registered by blacks during the 1980s. For example, three blacks were starting quarterbacks during the NFL 1988–1989 season: Doug Williams (Washington Redskins); Randall Cunningham (Philadelphia Eagles); and Warren Moon (Houston Oilers). Williams was the first black to start a Super Bowl game (his team won the 1988 championship and he was named the MVP of the game). Cunningham and Moon were the starters in the 1989 "Pro-Bowl." Other professional teams in 1989–1990 (e.g., Philadelphia Eagles) had a black as a back-up quarterback. At the intercollegiate level, black quarterbacks started the 1989 Rose Bowl and Fiesta Bowl games, and there were blacks in starting quarterback positions for several additional 1989 "bowl" teams representing almost all parts of the country.[31] Advancements of this sort attest to the progress made by blacks in sports that have substantially improved the economic status for some of them. High salaries and lucrative endorsements for a select few mask some of the more profound problems remaining in professional sports—even in the 1990s. For example, in those areas dominated by black players, blacks are generally excluded from ownerships, coaching, and managerial jobs. In the 1988–1989 NBA season, 22 percent of the managers (Don Chaney of Houston; Bernie Bickerstaff of Seattle; Wesley Unsoeld of Washington; Willis Reed of the New Jersey Nets) were black. In the 1989–1990 NBA season, the New York Knickerbockers appointed a black, Stu Jackson, as head coach of that team. Only 6 percent of the front officer management in the NBA was black. No black had ever been hired as a general manager of an NFL team and relatively few blacks remained as assistant coaches for professional football teams.[32] However, in 1989, the historic barrier against black ownership of professional sports teams fell when Bertram Lee and Peter Bynoe purchased the Denver Nuggets, an NBA team, for a reported $65 million, and Art Shell was named Head Coach of the Los Angeles Raiders, an NFL team. In 1990, a black woman, Elaine C. Weddington, was named assistant general manager of the Boston Red Sox—the first black female professional baseball executive.

Compared to basketball and football, professional baseball, even 43 years after Jackie Robinson broke the color barrier against players, has not progressed very far. Only in 1989 was the fourth black ever to manage a professional baseball team hired. The hiring of Cito Gaston to manage the Toronto Blue Jays meant that he and Frank Robinson of the Baltimore Orioles were the only blacks managing professional baseball teams. Blacks have extreme difficulty landing managerial jobs of "farm teams" for the major leagues and remain more likely to be hired in low-level front-office positions.

One explanation for the intransigence of baseball with respect to affirmative efforts to expand employment opportunities for blacks is the continued presence of decision-makers who adhere to demeaning stereotypes concerning the intellectual capacities of blacks and the dominance of brute force over their *thinking* capacity as rationalizations for excluding blacks from important positions. Another factor is the reliance on cronyism, friendship-cliques, and networks in the selection of incumbents for high-level baseball positions. As members of an organization of black ex-baseball players called the "Baseball Network" insist, blacks are generally excluded from access to the brokers of power and influence.

Following the widely covered Al Campanis statements on the ABC Nightline program in 1986 concerning the ability of blacks to perform leadership roles, Baseball Commissioner Peter Uberroth promised the American public that he would take aggressive action to increase the employment of blacks and other minorities in all aspects of baseball. One of his most immediate actions was his decision in 1987 to hire Harry Edwards, a major leader in the field of Sociology of Sport and then an Associate Professor of Sociology at the University of California/Berkeley, as his special assistant. It was expected that Dr. Edwards would develop a strategy by which more blacks would be hired as field managers and in other high level positions.

In 1988, Commissioner Uberroth reported that within the previous two years the employment of blacks in baseball jumped from only 2 percent to 10 percent. Uberroth's report was strongly criticized by Hank Aaron, the reigning "home run king" of baseball and one of the few blacks holding a major front-office position in baseball, for the misperceptions of progress generated by his report. However, Aaron conceded that while virtually no progress had been attained with respect to blacks in general or field manager positions, employment of blacks had increased in other areas. In other words, greater progress had been achieved in the hiring of blacks as chief financial officers, heads of departments ranging from accounting and advertising to ticketing.[33] Despite the progress evident in the selection of William "Bill" White in 1989 as the first black person to be President of a major league sport (The National Baseball League), even with the frequent firings of managers, blacks are not offered such jobs. Again, the combination of undue reliance on racist stereotypes, the entrenched cronyism, resistance by some owners, and the beliefs that some blacks may simply be "too nice" render baseball leadership as a white male bastion of exclusivity in the 1990s.

Blacks are also less likely to be selected as agents for athletes and entertainers. Selection of agents, although a personal choice by black and white athletes, is often a response to perceived racism among white owners and directors of player personnel. Athletes may not believe that black agents have sufficient clout, respect, experience, and skill as white agents that will result in the most lucrative contract for them. Such beliefs help to account for Nelson George's[34] observation that an overwhelming majority of black stars employ white agents. Attitudes expressed by athletes may also reflect an internalization of notions of white superiority by several athletes and entertainers.[35] Improvements in the employment of agents from the black population depend almost entirely on the efforts made by black athletes and entertainers themselves.

CORPORATE AND UNION EMPLOYMENT

It appears that blacks often gain positions of power and influence in institutions as they are in a phase of decline. This situation seems to be evident in the case of labor unions. In the early part of the 1980s, blacks constituted 15 percent of total union membership of approximately 20 million. By the end of the decade, it was reported that the 2.5 million black members of labor unions represented 26 percent of the total union membership of 17.7 million workers.[36] Black loyalty to unions continued to rise as white workers deserted unions following former President Ronald Reagan's successful effort to dismantle the Air Traffic Controllers Union. Loyalty combined with perceptions of unions as primarily responsible for gains in wages and other benefits helped account for the retention of blacks in unions and, consequently, their growing influence in leadership positions in some unions.

At the beginning of 1989, blacks served as president of the National Education Association (the largest union in the world), the National Union of Hospital and Health Care Employees, the American Federation of Government Employees, and the National Alliance of Postal and Federal Employees. Blacks were vice presidents of 19 major unions ranging from the American Federation of State, County and Municipal Employees (AFSME) to the United Steel Workers of America, and the International Ladies Garment Workers Union. In addition, these positions served workers in aerospace, agricultural implementation, auto employees, communication workers, postal employees, service employees, and retail, wholesale, and department store employees. A black was the Executive Director of the National Football Players Association and three were in the position of Secretary-Treasurer of their unions. Despite these achievements, as well as a tradition of union alliance with civil rights organizations, blacks have not been as successful in sharing leadership roles, power, and influence in the AFL-CIO, or in the garment and textile unions that traditionally have had Jewish leadership. However, blacks are in the forefront of the movement to change conditions for participants in the American labor force. Specifically, blacks are among the leaders who focus attention on "family issues" in negotiating contracts. Family issues include day care for workers, paid leave to care for sick members of their families, parental leave, housing benefits, and expanded health benefits.

The major corporations have rarely moved beyond tokenism in the employment of blacks. Davis and Watson[37] reported that in 1981 blacks represented only 4.2 percent of all U. S. Corporate officials and managers. By 1989, that proportion only approximated 5 percent.[38] However, 97 percent of all senior positions in corporations are still held by white males and less than 1 percent are held by blacks and other minorities.[39] Tokenism and exclusion have limited the numbers of blacks occupying positions of seniority in the corporate world. The entry of blacks into upper-level corporate management has been thwarted by the failure of white senior corporate executives to come to terms with new demographic realities. One of those realities is the increasing dependence of the nation on a workforce that is becoming more heavily weighted with blacks and other minority groups. But, tokenism is too widespread with respect to the upward mobility of blacks into senior management positions in the corporate world. Some researchers have pointed to "an artificial ceiling" on the number of blacks, other minorities, and white women who can penetrate top managerial and executive positions in the corporate world.[40] With the purchase of and change in management of TLC Beatrice International Holdings by Reginald F. Lewis, a black Wall Street financier, he became the first black Chief Executive Officer (CEO) of a Fortune 100 Company.

In recent years, several blacks have risen to important management positions in some of America's most prestigious corporations. Earl Graves' profile of the "twenty-five most powerful black managers in corporate America[41] showed that these *men* (no women made the list) have line authority over budgets and revenues totaling over $1 trillion."[42] They are employed at companies that have demonstrated a strong commitment to diversity in the workforce and locating the best available talent that enables these companies to achieve their own business and cultural objectives. These companies have not only articulated affirmative action as a policy but have more steadily moved toward aggressive implementation of such policies. For that reason, *Black Enterprise Magazine* published a list of the fifty best places for blacks to work in 1989 (Table 2.4). The American Bankers Association reported in 1989 that minorities occupied 15.9 percent of the top-level positions in America's largest banks. This organization also reported that whereas the number of minorities in professional positions rose from 12.3 percent in 1978 to 15.9 percent in 1988, the percent of black professionals in its institutions changed only slightly from 8 to 9 percent over the same period. The change in blacks holding positions as officials and managers, in toto, was only from 5.4 to 6.9 percent over a ten year period.[43] Clearly, blacks remain seriously underrepresented in upper-echelon management positions in the corporate world.

This underrepresentation may in part be attributed to the fact that only 5 percent of holders of MBA degrees are black and the pool of blacks eligible for management positions is relatively smaller than that of whites. While some truth is found in that assertion, such thinking masks the failure of corporations to select highly trained and experienced blacks for promo-

Table 2.4 BLACKS IN AMERICAN CORPORATIONS

Name of corporation	Number of employees	Number and percent black and/or minorities	Number of managers	Percent black and/or minorities as managers
AT & T	302,895	43,469 (14% = B)	121,915	9,446 (7.7% = B)
AMTRAK	22,031	5,481 (24.9% = B)	1,626	218 (13.4% = B)
Anheuser-Busch	41,000	8,393 (20.5% = M)	5,500	646 (11% = M)
Atlantic-Ritchfield	20,184	1,711 (8.5% = B)	4,344	153 (3.5% = B)
Avon Products	8,062	1,002 (12% = B)	4,207	348 (8% = B)
Chase-Manhattan	25,000[a]	5,995 (23% = B)	8,230	1,298 (8% = B)
Chrysler	90,000	(26% = M)		(11.4% = M)
Coca-Cola	9,337[a]	1,899 (20% = B)	1,522	116 (8% = B)
Coors	7,395	(4.4% = B)	877	(31% = B)
Eastman Kodak	75,324	5,574 (7.4% = B)	7,711	202 (2.6% = B)
Equitable	17,987	1,975 (11% = B)	5,760	319 (5.5% = B)
Exxon	41,410	5,844 (14.1% = B)	6,060	326 (5.4% = B)
Federal Express	56,098	13,650 (24% = B)	3,657	302 (8% = B)
Ford	180,500[a]	29,421 (16.3% = B)	N/A	N/A (7.5% = B)
Gannett	38,123	4,832 (12.7% = B)	5,352	389 (5.4% = B)
General Mills	71,773	10,534 (14.8% = B)	4,912	275 (5.6% = B)
General Motors	114,563	12,239 (9.4% = B)	42,616	4,309 (10.1% = B)
Hallmark	13,656	1,204 (9% = B)	1,569	58 (4% = B)
IBM	226,850	20,450 (9% = B)	N/A	(12.3% = B)
Johnson & Johnson[a]	29,500[a]	3,374 (11.4% = B)	5,778	302 (6.3% = B)
Kellogg	6,987	936 (13% = B)	836	69 (8% = B)
Kraft	37,453	4,567 (12.2% = B)	5,280	259 (4.9%)
McDonald's	118,159	30,659 (25.9% = B)	9,453	1,587 (16.8% = B)
Merck & Co.	15,000	1,456 (9.7% = B)	3,200	129 (4.0% = B)
N. C. Mutual	840	(99% = B)	13	(92% = B)
J. C. Penney	177,954	15,835 (8.9%)	23,520	1,372 (5.8% = B)
Pepsi-Cola	16,761	1,573 (9.4% = B)	2,685	159 (6.0% = B)
Philip Morris	68,500[a]	(27.1% = B)		(15.4% = B)
Port Authority	8,721	1,851 (21% = B)	1,364	187 (13.7% = B)
Ryder	32,473	4,655 (14.3% = M)	3,978	(6.5% = B)
J. E. Seagram	3,949	644 (16.3% = B)	1,400	157 (11.2% = B)
U. S. Armed Forces	2,100,000	(19.8% = B)		(6.6% = B)
Xerox	53,162	(13.8% = B)	7,191	(11.4% = B)
Aetna Life	41,023	5,033 (12.3% = B)	2,371	64 (2.7% = B)
Am. Airlines	65,154	5,595 (8.6% = B)	840	21 (2.5% = B)
Apple Computers	6,979	205 (3% = B)	1,492	26 (1.8% = B)
Bristol-Myers	34,100	(18% = M)		(10% = M)
Chevron	40,000	3,420 (8.5% = B)	6,000	200 (3.3% = B)
Digital	140,000	(16.6% = M)		(10% = M)
General Electric	198,550	21,760 (11% = M)	20,940	980 (4.7% = M)
Hewlett-Packard	57,328	(4% = M)	9,025	(10.6% = M)
Inner City Broadcasting	175	89 (50% = B)		
Mobil	33,259[a]	3,501 (10.5% = B)	5,077	277 (4.3% = B)
H. J. Russell	490	236 (48% = B)	62	36 (58% = B)
Sears	95,000	(18.8% = B)	3,240	(7.5% = B)
Stroh Brewery	4,800	(20% = M)	853	(10% = M)

Table 2.4 (Continued)

Name of corporation	Number of employees	Number and percent black and/or minorities	Number of managers	Percent black and/or minorities as managers
Time	22,800	4,020 (17% = B)	3,830	275 (7% = B)
US West	68,497	(4.4% = B)		(3.7% = B)
Soft Sheen Products	617	(99% = B)	89	(98% = B)

[a]Domestic employees.

B: Black employees.

M: Minorities.

Source: Adapted by permission from "The 50 Best Places for Blacks to Work," Black Enterprise (New York: The Earl E. Graves Publishing Co., February 1989): 73–91.

tion or to mount training programs that will enable their own junior level black employees to break through the "glass ceiling," have a modicum of a chance for upward mobility, and hire sufficient numbers of blacks and whites committed to acting as mentors to blacks who enter in lower-echelon positions. It ignores the fact that tokenism, exclusion of blacks from informal social networks, business conversation, limited interracial socialization and associations external to the workplace, and maltreatment as well as hostility, bigotry, and pernicious discrimination by some white associates often force blacks to abandon the corporate world. Alleviating these conditions will lead to a substantial increase in the numbers of blacks hired and retained in large corporations.

Without question, some corporations have initiated actions designed to address the problem of the underrepresentation of blacks in the corporate world. These actions include the implementation of more aggressive outreach and recruitment policies; the creation of "talent identification lists," the establishment of management seminars, workshops and training programs for employees and potential employees, and the re-structuring of their performance evaluation and promotion systems.[44]

FACTORS ASSOCIATED WITH EMPLOYMENT

The nature of the job market has changed radically since the 1960s. Evidence of this transformation is the shift in the proportion of jobs that require higher levels of education. As a result, it is estimated by the Hudson Institute of Indianapolis and the Bureau of Labor Statistics report, Projections 2000, that by the year 2000 the majority of all jobs will require post-secondary education at minimum.[45] In some areas, such as metropolitan Boston, where the economy is closely tied to high technology, that estimate reaches as high as 80 percent of jobs requiring post-secondary education.[46] Therefore, educational attainment occupies a central role in determining eligibility for employment. However, as will be subsequently discussed, the interplay between race and education is also crucial for blacks in job attainment.

The business community has taken the leadership in the effort to assure a better educated workforce. This action is in part motivated by vested interests and in part by a recognition of the urgency of the problem of poor quality education received by many young Americans. The National Center for Education Statistics estimates that 140,000 partnerships between public schools and the business community are in operation. Such collaborations are designed to effect educational reform, implement curriculum changes in public schools, and halt the staggering drop-out rates in urban high schools.[47]

Although many job-seekers may, indeed, be very well educated, their skills may not be suitable for the available jobs. Consequently, such persons are less competitive for some of the more lucrative and personally rewarding positions. Just as technical training programs are often necessary for the relatively unskilled, training programs are invaluable in cases of mismatch between job needs and the individual's current skills for more highly skilled workers.

Another salient factor associated with job attainment is the ability to make informed choices or decisions regarding jobs available. Making informed choices is a complex issue involving strength of interest in a specific type of work, job demands or expectations and confidence that the individuals are capable of meeting those demands, salary or wage structure, quality of the working environment, opportunities for upward mobility, job satisfaction, and belief in one's capacity to make significant contributions to the job.

In addition to such critical factors as education, available training programs and the interests that job-seekers have in taking advantage of them as well as the ability to make informed decisions or choices, the acquisition of a job is also related to such factors as transportation, presentation of self during interviews, location of the job, and many others.[48] However, most important for blacks, other minorities, and white women is the persistence of discrimination in the workplace. Race and gender discrimination continues to lock out such underpreferred groups from many jobs, thereby sustaining a situation of structural inequality throughout the United States.

By the year 2000, it is expected that the white labor force will have grown by 15 percent but, because the white population is aging and its birth rate is much lower than that of blacks, the growth of blacks workers in the labor force is estimated to be about twice that of whites.[49] It is further projected that the pattern of job creation observed in 1989–1990 will remain virtually unchanged. In other words, this means declining jobs in manufacturing, mining, and farming and expanded job creation in the catch-all service sector. However, the jobs created are likely to be low-paying ones. Research findings by Barry Bluestone and Bennet Harrison[50] show that there has already been a proliferation of low-wage jobs, a fact that was either disregarded or minimized by the Reagan Administration in its enthusiastic claims about growth in labor force participation and falling unemployment rates. For example, between 1979 and 1985, at the same time that many upper-echelon jobs were indeed developed, 44 percent of the "net new jobs created" were remunerated at poverty-level incomes.[51]

As this pattern rigidifies, two classes of workers, one core, the other peripheral and expendable, are being created.[52] Given the persistence of a systematic pattern of discrimination in the marketplace that has solidified racial stratification between the upper and lower tiers of the labor market, radical changes will be mandated to move increasing numbers of blacks into the category of "core" workers. It is also important to understand that 20 percent of American workers are classified as "contingent workers," or part-timers who either are unable to obtain full-time work or choose less than full-time employment. Blacks constitute a significant proportion of those persons who are not able to find a full-time job.

All the fastest growing jobs during the 1990s will require the American society to address head-on barriers to economic opportunity in order to meet the demands of a highly competitive global economy and strengthen the nation's need for competence, imagination, and ingenuity. As shown in Table 2.5, the fastest growing jobs include, inter alia, those in high technology (e.g., computer applications and electronic engineers). There will also be a continuing need for lawyers, nurses, and accountants.

Implicit in the projected need for so many correction officers and jailers is the assumption that the nation's prison population will substantially grow and more prisons will be constructed. The increase in the prison population may be, in fact, related to the persistence of structural inequality—poverty, low education, discrimination in the marketplace.

The fastest declining occupations are depicted in Table 2.6. These jobs reflect the anticipated greater automation of some types of work (e.g., perhaps robots replacing household workers, the increasing mechanization of agriculture, and automated postal operations). The anticipated slow-down in college and faculty hiring suggests declining enrollments associated with a slow population growth in the traditional college-going cohorts. However, blacks, particularly, should have a special interest in these projections. Because of their underrepresentation in the college and university teaching profession, the pressing demand for greater diversity in the nation's colleges and universities may stimulate accelerated recruitment and hiring of blacks for faculty positions. Here, as elsewhere, the question of how committed is the nation to reduce, if not eradicate, institutional racism and discrimination becomes the critical variable for determining the success or failure of black Americans to take advantage of jobs that will become available during the 1990s and into the twenty-first century.

Table 2.5   FASTEST GROWING OCCUPATIONS: 1984–1995 AND PROJECTED
1995 LEVELS
(In Thousands)

| | Employment[a] | | | |
| | | | 1995[b] | |
Occupation	1984	Low	Moderate	High
Total	106,843	117,268	122,760	128,718
Computer programmers	341	559	586	609
Computer systems analysts	308	498	520	539
Medical assistants	128	195	207	216
Electrical and electronic engineers	390	571	597	617
Electrical and electronics technicians	404	579	607	629
Computer operators excluding peripheral	241	337	353	366
Lawyers	490	635	665	691
Correction officers & jailers	130	171	175	180
Accountants & auditors	882	1,135	1,189	1,235
Mechanical engineers	237	303	317	329
Registered nurses	1,377	1,753	1,829	1,908

[a]Based on low, moderate, and high assumptions.

[b]Includes other occupations not shown separately.

Source: U. S. Bureau of Census, Monthly Labor Review, November 1985.

INCOME DISTRIBUTION BY RACE

By whatever measure employed, blacks continue to be paid substantially less money than whites for their labor. Not only is there a tremendous disparity between the races in income received, but the money gap between rich and poor is widening. This disparity may be illustrated by an analysis of racial differences in per capita income, median family income, in ownership of net wealth, and income differences between the poor and the rich.

As expected from the overall income gap between blacks and whites in the United States, per capita income of blacks has historically fallen substantially below that of whites. In 1981, for example, the per capita income for the nation as a whole was $8,306 (i.e., the amount of money per person for all the people in the United States). A year later, the per capita income for the nation as a whole was $8,898. Among blacks, the change in per capita income was from $4,937 in 1981 to $5,394 in 1982. Hence, the money income gap for blacks widened in a single year from $3,369 to $3,504. Between 1982 and 1988, per capita incomes in the

Table 2.6   FASTEST DECLINING OCCUPATIONS: 1984–1995 AND PROJECTED
1995 LEVELS
(In Thousands)

Occupation	Employment[a] 1984	1995[b] Low	Moderate	High
Total	106,843	117,268	122,760	128,718
Stenographers	239	136	143	148
Private household workers	993	778	811	840
Telephone installers, repairers	111	87	92	96
Sewing machine operators	676	534	563	586
Textile machine operators	279	223	235	247
Industrial truck and tractor operators	389	326	342	357
Farm workers	1,079	911	958	968
College and university faculty	731	636	654	875
Pressing machine operators, tenders	116	101	106	110
Postal service clerks	317	274	290	309

[a]Based on low, moderate, and high assumptions.

[b]Includes other occupations not shown separately.

Source: U. S. Bureau of Census, Monthly Labor Review, November 1985.

United States accelerated by virtue of the overall economic recovery that occurred during that period. In 1988, per capita money income for the nation reached an unprecedented high of $13,123; for whites per capita income was $13,896 while for blacks it was $8,271 or a widening gap of $5,625. The per capita money income for Hispanics was $7,956 in 1988.

The position of blacks in the labor force remains weak compared to that of whites even as their overall status improves in consonance with the economic expansion of the latter part of the 1980s. Andrew Brimmer argues that this weakness "translates into a sizeable deficit in black income."[53] This observation is illustrated by the fact that in 1982 the $146.2 billion in money income ("total sum of gross receipts") received by blacks represented 7.09 percent of the total money income of $2,061.7 billion. By 1987, the black share of money income for blacks had risen to $220 billion or 7.42 percent of total money income. But in 1982, blacks constituted 10.28 percent of the civilian labor force and in 1987, they constituted 12.25 percent. Brimmer's argument is that had the black share of income equalled their proportion in the civilian labor force, their money income would then have been $321.2 billion in 1987. Thus, the 1987 money income for blacks was $101.2 billion less than it should have been.[54]

Unmistakably, the rich are getting richer and the poor are getting poorer in the United States. Although this point will be amplified in a subsequent section in this chapter, some preliminary evidence may be offered in this context. As this nation came out of World War II, the concern for a more equitable distribution of income was apparent in the federal government. From that time up to about 1975, this movement toward greater equity in general income continued. In 1960, for instance, Brimmer noted that families who composed the lowest 20 percent of the population received 4.8 percent of money income. By 1975 that proportion had risen to 5.4 percent. However, during the same period, Brimmer's research showed that the money income of people in the middle income bracket dropped slightly from 17.8 percent to 17.6 percent in 1960 and 1975, respectively. A more noticeable decline was registered by persons in the top 20 percent of the income bracket since their proportion fell from 15.9 percent of the money income in 1960 to 15.5 percent in 1975.[55]

Beyond 1975 the trend toward reducing income disparities has come to a screeching halt. In fact, inequities between the rich and the poor became more pronounced after 1975, and will widen even further as a result of the enactment of the Economic Recovery Tax Act of 1982. With the nation plummeting into its fourth recession of the past decade, in 1980, the families in the top 5 percent of income groups received about three times (15.7 percent of total) as much money income as did the families in the lowest groups who received 5.3 percent of money income.[56] In effect, such gains through tax breaks, loopholes in the tax laws, and special deductions result essentially in a form of welfare for the rich that is not actually available to people in the poorer categories of the society. This situation is further demonstrated by data released in April 1984 by the nonpartisan Congressional Budget Office which showed that a family with an income of less than $10,000 would lose $390 and receive only a $20 tax cut in 1984, while a family with an income of $80,000 or more would gain $8,390 in tax benefits as a result of the Reagan tax cuts and welfare changes.

In 1986, the richest fifth of the population received 46.1 percent of all household income while the poorest fifth received only 4.7 percent.[57] Lardner[58] reported that a 1989 study by the House Ways and Means Committee revealed continuing income polarization. The study showed that between 1979 and 1987 the average household income of the richest families increased by 11.1 percent or from $61,917 to $68,775. During the same period, the average household income of the poorest fifth increased by only 6.1 percent or from $5,439 to $5,807 in 1987 dollars.[59] During that period, the standard of living for the bottom fifth of the population fell by 9 percent but increased by 19 percent for the upper, richest fifth of the population.[60]

How can this widening gap be explained? Passell[61] and Sege's separate interviews of leading economists in the United States indicate that income polarization between the poor and the rich may be explained by a combination of Reagan's economic policies and societal forces. They attribute the income gap to such factors as: (1) the continuing increase in households headed by single parents, (2) growth in the number of working women, (3) "an increasingly global economy," (4) an expanding income gap between the better educated, particularly college graduates, and high school graduates, (5) stabilized real wages among men, (6) the shift from an economy based largely upon manufacturing to one based on services, (7) increase in households in which both spouses are in the labor market, (8) the changing value of the American dollar which resulted in cheaper imports, (9) an increase in the number of small families among incumbents of professional occupations, (10) a fall in noncash government benefits for the bottom fifth parallelled by income gains generated by tax benefits for the more affluent top fifth of the population, (11) a 25 percent reduction in "state-determined AFDC payments to young parents," and (12) loss of net pay to the poor resulting from higher payroll taxes for Social Security.[62]

This analysis also showed that between 1979 and 1987, there was a 46 percent increase in the number of single-parent families below the poverty level. At the same time, the rapid increase in the participation of minorities and women in the labor force "depressed earnings for young, unskilled workers."[63] However, as Sawhill asserts, the more affluent top fifth experienced a significant rise in capital gains, investment income, dividends, interest, and private pension payments.[64] Such gains reflected the benefits accrued to the wealthy as a consequence of the Economic Recovery Act passed by Congress during the first Reagan Administration. Simultaneously, the value of a college degree rose significantly as we moved more and more toward a global economy. Research by Finis Welch showed that the value of a college degree over a high school diploma rose from 30 percent more in 1979 to 70 percent more in 1987.[65]

Similarly, the gap between blacks and whites can be attributed to a number of the factors mentioned above but, most important, to the fact that Reagan's economic policies were not as beneficial to blacks as they were to the white population (see also a following section on Reagan and blacks).

Median Family Income

Income polarization between the races is particularly apparent in the median income of blacks and whites. In 1971 census data showed that the median income of black families was $6,440 compared to $10,672 for white families. In that year, the median family income of black families was approximately 60 percent that of white families. The ratio of black to white median family income peaked in 1975 to 61.5 percent, declined to 56 percent in 1981, and has not shown significant improvements since. In 1986, the median family income of black families was only $18,247, compared to $31,935 for white families and $20,726 for Hispanic families. In that year, median family income for blacks represented 57.1 percent of that of white families. In 1987, while the median family income of whites rose to $32,274, that of blacks dropped to $18,098 (or 56.0 percent of that of whites) and median family income of Hispanics also declined to $20,306. The last year for which data are available on median family incomes by race is 1989.* In that year, white family median income was $33,915. However, the median family income of blacks stood at $19,329 or 56.9 percent that of white families. (Table 2.7). It is evident that, while the median family income of all races has improved significantly since the 1970s, black families have not been able to keep pace with white families.

Not unexpectedly, the distribution of wealth in the United States is heavily weighted toward the white population. According to Bureau of Census data, the net wealth of whites in the United States is more than eleven times greater than that of blacks and eight times greater than that of Hispanics. Net worth refers to one's assets (e.g., ownership of savings, houses, automobiles) minus one's debts. Using that formula, the Census Bureau concluded that the overall net worth of white families is $39,135 while that for black families is $3,397 and Hispanic families have a net worth of $4,913.

Median Income and Regions

Although substantially more blacks are concentrated at the lower rungs of the income ladder and considerably fewer are at the top compared to the white population, regional distinctions in this regard are also important. As shown in Table 2.8, four times as many black households (13.5 percent black and 3.2 percent white) have incomes under $5,000 per annum. More than twice as many black households as white households receive between $5 and $9,999 per year. Almost half of all black households, compared to less than one-fourth of white households, receive less than $15,000 a year. Blacks are less likely to live below the poverty line if they are residents of the Western part of the United States but more likely to have low incomes if they reside in the Midwest. Regional distinctions in money income do not appear to be significant for whites at the lower income levels.

At income levels above $35,000 per year, half (50.4 percent) of white households of the Northeast, compared to slightly more than one-fourth of black households in the same region, receive annual incomes in this range. About one-fifth of black households in the Midwest, in contrast to more than forty percent of white families in that region, receive money income of $35,000 and above. The same pattern is found between black and white families in the South in which whites are at least two times more likely to have family incomes in this range than black households. However, in the western region, the gap between black and white households

---

*This figure is as of March 1989.

at this income level approximates the rates observed in the Northeast (Table 2.8).

As stated earlier, there is a strong relationship between the amount of formal schooling attained and median family income received (Table 2.8). Among all groups, persons who have completed less than eight years of schooling are concentrated in poverty incomes (i.e., below $12,091* annual income range). However, this table also reveals the magnitude of salary/wage inequity between the races, particularly among persons who have completed high school and post-secondary education. Blacks with four or more years of college are twice as likely as whites with the same educational attainment to receive incomes in *each category* of less than $20,000 per year. A slightly greater proportion of black households than white households are concentrated in the $20,000 to $29,999 range among persons who have received four or more years of college education.

However, in the upper income levels, racial disparities among persons with four or more years of college education are profound. Three-fourths of all white households here have annual incomes above $35,000, compared to slightly more than half of black households. One in six white households, compared to one in four black households receive annual incomes of $50,000 or more if they have attained four or more years of college. However, despite the continued increase in the number of black families in the highest income range reported by the Bureau of the Census, two and a half times more white families than black families receive annual incomes of $50,000 or more. Again, this situation reflects a pattern of wealth concentration within the white population (Table 2.8). It is especially the case for white males since they are almost four and a half times more likely than black males (9.1:2.1 percent) to receive annual incomes of $50,000 or more.

The rigidity of systemic discrimination and racial stratification in the marketplace, often associated with both endogenous and exogenous patterns of prejudice and discrimination,[66] is reflected in the greater financial rewards accrued by the average white person with less formal education than blacks. This fact is especially apparent among blacks who have received four or more years of college education and white males with only a high school diploma.

Although the income disparity between blacks and whites in the United States is enormous, black Americans have a $300 billion consumer market. Tony Brown points out that this spending power is equal to or greater than the gross national product (GNP) "of Canada or Australia or the ninth largest nation in the free world."[67] A survey conducted by *Ebony* showed that black Americans annually spend $34.5 billion on food products; $14.3 billion on automobiles and trucks; $12.8 billion on clothing

---

*The Bureau of the Census reported in 1989 that the poverty level income for a nonfarm family of four was $12,091.

Table 2.7 MONEY INCOME OF FAMILIES—MEDIAN FAMILY INCOME IN CURRENT AND CONSTANT (1981) DOLLARS
By Race and Spanish Origin of Householder: 1950–1981

Year	Median income in current dollars				Median income in constant (1981) dollars				Average annual percentage change of median income of all families	
	All families[a]	White	Black	Spanish origin[b]	All families[d]	White	Black	Spanish origin[b]	Current dollars	Constant dollars
1950	3,319	3,445	1,896[c]	(NA)	12,548	13,025	7,066[c]	(NA)	3.1[d]	0.6[d]
1955	4,418	4,613	2,544[c]	(NA)	15,003	15,665	8,639[c]	(NA)	5.9	3.6
1960	5,620	5,835	3,230[c]	(NA)	17,259	17,919	9,919[c]	(NA)	4.9	2.8
1965	6,957	7,251	3,993[c]	(NA)	20,054	20,901	11,510[c]	(NA)	4.4	3.0
1970	9,867	10,236	6,279	(NA)	23,111	23,975	14,707	(NA)	7.5	2.3
1971	10,285	10,672	6,440	(NA)	23,097	23,966	14,462	(NA)	4.2	-0.1
1972	11,116	11,549	6,864	8,183	24,166	25,107	14,922	17,790	8.1	4.6
1973	12,051	12,595	7,269	8,715	24,663	25,777	14,877	17,836	8.4	2.1
1974	12,902	13,408	8,006	9,540	23,795	24,728	14,765	17,594	7.1	-3.5
1975	13,719	14,268	8,779	9,551	23,183	24,110	14,835	16,140	6.3	-2.6
1976	14,958	15,537	9,242	10,259	23,898	24,823	14,766	16,390	9.0	3.0
1977	16,009	16,740	9,563	11,421	24,027	25,124	14,352	17,141	7.0	0.5
1978	17,640	18,368	10,879	12,566	24,591	25,606	15,166	17,518	10.2	2.3
1979[e]	19,661	20,502	11,644	14,569	24,635	25,689	14,590	18,255	11.5	0.2
1979[f]	19,587	20,439	11,574	14,169	24,540	25,608	14,501	17,752	(X)	(X)
1980	21,023	21,904	12,674	14,716	23,204	24,176	13,989	16,242	7.3	-5.4
1981	22,388	23,517	13,266	16,401	22,388	23,517	13,266	16,401	6.5	-3.5
1982	23,433	24,603	13,598	16,227	26,116	27,420	15,155	18,085	4.7	-1.4
1983	24,674	25,837	14,561	16,930	26,642	27,898	15,722	18,280	5.3	2.0

Table 2.7 (Continued)

Year	Median income in current dollars				Median income in constant (1981) dollars				Average annual percentage change of median income of all families	
	All families[a]	White	Black	Spanish origin[b]	All families[d]	White	Black	Spanish origin[b]	Current dollars	
1984	26,433	27,686	15,432	18,833	27,376	28,674	15,962	18,505	7.1	2.8
1985	27,735	29,152	16,786	19,027	27,735	29,152	15,786	19,027	4.9	1.3
1986	29,458	30,809	17,064	19,995	30,534	31,935	18,247	20,726	6.2	4.2
1987	30,853	32,274	18,098	20,306	30,853	32,274	18,098	20,306	4.7	1.0
1988	32,491	33,915	19,329	21,796	32,191	33,915	19,329	21,796	—	—

Minus sign (−) denotes decrease.

NA: Not available.

X: Not applicable.

[a]Includes other races not shown separately.

[b]Persons of Spanish origin may be of any race.

[c]For 1950–1965, black and other races.

[d]Change from 1947.

[e]Population controls based on the 1970 census; see text, pp. 2 and 416.

[f]Population controls based on the 1980 census; see text pp. 2 and 416.

Source: U.S. Bureau of the Census, Current Population Reports, series P-60, No. 134, Tables 713 and 714, and earlier reports. See headnote, Table 713.

Note: For definition of median, see Guide to Tabular Presentation.

Table 2.8 MONEY INCOME OF FAMILIES—PERCENT DISTRIBUTION BY INCOME LEVEL, BY RACE AND HISPANIC ORIGIN OF HOUSEHOLDER, AND SELECTED CHARACTERISTICS: 1987

Race of householder, region, and education	Number of families (1,000)	Percent distribution of families, by income level								Median income (dol.)
		Under $5,000	$5,000–$9,999	$10,000–$14,999	$15,000–$24,999	$25,000–$34,999	$35,000–$49,999	$50,000–$74,999	$75,000 and over	
All families[a]	65,133	4.4	7.3	9.0	18.7	17.5	20.2	15.1	7.8	30,853
White, total	56,044	3.2	6.1	8.5	18.4	18.1	21.2	16.1	8.4	32,274
Northeast	11,855	2.9	5.6	6.9	16.5	17.7	21.9	17.7	10.8	35,262
Midwest	14,240	2.9	6.0	8.1	18.7	19.4	22.0	16.2	6.6	32,149
South	18,559	3.8	6.9	9.5	19.2	17.5	20.8	14.7	7.5	30,729
West	11,389	2.9	5.7	9.2	18.7	17.7	20.0	16.4	9.4	32,521
Householder completed[b]										
Elementary school:										
Less than 8 years	3,259	7.7	21.1	20.3	23.9	13.1	8.7	4.1	1.1	15,264
8 years	2,798	5.8	13.0	18.5	29.6	16.6	10.5	4.4	1.5	18,718
High school:										
1–3 years	6,036	5.0	10.3	13.4	26.1	19.1	15.5	8.2	2.5	22,653
4 years	20,020	2.7	5.0	8.2	20.5	21.7	23.6	14.1	4.1	30,958
College:										
1–3 years	9,184	1.9	3.2	5.6	15.1	19.4	26.9	20.2	7.9	37,324
4 years or more	12,398	.7	1.0	2.3	8.2	12.3	24.0	28.2	23.3	50,908
Black, total	7,177	13.5	16.4	12.5	21.8	13.6	12.8	7.0	2.5	18,098
Northeast	1,189	12.6	14.4	10.2	21.6	12.7	16.0	8.6	3.8	20,678
Midwest	1,389	15.1	18.6	11.7	18.8	14.0	12.9	6.1	2.7	16,755
South	3,972	14.3	16.6	13.4	21.9	13.5	11.6	7.0	1.7	17,302
West	627	6.2	14.5	12.3	27.6	14.7	14.4	5.6	4.8	20,627
Householder completed[b]										
Elementary school:										
Less than 8 years	821	11.2	28.2	20.2	20.6	11.6	5.4	2.3	.5	12,149
8 years	382	15.2	23.6	17.8	22.0	7.6	7.9	5.5	.5	13,210

Table 2.8 (Continued)

Race of householder, region, and education	Number of families (1,000)	Percent distribution of families, by income level								Median income (dol.)
		Under $5,000	$5,000–$9,999	$10,000–$14,999	$15,000–$24,999	$25,000–$34,999	$35,000–$49,999	$50,000–$74,999	$75,000 and over	
High school:										
1–3 years	1,306	18.1	23.6	15.5	19.4	10.4	8.8	3.6	.5	12,166
4 years	2,467	13.2	13.4	11.4	22.7	16.0	14.9	7.1	1.4	20,263
College:										
1–3 years	1,006	5.5	9.0	8.2	27.1	16.2	19.3	11.2	3.5	25,115
4 years or more	692	1.9	3.3	3.9	22.2	15.3	21.5	17.9	14.0	36,568
Hispanic,[c] total	4,588	8.5	14.4	14.7	21.9	15.7	14.0	7.9	2.9	20,306
Northeast	916	11.9	22.2	11.9	17.3	13.2	12.3	8.5	2.6	16,750
Midwest	306	11.4	13.7	8.5	22.5	18.6	13.7	9.1	2.6	21,985
South	1,477	10.4	14.5	15.6	21.9	14.5	13.8	6.4	2.8	18,798
West	1,889	5.0	10.6	16.3	24.0	17.4	14.9	8.6	3.2	22,142
Householder completed[b]										
Elementary school:										
Less than 8 years	1,165	10.7	23.1	21.6	22.0	13.3	6.0	2.8	.4	13,540
8 years	284	9.5	23.0	13.8	27.2	13.4	9.2	3.5	.4	16,319
High school:										
1–3 years	663	9.3	17.2	15.5	25.3	15.5	9.2	5.4	2.6	17,939
4 years	1,143	5.4	8.8	12.8	22.7	18.8	20.3	9.1	2.1	25,130
College:										
1–3 years	530	4.0	4.0	9.1	21.0	18.9	21.6	16.9	4.5	31,006
4 years or more	388	2.1	3.3	2.6	10.3	15.4	29.6	20.8	15.9	43,382

[a]Includes other races not shown separately.

[b]Restricted to families with householder 25 years old and over.

[c]Hispanic persons may be of any race.

Source: U.S. Bureau of the Census, Current Population Reports, series P-60, No. 161, and unpublished data. [Families as of March 1988. See headnote, table 720. See Historical Statistics, Colonial Times to 1970, series G1–8 for U.S. data on total, White, Black and other races.

and accessories; $6.2 billion on home furnishings and equipment; $3.5 billion on various types of insurance; $3.3 billion on personal care and services; $2.6 billion on nonalcoholic beverages; $2.4 billion on alcoholic beverages; and $880 million on nonprescription drugs and supplies.[68] Tony Brown asserts that black teens purchase 40 percent of all records sold in the United States and that blacks between the ages of 12 and 24 account for 50 percent of tickets sold at movie theatres. He also maintains that only 6.6 percent of income by blacks is actually *spent* on a black business or professional. The result is that blacks export 1.7 million jobs each year from black neighborhoods.[69] In the meantime, blacks continue to encounter prejudice and discrimination in their efforts to obtain jobs with businesses who are the beneficiaries of their spending power.

UNEMPLOYMENT AND RACE

The unemployment rate among blacks has remained two or more times as high as that for whites for more than 40 years. The unemployment picture is an extremely complex phenomenon that consists not only of those persons who are *traditionally unemployed* (persons reportedly looking for jobs who cannot find them) but also those who constitute the *subemployed* (those not fully employed who also desire to work full-time) as well as the *discouraged workers* (those persons who are so disenchanted that they stop looking for work and may not be counted in the statistics on unemployment). Whether unemployed, subemployed, or discouraged workers, the numbers and proportion of blacks in these categories reached a crisis stage in 1983 and has been only moderately alleviated in subsequent years.

The historic pattern of the ratio of black to white unemployment is portrayed in Table 2.9. In 1950, five years after the end of World War II, the unemployment rate of black and other races was 9.0 percent but the ratio of black and other races to white unemployment was 1.8. The 1950s were called by Jessie Bernard "an age of abundance"; however, as that decade unfolded the ratio of black to white unemployment worsened, and has never fallen to the 1.7 ratio registered in 1953. In 1989, almost three times as many blacks as whites were unemployed.

The lowest rate of unemployment registered by blacks between 1950 and 1989 was in 1953 when only 4.5 percent of all blacks ("and other races") were unemployed. In 21 of the 37 years since that year, the unemployment rate among blacks has been 10 percent or substantially higher but at no time during that period has the rate of unemployment within the white population reached 10 percent. The recession of the early 1980s was particularly devastating to blacks in the United States. By December 1982, the overall unemployment rate in the United States had reached a post-Great Depression high of 10.8 percent, but for blacks alone their 20.8 percent unemployment figure was higher than the 19.1 percent unem-

Table 2.9 AVERAGE UNEMPLOYMENT RATES FOR BLACK AND WHITE AMERICANS
AGED 16 AND OVER: 1950–1990

| Year | Unemployment rate | | |
	Black and other races (Percentages)	White (Percentages)	Ratio: black and other races to white
1950	9.0	4.9	1:8
1951	5.3	3.1	1:7
1952	5.4	2.8	1:9
1953	4.5	2.7	1:7
1954	9.9	5.0	2:0
1955	8.7	3.9	2:2
1956	8.3	3.6	2:3
1957	7.9	3.8	2:1
1958	12.6	6.1	2:1
1959	10.7	4.8	2:2
1960	10.2	4.9	2:1
1961	12.4	6.0	2:1
1962	10.9	4.9	2:2
1963	10.8	5.0	2:2
1964	9.6	4.6	2:1
1965	8.1	4.1	2:0
1966	7.3	3.3	2:2
1967	7.4	3.4	2:2
1968	6.7	3.2	2:1
1969	6.4	3.1	2:1
1970	8.2	4.5	1:8
1971	9.9	5.4	1:8
1972	10.0	5.0	2:0
1973	8.9	4.3	2:1
1974	9.9	5.0	2:0
1975	13.9	7.8	1:8
1976	13.8	7.0	1:9
1977	13.1	6.8	1:9
1978	12.4	5.5	2:3
1979	11.5	5.6	2:1
1980[a]	14.3	6.3	2:3
1982[a]	20.2	9.3	2:2
1983[a]	19.5	8.4	2:3
1987[a]	13.0	5.3	2:5
1988[a]	11.7	4.7	2:5
1989[a]	11.6	4.3	2:7
1990[a,b]	11.3	4.6	2:3

[a]Blacks only.

[b]Reported for July, 1990.

Source: Adapted from Table 47 in The Social and Economic Status of the Black Population in the United States, 1790–1978 (Current Population Reports, Series P-23, No. 80) (Washington, D. C.: U. S. Department of Commerce, 1979); Robert Hill, The Illusion of Black Progress (Washington, D. C.: The National Urban League, 1979), p. 33; Current Population Reports, P-23 Series, 1990.

ployment figure registered at the end of the Great Depression in 1941. Black Americans were mired in Great Depression unemployment and poverty levels during the early 1980s.

Unemployment among black *teenagers* reached an unprecedented high of 50.7 percent in August 1981. Until 1986, that rate had hovered at about 40 percent. Thereafter, the black teenage unemployment began to register significant declines; first to 34.7 in 1987 and then to 32.4 percent in 1988. Unofficial data collected by various local agencies in many cities across the country indicate that the black teenage unemployment rate is sometimes as high as 90 percent but more often in the 60 to 70 percent range. The Bureau of Labor Statistics reports that the situation is particularly grave for black male teenagers and that almost two-thirds of them are not in the labor force during any part of the year.[70] Blackwell's study of *Youth Employment and Unemployment in Massachusetts: Outreach Initiatives*[71] revealed that many white employers were highly suspicious of young black males and many rationalized their refusal to hire black males in terms that indicated a most perturbing internalization of the most negative and pejorative stereotypes about young black males. For example, some believed that white co-workers would fear them; that young black males might be inclined to sexually assault white females or be combative without provocation toward other workers; that they would be unreliable, and would come improperly dressed for work. In general, black teenagers are about three times more likely than white teenagers to be unemployed.

The overall teenage unemployment rate was 16.3 percent in 1990. It was 31.8 percent for black teenagers and 13.7 percent for white teenagers. With such a huge proportion of black teenagers outside the labor force, this problem continues at the crisis level. Without significant changes in the labor participation pattern of black youth in the immediate future, hundreds of thousands of them will reach adulthood without ever having attained work experience. The severity of black teenage unemployment could portend major difficulties of even greater vulnerability for the black population in the immediate future.[72] The nation as a whole will ultimately pay the price for this situation if it does not provide adequate education, training, and work experience at a time when the United States is undergoing a dearth of skilled workers.

In addition, the cost of this dereliction will continue to be reflected in the rising rates of other social problems. In fact, the gravity of the situation is evident currently in cocaine/crack-infested areas of several urban communities and in gang wars related to control of drug trafficking. Many young people are lured into the highly lucrative drug marketing business simply because the remuneration is so enormous for what they perceive as "little or no effort." A twelve- or thirteen-year-old can earn as much as $1,500 a day simply as a "look-out" or a "runner." Substantially more can be earned as a "dealer." That income is sometimes used to support a single mother living in abject poverty or to purchase consumer goods and services that will enhance that person's status among his or her peers.

From Boston to Washington, D. C., to Los Angeles, reports indicate that youthful drug merchants drive expensive automobiles, wear expensive clothing, "lots of gold," and designer sneakers heavily advertised in black ghettos all over the United States, and buy other goods that emulate the television version of the "good life" in America. For many of these youngsters and young adults, employment as a hamburger flipper in Burger King, Wendy's, or McDonald's remunerated at $5 or $6/hour is not particularly appealing. Participants in this aspect of the underground economy are neither impressed by efforts to either defer gratifications until they can be fulfilled through legitimate pursuits nor by pronouncements concerning socially acceptable work ethics. Their newfound value construct or the internalization of a value system that is not antithetical to this type of venture renders it relatively easy to become involved in such illicit, anti-social, and dangerous activity. This topic will be further explored in Chapter 12.

Another aspect of the unemployment issue is the distinction between *cyclical* and *structural* unemployment. Martin Feldstein, who served as head of the President's Council of Economic Advisors during the Reagan Administration, maintains that cyclical unemployment is due to such conditions as back-to-back recessions, illustrated by those that occurred in the United States during 1979–1980 and 1981–1982. In his view, this type of unemployment accounted for about 40 percent of the more than 12 million people who were unemployed at the end of 1982, for example. On the other hand, *structural unemployment* is the result of such factors as age, sex, race or minority status, educational attainment, work experience, and sectoral (specific industries) conditions.[73] Structural unemployment, in Bernard Anderson's view, is the difference between such factors as job chances, seasonal variations resulting in layoffs, and reduced job demands resulting from a "slowdown in the economy" *and* "the total amount of unemployment."[74]

Anderson also identifies three types of structural unemployment: (1) the type that stems from people searching for jobs without appropriate qualifications, (2) the type that results from economic dislocation induced by foreign competition and automation and similar factors, and (3) the type that results from untrained workers in search of jobs. In effect, structural unemployment is applicable to the major factors that contributed to particularly high rates of unemployment at varying points throughout the 1980s. For instance, it is associated with black and Hispanic teenagers, and with those persons who lost jobs to overseas workers who are paid lower wages than their American counterparts, as well as to those workers displaced by automated machines.[75]

Contributing Factors and Consequences

Without question, the primary contributing factor to the seemingly uncontrollable unemployment rate in the United States witnessed from the late 1970s and well into the 1980s is the sluggish state of the economy. In the first place, the American economy suffered during the 1970s from unprecedented levels of inflation and, in effect, began to pay a major price for deficit spending caused by the Vietnam War. The fiscal and monetary policies of the 1970s, based upon a Keynesian approach, coupled with a worldwide economic decline fueled in part by the escalation of oil prices, helped to further weaken the American economy. Double-digit inflation rates combined with rising unemployment rates to produce what became known as "stagflation".[76]

Indeed, the dismal state of the American economy in 1983 was attributed to the following factors as they impacted on the overall unemployment rate: (1) the restructuring of the American economy, (2) the energy crisis that began in 1973, (3) inflation policy, (4) escalating consumer prices, (5) reductions in the federal government work force, (6) immigration, and (7) the failure of the federal government to enact a broad-based job creation program designed to stimulate full-employment.

As previously stated, the American economy is undergoing a major restructuring process. This process is evidenced in the shift of manufacturing from cities to suburbs within the United States, huge foreign investments in this country,[77] the "deindustrialization of the United States,"[78] through the relocation of major industries (steel, automobiles, and several manufacturing companies) to foreign countries, increased movement toward high technology supported by service industries in the United States, imbalances between imports and exports resulting in a balance of trade deficit, reduction in factory output in the United States, a tax structure that favors the well-to-do, and a slowed growth in the country's gross national product (GNP). In varied ways, all these factors have combined to increase the unemployment rate in the United States.

For instance, in 1970, imports composed 14.7 percent of the total number of automobiles sold in this country but in 1980, imports represented 26.9 percent of cars sold in the United States. In that 10-year interim, there was a 9.1 percent decline in the number of workers employed in the auto industry in the United States. That drop represented a loss of 1 million jobs. This situation took a heavy toll on blacks who had been quite successful in finding work in the auto industry. Between 1970 and 1980, about one-fifth of all blacks employed in the auto industry lost their jobs. This deterioration deepened well into the 1980s as the unemployment rate in Michigan rose to over 16 percent and the rate for blacks in an autoproduction center such as Detroit climbed to over 25 percent.[79]

Similarly, there was an 8.5 percent decline in the basic iron and steel industry in this nation between 1970 and 1980. As with the auto industry, a large proportion of this drop was due to foreign competition or an increase in foreign imports.[80] Again, blacks experienced a serious job loss among its workers in the steel industry, that is, from 184,000 in 1970 to 179,000 in 1980.[81]

The sluggish American economy is also attributed to "the slow growth rate of the U.S. industrial production."[82] In 1983, its sluggishness was second only to that of Great Britain among the major industrial nations. The American growth rate of production declined from 4.5 percent for the 1953–1969 period to 2.7 percent for the 1973–1979 period. This nation increased the amount of imports as the dollar value increased, triggered by an upsurge in interest rates in the United States. This change made it easier to purchase and import foreign goods. As a result, domestic production suffered and declined markedly. This situation inevitably led to low profits followed by low investments, factories working at less than 70 percent capacity, and higher unemployment. It is particularly devastating for blacks. They have heavy employment in precisely the industries most seriously affected by job dislocations, layoffs, the closing of plants, relocation of plants (because they do not have the necessary funds required for relocation), and by the import-export imbalance in such areas as textiles, shoe manufacturing, and other consumer goods.[83]

That restructuring process continues into the 1990s. Losses in manufacturing jobs have not been halted significantly. The national debt was about $189 billion in 1989 and the country's economy is increasingly dependent upon foreign capital and loans. Foreign investments in the United States have occurred at such an accelerated rate that newspaper headlines frequently scream such captions as "America for Sale." Such concerns may be supported by data reported by Leonard Silk. His research showed that between 1982 and 1988, to take one period during the Reagan years, foreign private holdings of United States Government securities grew from $29 billion to $121.5 billion. During the same period foreign private holdings of United States corporate bonds skyrocketed from $41 billion to $178 billion and their claims on American holdings climbed from $76 billion to $172 billion.[84]

In effect, the American economy is being propped up by foreign investors and money-lenders. In addition, some of the most famous structures, such as Watergate and the building that houses the U. S. Department of Justice, as well as prime land in cities such as New York, Los Angeles, and Houston are foreign owned. It is estimated that 64 percent of the real estate in downtown Los Angeles and more than a third (39 percent) of that in downtown Houston is now owned by foreign investors. Canadians own one-third of the office space in Minneapolis and the British are heavy investors in prime land and buildings in Washington, D. C. It was estimated in 1989 that foreign ownership of American firms, factories, banks, businesses, and other assets exceeded $1.5 trillion.[85]

The issue here is not the foreign ownership of property and assets in the United States but the impact of that ownership on equal employment opportunity and the participation of blacks in those areas controlled by foreign ownership. For that reason, the action of Japanese investors achieves a special salience.

It is estimated that Japan has invested some $33 billion in the United States. This amount includes, inter alia, a 50 percent ownership of 489 assembly and production plants, 6 automobile assembly plants, and 150 auto parts suppliers.[86] Under the Federal Contract Compliance Program established by the U. S. Congress, any firm, including foreign investors in the United States, must comply with U. S. affirmative action laws and guidelines. While the Japanese do not hold the majority of foreign investments in the United States, what they do own has profound and immediate implications for employment opportunities for blacks. For several years, Japanese firms operating in the United States have come under severe criticism for violations of U. S. affirmative action guidelines. Specifically, they have been accused of discrimination against blacks in their hiring policies and Japanese political leaders have had to apologize for racist remarks about black Americans.

For example, the Hitachi Consumer Products Company, located in Compton, California, a city that is 80 percent black and constantly registers an unemployment rate of from 20 to 40 percent, was accused of such discrimination. Subsequently, the settlement reached by Hitachi with the California Fair Employment and Housing Department called for the company to take immediate corrective actions. Hitachi agreed to pay a quarter of a million dollars in damages to those persons who had applied and were refused jobs during the first ten months of 1981. Hitachi also agreed to "initiate an immediate affirmative action program."[87] Honda, Toyota, and Sony have also been accused of anti-black discrimination for refusing to hire blacks or allow them to obtain dealerships.

Robert Coles' study of 100 sites of automobile manufacturers and suppliers further illuminated the magnitude of discrimination by Japanese firms against blacks in the United States. One pattern Cole observed was the tendency of Japanese firms to locate in areas underpopulated by blacks and then to hire fewer blacks than they should have in terms of the number of blacks in the population. For example, a Honda plant was located in Marysville, Ohio, an area in which blacks constitute 10.5 percent of total population. However, blacks are a mere 2.8 percent of Honda's workforce. Smyrna, Tennessee, has a black population of 19.3 percent. However, blacks represented 14 percent of the employees in the Nissan plant located there. (It is noteworthy that in 1989 the United Auto Workers failed in its effort to unionize workers at the Smyrna facility.) Similarly, blacks represented only 14 percent of the employees in the Madza plant located in Flat Rock, Michigan, but constituted 29 percent of the areas' population.[88]

In 1988, Honda of America Manufacturing was ordered by the Equal Employment Opportunity Commission (EEOC) of the U. S. Government to pay $6 million to 377 blacks and women for hiring discrimination against them.[89] Subsequently, Nissan Motor Corporation in California also agreed with an EEOC order to pay $605,600 in back pay to 92 workers who had been discriminated against on the basis of race or age. Under the terms of this settlement, Nissan also agreed to increase opportunities for high-level sales and management positions for minorities and women as well as to revise its recruitment and hiring practices in ways that would not be discriminatory.[90]

Many Americans, including black citizens, Japanese-American Congressmen, and other political leaders, reacted sharply to racist comments made by Japanese Prime Minister Yasuhiro Nakasone in 1986, and to similar remarks made by the then chief of Japan's ruling Democratic Party, Michio Watanabe, in 1988. Nakasone asserted that the presence of blacks and Hispanics lowered the intelligence of the United States. Watanabe claimed that blacks have no aversion to declaring bankruptcy because by so doing blacks feel "now we don't have to pay anything back."[91] Both men later apologized following widespread protests in the United States. Such racially insensitive comments were followed by revelations of equally disturbing practices of other Japanese business companies.

The Sanrio Toy Company manufactured the extremely popular "Little Black Sambo" dolls and distributed them on the Japanese market. The Yamato Mannequin Company manufactured mannequins that stereotyped blacks as "having grotesquely large lips," and bulging eyes, features once common in American minstrels. These mannequins were displayed at the Sogo Department store in Tokyo.[92] One of the most popular toothpastes in Japan was called "Darky." Its logo was an offensive depiction of blacks. Subsequently, the name was changed to "Darlie" and the logo showed blacks dressed in tuxedos. Many Americans also expressed outrage over the fact that, at the time when American businesses are responding to pressures against the racist apartheid government of South Africa by disinvesting from that country, Japan has become that country's leading trading partner.[93]

In response to criticisms against Japanese government officials and to business practices, Sanrio apologized, recalled the "Little Black Sambo" dolls, and donated more than $250,000 in toys to San Francisco's poor children. Honda, Toyota, and Sony began either to contribute or advertise their contributions to major black civil rights organizations, namely the National Association for the Advancement of Colored People (NAACP), the National Urban League (NUL), and the United Negro College Fund (UNCF). These companies increased their advertisements in black-owned publications, particularly *Black Enterprise Magazine,* and *Ebony.*

Another important response was directly from the black community itself and several of its prominent leaders. Attention was called to the consumer market power of the black community and the sizeable amount of money spent by blacks on Japanese manufactured products. It is estimated that blacks in the United States account for 25 percent of the purchases of Japanese-made automobiles, and 10 percent of Japanese VCRs, TVs, and audio equipment.[94] Black leaders all across the nation, from Boston to Los Angeles, called for a boycott of all Japanese manufactured products sold in the United States. In August 1988, following a meeting of black political, business, and civil rights organizations, a "Buy American" campaign was initiated.

The Congressional Black Caucus reminded the Japanese government and business community of the possibility of escalation of intergroup conflict generated by episodes described above as well as by the lingering animosity resulting from the loss of jobs by auto and steel workers to Japanese industries and the hiring policies of Japanese firms operating in the United States.[95] Further, several prominent leaders from the black community, including U. S. Congressman Mervyn Dymally (then President of the Congressional Black Caucus), the Rev. Jesse Jackson, and Atlanta's Mayor Andrew Young, held talks with Japanese business leaders and government officials. These meetings were designed to increase employment opportunities for blacks in Japanese firms operating in the United States, to establish or strengthen commercial links between Japanese and black-owned businesses in the United States, and to foster a more harmonious relationship between the Japanese and minority groups.[96]

Inflation Policy

With the consumer prices rising monthly and double-digit inflation becoming normative, the federal government embarked on a program to reduce inflation by slowing down the growth of the money supply.[97] The Reagan Administration, in cooperation with the Federal Reserve Board, substantially reduced inflation between 1981 and 1983 below double digit levels.[98] However, by reducing inflation, the cost of borrowing accelerated to enormously high rates which, in turn, decelerated the demand for automobiles, machinery, housing, and costly consumer products.[99] One consequence of low demand for goods and services was the loss of countless thousands of jobs. Since 1983, the nation has not recovered losses in jobs triggered by policies initiated in the early years of the Reagan Administration. This loss is especially evident in manufacturing, the automobile industry, and related services. More than 3 million manufacturing jobs and more than 2 million in related services had been lost by 1987, according to Economic Policy Institute of New York University.

Such losses are also triggered by the massive trade deficit and a potentially dangerous debt structure in the United States. Leonard Silk reported that between 1979 and 1988, total private and public debt in the United States grew from $4.2 trillion to $10.9 trillion. This change represented an increase of 157 percent but inflation accounted for a third of that increase. During the same period, the federal debt climbed from $663 billion to $2.1 trillion while private debt (consisting of households and nonfinancial institutions) jumped from $$2.9 trillion to $6.7 trillion.[100]

Under President Reagan, the United States shifted from the world's largest creditor nation to the world's greatest debtor nation. The national debt, which reduces money available for social programs and for job creation, is sustained in no small measure by the mammoth defense build-up under Reagan and Secretary of Defense Casper Weinberger. While the huge outlays for defense mounted, a procurement contracts scandal, involving Pentagon officials and contractors or other civilians, unfolded. That episode revealed enormous wastage, kickbacks, and payments of as much as $924 for a plastic chair boot that would be ordinarily marketed for about twenty-five cents.

If such wastes were eliminated, it would not only reduce the DOD's budget but would save and make available significant amounts of money for curbing unemployment and poverty. Increases in the DOD budget do not result in increased employment for blacks. On the contrary, they depress the total amount available in those sectors in which blacks are more likely to be employed.

Reductions in Force

Another contributor to the high unemployment rate among blacks between 1981 and 1983 was President Reagan's success in persuading Congress to enact every proposal he requested in 1981 under the label of "supply-side economics," also called "Reagonomics." Inevitably, this meant, among other things, layoffs of thousands of workers, especially in the public sector.

At the federal level, budget cuts and recessions resulted in widespread reductions-in-force (called "riffs"). These job losses had a harsh impact among blacks for two reasons. First, under most seniority rules, the "last hired, first fired" policy is enforced. Since blacks entered the higher paid job market later than whites, they have been not only the first to be dismissed but they have borne the greater burden of "riffs." The second reason why "riffs" seriously affected blacks is because the ascent to middle-class status for many blacks was achieved through the acquisition of relatively secure employment with the federal government. Significant inroads were made in the attainment of such positions during the late 1960s and early 1970s. By virtue of affirmative action policies, they and other minorities held 550,000 of the 2.1 million federal jobs in 1980. However, the cutbacks ordered by President Reagan resulted in the downward mobility of many black Americans.[101]

According to a 1982 report by the Federal Government Civil Service Task Force, the rate of job loss, through "riffs" ordered by President Reagan, for blacks and other minorities was about double the proportion of their representation in federal jobs. In 1981, blacks and other minorities composed about 20 percent of all federal employees. However, in the six-month period between October 1, 1981, and March 31, 1982, about 40 percent of all persons laid off from federal jobs were blacks and other minorities.[102]

As President Reagan's budget cuts were implemented in late 1981 and 1982, they impacted most heavily on those agencies and departments in which blacks were employed. Reductions-in-force amounted to 25 percent in the Department of Commerce; 24.5 percent in the Department of Education; 19.6 percent in the Department of Labor; 12.9 percent in the Department of Housing and Urban Development, and 6.2 percent in the Department of Health and Human Services.[103] Some programs, such as those under the Comprehensive Employment and Training Act (CETA), which employed as many as 24 million persons between 1974 and 1982, were abolished.[104] Units such as the Community Service Agency were also obliterated by the Reagan-ordered budget cuts. These job losses were not compensated by job replacements at the state level. In fact, because of reductions in federal revenue, almost half the states had to cut back their own budgets; unemployment increased, and many states ran out of unemployment compensation funds and were forced to borrow federal monies to meet their own needs.

As the national economy improved, the better trained and least expendable workers of all races were able to find new jobs. President George Bush committed himself to a "kinder, gentler society," implying greater economic opportunity for all Americans. However, during the first year of his administration, the unemployment rate for blacks, while declining, remained twice that of whites. One conclusion of this finding is inescapable: Black Americans have not benefited as greatly as white Americans from the economic expansion of the latter part of the 1980s. Without major transformations in economic policies at the federal level, this inequity is not likely to diminish.

Impact of Immigrants

The influx of millions of legal and illegal aliens into the United States since 1970 fueled a long-standing debate about the impact of immigrants on the American economy. As the economy plummeted during the recessions of 1974–1975, 1979–1980, and 1981–1983, and was accompanied by depression level unemployment rates, the volatility of this debate permeated the American society. There are at least two dominant points of view concerning the impact of immigrants on the economy. On the one hand, there are those who claim that the recent immigrants are an important source of inexpensive young workers who may take on jobs no longer desired by American citizens. Moreover, many of these immigrants are filling voids by supplying needed services to the communities in which they have settled. In this view, there is a strong respect for the American tradition that advocates a long-standing and fundamental commitment to accept people from other shores who desire freedom and the opportunity to establish a better life in this country.[105]

On the other hand, there is the belief, held by a substantial portion of the American society, that immigrants are "displacing domestic workers and depressing wages and working conditions," especially in the lower tier of the split-labor market.[106] The magnitude of this belief is reflected in the results of a Roper survey of 1980 which showed that 82 percent of blacks and 80 percent of whites agreed with the statement that the United States should curtail the number of legal immigrants admitted annually. In the same survey, 92 percent of the white participants and 88 percent of black participants agreed that the United States should exert the strongest possible effort to stop illegal immigration.[107]

It was estimated in 1981 that about 659,000 legal immigrants and refugees and another 500,000 illegal immigrants entered the United

States. About seven of every ten new immigrants settled in California, Florida, Illinois, New Jersey, New York, and Texas. These six states happen to have huge urban populations and enormous concentrations of blacks. This settlement pattern ignited a long-standing resentment among many blacks that the United States is considerably more interested in improving the lot of foreign persons, especially if they are white, than it is in making resources available to American-born black citizens who also wish to "live a better life."[108] Many blacks believe that black Haitians, in contrast to white Cubans, for instance, are treated unfairly and denied even a minimum of social and economic opportunity.

This problem is further exacerbated by the tendency of many new immigrants from Indochina, Asia, and the Caribbean to settle in black communities. This seems particularly so in such cities as New York, Washington, D. C., Compton, California, New Orleans, and Miami. Many new immigrants have opened businesses in the black community. For example, Koreans have established most of their 300 businesses in Washington, D. C., in black communities as well as 58 stores on Harlem's 125th Street alone, which is located in the heart of Harlem in New York City.[109] The problem is not the establishment of businesses by Koreans, Vietnamese, Arabs, Indians, Pakistanis, Filipinos, and Cubans. It is the strongly held belief among black hardliners that many of the new immigrants are essentially sojourners who plan to remain in the black communities only until such time as they have accumulated sufficient capital that will enable them to relocate elsewhere. In this view, not only are the new immigrants without a long-standing commitment to return some of their profits for the economic improvement of the black community, they are perceived as exploiters of blacks, and similar to white capitalists. Many blacks allege that the new immigrants either enter the country with prejudices against blacks or that they soon internalize what they perceive to be the perspectives of the dominant group about blacks; they proceed to discriminate against them and refuse to interact with the black population.[110]

Overlooked in such assertions is the fact that many new immigrants are frequently victimized by pernicious racism and discrimination in the marketplace and in housing. Countless numbers are brutalized by vicious physical assaults by whites who resent their presence, competition, real or imagined, and their accomplishments.

Nevertheless, other suspicions, real or imagined, prevail among many blacks about the ability of the new immigrants to raise large amounts of capital to establish business enterprises. There are allegations that the federal government provides special assistance to the newcomers that enables them to open up small businesses, such as restaurants, clothing shops, newsstands, grocery stores, or motels. Such allegations, as well as those that the new immigrants are reaping the benefits of affirmative action in ways denied to blacks, are denounced by the federal government, some blacks, and many social scientists.[111] Be that as it may, the problem of strain between many new immigrants and members of the

American population of all races is a reality. That problem, with respect to the black community, was especially exacerbated by the influx of such large numbers of immigrants at a time when so many blacks believed that discrimination against them was rising, and that President Reagan was doing very little to curtail structural discrimination.

POVERTY AND HUNGER AMONG BLACK AMERICANS

The severe downturn in the American economy between 1981 and 1983 and the high rates of unemployment that were the results of this decline have taken their toll on the American population as a whole. There was an increase in family stress, family violence, an acceleration of mental health deterioration, an escalation of suicide rates among both young and old, and an upturn in the rates of drug addiction, separation, and divorce. Not only did many people become more aggressive in their treatment of others, or have debilitating states of anxiety and depression, they lost personal possessions. People missed payments on homes and lost them, skipped payments on cars and had them repossessed, and many went on welfare as an act of last resort.[112] More and more Americans of all races are now deeply mired in poverty, and almost unprecedented numbers of American citizens are hungry and homeless. Unfortunately, several of the Reagan administration's policies led many persons to conclude that the President of the United States "seems willing to forget the poor," the very people who are victimized most by the recession/depression of the 1980s.[113]

As a result of relegation to the bottom rungs on the occupational ladder, which are characterized by the lowest incomes and the highest unemployment, a disproportionate number of black Americans are living in poverty as the decade of the 1990s begins. Poverty is defined by the U. S. Department of Commerce on the basis of the estimated income needed to maintain a nonfarm family of four in the United States. However, the poverty income level rises steadily from year to year, may vary from region to region, and is a significant indicator of the cost of living in various regions and cities. Therefore, while the national poverty income may be set at one figure, the poverty income in a high cost of living area may be substantially higher than the national poverty income level.

In 1971, the poverty income level was set at $4,137. By 1981, because of the gigantic leap in the cost of living, this figure had more than doubled to $9,287. Throughout the 1980s, the poverty threshold income level continued to rise. By 1985, it had reached $10,989 and by 1988, it was set at $12,091.[114]

As the poverty income threshold rose, the number of Americans below the poverty level, especially blacks and Hispanics, increased at a Depression pace. For example, in 1980, the poverty rate for the nation as a whole was 13.2 percent; for whites, 10.4 percent, and for blacks, 32.4 percent. In that year, 29.6 million Americans were in poverty. In 1983, the national poverty rate reached 15 percent and 34.4 million people were classified as poverty-stricken. Thirty-six percent of all blacks; 28.1 percent of the Hispanics, and 12.2 percent of the white population were living in poverty. The 15 percent national poverty rate was the highest proportion of American people living in poverty since 1965. Thereafter, with improvements in the overall economy, the absolute number of persons in poverty began to fall. However, as recently as 1988, it is estimated that the national poverty level was 13.1 percent; 10.1 percent for whites, 31.6 percent for blacks, and 26.8 percent for Hispanics. The total number of Americans in poverty is approximately 32 million.[115]

Significantly, blacks are about three times as likely to live in poverty as whites are. However, about two-thirds (65.8 percent in 1988) of all poor people in the United States are white; 29.8 percent are black, and 4.5 percent are Hispanic and other races. Although more whites than blacks or Hispanics are poor, blacks and Hispanics are overrepresented among America's poor.

Not only is poverty unevenly distributed along racial lines, it varies enormously by geographic regions and in metropolitan compared to non-metropolitan areas. The U. S. Bureau of the Census reported that the South has the highest poverty rate of any region (16.1 percent). It is followed by the Midwest and West, each with a 12.7 percent rate; the Northeast region, with a poverty rate of 11 percent, has the lowest regional rate in the United States. More than half (58.8 percent) of poor people in the United States live in central cities. More than one-fourth (28.2 percent) live in nonmetropolitan areas; about one in every eight (12.9 percent) reside in suburban communities and about the same ratio (12.6 percent) of all farm residents are poverty-stricken.[116]

In general, most attention is focused on the urban poor, but blacks, as well as whites, in rural areas often suffer from debilitating poverty conditions. Joyce Allen estimates that there are more than 2 million poverty-stricken blacks in rural areas of the United States.[117] Allen's research shows that the black rural poor are likely to be concentrated in the South, where they account for 97 percent of the rural poor. By contrast, the poverty rate for southern blacks as a whole is 44 percent. Although black farmers account for only 3 percent of rural blacks, they have a poverty rate of 45 percent. Allen also reported that 52 percent of the rural poor live in female-headed families while 32 percent live in two-parent and other families. Black rural poor children are seriously victimized by poverty. Approximately six of every ten black children under the age of six in rural areas is in poverty and more than eight of every ten of children of the same age living in a female-headed family is poverty-stricken. By contrast, white children in rural areas under the age of six constitute 22 percent while among those living in a female-headed household the poverty rate is 65 percent.[118]

Although the poverty rate among America's elderly has fallen sharply in recent years, especially in response to higher Social Security benefits, the rural black elderly have a poverty rate of about 42 percent. By contrast, the poverty rate for the rural white elderly, persons aged 65 and older, is about 16 percent. Again, poor elderly blacks living in rural areas have a poverty rate two and a half times higher than that of rural elderly whites.[119]

Gender and Children

Irrespective of race, chances of living below the poverty line in the United States reflect both gender and age level. Specifically, women and children are significantly more likely to be impoverished financially than males and persons above the age of 18 (see Chapter 3). Women more so than men are likely to be victimized by poverty. In general, women are two times more likely than men to live below the poverty line. Hardest hit by poverty are single women with children, especially black female heads of households. In 1981, over a third of all female householders lived in poverty compared to one in ten male householders. More than half of all black female householders (52.9 percent) and Hispanic female householders (53.2 percent) were living in poverty in 1981, compared to more than one-fourth (27.4 percent) of white female householders. At the same time, one in five (19.9 percent) of black male householders, one in five (19.2 percent) of Hispanic male householders, compared to less than one in ten (8.8 percent) of white male householders, were poverty-stricken.

More recent data shows that disparities in poverty rates between the sexes have not abated. Although the term "feminization of poverty" may mask the pervasiveness of poverty among two-parented families, it does capture the essence of poverty among poor women. For example, in 1988, Bureau of the Census data showed that 53 percent of female-headed households were in poverty. The rates for black, Hispanic, and white women in this category were 49.0%, 49.1% and 26.5% , respectively.

How can gender differences in poverty rates be explained? Such variations in part may be attributed to the rise in divorce rates and the failure of men to pay alimony or child support. Almost fifty percent of all marriages now end in divorce. David Ellwood maintains that only one-third of all single mothers receive child support and when they do their average payment is only $2,300 per year.[120] The rise in teenage single parents who establish a separate household is another explanatory factor. Discrimination in the marketplace—whether in occupations attained or income paid to women (compared to wages received by men in addition to the fact that women are more likely to enter at lower levels)—combine to reduce the overall wages of working women. As a result, women are more likely to receive poverty-level incomes. Full-time working women earn only about 65 percent of the income earned by full-time working men. Of course, gender disparities in poverty rates may be attributed to other factors but these conditions account for a considerable amount of those differences.

The issue of children in poverty seems finally to have captured the attention of the nation's political leaders. During the 1988 presidential campaigns, the leading candidates from both parties committed themselves to the elimination of this problem. Whether their pronouncements were nothing more than political rhetoric designed to capture votes or a sincere commitment to address this problem remains to be seen in 1990. In the meantime, poverty among children continues at a most alarming pace. It is not exclusively a condition affecting single, welfare mothers.[121] Twelve million American children are in poverty. This figure means that one of every five American children lives in poverty and not all of them are in single-parent welfare households. David Ellwood states that 40 percent of American poor children live with two parents and that in many of those households at least one parent works.[122] They are found among the growing legion of the working poor families in the United States. Many poor children are in homes fractured by divorce and involuntary separation such as the death or imprisonment of a spouse. It is estimated that 50 percent of the children born in 1989 will live with only one parent at some point in their lives before they reach the age of 18.[123] Undoubtedly, a significant proportion of children in that group will be victimized by poverty as well.

A black child in the United States is three times more likely to live in poverty than a white child. An Hispanic child is twice as likely as a white child to be in poverty. Notwithstanding, the problem of poverty is widespread among all three groups of children. Almost fifty percent of all black children and 33 percent of all Hispanic children are in poverty. By contrast, one in six white children are victimized by poverty. The Children's Defense Fund reports that during the 1980s the poverty rate for all children, irrespective of race, climbed dramatically. However, the poverty rate for black and Hispanic children outdistanced that of white children. That fact accounts for the increased severity of poverty among those two groups.[124] Given the ubiquitousness of poverty among the young, it is clearly in the nation's best interests to devise and implement social policies far beyond quick-fix solutions that will ameliorate this condition and provide a chance for these youngsters to become full and equal participants in the opportunity structure.

CONSEQUENCES OF POVERTY

Poverty takes a devastating toll on its victims. Although millions of individuals and families do escape poverty either through their own hard work, determination, and ambition or with the assistance of government-supported social programs and become highly productive and important contributors to society, others live a life of despair, hopelessness, and daily trauma. The poor are too often regarded as outsiders and pariahs in American society. They are victimized by a loss of autonomy or a sense of control over their lives; by a feeling of powerlessness, and by a deprivation that interweaves throughout all aspects of their lives.

The poor are more likely to suffer from hunger, malnourishment, hopelessness, and inadequate housing. In 1989, for example, the Department of Housing and Urban Development (HUD) reported that 2.7 million people or about one in every five poor households lived in substandard housing. One-third of all poor blacks, compared to 27 percent of poor Hispanics and 14 percent of poor whites, lived in substandard housing.[125] The poor are also more likely to be victimized by chronic illnesses, less likely to seek out medical assistance, more likely to become mentally ill, less likely to hold health insurance, and have a higher infant mortality rate than the non-poor in the United States.[126] The life span of the poor is shorter. The poor in America have more than their share of family violence, crime and crime victimization, divorce and separation, suicide, and illegitimacy. They are isolated, physically and psychologically, from the more well-to-do in American society—an isolation that sometimes expresses itself in distrust, mutual hostility, and fear. It is, however, essential to keep in mind that America's poor are not a homogeneous group and that all too frequently the poor are victimized by unfounded myths.[127]

One of the most serious consequences of poverty is hunger. It is often difficult for Americans who have never been poverty-stricken and never had to go to bed hungry to understand how pervasive this problem is. For many such persons, discussions of hunger elicit mental images of starving refugees from the scourges of war and drought in places like Indochina, sub-saharan Africa, or of the efforts of the late Congressman Mickey Leland to bring relief to hunger-stricken people in Ethiopia, Eretrea, and Sudan. However, the events of the 1980s associated with the ravages and deprivations of unemployment focused on an alarming increase in hunger, malnourishment, and infant mortality among American citizens. A report by the U.S. Conference of Mayors in 1983 underscored the pervasiveness of the hunger problem in major cities all across the country. The media graphically portrayed long lines of people, individuals and families alike, queuing up in front of a growing number of soup kitchens, for their only meal of the day. Churches, agencies such as the Salvation Army, and other voluntary associations attempted to help alleviate the hunger problem by the extension of services to larger and larger numbers of people, while President Reagan and his administration curtailed child nutrition programs, attempted to classify ketchup as a vegetable, and pronounced that the poor could eat cheese!

Some cities established "Emergency Relief Committees" (e.g., Detroit), other emergency food programs (e.g., Cleveland and San Antonio), and appealed to the U.S. Department of Agriculture (USDA) to release more of its stored powdered milk, cheese, butter, cereal, and spaghetti to help them alleviate a mounting problem. According to the U.S. Conference of Mayors, there was a 222 percent increase in the number of requests for food during the first nine months of 1982 in New Orleans, compared to the same period in 1981. Detroit reported a 500 percent increase in the number of people accommodated by its emergency food program during the 1980–1982 period. Between 1981 and 1982, there was a 112 percent increase in the number of people who requested food assistance in Cleveland, and a 75 percent increase in the number of soup kitchens opened in Rochester, New York, in 1982. Requests for family assistance in Nashville rose by 66 percent in 1982 over the 1981 period, and a 33 percent increase was noted in the number of people served in the food program of Oakland during the same period.[128] Essentially, the problem of hunger had become so widespread by mid-1983 that city leaders were demanding stronger support from the federal government to alleviate the situation. Yet, the President's Commission on Hunger subsequently claimed that hunger was not as widespread as publicized in the media. This position was disputed and strongly criticized by the Physicians' Task Force on Hunger as a result of its investigations in 1984.

As almost unprecedented numbers of Americans were being ravaged by poverty, hunger, destitution, and homelessness, the Reagan Administration successfully engineered massive cutbacks in social programs that were constructed to alleviate such problems. For instance, by virtue of the budget cuts ordered in 1981, there was a 20 percent reduction in federally aided social programs, which included those that financed day-care centers, and many were forced to close. Working mothers who depended upon them were compelled to find other alternatives. About 687,000 of the 3.9 million family recipients of public welfare were removed from the welfare rolls. Approximately 408,000 Aid to Families with Dependant Children (AFDC) recipients, many of them black, were denied AFDC assistance. Approximately one-fifth of the losses in Medicaid programs were suffered by blacks, and about 400,000 blacks were removed from the food stamp program.[129]

Although a substantial number of blacks suffered excessive losses consequent to fiscal year 1981 and 1982 cutbacks in the "New Federalism" budget, several myths persist concerning blacks and public welfare. These myths center around the proportion of blacks receiving various forms of federal assistance, food stamps, Medicaid, Supplementary Security Income (SSI), and housing. Blacks are, of course disproportionately represented among recipients of public assistance since 22 percent of all black families benefit from such programs.[130] But blacks are disproportionately represented in the lower tier of the split-labor market, among recipients of low income, high unemployment, and poverty areas. About 83 percent of all eligible blacks, compared to 89 percent of the eligible white population, are covered by Social Security.[131]

Nevertheless, about 25 percent of black households receive food stamps and about the same proportion are on welfare; half of all black households do not receive either food stamps, welfare, or Medicaid. This assistance is confined to the truly needy and rarely to "welfare queens" who are manifestly illegal recipients of governmental largesse.[132]

However, there are different forms of welfare—welfare for the poor and welfare for the rich. It is possible to think of governmental bailouts for major corporations such as Lockheed and Chrysler (to whom the federal government made a loan of $1.3 billion in 1981) as a form of welfare for the rich. It is also possible to regard the Economic Recovery Act of 1981 (ERTA) as a form of welfare for the rich since the results of that act benefitted the well-to-do more so than persons at the lower end of the wage/income scale. This act actually increased inequities in after-tax, disposable income since persons earning over $1 million annually gained 26.1 percent in disposable income compared to less than one percent for persons earning under $5,000 per year. Further, the law permitted persons at the upper-income levels to benefit from a wide range of deductions—unlike persons at the lower end—including mortgage interest and property deductions, capital investments, benefits from inheritance tax relief, special investment credits, and capital gains subsidies.[133]

What is needed to effect more equitable income distribution and employment opportunities are sound programs organized and financed by both the public and private sectors.

SPECIAL PROGRAMS

The "War on Poverty" initiated during the Kennedy-Johnson Administrations, which encompassed what was called "Great Society" legislation, created a plethora of programs designed to alleviate the problems of unemployment, poverty, hunger, and discrimination in the attainment of jobs. Throughout the 1980s, it seemed to have become almost fashionable to conclude that that legislation did not work. While the results of the Great Society Programs were, indeed, mixed, it is erroneous to assume that none of those programs worked. Under the Economic Recovery Act of 1964, the centerpieces of the anti-poverty program were enacted. However, the overall effort included the Job Corps, VISTA, Head Start, Medicare and Medicaid, the Food Stamp Program, Manpower Training Programs, low-income housing, educational assistance programs, Upward Bound, Community Action, Foster Grandparents Program, the Legal Aid Corporation, and others. All these programs helped millions of poor people; many continue to provide much needed assistance to them in the 1990s. As Hyman Bookbinder asserts, "the War did not fail but society tired of the war too soon."[134]

By far the most controversial of all these programs, initiated during the 1960s, is affirmative action. It was under President Richard Nixon that the first federal guidelines for affirmative action were promulgated. In general, these guidelines called for "floor targets" of a specified number of underutilized groups—such as blacks, other minorities, and women who ought to be hired—and specified that "good faith" efforts must be demonstrated toward the attainment of these floor targets. The numbers proposed were interpreted by some persons and groups previously allied with civil rights organizations, such as many Jewish organizations and organized labor, as "quotas" to which they were unalterably opposed.

Nevertheless, primarily due to the enforcement powers of the federal government and the moral persuasion employed by several high-level federal administrators, affirmative action programs were implemented by thousands of business firms and institutions, in both the public and private sectors, throughout the United States. It was the existence of these programs that fostered the upward movement of blacks in the occupational structure, the hiring of larger numbers of blacks in colleges and universities, in the corporate world, and in managerial and professional positions in unprecedented numbers during the 1970s.

The issue of minority hiring was tested in several cases before the U.S. Supreme Court, and usually resulted in a firm commitment to the principles of equal employment opportunity. Such was the situation in the case of *Weber* v. *Kaiser Aluminum* (1979) in which the company's right to implement a voluntary program for the promotion of blacks with less seniority than whites was sustained. The right to "set aside" a prescribed number of jobs for blacks who had been previously denied employment opportunities was supported in *Fullilove* v. *Kluznick* (1980), and the right of a city or state to designate a fixed proportion of local residents who should be hired by public works contractors was upheld in the case of *White* v. *Massachusetts Council* (No. 81-1003) in 1983. However, the U.S. Supreme Court seemed willing to dodge the troubling issue of seniority by declaring the plaintiffs' arguments moot in *Boston Firefighters Unit, Local 718* v. *Boston Chapter, NAACP* (No. 82-185), which involved Boston employees who wanted to declare unconstitutional any layoff policy not based strictly upon seniority. Yet, the Supreme Court agreed in the spring of 1983 to hear a similar case from Memphis that involved firefighters laid off and rehired under circumstances similar to the situation in Boston. But later that year, it upheld affirmative action regarding police layoffs in Detroit since the plan, which protected blacks, was voluntarily implemented by the city. In June 1984 the U.S. Supreme Court ruled by a 6–3 decision in the Memphis case *Firefighters* v. *Stotts* (No. 82-206, 1984) that seniority takes precedence over affirmative action in layoffs. In other words, recently hired blacks cannot be protected at the expense of whites with more seniority when determining job layoffs. The implications of this decision are enormous for all minorities and women.

Since the U. S. Supreme Court handed down its momentous decision of 1954 in *Brown* v. *Board of Education of Topeka, Kansas,* blacks, other minorities, and women have looked to that body for relief from all forms of discrimination whether in terms of access to jobs, discrimination on the job, or in housing and other areas. However, when Ronald Reagan assumed the presidency following the election of 1980, it was evident that he was determined to turn back the clock on the civil rights gains of the previous quarter of a century. One of his most effective methods in implementing a conservative agenda was to replace vacant positions on the U. S. Supreme Court with justices who shared his ultra-conservative ideology and who would become activists in support of his efforts. Despite the resistance of the Supreme Court to efforts by President Reagan, Attorney General Edwin Meese and Assistant Attorney General for Civil Rights William Bradford Reynolds to undermine established affirmative action precedents, in case after case President Reagan attacked affirmative action and other civil rights gains even though he did not have a majority on the Court who supported his positions.

However, the third and final appointment to the Court made by President Reagan in the waning days of his second term, Associate Justice Anthony Kennedy, ultimately gave him the 5–4 conservative dominance he sought. As a result, it appears that Reagan was successful in structuring a Supreme Court that is either anti-civil rights or bent on reversing previous decisions that supported efforts of blacks, other minorities, and women to achieve economic, political, and social justice.

RECENT SUPREME COURT DECISIONS

Several decisions rendered by the U. S. Supreme Court in 1989 are instructive with respect to a major shift of the Court toward highly conservative interpretations of law. First, is *City of Richmond* v. *J. A. Croson Co.* This case was of special importance since Richmond, Virginia, like some 36 states and approximately 200 local governments, had voluntarily implemented minority set-asides in awarding construction contracts. That is, a specific percentage of contracts awarded must be assigned to minorities and women or to contractors who would subcontract a specific portion of their work to minority and women contractors. In 1983, the Richmond City Council enacted a 30 percent set-aside because its evidence showed that during the previous five years only two-thirds of one percent of its construction contracts had been awarded to minority-owned businesses.[135] When it was not awarded a bid to supply toilets for the city jail because it did not show that a minority subcontractor would be used on the $126,000 project, the white-owned J. A. Croson company sued on the grounds of reverse discrimination.[136]

Using the "doctrine of strict scrutiny" as justification for its decision, the Supreme Court ruled that the Richmond ordinance "violated the rights of white contractors," and did not prove "identified discrimination." By "strict scrutiny" is meant that the same constitutional test must be used to judge laws favoring blacks over whites as those involving whites over blacks. In effect, statistical evidence showing the absence of minority persons hired or given contracts in the past does not ipso facto *prove* that specific individuals had been the victims of discrimination.[137]

Among the dissenting voices against this decision were those of Associate Justice Thurgood Marshall and Associate Justice Harry Blackmun. Justice Marshall wrote:

A profound difference separates governmental actions that themselves are racist, and governmental actions that seek to remedy the effects of prior racism or to prevent neutral governmental activity from perpetuating the effects of such racism. . . . In concluding that remedial classifications warrant no different standard of review under the Constitution than the most brute and repugnant forms of state-sponsored racism, the majority of this Court signals that it regards racial discrimination as largely a phenomenon of the past and that governmental bodies need no longer preoccupy themselves with rectifying racial justice.[138]

In the same line of thinking, Associate Justice Blackmun said:

I never thought that I would live to see the day when the city of Richmond, Virginia, the cradle of the Old Confederacy, sought on its own, within a narrow confine, to lessen the stark impact of persistent discrimination. . . . But Richmond, to its credit, acted. Yet, this Court, the supposed bastion of equality, strikes down Richmond's efforts as though discrimination had never existed or was not demonstrated in this particular litigation. Justice Marshall convincingly discloses the fallacy and the shallowness of that approach. History is irrefutable, even though one might sympathize with those who though possibly innocent themselves benefit from the wrongs of the past decades.[139]

This decision opened the doors for challenges from white contractors who had been denied city/government contracts under the minority set-aside programs which had been a most effective tool for expanding job opportunities for blacks, other minorities, and women. Following the decision in the Richmond case, the Georgia Supreme Court relied on the decision in the Richmond case to rule unconstitutional the Atlanta set-aside program. Atlanta's program had established a goal of 35 percent participation of minorities and women on all city-financed projects. As a result of its effective implementation, the proportion of minorities receiving city contracts had risen from a mere 1 percent in 1972, when minorities received only $40,000 in contracts, to over 35 percent in 1989 with minorities receiving contracts totalling some $29 million.[140] Challenges followed in other cities, including Boston, while other municipalities vowed to find ways of maintaining affirmative action programs that had proven beneficial to them.[141]

The second and third decisions were handed down by the U.S. Supreme Court in March 1989. In the first of these two the Supreme Court urged a federal appeals court in Florida to "consider dismantling a Miami plan" that required a 5 percent set-aside for minorities and women. The Court in Florida had dismissed a challenge to the Metropolitan Dade County Plan under which officials had awarded a contract to a bidder who met specific guidelines for participation in its program. The project involved was financed with 80 percent federal money. However, the H. K. Porter Company sued, alleging reverse discrimination. The U. S. Supreme Court essentially agreed with that company. The second of these two decisions grew out of a challenge to the Michigan Minority Set-Aside program by the Michigan Road Builders Association. The Michigan set-aside program required by law that 7 percent of all state contracts be awarded to blacks and other minorities and that 5 percent be awarded to women. The challenge was successful at the level of the 6th U.S. Circuit Court of Appeals and the U. S. Supreme Court declared the Michigan law unconstitutional without issuing a written opinion on the case.

With those two cases decided, a pattern emerged in Court actions which suggested that the Court intended to make it particularly difficult for local and state governments to justify minority set-aside programs.

The fourth case, *Patterson* v. *McLean Credit Union* (87-107), involved a challenge to a precedent decision rendered in 1976 by the Burger Court in *Runyon* v. *McCrary.* In the *Runyon* case, the Supreme Court relied upon an 1866 law to protect the rights of citizens against harassment on the job and which outlawed discrimination in private contracts. Although no one had apparently requested the Supreme Court to reconsider this precedent, it decided in 1988 that it wished to hear testimony as to why that decision should not be overturned. Forty-seven of the 50 states Attorney Generals, 171 members of Congress, and 100 civil rights organizations signed petitions urging the Supreme Court not to overturn the Runyon decision. Although the decision in *Patterson* v. *McLean Credit Union* unanimously was against overturning that portion of *Runyon* which made it illegal to discriminate in private contracts, by a 5–4 margin the Court stated that that law was not applicable to racial harassment.

In a fifth decision, *Price Waterhouse* v. *Hopkins,* rendered in May 1989, the Supreme Court ruled that employers must prove that they have legitimate reasons for refusing to hire or promote a person and that refusal is not based upon discriminatory reasons. Yet employers can establish their own standards of appearance and conduct for their employees. Then, in June, the Supreme handed down two decisions that had far-reaching implications for established consent decrees and efforts by white men to use the allegation of "reverse discrimination" as a basis for rehearing if not overturning previous court actions. In *Martin* v. *Wilks,* the Court ruled that white firefighters in Birmingham, Alabama, have the right to challenge existing court orders and consent decrees which they believe to be reverse discrimination even eight years after a consent decree had been accepted. In other words, even though they did not challenge the consent decree at the time it was implemented, it was constitutionally within the rights of white men to wait eight years to legally assault such decrees. But in *Lorance* v. *A.T.&T.* in which three white women challenged what they believed to have been bias in changes implemented in A.T.&T.'s seniority system, the U. S. Supreme Court ruled that suits must be filed no later than *300 days* after those changes were made. In essence, the Court said that it is "never too late for white men"[142] who did not intervene at the time the consent decree was reached but for women, and presumably minorities, challenges must be immediate. Perhaps the most apparent effect of the Birmingham decision was to open up the possibility of a floodgate of white male challenges to consent decrees that have been in effect for several years and by which discrimination against minorities and women has been reduced.

In *Wards* v. *Atonio,* the Court ruled that statistical evidence which showed employment discrimination against minorities by concentrating them in low-paying jobs and whites in high-paying positions did not prove that employers did not have justifiable business reasons for their practices. The burden of proof to show otherwise was the responsibility of the employees and not of the employers. This ruling was a sweeping reversal of civil rights legislation. Previously, in 1971 in the case of *Griggs* v. *Duke Power,* the Supreme Court, presided over by Nixon appointee Warren Burger, unanimously said that it was unconstitutional for employers to utilize measures that had a racially discriminatory impact on hiring and promotions; in such challenges, it was the responsibility of the company to prove that its actions were not discriminatory. In the 1989 *Wards Cove Packing* v. *Atonio* decision, the Court shifts the burden of proof from the business company to the employees and the employer need only provide evidence that a valid business reason explained the employer's actions. Importantly, the Rehnquist Court disrespected a precedent that has become a cornerstone of civil rights law by rejecting the ruling rendered in 1971.

In *Jett* v. *Dallas Independent School District, No. 87-2984,* the U. S. Supreme Court ruled in June 1989 that Section 1981 of the Civil Rights Act of 1866 cannot be used to sue state or local governments for racial discrimination. As in most of the 1989 decisions, the vote was 5–4 and the lineup reflected the power of the conservative majority and of the Reagan appointees to the Court. One dissenter, Associate Justice Brennan, stated that "all lower Federal courts have interpreted Section 1981 as permitting damage suits against state and local governments."[143] This section had proven an effective remedy against discrimination by state and local governments.[144]

Civil rights organizations opposed these Supreme Court decisions and mounted an effort to persuade the U. S. Congress to enact measures that would overturn such Court actions. Leaders of these organizations attempted, without success, to enlist the support of President Bush in their efforts and persuade him to speak out against the dramatic shift of the Court to its more conservative interpretation. Specifically, civil rights organizations wanted President Bush to join them in their plan to persuade Congress to enact new legislation that would protect minorities and women from dismantlement of statutes and regulatory procedures that had been successful in facilitating greater economic opportunity for all citizens. President Bush initially responded only in noncommittal platitudes such as his opposition to prejudice and discrimination against anyone. However, Benjamin L. Hooks, Executive Director of the NAACP, said in his address before the delegates to the 1989 national NAACP convention in Detroit that the U. S. Supreme Court "is more dangerous to the legitimate hopes and aspirations of black people in this nation" than the segregationist foes of the civil rights movement."[145] Many blacks and other minorities who looked to the Supreme Court for protection of their constitutional rights now, in the early 1990s, are convinced that such support can no longer be taken for granted. The lobbying efforts of civil rights groups against the six 1989 U. S. Supreme Court decisions eventually persuaded the U. S. Congress to enact the Civil Rights Act of 1990. This Act was designed to safeguard and protect employment rights of minorities and women that were weakened by 1989 Supreme Court decisions.* Ironically, many civil rights lawyers sense that the greatest safeguards against discrimination will be found in state action.

Between 1954 and 1989, but especially in the pre-Ronald Reagan years, the NAACP, with the support of the EEOC, was successful in gaining compliance with federal employment guidelines. Many of the nation's largest firms and municipalities were persuaded to hire and promote minorities and women in greater numbers, to make back payments for past acts of discrimination, and to develop more aggressive affirmative action programs. Despite various subterfuges and insincerities in some areas, individual companies or institutions, affirmative action worked all too well. It came under relentless attack during the 1970s by various groups of people including some Jews who believed themselves justifiably (based upon their past experiences with discrimination) opposed to quotas, as well as those who actually resented federal intervention in the hiring process and also wished to maintain the status quo in their hiring practices. As a result, especially since 1981, when Reagan entered the White House, there was a steady retrenchment from affirmative action by many employers and an erosion of many gains achieved consequent to the more positive actions taken during the late 1960s and early 1970s.

One explanation for this situation is the fact that President Reagan vigorously opposed affirmative action. Under his administration, EEOC enforcement slackened and many employers firmly believed that the Reagan Administration that was so hostile to civil rights would not enforce punitive action against persons who either violated EEOC and federal guidelines or would ignore requests for assistance from aggrieved minorities and women.

OTHER ANTI-POVERTY PROGRAMS

According to a 1988 study by the U. S. Bureau of the Census, the most effective program for attacking poverty has been Social Security. More than the tax system, Social Security is most effective for reducing inequality.[146] This report claimed that through the Social Security program, between 1978 and 1986, the number of poor people fell from 50.6 million to 35.5 million and that 15.1 million people were able to escape poverty in 1986 alone.[147] The elderly population, particularly, benefited from So-

---

*Undoubtedly bowing to pressure from ultra-conservative Republicans and the white business community, President Bush vetoed this Act. Thus, he follows Presidents Reagan and Andrew Johnson as the only presidents to ever veto a civil rights act.

cial Security since their poverty rate registered a particularly sharp decline from 47.5 percent to 14 percent over that period.[148] Cash welfare programs were comparatively less effective in reducing poverty since only 2.1 million people rose above the poverty line by virtue of cash welfare benefits.

How are government benefits (including housing subsidies, Medicare, Medicaid, and food stamps) distributed by race? How are these benefits related to the taxes paid by various segments of the population? The Bureau of the Census study cited above indicated that American households paid $581.6 billion in taxes but received $298.1 billion in benefits. White households, composing 86.4 percent of all households, received 86.1 percent of all benefits. These households paid $530.7 billion in taxes and obtained $256.6 billion in benefits. By contrast, black households, representing 11.1 percent of the total number, were the recipients of 12.1 percent of government benefits. They paid $34.2 billion in taxes and obtained $36 billion in benefits. Hispanic households composed 6.1 percent of the total number, paid 3.8 percent of the taxes, and but received 5.2 percent of the benefits. The dollar value of their benefits ($15.4 billion) was significantly less than the $22 billion that Hispanic families paid in taxes.

By far, the elderly population received a greatly disproportionate share of the benefits either in terms of their representation in the total population or actual taxes paid. The elderly of all races, who make up 23.4 percent of all households and paid $60.7 billion in taxes, received more than two-thirds (68.4 percent). Slightly more than one-fifth (21.5 percent) of government benefits went to families with children (Table 2.10).

Not explicit in such benefits is welfare for the rich. They gain from tax breaks, loopholes in tax law, and gigantic and costly corporate bail-out programs. For example, conservative estimates of the 1989 government-financed bail-out bill for the nation's faltering Savings and Loan Associations is at least $326 billion. Taxpayers of all races will undoubtedly subsidize the greed, avarice, and mismanagement of the more well-to do which were components in the S & L problems.

Table 2.10   WHO BENEFITS FROM GOVERNMENT PROGRAMS?

Household type	Percent of household	Taxes paid	Percent of total	Benefits (in billions)	Percent
All	100	$581.6	100	$298.1	100
White	86.4	$530.6	91.2	$256.6	86.1
Black	11.1	$34.2	5.9	$36.0	12.1
Hispanic (all races)	6.1	$22.0	3.9	$15.4	5.2
Elderly	23.4	$60.7	10.4	$204.0	68.4
Family w/children	37.8	$242.2	41.6	64.2	21.5

Source: U.S. Bureau of the Census.

THE REAGAN ADMINISTRATION AND BLACKS

President Reagan was considered among many black Americans as an enemy to the cause of racial justice, economic and educational opportunity, and equality. He symbolized all the efforts "to turn back the clock" to the days when overt discrimination and racial hostility were the norms in American society. He vigorously opposed affirmative action, quotas in hiring, busing for school desegregation, and other remedies against past and current discrimination. He was almost vehement in his attacks on the Legal Aid Corporation which served the needs of poor people and tried unsuccessfully to totally destroy it. He attempted to use the U. S. Commission on Civil Rights as an instrument for the implementation of policies consistent with his own conservative ideology. His administration filed amicus briefs in support of plaintiffs who alleged reverse discrimination and had government attorneys shift support from litigants who had been successful in gaining anti-discriminatory consent decrees to support others who claimed reverse discrimination (e.g., Birmingham firefighters). He steadfastly refused to meet with members of the Congressional Black Caucus throughout his entire eight years in office, even to discuss problems of economic and social justice for all American citizens. He was the only President who refused to meet with the Congressional Black Caucus in the 20 years since its formation.

During the course of a president's four-year term, a president may make approximately 1,000 appointments to such positions as department secretaries, undersecretaries, assistant secretaries, other executive branch agency heads, U. S. Attorneys, judges, and ambassadors.[149] The differences between former Presidents Reagan and Carter in this regard are striking. President Carter, in his first year in office, selected minorities for 14 percent and women 12 percent of such appointments, both full-and-part-time. These proportions rose to 21 and 22 percent, respectively, for minorities and women, by the end of his four-year term. President Carter appointed the first black male as U. N. Representative for the United States, the first black to serve as Secretary of the Army, and the first black woman to a Cabinet position. Of the 1,192 appointments made by President Carter during his four-year term, 12.2 percent were black, compared to 4.1 percent of the 980 appointments made by former President Reagan during his first two years in office.

Goldman's analysis of federal appointments covering the administrations of former Presidents Johnson, Nixon, Ford, Carter, and Reagan revealed that the Reagan first-term record was the worst of all five administrations in the recruitment and hiring of blacks. The Reagan Administration was second only to the Carter Administration in terms of appointments of women and Hispanics but there was little apparent effort to embrace blacks for administrative or judicial appointments. Only 0.8 percent of Reagan's U. S. District Court appointees were black, compared to 13.9 percent for Carter, 5.4 percent for Ford, and 3.4 percent for Nixon.[150] Under President Carter, 16.1 percent of all appointees to the

Court of Appeals were black but under President Reagan only 3.2 percent were black.[151]

By late 1986, 290 federal judges had been appointed during the first six years of the Reagan Administration. Of that number, five or less than 2 percent were black. During the same period, only two of the 93 U. S. Attorney appointees were black.[152] The Office of Attorney General under Meese and William Bradford Reynolds was opposed to affirmative action and, apparently, did not recommend a representative number of blacks for positions in the Justice Department. Following the embarrassment of the Iran Contra affair and the resignation of his National Security Adviser, President Reagan did appoint General Colin Powell, a well-respected military man who happened to be black, to that important and crucial position. Nevertheless and without question, very few blacks served in the Reagan Administration. For all these reasons, black Americans had very little faith or trust in former President Reagan.

In summary, the conditions of low income, inaccessibility to high-paying occupations, widespread unemployment, and pervasive poverty are dominant in the black community today. If allowed to continue unchecked, they will have major consequences for the quality of life not only in the black community itself but for America as a whole. These conditions have a profound impact on the stability of the family, and on those who are forced to seek public assistance and must suffer severe psychological trauma in the process. They create invidious stratification systems, inhibit the mobility of people from one social stratum to another, and determine to a large degree who will not be educated. They combine with racism to keep blacks contained in the concrete ghettos of the inner cities or isolated in rural areas or spatially separated in the South and in the North restricted to areas surrounded by white suburbanites who continually seek to block their exits. Low income, unemployment, and poverty effectively unite with racist practices to reduce the availability of black capital necessary for the construction and survival of black business. This situation, in turn, undermines the potential political power that could be generated in several black communities. For power is not only the possession of resources; among other things it is also a function of the mobilization of those available resources. Mobilization requires money. Finally, the problems of low income, poverty, unemployment, and racism may be directly interconnected to expressions of deviant behavior, whether in the forms of psychological disorders or alcohol and drug abuse.

NOTES

1. For the pros and cons of this topic, see Charles V. Willie, *The Class Caste Controversy* (Bayside, N. Y.: General Hall, 1979).
2. Cf. James E. Blackwell, "Persistence and Change in Intergroup Relations: The Crisis upon Us," *Social Problems* 29:4 (April 1982): 325–346, and Manning

Marable, "Reaganism, Racism and Reaction: Black Political Realignment in the 1980's," *The Black Scholar* 13:6 (Fall 1982): 2–15.

3. Paul Blumberg, *Inequality in the Age of Decline* (New York: Oxford University Press, 1980), p. 17.

4. *Ibid.*, p. 32.

5. Sethard Fisher, *Power and the Black Community* (New York: Random House), p. 217 and Chap. 29.

6. Lerone Bennett, "The Making of Black America: The Black Worker, Part X," *Ebony,* 27 (December 1972): 73–79, and (November 1972): 118–122.

7. Gunnar Myrdal, *An American Dilemma* (New York: Harper & Row, 1945).

8. Joseph F. Brooks, "The Decline in Black Landownership," *Focus,* 11:5 (May, 1983): 6.

9. *Ibid.*

10. Quoted in Christopher C. Williams, "Advising the New Administration," *Black Enterprise* (January 1989): 49–53.

11. James E. Blackwell, *Mainstreaming Outsiders: The Production of Black Professionals,* 2nd ed. (Dix Hills, N. Y.: General Hall, 1987).

12. Edna Bonacich, "A Theory of Ethnic Antagonism: The Split Labor Market," *American Sociological Review* (October 1972): 547–559.

13. Cf. E. Newton and U. Gupta, "Fighting Back in Hollywood," *Black Enterprise* (September 1982): 35–39, and "Blacks and the Mass Media," *Crisis* (June/July, 1989).

14. Newton and Gupta, *ibid.*

15. *Ibid.*

16. "Blacks in Hollywood: What Roles Do They Play?," *West 57, CBS Program* (May 27, 1989).

17. *Op. cit.*

18. Cited in Erwin Washington, "Why? And What Can Be Done?," *Crisis* (June/July 1989): 34–40, 66.

19. *Ibid.*

20. *Ibid.*, p. 40.

21. *Ibid.*

22. Cited in *Jet Magazine* (July 5, 1989): 25.

23. Newton and Gupta, *op. cit.*, p. 35.

24. Noah W. Griffin, "Broadcasting," *Crisis* (June/July 1989): 28–32, 66.

25. *Ibid.*

26. Cf. Benjamin L. Hooks, "Publisher's Foreword," *Crisis* (June/July 1989): 4; David Hatchett, "Blacks and the Mass Media," *Crisis* (June/July 1989): 18–26, 68; "Minorities in Newsrooms Are Now at Crisis Stage," *Jet* (July 31, 1989): 18; and "Newspapers: Minority Hiring Weak," *USA Today* (August 25, 1988), p. 28.

27. Hatchett, *op. cit.*

28. Telephone discussion with Harry Edwards, April 5, 1983.

29. Murray Chass, "Highest-Paid Player, It's Your Pick," *New York Times* (February 12, 1989), Section 8, p. 3.

30. Arthur Ashe, *A Hard Road to Glory: A History of the African-American Athlete, Vol. One: 1619–1918* (New York: An Amistad Book—Warner Book, 1988); NBC Nightly News Report (July 10, 1989); "U. S. Blacks a Minority in Major League Baseball," *Jet* (June 26, 1989): 50; Frank Robinson, *Extra Innings: My Life in Baseball* (New York: McGraw-Hill, 1988).

31. David Halberstam, "Champions We Never Knew," *New York Times* (December 4, 1988), p. 11.
32. Arthur Ashe, *op. cit.,* and *NBC Nightly News, op. cit.*
33. Murray Chass, "Baseball Salaries Are Reaching the Upper Deck," *New York Times* (December 13, 1988), p. B-9; David Halberstram, *op. cit.;* and Larry Whiteside, "Fading Dreams: Minority Development More Mirage Than Reality," *Boston Globe* (November 15, 1988), p. 77.
34. Nelson George, "The New Bidding Game in Sports," *Black Enterprise* (January 1983): 28–32.
35. *Ibid.*
36. Cf. Steve Askin, "Turmoil in the Ranks," *Black Enterprise* (September 1982): 59–64, and Douglas C. Lyons, "Black Labor Leaders, *Ebony* (June 1989): 42–47.
37. George Davis and Glegg Watson, *Black Life in Corporate America* (New York: Doubleday, 1982), p. 60.
38. Cf. Peggy Schmidt, "Women and Minorities: Is the Industry Ready?," *New York Times* (October 16, 1988), p. F-5.
39. Patti Doten, "Beyond Corporations' Glass Ceiling," *Boston Globe* (August 31, 1989), p. 77.
40. Cf. John W, Work, *Race, Economics and Corporate America* (Wilmington, De.: Scholarly Resources Inc., 1984).
41. See *Black Enterprise Magazine* (February 1988).
42. Earl Graves, Address to the 78th Annual National Urban League Convention, Detroit, Michigan; August 2, 1988, unpublished.
43. Peter Ramjug, "Minority, Women Management Jobs Rising at Banks," *Boston Globe,* (August 28, 1989), p. 10.
44. Schmidt, *op. cit.*
45. Cited in *New York Times* (August 20, 1989), p. F-3; see also Bureau of Labor Statistics, *Projections 2000* (Washington, D.C.: U. S. Government Printing Office), 1989.
46. James E. Blackwell, *Youth Employment and Unemployment in Massachusetts: Outreach Initiatives* (Boston: William Monroe Trotter Institute, University of Massachusetts/Boston, 1987).
47. *Ibid.* and *op. cit.*
48. *Ibid.* and James E. Blackwell, *Youth and Jobs* (Boston: William Monroe Trotter Institute, University of Massachusetts/Boston, 1987).
49. "Careers and Opportunities in 1989," *Black Enterprise* (February 1989): 67–70.
50. Cf. Barry Bluestone and Bennett Harrison, "The Grim Truth About the Job Miracle," *New York Times* (February 1, 1987).
51. *Ibid.*
52. Louis Uchitelle, "As Jobs Increase, So Does Insecurity," *New York Times* (May 1, 1988), p. F-25.
53. Williams, *op. cit.,* p. 51.
54. *Ibid.,* pp. 51–52.
55. Cf. John Herbers, "Census Data Reveal 70s Legacy, Poorer Cities and Richer Suburbs," *New York Times* (February 27, 1983); James E. Blackwell and Philip Hart, *Cities, Suburbs and Blacks* (Bayside, N. Y.: General Hall, 1983); and James E. Blackwell and Philip Hart, *Race Relations in Boston: Institutional Neglect, Turmoil and Change* (Boston: The Boston Committee, 1983).

56. Herbers, *op. cit.*
57. Robert Pear, "U. S. Pensions Found to Lift Many of Poor," *New York Times* (December 20, 1988), p. 1.
58. James Lardner, "Rich, Richer; Poor, Poorer," *New York Times* (April 19, 1989), p. A-27.
59. *Ibid.*
60. Peter Passell, "Forces in Society, and Reaganism Helped Dig Deeper Hole for Poor," *New York Times* (July 16, 1989), p. 1, and Irene Sege, "Growing Gap Shown Between Rich, Poor," *Boston Globe* (May 15, 1989), p. 17.
61. *Op. cit.*
62. *Ibid.* (*Note:* These writers interviewed such economists and other social scientists as Frank Levy, Sheldon Danziger, Isabel Sawhill, Barry Bluestone, Robert Reich, Fenis Welch, and Christopher Jencks).
63. *Ibid.,* and Passell, *op. cit.*
64. *Ibid.*
65. *Ibid.*
66. Cf. James E. Blackwell, "Persistence and Change: The Crisis Upon Us," *Social Problems* 29:4 (April 1982): 325–346.
67. Cf. Tony Brown, "Economics: The Final Stage of the Civil Rights Movement" (An address given before the Commonwealth Club of California; February 20, 1987); Terri Jones, "Japan's Hiring Policies Blasted," *Boston Globe* (January 1, 1989) p. 17, and "Don't Ignore Impact of Ethnic Market on U. S. Economy: NAMD Prexy," *Jet* (June 26, 1989): 23.
68. "Backstage," *Ebony* (May 1989): 2.
69. *Op. cit.*
70. Margaret C. Simms, "Black Youth Face Uncertain Jobs Future," *Focus* (April 1988): 6.
71. Blackwell, *op. cit.* (1987a).
72. Blackwell, *op. cit.* (1987b).
73. Bernard Anderson's comments cited in Elliot D. Lee, "The Black Enterprise Board of Economics Look Into the Future," *Black Enterprise* (June 1982): 192.
74. *Ibid.*
75. Blumberg, *op. cit.,* p. 5.
76. *Ibid.*
77. *Ibid.*
78. Andrew F. Brimmer, "Foreign Employment and Economic Welfare," *Black Enterprise* (April 1982): 28.
79. *Ibid.*
80. *Ibid.*
81. Sir Arthur Lewis, "Black Americans and the Changing World Economy," *Black Enterprise* (March 1983): 36.
82. *Ibid.*
83. Cf. Frederick V. Boyd, "Black Enterprise Board of Economics Report: Unemployment," *Black Enterprise* (March 1983): 63–66, and Blackwell and Hart, *loc. cit.*
84. Leonard Silk, "Economic Scene: Reasons to Fear A Recession," *New York Times* (August 25, 1989), p. D-2.
85. Jack Anderson, "Who Owns America?," *Parade Magazine* (April 16, 1989): 4–6.
86. "Japanese Slurs on Blacks Causing Rifts Between Them," *Jet* (October 31, 1988): 12.

87. Joint Center for Political Studies, "Immigration and Black America," *Focus* 3 (February 1983): 1–4.
88. Terri Jones, *op. cit.*
89. *Ibid.*
90. "Nissan to Pay $605,600 to Settle Race and Bias Case," *New York Times* (February 4, 1989), p. 8.
91. Quoted in "Japanese Racial Insensitivity—Again," *Focus* (July 1988): 2.
92. *Ibid.*
93. Terri Jones, *op. cit.*
94. *Focus* (July 1988), p. 2.
95. *Ibid.*
96. *Ibid.*
97. Herbers, *op. cit.*
98. Robert Pear, "Reagan Asks Wide Cuts in Programs to Aid Poor," *New York Times* (January 29, 1983), p. 6.
99. NBC Nightly News (June 17, 1983).
100. Silk, *op. cit.*
101. Isiah Poole, "The Disappearing Civil Servant," *Black Enterprise* (February 1983): 91–94.
102. *Ibid.*
103. Robert Pear, "Broad Recovery Called Essential to Job Creation," *New York Times* (November 28, 1982), p. 28.
104. Joint Center for Political Studies, *op. cit.*
105. Gupta, *op. cit.*
106. *Op. cit.*
107. *Op. cit.*
108. *Ibid.*
109. *Ibid.*
110. *Ibid.*
111. Adam Clymer, "Joblessness Causes Stress and Gloom About Nation," *New York Times* (February 2, 1983), p. A-19.
112. Editorial, *New York Times* (January 7, 1983).
113. Bureau of the Census, *Characteristics of the Population Below the Poverty Level: 1981,* U. S. Department of Commerce, Current Population Reports, Series P-60; No. 138 (March 1983).
114. Cf. Current Population Reports for specified years.
115. Felicity Barringer, "Number of Nations' Poor Remains at 32 Million for a Second Year," *New York Times* (October 19, 1989), p. A-24.
116. Cf. "Poverty: Who Are The Poor?," *USA Today* (September 1, 1988), p. 8A.
117. Joyce E. Allen, "The Forgotten Poor: Blacks in Rural Areas," *Focus* (July 1988): 5–6.
118. *Ibid.*
119. *Ibid.*
120. David T. Ellwood, *Poverty in the American Family* (New York: Basic Books, 1988).
121. Irene Sege, "Poverty's Grip on Children Widens," *Boston Globe* (March 12, 1989), p. 1.
122. Cited in *ibid.*
123. *Ibid.*
124. "Report Finds Poverty Among Children Up," *New York Times* (February 2, 1989), p. C-13.

125. E. J. Dionne, "Poor Paying More for Their Shelter," *New York Times* (April 18, 1989), p. A-18.
126. Robert H. Lauer, *Social Problems and the Quality of Life*, 4th ed. (Dubuque, Iowa: William C. Brown, 1989), Ch. 8.
127. *Ibid.*
128. Blackwell and Hart, *Cities, Suburbs and Blacks*, pp. 191–192.
129. Harry A. Ploski and James Williams, *The Negro Almanac: A Reference Work on the Afro-American*, 4th ed. (New York: John Wiley and Sons, 1983), pp. 659–661.
130. *Ibid.*
131. *Ibid.*
132. John K. Scholtz, "Reforming the Tax Structure," *Focus* 11:4 (April 1983): 5.
133. Cf. Blackwell and Hart. *op. cit.* and Manning Marable, *op. cit.*
134. Hyman Bookbinder, "Did the War on Poverty Fail?," *New York Times* (August 20, 1989), p. E-3.
135. Linda Greenhouse, "Court Bars a Plan Set Up to Provide Jobs for Minorities," *New York Times* (January 24, 1989), p. 1.
136. *Ibid.*
137. *Ibid.*
138. *Ibid.*
139. Quoted in *ibid.*
140. Ronald Smothers, "Atlanta's Minority Plan Is Struck Down," *New York Times* (March 3, 1989), p. A-14.
141. Cf. Martin Tolchin, "Officials in Cities and States Vow to Continue Minority Contractor Programs," *New York Times* (January 25, 1989), p. A-18; Smothers, *op. cit.;* and Ronald Smothers, "Affirmative Action Booms in Atlanta," *New York Times* (January 27, 1989), p. A-10.
142. This is the heading of an editorial on this subject: *New York Times* (June 15, 1989), p. A-26.
143. Quoted in Linda Greenhouse, "New Limit Is Placed on Scope of 1866 Civil Rights Law," *New York Times* (June 23, 1989), p. A-8.
144. Cf. *op. cit.* and Frank R. Parker, "The Supreme Court: Which Way on Civil Rights?," *Focus* (October 1988), 4–8.
145. Quoted in Julie Johnson, "High Court Called Threat to Blacks," *New York Times* (July 10, 1989), p. A-14.
146. *Ibid.*
147. *Ibid.*
148. *Ibid.*
149. Quoted in *ibid.*
150. *Ibid.*
151. Sheldon Goldman, "Reagan's Judicial Appointments," *Focus* (March 1985): 4.
152. Cf. "Political Trend Letter," *Focus* (March 1987): 7–8.

Chapter
3

The Black Family in American Society

*T*his chapter examines the family as the basic social unit in the structure of the black community. The major argument here is that, both structurally and functionally, the black family system further exemplifies the high degree of differentiation within the black community referred to earlier. Attention will be devoted to such topics as: (1) the impact of slavery on black family life, (2) patterns of family life, (3) interracial marriage, (4) controversial issues such as illegitimacy, divorce, and the black matriarchy, and (5) urbanization and the changing family. The reader is cautioned here regarding the author's use of the definite article *the* in reference to black families. It is employed here purely for the sake of convenience and not as a description universally characteristic of black persons or families.

THE IMPACT OF SLAVERY ON THE BLACK FAMILY

Some sociologists argue that the black family in contemporary America is heading toward increasing disintegration and that this process has its roots in slavery. The most common element in their theories is to regard slavery as the cause of all the pathologies that they say are "characteristic" of the black family today.[1] Undoubtedly, slavery did leave its mark upon black family patterns but not with the magnitude claimed by Frazier and Moynihan. It has never been satisfactorily demonstrated that slavery is directly and exclusively accountable for *all* the present-day attributes of the black family life. Slavery was responsible, however, for establishing a caste system that relegated blacks to an inferior status. The detrimental effects of this status, from which they have never fully recovered, profoundly affect black family life.

Slavery undermined the family as the fulcrum of the social order that blacks had known in West Africa, from which most slaves came, even though it never *completely* destroyed marriage and the family as important social institutions. The process of family erosion was slow and insidious but quite effective, nonetheless. To begin, some slaves did marry, of course. However, it is inescapable that whether or not marriages were voluntary, they affected black peoples' chances of remaining together until death. Their opportunities for relatively stable sexual unions outside the institution of marriage not only varied from region to region but also depended upon the willingness of slaveowners to adhere to the law regarding these unions. Whites in New England, for example, applied far more stringent regulatory norms to black people and to whites themselves than did whites in most of the southern regions. Consonant with the Puritan ethic, they expected all who engaged in heterosexual activities to do so only after they had taken marital vows. The publishing of marital bans prior to marriage, which was conducted by a magistrate, was a further effort to regulate sexual norms. There is considerable evidence to support Franklin's argument that this explicit respect for the institution of marriage and the implicit regard for the family prevailed throughout New England.[2] Not unexpectedly, black people were eager to conform to these societal and legalistic expectations, since they had come from areas having carefully delineated proscriptions for the institution of marriage and the family. It was in the South, however, more so than in any other region, where Frazier's comment about the inimicality of economics for black family life takes on more explicit meaning. During the early stages of the slave trade, more men were recruited than women, largely because of the need for strong men to till the soil and work the land. This created a highly distorted sex ratio, but in time more black women were forced into American slavery, which not only balanced the sex ratio better but proved to be economically more profitable for slaveowners.

In the South and Middle Atlantic states, particularly, experiments with different forms of slave unions, both in and out of wedlock, occurred but largely as a means of strengthening economic life among large slaveowners. Thus legal marriages, casual unions, and stud farms—whose main purpose was the production and subsequent marketing of children like cattle—were sanctioned by the prevailing social system. During this process, there developed a myth of black licentiousness and animalistic sexual behavior overlaid with a disdain for formalized marital unions. This myth was created by slaveowners who structured social situations that facilitated a self-fulfilling prophecy of sexual behavior between black men and women. It was convenient to rationalize, for instance, that blacks had no regard for marriage while whites were simultaneously forcing them into sexual unions on stud farms, often without benefit of marriage. Not infrequently, young girls of 13 became mothers. Once their fecundity had been established, they were used to bear more children with amazing regularity so that by the time they reached 25 at least a dozen children had been born.[3] Many of the children were traded or sold and separated from their families. Many fathers were never permitted an opportunity to play the role of husband-father. Casual, if not brittle, familial relationships were common. In many instances the extirpation of family life as we know it among slaves was a *sine qua non* for maintenance of the economic system of slavery. Therefore, innumerable family units were destroyed by the persistent practice of selling fathers or mothers separately and children as well, or by trading children for other property or cash.

The contempt for black family structures displayed by white slave-owners and overseers was engendered by a system that simultaneously made black women easily accessible to white men. In the American population the diversity of color found among persons legally identified as black is evidence of the extent to which cohabitation between the races occurred in the past. White men exploited their superior group status in taking advantage of black women. They began the practice of bedding black women, impregnating them, and then deserting them, leaving them to fend for themselves and their offspring. (White women, too, occasionally initiated secret liaisons with black mandangoes, sometimes at great personal risks to themselves and the black males.)

When black men did leave their families, historical and sociological evidence shows that they usually did so under duress. The only alternative to forced separation was instant death. Indeed, numerous slave escapes were undertaken because of the unfailing determination of black men to reunite with their family members. Even their success at this endeavor *fails* to confirm the viewpoint that slaves welcomed separation because it permitted greater freedom to establish new sexual liaisons. Although white disregard for the black slave family seems to have been the norm, there were exceptions. In the South and Middle Atlantic states, for example, usually depending upon the size of the plantation, some slaveowners did make valiant attempts to protect and preserve the sanctity of the institution of the family among slaves. Smaller plantation owners were often more diligent in this regard than larger owners, among whom a callous disregard for black family life was particularly characteristic.[4]

Without question, slavery left an enduring impact on black family life. In the 1990s, however, it is necessary to look for additional explanations for the changing characteristics of black families in the United States. In the first place, it is necessary to stress that profound changes are occurring in the structure, composition, and other characteristics of both white and black families. In fact, some conditions that once dominated the literature as evidence of the unique family disorganization within the black community are increasing at extremely rapid rates in the white community. For instance, there are more white women in the labor force in 1990 than black women, creating the necessity to look for alternative child care arrangements; the battered wife syndrome and child abuse are no longer the exclusive domain of the black working class. The white teenage pregnancy rate is showing a steady, significant upturn while the black teenage pregnancy rate is decreasing (even though the black teenage pregnancy rate is still alarmingly higher), and the highest increase in female-headed households registered during the decade of the 1970s was by college-educated women. Further, more and more white females are gravitating toward other patterns that once seemed to have been far more characteristic of black families. For instance, many white females are deciding to keep children born out of wedlock as most black women have always done under similar circumstances.[5]

As Hill points out, it is vital to examine the degree to which other factors contribute to these changing characteristics of both black and white families. Blacks remain unique with respect to the magnitude of American racism; relentless discrimination and prejudice have thwarted their efforts to sustain viable family units. It is, indeed, a measure of the resilience of the black community that the family has survived in the face of so much racial hostility and discrimination within the American society. Both blacks and whites suffer from high rates of unemployment and poverty, and such economic instability is highly correlated with marital instability.[6] However, since the black unemployment rate is usually twice that of the white population (even higher in some cities) and the black teenage unemployment rate is some three times that of white teenagers, and since blacks are still more likely to be relegated to the lower tier of the split-labor market with a fraction of the wages paid to white workers, it should not be unexpected that they would be doubly impacted by those factors associated with family instability.

PATTERNS OF FAMILY LIFE

It is from the conditions mentioned in Chapter 2 and above that the diversity in black family life emerges. As we shall see, black family life varies by types of marriage, authority structure, household patterns, family functions, and the degree of stability. Chapter 4 will extend this diversity to include social class attributes and mobility patterns. Despite their persistent variation, these factors collectively become crucial elements in a family system.

Marriage Types

Monogamy is, of course, the norm among black families in America; that is, almost all black people conform to the law permitting one spouse at a time. Variations from this pattern represent aberrations to traditional patterns. *Serial monogamy* is a series of marriages of relatively short duration between a man and a woman. While serial monogamy is quite widespread throughout the American society, with many persons having second or third marriages within the black population, it appears to be more characteristic of lower socioeconomic groups than others. It also occurs among black Americans, especially consequent to the advent of more permissiveness and freedom in obtaining divorces which appears to have accompanied the so-called sexual revolution and the counterculture movement of the 1960s and 1970s.

Common-law marriages are informal marriages between a man and a woman who decide to live together as husband and wife without the benefit of more formalized marital sanctions such as a marriage license. Except in a few states, common-law marriages are not recognized as legal and the children from such unions may not be considered legitimate unless paternity is legally acknowledged. Common-law marriage is similar to the practice of "taking up" with someone, in which case an unmarried couple may live in marital arrangements for an indefinite period of time. The various forms of boyfriend-girlfriend arrangements, discussed in a later section of this chapter, may be a derivative of the "taking-up" phenomenon. Similarly, casual living arrangements of unmarried couples, which increased at relatively high rates during the 1970s so that 1.8 million households were counted by 1981, are also a variation on this theme.

Interracial marriages are legal unions between persons of different races. As discussed in a subsequent section, most marriages in the United States involving blacks and whites are those in which a black male is married to a white female. Given the imbalanced sex ratio in the black population, that is, a higher number of black women than black men, the marriage of black men to nonblack women not accompanied by a equal number of "other race" men available to black women reduces their chances of getting married.

Marriage Rates

One particularly notable trend with respect to marriage during the 1970s and 1980s was an increasing tendency for Americans to postpone the age of first marriage. Between 1970 and 1981, the median age of first marriage increased by 1½ years or to 22.3 years for women and 24.8 years for men. By 1985, the figures were 23 and 24.8, for men and women, respectively. Blacks tend to postpone marriage to a later date than whites, a pattern observed since 1960. In 1960, among persons aged 20 to 24, 56 percent of black men, compared to 53 percent of white men, were never married. In 1970, the figures were 57 percent for black men and 56 percent for white men. By 1980, 79 percent of all black 20–24-year-old-men were never married in contrast to 69 percent of white males in the same age cohort. However, by 1989, almost eight of every ten (76.0 percent) of all 20 to 24 year old white males, compared to 84.9% of black males, were single, never married individuals. Among females in the same age cohort, the percentages of never married black females were 36 in 1960; 43 in 1970, 69 in 1980 and 77.9 in 1989. By contrast, among white females never married, the percentages were 29,36,50 and 59.9 for 1960, 1970, 1980, and 1989, respectively.[7] These changes probably reflect college attendance patterns as well as postponement of marriage due to such factors as uncertain job prospects, lower beginning salary/wage rates and fears of a recession, military service, imprisonment, rising housing costs, and the increasing proclivity of young people to live in a trial marital arrangement before legally consummating marriage, if ever. Race notwithstanding, the average age of first marriage for men in the United States is 26 while that for women is almost 24. The number of unmarried couples living together quadrupled between 1970 and 1987. The numbers of such couples climbed from 523,000 in 1970 to 2,334,000 in 1987. The latter figure included 1,315,000 never married men and 950,000 never married women, or 97 percent of all such couples.[8] While Bureau of Census data do not disaggregate these figures by race, it is not unreasonable to assume that all races are represented among persons living in trial marriage arrangements as well as among those persons living together but who have no intention of every marrying their living partners.

The pattern of declining proportions of married persons in the black population continues. The most recent data, published in 1989, show that the percent married in the 18 and over black population is 47.7. Approximately half (50.9 percent) of all black men and 45 percent of all black women in this age cohort are married.[9]

Interracial Marriages

Between 1660 and 1967, blacks and whites were often prohibited from marrying each other in many colonies and states. This restriction was imposed as a boundary-maintenance system designed to maintain racial separation of the sexes and, most particularly, to restrict sexual congress between black men and white women. While most states imposed such restrictions at one time or another during that period, they did very little to prevent the sexual exploitation of the black female by the white male. It was virtually unheard of to convict a white male of raping a black woman but countless numbers of black men were convicted and lynched due to allegations of rape, attempted rape, or "thoughts of raping" white women. These actions did in fact reduce sexual contact between black men and white women but, again, did not deter those white men who desired black women as concubines, mistresses, or secret lovers from having them.[10]

Legal restrictions against interracial marriages existed in 29 states in 1960; most of these states were in the southern and border regions. The number of states with such prohibitions declined to 19 within a four-year period (1964) probably because of pressures for change as well as by virtue of the fact that many young people involved in the spirit of the 1960s were ignoring state regulatory norms. In 1967 the case of *Loving* v. *Virginia* reached the United States Supreme Court in which a white male and a black female petitioned to overturn a Virginia law that banned interracial marriages. The Supreme Court agreed with the Lovings that such statutes violated their constitutional rights and declared unconstitutional all existing legal restrictions against interracial marriages. Thus the laws remaining in some 16 states were declared unconstitutional.[11]

Even though legal barriers against interracial marriages were removed by virtue of the Supreme Court's action in *Loving* v. *Virginia*, rigid social customs and taboos still prevent many persons who may desire to transcend racial boundaries from marrying across racial lines. However, small increases in interracial unions were noted in the years following the Loving decision. Between 1960 and 1970, black/white marriages rose from 0.44 percent to 0.70 percent of all marriages in the United States.[12]

The absolute number of interracial marriages has continued to climb since 1970. For instance, in 1970 the number of such couples was 310,000. By 1977 it had climbed to 421,000 and by 1980 the absolute number of 613,000 almost doubled the 1970 figure. However, the 799,000 interracially married couples were approximately two and a half times greater than the 1970 figure. The general pattern in black/white marriages is a dyad of black male/white female. In 1970, 63 percent of all black/white marriages involved such unions. By 1977 black male/white female couples represented 76 percent of all black/white marriages. This arrangement declined slightly to 72 percent in 1980 and dropped significantly to 68.3 percent by 1987. Blacks have not married into other groups as frequently as they have united with white persons. In general, minorities who marry across racial lines tend to marry white persons more frequently than members of other minority groups. However, as shown in Table 3.1, the number of black men married interracially to other than white women more than quadrupled between 1970 and 1987. The number of black women who married interracially to a spouse who was not white rose from 4,000 in 1970 to 14,000 in 1980 but fell dramatically to 8,000 in 1987.

Because of the castelike nature of the American society which relegates blacks to a lower social status position than whites, the general tendency is to regard blacks who marry whites as having married hypergamously or upward. This view reflects social perceptions and may totally disregard the fact that intermarriages may involve equal status unions, if considered in terms of socioeconomic status variables, or they may be hypogamous or downward marriages if the black person ranks higher on standard socioeconomic status measures. However, in the view of some persons, any white person who marries a black person has married hypogamously, but that view, once again, reflects a prejudiced social definition that has little or nothing to do with objective reality.[13] More often than not, in terms of class origins of the partners, interracial marriages are between equal-status partners.[14]

One explanation for the greater proportion of black males than white males who marry across racial boundaries is that many black males are seduced by the highly publicized "somatic norm image" which accentu-

Table 3.1 INTERRACIAL MARRIED COUPLES BY YEAR: 1970–1987
(In Thousands; 1979, Persons 14 Years and Older; 1980 and 1987, Persons 15 years and older)

Types	Years			Types	Years		
	1970	1980	1987		1970	1980	1987
Total married couples	44,597	49,714	52,286	Other interracial married couples	245	484	622
Interracial married couples	310	651	799	Husband black	8	20	33
All black–white married couples	65	167	177	Wife black	4	14	8
Husband black–wife white	41	122	121	Husband white	139	287	358
Wife black–husband white	24	45	56	Wife white	94	163	223

Source: U. S. Bureau of the Census. Census of Population, 1970, Marital Status, PC(2)–4C; Current Population Reports, Series P-20, No. 424 and other reports.

ates the desirability of Nordic features, especially lightness of skin.[15] Some black men find the white female more attractive and are drawn to the "once-forbidden" or aganathamous partner. For some black men, a white female partner is a matter of ego-enhancement and status attainment. For others, it is strictly a marriage of love for a person and is not restrained by irrelevances of race. Many white males, on the other hand, eschew public interracial liaisons and marriage with a black partner because of fear of social disapprobation, stigmatization, and economic/occupational penalties. Specifically, they may fear that marriage with a black woman may be an impediment to upward mobility within the occupational structure or a barrier to other social dimensions of status attainment.[16]

These marriages meet with far less disapprobation in the black community than in others. The upward trend in interracial marriages previously noted is likely to continue as black/white contact increases in the marketplace and through expanded opportunities for social interaction. Those opportunities will occur through increasing school and college desegregation, diversity in employment opportunities for black and white females, as well as through desegregation of housing. Such changes accelerate propinquity and permit persons of different races to interact more frequently, come to respect each other's individuality, and identify those particular attributes that may draw them together. However, even when individuals of different races are attracted to each other, one or both partners may not be able to disregard the intense pressures brought against their potential marriage by such significant others as members of their reference groups. These pressures, combined with such factors as in-group loyalty, exclusive attraction to members of one's own racial group, and the belief that one should not marry across racial lines, may help to depress the actual numbers of interracial marriages for an indefinite period of time despite the upward trend observed in the 1980s. Yet differences in the success rate of intragroup and interracial marriages appear to be negligible.

AUTHORITY STRUCTURE

Black families vary considerably in the structure of family authority. The authority figure may be either the male or female, or both may equally share authority. If authority and decision-making responsibilities are either vested in or assumed by the husband or father, the family is patriarchal. If the wife or mother is the head, then the family is martriarchal. If both husband and wife share equally in these responsibilities, the family is equalitarian. Black families in America are characteristically stereotyped as matriarchal, but the equalitarian family pattern is actually the most common authority pattern found. Even at the low-income levels equalitarianism precedes in importance both matriarchy and patriarchy as dominant family types.[17] The trend toward equalitarian family structures has developed over a long period. Basically, the movement has been away from the traditional patriarchal structure, once characteristic of most American families, white and black, in which an overpowering male potentate rules without much challenge from other family members. As patriarchies disappear, they are being replaced by egalitarian family structures, single family units, and increasing numbers of families headed by women, in which case matricentric authority may or may not prevail. Whether or not a matriarchy or purely matricentric situation exists may be a function of the type of living arrangement the woman in question may have with a male companion, if any. However, the existence of a black matriarchy dominating black family life continues to be a matter of debate. Sociologists like Andrew Billingsley,[18] Robert Hill,[19] Harriette Pipes McAdoo[20], and Robert Staples[21], argue against notions of the universality of the black matriarchy and assert that female dominance is by and large class linked. And if David A. Schulz is correct, there is reason to question the notion of female dominance even in lower socioeconomic status groups, especially when the quasi-father and the boyfriend exist as male norms.[22]

HOUSEHOLD PATTERNS

Family patterns among black Americans vary in terms of household composition. Billingsley identifies three primary family types: (1) basic, characterized by the presence of the husband and wife only; (2) nuclear, consisting of husband, wife, and children; and (3) attenuated nuclear families, characterized by the absence of one of the marital partners. He subdivides these primary types into extended families, subfamilies, and augmented families. Extended families are composed of one or more relatives as members of the nuclear or basic families. Subfamilies consist of relatives who join another family as a basic family unit (e.g., parents and children joining another nuclear family in the latter's residence). Augmented families form when persons having no consanguinal ties to the family join the family unit. These persons may be boarders, roomers, or extended guests. In addition, combinations and derivations of the primary family and their subtypes may arise. The most important feature of this typology is that it depicts the tremendous diversity in types and composition of black family structures. The apparent heterogeneity among black family structures is an attempt to adopt and survive in what has been an alien and hostile environment for a sizeable proportion of the black population in America.[23]

Of all the types mentioned by Billingsley, the simple nuclear family— father, mother, and *their children* under one roof—is the universally accepted model to which Americans of all races are expected to aspire. Within the American population as a whole, this type of family structure represents less than half of all black families in the United States. Although this structure may be regarded as an ideal type, it has not been achieved by a majority of the black families. One explanation for this situation is simply that a significant number of black family units are either extended, subfamilies, or of one or more of the 12 family types identified by Billingsley.[24] Other factors to be considered are the mounting rates of marital dissolution and enormously high rates of single parent families within the black community.

The actual number of black families increased from 5.3 million in 1970 to 6.0 million in 1980 and to 7.09 million by 1987. Although family structure within the black family is changing, the latest available data continue to show that more than half (53.7 percent) of all black families are of a married couple with or without children.[25] Nevertheless, this proportion of married couple families represents a dramatic downturn from the 70 percent black married couple families observed in 1970. This change in family structure is a major factor in assertions by some scholars, policymakers, and journalists that the black family is "in trouble."[26]

Two-Parent Families

When people refer to the simple nuclear family as the norm, they really mean that a high premium is placed on families in which both parents are present. Thus two-parent families are regarded as the singularly most powerful indicator of family stability. It is assumed that such families can best serve the various functions of family units and meet the needs of individual members. Such family structures are less likely to be encumbered with social problems, and, even when problems occur, presumably, two-parent families have the wherewithal necessary for problem solving with minimal trauma. A logical corollary of this argument is that the attenuated nuclear family, in which only a single parent is present, is the opposite of the two-parent structure in terms of stability and finding meaningful solutions to the problems of daily life. A further extension of this argument is that single-parent families are a strong indicator of family disorganization or disintegration. This is a controversial viewpoint and one vigorously rejected by feminists who see strengths in single-parent structures. Although the issue is provocative, we will now concentrate on two-parent structures in the black community.[27]

Between 1980 and 1987, the proportion of *two-parent families* in the black community with children under the age of 18 dropped from a majority (55.5 percent) to less than half (41.5 percent). That decline continued a pattern that proceeded at a steady but alarming pace since the end of World War II. In 1950, almost eight of every ten (77.7 percent) black families was two-parented; even two decades later (1971), two-thirds (67.4 percent) of all black families were two-parented. Just as this type of family declined dramatically in the black community, it also fell, though not as precipitously, in the white community. Among white families, the percent two-parent was 88 and 82.4 in 1971 and 1980, respectively. However, by 1987, slightly more than three-fourths (78.3 percent) of all white families could be described as two-parented (Table 3.2). This dramatic transformation of black family structure characterized by the presence of both parents to one increasingly headed by women leads many observers to assert that the matriarchy is the dominant structural pattern of black families in the United States.

Female-Headed Households

The proportion of American families headed by women more than doubled between 1970 and 1987. In 1970, such families constituted 9.9 percent of all households with children. However, by 1987, almost one in every five (19.7 percent) American households was headed by a woman. By contrast, in the same year, 3 percent were male-headed and 77.3 percent of all American households with children were two-parented.[28] Included in the category female-headed are all types of marital statuses (e.g., single, never married; married, spouse absent; widowed; and divorced). Selective perception induced by the electronic media would lead many persons to conclude that all female-headed households are single, never-married teenage mothers of small children. Such impressions are false. The median age of a black female-headed householder with no spouse present is 37.3 in contrast to a median age of 42.1 for white female-headed households.

Between 1970 and 1987, the proportion of black female-headed households categorized as a single (never-married) person more than doubled from 16.2 (1970) to 37.3 percent (1987). Similarly, the proportion of such families in the white community also climbed significantly from 9.2 percent in 1970 to 13.8 percent in 1987. Approximately one in five (20.7 percent) of black female-headed households was headed by married women whose spouse was absent. By comparison, about one in six (16 percent) of white households were in this category. Eighteen percent of all female-headed households among black Americans, in contrast to 27.8 percent of white female-headed families, were widowed. Almost one-fourth (24 percent) of black female household heads were divorced; so were 42.4 percent of all white families headed by women. Two-thirds (68.3 percent) of black female-headed families and 57.3 percent of white female-headed families incorporated their own children into their family structure. The average number of children under the age of 18, in 1987, per female-headed family was 1.25 per black family and .96 per white family (Table 3.3).

Male-Headed Households

In 1970, 2.9 percent of all households in the black population were headed by men. That proportion remained relatively stable for the next ten years when in 1980, males headed 3.0 percent of all households. However, by

Table 3.2 FAMILY GROUPS WITH CHILDREN UNDER 18, BY RACE AND TYPE: 1970, 1980, AND 1987

Presence of parents and marital status	1970 total (1,000)	1980 total (1,000)	Number (1,000)			Percent distribution			Percent, by type			
			Total[a]	White	Black	Total[a]	White	Black	All family groups	Family households	Related subfamilies	Unrelated subfamilies
Total with children under 18	29,631	32,150	34,242	28,180	4,963	100.0	100.0	100.0	100.0	93.2	5.6	1.2
Two-parent family groups	25,823	25,231	25,005	22,076	2,058	73.0	78.3	41.5	100.0	98.6	1.4	.1
One-parent family groups	3,808	6,920	9,236	6,104	2,904	27.0	21.7	58.5	100.0	78.5	17.0	4.4
Maintained by mother	3,415	6,230	8,128	5,190	2,747	23.7	18.4	55.3	100.0	77.5	17.9	4.7
Never married	248	1,063	2,575	1,015	1,512	7.5	3.6	30.5	100.0	61.3	34.7	4.0
Spouse absent	1,377	1,743	1,734	1,116	563	5.1	4.0	11.3	100.0	83.7	13.6	2.8
Separated	962	1,483	1,512	970	499	4.4	3.4	10.1	100.0	84.8	12.2	3.0
Divorced	1,109	2,721	3,309	2,708	535	9.7	9.6	10.8	100.0	84.4	9.0	6.6
Widowed	682	703	511	353	139	1.5	1.3	2.8	100.0	93.0	5.1	2.0
Maintained by father	393	692	1,107	914	157	3.2	3.2	3.2	100.0	86.3	11.1	2.6
Never married	22	63	209	148	55	.6	.5	1.1	100.0	73.7	23.9	2.4
Spouse absent	247[b]	181	252	209	29	.7	.7	.6	100.0	84.1	15.1	.8
Divorced	(NA)	340	576	497	65	1.7	1.8	1.3	100.0	90.3	6.1	3.6
Widowed	124	107	69	58	7	.2	.2	.1	100.0	100.0	—	—

—: Represents or rounds to zero.

NA: Not available.

[a]Includes other races, not shown separately.

[b]Includes divorced.

Source: U.S. Bureau of the Census, *Current Population Reports,* series P-20, No. 24 and earlier reports.

Table 3.3   CHARACTERISTICS OF FEMALE HOUSEHOLDS WITH NO SPOUSE PRESENT, BY RACE AND YEAR: 1970–1987

Characteristics	Unit	Race White					Race Black				
		1970	1980	1985	1986	1987	1970	1980	1985	1986	1987
Female family householder	1,000	4,185	6,052	6,941	7,111	7,227	1,349	2,495	2,964	2,874	2,967
Percent of all families	Percent	9.1	11.6	12.8	12.9	13.0	28.3	40.3	43.7	41.5	41.8
Median age	Years	50.4	43.7	42.7	42.4	42.1	41.3	37.4	38.0	37.9	37.5
Marital status:											
Single (never married)	Percent	9.2	10.6	11.9	12.8	13.8	16.2	27.3	33.4	35.4	37.3
Married, spouse absent	Percent	18.5	16.9	16.0	15.8	16.0	39.7	28.6	21.1	21.2	20.7
Separated	Percent	11.4	13.9	13.8	13.5	13.8	33.8	26.8	19.3	19.7	18.6
Other	Percent	7.2	3.0	2.1	2.3	5.9	1.8	1.7	1.5	2.1	2.1
Widowed	Percent	47.0	32.7	28.3	28.6	27.8	29.9	22.2	21.2	18.4	18.0
Divorced	Percent	25.3	39.8	43.8	42.8	42.4	14.2	21.9	24.5	25.1	24.0
Presence of children under 18:											
No own children	Percent	52.0	41.2	43.5	43.2	42.7	33.5	28.1	34.5	32.7	31.8
With own children	Percent	48.0	58.8	56.5	56.8	57.3	66.6	71.9	65.5	67.3	68.3
1 child	Percent	18.8	28.1	28.9	29.3	29.6	19.1	26.3	27.5	25.0	29.2
2 children	Percent	15.0	19.9	18.6	19.2	19.1	14.4	23.2	21.6	22.8	22.1
3 children	Percent	7.8	7.4	6.4	5.9	6.3	12.5	11.1	10.1	11.7	10.0
4 or more children	Percent	6.4	3.4	2.6	2.4	2.3	20.6	11.3	6.3	7.8	6.9
Children per family	Number	1.00	1.03	.96	.95	.96	1.83	1.51	1.29	1.34	1.28

Source: U. S. Bureau of the Census, Current Population Reports, series P-20, No. 24 and earlier reports. Date as of March 1970, covers persons 14 years old and over; beginning 1980, covers persons 15 years old and over. Based on Current Population Survey; see headnote, Table 68.

1987, as the overall number of black households climbed to almost 10 million, the 386,000 households headed by black men represented 3.9 percent of the total number. In 1987, white males headed 2.6 percent of white households while Hispanic males, heading 4.7 percent of their households, were significantly more likely than either black or white males to be heads of households with no wife present.[29] Black male heads of families are somewhat less likely than female household heads to live in central cities. Male-headed families are more often found in cities with a population in excess of 3 million inhabitants. About 36 percent of all such families residing in SMSAs live in the larger metropolitan communities of the United States compared to 5.2 percent whose homes are established in cities with a population under 250,000.[30]

RESIDENCE OF CHILDREN

Among white, black, and Hispanic families, the proportion of children under the age of 18 living with both parents has been on a downward spiral since 1970. Less than three-fourths of all American children actually live in homes with both parents present. While slightly more than one in five children under age 18 live only with their mother, children are almost as likely to live with neither parent as to live with their fathers (Table 3.4). Within the white population, 89.5 percent of children under the age of 18 lived with both parents. However, by 1987, 79.1 percent of white children resided with both parents. In the black community, 58.5 percent of under-age children lived with both parents in 1970 but by 1987 six of every ten black children resided in a different family structure. Among Hispanic families, 77.7 percent of children under that age lived with both parents in 1970. In 1987, approximately two-thirds (65.5 percent) of Hispanic children had residence with both parents (Table 3.4). Such data underscores a pattern previously addressed; that is, the American family structure, irrespective of race, is undergoing such profound change that the traditional two-parent family is becoming noticeably less universal.

Blacks, Hispanics, and whites differ with respect to the average size of the family. Among these three racial groups family size declined between 1970 and 1987. In black families, the average family size dropped from 4.13 in 1970 to 3.67 in 1980 and then to 3.52 in 1987. In white families, average family sizes were 3.52 (1970), 3.23 (1980), and 3.13 in 1987. Although comparable data were unavailable for Hispanic families in 1970, the Bureau of Census reported in 1980 that the average size of Hispanic families was 3.90 and declined to 3.83 by 1987.[31]

Racial differences in the living patterns of children are highly significant. Table 3.5 not only reveals the steady decline in the proportion of white and Hispanic children living with both parents, it also shows that slightly more than half of all black children reside exclusively with their

Table 3.4 CHILDREN UNDER 18 YEARS OLD, BY PRESENCE OF PARENTS AND YEAR: 1970–1987

Race Hispanic origin, and year	Number (1,000)	Both parents	Mother only					Father only	Neither parent
			Total	Divorced	Married, spouse absent	Single[a]	Widowed		
All races[b]									
1970	69,162	85.2	10.8	3.3	4.7	.8	2.0	1.1	2.9
1980	63,427	76.7	18.0	7.5	5.7	2.8	2.0	1.7	3.6
1985	62,475	73.9	20.9	8.5	5.4	5.6	1.5	2.5	2.7
1986	62,763	73.9	21.0	8.5	5.3	5.7	1.4	2.5	2.6
1987	62,932	73.1	21.3	8.5	5.2	6.3	1.3	2.6	2.9
White									
1970	58,790	89.5	7.8	3.1	2.8	.2	1.7	.9	1.8
1980	52,242	82.7	13.5	7.0	3.9	1.0	1.7	1.6	2.2
1985	50,836	80.0	15.6	8.1	4.1	2.1	1.3	2.4	2.0
1986	50,931	79.9	15.7	8.2	4.1	2.3	1.2	2.5	1.9
1987	51,112	79.1	16.1	8.4	4.0	2.7	1.1	2.6	2.2
Black									
1970	9,422	58.5	29.5	4.6	16.3	4.4	4.2	2.3	9.7
1980	9,375	42.2	43.9	10.9	16.2	12.8	4.0	1.9	11.9
1985	9,479	39.5	51.0	11.3	12.4	24.8	2.5	2.9	6.6
1986	9,532	40.6	50.6	11.1	12.0	24.9	2.6	2.4	6.3
1987	9,612	40.1	50.4	9.6	12.0	26.3	2.6	2.5	7.0

Percent living with

Table 3.4 (Continued)

Race Hispanic origin, and year	Number (1,000)	Both parents	Percent living with					Father only	Neither parent
			Mother only						
			Total	Divorced	Married, spouse absent	Single[a]	Widowed		
Hispanic[c]									
1970	4,006[d]	77.7	(NA)	(NA)	(NA)	(NA)	(NA)	(NA)	(NA)
1980	5,459	75.4	19.6	5.9	8.2	4.0	1.5	1.5	3.5
1985	6,057	67.9	26.6	7.3	11.1	6.5	1.7	2.2	3.3
1986	6,430	66.5	27.7	8.6	10.7	7.0	1.4	2.7	3.1
1987	6,647	65.5	27.7	8.0	9.3	8.8	1.6	2.8	4.0

NA: Not available.

[a]Never married.

[b]Includes other races not shown separately.

[c]Hispanic persons may be of any race.

[d]All persons under 18 years old.

Source: U.S. Bureau of the Census, Current Population Reports, series P-20, No. 423 and earlier reports. (As of March 1988. Excludes persons under 18 years old who maintained households or family groups. It is likely that most of the sizeable increase in children living with never-married mothers is the result of new and more definitive coding procedures introduced by the Census Bureau in 1982. Based on Current Population Survey; see headnote, table 68.)

Table 3.5 POVERTY STATUS OF FAMILIES BY TYPE OF FAMILY. PRESENCE OF RELATED CHILDREN UNDER 18 YEARS OLD, BY RACE AND HISPANIC ORIGIN: 1959–1987

Numbers in Thousands Families as of March of the following year.

White

With children under 18 years

	All families below poverty			Married couple families below poverty			Male householder, no wife present below poverty			Female householder, no husband present below poverty		
	Total	Number	Percent	Total	Number	Percent	Total	Number	Percent	Total	Number	Percent
1987	27,912	3,463	12.4	22,407	1,568	7.0	997	151	15.1	4,508	1,744	38.7
1986	27,929	3,637	13.0	22,466	1,692	7.5	911	132	14.5	4,552	1,812	39.8
1985	27,795	3,695	13.3	22,399	1,827	8.2	926	138	14.9	4,470	1,730	38.7
1984	27,380	3,679	13.4	22,181	1,879	8.5	862	117	13.6	4,337	1,682	38.8
1983	27,303	3,859	14.1	22,361	2,060	9.2	732	123	16.8	4,210	1,676	39.8
1982	27,118	3,709	13.7	22,390	2,005	9.0	692	120	17.4	4,037	1,584	39.3
1981	27,223	3,362	12.4	22,334	1,723	7.7	652	75	11.6	4,237	1,564	36.9
1980	27,416	3,078	11.2	22,793	1,544	6.8	628	100	16.0	3,995	1,433	35.9
1979	27,329	2,509	9.2	22,878	1,216	5.3	584	82	14.1	3,866	1,211	31.3
1978	26,907	2,513	9.3	22,601	1,185	5.2	526	60	11.4	3,780	1,268	33.5
1977	26,924	2,572	9.6	22,703	1,256	5.5	486	55	11.3	3,735	1,261	33.8
1976	26,812	2,566	9.6	22,872	1,242	5.4	484	64	13.2	3,456	1,260	36.4
1975	26,975	2,776	10.3	23,134	1,456	6.3	435	48	11.0	3,406	1,272	37.3
1974	26,890	2,430	9.0	(NA)	(NA)	(NA)	(NA)	(NA)	(NA)	3,244	1,180	36.4
1973	26,694	2,177	8.2	(NA)	(NA)	(NA)	(NA)	(NA)	(NA)	2,988	1,053	35.2
1972	26,763	2,238	8.4	(NA)	(NA)	(NA)	(NA)	(NA)	(NA)	2,748	970	35.3
1971	26,745	2,372	8.9	(NA)	(NA)	(NA)	(NA)	(NA)	(NA)	2,664	982	36.9
1970	26,256	2,219	8.5	(NA)	(NA)	(NA)	(NA)	(NA)	(NA)	(NA)	(NA)	(NA)
1969	26,307	2,089	7.9	(NA)	(NA)	(NA)	(NA)	(NA)	(NA)	(NA)	(NA)	(NA)
1968	25,803	2,176	8.4	(NA)	(NA)	(NA)	(NA)	(NA)	(NA)	(NA)	792	36.0
1967	25,531	2,276	8.9	(NA)	(NA)	(NA)	(NA)	(NA)	(NA)	(NA)	748	34.9
1966	(NA)	2,400	9.5	(NA)	(NA)	(NA)	(NA)	(NA)	(NA)	(NA)	803	38.4

Table 3.5 (Continued)

	All families below poverty			Married couple families below poverty			Male householder, no wife present below poverty			Female householder, no husband present below poverty		
	Total	Number	Percent	Total	Number	Percent	Total	Number	Percent	Total	Number	Percent
1965	(NA)	2,858	11.5	(NA)	(NA)	(NA)	(NA)	(NA)	(NA)	(NA)	867	43.2
1964	(NA)	3,205	12.8	(NA)	(NA)	(NA)	(NA)	(NA)	(NA)	(NA)	814	40.3
1963	25,056	3,328	13.3	(NA)	(NA)	(NA)	(NA)	(NA)	(NA)	(NA)	882	45.0
1962	(NA)	3,673	14.7	(NA)	(NA)	(NA)	(NA)	(NA)	(NA)	(NA)	908	49.2
1961	(NA)	3,785	15.4	(NA)	(NA)	(NA)	(NA)	(NA)	(NA)	(NA)	892	46.4
1960	(NA)	3,690	15.3	(NA)	(NA)	(NA)	(NA)	(NA)	(NA)	(NA)	905	47.1
1959	24,146	3,812	15.8	(NA)	(NA)	(NA)	(NA)	(NA)	(NA)	(NA)	948	51.7
Black												
With children under 18 years												
1987	4,867	1,817	37.3	2,210	301	13.6	219	65	29.6	2,437	1,451	59.5
1986	4,806	1,699	35.4	2,236	257	11.5	185	58	31.5	2,386	1,384	58.0
1985	4,636	1,670	36.0	2,185	281	12.9	182	53	29.0	2,269	1,336	58.9
1984	4,512	1,758	39.0	2,001	331	16.6	175	62	35.5	2,335	1,364	58.4
1983	4,482	1,789	39.9	2,052	369	18.0	186	58	31.1	2,244	1,362	60.7
1982	4,470	1,819	40.7	2,093	360	17.2	178	58	32.7	2,199	1,401	63.7
1981	4,455	1,652	37.1	2,202	357	16.2	135	34	25.0	2,118	1,261	59.5
1980	4,465	1,583	35.5	2,154	333	15.5	140	34	24.0	2,171	1,217	56.0
1979	4,297	1,441	33.5	2,095	286	13.7	139	26	18.4	2,063	1,129	54.7
1978	4,159	1,431	34.4	2,056	247	12.0	157	40	25.5	1,946	1,144	58.4
1977	4,107	1,406	34.2	2,088	295	14.1	141	30	21.3	1,878	1,081	57.5
1976	4,047	1,382	34.2	2,146	311	14.5	120	28	23.3	1,781	1,043	58.6
1975	3,878	1,314	33.9	2,119	349	16.5	108	16	14.8	1,651	949	57.5
1974	3,915	1,293	33.0	2,187	317	14.5	105	27	26.2	1,623	949	58.5
1973	3,831	1,280	33.4	(NA)	(NA)	(NA)	(NA)	(NA)	(NA)	1,538	905	58.8
1972	3,650	1,303	35.7	(NA)	(NA)	(NA)	(NA)	(NA)	(NA)	1,494	912	61.0
1971	3,660	1,261	34.5	(NA)	(NA)	(NA)	(NA)	(NA)	(NA)	1,369	821	60.0

Table 3.5 POVERTY STATUS OF FAMILIES BY TYPE OF FAMILY. (Continued)

	All families below poverty			Married couple families below poverty			Male householder, no wife present below poverty			Female householder, no husband present below poverty		
	Total	Number	Percent	Total	Number	Percent	Total	Number	Percent	Total	Number	Percent
1970	3,470	1,212	34.9	(NA)	(NA)	(NA)	(NA)	(NA)	(NA)	(NA)	(NA)	(NA)
1969	3,386	1,095	32.3	(NA)	(NA)	(NA)	(NA)	(NA)	(NA)	(NA)	(NA)	(NA)
1968	3,218	1,114	34.6	(NA)	(NA)	(NA)	(NA)	(NA)	(NA)	(NA)	(NA)	(NA)
1967	3,200	1,261	39.4	(NA)	(NA)	(NA)	(NA)	(NA)	(NA)	(NA)	(NA)	(NA)
Hispanic[a]												
With children under 18 years												
1987	3,213	1,032	32.1	(NA)	(NA)	(NA)	(NA)	(NA)	(NA)	854	518	60.7
1986	3,080	949	30.8	(NA)	(NA)	(NA)	(NA)	(NA)	(NA)	822	489	59.5
1985	2,973	955	32.1	(NA)	(NA)	(NA)	(NA)	(NA)	(NA)	771	493	64.0
1984	2,789	872	31.3	(NA)	(NA)	(NA)	(NA)	(NA)	(NA)	711	447	62.8
1983	2,697	867	32.1	(NA)	(NA)	(NA)	(NA)	(NA)	(NA)	660	418	63.4
1982	2,458	802	32.6	(NA)	(NA)	(NA)	(NA)	(NA)	(NA)	613	391	63.8
1981	2,428	692	28.5	(NA)	(NA)	(NA)	(NA)	(NA)	(NA)	622	374	60.0
1980	2,409	655	27.2	(NA)	(NA)	(NA)	(NA)	(NA)	(NA)	(NA)	(NA)	(NA)
1979	2,209	544	24.6	(NA)	(NA)	(NA)	(NA)	(NA)	(NA)	502	288	57.3
1978	2,002	483	24.1	(NA)	(NA)	(NA)	(NA)	(NA)	(NA)	(NA)	(NA)	(NA)
1977	2,057	520	25.3	(NA)	(NA)	(NA)	(NA)	(NA)	(NA)	(NA)	(NA)	(NA)
1976	1,899	517	27.2	(NA)	(NA)	(NA)	(NA)	(NA)	(NA)	(NA)	(NA)	(NA)
1975	1,891	550	29.1	(NA)	(NA)	(NA)	(NA)	(NA)	(NA)	(NA)	(NA)	(NA)
1974	1,834	462	25.2	(NA)	(NA)	(NA)	(NA)	(NA)	(NA)	(NA)	(NA)	(NA)
1973	1,726	410	23.8	(NA)	(NA)	(NA)	(NA)	(NA)	(NA)	(NA)	(NA)	(NA)
1972	1,700	416	24.5	(NA)	(NA)	(NA)	(NA)	(NA)	(NA)	(NA)	(NA)	(NA)

[a]Hispanic persons may be of any race.

Note: Prior to 1979 unrelated subfamilies were included in all families. Beginning in 1979 unrelated subfamilies are excluded from all families.

Source: U.S. Bureau of the Census. Current Population Reports. Series P-20, No. 24 and earlier reports.

mothers. Less than four of every ten black children live with both parents. In fact, black children are more than twice as likely to have residence with neither parent as to live only with their fathers. However, irrespective of race, children are far less likely to reside with their fathers than with their mothers. Again, this pattern undoubtedly results from such factors as child custody arrangements, the rising rate of unwed mothers, and family separation due to death, divorce, or imprisonment. When children do not reside with either parent, residence is usually with other relatives such as grandmothers, grandparents, aunts/uncles, or older siblings. In either case, the primary responsibility for children under age 18 not living with both parents is assumed by women.

As stressed in Chapter 2, American children are increasingly vulnerable to a life of poverty. Evidence shows that, while the poverty status of white children is hardening, black and Hispanic children are at greater risk. In married couple families with children under the age of 18, in 1980, 15.5 percent of such families were poverty stricken. During the recession years of 1981–1983, that proportion rose to 18.0 percent; however, by 1987, even as it declined to 13.6 percent, one in seven black children residing with both parents is in poverty. About one in three (29.6 percent) of black children living with the father only is in poverty. The situation worsens when the black child lives in a female-headed household. In this case six of every ten (59.5 percent) of all black children residing with their mothers are living below the poverty line. About one-third of all Hispanic families (32.1 percent) suffer from poverty but 60 percent of the children under the age of 18 residing with their mothers live below the poverty line. In the white community, while 12.1 percent of families with children under 18 are poverty stricken, only 7.0 percent of children living with both parents and 15.1 percent of those residing with their fathers live below the poverty line. On the other hand, 38.7 percent of white children with their mothers live a life of poverty (Table 3.5). It is because of such disparities in the condition of children in relationship to the family structure in which they reside that the term "feminization of poverty" captures a harsh reality of gender-based inequities and the life of a huge number of women and children, irrespective of race, in the United States.

The differences in residential patterns of black children demonstrate the need of black families for financial assistance and social services in caring for their children and meeting their functions as family heads. Unable to meet these needs, some parents allow their children to live with other family members for a time until their economic situation improves. Thus such arrangements are often temporary ones and, perhaps, help to explain the increase in the proportion of children living with their own parents at the upper-income levels. The absence of children from the households of their parents may be further explained by family dismemberment because of death, desertion, divorce, or involuntary separation. It may also be due to a temporary arrangement whereby grandparents and other relatives take care of children while natural parents are working, or hospitalized, or in prison, or taking up with girlfriends or boy-friends.

Augmented Families and Boyfriends

Some husbandless women, in time, feel compelled to make more depend-able arrangements to meet their emotional or affectional needs as well as to augment their capacity to care for their children when the husband-father is absent. Similarly, some men who wish to avoid formalizing a liaison with women through marital bonds make tentative arrangements as boyfriends. One of the more important research studies in this area demonstrates that the diversity of the black family structure extends to the roles of boyfriends.

David Schulz addresses himself to liaisons between black men and women in the lower class.[32] Contrary to popular belief, he argues, such liaisons are much more stable than is commonly assumed. Black men and women are able to establish a kind of quasi-familial relationship in which men do express great concern for women and the care of their children. In this view, the establishment of a boyfriend relationship is an adaptive response to oppression and deprivation experienced in the larger society. But boyfriends are obviously not all the same; they are dissimilar in the degree of financial and emotional support they bring into the relationship. They also vary in the types of relationships that they establish. Thus Schulz identifies four different types of boyfriends: (1) the quasi-father, (2) the supportive biological father, (3) the supportive companion, and (4) the pimp.[33]

A brief description of each type will help demonstrate the variations in degrees of concern for women and their children, and will illuminate other distinguishing features as well. The *quasi-father* seems in many ways to epitomize certain aspects of exchange theory in sociology. He gives and expects something in return. There is kind of quid pro quo in his relationship with women that suggests that he is bargaining for more than a woman in a family context. In general, his distinguishing features are as follows: (1) regular and sustained support for his girlfriend and her children; (2) the establishment of an affective relationship with his girl-friend's children, as, for example, through provisions for spending money, attempts at disciplining them, and engaging in various forms of recreation and entertainment with them; (3) intermittent visits with family, since he may or may not take up a permanent residence with them; and (4) an open relationship. That is, the relationship between the quasi-father boyfriend and his girlfriend is not clandestine. Other members of her family may have full knowledge about their arrangement with each other. What re-wards does the quasi-father obtain from this situation? According to Schulz, he obtains at least four assurances from his partner. First, he has the assurance that his food will be prepared for him. Second, his laundry will be done for him. Third, he has assurances of sexual gratification. And, fourth, he can expect familial companionship. Therefore, this type of relationship assures its participants both the instrumental and the expressive family functions.[34]

The *supportive biological father* has basically the same concern as the biological mother—support for the children even though both the mother and father do not entertain the probability of marriage to each other. Indeed, the man may already be married to someone else when the woman is impregnated or when the child is born. His support of his child or children is acknowledgment of paternity and an acceptance of its responsibilities, but neither the man nor the woman agrees to marriage. The duration of this support is uncertain and may or may not be sustained for a long period of time.[35]

The *supportive companion's* principal concern is having a good time with "a clean woman." On the other hand, the woman's primary wish is for support and reasonable companionship. This is a somewhat fragile relationship, but as Schulz cautions, it is not synonymous with prostitution. (A similar feature in white culture is the mistress.) Their relationship is not an impersonal business transaction, such as prostitution tends to be, but a mutual effort to obtain intimacy under severe economic and emotional difficulties. This type of relationship is characteristically found among men in their twenties and thirties and substantially younger unwed mothers. The older man may at first be perceived as someone who rescues the woman or girl from an extremely difficult situation. He provides her with a good time, emotional support, and spending money. He enjoys her companionship and sexual favors but does not desire family responsibility. Thus if and when a child is conceived as a result of their liaison, he abandons the woman and her offspring.[36] Undoubtedly, the supportive companion is the source of the current stereotype of the lower-class black male as a man of insatiable sexual appetite who exploits and deserts his childbearing woman and is either unwilling or incapable of serving instrumental parental functions.

The *pimp* is also the source of an exploitative image of the black male. Certainly, this image is perpetuated not only in popular novels but in black "sexploitation" movies of the 1970s, and TV, and the theater. Schulz distinguishes, quite correctly, between the traditional and the more contemporary usages of the term *pimp.* Classically, the term depicts a relationship in which a man lives off the earnings of one or more prostitutes who provide him with an elaborate life style, while he, in turn, provides them with police protection, bail money, if they are arrested, and some degree of social status in a subterranean life. Schulz employs the term to describe a stud or gigolo—a younger man who exploits well-financed, fading older women by providing sexual favors for them in return for a stylish life for himself. Although they are, in fact, "kept men," studs are not pimps in the classical or professional sense of the term.[37]

The role of the pimp, whether perceived in the classical or contemporary sense, appears to be glamorous. Impressionable ghetto blacks frequently wish to emulate pimps. These perceptions of pimps develop in a social context in which material acquisitions are highly prized and the legitimate avenues for achieving them are not equally accessible to ghetto black youths. They are impressed by the pimp's long "hog," or flashy automobile, and the excesses of his expensive clothing, called "threads" in black vernacular. They esteem the pimp's life style, at least as overtly manifested, as an easy way of "making it" in "the man's world." The pimp's employment, in their view, is legitimate as a way of making it, and making it quickly, with a minimum deferment of gratifications. Their heroes may be the "superflies" of the lower-class black community; the ghetto youth may come to idealize similar characters when they are portrayed in films. Thus the socialization that begins with the impressionable youth's own observations of objective reality is reinforced by the fantasies of the motion picture world. However, the duration of the classical pimp's role is subject to extreme variation depending upon his prowess in managing his stable of prostitutes, on the one hand, and the degree to which the indiscretions of the stud or kept man will be tolerated by a woman who, on the other hand, feels that her powers of persuasion are dimming. Schulz claims that the classical pimp may in time become enamored of one of his prostitutes, marry her, and settle down to family life. But there is little reason to assume that the stud role is anything but transitory or that pimps in general have a real concern for their women. Men who play this role are likely to be peripatetic and transient and are not likely to marry women who have kept them.[38]

The research conducted by Schulz is important. Not only does he demonstrate the concern of lower-class black men for their women and their families, uneven though it may be, but his view is also clearly at variance with the orthodox sociological perspective advanced in the literature on family disorganization and revived in some of the more popular urban anthropological studies of the black underclass. The stereotype of the lower-class black stud as a veritable wellspring of raw sexuality, moving from bed to bed, leaving a flock of children in his path and abandoning them for support through public assistance is subjected to serious question here.

FAMILY FUNCTIONS

In other sections of this chapter we have referred to the capacity of black families to serve varied functions. We need now to specify and describe the different types of family functions. Billingsley, borrowing from Parsons and Bales, differentiates between instrumental and expressive functions in his analysis of black family life. The following discussion is based upon his insights and theoretical analysis of family functions in his provocative study *Black Families in White America.*[39]

The *instrumental functions* of the family facilitate and assure its maintenance as a physical and economic unit. They include such activities as providing for the economic well-being of family members and for physical and social sustenance. Instrumental functions also contribute to the stability of the family when meeting the basic needs of food, housing, clothing, and health care. The ability to meet such fundamental needs presumes access to such essentials as a dependable job and sufficient income, which constitute the fulcrum for performing instrumental family functions. Given the disadvantaged income and occupational structure in the black community, as compared to the white population, black families are predictably less effective in instrumental function performance. Here effectiveness depends upon conditions external to the black family structure—those uncertain opportunities in the larger social system.[40]

Expressive functions deal with emotional states—social relations and feelings *between* family members and their psychological well-being. It is in the realization of expressive functions that individual members come to share in what W. I. Thomas once labeled "a fulfillment of the four wishes." By that he meant that by virtue of membership in a reference group like the family the fundamental social desires for love and affection, a sense of belonging to a group, companionship and group acceptance, and self-recognition are met. This is precisely what black leaders like Reverend Jesse Jackson intend when they cajole blacks into repetitive recitations of "I am somebody," "I am important," "I am worthy, and "I am of value." Thus expressive functions are largely internal to the family system and depend upon the quality of reciprocal relationships among individual family members.

In some instances, as Billingsley observes, the lines between expressive and instrumental functions are blurred and indistinctive, as, for example, in sexual behavior, reproductive functioning, and socialization. Both instrumental and expressive functioning are involved in each process. However, with respect to pleasurable sex (irrespective of opposite views communicated in films, television, and novels), it is only through the institution of marriage that such acts are officially condoned or received widespread social approbation. This belief system prevails even though the number of sexually active blacks and whites in the teenage population, for instance, is rising at a rapid rate. An increasing number of unwed black mothers, for example, continue to keep their children rather than place them for adoption. Yet the tendency is to still view such children as illegitimate, and procreation by a married couple remains most highly valued. Given the fact that an increasing number of well-educated women, black and white, whose annual income is above the poverty level, also have children out-of-wedlock, it is no longer clear-cut that what may have once been labeled idiosyncratic behavior among whites is decidedly class and race linked.[41]

In discussing family roles and functions, Hill identifies five major strengths of black families: (1) strong kinship bonds as manifested in the capacity to absorb other individuals into the family structure and informal adoption; (2) a strong work orientation; (3) adaptability of family roles; (4) high achievement orientation; and (5) a religious orientation. These strengths account for the ability of black families to survive as going concerns. To provide support for his position Hill draws attention to observations such as the following:

- The large-scale incorporation of minor children, elders, and sub-families into one's family structure. This supports the notion of strong family bonds and provides evidence of techniques employed to perform both instrumental and expressive family functions.
- The greater likelihood for black children rather than white children, born of unwed mothers, to remain within the family of procreation rather than to be adopted outside the family. In other words, some blacks may not view illegitimacy as socially stigmatizing as some white families do.
- A strong work orientation among black people.
- High flexibility of black families in role performance and the greater likelihood of an egalitarian authority structure.[42]

Hill also shows how exchanges occur between husbands and wives in terms of traditional role expectations. These exchanges may be essentially role reversals structured by the social situation in order to get the job done. Thus husbands may change diapers or cook or do heavy housework, depending upon social class affiliation. Wives may mow the lawn, clean the house, and repair things around the house. These exchanges and flexibility of roles may serve to keep the family intact when it is confronted with the crisis situation of involuntary family dismemberment.[43] They are also characteristic of egalitarian families. Many of Hill's observations are shared by other social scientists, notably McAdoo, Ladner, and Wilkinson who also wrote of strengths in the black family.[44]

CONTROVERSIAL FAMILY ISSUES IN THE BLACK COMMUNITY

The status of the black family in contemporary America is the subject of considerable controversy among academicians, activists, bureaucrats, and journalists. Although the controversy is somewhat amorphous in character, it focuses on several points: (1) teenage pregnancy and unwed motherhood; (2) abortion; (3) divorce; (4) the position of the black male; (5) the black matriarchy; (6) welfare; and (7) the impact of urbanization and the lingering effects of slavery on the black family. These factors are essentially contravening variables because they are believed by many to not only adversely affect family stability in general but to have created a state of disorganization within urban black communities. In this context, even as the magnitude of some of these problems within the black community is recognized, there is a major risk of resorting to what some sociologists refer to as a "fallacy of dramatic instance"[45] with overgeneralizations of attributes of the underclass to the entire black population. Since constraints of space preclude a detailed treatment of each of these areas, the discussion that follows will be, at best, an introduction to the major issues involved in the controversy.

Teenage Pregnancy and Unwed Motherhood (Illegitimacy)

Traditionally, illegitimacy in the United States is regarded as a black lower-class phenomenon and, therefore, as a strong measure of family disorganization. In this view the greater the proportion of children born outside the bonds of marriage, the greater the likelihood that the family is in a state of disarray. When we speak of the illegitimacy rate, we mean the number of illegitimate births per 1,000 unmarried women. This rate is much larger for blacks than for whites, even though in the 10-year period beginning in 1962, as the rates for blacks have shown a steady decline, the rates of illegitimacy in the white population have shown a steady increase in every age group. Between 1940 and 1961 the illegitimacy rates among black women almost tripled, but during the 1961–1968 period, the rates for this group declined by as much as 14 percent. Significantly, during the same period the white illegitimacy rate tripled. Between 1940 and 1961 the black rate climbed from 35.6 to 98.3 while the white rate rose from 3.6 to 9.2. But between 1960 and 1968, as rates for black women declined to 86.6, the rates for whites increased to 13.2.[46]

In 1970 1 of every 10 babies born in the United States was to an unwed mother. By 1979 the rate had increased to 1 of every 6.[47] The rate of increase is largely attributed to sexually active unmarried white teenage females. Gutenmacher's 1981 findings showed that, at the then current rate of teenage pregnancies, 4 of every 10 girls in the United States aged 14 would become pregnant at least once during her teenage years, and 2 of them would give birth; one of every 7 would have an abortion. He also reported that the number of sexually active teenagers increased by about two-thirds during the 1970s—a fact associated with the dramatic climb in the number and percentage of unwed teenagers.[48] His data also showed that sexually active teenagers account for 18 percent of women "capable of becoming pregnant," 46 percent of all out-of-marriage births, and 31 percent of the abortions. Although black teenagers are more sexually active than whites, on an age-for-age basis, the gap between the races is rapidly closing.[49] Further, Ventura's research also showed that the upsurge in the number of children born out of wedlock during the 1970s was significantly attributed to a higher rate of increase in out-of-wedlock births among white teenagers.[50]

Attention to the problems of unwed motherhood became substantially

more widespread during the 1980s. Although media treatment of illegitimacy and teenage parenting often presents this problem as if it were
confined exclusively to blacks, Elise F. Jones and her colleagues, in a study
of teen pregnancy in 37 nations, indicated that the illegitimacy rate of
white females in the United States is at least twice the rate found among
women in five other industrialized nations of Europe and North America.[51] The birth rate to unmarried white women between the ages of 15
and 44 rose from 17.6/1,000 unmarried women in 1980 to 23.2/1,000
unmarried women in 1986. During the same period, the birth rate for
unmarried black women in the same age cohort declined slightly from
81.4/1,000 unmarried women to 80.9/1,000 unmarried women. Even so,
black unmarried women are four times more likely to give birth out-of-
wedlock than are unmarried white women.[52]

It is estimated that more than one million teenagers become pregnant
each year. Henshaw and Van Fort reported that about 31,000 of such
pregnancies are among girls under the age of 15. About a half million
teenagers per year give birth; the remainder of the one million pregnancies are either terminated through abortions, miscarriages, or do not result
in unwed motherhood because the child is legitimated before birth.[53]
Cutright and Smith's examination of nonmarital fertility rates by race
revealed significant differences between blacks and whites with respect to
an overall pattern of sexual activity as well as increasing similarities between them with increasing age. Blacks tend to become sexually active at
a slightly younger age than whites. However, the gap between blacks and
whites is closing. The out-of-wedlock-conceived birthrate (OWCBR) as
well as the actual illegitimacy rate are substantially higher for blacks than
whites in every age cohort. For example, black 15- to 19-year-old females
have an OWCBR of 95.5/1,000 compared to an OWCBR rate of 31.6 for
whites in the same age category. In this age cohort, the illegitimacy rate
for blacks is 89.7/1,000 while that for whites is 16.8 or a black to white ratio
of 5:34. In the 20–24 age group, young black women have an OWCBR of
121.1 and an illegitimacy rate of 116.7. By contrast, white women in this
age group registered an OWCBR of 36.4 and an illegitimacy rate of
24.5/1,000. The gap between the OWCBR and the illegitimacy rate closes
for both races in the 25–29 age cohort. Among black women, the OWCBR
is 85.7 while the illegitimacy rate is 82.7. White women in the same age
group showed an OWCBR of 27.4 and an illegitimacy rate of 20.5/1000.
Their study was based upon data reported in 1979 and 1980.[54]

Henshaw and Van Fort, using more recent data in which the "nonwhite" category was not decomposed, showed that the pregnancy rate
among white teenagers between the ages of 15 and 19 was 92.9/1,000
while that for nonwhite 15- to 19-year-olds was 185.8 or about twice that
of white teenagers. Similarly, the actual birth rate for nonwhite 15- to
19-year-olds at 89.7/1,000, was slightly more than twice that for white
teenagers (42.8/1,000).[55]

Racial differences, as reported by Cutright and Smith, in fertility and
births outside of marriage can be attributed to four factors: (1) differences

in sexual activity between the races, or "exposure to risk"; (2) differences in abortion, both spontaneous and induced; (3) differences in the use of contraceptives or what they label "method efficacy"; and (4) differences between the races in legitimation or marriages before the child's birth.[56] Among black and white women, the percent "sexually active" rises significantly with each age cohort from 15–19, to 20–24 up to 25–29. However, the black/white ratio with respect to sexually active females declines from 1.75 in the 15- to 19-year-old cohort to 1.16 among 20- to 24-year-olds but rises to 1.33 in the 25–29 age group. With respect to the percent not using contraceptives, the black/white ratio rose from 1.21 among 15- to 19-year-olds to 1.97 and then to 2.0 among 20–24 and 25- to 29-year-old women, respectively. In every age group, these researchers observed that unmarried white women are significantly more likely than black women to abort a fetus. The black-white ratio rose from 0.64 to 0.78 between the age categories of 15–19 and 25–29, respectively. Similarly, they found that white 15- to 19-year-olds were more than seven times more likely to legitimate a child before birth than were black teenagers.[57] Only about 10 percent of the racial differences in nonmartial fertility rates were attributed to racial differnces in the use of contraceptives while the remaining three factors accounted equally for the remaining 90 percent of those differences.[58]

The problem of "children having children" in the United States was elevated to a level of serious public debate during the 1980s. This debate called attention to conditions or situations that can produce devastating consequences of unmarried teenage motherhood. For example, these young mothers are likely to: begin their new status of motherhood in poverty; receive little and often improper pre-natal care; obtain improper, if any, post-natal care; bear children who will suffer from low birth weight and who will have higher rates of illness and infant mortality. There is also evidence that their children are substantially more likely to be victimized by child abuse and, later in their lives, to suffer emotional and educational problems reflected in a higher school drop-out rate as well as other social problems. These young mothers often drop out of school and many are forced to rely on some form of public assistance, especially Aid to Families with Dependent Children (AFDC), since many of their teenage fathers do not help and cannot provide financial support due to their inability to land a job. Inasmuch as the teenage mother is likely to be unskilled and untrained, the opportunities for her to obtain a job capable of supporting herself and her child are severely limited. Consequently, more often than not, working teenage mothers are confined to low-paying, unskilled, unrewarding dead-end jobs. The poverty experienced combined with the desperation so often felt coupled with the demanding requirements of motherhood for which she was not prepared create for many a deepening well of loneliness and disillusionment. Among those who do legitimate their child before birth, their chances of experiencing a divorce are two to three times greater than the national average.[59]

Aside from the contributing factors to unwed motherhood among teenagers identified by Cutright and Smith, what other explanations can be offered for the escalating rate of teenage pregnancies in the United States, especially in the black community? The Children's Defense Fund maintains that poverty is a major contributing factor to teenage pregnancy.[60] In such conditions of poverty, many young girls feel a sense of economic and emotional deprivation induced by lack of money to meet ordinary human needs as well as acquire material possessions observed among the more affluent. Many in this group, as well as the sexually active young population in general, have neither familiarity with nor the most rudimentary understanding of such contraceptives as diaphragms, IUDs, or condoms. Like so many American teenagers, irrespective of race, they have not had parents who would talk frankly about human sexuality with them. At the same time, many American teens are subjected to inordinate peer pressure to "lose their virginity" and adolescent boys are often compelled to believe that their masculinity depends, at least in the eyes of their peer group, on their frequent reports of "scoring" and to have confirmation that they have "not shot blanks" as evidenced by the fact that their mates became pregnant.

Some reports place a considerable blame for the rise in teen pregnancy on the way that unwed motherhood is glamorized by popular stars in the entertainment world and the manner in which sex without responsibility is seemingly promoted on television—in daytime soaps and on prime-time shows—in movies, magazines, and music. Indeed, there is little argument against the assertion that young Americans are constantly bombarded with sexual messages in both the electronic and print media.[61] Yet, many teenage persons are abysmally ignorant about reproductive biology and think that pregnancy can only result from frequent sexual relations and not "the first time." Some observers of the teenage pregnancy phenomenon have blamed its escalation on welfare. They claim that young women "deliberately get themselves pregnant" in order to establish independence from their parents due to the availability of welfare. This assertion is refuted in studies reported by the Alan Guttmacher Institute which claimed no substantive support for such views.[62] However, there is some evidence that some teenage mothers have reported that they were so lonely, felt so dispossessed that having a baby was the only way to be assured of "having something of my own."[63] Another factor affecting higher rates of unwed motherhood is the changing American morality. Illegitimacy is no longer the ruthless stigma that it once was in American society. In earlier times, the rate was held in check by the internalization of family moral values that prohibited or condemned premarital sex; the fear of church and community sanctions; informal mechanisms of social control such as gossip that labeled the pregnant mother as sinful, depraved, or by other pejorative terms, and the father as totally irresponsible. The only way, in that context, to salvage one's reputation when pregnancy outside marital bonds occurred was through a "shotgun marriage." Such hurriedly arranged marriages are not so commonplace; more and more unmarried women are not opting to place their child in an adoption agency and elect to keep the child themselves.

The Reagan Administration mounted "Just Say No" campaigns not only as a prevention strategy against drug abuse but against premarital sexual relations as well. Religious bodies are also in the forefront of the movement to encourage abstinence as the most efficacious prevention strategy. On the other hand, some persons argue that, while abstinence must be encouraged, it is also important to recognize the fact that a significant proportion of teens are sexually active but uninformed about reproductive biology. Consequently, sex education in public schools is advocated with increasing fervor.

Sex education programs advocates tend to focus on reproductive biology, prevention of pregnancy and sexually transmitted disease through the use of condoms and other contraceptives, counseling to individuals who wish to maintain their virginity or postpone sexual activity until marriage, and on individual responsibility for their own behavior. Several municipal and state governments have developed programs for counseling pregnant teens as well as programs described as "Pregnancy and Parenting Programs." In the black community, major organizations, such as the National Urban League, the National Council of Negro Women, and Delta Sigma Theta Sorority have organized pregnancy prevention programs as well as programs that focus on the black unwed father. The Children's Defense Fund sponsors television educational "ads" designed to prevent teen pregnancy and some black stars of popular music, such as Jermaine Stewart, have used their songs to persuade young black men and women that "We Don't Have to Take Our Clothes Off." The effectiveness of these efforts has yet to be adequately measured or empirically tested.

Black Unwed Fathers

During the 1980s, the young black male, parents and nonparents, became the focal points of specialized programs designed to curtail the rate of unwed motherhood among black teens and young adult females. Programs sponsored by such black service organizations as the National Urban League attempt to inculcate within black male teenagers a sense of responsibility in the event that they are or do become teen parents to children out of wedlock, familiarize them with family planning procedures, and facilitate their understanding of the roles they could play in nurturing their offspring.

Sargent calls attention to two pervasive myths about black unwed fathers. First is the myth that the majority of them are themselves teenagers. He cites data from a study released by the Children's Defense Fund which shows that only 6 percent of black teenage fathers are under the age of 18 but at least 55 percent of them are in their early 20s. Twenty-four percent of these fathers are 18- to 19-year-olds and 11 percent of fathers to children born to teenage black females are between the ages of 25 and

29.[64] The second myth asserts that fathers of children born to teenage mothers are "totally irresponsible," uncaring and without love for their children. As Sargent stated, while some fathers' behavior does conform to the stereotype, the behavior of most fathers refutes that stereotype.[65] Consistent with findings from a Ford-Foundation-sponsored program conducted by Bank Street College in New York City, many of these fathers do express love, concern, and emotional support for their children. Inasmuch as many are school drop-outs themselves, have difficulty obtaining work, or have extremely low-paying jobs, it is particularly difficult for them to provide the kind of financial support needed either for the care of a newborn or the child's early development.[66]

Abortion

Abortion has never been as popular within the black community as in the white community and blacks have not been as demonstrably active in the abortion rights movement. This difference or reticence may be explained by the strong influence of religion and of religious leaders who frown upon abortion in the black community as well as the widespread belief that abortion is tantamount to genocide. Another factor is the cost of abortion which, until the advent of the *Roe* v. *Wade* decision in 1973, and subsequent governmental assistance to poor women who sought abortions, was often too prohibitive for many black women. Black women were substantially more inclined to incorporate the child of the unwed mother into the basic family structure, sometimes explaining the newborn as the child of its grandmother, or as a relative's child being reared by the mother's parents.

Divorce

Another factor that contributes to the changing structure of the black family is the unparalleled rise in the rate of divorce. In 1970, the divorce rate among black males of 62/1,000 married persons nearly doubled the 32/1,000 persons divorced in the white male population. Between 1970 and 1987, while the divorce rate among black males spiralled upward by almost 300 percent (i.e., 184/1,000 married persons), the rate for white males rose at a somewhat faster rate to 102/1,000 married persons. Similarly, the divorce rate for black women (104/1,000) was approximately twice the rate for white women (56/1,000). By 1987, the divorce rate for black women also climbed by more than 300 percent (317/1,000) while that for white women (142/1,000) rose by two and a half times over their 1970 rate. An examination of Table 3.6 shows that within each race, the divorce rate for women is significantly higher than that for men.

As stated earlier, the median age for marriage in the United States is rising and in 1989 was 26.2 years. Blacks tend to postpone marriage to a somewhat later time than whites. Since most social science research shows

Table 3.6 DIVORCED PERSONS PER 1,000 MARRIED PERSONS WITH SPOUSE PRESENT, BY SEX, RACE, AGE, AND YEARS: 1970–1987*

Year	Total	Male	Female
1970	47	35	60
1975	69	54	84
1980	100	79	120
1983	114	91	137
1884	121	96	146
1985	128	103	153
1986	131	106	157
1987	130	107	154

| Sex and Year | Race | | Age | | | |
	White	Black	15–29 years	30–44 years	45–64 years	65 years old and over
Male 1970	32	62	[a]28	33	40	32
1980	74	149	78	104	70	48
1985	98	179	100	138	93	49
1987	102	184	101	137	100	57
Female 1970	56	104	[a]46	61	66	69
1980	110	258	108	147	112	89
1985	142	326	117	190	151	111
1987	142	317	116	184	159	111

*Between March 1970 and 1975, persons 14 years and older; From 1980 on, 15 years old and over.

[a]14–29 years.

Source: U. S. Bureau of the Census. Current Population Reports, Series P-20, No. 423 and earlier reports.

that the first seven years of marriage are the most vulnerable and fragile time,[67] it is not unexpected that the modal age cohort for divorces is that of 35 to 44 years (Table 3.6).

Divorce is traumatic not only for the previously married couple but especially for children who may not be prepared to cope with this type of family disruption. Broderick reports that about half of all American children can expect to lose one parent by the age of 18.[68] Given the fact that so many parents of black children never marry, the proportion of black children who will always live with no more than one parent prior to the age of 18 will undoubtedly be substantially larger than the fifty percent projected for American children as a group. Inasmuch as many divorced parents do marry again following a divorce, some children will ultimately live in a "reconstituted family," and may be faced with intrafamily conflicts and difficult adjustment problems.[69] Inasmuch as 70 percent of all women who are awarded alimony never receive it, the children of divorced parents often experience severe economic difficulties following the separation of the father from the household. Only 7 percent of black women are awarded alimony in connection with their divorces and less than one-third are awarded child-support payments. Consequently, they are compelled to rely on other means of support for themselves and their children.[70]

Some portion of the rising divorce rate can be attributed to changing social attitudes toward marriage and the ease with which divorce can be attained (especially with "no-fault" divorce laws and catch-all grounds such as "irreconcilable differences"). However, the economic and social stress experienced by blacks across all social lines may be an even more compelling explanatory factor. Some unemployed husbands simply leave their families to make them qualified for certain governmental benefits. Some leave out of shame triggered by their inability to care for their families. Some recent arrivals into middle-class status cannot adjust to the demands and stresses often associated with middle-class life styles. Other upwardly mobile blacks respond to impulses and beliefs that extramarital "affairs" are fashionable until uncooperative spouses discover the relationships and decide to terminate the marriage.

Further, there is a major bind that confronts many well-educated black women—the shortage of eligible black men in terms of educational attainment and occupational status. In order to be married, some women in this group marry hypogamously, or "down." The divorce rate in hypogamous marriages of black women has escalated. The higher her level of attainment, the more likely is the black woman to become divorced. She, like her white counterpart, is less likely to remarry than is her ex-husband.

Albeit, divorce rates have continued to climb within the black population. They seem to be correlated with increasing urbanization and economic instability, as well as with inadequate preparation for marriage. This increasing pattern points to the relentless stresses on the black family in its efforts to maintain intact families. It takes its toll on the ability of the divorced family to meet both instrumental and expressive functions, and may have deleterious consequences on the psyches of both parents and children.

The Black Male

Just as "the black community" in American society is not a monolith—a homogeneous structure whose characteristics are shared by all members—neither is the black male. There is as much variation in the socioeconomic characteristics of the black male or in his commitment to family responsibilities as one will find among males in the white community. Nevertheless, the search for answers to some of the more perplexing problems confronted by the black family inevitably raises questions about the status of the black male in white America. His status is as much a function of how he is perceived and treated in the American society and of his chances for equal participation in the opportunity structure as it is for his failure to seize those opportunities available to him or his ability to develop the necessary coping strategies that permit him to deal with the racism he constantly confronts in American society.

As pointed out in Chapter 2 and mentioned again in subsequent chapters, high achievers and success stories among black males are legion. From the period of slavery into the 1990s, the struggle of black men to nurture and provide care and sustenance for their families is evident by the overall accomplishments of black Americans in an America that has brutalized blacks with bigotry; hatred based purely on differences in skin color and false notions of white superiority; discrimination and segregation. Despite their experiences with prejudice, discrimination, and segregation, black males have triumphed as educators, jurists, physicians and surgeons, businessmen, leaders in the religious community, politicians, athletes, entertainers, leaders in labor unions, and as functioning members of a labor force through which they contribute to the social and economic foundation of the total American society, and as parents, fathers, grandparents, and role models who have inspired generations of young people to succeed.

However, that characterization of the black male is not the image projected through the mass media. It is rare, except for the recent success of the *Bill Cosby Show,* to observe presentations of the black father as a responsible, loving, caring provider. The media image of the black male is a conglomerate of "week-end gladiator," an athlete often described in animalistic terms by sports announcers but not intimidating because he is in a controlled situation; a nonthreatening entertainer; an irresponsible unwed father measuring his masculinity by the number of children he has fathered while not caring about providing financial support for them because "they can get welfare"; as rapists brutally assaulting white women; the hustler plotting to get by without engaging in hard work; criminals undermining the social fabric of white society or as addicts, drug pushers, and the dominant force in gang wars. Only in the latter part of the 1980s did the media turn its attention to the way that battles for control over the sale and distribution of drugs can tear apart or destroy what had been safe communities for law-abiding black citizens.

Without question, as we approach the end of the twentieth century, despite the progress and accomplishments of millions of black men against the odds they face in American society, the position of black males is precarious.[71] Why? About one-fourth of black male youngsters drop out of school before completing a high school diploma; they have the highest rates of suspensions and push-outs of school; the unemployment of young adult black males is constantly in the area of 40 to 50 percent; the homicide rate of black males is nine times that of white males; indeed, homicide is the leading cause of death among black males between the ages of 20 and 29; suicide is the third leading cause of death among black men in the same age cohort. Although black males constitute only 6 percent of the total American population, they compose about 50 percent of the prison population. The senseless, wanton killings of black men, primarily teenagers and young adults, by other black men resulting from intergang conflicts and efforts to control the highly lucrative drug trafficking in communities' gangs have captured and all but destroyed also are a persuasive argument supporting the position that the young black male is "an endangered species."

As already mentioned, the conditions that give rise to the precarious status of many black men in American society lie in the social structure of that society, its perceptions and treatment patterns of black men, and, to a lesser degree, imperfections in the character of persons categorized as social deviants. For example, several observers point out that "to be born black and male is double jeopardy."[72] He will suffer both from the prejudices experienced by the whole of black people in the United States, irrespective of class or social standing, as well as from the perceived threats of "the black male" to the white community.

Alienation from the social system begins, for many black boys, in elementary school. Often teachers, who are either uncaring or do not understand nuances of black experiences in a subculture isolated from mainstream society, affix stigmatizing labels to black boys from which it is difficult to extricate themselves. Such labels as "hyperactive," slow learners," "disciplinary problem," "hostile," and a "candidate for special education" take on a special meaning when attached to certain categories of children and when other teachers blindly accept them as substantiated truths. Sometimes, black boys are shunted off to "special ed" purely on the basis of their physical size or on criteria that have absolutely no educational validity. Because of such treatment, many black boys, especially those without proper parental guidance or the inner strength to cope with an unhappy situation, become "turned off" by school and education early in life. Many look at the deprivation in their family despite the hard work of their parents and question the ultimate value of education as well as the work ethic espoused by their parents. As they move through secondary school, many will experience varying degrees of prejudice and discrimination in gaining access to a college or university and, later, to a graduate or professional school as well as in their efforts to progress through the higher education system in general. Disillusionment and alienation, rather than determination to achieve despite subtle and overt manifestations of prejudice and discrimination, may engulf and cripple them.

Although many black males, like a substantial number of men in every racial group, are bent on self-destruction through their involvement in crime and the drug culture, as will be evident in Chapter 11, black males are also victims of inequities in the criminal justice system. Inasmuch as discrimination in employment was discussed in Chapter 2, the untold effects of economic injustice on the black male's efforts to help provide for his family need not be repeated. However, it is important to reiterate an observation made in Chapter 2: from pre-teenage through teenage and into adulthood, the black male in American society is often perceived as an intimidating threat to white men and women; sexually aggressive, hostile, and potentially violent. Among those who are intellectually gifted or highly competent, the same behavior often applauded in white males will be deemed as "arrogant," "super-sensitive," or a "difficult personality." Their successes are rationalized as atypical or as "exceptions," not as refutations of demeaning stereotypes about them. Despite these untoward situations and the negative images portrayed through the media, the majority of black men in America continue to be law-abiding citizens, responsible and caring fathers, sons, or brothers, and contributing members of the American society and its black community.

The Black Matriarchy

Especially since the 1965 publication of Moynihan's *The Negro Family: The Case for National Action,* social scientists have devoted considerable energies to the issue of a rising black matriarchy. This research and discussion have usually focused on the presumption that such family structures generally induce pathological outcomes within the family unit (e.g., severe economic disabilities, enormously higher rates of poverty, illegitimacy, high rates of crime and delinquency, and so on) than in traditional two-parent families. Another component of the argument centers about authority and decision-making within the home. According to this viewpoint, the matriarchy is dominant within black family life because black women are the chief decision-makers by virtue of their greater participation in the work force and their capacity to earn a disproportionate share of the income. Each of these arguments is debatable and the evidence to support the first of them is inconclusive.

However, as stated earlier, the number of two-parent families in the black community has plummeted over the past two decades, down to only 41.5 percent, while the number of such families in the white population has hovered about 78 percent since the 1960s. Nevertheless, married-couple two-parent families still constitute a majority, however fragile, of all black family structures. Moreover, this statistic regarding the black community does not consider the sizeable number of black men who are literally forced to leave their families so that their families qualify for greatly needed governmental benefits because they cannot find gainful employment. This fact may help to explain the extremely high proportion (60 percent) of families headed by black women that are poor. Thus, increasingly such families are poverty stricken, and many are in a daily struggle to meet the most fundamental survival needs. As already asserted, a major share of the black female poor population is the result of the increase in the number of unmarried teenage mothers. That increase helps to depress the number and percentage of families headed by both parents. Similarly, the fact that black divorced women do not remarry at the same rate as black divorced men, as is the case in the white population, and because there are simply more of them, divorce also depresses the number of two-parent families. These factors heighten the statistical representation of families headed by women in the population. They also help us to understand how the conditions of the American social structure, as they exist in the 1990s, have such a profoundly negative impact on families, especially black families.

Welfare Revisited

As mentioned in Chapter 2, a number of misconceptions have developed about blacks and public welfare. So pervasive are the myths that the word "welfare" had become, until the severe economic downturn of 1981, a political code for antiblack sentiments, and the white population had been misled into believing that the myths were reality. Even with the huge influx of thousands of laid-off white workers onto the welfare rolls in the 1980s, many still perceive that arrangement as a temporary phenomenon and that the newcomers will remove themselves from the welfare rolls when the economy improves and they are rehired. Thus many persons who have shared the untoward experiences of other welfare recipients of long-standing may or may not change their beliefs about public welfare.

Four misconceptions are especially at fault regarding blacks and welfare. First, there is and always has been a disproportionately large number of blacks on public relief. Second, the majority of people on public welfare are able-bodied, lazy, shiftless, street-corner blacks. Third, black people do not wish to work but spend their time loafing. Fourth, black people deliberately have illegitimate children in order to collect public assistance. Each of these myths will now be examined.

Blacks are relatively newcomers to the public welfare system because of the long-standing patterns of discrimination in many states that disallowed relief for large segments of the black population. Frances Fox Pivin and Richard Cloward maintain that blacks did not, for example, appear in significant proportions on Aid to Families With Dependent Children (AFDC) rolls until 1948. Increases in the proportion of blacks receiving AFDC benefits had nothing to do with black family structure; rather they were a consequence of pressures exerted by the federal government, particularly on southern states, to reduce discriminatory practices against blacks as well as of the migration of blacks to more liberal states.[73] Even these factors did not result in appreciable increases in the proportion of blacks receiving only this form of public assistance until after 1964.

More than 32 million Americans are officially below the poverty-income level. Only about 60 percent of poverty households received some form of noncash welfare benefits. To alleviate the problems of the unemployed, subemployed, and discouraged workers, two kinds of direct cash or income maintenance programs have been established: (1) social insurance programs (e.g., Social Security and unemployment compensation) and (2) public assistance (e.g., AFDC, AFDC Unemployed Parents, Supplemental Security Income or SSI).

Hill's analyses showed that very few blacks are "multiple participants" in these programs, and that whites represent the overwhelming majority of the recipients of all forms of public assistance.[74] For instance, blacks compose 10 percent of the 22 million Social Security recipients but whites are 88 percent of all such recipients. However, 31 percent of blacks (3,528,000 persons) receive Social Security benefits compared to 30,533,000 or 20 percent of the public population.[75]

The dominance of the white population as recipients of governmental benefits is supported by additional empirical data. For example, they account for 60 percent of all public assistance benefits, 64 percent of all Supplemental Security Insurance recipients, 67 percent of all Medicaid, and 63 percent of all food stamp beneficiaries.[76] In addition, 58 percent of all recipients of public or subsidized housing are white; so are approximately 80 percent of all children who receive Social Security benefits.[77]

Ploski and Williams point out that more than half of all poor black families received no welfare at all in 1980 and that 70 percent of all unemployed blacks did not receive jobless benefits.[78] Their analyses showed that of the 3,523,000 AFDC families, 43 percent were black. In other words, of the more than 6 million black families, 1.5 million were recipients of AFDC monies. Of that 1.5 million, some 720,000 were headed by black mothers under the age of 30.[79] Less than one-fourth of the AFDC mothers were high school graduates—a situation that restricted, if not totally eliminated, their employability. Many of these young women were teenagers who never set out to deliberately become pregnant and had only one child.

It should be stressed that welfare recipients of all races are likely to be limited in marketable skills, have poor education, and in poor health. They include a majority of people who are the underaged poor children, elderly men and women, and the disabled and blind. Although blacks are disproportionately represented in public assistance programs due to employment and income disabilities, discrimination in the marketplace, and averaged lower levels of educational attainment, they do not constitute a majority. Furthermore, there is no reliable evidence to support the allegation that most welfare recipients are able-bodied men who do not wish to work. To the contrary, they are likely to be mothers forced to rely on welfare to support themselves and their children.

THE IMPACT OF URBANIZATION ON THE BLACK FAMILY

It was stated earlier that the black population in the United States is now predominantly urban. More than 80 percent of all blacks live in cities. The process of urbanization among blacks, as in the case of the American population in general, occurred largely within the last century since a century ago the United States was still quite fundamentally a rural nation. However, in the case of the black population, this transformation from rural dwellers to city dwellers had its most auspicious beginning at the end of the first decade of the twentieth century. It has continued at such an unabated pace that the trend now seems irreversible. As a process, the urbanization of American blacks occurred as America itself was transformed from an agricultural nation into an industrial one. Industrialization was accompanied by a population explosion in strategic areas, mainly from an influx of people from the farm to the city in search of a new life and higher standards of living. It also signaled basic changes in patterns of work and the development of a more complex division of labor. Thus even though the city was to become a profoundly unique experience for the migrant rural peasantry, black and white, its effect upon the black family would in time prove to be particularly notable.

At least two schools of thought prevail regarding the impact of urbanization on the black family. First is the deterioration theory as represented in the early works of Frazier[80] and the more recent but highly controversial arguments advanced by Moynihan.[81] The basic assumption that underlies the family deterioration theory is that urbanization has wreaked an almost uncontrollable disorganization upon the black family—a process stemming from the mass movement of a woefully unprepared sharecropping, tenant farming, and unskilled population into a highly complex social structure. This lack of preparation for city life, coupled with the rapidity of their infiltration into urban settings, rendered blacks incapable of making satisfactory adjustments to urban complexities. Neither individuals nor families could cope with the myriad problems that confront the experienced urban dweller—problems of anonymity, personal isolation, limited primary group affiliations, impersonality, earning a living, finding suitable housing, obtaining basic health care, and establishing social bonds or developing a sense of group solidarity. Failing to make these adjustments, the family became disorganized, a condition most directly revealed by divorce, desertion, separation, illegitimacy, matriarchal family structures, sexual immorality or casual sexual relations, delinquency,

criminality, high rates of unemployment, alienation, and general norma-
lessness.

Frazier advanced this position in a 1939 prize-winning study, *The
Negro Family in the United States*. As a point of clarification, it should be
stressed that Frazier's analysis of what he called the disorganization of the
Negro family was not intended to make black people culpable for their
condition, as he defined it; rather, he was identifying those situations
within urban social structure and the American experience that generated
family deterioration. Of primary importance to him was the legacy of
slavery, which, as a sustained institution, had numerous deleterious consequences for the black family. He saw in slavery and its consequences major
structural divergencies from the normative patterns of American middle-
class family life. These variations persisted through urbanization and
were, in effect, viewed as atypical behavioral patterns. However, it is
particularly significant that Frazier attributed a major responsibility for
whatever disorganization he observed with black family structures to the
pernicious elements of prejudice, discrimination, and white racism and
not to callous blacks. These were the factors that accounted for large-scale
unemployment and abject poverty, that fostered impoverished conditions, and that constituted the main impediments to the inclusion of blacks
in the opportunity structure on an equal basis with the white population.
Irrespective of these explanations, social scientists have often cited
Frazier's position to support the general theory of black family disorganization. Almost as frequently as it has been cited, it has been quoted out
of context and in such a manner as to support prevailing stereotypic and
racist ideologies concerning black family blight.

Perhaps it is the persistence of misconceptions about black family life
interfaced with intellectual racism that helps to explain the vituperative
reactions among many practitioners and academicians to the publication
of the Moynihan Report on the black family in 1965. In a way, Moynihan's
analysis of the conditions of contemporary black families is similar to that
of Frazier. Both give similar explanations of the so-called family disorganization or deterioration. Significantly, the Frazier–Moynihan perspective
diverges in the level of consciousness with which racism, discrimination,
and prejudice are viewed as contributing factors to the condition specified
as disorganization. Frazier's position on this subject was clearer than
Moynihan's. The contexts in which their publications appeared, however,
were quite dissimilar. For many American people Moynihan failed to
specify clearly that Americans must devise effective means of first controlling prejudice and racism, which are the manifest springboards for discrimination, before any national effort of substantial credibility can be
mounted to strengthen the black family. He did, however, stress the need
to strengthen the role of the black male to halt further deterioration. The
"tangle of pathology" he describes, assuming that it has partial merit, is
a function of inequities in the opportunity structure between blacks and
whites—disparities so pervasive as to relegate blacks into an almost ines-

capable subordinate status. Moynihan does not sufficiently clarify this essential point.

A second school of thought maintained by Billingsley,[82] Hill,[83] Staples,[84] and others holds that many of the conditions characterized as disorganization may be viewed as either strengths or as new modes of adaption to untoward situations. It is also argued that the black matriarchy is a myth.[85] In this view the impact of urbanization on the black family is neither totally nor necessarily deleterious. It may not even be particularly dysfunctional as a process, but an ethos of racism permeating the nation and forcing blacks into a subordinate status can be quite detrimental to black family life. The fact that black families remain relatively organized around differentiated role-specific and role-general functions is a strength,[86] and the existence of extended family systems as a welfare family function is a significant adaptive response to urbanism.[87]

Regardless of the position or school of thought that one accepts, certain fundamental observations can be made concerning the urbanization of black families. First, as the earlier black population shifted from the farm to the city, they did not differ noticeably from earlier American immigrants except in terms of limited access to the opportunity structure and in the color of their skins. But these were profound differences, for they were to shape the character of the black family's experiences in the city. For example, being outside the opportunity structure placed them in a disadvantaged position within an increasingly complex labor force. Discriminatory practices prevented even the best trained men, with some notable exceptions, from obtaining high-salaried positions. Therefore, since they were largely laborers, occupational diversity was seriously curtailed, which, in turn, limited income that could be earned legally. In many instances, unemployment led to poverty, which also engendered numerous personal problems.

Second, the isolated and impersonal conditions under which early black urban migrants existed, coupled with the freedom from powerful, if informal, structures of social control, permitted experimentation with social relationships between the sexes that would have generated severe social disapprobation in a rural setting. Thus urbanization fostered another interpretation of machismo or manhood—freedom to embrace a double standard of morality. Some may argue, as have Elliott Liebow[88] and Charles A. Valentine,[89] that this process is a sociopsychological response to failure as a man in an economic world in which the lower-class black male cannot earn his way and provide for his family as he basically desires. It is not an essential element in a culture of poverty. This is, of course, a point of continuing debate; however, there is general agreement that the urbanization of blacks is continually accompanied by increasing divorce rates. Even this observation does not solve the dilemma for protagonists of the two schools of thought described previously, inasmuch as those in the first school would perceive divorce as an index of disorganization, whereas those in the second school would undoubtedly view it as a mode of adaption that allows extrication from an intolerable situation.

Third, urbanization generated a transfer of several family functions to other institutional structures, either in part or in toto. Thus socialization is shared with educational institutions, protection with law enforcement agencies, and religious training with the established church, while recreational functions are dispersed among a wide array of secondary enterprises and voluntary associations, and economic functions are not now the exclusive responsibility of the family. The family is no longer primarily a producer but a consumer. But it is this transfer of economic functions that has facilitated an increase in independence among women and removed many of them from the home into the labor market.

One consequence of the independence of women is evident in a fourth observation—the breakdown of the traditional patriarchal structure. As stated in the discussion of household patterns and authority structures among the black population, a shift from patriarchy to egalitarianism has occurred among black families. This transformation coincided with increasing urbanization and appears to be the most prevalent authority structure among present-day urban blacks in the United States when all forms of household arrangements are taken into consideration.

One final observation is that of the impact of ghettoization on black families. Although inner-city life is often highly stratified, many blacks are restricted to harsh, disorganizing living conditions each day of their lives, especially those at the bottom end of the socioeconomic scale. Many are in homes devastated by income disabilities, overcrowded living conditions, and homes in which a sense of hopelessness and despair about their future prospects is normative. Many young people are left fending for themselves because their parents no longer have funds for child-care arrangements. Unsupervised teenagers, with no organized recreational pursuits to occupy their time and no parents available to demand that more time is spent on formal educational endeavors, are more vulnerable and likely to become involved in deviant behavior. Many come from homes in which parents do not assert authority and discipline that would encourage children to increase schooling and marketable skills and, sadly, many do not know how to be good parents. Some have neither appropriate male or female role models. They grow up in a life of negation and deprivation which is oftentimes transmitted to their own offspring. The black family structure is, in fact, weakened. All these conditions are compounded by the severe lack of city services. Consequently, many black children, mothers, and fathers come to believe that no one really cares.[90]

In conclusion, it should be stressed that even though the black population continues to shift from the rural areas and small towns to the large cities, we cannot assume that the migrant blacks are ignorant, unprepared peasants cluttering already overcrowded slums. More and more black immigrants are moving from one large city to another, and many are higher achievers than many blacks and whites already residing in the cities to which they migrate. Urban life is a highly complex one that requires adjustments, adaptations, resilience, and both formal and informal support structures. Other problems related to urban life, such as deviance, will be given more attention in Chapters 11 and 12.

Finally, because of the widespread alarm created in the black community and the nation as a whole and the media attention to forces destructive to the black family, various leaders and organizations within the black community have given priority to improving the status of the black families. For example, in 1984, the NAACP and the National Urban League convened approximately 200 representatives of more than 100 black organizations for a Black Family Summit at Fisk University in Nashville, Tennessee. This summit was followed by conferences in 43 cities, sponsored by a predominantly black Greek Letter Organization, Delta Sigma Theta Sorority, in which the focus was on some of the issues from the Nashville Summit. These two events represented a public acknowledgment by black leaders that the traditional black family was in trouble and that blacks themselves have a compelling responsibility to initiate concrete steps to alleviate the oppressive conditions that have a negative impact on the black family.

Since those early conferences, leadership roles in calling attention to the strengths and prevailing traditional values of the black family as well as the construction of programs addressing problems that undermine basic family structure and functions have expanded. Among groups in the forefront of this endeavor are the National Council of Negro Women, the Children's Defense Fund, the National Urban League, the NAACP, the Joint Center for Political and Economic Studies, the Black Church, Black Greek Letter organizations, and service groups such as the Links and the Jack and Jill Organization. Reverend Jesse Jackson has continued to encourage black youth to avoid drugs and stay in school as well as to abstain from premarital sexual relationships. Black organizations, of the types mentioned above, have developed a number of blueprints for attacking the problems of teenage pregnancy, unemployment and low income, marital instability, problems of the elderly, housing, and crime and violence. Black leaders are still in the forefront of the movement to create full employment and to reduce, if not eliminate, discrimination in the labor force; to establish new educational systems that would address the needs of black, other minority, and poor white children; the allocation of funds to support social programs of benefit to outsider groups; and the establishment of a national child-care policy.

Foundations now support a number of pilot programs and demonstration projects designed to move more and more young people into the work force, to enable parenting teens to become more responsible parents, obtain higher education, and be participants in the labor market as well as programs oriented toward pregnancy prevention among teenage girls. However, in the final analysis, the strength of the black family will continue to be intricately linked to the ability of black Americans to be active and equal participants in economic institutions that do not use race or gender as instruments for denial of opportunity and discrimination.

NOTES

1. For a discussion of the pathologies of black families, cf. E. Franklin Frazier, *The Negro Family in the United States* (Chicago: University of Chicago Press, 1939); Alphonso Pinkney, *Black Americans* (Englewood Cliffs, N.J.: Prentice-Hall, 1969), Chap. 5; and Daniel P. Moynihan, *The Negro Family: The Case for National Action* (Washington, D.C.: United States Department of Labor, 1965).
2. Cf. John Hope Franklin, *From Slavery to Freedom* (New York: Alfred A. Knopf, 1948), p. 108, and John W. Blassingame, "Status and Social Structure in the Slave Community," in Randall M. Miller (ed.), *The Afro-American Slaves: Community or Chaos?* (Malabar, Florida: Robert E. Krieger Publishing Co., 1981).
3. *Ibid.*
4. *Ibid.*
5. Robert Hill, *Economic Policies and Black Progress: Myths and Realities* (Washington, D.C.: National Urban League Research Department, 1981), p. 101, and telephone interview with Robert Hill, June 15, 1983.
6. *Ibid.*
7. U. S. Department of Commerce, *Marital Status and Living Arrangements, March 1981* (Washington, D.C.: Bureau of the Census, Current Population Reports, Series P-20, No. 372, June 1982), p. 2. *Statistical Abstracts of the U. S., 1989,* p. 42; and Bureau of the Census, *Marital Status and Living Arrangements:* March 1989 (Washington, D. C.: U. S. Department of Commerce, Series P-20, No. 445, June 1990), p. 9.
8. See *Statistical Abstracts of the United States 1989.* Table 56, p. 44.
9. *Ibid.,* Table 54, p. 43.
10. Cf. James E. Blackwell, "Social and Legal Dimensions of Interracial Liaisons," in Doris Y. Wilkinson and Ronald Taylor (eds.), *The Black Male in America* (Chicago: Nelson Hall, 1977), pp. 219–243; Gunnar Myrdal, *An American Dilemma* (New York: Harper & Row, 1944); and Charles Stember, *Sexual Racism* (New York: Elsevier Publishers, 1976).
11. Blackwell, *op. cit.*
12. *Ibid.*
13. *Ibid.* See also Ernest Porterfield, *Black and White Mixed Marriages* (Chicago: Nelson Hall, 1978).
14. *Ibid.*
15. Stember, *op. cit.*
16. *Ibid.* See also Frank A. Petroni, "Interracial Dating: The Price Is So High," in Irving Stuart and Lawrence Abt (eds.), *Interracial Marriage* (New York: Grossman Publishers, 1973), and Doris Y. Wilkinson, "The Stigmatization Process: The Politician of the Black Male's Identity," in Doris Y. Wilkinson and Ronald Taylor (eds.), *supra,* pp. 145–158.
17. Andrew Billingsley, *Black Families in White America* (Englewood Cliffs, N.J.: Prentice-Hall, 1968), pp. 143–144.
18. *Ibid.*
19. Robert Hill, *The Strengths of Black Families* (New York: Emerson Hall Publishers, 1972), p. 9.
20. Harriette McAdoo, (ed.), *Black Families* (Beverly Hills, Calif.: Sage, 1980).

21. Robert Staples, *The Black Family: Essays and Studies,* 2nd ed. (Belmont, Calif.: Wadsworth Publishing Co., 1978), pp. 149–159.
22. David A. Schulz, "The Role of Boyfriend," in *Coming Up Black: Patterns of Ghetto Socialization* (Englewood Cliffs, N.J.: Prentice-Hall, 1969), pp. 136–144.
23. Billingsley, *op. cit.,* pp. 18–25.
24. *Ibid.*
25. *Statistical Abstracts of the United States 1989,* Table 68, p. 50.
26. Cf. CBS REPORTS, "The Vanishing Family: Crisis in Black America," correspondent Bill Moyers; January 25, 1986 and March 25, 1986.
27. Cf. Staples, *op. cit.,* La Frances Rodgers-Rose (ed). *The Black Woman* (Beverly Hills, Calif.: Sage Publications, 1980); and Charles V. Willie, *A New Look at Black Families* (Bayside, N. Y.: General Hall, Co., 1981).
28. *Statistical Abstracts of the United States, 1989,* p. 51.
29. *Ibid.,* p. 46.
30. U. S. Department of Commerce, *Household and Family Characteristics March 1980* (Washington, D. C.: U. S. Department of Commerce, 1980), p. 18.
31. *Op. cit.,* Table 69, p. 51.
32. Schultz, *op. cit.*
33. *Ibid.*
34. *Ibid.*
35. *Ibid.*
36. *Ibid.*
37. *Ibid.*
38. *Ibid.*
39. Billingsley, *op. cit.,* p. 22.
40. *Ibid.*
41. Hill, *op. cit.,* 1981, 1983.
42. Hill, *op. cit.,* 1972, pp. 5–36.
43. *Ibid.*
44. Joseph Julian and William Kornblum, *Social Problems,* 4th ed. (Englewood Cliffs, N. J.: Prentice-Hall, 1983), pp. 33–332, 419–420.
45. Robert H. Lauer, *Social Problems and the Quality of Life,* 4th ed. (Dubuque, Iowa: William C. Brown Publishers, 1989), p. 38.
46. *The Social and Economic Status of the Black Population in the United States,* 1971, *loc. cit.,* p. 111.
47. Stephanie Ventura, "Trends and Differentials in Births to Unmarried Women, United States, 1970–1976" (Hagerstown, Md.: National Center for Health Statistics, 1980, November 1981), pp. 1–10.
48. Alan Guttmacher, *Teenage Pregnancy: The Problem That Won't Go Away* (New York: Alan Guttmacher Institute, March 1981).
49. *Ibid.*
50. Ventura, *op. cit.*
51. Elise F. Jones, et al., "Teenage Pregnancy in Developed Countries: Determinants and Policy Implications," *Family Planning Perspectives,* 17:2 (March/April 1985): 53–63.
52. Cf. Elise F. Jones, *op. cit.;* Stanley K. Henshaw and Jennifer Van Fort, "Teenage Abortion, Birth and Pregnancy Statistics," *Family Planning Perspectives,* 21:2 (March/April 1989): 85–89; and Phillips Cutright and Herbert L. Smith, "Intermediate Determinants of Racial Differences in 1980 U. S. Nonmarital

Fertility Rates," *Family Planning Perspectives,* 20:2 (May/June 1988): 119–123.

53. *Op. cit.,* p. 85.
54. *Op. cit.,* Table 1, p. 120.
55. *Op. cit.,* Table 1, p. 85.
56. *Op. cit.,* p. 119.
57. *Ibid.*
58. *Ibid.*
59. Cf. James R. Kelly, "Numbers Versus Moral Realism and Teen-age Pregnancies," *America* (February 14, 1987): 131–136; "Interview With Nathan Hare," *Crisis* (March 1986): 30–35. Edward Sargent, "Unwed, Absent Fathers," *Sisters* (Fall 1988): 28–31; "Mothers Raising Mothers," *U. S. News and World Report* (March 17, 1986); "Children Having Children," *Time* (December 9, 1985): 78–90.
60. *Adolescent and Young Adult Fathers: Problems and Solutions.* (Washington, D. C.: Children's Defense Fund, 1988).
61. Cf. Studies cited in *Time* (December 9, 1985).
62. Cf. Elise F. Jones, et al., *op. cit.*
63. Cf. Children's Defense Fund Study; Edward Sargent, *op. cit.* and *Time* (December 9, 1985).
64. Sargent, *op. cit.*
65. *Ibid.*
66. "The Missing-Father Myth," *Time* (December 9, 1985): 9, 90.
67. Julian and Kornblum, *op. cit.,* p. 414.
68. Carfred B. Broderick, "Marital Stability," *Marriage and the Family,* 2nd ed. (Englewood Cliffs, N. J.: Prentice-Hall, 1984), p. 12.
69. Lauer, *op. cit.,* p. 448.
70. Harry Ploski and James Williams, *The Negro Almanac: A Reference Work on The Afro-American,* 4th ed. (New York: John Wiley and Sons, 1983).
71. For a detailed discussion of the status of the black male, see Kenneth M. Jones, "The Black Male in Jeopardy," *Crisis* (March 1986): 17–21; James McGhee, *Running the Gauntlet: Black Men in America* (New York: The National Urban League, 1985); Nathan Hare and Julia Hare, *The Endangered Black Family* (San Francisco: The Black Scholar Press, 1986); Nathan Hare, *Bringing the Black Boy to Manhood* (San Francisco: The Black Scholar Press, 1986); Robert Staples, *Black Masculinity: The Black Male's Role in American Society* (San Francisco: The Black Scholar Press, 1982); Robert Staples, "Black Male Genocide," *The Black Scholar,* (May/June 1987): 2–9; Manning Marable, "Open Season on Blacks—Again," *Los Angeles Sentinel,* January 8, 1987, p. A-7, and Alvin F. Poussaint, "Black Men Must Organize," *Black Scholar* (May/June 1987): 12–15.
72. Leland Hall cited in Kenneth Jones, *op. cit.*
73. Frances Fox Pivin and Richard Cloward, *Regulating the Poor* (New York: Vintage Books, 1971), pp. 189–190.
74. Hill, *op. cit.,* 1981, p. 47.
75. *Ibid.*
76. Ploski and Williams, *op. cit.,* p. 663.
77. *Ibid.*
78. *Ibid.,* p. 479.
79. *Ibid.*

80. Frazier, *op. cit.*
81. Moynihan, *op. cit.*
82. Billingsley, *op. cit.*
83. Hill, *op. cit.*
84. Staples, *op. cit.*
85. *Ibid.*
86. Hill, *op. cit.*
87. Staples, *op. cit.*
88. Elliot Liebow, *Talley's Corner: A Study of Negro Street Corner Men* (Boston: Little, Brown, 1966).
89. Charles A. Valentine, *A Culture of Poverty* (Chicago: University of Chicago Press, 1968).
90. Blackwell and Hart, *op. cit.*

Chapter
4

Stratification and Social Mobility

As a result of occupational, educational, and income advances achieved by members of the black community during the 1960s and 1970s, many persons began to speak of a "new black middle class," as if stratification and social differentiation were new dimensions of the black community. Such views disregard the fact that social differentiation has a long history in the black community. Though the roots of this system can be traced to slavery, its present dynamic character is a result of major transformations within our industrialized society. It is also evidence of increasing shifts from ascription to achievement as the basis for stratification and mobility. Both traditional socioeconomic status (SES) and class variables facilitate social differentiation and upward mobility as in the larger society. A new variable, "blackness," was a powerful determinant of access to important jobs, which generally accelerated upward mobility during the late 1960s and early 1970s. The primary impetus for its significance was the black power movement with its emphasis on cultural nationalism. However, its importance in the 1990s as a determinant of upward mobility has probably lessened. These observations will be elaborated next.

PERCEPTIONS AND INDICES OF SOCIAL CLASS

Contemporary views about social stratification draw upon the rich legacy provided by the seminal works of Karl Marx and Max Weber, so much so that when we think of social classes, we almost automatically fix in our minds concepts such as property, prestige, power, life styles, and economic base. These concepts are widely used in explications of social class by contemporary sociologists.

At the risk of oversimplification, Marx's views may be briefly summarized as follows. Classes are groups of people, rather than specific individuals, who are united around commonly shared experiences in relationship to the means of production. The relationship to the means of production is dichotomized: Either people own these means (the bourgeoisie) or they sell their labor (the proletariat). The bourgeoisie is exceedingly powerful but limited in number, whereas the proletariat is considerably larger in size but limited in power. This disparity in the economic structure forms the basis of all social classes and determines one's place in the society as a whole. For Marx, economic position becomes the basis for quality of family life, prestige, status, and political power.

A second perspective on social class was provided by Weber, who, in effect, expanded and modified Marxian thought. For Weber three principal factors serve as the foundation of social stratification—the economic order, the social order, and the political order. These orders are generally interpreted as class, status or prestige, and power, respectively. Weber's use of the concept social order closely corresponds to the Marxian meaning of class; and it was, quite importantly, based upon the life chances and opportunities provided a person in terms of economic position. It should be clear that Weber stressed the independent nature of the three factors of class, status, and power even though they do intersect at crucial points within societies and subcommunities. By this is meant that the possibility of relatively powerless well-to-do and high-prestige relatively poor did exist within Weber's theoretical formulation. In fact, they exist in everyday life.

Both perspectives generated schools of thought among social scientists about the formation of social class[1] and, most significantly, identified elements that should be specified when developing class distinctions. Thus the conceptual tools of property, power, prestige, and economic base are among the more common indicators of class position and determinants of mobility employed today.

Property refers to possessions and the implicit right to dispose of them as the owner sees fit. It is derived from group membership, exchanges of scarce values, capital investments, inheritance, and outright gifts. Its acquisition may be highly correlated with one's position in the economic, social, or political order.[2]

Although there are numerous conceptualizations of the term "power," for our purposes it may be viewed simply as the ability to control the decision-making apparatus and shared values of the social system. This ability may rest with one or more individuals, or it may be vested within certain groups under certain conditions. Group power, as perceived by Robert Bierstedt, may have its source in (1) numbers or the size of the group, (2) the degree of the group's social organization, and (3) the amount and types of resources available to the group.[3] Expanding upon Bierstedt's formulation, Hubert Blalock suggested that a critical variable in the acquisition and maintenance of group power is the ability of the group to mobilize its resources over time until it reaches its goal.[4]

On the other hand, *individual* power may be derived from the roles performed by individuals (their institutional positions); implied or actuated force; the acquisition of property, which enables the individual to control the distribution of certain aspects of scarce resources; or from what Weber correctly called "charisma"—those personal qualities that permit certain people to influence, persuade, and charm others into complying with their wishes.[5] The sources of individual power are virtually identical to those that generate prestige or what Weber identified as social honor. However, it is imperative to stress the independent nature of variables such as prestige, power, and property, for the possession of one does not and should not imply the automatic possession of the other. Their independence of operation creates considerable status inconsistency in the American society—ranking high on one status dimension and low on another—and especially among black people in relation to the larger society. Regional and community variations may be missed entirely if categorical or uniform perceptions of power and prestige, for example, are taken as a norm in social class analysis. To illustrate, the amount of prestige awarded a college professor may be substantially greater in Walla Walla, Washington, a small college town, than would be accorded such a person in New York City. Moreover, the mere acquisition of property, for example, does not necessarily assure concomitant power and privilege. Some people in the United States, black and white, are more concerned with *how* one attains property or wealth than with the actual possession of it. Nevertheless, the acquisition of power, prestige, and property and a solid economic base may, as we will see, facilitate upward mobility in the stratification system.

It is also possible for a discontinuity to arise between a person's objective class position and the person's subjective position in the social structure. By definition, the objective class position refers to the real rank the person holds in a society according to some predetermined and somewhat universalistic criteria. The subjective class, on the other hand, refers to the rank one feels or thinks one holds. The two may or may not be congruent. But the disparity between these two viewpoints—how others see an individual and how the individual sees him- or herself—often results in eccentric behavior among certain individuals.

ETHNIC STRATIFICATION

So far, we have stressed class as a fundamental basis for stratification in the American society. However, social class is only one of the two major systems of stratification in the United States. A second and equally powerful system is ethnic stratification.[6] This system by and large expresses where a particular group falls on a social distance scale, that is, how closely it approximates conventional norms and standards of social acceptability of the white Anglo-Saxon society in the United States. In every social distance scale, ethnic groups, particularly the so-called new ethnics— blacks, Chicanos, Puerto Ricans, and Asians to a lesser degree—are relegated to the bottom positions. European immigrants, including new European groups such as Italians, Jews, and Poles, rank above new minority ethnics in the eyes of most of the predominant society. Because of color, however, the new ethnics have greater visibility, which helps to identify them and set them apart from white Anglo-Saxons. Their greater visibility may also function to restrict advancement within the opportunity structure and thereby retard upward mobility in a class system. Since they are set apart from the rest of the members of the larger society, and are excluded from full participation in that structure, they tend to develop a stratification system of their own, superimposed on and overlaid by the larger one.

The process of ethnic classification and subsequent stratification is more or less inescapable in a pluralistic society in which power is unequally distributed. Unequal access to scarce values and to goods and services by which they are identified, classified, and positioned within the social structure accompanies limitations of power. Whenever the color variable enters into the classification schema, it is almost axiomatic that the more closely a person or a group approximates whiteness, the higher his or its rank in the larger system. The same principle often holds true within some ethnic groups in their own stratification system. Color, therefore, has both a divisive and unifying effect. The dominant group uses it, on the one hand, to distinguish itself from subordinates or less favored individuals. On the other hand, members of the subordinate group who approximate the dominant one in color employ it to establish positions of privilege within the subordinate structure. Moreover, because all members of the subordinate group are lumped together, color becomes the unifying force in the face of externally imposed sanctions, categorical treatment, intergroup conflicts, and denials of access to highly prized scarce resources, goods, and services.

THE FORMATION OF SOCIAL CLASSES IN THE BLACK COMMUNITY

Chapter 1 showed how a stratification system formed among American blacks from the distinctions made between house servants and field hands during the period of slavery. House servants, for the most part, were mulatto offspring and the descendants of unions between white men and black slave women. During slavery, house servants were able to acquire a distinctive level of living that set them apart from the field hands. As we noted previously, they were also socialized into the cultural mandates and life styles of the white ruling class in a manner not available to other groups of slaves. The differences that emerged between house slaves and field hands were further widened because of the value placed upon white ancestry and the social status resulting from this value. The work done by house servants compared to that done by field hands also maximized distinctions based upon color and rank. The skills that house servants learned were predictably beneficial because they helped transform these slaves into freemen. Indeed, many house servants were manumitted; others were able to buy not only their own freedom but also the freedom of other members of their families. Through this process a class of free blacks became the founders of a propertied "aristocracy of color" among American blacks.

Black field hands, who either attempted to hold on to the rudiments of a rapidly disappearing culture or desperately tried to accommodate to sketches of the new white culture, were forced to become America's underclass—the lumpen proletariat of society. Primarily unskilled and untrained, they worked with their hands, engaged in menial tasks, and supplied the brawn and labor necessary to build many of the physical structures of the American republic. They suffered the abuses of low status and low esteem. They were forced to internalize white perceptions of their value and to deny the worth of their color. Thus slavery produced a twofold class system among black Americans: an upper class based almost exclusively upon color and a lower class that consisted primarily of the sons and daughters of field hands.[7] It also originated a dual stratification system.

In time, as opportunities expanded through industrialization and shifted away from a paternalistic agricultural slavery system, stratification within the black population would somewhat parallel that of the larger American social structure. Earlier, black codes were promulgated to keep slaves in their place; later, varying legislation was enacted to restrict freemen and subordinate them into a kind of caste arrangement in the American social structure. The post-emancipation period and particularly the post-Reconstruction period witnessed a proliferation of legal restraints aimed at preventing the emergence of an independent group of blacks— all of which fostered a dual social structure and, inevitably, a parallel system of stratification.[8] This observation supports the assertions by conflict theorists that social classes are man-made and subject to man-made change. The articulation of a *structure of privilege* versus a *structure of want,* for example, was indeed made by people who undoubtedly believed that their acts were rational. The mythical men of power not only created a system of inequality within the larger society and between the white members of that society and the black nonmembers; they also established a model that blacks would in time emulate for creating social differentiation among themselves.

Slavery, Color, and Stratification

The color variable, often labeled "family background," persisted as the most important criterion for admission to the black upper class through most of the Reconstruction period and, in some circles, until the 1940s. The importance of the degree of color lightness in conferring higher status among blacks began to wane with expanding educational opportunities, which occurred during Reconstruction and afterwards. This process was stimulated by two major sources, the Freedmen's Bureau and white philanthropists.

The U.S. Congress established the Freedmen's Bureau in 1865 to provide economic, social, and educational rehabilitation for the newly emancipated slaves and refugees of the slavery period. Under its aegis some blacks were fed, clothed, and given medical treatment and other social services. The bureau also established schools that gave rise to a more literate class among the darker-skinned blacks and allowed many of them to lease land in order to get a head start toward economic betterment. The work of the Freedmen's Bureau only partially undermined the aristocracy of color. The same effect resulted from the work of the numerous philanthropic organizations, voluntary groups, and individuals concerned about the plight of the masses of black people. Institutions such as the American Missionary Association and religious bodies like the Methodist Episcopal Church, the Presbyterians, the Episcopalians, the Baptists, and, to a lesser degree, the Catholics founded institutions for the educational development of blacks. George Peabody, John D. Rockefeller, John F. Slater, Anna T. Jeanes, and Caroline Phelps-Stokes were among a fairly large aggregate of individuals who came forward with substantial financial aid to expand educational opportunities for black people. Over a period of three decades approximately 121 colleges and universities would be founded for educating the black masses. The establishment of black secondary schools, colleges, and universities increased the likelihood that darker-skinned members of the black population would become educated, which, in time, facilitated the erosion of the aristocracy of color.

Family Background and Prestige

Family background was the second most important criterion for high status and upward mobility within the black community. The importance attached to one's family background, although diminished in broad significance since World War II through expanded economic and occupational opportunities, still persists in many segments of black social life. Regardless of the acquisition of wealth by the new black bourgeoisie[9] and the new black Anglo-Saxons,[10] admission to the pinnacle of the black social class structure is still largely a function of family name, social honor, and prestige. In several communities prestige continues to be accorded to persons whose families were respected in times past even though they themselves may have only modest means. Such families retain social honor for any number of reasons, including leadership roles in the community, positions held or services performed in the church, a lengthy history of unimpeachable character, relationships with white people, and respected personal attributes. In most instances, however, these preferred families have or once had considerable property, were never on welfare, kept their children out of trouble with white people and the law, and traditionally valued education. Today, these families often know each other because they have an extended and persistent network throughout the United States.

Educational Attainment

Perhaps the one factor that emerged as the most potent instrument for effecting major changes in the class structure within the black community was educational attainment. Formal schooling especially helped to delineate a black middle class. This class was formed by people sufficiently literate to perform important roles and functions required within the larger social structure and within the black community. Originally, schoolteachers, undertakers, postal workers, businesspeople, insurance agents, and real estate workers composed the black middle class. But the status of incumbents of these occupations varied from community to community and from region to region; often, though, some of these persons were included in the upper-class structure of the black society because of the convergence of a worthwhile occupation, a good family name, and the proper degree of education. What is of special importance here is that blacks, like many other low-status minority groups, placed a recognizably high value on educational attainment. So great was the value placed on educational achievement that black mothers were domestic servants to white people and fathers labored at low wages for white people in order to send their children to college and professional schools. Countless numbers of black young men and women deferred gratifications and sacrificed ordinary pleasures to raise money to attend college, often not knowing how they could afford to remain once admitted. Numerous black professional men and women of today did not come from well-to-do families that were able to support them throughout the period of college or professional training. But their eagerness to obtain an education moved them to work at service jobs for the white population to raise the necessary funds. Black students could be found working as waiters at country clubs or in the more genteel restaurants, as caddies, bellhops, and doormen in the larger hotels where tipping was generous, as janitors, laundrymen and women, cooks, domestic workers, part-time carpenters, bricklayers, and construction workers. Once education was attained, upward mobility within the black stratification system was considerably less difficult to attain.

As more black youth became educated and later as their economic positions improved, parents and brothers and sisters often shared in the benefits. Unfortunately, some who achieved success later spurned their hard-working mothers and fathers and others who had sacrificed in their behalf. These sons and daughters were, to put it bluntly, ashamed of their lowly origins; they often manufactured elaborate fabrications of family origins and falsehoods about their prestige and power within home communities. This pattern reflected a deeply rooted personal insecurity and an inability to express pride in achievements in the American tradition of the self-made man or woman. Many successful blacks today, however, do not shy away from knowledge of their humble backgrounds.

The importance of education as a cherished value within the black community can also be observed in the gross exaggerations of educational attainment and the importance attached to degrees obtained from certain institutions. Frazier once spoke of this situation in terms of the role of the black press in creating a make-believe world among black people.[11] Although present-day facts and more empirical investigations contradict much of what Frazier wrote in 1957, he was correct in his assertion that the black press frequently exaggerates the educational achievements of black people. The acquisition of a baccalaureate degree, especially from a prestigious predominantly white university, used to be reported as though it were a much higher degree. To some extent this is still true today. However, erroneous reporting has substantially lessened as a consequence of increasing sophistication and greater competence among black journalists. More attention and more coverage, though, are still given to graduates of predominantly white institutions than to graduates of predominantly black colleges and universities.

In general, it can be stated that at least until World War II the convergence of color, family background, and education formed the basic features of social stratification within the black community. The right combination of these elements differentiated various levels of social acceptability, status recognition, and special privilege observed within black communities throughout the United States. That system would undergo profound changes with improvements in the economic opportunities of black people and with the development of an expanded occupational structure that admitted an increasingly large and diverse group of blacks at the middle and upper ranges, both within the black community and the larger social structure, though to a far lesser degree. But these changes did not appreciably alter the subordinated status of the black social class system.

Occupation

The desegregation movement that followed the decision of the United States Supreme Court in the case of *Brown* v. *Board of Education of Topeka, Kansas,* in a large measure, focused on expanding economic opportunity for black Americans. This drive to access jobs propelled many talented blacks, previously excluded by virtue of systemic segregation and discrimination, into higher level occupations, and in unprecedented numbers. Economic institutions, public and private, responded in positive ways to the new demands for equality of access and to federally mandated policies of affirmative action in the marketplace. Well-educated blacks moved into professional, managerial and administrative positions—occupations that automatically conferred a new social status on them. Possessing higher status jobs, these blacks were able to purchase goods and services that changed their life styles, place of residence, and much of their social behavior in ways that conformed to a new social class position.

Between 1970 and 1980, there was a 59 percent change in the proportion of blacks who held higher level occupations (e.g., managers, professional occupations), a 19 percent growth in the proportions of blacks with medium-level occupations (e.g., clerical, operatives, and sales), and only an 8 percent growth in the number of blacks who were in the lower-level jobs (e.g., laborers, service and private households).[12] Occupations, rather than income, became a more fruitful way of determining class distinctions because many incumbents of lower-status jobs began to earn considerably more income than many incumbents of higher-status occupations. For instance, due to sustained successes in increasing wages through union contracts, many black members of crafts unions, or persons who are employed as bus drivers, or as garbage collectors are paid higher salaries than many public school teachers. Yet, on standard indexes of occupational status, teachers rank higher than craftsmen, garbage collectors, and bus drivers. Teachers have more prestige, social honor, and probably greater community influence than garbage collectors. It is precisely because of such diversity in income and status differentiation by occupations that each stratum within the class hierarchy has considerable overlap. Nevertheless, by the late 1960s and 1970s, and certainly in the 1990s, perhaps more so than ever before, occupations are a major determinant of class position within the black community. Scholars, such as Sampson[13], Levitan[14], McAdoo[15], insist that any assessment of social class in the black community must take into consideration this factor of occupational diversity.

Index of Social Class

What, then, are the measures of social class within the contemporary black community? In many respects the determination of social class among blacks is quite similar to that among whites. They differ in the degree to which some factors are more highly valued than others and, perhaps, *how* measures of social class are employed in daily life. Traditionally, sociologists associate class position with one's standing in relation to SES variables of occupation, education, and income. These variables are primary—possessing almost universal applicability. They are also associated with what we may now call secondary variables: family background, place of residence, status symbols, membership in formal and informal associations, voluntary groups, friendship cliques, church membership, and life styles. With the possible exception of church membership and family background, these factors are secondary in the sense that they are derived from the primary sources of class identity. In a society that is ethnically stratified, the factor of skin color becomes a further index of status and social class. Blackness may possibly supplant whiteness in the black community as a variable that defines class identity. Its value now is primarily symbolic.

Within the black community all the foregoing determinants of social class function in social differentiation. It is the interplay among them that characterizes and distinguishes the system; however, primary variables are interrelated and often affect secondary outcomes. For example, the interplay of education and occupation has had a profound consequence on the amount of legitimate income received per year by black Americans, which, in turn, decidedly affects ability to attain status symbols and conspicuous life styles. *The crystallization and interaction of these variables in terms of role-sets and status rewards resulted in the elaboration of a class structure that is nonetheless definitive though imperfectly formed. However, the presence of such a system exemplifies the diversity within the community and destroys the myth of the black population as a monolithic homogeneous unit.*

SOCIAL STRATIFICATION WITHIN THE BLACK COMMUNITY TODAY

Two stratification subsystems prevail in the black community today: One is a socially approved class, whereas the other has its roots in illegitimate structures such as the underworld of crime and vice. Our attention is focused primarily upon the first, although, paradigmatically, this subterranean underworld social structure can be superimposed onto the legitimate class structure in much the same way as the overall black stratification system can be superimposed onto the larger system within the American society. Figure 4.1 illustrates this structure.

The legitimate social structure consists of three broad commonly accepted classes or strata: upper, middle, and lower. As indicated in Figure 4.1, each of the three broad social classes is further subdivided into two or more subclasses. The type of structure depicted in the illustration demonstrates the immense variation in status and behavior characteristic of the black community. Some of the more extensive studies of the class structure within the black community were the earlier works of Frazier[16], Cayton and Drake[17], and Gunnar Myrdal[18]. More recent analysis of various dimensions of class structure within the black community have been provided by Billingsley[19], McAdoo[20], Landry[21], Sampson[22], and Stack[23]. A systematic analysis of these studies would reveal changing determinants of class position, described previously, from one generation to another.

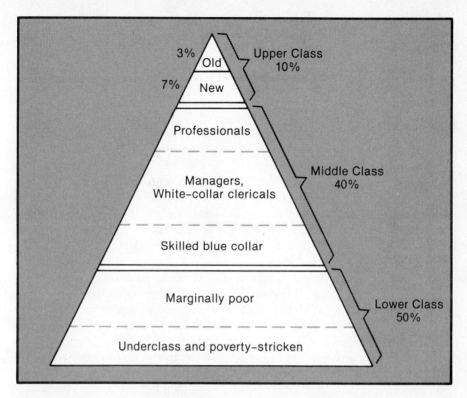

Figure 4.1 *THE SOCIAL STRUCTURE OF THE BLACK COMMUNITY.* Solid lines denote relatively stable divisions between classes whereas broken lines indicate that demarcations between substrata are often blurred.

The descriptions that follow depend heavily on insights gleaned from their contributions to this area of social life among black people. As stated earlier, because of the emphasis placed on prestige associated with occupations and income diversity based upon types of jobs held, there is considerable overlap in some elements of social behavior and life styles between the various strata.

The Upper Class

Regardless of the criteria used to assign social class position, the black upper classes are significantly smaller in size than all other social classes in the black community. In fact, many persons write as if no true black upper class has ever existed. Rather, these persons are lumped together as one broad but highly diversified "black middle class."[24] This assessment departs from that view and holds that the upper tier of what some may label a middle class actually contains the principal attributes of a diversified upper class. It is further posited here that, irrespective of some degree of convergence apparent among blacks of all social classes, especially in their beliefs about the persistence of discrimination against blacks and commonalities in some aspects of their political behavior[25], the upper tier of the black stratification system will probably expand. Whether it does or not depends upon the degree to which blacks are successful in obtaining higher paying, high-status positions, and high levels of educational attainment even in the face of racism and occupational discrimination. In 1990 the upper classes comprise roughly 10 percent of the black population.

The upper class is subdivided into two hierarchical strata: the old upper class and the newly arrived. The distinctions between the two substrata have created superordinate-subordinate boundaries between them. The old upper class includes persons with an enduring family name, high prestige, and respectable families. Its members are generally characterized by a long-established tradition of education, respectable occupations, dependable income, and unimpeachable reputations. Until the 1940s this group represented an aristocracy of color composed particularly of those individuals whose families were descendants of free men and women who lived during the slavery period. Extremely color conscious, they often went to elaborate lengths to avoid interaction or social encounters with darker-skinned brethren and limited contacts with them. In some parts of Louisiana, for example, they established a separate elementary school system for themselves—apart from the already existing dual school system. Their marginality and existence as a third force in such communities that did not provide them with a high-school system compelled them either to send their high-school and college-age children to out-of-town schools or to schools where they could become *passe pour blanc* or *pasa blanche* ("passed for white") or to discontinue formal education at the grade-school level. Those with a sufficient income chose the pasa blanche alternative, thereby losing a black identity and intermixing with the white population.

The color aristocrats formed a tenuously closed system strengthened by family and group restrictions against exogenous marriages to persons easily identified as black. This is still characteristic of many of these old families, who cling to memories of their glorious past when they were respected for their white ancestry. In time, however, this group was subjected to ridicule by less fortunate blacks and to abusive epithets such as "high yaller," "half-white bastards," and so on. Undeniably, this group received the benefits of special advantages because of the privileges associated with their color caste. A self-fulfilling prophecy prevailed since those who were light-skinned received higher education, and the highly educated were in turn likely to be light-skinned and receive the better paying jobs. This aristocracy of color was undermined, however, by factors mentioned earlier, and in time education, occupation, and income preempted the relative importance of color as the major attribute for upper-class identification. Although this view has been discredited, on a purely subjective level, the importance of the color variable is highly significant even among some young black persons. For instance, the author interviewed a young, black woman who had convinced herself that her light skin and Harvard degree automatically conferred "upper-class status" on her even though she was employed essentially in a middle-level managerial position.

The old upper class, comprising roughly 3 percent of the total number of black families, consists of persons in the following occupational groups: established physicians, surgeons, dentists, attorneys, judges, ambassadors and high-ranking government officials, wealthy bankers and insurance executives, college presidents, and ministers of the larger, well-known churches. These are likely to be people whose families were able to provide them with what Billingsley calls "screens of opportunity"[26] when they were young that consisted of financial and emotional support, a legacy of achievement, and high motivation for success. As adults they, too, are able to support their families on a high plane.

Placing considerable value on marital stability, the old upper class tends to avoid divorces and separations, and adheres to a strongly paternalistic family structure. They are often puritanical in public yet foster a double standard for men, since men are supposed to enjoy certain prerogatives not granted to women. They encourage excellence in manners and social intercourse and send their children to the better schools, often to private elementary and secondary schools as well as to private colleges and universities. Whereas their parents took pride in sending them to prestigious black colleges in the past (e.g., Howard, Fisk, Morehouse, Spelman, Talladega, Bennett, and Xavier), the sons and daughters of the old aristocracy now place a higher premium on having graduates of Harvard, Radcliffe, Princeton, Yale, Smith, Vassar, and Bryn Mawr. A few, motivated by loyalty and a commitment to blackness and enhancing the opportunities for their children to find suitable marital partners from old families of the black professional class, still send their sons and daughters to prestigious black colleges and universities.

There is an extensive, nationwide network of social relationships among old upper-class families. The degree of familiarity among prominent black families may reinforce the stereotype among many white people that all educated blacks know each other. Although the stereotype is false, there is much truth in the small world syndrome with respect to prominent black families. Like the white elite, the black elite do attempt to maintain social intimacy with each other and assure that their children interact with each other. Although less so in the 1990s than in the recent past, one may still read about their jet-set activities as well as those who try to emulate them in the society section of the 194 weekly black newspapers, such as the *Louisiana Weekly,* or one of the few black newspapers with national editions (the *Pittsburgh Courier* and the *Afro-American*), or in one of the three daily black newspapers (the *Atlanta Daily World,* the *Chicago Defender,* and the *Daily Challenge* in Brooklyn). Social interaction among the members of the old upper-class families is facilitated by quick modes of transportation and comfortable financial situations. Thus it is not uncharacteristic for members of this group to travel great distances to attend a social function hosted by their counterparts in another city. Their children will travel from Atlanta to Charleston to Los Angeles or from San Francisco to New Orleans and Washington, D.C., to participate in the weddings of their friends, who will honeymoon, not in a black-owned motor lodge in Houston, but, probably, in an exclusive hotel in Honolulu, Acapulco, Cancun, Paris, Rome, or Rio. Like their white counterparts, announcements of these activities are discreetly placed in leading black publications, such as *Ebony* and *Jet,* and, occasionally, in the local white daily—but rarely do they ever make *The New York Times.*

The members of the old upper class are conspicuous consumers but stress good taste. Clothing is likely to be expensive, often specially designed and stylishly conservative; automobiles are selected for durability and are less ostentatious than those purchased by the new upper class; and residences are usually unpretentious structures set on sizeable lots. Whether in the suburbs or in segregated areas of the city, their residences are likely to be located in the "more respectable" neighborhoods. Richly furnished, spacious rooms characterize these homes.

Their leisure-time activities are no longer centered on the playing of poker, as Frazier claimed,[27] if indeed that ever was their focal concern, but are highly diversified. There is, however, a network of secret social clubs and bridge clubs that reveals who is admitted to class membership from time to time. They patronize the arts, enjoy the theatre, opera, and the local symphony. The musicians whose works they enjoy range from Bizet, Mozart, Rachmaninoff, Chopin, Leontyne Price, Marion Anderson, to Duke Ellington. Entertainment is often done in the home, usually with members of cliques or to promote professional activities. Occasionally, members of the old upper-class sponsor events or fund-raising activities for charitable purposes, and these benefits may take place either in their homes or in some reputable public place. In the Washington, D.C. area, many old upper-class families, as well as the new upper class and professional middle class, take considerable pride in participating in the diplomatic cocktail circuit. The African embassies are especially open and hospitable to black Americans—reflecting mutual efforts to establish linkages and psychological identities with other black people. The diplomatic staffs of the nonblack embassies, on the other hand, do not differ appreciably from the upper echelons of the State Department and the federal government—in general, they often make an effort to assure only token integration at their social functions. For some blacks it is considered a privilege to be invited to socialize with functionaries of foreign nonblack governments and with high-level white government officials. These associations provide one mechanism for ensuring high social status.

In addition to these leisure-time activities, the old upper class travels a great deal, taking two or three vacation trips per year; a special colony of "black brahmins" goes to Cape Cod as do the upper-class blacks of the underworld. Many play golf and tennis and swim in their own pools, and ski. Others enjoy the spectator sports of football and basketball, and, if it is a major social event, several will "turn out" for a prize fight. Although fraternities and sororities have diminished in social significance for them, the members of this class do join a variety of social clubs and voluntary associations or support major civil rights organizations such as the Links, the NAACP, the National Urban League, and similar predominantly black groups. They do not easily join white organizations because white organizations still engage in exclusionary practices that deny them equal access. Since there is considerable latent hostility in this class against white people, it is not likely that they would be eager to join them in social activities even if the opportunities were available. Cotillions in New York, New Orleans, and the San Francisco Bay area, for example, are still popular as a means of introducing their young to society, although, increasingly, the old upper-class families are sponsoring private coming-out parties for their daughters and abandoning the more public functions to the *nouveau riche* and social climbers.

The church has always played a significant role in the lives of black people; and the upper class is no exception. The members of this class are quite religious and committed to church membership. Not only do they tend to be members of Episcopalian, Congregational, and Presbyterian churches, but they also provide substantive financial support for them and attend services regularly. In many parts of the United States the old upper-class family members play prominent roles in the activities of these churches, serving on boards of deacons, as members of financial committees, and sponsors of charitable activities endorsed by the church. Affiliation with these churches is further evidence of this class' high status and of their differences from folk blacks. They enjoy the relatively quiet and unemotional services of the Congregationalists, Presbyterians, and Episcopalians. The Catholic church has increasingly attracted membership from the black upper classes. Undoubtedly some of the 300 black priests have upper-class origins. It was and continues to be the dominant church of the old aristocracy of color, particularly in Creole New Orleans, the southern portions of Louisiana, and the easternmost portions of Texas.

As a rule, the old upper class tends to be conservative on the issue of race relations, preferring not to be active participants in civil rights activities. They are also disposed toward biracial politics and bilateral agreements. They would rather provide financial support and ideas but avoid direct involvement. They are neither prone to the extremes of political radicalism nor disposed toward modern-day Uncle Tomism. However, their lack of involvement may reflect their desire to protect their privileged positions and their vested interest in maintaining the status quo.

With incomes ranging generally from $50,000 to more than $1 million per year, the members of this class are in a position to support the style of life just described. Since so many are self-employed and are not dependent upon a fixed salary, they are in a better position to sustain this life style for a much longer period of time than are the new upper-class blacks. Thus there is a far greater degree of permanence attached to their social position.

The New Upper Class

Although the members of this class may have higher incomes, which generally range from $40,000 to more than $1 million per year (made by mostly entertainers, a few athletes, and "shadies"), they by no means parallel the old upper-class black family structure. Their income is transitory; that is, it is not necessarily based upon secure occupations and high educational attainment. They are, therefore, only able to sustain an upper-class life style for a relatively short period of time, depending upon the care with which their financial holdings are invested or upon the permanence of their occupations. The exception is found in those whose new class position is grounded on substantive educational achievements that have enabled them to move upward in the occupational structure and earn substantial incomes either on the job, through investments, or through personal attributes.

This class provides evidence of the dynamic characteristics of the class structure within the black community. And in many ways, as in the case of the old upper class, the behavior of its members mirrors that of their counterparts in the white social class structure. The members are relatively new to prominence, fame, and money. Some have attained their positions through achievement rather than ascription, and some have managed to parlay special talents into financial success that enables them to purchase or literally buy upper-class status. Some, however, especially in the small towns of the South and in nonsouthern communities where the black population is scarce, may also have the advantages of a notable family name and respectability. But most members of this class are reminiscent of the Horatio Alger rags-to-riches myth.

New upper-class members are likely to be relatively new to high political office and/or government office. They are self-made men and women who through hard work and ability to capitalize on opportunities have made it almost to the pinnacle of the black social structure, especially through benefits generated by the civil rights movement. Included in the new upper class are people such as Mayor Thomas Bradley of Los Angeles; a former mayor of Cleveland, Carl B. Stokes, and his brother, Congressman Louis Stokes; Mayor Richard Hatcher of Gary, Indiana; and William Goode of Philadelphia. As a group, their meteoric rise can be attributed to educational achievement, present and past occupations, and charisma. Besides being comprised of politicians, congressmen, and state and local officials, this class also includes a large array of entertainers, actors and actresses, and athletes. This money is new, their incomes and social positions are transitory, and they are less likely to have either middle- or upper-class origins. Although these professions enjoy a certain amount of

prestige within some elements of the black community, the status conferred upon incumbents of such professions is highly selective. In this case
status depends upon what services are performed for the welfare of less
fortunate blacks, the leadership roles members of this class actually carry
out, the extent of their commitment to civil rights activities, and whether
or not their behavior conforms to idealized expectations of propriety and
conventional norms. Thus it cannot be assumed that simply because a
black actor earns in excess of a million dollars per year, or because an
athlete is highly touted or a singer earns more money and is more widely
known than a Detroit judge or a black college president, that the latter
people are less important, less esteemed, or have lower prestige than any
of the former. This is not the case in the black social world. Yet this
erroneous assumption is often made by persons who do not understand the
black social structure. In fact, the majority of the old upper-class black
families and many of the established middle-class black families would not
welcome into their families either entertainers, athletes, or actors who are
not of similar class origins regardless of the amount of money these glamorous people make.

Billingsley cites evidence that shows that entertainers and athletes,
male and female, are less likely to have old upper-class origins than black
professionals. He observed that 80 percent of the professional blacks have
family origins in either the middle or upper classes. He also concludes,
from his analysis of data drawn from *Current Biographies,* that 59 percent
of the male and 50 percent of the female entertainers had old upper-class
origins, whereas only one-eighth of the male athletes were originally from
this class.[28] By contrast, Hill's research, which focused largely on economic
differentials, showed that 80 percent of middle-class black men came from
lower-status origins, and only 18 percent had "middle-class" origins.[29]
Inasmuch as unprecedented numbers of blacks have entered such professional sports as basketball, football, and baseball plus the fact that so many
of those now playing entered these sports under the so-called "hardship
rule," the percentage of athletes with old upper-class or new upper-class
origins is probably much lower than was the case when Billingsley made
his analysis.

A high percentage of entertainers, male or female, with upper-class
origins is also highly unlikely now than was the case earlier. Despite
improvements in their economic status, even in 1990, blacks are less likely
to become professional skiers or hockey or tennis players. These sports
require a great deal of money for training and travel. That is probably why
only a few blacks, such as Arthur Ashe, Althea Gibson, Zena Garrison,
Laura McNeil, and Chip Cooper, have risen to national prominence in
tennis. This is not the case for other spectator sports. Invariably, championship teams in baseball, football, or basketball will be composed of
"black stars." Basketball has its Earvin "Magic" Johnson, Isaiah Thomas,
Michael "Air" Jordan and such legends as Kareem Abdul Jabbar, Julius
"Dr. J" Erving, Bill Russell, and Wilt Chamberlain. Baseball has its stars,

past and present, such as Willie Mays, Hank Aaron (the all-time home-run king), Reggie Jackson, Bob Gibson, David Winfield, Tony Gwynne, and many, many more. In 1989, professional football could claim four blacks as starting quarterbacks: Warren Moon, Doug Williams, Randall Cunningham, and Rodney Peete. Professional football also has its Jerry Rice, Hershel Walker, and Earl "Too Tall" Jones. All these individuals, and countless others like them, used professional sports as a means of marketing their special talents to facilitate a rise in the social class structure—especially in terms of life styles.

Similar breakthroughs, commensurate with the breakdown of racial and discriminatory barriers, have occurred in the entertainment world. The success of recording artists, a few television performers, and movie people illustrate the possibilities of emulating the life styles of persons in upper and middle classes regardless of class origins. Hence they can purchase a house in Malibu or an apartment on Central Park or buy Rolls Royces and Mercedes. The insecurity of this group in social behavior often reflects the precariousness of their position. All too many experience the pains of downward mobility after their professional career has ended. However, some black athletes and entertainers reportedly have taken measures designed to safeguard and protect their social class status in the future, and some have already become well recognized for their business acumen. For instance, Willie Davis, a former football player with the Green Bay Packers, is a millionaire owner of several businesses, franchises, and radio stations in Los Angeles. Smokey Robinson is vice-president of the highly successful recording and production company, MoTown; Bill Cosby, a multimillionare extremely popular television star who almost singlehandedly catapulted NBC into the number one position for night-time television, is a businessman who holds a doctorate in Education from the University of Massachusetts/Amherst. David Winfield, Franco Harris, Brady Keys, and several other athletes are owners of franchises of fast-food chains. "Magic" Johnson co-owns with publisher Earl Graves a Pepsi Cola Bottling Company in Washington, D. C. Julius Erving, another basketball star, co-owns with Bruce Llewellyn a Coca Cola Bottling Company in Philadelphia. Walter Payton, former football star of the Chicago Bears, is the co-owner of at least 30 restaurants and nightclubs. He is also owner of the food and beverage contract for the Houston Intercontinental Airport. Mel Farr, another former football player, owns three auto dealerships. Several additional black musicians, professional athletes, and entertainers also own auto dealerships, restaurants, recording companies, other business enterprises, and have made what appears to be sound investments as a means of safeguarding their present social and economic status for the future. But their status is a function of income rather than occupational attainment.

The new upper class also includes a number of newly arrived physicians, lawyers, college professors, some business executives, and members of managerial groups. The likelihood of class permanence and/or move-

ment to the top is substantially greater for this group than it is for entertainers, actors, and athletes. Many, in fact, are blessed with a middle-class
origin, solid family names, and have originated from intact nuclear families. Several possess impeccable educational credentials and have impressive security and confidence in the presence of the old upper-class families. Indeed, according to much of the criteria, many of them are often
indistinguishable from the old upper class.

The members of this class emulate the old upper class in life style as
closely as possible. This effort to be like people at the top often results in
exaggerated behavior. They are frequently among the most conspicuous
consumers, wearing dazzling clothing, displaying a preference for expensive cars and for jewelry and furs. Their houses are usually lavishly furnished and located in the more expensive suburbs, wherever they have
been able to break through the barriers of housing discrimination. Not
infrequently, they will use the help of white friends to purchase houses for
themselves in the more "exclusive" neighborhoods, especially when confronted with racial bigotry among real-estate personnel. Often, they are
forced to pay prices far in excess of what a white person would pay for the
same house. Occasionally, they are also victimized by excessive fees
charged by black real-estate brokers who, using the rights of multiple
listings and membership in real-estate associations, exploit the desire for
owning a house in the "right" neighborhood. They also take inordinate
pride in entertaining friends as well as friends of friends, taking special
efforts to assure that announcements of these functions will be accompanied by excellent press coverage. Their entertainment practices are intended to be overt manifestations of success and high status; their purpose
is to heighten social recognition and demonstrate their rights to belong to
the upper class.

Members of the new upper class differ from those of the old upper
class in the excessiveness of their social activity and with regard to the
public nature of much of their behavior. They seem to be more tolerant
of divorce and more indulgent in the treatment of their children. Although they tend to join the same churches as the old upper-class families
or may also hold membership in the better-known Methodist and Baptist
churches, their commitment to organized religion may be questioned.
They are less likely to engage in the more formalized leisure-time activities observed in the old families, and less likely to have similar tastes in
reading materials.

The Middle Class

The diversity in the social class structure of the black community is also
reflected in the trichotomy of the black middle class: upper middle-class
professionals, middle-class white-collar and clerical workers, and skilled
blue-collar workers. These groups share in common high achievement
motivation, a tradition of family stability, high religiosity, high regard for

property ownership, a sustained history of political participation and activism, social striving, and consumption of durable goods. The subclasses differ in occupations, income, interracial attitudes, religious practices, educational attainment, and some aspects of political behavior. Because of these differences, and contrary to previous studies that treated this group as a more homogeneous class, the three substrata should be treated separately.

One of the weaknesses in Frazier's highly regarded and much acclaimed study, *Black Bourgeoisie,* is that it suffers from the pitfall common to most sociological studies at the time: the failure to make refinements in interpretations of social differentiation among black people. Thus he categorized all persons who are here identified as members of the old and new upper classes and the trichotomized middle classes as belonging to one relatively large bourgeoisie. Although that description may have been appropriate at one time (and this is a generous assumption), the exigencies of time and the salient changes in the socioeconomic conditions of blacks necessitate descriptions based upon more definitive demarcations. The black middle class is smaller than the lower classes but substantially larger than the black upper classes. Even with these observations in mind, it takes little more than common sense to recognize that the lines between each stratum within the middle classes, as well as those between the middle and upper classes, are often undefined. Wilensky and Lebeauz,[30] McAdoo,[31] Levitan,[32] and Sampson[33] asserted that the lines between those employed in occupations identified as the upper working class and the lower middle class are blurred. They were speaking about foremen, craftsmen, and high-paid operatives as opposed to clerks, salesmen, small entrepreneurs, and managers characteristic of the lower middle class. And they were referring largely to the overall American class structure rather than specifically to the black social class structure. Basically, though, the lines that separate the classes are not always distinct but are sufficiently formed to allow for certain types of classifications for analytical purposes.

Middle-Class Black Professionals

The upper levels of the black middle class consist of those black professionals who have not yet qualified for admission to the new upper class. On a strictly subjective dimension, many of these persons *feel* that they enjoy a higher social status than many members of the noveau rich in the newer black upper class. For that reason the income variable alone is an inadequate measure of class standing or social status within the black community. They are the proprietors, managers and supervisors, accountants, established teachers and lawyers who have not quite made it into the upper levels, as well as ministers of middle-range congregations. Their status, like that of many of those in the upper-class levels, is considerably higher than it would be in the white community simply because blacks confer higher social rewards on such achievements than the white social structure does. Their occupations generally require a college education, which, coupled with family income, accords them a relatively high rank in the black social structure.[34] Their income range from $25,000 to $50,000 per annum.

As shown in Table 2.1, the paucity of blacks in the higher occupational levels is shockingly clear. Hence it provides little comfort to know that blacks have made stunning economic progress and occupational mobility over the past 35 years when, despite the gains made during the civil rights and black power movements, blacks remain so critically underrepresented in the professions. If only 6.6 percent of the professional workers, 2.1 percent of the nation's engineers, 2.0 percent of the physicians, 2.3 percent of the dentists, and 9.3 percent of the clerical and kindred workers are black in the 1990s, then deprivations and inequities in the distribution of occupations and attendant incomes are obvious and, consequently, provide ample ammunition to dismantle arguments against affirmative action programs and compensatory hiring.

Upper middle-class professional families in the black community are likely to be relatively stable and more equalitarian than patriarchal. Infidelity and illegitimacy are not condoned. The divorce rate is still relatively low even though it has increased since 1970. The average number of children is two. Males in this group prefer marriage partners of the same shade of color as themselves or somewhat lighter in complexion; hence showing once again the persistence of the aristocracy of color syndrome.

Religion for this group is more staid and serene when compared to observances in classes below it in the hierarchy. Their religious affiliations are with the Catholic, Methodist, Baptist, Episcopalian, and Presbyterian churches. As they moved up the social ladder, they in all probability changed their religious affiliations to those with higher prestige. The character of the church may also change as more members become middle class. In some instances, membership may be held in two churches as a means of accommodating both professional interests and social needs.[35] People in this group are social strivers who also emulate, as far as financial stability will permit, the life style of the members of the upper classes. This pattern of emulation extends to purchasing consumable goods and services, clothing, housing, and other evidence of the attainment of high social status. A high premium is placed on friendship cliques and on membership in service, Greek-letter organizations, and voluntary associations. They also enjoy occasional theatre, both jazz and classical concerts, public lectures, and a relatively broad range of reading materials.

If they have become suburbanized, like many others in the middle and upper classes, they often pay a heavy price in alienation, social isolation, and loneliness in their new communities. While they may be quick to invite white neighbors into their homes, they may find that it is quite rare for white suburbanites to reciprocate either by inviting blacks into their homes or to participate in any social and recreational activities with them. Research by Blackwell and Hart showed that either by choice or the peculiarities of their circumstances, many blacks in these classes maintain social bonds and contacts with blacks in the central city or other suburbs.[37] In many instances, suburban middle- and upper-class blacks engage in a type of "avoidance behavior" with other blacks in suburbia, as if they *should not* be on friendly relationships with them.[38]

Politically, they tend to affiliate with the Democratic party or classify themselves as Independents. Although regional variations in this tendency may surface, by and large, blacks are not dissimilar from other ethnic groups in supporting one of their own people regardless of party affiliations. Hence they can be counted on to vote. Having provided the major leadership for the civil rights movement, they can be characterized as political activists, picketing and demonstrating when needed. Membership in traditional organizations such as the NAACP, the National Urban League, and CORE has now extended to the Southern Christian Leadership Conference and to People United to Serve Humanity (PUSH). But their children are likely to be enthralled with the militancy of black student-union and Afro-American societies.

White-Collar Clericals

White-collar and clerical workers form the middle stratum of the black middle class. They can be grouped, occasionally, into clerical and kindred workers, sales workers, small entrepreneurs, and some entertainers who have yet to become established and recognized. Blacks compose 3.8 percent of all sales workers and 9.3 percent of all clerical and kindred workers in the United States. Their salaries range from $15,000 to $25,000. Inasmuch as their life style and general behavior are not distinct from that of the professional middle-class group, we shall not dwell on this group.

Skilled Blue-Collar Workers

Blue-collar blacks are the skilled, stably employed craftsmen, foremen, mechanics, repairmen, metal craftsmen, construction craftsmen, and operatives. Their personal income range is from $12,000 to $25,000 per year. Although their families are likely to be upwardly mobile, family background in the traditional sense and education are not the crucial variables for social advancement. This is not to imply that these people do not place a high premium on the education of their children. On the contrary, though they are less likely to be college graduates or to have attended college, they are willing to sacrifice themselves for the educational advancement of their children.

Blue-collar workers commonly stress family stability, which has held the marital dissolution rate to a relatively modest level; thus, these families are still nucleated and intact. They tend on the average to have no more than two children per family and to be identical to the white-collar professionals in their color preferences among marriage partners.[39] They are more akin to the working poor and other lower classes than to the upper classes in their church preferences and religious activities. They belong to Baptist and some Methodist institutions that encourage emotional fulfillment and individual expression through active participation in religious services. Although almost half the members in this group are undoubtedly lifelong Baptists, if the men marry higher-status women, they may change to the religion of their wives. This tendency accounts for the increasing presence of Methodists, Catholics, and Congregationalists among this group.

The members of this stratum consume as much as money can buy and, like so many white Americans similarly classified, rely upon good credit ratings as a means of purchasing consumable goods. However, they are not able to save very much money, not only because of their consumption patterns but also because so much of their income is spent on meeting instrumental family needs: housing, food, clothing, and transportation. Color televisions, house parties, card playing, dances, night clubbing, bowling, and professional spectator sports are major forms of recreation. Whites in the same classification generally earn more money than blue-collar blacks, but it is likely that they spend proportionately less on recreation and less on instrumental needs and are, therefore, likely to save more for the future.

Politically, this group is likely to be Democratic and have voted in the most recent national, local, and statewide elections. They do not tend to be as politically active in civil rights movements as the classes above them, and their support is comparatively uncertain and sporadic. Yet, blue-collar workers and blacks in the classes below them rage with bottled-up hostility against whites, which may account for their increasing attraction to separatist groups in the black liberation movement (see Chapter 13).

The middle classes, taken as a whole, are more disposed toward bilateral measures (i.e., many forms) of discipline for their children than are those in lower social strata. Thus they are less punitive and more inclined to employ persuasive approaches to elicit obedience and conformity than to rely upon coercion and physical punishment. Yet they do demand respect for parental authority.

The Lower Social Strata

The lower classes constitute about 50 percent of the entire population. In 1989, about 45 percent of the black population was "economically poor" even though approximately one-third of all black families were officially below the poverty line. The Bureau of Labor Statistics (BLS) uses economic measures to differentiate families in terms of family budget standards which take into consideration diversity in standards of living. Hence, families at the lower budget level are classified as poor people; those at the lowest rung of this level are the actual underclass.[40] Status in this level, as well as at the lower rung of the middle-class group, is complicated by the job insecurity of wage-earners. A loss of income of any magnitude may force these families into a downward spiral resulting in downward mobility and further deprivation of their life chances. Nevertheless, we are reminded that poverty level is not only a matter of receiving an annual income no more than $12,091 (the 1989 poverty level) but encompasses how people feel about themselves and their future levels of upward mobility.

The range of occupations within this group includes garbage collectors, laborers, small-scale farmers, service workers, and private household workers. Blacks constitute 53 percent of all American private household workers, 21.8 percent of the janitors and cleaners, and 17.3 percent of nonconstruction laborers. Thus, black Americans continue to be over-represented in the lower-paying, lower-prestige, and lower-tier occupations in a dual labor market system.

The majority are not receiving any form of public assistance; they are hard-working ordinary citizens. They are Ralph Ellison's invisible men in the sense that others refuse to see them and recognize them for their values and their value to the total American community. They are the group most often studied by social scientists, misunderstood, and used as the basis for arrogant generalizations about the whole black community. The overwhelming majority of the black lower classes are people of integrity who basically and fundamentally want to survive in what they know to be an extremely difficult and hostile society. They have no great illusions about themselves or their personal accomplishments other than that they have survived, but they do have aspirations for their children. They, too, dream great dreams and even have high hopes of "making it" in the white man's world.

The Marginally Poor   The marginally poor are at the top of the hierarchy in this strata. They are the semiskilled, steadily employed industrial workers. They comprise the largest portion of America's black truck drivers, foremen, mechanics, and lower level transport-equipment operators. The lower end of this group comprises the unskilled laboring occupations: farm laborers, migrant workers, service workers, porters, janitors, and domestic household workers who can barely maintain even a poverty-level income. These families struggle to keep their households together. Both spouses work, whenever employment is available, to meet the instrumental needs of the family. It seems for them that the harder they try and the more they work the more difficult it is for them to stay afloat. They are among those who often feel the brutal impact of economic downturns, inflation, and high unemployment. Hence there is a tremendous amount of alienation, disillusionment, and despair in this group, especially among those who see so little progress and even fewer possibilities of breaking out of the throes of economic and social deprivation. They want their children to succeed and still rest their hopes on the possibility that their children will attain an educational level that will enable them to rise above poverty.

Although they are among the economic powerless, they have enormous political power were their numbers translated into votes.

It is increasingly difficult for the poor to maintain intact families. They are experiencing higher levels of female-headed households but a significant proportion of all the families in this stratum are likely to include subfamilies and/or an extended family network. When in economic straits, they look to other family members for assistance. The family is the most important element in the structure of social relationships. The performance of affective family functions depends heavily upon kinship interactions.

Friendship cliques are likely to be drawn from a circle of church members, the social community clubs to which they may belong, the workplace, neighborhood taverns and pool halls. They are members of the Baptist and Holiness churches, lodges, the Elks, Masons, Ladies of the Sharon Star, and the Democratic Party. Women in this group are active participants in and loyal supporters of the church, often attending church activities as many as five times per week. They are choir members, ushers, and fund raisers through raffles, fish frys, suppers, and potluck dinners. Their desire for status and recognition is often manifested in the type of automobile they may be able to purchase, how frequently cars are bought, and in their personal appearance at public functions. Within their stratum and friendship cliques, status may be granted by the achievements of those members of their family, a brother, sister, son or daughter, who has "made it" into the middle classes. They are being drawn with increasing regularity into the ranks of political activists, and various subgroups of black nationalists.

The Black Underclass   The black underclass is the subject of increasing concern among the American public. This attention can be attributed in the main to characteristics associated with the underclass that will be described below. This group is at the very bottom of the social structure—the group that Marx once described as the lumpen proletariats of society. Within the black community, the black underclass constitutes a wasteland of manpower and potential resources as depicted in Kenneth Clark's *Black Ghetto* and Elliot Liebow's *Tally's Corner.* They rank lowest in income, occupational skills, employment, education, family stability, and the acquisition of status symbols through legitimate means. They are an integral component of Michael Harrington's *Other America;* the downtrodden described by Andrew Billingsley in *Black Families in White America,* and by Douglas Glasgow in *The Black Underclass.* But in 1990, the public's concern about the black underclass seems more motivated by the *fear* of this group than by finding realistic solutions to the problems faced by its members.

Who are they? Members of the black underclass earn less than $5,000 per year, often considerably less and sometimes substantially more, depending upon their involvement in an underground economy or illicit means of financial support. The family head characteristically has a sixth-grade education or less. Young people in this group comprise a higher proportion of school drop-outs than any other segment of the population. The underclass are the laborers in the lumpen proletariat; they work at odd jobs, doing sporadic day work or serving as waitresses in low-paying cafes and bars. Migrant farm workers are also found here. The underclass constitutes the bulk of the welfare recipients within the black population, including many teenage mothers whose children are abandoned by their fathers; teen fathers who cannot find employment; many discouraged workers; and many infirmed elderly. Suffering from the lowest life chances and minimal health care, they are inevitably condemned to delapidated housing in the urban slums and, quite frequently, to the concrete public-housing ghettos of the deteriorating inner cities of America. Abject resignation to insufferable conditions permeate lives compounded by a persistently nagging sense of despair, hopelessness, and frustration. Confronted with the stark reality that they are not likely to escape the ghetto and a rejection of traditional escape routes that have lifted legions of their predecessors from a life of poverty, they show their machismo and their femininity through sexual expression. Many young men from the under-class, while knowledgeable about the use of condoms, eschew birth control measures because they either want to be reassured that they are "not shooting blanks," or because they dislike them or because they cannot afford to purchase them. Many young women in this group are victims of ignorance about birth control devices as well as misinformation about the high probability of becoming impregnated after their first sexual encounter. Most single parent female-headed families are in this class. However, all types of family patterns are observable here just as they are found in all strata of the entire American society: nuclear, extended, attenuated, segmental, female-headed, male-headed, and intact families.

Members of the underclass are folk blacks described a half century ago by Charles S. Johnson. They are less likely to be assimilated into mainstream American life, not because they do not want to be assimilated but because they are so far removed from it. (It is their life style that many, including some white radical intellectuals, romanticize as the authentically black experience in American life. It is that life style that so much of white America seems to have internalized as "the way all blacks live" which permits them to deny the existence of a viable middle- and upper-class community among the black population or think of them as an imitation of white America.) In recent years, this life style has been even more so than ever before characterized as the life of a deviant population, however, or as a unique culture. This group's customs, beliefs, and values center on a fundamentalist religious perspective; "just making it" in the white man's world; sexual freedom, toleration of illegitimacy; trying to have a good time, and communication through "the blues." All these features, it may be argued, express a basic and compelling effort to adapt to a world that has excluded them or which they are not prepared to enter. The focal points of the public concern in the 1990s are on welfare dependency, extensive drug abuse, gang violence associated with drugs, explosive criminal and delinquent activity—all of which raised community fear to higher levels when revealed through sensationalized media accounts of underclass violence.[41] People in the underclass are more vulnerable to delinquency and criminality than they are to participate in it. They are more likely to be victimized by the underworld and its aggressive violence than to be perpetrators of that activity. Nevertheless, these conditions, whenever observed or revealed, serve to reinforce the stereotype of "the bad nigger," the shiftless black male who is slightly more than a keg of dynamite waiting to explode at the most minute provocation.

For many people in the underclass, religion is an important part of their lives. It is an escape from the insurmountable burdens of daily existence. Therefore, the shouting, dancing, and handclapping characteristic of storefront churches, various religious sects, and of the fundamentalist groups provide opportunities for a kind of catharsis—a ventilation of feelings, emotions, and imaginative communication with others who share so much in common. The church also offers them social contacts, recreation, and an opportunity for leadership positions as ministers, deacons, ushers, and other functionaries.

The underclass tends to use unilateral techniques in disciplining its children relying upon the heavy hand of authority and punishment to coerce obedience and conformity. Frequently, there is no control and no consistent authority structure to build discipline and respect for either authority or self. There is a further problem of child abuse, neglect, and abandonment that is found among many families in this subclass, especially, seemingly, among parents addicted to crack, heroin, and cocaine as well as among some unwed mothers whose boyfriends eschew responsibilities of adequate child care and parenting.

STRATIFICATION AMONG THE SUBTERRANEANS

There is a subterranean class structure that exists in the black community about which little is known or has been written. This world of the *shadies*, a term used by Cayton and Drake[42] and Billingsley,[43] has, of course, its prototype in the white population, as Figure 4.2 shows, but our attention is directed to the black group. Impressionistic evidence suggests that this subterranean class structure can also be divided into three broad strata that parallel the legitimate system. Each system has social characteristics and mobility patterns similar to those found in the legitimate stratification system of America's blacks.

This extralegal group theoretically operates underground and is, of course, external to the legal structure. In the large cities of the United

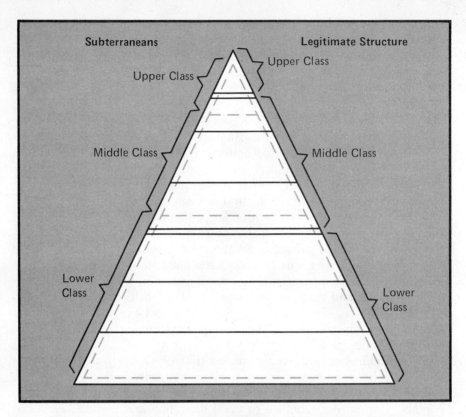

Figure 4.2 *The Black Subterranean Class Structure: The World of Shadies and the Underworld* (superimposed onto the legitimate black social structure). Broken lines denote subterranean class structure and blurred divisions between classes. Note that the upper and lower strata among subterraneans are somewhat larger than the legitimate upper and lower strata, but the middle-level subterraneans are fewer in number than middle levels in the legitimate black social structure.

States it has a certain amount of control over organized vice, prostitution, gambling, narcotic trafficking, and various types of businesses that receive police protection. This control is only partial, since it is commonly held in the working class and lumpen proletariat black ghettoes that the man— white people—actually controls organized crime in the black communities. The pimps, the pushers, the hustlers, and the vice lords are the fronts for white rulers who live in the suburbs and conduct legitimate businesses in the cities.

The upper class in this group consists of those "big-time" drug traffickers and gamblers, racketeers, numbers kings, and shady businessmen who have made it to the top in terms of income and life style. They resemble the new upper class in their consumption patterns and overall life styles. They attempt to establish close social relationships with the new and old upper classes as well as with the middle classes, but with limited success even at the most superficial level. They are concerned about their status in the community as well as the status of their children. Thus they attempt to conceal the nature of their work or refer only to the legitimate work they are associated with. They may live in the same neighborhoods as upper-class black families, but, if their subterranean activities are known or suspected, they will be excluded from membership in the social circles of the upper and middle classes. Their money and stylish life do not enable them to gain entry into legitimate black society.

The middle class in this group is comprised of the more successful pushers, bookies, pimps, hustlers, call girls, and gamblers. The lower class is comprised of flunkies, runners and look-outs for drug dealers, junkies, and less successful prostitutes. They, too, follow the same life styles as their counterparts in the legitimate black stratification system. But the people in the middle and upper groups are perhaps more visible, for they frequent bars, restaurants, nightclubs, and other places that heighten their visible success. They drive long "hogs," wear expensive clothing and jewelry, and evoke the appearance of having "made it" without working. As noted earlier, they become models for and are the source of considerable envy by lower-class black youths, who learn to regard their way of life as a means of escaping from poverty and living the good life.

MOBILITY PATTERNS

We have already inferred and suggested a number of factors affecting the probability of upward mobility or improvements in status and rank within the black community. In a society that is ethnically stratified, as the American society is, it is extremely difficult for minority groups to experience sustained upward mobility. This is historically and readily apparent for the major portion of the black population. No matter how successful they become as individuals or within the subsystem of stratification of the black population and no matter how successful they are in learning whatever is specified as American culture or in acquiring those characteristics attributed to the more refined and cultured whites, blacks still carry the physical signs of their biological inheritance, which give them a subordinate social status in the larger society. Only exceptional blacks can contradict or transcend that process and are tangentially accepted into the social world of high-status whites. Often this acceptance is a function of reverse status conferring, which blacks of higher occupational status or social prestige can bestow on some whites by their presence at white social functions. Or, in the case of some "superstar" athletes and entertainers, some whites may enjoy a temporary status attainment by demonstrating to others that they have a certain familiarity with black "superstars." This type of shallow social activity, which may mask the real sense of superiority felt by some white persons in such situations, has led such blacks to believe their own self-importance has been heightened—a belief their admirers share.[44]

Mobility also depends upon the acquisition of highly visible status symbols, which act as indicators to others of what the person has already achieved or believes he has achieved; that is, he shows he is economically successful whether or not he comes from an established, highly esteemed family. This display of status symbols and pecuniary gain may become crucially significant as determinants of how a person is treated and where the person is placed by others in the stratification schema. Thus wealth and property may generate prestige. The converse of this principle was illustrated in the case of the subterranean classes. It has also been suggested that, in some instances, high status may be found among those having excellent family backgrounds but limited wealth.

The factors of wealth, property, power, and prestige do behave independently and can exist separately and apart. By the same token, because an individual may rank higher on one of these dimensions, as, for example, higher on property than on prestige, some individuals find themselves in a state of status inconsistency.[45] This pattern influences the nature of their social participation and may lead status-inconsistent persons to feel undervalued in the stratification system. At a subjective level these people tend to rate themselves more highly than their objective position on an SES scale indicates. Thus some blacks feel rejected by a social world in which they subjectively believe they belong.

Even though blacks experienced upward mobility in larger numbers during the 1960s, 1970s, and late 1980s, they remain the most seriously impacted by recessions and a depression in the economy. As stated earlier, in the early 1980s, they accounted for a significant proportion of the layoffs in the civil service, the federal government, and in industry. For many, the rise into the middle and upper classes, as determined by economic conditions, was contingent upon the presence of dual salaries or wages. The loss of either one, for many black families, meant slippage back into a lower socioeconomic stratum and the loss of many of the status symbols of "having made it." Further, as Hill stresses, another sign of downward mobility is the escalating number of middle-class black women who have become single parents either by virtue of illegitimacy, divorce, or widowhood. In this sense, he argues, there is a growing convergence between the social classes in the black community, despite the tendency to rationalize illegitimacy as an "alternative life style" or the "single-parent experience."[46]

Marriage, a chance to use native intelligence, personal attributes, high achievement, and many previously discussed factors all coalesce systematically to make the black society and its stratification system viable, dynamic, and increasingly open.

BLACKNESS AS A VALUE IN STATUS AND MOBILITY

During the decade of the 1960s and perhaps at the apex of the new black revolution, another dimension to mobility and social acceptance emerged. We are speaking here of the concept of blackness, which has no single meaning that can be easily explained. Blackness has several dimensions but its single most important one remains a high level of consciousness of one's own identity. It has also come to mean racial pride and solidarity, and acceptance of the self as it is but with a full understanding that one can parlay personal abilities into high achievement both within the black and white worlds. Earlier on, much more so than in the 1980s, it was expressed in aspects of physical appearance such as the wearing of Afro hair styles, dashikis, and African jewelry. It was also manifested in unique handshakes ("daps," "high fives") attributed to soul brothers and sisters, body English, and the manner in which blacks genuinely greet other black people. For some, it meant a rejection of Standard English, entirely or selectively, depending upon the racial composition of the audience. It was also evident in the rhetoric of black militancy couched in terms that communicated the speaker's intent to "take no guff from either 'white honkies' or black 'Uncle Toms and oreos.' " These efforts sometimes bordered on the brink of absurdity, as, for example, the refusal of some "black blacks" to shake hands with light-skinned blacks whose happenstance of color made them less than "true black." For some, it meant a rejection of those often labeled "plastic blacks" who presumably purchased conspicuous status symbols with credit cards. This determination to articulate one's own blackness and communicate it to the outside world led to what may be called outblacking blacks or what George Napper has aptly called *Blacker Than Thou.* [47] Force or threats of intimidation and bodily harm were used to enforce conformity to newly defined black norms. One of the manifest consequences or payoffs of this orientation toward blackness was increasing access to shared values. This led, in turn, to access to more competitive resources (that is, better-paying jobs, higher incomes, and upward mobility in the stratification system). The more vocal individuals proclaimed their blackness, the more they gained control of certain jobs in the black community, whether trained for them or not, and others became "academic hustlers" in some of the more disreputable Afro-American studies programs. Responsibility was not infrequently abandoned for fear of reprisals from excessively militant blacks. The downfall of a few Afro-American programs, which, in fact, have as much legitimacy as a source of scientific inquiry as Slavic studies, Jewish studies, or American studies, can, in part, be attributed to this phenomenon. It may also be attributed to a shift in focus toward career-oriented curricula.

The concept "blackness" has taken a curious route to social acceptability. It has wide acceptability among all but the traditionalists and die-hards of the aristocracy of color in the United States, who refute both its ideological meaning and its implications regarding biological heredity. This is particularly so, since the word "black" has had such a negative connotation in the English language. For instance, we use terms such as "black lie" to illustrate the worst form of mendacity, "black sheep" to suggest a social misfit, "blackmail" to mean extortion, and "blacklist" to mean the censure of a person for suspected nonconformity. The color black is associated with evil and most of the ethnophaulisms—derogatory terms directed against a group—are associated with the word "black." For many black children a dark color was a badge of inferiority, and, as young adults, until recently, they spent enormous sums of money attempting to erase that badge by the use of bleaching creams and hair processing. Even today, blacks are as conscious of color variation among themselves as whites are about theirs. Instead of differentiating their members on the basis of hair color, blacks differentiate among each other on the basis of varying hues of skin color. Thus one is very light, almost white, quite light, brown, medium, dark brown, dark, or very dark. These differentiations exist because they refer to external characteristics rather than to ideological positions or beliefs. As we will see in subsequent chapters, one can be politically black and a biologically white-skinned black; this is further proof that how a person is treated is not necessarily a function of what one is, but how one is defined.

In 1988, Reverend Jesse Jackson took the leadership to change identities from "black" to "African-American." The latter term already had long-standing preference in the intellectual community. Reverend Jackson, and those who share his rationale for the change in nomenclature, are convinced that most black Americans now wish to be identified as "African-American." The identification, it is claimed, will provide this ethnic group an historical cultural reference tied to a definite geographic base similar to that observed among other ethnic groups in the United States.[48] This shift from a racial description that once represented a triumph of "political self-assertion," to African-American, it is argued, will enhance racial dignity and individual self-esteem.[49] As of 1990, while the term African-American appears to be increasingly accepted, resistance to this shift in ethnic identity remains widespread. Opposition is evident among many integrationists who had a difficult time accepting the change from "Negro" to "black"; from those who resent what they believe to be an imposition by political leaders and individuals in the intellectual community who may have little evidence to support their claims; from persons who still do not identify themselves with the African continent; and among those who believe as W. E. B. DuBois once warned that undue emphasis should not be placed on what something is called, or Bayard Rustin's observation that "the real problems lie beneath the surface."[50] Nevertheless, the major focus is on self-identity, the determination of self-esteem, positive valuations of self, and full appreciation of the contribution of this ethnic group to American life.

It should also be stressed that racism in America has a deleterious effect upon the self-images of many black children. Racism and discrimination can be devastating to those black children who are not supported by familial strengths and coping mechanisms. Indeed, children come to understand the forces of racism, segregation, and discrimination through the world of their family. Their interactions with other family members affect their understanding of their identity and self-realization. It is through the family, whether upper, middle, or lower class, that children come to understand who they are and what they are becoming through the process of maturation. Thus it is the concept of what one learns during the socialization process that affects self-perceptions and identity. If one comes to see oneself as a source of scorn and disparagement rather than a worthy human being, the black child will, of course, tend to internalize these negative definitions. This is one condition that blackness as an ideology and as a source of pride seeks to correct. It attempts to provide an environment of personal worth and acceptance and to heighten one's self-esteem, self-evaluation, and higher aspirations for achievement. For blackness or African-American identities to be effective, resocialization of parents is necessary in order to counteract those negative definitions that the black child still confronts through other socializing agents, most particularly the school. It should be noted that the position that the child's parents occupy within the class hierarchy will have a determining impact on any degree of success achieved. The relationships between social class and other life chances will be further elaborated in subsequent chapters.

IMPLICATIONS OF SOCIAL STRATIFICATION FOR BLACK UNITY

One consequence of a class structure within the black community is the possible isolation of the upper classes from the lower ones. Wherever this has occurred, evidence seems to indicate that intensified stresses, strains, and intragroup conflicts have ensued. What makes this situation crucial is that it portends structural, organizational, and philosophical divisions among groups who theoretically are bound together in the pursuit of a common goal—achieving status as first-class citizens in American society.

One of the manifestations of class-linked disunity is the tendency of members of the upper classes to blame the most obvious victims of racial bigotry, the black lower classes, for the present status of all black people. The black upper classes particularly blame the black lower classes for the failure of the latter to become fully incorporated, if not fully assimilated, as equals in the larger stratification system. Thus blaming the victim pervades this class and is often articulated in expressions such as "you (lower-class blacks) make it difficult for us (upper- and middle-class blacks)" or "if it weren't for you, our race would be much further ahead than it is now" or "I've got mine; now get yours!" In many ways persons who engage in this type of behavior mirror the raw prejudices and categorical treatment of blacks so pervasive among nonblack racial bigots. Therefore, a major problem emerges. Lower-class blacks maintain that whatever economic and social leverage black upper classes may possess is not adequately transformed into advantages for the black masses. Neither is that power used to substantially promote the social and political causes of the black population as a whole. On the contrary, they argue, the social, economic, and political advantages of the black middle and upper classes are used all too frequently to promote self-interest. Moreover, specific individuals relish the notion of being "a black first" without due appreciation for the possibilities of exploiting this advantage, however limited it may be, for the good of the black community. If these allegations are substantially true, this situation undoubtedly emanated from upper- and middle-class self-definitions as a separate and more privileged group whose status resulted from individual accomplishments rather than from any specific group quality.

The fact remains that lower classes are highly suspicious of middle- and upper-class blacks whose contributions to the larger black community are not well known. This suspicion often leads to generalizations concerning the interest of middle- and upper-class blacks in promoting broader interests than self, of substantive involvement in social action programs, and of demonstrated willingness to work in lower-income black neighborhoods. Suspicion is, furthermore, exacerbated by the role played by color, the residue of historical resentment and animosity among blacks of darker hues against lighter-skinned blacks. Another apparent consequence has been the lack of grassroots social action programs among lower-class blacks in the past. The prevailing mood of inaction, stimulated by the feeling of little or no support from the financially well-off, forced the less well-off to resign themselves to inaction and nonparticipation even in causes designed to bring relief to the black poor. These inconsistencies led to structural alterations in the civil rights movements and an articulation of new motivational techniques for broadening the basis of participation in the black liberation movement.

As we inferred earlier, an inordinate amount of financial resources seem to be allocated to status-seeking endeavors by affluent black people. This automatically reduces the total sum available for social welfare assistance to less fortunate blacks. A major dilemma faced by the middle- and upper-class blacks is: What is their responsibility to less advantaged blacks? How much of their resources can they or should they sacrifice for assisting those who, for whatever reason, have not become as fortunate as they? Should they follow the model established by Jews, for example, by creating viable and extensive associations of black charities all consolidated under one single organization? Or should they continue already established mechanisms for assisting blacks who are in need of help such as voluntary organizations (e.g., churches, fraternal organizations like the Elks and the

Masons, private social clubs like the Links, Jack and Jills, fraternities and sororities, and other formal institutions) as has been done in the past? Should they assume that their first responsibility is to their own families for guaranteeing their success and personal development, or should they distance themselves from their families, or disavow status rewards by making more substantive financial contributions to the less well-off blacks in the anticipation that the latter group will be brought into the mainstream of American society?

Partial answers to these questions have already been provided by the activities, social and political behavior of blacks in the recent past. Many black charities or philanthropies are quite viable and increasing their capacity to deliver important services to needy blacks. A case in point is the Black United Appeal which had to fight both the federal government and United Way in the courts in order to permit potential contributors to have their contributions allocated to this organization through standard payroll deductions. Many black social groups, such as the Links, fraternities and sororities, women's auxiliary groups of medical, dental, and legal organizations, have contributed millions of dollars to organizations such as the United Negro College Fund, the National Urban League, and the NAACP to promote their work.

Many black professionals, physicians, dentists, lawyers, and university professors provide free services and expertise to economically distressed blacks and to grass-roots organizations in the black community. Many black college students serve as wholesome role models for thousands of black children by participating in "big brother" and "big sister" programs, and many are actively involved in voter registration campaigns underway in poor black communities throughout the United States. In fact, the involvement of black college students in the 1983 mayoralty election in Chicago was particularly instrumental in increasing the numbers of young blacks from poor neighborhoods who voted and helped elect Harold Washington as the first black to become mayor of Chicago.

Emmett Carson's research on black philanthropy revealed that black Americans have had a long history of "giving." Slightly more than two-thirds (67.3 percent) of donors in his survey contributed funds to a charitable organization but 68 percent of their contributions went to their own church. Lesser sums were allocated to religious organizations, hospitals, social welfare organizations, educational organizations, and political organizations. However, more than half of all blacks surveyed by Carson reported having donated food, clothing, property, service to the homeless, the poor and needy relatives, friends, or neighbors. Significantly, his data showed that the higher the income of the respondent the more likely was the person to donate money as a charitable contribution.[51]

The most highly publicized and largest philanthropic contribution by a black American to a black institution was the $20 million donated by Bill and Camille Cosby to Spelman College, an historical black women's college in Atlanta. This gift followed a tradition of donations to black educational institutions that characterizes much of the Cosby's philanthropic outlays. For example, the Cosbys had already donated significant monies to other historical black colleges and universities (HBCUs) including $325,000 to Howard University; $750,000 to Bethune-Cookman College; $1.3 million to Fisk University; $1.3 million divided equally between Central State University, Florida A & M University, Shaw University, and Howard University. While their gifts to HBCUs is without precedent, it is difficult to determine the degree of influence they have had on other blacks in ways that stimulate increased charitable contributions to black educational institutions. It is known that some HBCUs, such as Xavier University of New Orleans and Hampton Institute in Virginia, have mounted particularly successful fund-raising campaigns involving their alumni.

Several black entertainers and athletes achieved deserved recognition during the 1980s for their contributions and fund-raising activities in behalf of HBCUs, especially to the 42 United Negro College Fund (UNCF) institutions. For example, Lou Rawls annually hosts the major fund-raising telethon for the UNCF. "Magic" Johnson annually sponsors a basketball game (or tour of games) and dinner that raised about $3 million in the 1980s for the UNCF. Such basketball luminaries as Dominique Wilkins, Michael Jordan, Isaiah Thomas, Charles Barkley, James Worthy, and others not only contribute their talents for this benefit but assist Johnson by their presence at the "black-tie" dinner which follows the game. Another major contributor to HBCUs is television talk show host Oprah Winfrey. She has made significant contributions to her own alma mater, Tennessee State University, as well as to the Medical School of Morehouse College. Whitney Houston and Michael Jackson donated their profits from benefit concerts in 1988 to the UNCF and to provide low cost housing in depressed black neighborhoods. Bryant Gumbel raises funds for the UNCF.

Many middle- and upper-class blacks, young and old, are active participants in mentor programs for the underclass as well as in tutorial programs designed to improve educational skills among young people in the underclass. Black sororities and fraternities as well as self-help organizations such as the National Urban League sponsor on-going projects that help to reduce teen-age pregnancy, increase knowledge of effective parenting, and help young black teen fathers assume greater responsibility for their children.

While it is true that some upper- and middle-class blacks wish to distance themselves from the black downtrodden and attempt to avoid recognition of their class origins, others are sympathetic to the needs of the poor and underclass. Even those who wish to deny their "blackness" share two things in common with blacks in all social classes—the knowledge that, although the intensity may not be as strong in some classes as in others, blacks of all classes *feel* racial discrimination in American society. They also share a certain political unity. This sense of unity was further illustrated by the ability of presidential candidate Reverend Jesse Jackson to appeal to a major cross section of all socioeconomic groups within the black community during the Democratic primaries of 1984 and 1988. His candidacy seemed to have persuaded blacks of all social class groups that he could have a significant impact of the effort to deal a death blow to Reaganism.

NOTES

1. For varying dimensions of social class and theoretical formulations cf. Karl Marx, *Capital*, Max Eastman (ed.) (New York: Modern Library, 1968); *The Communist Manifesto* (Chicago: Regnery, 1969); *Pre-Capitalist Economic Formations*, Eric Hobsbawm (ed.), O. Jack Cohen (tr.) (New York: International Publishers, 1921); and Max Weber, *The Protestant Ethic and the Spirit of Capitalism*, Talcott Parsons (tr.) (New York: Scribner, 1930); *The Theory of Social and Economic Organization*, A. M. Henderson and Talcott Parsons (trs.) (Glencoe, Ill.: The Free Press, 1947). The functionalist aspect is explained by Kingsley Davis and Wilbert E. Moore, "Some Principles of Stratification," *American Sociological Review*, 10 (1945): 242–249. The conflict school is elaborated in Ralf Dahrendorf, *Class and Class Conflict in Industrial Society* (Stanford, Calif.: Stanford University Press, 1959).
2. Cf. Reinhard Bendix and Seymour Lipset (eds.), *Class, Status and Power* (New York: Free Press, 1966) and Lucile Duberman, *Social Inequality: Class and Caste in America* (Philadelphia: Lippincott, 1976).
3. Robert Bierstedt, "An Analysis of Social Power," *American Sociological Review*, 15 (December 1950): 730–738.
4. Hubert M. Blalock, Jr., "A Power Analysis of Racial Discrimination," *Social Forces*, 39, (1960): 53–69, and *Toward a General Theory of Inter-Group Relations* (New York: Wiley and Sons, 1967).
5. Roger G. Emblen, *Society Today*, 2nd ed. (Del Mar, Calif.: CRM Books, 1973), pp. 196–198.
6. T. Shibutani and L. M. Kwan, *Ethnic Stratification: A Comparative Approach* (New York: The Macmillan Company, 1972), pp. 33–34.
7. Gunnar Myrdal, *An American Dilemma* (New York: Harper & Row, 1944), Chap. 32 and p. 689.
8. *Ibid.* Also see C. Van Woodward, *The Strange Career of Jim Crow* (New York: Oxford University Press, 1957).
9. For a discussion of the black middle class, cf. E. Franklin Frazier, *Black Bourgeoisie* (New York: The Free Press of Glencoe, 1957); Sharon M. Collins, "The Making of the Black Middle Class," *Social Problems* 30:4 (April 1983): 369–382; and Richard Freeman, *The Black Elite* (New York: McGraw-Hill, 1976).
10. Nathan Hare, *The Black Anglo-Saxons* (New York: Macmillan Company, 1970).
11. Frazier, *op. cit.*, Chap. 3.
12. Robert Hill, *Economic Policies and Black Progress: Myths and Realities* (Washington, D.C.: National Urban League Research Department, 1981), p. 101.
13. William A. Sampson, "New Insights on Black Middle-Class Mobility," *Urban League Review* 5:1 (Summer 1980): 21–24, and William A. Sampson, and Vera Milam, "Interracial Attitudes of the Black Middle-Class: Have They Changed?" *Social Problems* 23 (December 1975): 53–65.
14. Sar A. Levitan, William B. Johnston, and Robert Taggart, *Still A Dream: The*

Changing Status of Blacks Since 1960 (Cambridge,: Harvard University Press, 1975), pp. 190–192.

15. Cf. Harriette Pipes McAdoo, (ed.), *Black Families* (Beverly Hills, Calif.: Sage, 1981), and "Youth, School and Family in Transition, *Urban Education* 16 (October 1981): 261–277.

16. Cf. Frazier, *ibid.*, and *The Negro Family in the United States,* rev. ed. (New York: The Macmillan Company, 1957).

17. Horace Cayton and St. Clair Drake, *Black Metropolis: A Study of Negro Life in a Northern City* (New York: Harper & Row, 1945).

18. Myrdal, *op. cit.*

19. Andrew Billingsley, *Black Families in White America* (Englewood Cliffs, N.J.: Prentice-Hall, 1968).

20. McAdoo, *op. cit.*

21. Bart Landry, "Growth of the Black Middle Class in the 1960s," *Urban League Review* 3:2 (Winter 1978), and Bart Landry and Margaret P. Jendrek, "Employment of Wives in Middle-Class Black America," *Journal of Marriage and the Family* 40 (November 1978): 787–797.

22. Sampson, *op. cit.*

23. Carol Stack, *All Our Kin: Strategies for Survival in a Black Community* (New York: Harper & Row, 1978).

24. Cf. Carl Gershman, "A Matter of Class," *New York Times Magazine,* October 5, 1980; Carl Gershman, "The Black Plight, Race or Class?," *The New York Times Magazine,* June 27, 1980; Earl Caldwell, "The Rising Status of Commitment," *Black Enterprise,* (December 1978): 38–42; James A. Moss, "Brashler's Black Middle Class: A Rebuttal," *The Crisis* 86:7 (August/September 1979): 307–310; Harriette Pipes McAdoo, "Black Kinship," *Psychology Today* (May 1979): 67–79, 110; and Ordie Coombs, "Still Without the Substance of Power," *Black Enterprise,* (December 1978): 28–33.

25. Cf. James E. Blackwell and Philip Hart, *Cities, Suburbs and Blacks* (Bayside, N.Y.: General Hall, Inc., 1982), *passim,* and The National Urban League, *The Black Pulse Survey Report* (Washington, D.C.: Research Department of the National Urban League, 1980), pp. 1–2.

26. Billingsley, *op. cit.* p. 129.

27. Frazier, *op. cit.,* Chap. 9.

28. Billingsley, *op. cit.*

29. Hill, *op. cit.*

30. Harold Wilensky and Charles Lebeaux, *Industrial Society and Social Welfare* (New York: Russell Sage Foundation, 1958), pp. xxvi–xxvii.

31. McAdoo, *op. cit.,* 1980 and 1979.

32. Levitan, *op. cit.*

33. Sampson, *op. cit.,* 1980.

34. Cf. Levitan, *op. cit.,* Hill, *op. cit.,* and McAdoo, *op. cit.,* 1979.

35. Billingsley, *op. cit.*

36. Cayton and Drake, *op. cit.,* p. 524.

37. Blackwell and Hart, *op. cit.,* Chapter 6.

38. *Ibid.*

39. Sidney Kronus, "Some Neglected Areas of Negro Class Comparisons," in Edgar Epps, (ed.), *Race Relations* (Cambridge, Mass.: Winthrop Publishers, 1973), pp. 236–249.

40. Hill, *op. cit.,* p. 40.

41. For an extensive discussion of various perceptions and components of the black "underclass," see such references as Myron Magnet, "America's Underclass: What to Do?," *Fortune* (May 11, 1987): 131–150; William Kornblum, "Lumping the Poor: What is the 'Underclass?' " *Dissent* (Summer 1984): 295–302; Douglas Glasgow, *The Black Underclass* (San Francisco: Jossey-Bass Publishers, 1980); Andrew Billingsley, *The Black Family in White America* (Englewood Cliffs, N.J.: Prentice-Hall, 1968); Kenneth Clark, *Dark Ghetto* (New York: Harper & Row, 1965); and Katherine McFate, "Defining the Underclass," *Focus* (June 1987), 8–9, 11.

42. Clayton and Drake, *op. cit.,* p. 524.

43. Billingsley, *op. cit.,* pp. 138–140.

44. Blackwell and Hart, *op. cit.*

45. Cf. Gehard Lenski, *Power and Privilege: A Theory of Stratification* (New York: McGraw-Hill, 1966) for an elaboration of status inconsistency theory.

46. Hill, *op. cit.,* 41.

47. George Napper, *Blacker Than Thou: The Struggle for Campus Unity* (Grand Rapids, Mich.: William B. Eerdmans Publishing Co., 1973).

48. Cf. "Negro, Black and African-American," *New York Times* (December 22, 1988), p. A-22; Isabel Wilkerson, "Many Who Are Black Favor New Term for Who They Are," *New York Times* (January 31, 1989), p. 1; Bayard Rustin, "What's in a Name?," *New York Times* (February 1, 1989), p. A-25.

49. *Ibid.*

50. *Ibid.*

51. Emmett D. Carson, "Despite Long History, Black Philanthropy Gets Little Credit as "Self-Help" Tool," *Focus* (June 1987): pp. 3–4, 7.

Chapter
5

The Church and Religion in the Black Community

Second only to the family, the church is the most important social institution in the black community—it is the only institution over which black Americans have had complete independence, autonomy, and control.[1] From its founding during the 1770s, the church has undergone profound institutional change. This chapter explores some of those changes and analyzes the role of the black church in contemporary American society.

HISTORICAL OVERVIEW: INSTITUTIONAL CHARACTERISTICS

Blacks forced into involuntary servitude in America brought from their African heritage various forms of religious beliefs and practices. Therefore, it is not unexpected that an immense variety of religious workers were among enslaved blacks. These included high priests and priestesses, diviners, and root doctors.[2] Through their efforts, not only were there many African influences in the religious experience and orientations of blacks but they also served as the trustees of a folk religion that became deeply rooted in the black American experience.

Early missionaries in the American colonies introduced slaves to Christianity. These missionaries regarded such religious expressions as voodoo rites, reliance on the medicine man, and freely expressive behavior as primitive behavior, heathenism, and incompatible with Christian tenets.

Undoubtedly, there was also a fear that so long as black slaves adhered to beliefs that were antithetical to Christianity, bonding them to slavery would be substantially more difficult. Thus, missionaries had at least a twofold purpose for introducing blacks to Christianity. On the one hand, their efforts were designed to convert them from what the missionaries perceived as "heathenism." On the other hand, missionaries were an instrument of the prevailing capitalistic forces that dominated a plantation economy. Slaves had to be convinced that enslavement was God's will and that the enslaved on earth would find paradise in the next life. Rejection of that teaching meant that one would run the risk of angering God let alone slave masters who, like missionaries, were the instruments of God on earth.[3] The success of this teaching meant less difficulty in institutionalizing slavery in the New World.

Literal interpretations of biblical passages such as the Ephesisan (6:5) mandate for "servants to be obedient to their masters" were widely employed to persuade blacks to accept their inferior status.[4] A few "radical" white ministers did, however, infuse their preaching with notions of the fundamental equality of people "in the eyes of God" as well as with subtle messages emphasizing the incompatibility of the institution of slavery with equality of humankind.

Initially, slave masters/owners were reluctant to permit slaves to participate in organized religious activity. However, when they recognized that such activity provided another social control mechanism and a means by which the movements of their slaves could be monitored, many allowed religious worship on their plantations.[5] Thus all-black congregations were established on large plantations and in such towns as Richmond, Charleston, and Lexington.[6] The number of black preachers proliferated to serve the needs of these new congregations as well as the religious needs of slaves unattached to church groups. With increasing freedom to worship, to pray, sing, and understand the moral tenets of the new religion, Christianity spread rapidly among black slaves and free people of color.

Black preachers were responsible for the development of a folk religion among slaves. This religion emphasized spirituality, love, human kindness, joyful noises, militancy sometimes and resignation to life as it is at other times, and sometimes a literal interpretation of the Bible. Wilmore maintains that this black folk religion, formed during slavery, "was the spirit that created independent black churches" and gave the religion of black people in America a uniqueness of style. This folk religion became a "theology of liberation."[7]

The movement toward liberation was precipitated by actions and restrictions imposed upon blacks by white slaveowners.[8] For instance, in some areas, blacks were not permitted to conduct religious services without the presence of a white person.[9] In other instances, black preachers were beaten or imprisoned. Sometimes, black preachers were forbidden to preach at all, especially as these preachers were accused of spreading the social gospel of freedom of all humankind and that slavery of human beings was not consistent with Christian principles.[10]

It was in the black churches of the South that African traditions survived and nurtured a desire for freedom on earth, ultimately giving rise to slave revolts, insurrections, and the separation of blacks from the white Christian church in the North. In fact, a small number of black independent churches sprang up in various parts of the South almost a century before the Civil War.[11] The move for actual separation in the South first arose among black Baptists under the leadership of George Liel and his protégé, Andrew Bryan. He founded a Baptist church in Savannah, Georgia, in 1779 which became "the nucleus for the organization of black Baptists throughout Georgia." Whites had attempted to disestablish the black church by imprisoning their preachers and whipping their members. Black Baptist churches were organized, occasionally with the assistance of white ministers, in other cities including Williamsburg (1785), Richmond, and Petersburg, Virginia (1776).[12]

Wherever blacks were permitted to worship with whites, segregated seating arrangements were often customary. Thus, blacks were confined to "Nigger heaven," a balcony area reserved for blacks, or the "African Corner," or some other area within the church.[13]

The independent black church movement in the North was led by Richard Allen and his followers (Absalom Jones and James Varick) in Philadelphia. In 1786, at the time Allen was converted to Christianity, blacks were allowed to worship with whites in white northern churches. However, after beginning his own ministry, Allen saw no need for blacks to be subservient to whites in the name of God and sought to establish an independent church. When Allen, Jones, and William White were "pulled from their knees" by white church officials as they sought to pray, Allen was more determined than ever to establish an independent black church.

Richard Allen organized the Free African Society from which sprang the Bethel Church in 1794. This church became known as the Bethel African Methodist Episcopal (AME) Church, the first AME black independent church in America. Branches of this church were organized in several communities early on, especially along the Eastern seaboard in such cities as Baltimore and Wilmington and in cities in Pennsylvania and New Jersey. The AME church became the most influential body among black Methodists.[14]

In 1796, black members of the John Street Methodist Episcopal Church in New York also became disenchanted with new manifestations of bigotry and domination by white church officials. Under the leadership of Peter Williams, they broke away from the white church and established one of their own. From this group came the African Methodist Episcopal Zion (AMEZ) Church. Reverend Thomas Paul, who organized the Negro Baptists of Boston in 1809, later assisted in the organization of the Abyssinian Baptist Church in New York[15]—a church that became known for its leadership in the black community and for the political activity of its most famous minister, Reverend Adam Clayton Powell.

However, the movement led by Richard Allen with his establishment of the Free African Society is singularly important in the history of the black church in the United States: It became the model for the black church. Wilmore asserts that this pattern has a dual focus: (1) "free and autonomous worship" in the way that black people desire to worship God, and (2) a pattern of unity and concern for the welfare of black people.[16] Both the AME and the AMEZ churches were outspoken in their opposition to slavery. The Allenites were accused of aiding Denmark Vesey in his insurrection in 1822 and the AMEZ congregations along the Mason and Dixon Line were "known as Underground Railroad Stations for escaped slaves."[17]

In 1870, the Colored Methodist Episcopal (CME) church was formed as a third black separatist body from the Methodist church. The fervor for independence that characterized Baptists and Methodists was missing among black members of the Presbyterian, Congregational, and Episcopalian churches. Wilmore identifies three reasons for their acceptance of their status or position in these denominations: (1) black membership in these churches was considerably smaller than in Baptist and Methodist churches, therefore, they could not perpetrate the kind of crisis as the latter could and did; (2) these churches attracted primarily mulattos and octoroons, persons closer in complexion to whites than was the case in Baptist and Methodist Churches; and (3) the Presbyterians, Episcopalians, and Congregationalists insisted upon an educated ministry—a fact that depressed the number of black ministers in these churches who could form an independent body.[18] Black preachers during slavery, often forbidden to learn to read and write, were often illiterate and, in general, relied on their ability to memorize texts they heard from the more educated white ministers and from the art of "talking" they had brought with them from their African past.

Black independent churches continued to grow and expand throughout the United States. Prior to the Civil War, they were an effective voice against the institution of slavery. They joined forces with white abolitionists to undermine that institution and provide care for runaway slaves. During Reconstruction, the black church, perhaps more so than before, fulfilled a welfare mission. It provided social services for the newly emancipated blacks and was instrumental in founding schools and colleges for blacks. Their edifices, tabernacles, and houses of worship continued to be a place of refuge from white supremacy and racism.

After the U. S. Supreme Court issued the famous "separate-but-equal" decision in the *Plessy* v. *Ferguson* case, overt manifestations of prejudice, racism, and bigotry became more blatant and indelibly imprinted in Jim Crow legislation. As amplified in subsequent chapters, the dominant white community created a plethora of boundary-maintenance structures to rigidly separate the races and institutionalize discrimination as a way of life in the United States. In the early part of the twentieth century, blacks were terrorized by the Ku Klux Klan and other renegade white supremacy groups. Lynching of blacks by white mobs became commonplace as whites used violence as an instrument of domination.

The militancy that had characterized so much of the black church in the period prior to slavery was abandoned for a philosophy of accommodation and a retreat to an old doctrine that suffering on earth would result in better rewards in the afterlife. Simultaneously, many black churches attempted to instill pride among blacks in their heritage, encouraging them to take advantage of existing opportunities and hope for the best in a segregated society. Most black churches had rejected black nationalistic movements and had begun to imitate orthodox Christianity and all its bourgeois trappings. Membership in the black church grew to unprecedented levels as the church performed the role of a safehaven, a refuge, a place where leadership could be developed and freedom of expression could not be denied.

THE BLACK CHURCH, URBANISM, AND MIGRATION

As stated in Chapter 1, the black population of the South began a massive exodus to the North in 1915. Blacks left the farms of Alabama, Georgia, and Mississippi and the agrarian areas, cities, and towns of the Carolinas and Virginia for what they believed to be a better and more prosperous life in cities like New York, Chicago, Cleveland, and Detroit.

This segment of the population included a huge number of blacks whose roots were in folk traditions and the more fundamentalist expressions of Protestantism. They were the outsiders, economically depressed, less educated, and determined to escape the brutalities of white racism. These people were excellent candidates for the new manifestations of black folk religion that was being rekindled in the urban North. These were people who had a thirst for economic, political, and social justice—a "yearning" that had been betrayed by accommodationist black preachers.[19]

Thousands flocked to the new cults or sects which had separated from larger denominations because they had lost sight of the fundamental roots of religion in the black community or because their members no longer felt comfortable in the older established and formal churches where emotionalism was diminishing. In this period, between 1896 and the two world wars, such black religious bodies arose as the Black Pentecostal and Holiness churches: the House of Prayer, the Church of God in Christ, the Apostolic Overcoming Church of God, and the Christian's Church of the Living God; Mt. Sinai Holy Church of America (Philadelphia); the United House of Prayer for All People (led by "Daddy Grace"); Father Divine's Peace Mission (New York); the Moorish Science Temple of America; the Church of God (Black Jews); Triumph the Church and Kingdom of God in Christ; the African Orthodox Church; the National Baptist Evangelical Life and Soul-Saving Assembly of the U. S. A., and the Nation of Islam.

Almost all operated as storefront establishments where ministers could be women as well as men.[20]

In the meantime, the largest body of black Christians in the United States, the National Baptist Convention, was split into the National Baptist Convention and the National Baptist Convention of America.[21]

Cults attracted members for several reasons. The majority of their members were recruited from recent arrivals from the South and they provided an emotional outlet, a freedom of religious expression, a place of adjustment as the new folk people sought a new life in the strange, crowded, anonymous urban ghetto. Black Jews believed that they "were the true Jews of the Bible," and that white Jews "were a fraud."[22] Father Divine appealed to the poor, the moralistic, and persons committed to civil rights and social welfare and preached the abolition of lynching and Jim Crowism. Father Divine distributed food and clothing to the poor and provided housing to the needy. Other cults practiced faith healing, some practiced spiritualism, and all offered opportunities for their members to "feel good about themselves" and the probabilities for better living in the immediate future.

ROLE OF THE BLACK CHURCH AND THE CIVIL RIGHTS MOVEMENT

Over time, the black church has been militant, radical, accommodationist, moderate, and reactionary. Its ministers have been accused of being insurrectionists or of plotting insurrections; servants or tools of the white establishment for the maintenance of a racially segregated society; impediments to social and economic progress for the masses while they filled their pockets with the fruits of the labors of their parishioners; Uncle Toms; Oreos; martyrs and true leaders of black people toward the ultimate goal of black liberation. At one point or another between 1950 and 1990, all these characterizations have been attributed to black ministers and their churches.

Aldon Morris in his prize-winning book, *The Origins of the Civil Rights Movement,* and Herbert Haines in *Black Radicals and the Civil Rights Mainstream, 1954–1970* independently point to the role of the black church and black ministers in the Civil Rights Movement. Morris systematically and painstakingly documents the roles performed by such ministers as the Reverend Martin Luther King, Jr., Reverend Ralph David Abernathy, Reverend Andrew Young, Reverend Jesse Jackson, Reverend T. J. Jemison, Reverend Fred Shuttlesworth, Reverend James Farmer, Reverend John Lewis, Reverend Douglas Moore, Reverend C. T. Vivian, Reverend Charles Sherrod, Reverend Wyatt Tee Walker, the Reverend Charles K. Steele in the bus boycotts of Louisiana and Alabama.[23] Even this list does not exhaust the hundreds of black ministers across the nation who played grassroots leadership roles in supporting the Civil Rights Movement.

Reverend Martin Luther King, Jr.'s name is synonymous with the Civil Rights Movement. By far, he was the most prominent civil rights leader at the national level between 1956 and 1968. Without question, his leadership, commitment to a philosophy of nonviolence at a time when white bigotry was often expressed in inhumane treatment by people who espoused "Christianity" and who often advocated or were indifferent to brutal forms of violence, and his inspirational oratory convinced legions of white Americans that the time had come to dismantle the most rigid barriers to desegregation in American life. However, as the list of ministers suggests, the church and their ministers played a major role in organizing and sustaining formal protest against racial injustice in Montgomery and elsewhere.

Dr. King was instrumental in founding the Montgomery Improvement Association (MIA) which organized a successful bus boycott against the company that segregated blacks in seating arrangements in Montgomery, Alabama. Prior to the formation of the Montgomery mass boycott, in 1953, Reverend T. J. Jemison, pastor of the Mt. Zion Baptist Church, had been the official leader of a mass boycott against segregated buses in Baton Rouge, Louisiana. That boycott was organized and directed through black churches in Baton Rouge and the organization established there to attack segregation, the United Defense League (UDL). Its massive protest movement served as a model for the bus boycott that elevated Dr. King to international prominence.

While Haines[24] stresses the financial support of the black church for the movement, Morris emphasizes total institutional support of the church. For him, the church was the "institutional center" of the movement; it provided an organizational base, a spiritual support that grew out of the black experience in songs, oratory, and testimonies of uplift and sharing; it was a leadership structure, a resource management and meeting place where planning strategies and tactics could be mobilized.[25] The church offered a place where an oppressed people could openly discuss and ventilate their feelings and find relief from that oppression through singing, praying, and shouting.[26]

Although Morris' observations are supported by a plethora of evidence, his analysis has special salience for the small cadre of Baptist ministers and churches that formed the Southern Christian Leadership Conference and who spearheaded the Montgomery Bus Boycott—the origins of the civil rights movement. It is also true that many churches and their ministers were initially reluctant to commit themselves to what they believed to be an extremely radical undertaking and many did not provide much more than lip service to the movement. In *Stride Toward Freedom* Dr. King expressed his dismay over the reluctance of the black church to become more activist in raising its public voice against racism, prejudice, discrimination, segregation, and white domination. King argued that it had always been the responsibility of the church to "challenge the status quo" but the black church, at that time, was not rising to that challenge. But black churches seemed more concerned with life in the future than in the present.[27]

As Wilmore also points out, King could not be confident that the majority of "black preachers and their congregations" would do more than make "polite gestures in his direction."[28] He also observed that the masses of black churches were like the masses of white churches—spectators rather than participants in the Movement.[29] In the meantime, hundreds of marchers aligned to or supporters of the Southern Christian Leadership Conference, the Congress of Racial Equality, or the Student Non-Violent Coordinating Committee were attacked, imprisoned, and prayed that someone would provide bail money. More often than not, it was not the black church that came to their rescue until the church became radicalized.[30] That radicalization did not occur until after the March on Washington in 1963 for it added a new legitimation to black grievances and respectability to the protest movement.

Radicalization took a variety of forms ranging from James Foreman's demands for "reparations" to the victims of slavery to James Cones' formulation of a "black theology"[31] to Albert B. Cleage, Jr.'s claims that "Jesus is the Black Messiah,"[32] to the insistence of black church people that the black church take a more active role in their struggle for liberation from racial discrimination. Since the 1970s, in response to profound changes in the black community that have threatened its institutional infrastructure, the church has become more activist and responsive to the current needs of its people.

THE BLACK CHURCH IN CONTEMPORARY AMERICA: MAJOR FUNCTIONS

The black church in contemporary American society is more directed toward immediate social changes and alterations in relations between blacks and whites in ways which, in the view of ministers and parishioners alike, reflect the broad view of the community. In this sense, functions performed by the black church of the 1990s are consistent with the kinds of community functions attributed to Warren and outlined earlier in Chapter 1.

At least seven functions of the contemporary black church may be identified at this point:

1. It provides a cohesive institutional structure within the black community.
2. It is an instrument for the development of black leadership.
3. It is a base for citizenship training and community social action.
4. It performs major educative and social roles.

5. It acts as a charitable institution.
6. It is an agency for the development of black business structures or ventures.
7. It serves as an index of social class.

Not unlike earlier times, social cohesion is a primary function of the black church in the 1990s. This role is especially critical at a time when the black family has undergone profound social changes evidenced by poverty, marital discord, separation, divorce, and an inordinately high rate of illegitimacy. The church stresses family values, mutual aid, and responsibility. There is still a tendency for the black community to look to the church for a sense of direction, for psychological support and coping strategies for dealing with persistent racial prejudice, discrimination, and social stress encountered in everyday life. The black church remains as an institution that instills racial pride in the achievement of the individual. It creates a sense of collective achievement from the accomplishments of other blacks. It continues to be a place in which, irrespective of one's station in life, a person can be treated with dignity and respect for one's own individuality and be made to feel, as Reverend Jesse Jackson often reminds his audiences, "like somebody." Hence, members have few reservations about active participation, and many young persons are exposed to invaluable role models by virtue of their involvement in the social and religious activities of the church.

The leadership role of the black church remains one of its important contributions. Largely because of the tremendous emphasis on active participation of members and the status rewards obtained thereby, the church is the training ground for a significant proportion of the black leadership structure. Moreover, by virtue of its socialization process to which active members are exposed, many are indoctrinated into the practical application of political and economic structures and given numerous opportunities for public speaking, the honing of organizational skills, and vocal training. These facts, coupled with the tendency in times of crisis to look to ministers for leadership should make it obvious why so many leaders and entertainers from the black community have a strong church identification. Among these leaders were the late Dr. Martin Luther King, Jr., the late Reverend Ralph David Abernathy, and the late Adam Clayton Powell, former member of the U. S. House of Representatives.

Current leaders include Reverend Jesse Jackson, candidate for President of the United States in 1984 and 1988; Reverend Andrew Young, U. S. Ambassador to the United Nations during the Carter Administration; Reverend William H. Gray III, former Chair of the Budget and Finance Committee of the House of Representatives and the Democratic Whip in the U. S. House of Representatives; Reverend Floyd Flake, member of the U. S. House of Representatives; the Reverend Walter Fauntroy, Congressional Delegate to the U. S. House of Representatives from the District of Columbia; John Lewis, former seminarian and member of the U. S. House

of Representatives; Reverend Leon Sullivan, Founder of Opportunities
Industrialization Centers of America and author of "The Sullivan Princi-
ples"—an anti-apartheid position for corporate America doing business in
South Africa; Reverend Benjamin Hooks, Executive Secretary of the
NAACP; Reverend Joseph Lowery, President of the Southern Christian
Leadership Conference, and others at the local level.

In addition, several performing artists have revealed the value of their
early training received in the choirs of black churches in the development
of their talent. Persons in this group include, for example, Leontyne Price,
a luminary in the annals of the Metropolitan Opera Company, and highly
acclaimed soul singers like Aretha Franklin and Gladys Knight and the
Pips.

Inasmuch as the black community is confronted with a broad array of
devastating social problems, the black church is broadening its roles of
preparation for citizenship, social action, and social welfare that characterized its early folk traditions and its role during the Great Depression. Of
special importance are church activities in anti-drug programs; housing
for the poor and the homeless; social welfare services for the hungry;
programs to combat teen pregnancy; AIDS education programs; economic development and job training; "stay in school" programs; family life
and day-care centers; and programs to promote family and social cohesion.
In addition, black church leaders often are in the forefront of efforts to
eliminate police brutality and bring police officers who maim or murder
innocent blacks and black persons suspected of a crime to justice.

The first National Conference on The Black Family/Community and
Crack Cocaine was organized by Reverend Cecil Williams of the Glide
Memorial United Methodist Church in San Francisco in 1989. As a result
of this conference, a national network was established in black churches
across the nation to develop anti-drug abuse interventions and strategies.
Specific programs were motivated by the fear that a large proportion of
the current generation of black youth could be lost to society by virtue of
their entrapment in the drug subculture. These programs included expanded job training opportunities, tutorials to prevent school dropouts,
sports activities, mentoring and Big Brother programs, peer counseling
workshops on "saying no to drugs," and instruction in moral values.

Similar programs were established in more than 100 churches in South
Carolina as a result of the Project A. D. A. M or Anti-Drug Abuse Movement. From San Diego to Cleveland, Philadelphia, and New York, black
churches have organized anti-drug campaigns. It is believed by their participants that such programs are a successful preventive intervention in
the war on drugs in the black community.[33]

Social services of black churches are, of course, broad and diversified.
Some are oriented toward strengthening black families and enhancing
positive development of children and youth.[34] Some churches have also
established Quality of Life Centers as a way of combatting the deterioration of black families. These centers offer day care, preschool programs,

nursery schools, programs in parenting, and family counseling. Some are substantially more comprehensive and provide remedial education, drug abuse prevention, employment training, and remedial activities.[35] Such programs and services can be found, for example, in New York at the AMEZ Church, the Abyssinian Baptist Church, St. Philip's Protestant Church, Bridge Street AME, and the Concord Baptist. In Chicago, they can be found at Olivet Baptist Church; in Detroit at Detroit's Second Baptist, and in Washington, D. C., at the Shiloh Baptist Church.

Social services also include programs to teach young men responsibilities of parenting and of adulthood and pride in being a black male (e.g., United Methodist Church in Chicago; the Project Image of 10 Chicago black churches) and programs to facilitate the adoption of black children (e.g., that run by Father George Clements of the Holy Angels Church in Chicago). The adoption model established by Father Clements is being replicated in other parts of the nation. For example, "Ministers for Adoption" was established in Jackson, Mississippi.[36]

The black church has expanded its efforts to provide affordable housing for the black elderly and other black people in need of housing. Thousands of units have already been constructed by black churches (e.g., Boston's St. Paul AME, Allen Temple Baptist Church in Oakland, United House of Prayer in Washington, D. C., Wheat Street Baptist Church in Atlanta, and the Church of the Good Shepherd in Chicago).[37]

As pointed out in Chapter 11, the black community was for a long time reluctant to recognize the number one public health problem in the United States as a problem found in the black community: Acquired Immune Deficiency Syndrome (AIDS). This pattern of denial originates in the fact that the black church, like many other Christian churches, considers homosexuality a sin. Therefore, there has always been an extraordinarily strong social taboo against homosexuality. To admit the presence of AIDS and the responsibility of the church to reach out to all people was extremely difficult for many churches. Not until 1989, when public health officials and some social service workers publicized the degree to which AIDS had attacked the heterosexual black community because of its transmission through dirty needles of drug users, did churches in metropolitan areas like New York City and Boston begin to organize efforts to deal with this problem. Subsequently, more ministers across the country have become involved in AIDS education programs. Nevertheless, the current position of the black church on this disease can probably best be characterized as one of ambivalence.

The black churches in the United States operate hundreds of soup kitchens, distribute clothing to the needy, and some operate hospices (e.g., Christ the Good Shepherd Church in Los Angeles) while others maintain a thriving credit union (e.g., Manhattan's Church of the Intercession).[38]

But as Reverend James Cone points out, despite filling the gap created by problems in the infrastructure of the black community, there is a pressing need for more ministers and black parishioners to reach out to persons in dire need of assistance.[39] Outreach activities on a wider scale would be most consistent with the extensive religiosity found among black people as observed by researchers such as Taylor[40], McAdoo[41], Taylor, et al.,[42] and Brown and Walters.[43] These studies report that at least two-thirds of all blacks say they are church members and seven of every ten claim to attend church weekly.

Again, in reference to the function of preparation for citizenship, it should be stated that thousands of black churches became actively involved in voter registration campaigns or are active participants in Operation Big Vote (a program designed to register millions of black voters and persuade them to actually vote in presidential campaigns). Jesse Jackson's presidential campaigns did in fact galvanize millions of black voters and his message of hope was often delivered from the pulpits of black churches. As in the heyday of the Civil Rights Movement, the black church continues to serve as an institutional community base of operations for civic groups within the black community. It has always served an educative function as indicated by the fact that more than half of the historically black four-year colleges were founded by black religious bodies and their supporters. Collectively, these institutions are currently of enormous value as socializing agents, places for mate selection, and for leadership training.

The contemporary black church is an instrument for the development of black business ventures and other community outreach programs. For instance, the leaders of 25 black religious bodies convened in late 1983 to establish a National Assembly of Black Churches (NABC). The central purposes of this group of denominations—which covered some 50,000 congregations—were to develop coherent implementable strategies for expansive economic development, to strengthen political organization in ways that would enhance the power of the black vote, and to expand educational training among young blacks. As stated above, hundreds of congregations across the nation are participants in social action and social service endeavors.

Several congregations of the American Muslim Movement operate grocery stores, restaurants, and cooperatives. Many Muslim congregations regularly purchase food, clothing, and appliances at wholesale prices and, in turn, sell them at low prices within their respective black communities. In addition, Iman Louis Farrakhan speaks a language of self-help, pride, and determination, despite criticisms against him for his position about Israel and Jews in America, that appeals to thousands of followers.

A final function of the black church is somewhat more complex. As explained in Chapter 4, church affiliation is often employed as an index of social status. However, one must be cautious about overgeneralizations in this regard since membership in the same denomination in one community, city, or section of the country may take on an entirely different social meaning in another location. Nevertheless, some denominations, in general, are more often associated with specific social classes while others may cut across all class lines.

MAJOR DENOMINATIONS

The majority of black Americans are affiliated with the Baptist churches. The largest segment of this denomination is represented by the National Baptist Convention U.S.A., Inc., with about 6.8 million members; the National Baptist Convention of America with approximately 3.5 million members; the 1 million member Progressive National Baptist Convention, Inc.; and the 450,000 member National Primitive Baptist Convention. The second largest group of churches are the Methodists whose combined membership is approximately 6 million. These include the African Methodist Episcopal Church, the African Methodist Episcopal Zion Church, the Christian Methodist Episcopal Church, and the United Methodist Church. Although it is estimated that there are about 2 million followers of the Muslim faith, accurate numbers are difficult to determine. It is probably more accurate to state that the American Muslim Mission (AMM) has about 100,000 members. It was organized in 1975 by Iman Warith D. Muhammad, son of the late Hon. Elijah Muhammad, with a philosophy viewed as an important departure from the original Nation of Islam by its opening of membership opportunities to non-blacks. However, the Nation of Islam, which is the more orthodox group of Muslims, probably has a membership of about 5,000 to 10,000. In 1977 the Nation of Islam broke from the AMM and regrouped under the leadership of Minister Louis Farrakhan.

In addition to the preceding denominations, significant numbers of blacks are members of such interracial religious bodies as the Roman Catholic Church, United Church of Christ, American Baptist Convention, Congregational Church, Presbyterian Church, Episcopal Church, Unitarian Church, Disciples of Christ, Jehovah Witnesses, Seventh Day Adventists, Holiness churches, and largely fundamentalists storefront Christian and spiritualist churches. Although membership in most of these churches is of long standing among members of the black community, only recently have many blacks been able to forge important linkages with these bodies or to rise up to high-level positions within the church hierarchies.

BLACKS AND THE CATHOLIC CHURCH

Blacks have never occupied a central role in the Catholic Church. There was a time when, in many churches, blacks were subjected to segregated seating arrangements and the Church exercised total indifference to the needs of black Catholics.[44] However, as the black proportion of th Church expanded and as whites abandoned the industrial cities for the suburbs, the Church found itself in a position that necessitated outreach to black Catholics.

Of the 53.4 million Catholics in the United States, approximately 2 million, somewhat less than 4 percent are black.[45] There are only 13 blacks serving as bishops, including one elevated to the level of archbishop but resigned his post in 1990. Less than 300 of the 54,000 priests in the Catholic Church are black and approximately 1,000 of the Church's 20,000 parishes have a predominantly black congregation but most of these are headed by white pastors.[46] Because of such arrangements, coupled with the paucity of blacks in high level positions in Church hierarchy, some continue to refer to a "plantation mentality" within the Catholic Church.

In 1990, however, the Church is attempting to be more responsive to the wishes of many black parishioners. Special attention is given to "self-expression" in which church services include "gospel choirs, spirited liturgies, African vestments for priests"[47] and other ceremonies reminiscent of the Protestant Church from which many black Catholics originated. It should be stated, however, that all black Catholics are not pleased with this turn of events. They prefer the traditional liturgies and services, often regarding the black orientation of some Masses as segregative and insulting.

In other denominations, modest steps are being made to include more blacks in higher church positions. For example, in 1989, Reverend Barbara Harris, a black, became the first woman ordained a bishop in the history of the Episcopal Church. Prior to that event, blacks had served as head of various councils of churches such as the 1984 selection of a black bishop from the AME Church as the leader of the National Council of Churches, a predominantly white body. This type of service represents a significant outreach from the black community and integration into multiracial religious organizations.

In conclusion, the history of the black church in America reveals an immense religious diversity within the black community that is longstanding. Despite criticisms against the black church, especially the accommodationist and conservative positions assumed by its leadership at crucial periods in the history of black Americans, it remains a major, important, and vital social institution in the black community. Throughout its history, the functions served by the black church were and are in the 1990s significant responses to urgent concerns of black people. That pattern continues as the black church accelerates attention to such troubling issues as indices of instability of the black family; widespread teen pregnancy and out-of-wedlock births; problems confronting black males; illiteracy; unemployment, hunger and homelessness; substance abuse; neighborhood fear, and AIDS. Of equal importance are the social bonds forged by the church that are a vital force for the sense of community shared by black Americans.

NOTES

1. Gayraud S. Wilmore, *Black Religion and Black Radicalism* (Garden City, N.Y.: Doubleday Anchor Books, 1973), Chap. 1.
2. Cf. *ibid.* and John Hope Franklin, *From Slavery to Freedom* (New York: Alfred A. Knopf, 1952), p. 200.
3. *Ibid.*
4. *Ibid.*, p. 34.
5. *Ibid.*, 36.
6. *Ibid.*, p. 198
7. *Op. cit.*, p. 36.
8. *Ibid.*, p. 105.
9. *Op. cit.*, p. 60.
10. *Ibid.*, p. 104.
11. *Op. cit.*, p. 160.
12. *Op. cit.*, p. 126.
13. *Ibid.*, p. 162.
14. *Ibid.*
15. *Op. cit.*, p. 114.
16. *Ibid.*, p. 121
17. *Ibid.*
18. *Ibid.*, p. 126
19. Joseph Washington, *Black Religion* (Boston: Beacon Press, 1964).
20. Franklin, *op. cit.*, p. 546, and Wilmore, *op. cit.*, pp. 210–225.
21. *Op. cit.*, p. 546.
22. *Op. cit.*, p. 216.
23. Aldon Morris, *The Origins of the Civil Rights Movement* (New York: The Free Press, 1984).
24. Herbert H. Haines, *Black Radicals and the Civil Rights Mainstream, 1954–1970* (Knoxville: University of Tennessee Press, 1988).
25. *Op. cit.*, pp. 4–16.
26. *Ibid.*, p. 4
27. Martin Luther King, Jr. *Stride Toward Freedom* (New York: Ballentine Books, 1960), pp. 167 ff., and Wilmore, *op. cit.*, p.245.
28. *Ibid.*
29. *Ibid.*
30. *Ibid*, pp. 241–249.
31. James H. Cone, *Black Theology and Black Power* (New York: Seabury Press, 1969) and James H. Cone, *A Black Theology of Liberation* (Philadelphia: J. B. Lippincott, 1970).
32. Albert B. Cleage, Jr., *The Black Messiah* (New York: Sheed and Ward, 1968).
33. "Ministers Mobilize Against 'The Death of a Race'," *Ebony* (August 1969):160–164.
34. Robert B. Hill, et al., *Research on the African-American Family: A Holistic Perspective* (Boston: William Monroe Trotter Institute of the University of Massachusetts/Boston), 1989, pp. 65ff.
35. B. Alexander, "The Black Church and Community Empowerment," in R. L. Woodson (ed.), *On The Road to Economic Freedom* (Washington, D. C.: Regnery Gateway, 1987), pp. 45–69, and D. R. Brown and R. W. Walters, *Explor-*

ing the Role of the Black Church in the Community (Washington, D. C.: Institute for Urban Affairs of Howard University, 1979).

36. Hill, *op. cit.*, and Derrick Z. Jackson, "An Urgent Role for Black Church," *Boston Globe* (February 19, 1989), p. A-26.
37. *Ibid.*
38. *Ibid.*, and James H. Cone, *For My People: Black Theology and the Black Church* (Mary Knoll, N.Y.: Orbis Books, 1984).
39. *Ibid.*
40. R. J. Taylor, "Correlates of Religious/Non-Involvement Among Black People," *Review of Religious Research* 30: 2 (1988): 126–139.
41. Harriett McAdoo, *Black Families* (Beverly Hills, Calif.: Sage Publications, 1981).
42. R. L. Taylor et al., "Black Americans' Perceptions of the Socio-Historical Role of the Black Church," *Journal of Black Studies* 18:2 (1987): 123–137.
43. Brown and Walters, *op. cit.*
44. Anthony DePalma, "Catholic Churches Move to Embrace Blacks," *The New York Times* (January 24, 1989), p. B-1.
45. *Ibid.*
46. *Ibid.*
47. *Ibid.*

Chapter
6

Contemporary Issues in Education

*T*he black population has, for more than a century, focused on achieving equality primarily through high educational attainment. This is because blacks strongly believe that education is at the cutting edge of broad social changes as well as the most effective route to upward mobility. To achieve this goal blacks have employed a variety of adaptive techniques and strategies during this period of time including accommodation to segregation, accepting benefits from white philanthropists and philanthropic organizations, aggressive litigation, and militancy. Although the historical underpinnings of present conditions are extremely important, the primary focus of this chapter is on contemporary issues in education affecting the black community.

SEGREGATION IN THE PRE-1954 PERIOD

The education of blacks has always been subjected to the largess of the white population. This principle prevailed through the period of slavery, when sympathetic whites violated restrictive codes against teaching rudimentary educational skills to slaves; religious groups in the North and Middle Atlantic states made efforts to formalize the inclusion of blacks in integrated school systems prior to the Civil War; the Freedmen's Bureau, created in 1865, also had educational goals, and under its auspices federally supported Howard University was established in Washington, D.C.; and, finally, enormous financial and manpower support was provided by philanthropic organizations and individuals as was mentioned in Chapter 4. As a direct consequence of these efforts, coupled with the momentum given to education by "black reconstructionists" (these were largely the black elected officials in Congress and state and local governments), by 1880 more than 700,000 black children were enrolled in school in ten Southern states and almost a million by the turn of the century.[1] Blacks seemed headed toward full incorporation into the educational structure of American society.

Plessy v. Ferguson

Undoubtedly, the most serious blow to this effort was the momentous decision rendered in the *Plessy* v. *Ferguson* Supreme Court case of 1896. Applied first to public transportation, it enunciated the principle of "separate but equal," which had implications extending far beyond public conveyances into the entire institutional structure of American society. This decision justified racial segregation, legitimated educational apartheid and institutional duality, and reestablished the traditions of white supremacy with black inferiority and structured privilege based upon color.

Plessy v. *Ferguson* resulted in a dual system that was indeed separate but manifestly unequal. Inequalities occurred, for example, when new facilities were constructed for white students, while black students inherited the deteriorating schools vacated by whites or remained in dilapidated, often overcrowded, and sometimes widely dispersed schools. Black students often had to walk 15 to 20 miles to schools while buses passed them en route, transporting white pupils to school. Inequities also occurred in the availability of educational resources (for instance, textbooks, supplemental reading materials, libraries, musical instruments, laboratories, and physical education facilities), some of which were transferred to black schools after whites had discarded them or were either outdated, underallocated, or totally absent. The only exceptions to the inequities came when white benefactors and concerned blacks were able to raise monies to acquire educational resources. How many black children learned the rudiments of physics without ever experiencing the pleasures of seeing electricity or mechanics demonstrated in a classroom? How many learned the foundations of chemistry without ever seeing a test tube or a Bunsen burner?

As a further consequence of *Plessy* v. *Ferguson,* the dual educational system often led to separate curricula for blacks and whites constructed to maintain a system of segregation and patterned superordinate-subordinate relations between the races. Hence whites were generally offered a college-preparatory curriculum, whereas blacks were given a less well-developed liberal arts curriculum adequate for their admission to predominantly black colleges or to industrial/vocational education in which blacks were to acquire skills required to serve mainly the white community. Industrial arts education for blacks was rationalized in the North on the basis of notions about the inability of blacks to handle a rigorous academic curriculum or on the futility of such offerings to blacks, since they were unlikely to be admitted to colleges anyway. Often, northern blacks received college-preparatory training only after insisting upon it as an inalienable right. In both the North and the South, less sums of money were expended by school systems on the education of black children. In some southern states the amounts expended per black child varied from one-fifth to one-third of the amount for white children,[2] and worsened to one-seventh before substantial improvements would be forthcoming. Inequalities in educational expenditures would continue, though not with the same magnitude, in the North[3] into the late 1960s and especially in those 30 states containing three-fifths of all black public school students.[4] Financial inequities also extended to the lower salaries paid to black teachers despite the heavier workloads demanded of them. It was not until 1940 in the U. S. Supreme Court case of *Alston* v. *School Board of the City of Norfolk* that black teachers were granted relief from salary inequities, and not until 1954 that salaries of black teachers approached parity with those of white teachers.

Corrective Steps

Philanthropists and philanthropic organizations made the first frontal attacks against educational inequalities and took major steps toward ameliorating the conditions created by *Plessy* v. *Ferguson*. Hence through the efforts of foundations such as that of George Peabody, John F. Slater, Anna T. Jeanes, Julius Rosenwald, Phelps Stokes, Andrew Carnegie, and the Dukes and Du Ponts, education for blacks immeasurably improved. The foundations sponsored teacher-training programs, expanded education into neglected rural areas, constructed school buildings and libraries, and provided educational resources for black secondary schools and colleges, thus creating a significant force of highly trained blacks despite enforced segregation. Their efforts stimulated public school attendance by blacks, so much so that the number of black pupils doubled between 1900 and 1940 (from 1 million to 2,698,901, or 6.4 percent of school-age children) and reached 5 million by 1950. An irreversible trend had been established in black education.[5]

In the five-year period prior to 1954 several states had also taken corrective steps to improve the quality of education, school buildings, and other facilities for black children. The primary purpose of this flurry of activity was to refute the claims argued increasingly before the various courts by the NAACP that segregated schools were universally unequal. White officials hoped to convince the courts that new schools, libraries, and science laboratories demonstrated their commitment to improvements in education for black people, but in an apartheid structure.

The NAACP maintained a relentless pressure to force social change by attacking segregated educational institutions, which were probably the most sacred segregationist institutions within the white community except possibly the family and finance.[6] To test the constitutionality of segregation the NAACP selected cases that were representative not only of geographical regions but also of the persistent problems stemming from the separate-but-equal decision. A brilliant cadre of black lawyers, including Thurgood Marshall, now a justice of the U. S. Supreme Court, and James W. Nabritt, argued these five cases: *Brown* v. *Board of Education of Topeka, Kansas, Briggs* v. *Elliot* (South Carolina), *Davis* v. *County School Board of Prince Edward County* (Virginia), *Gebhart* v. *Belton* (Delaware), and *Bolling* v. *Sharpe* (District of Columbia). Armed with voluminous and convincing evidence from social research, they persuaded the Supreme Court to respond favorably. In the lead case, *Brown* v. *Board of Education of Topeka, Kansas,* the Court decreed that the segregation of black and white children was unconstitutional and that the separate-but-equal doctrine did not apply to education. No other decision of the Supreme Court since *Plessy* v. *Ferguson* has had the impact of the *Brown* case nor carried with it such great potential for both positive change and racial conflict.

Predictably, reactions to the 1954 decision were mixed. The white South was stunned, angered, and somewhat apoplectic. White southerners were psychologically unprepared for this revolutionary decision. They could envision the long-range effects that the destruction of segregation in education would portend for the survival of white privilege and power. In short, the decision had dealt the "southern way of life" a death blow. The white North applauded the outcome of the case not only because it approved the decision but also because the case focused attention specifically in someone else's backyard. The decision was greeted as a momentous victory for and by the black community of the United States. For the first time many black people had a spark of hope that first-class citizenship was a possibility. Not all black people were enthusiastic, however, especially those who had for so long profited by the maintenance of dual structures and parallel institutions. Several persons in this group who were motivated by personal aggrandizement viewed the 1954 Supreme Court decision with almost as much animus as did the rank-and-file southern white person who saw southern culture crumbling. Indeed, Uncle Tom college presidents admonished "their" black students against applying for admission to the bastions of white supremacy—the state universities—for to do so, they cautioned, "would only cause trouble" and, besides, "we have our own colleges right here." They *feared* integration and desegregation because they implied a threat against personal survival.

The white South decided that it would never dismantle white educational privilege and control. It embarked upon a campaign to circumvent the Supreme Court's decision of 1954 and the stipulation to desegregate "with all deliberate speed," which was decreed by the Court in 1955. Hence, immediately after the 1954 decision, the South evolved a number of delaying tactics for noncompliance. Among them were: (1) nullification and interposition in Virginia; (2) massive resistance throughout the South; (3) legal maneuvers; (4) threats against and intimidation of blacks and white sympathizers; (5) resistance to desegregation by white southern congressmen as reflected in the *Southern Manifesto;*[7] (6) violence against integrationists and their property; (7) personal intervention by respected state officials who attempted to block the entry of black children into previously all-white schools; (8) the closing down of schools to prevent desegregation; and (9) the use of state funds to establish private schools for whites.

INTEGRATION AND DESEGREGATION: POST-1954

Because of the success of the nine strategies of noncompliance, integration and desegregation proceeded at an extremely slow pace. For a while it appeared that the more resistant elements in the southern white community had won the struggle to preserve their dual system. By 1957 in Arkansas, for example, where Little Rock had become a symbol of both white resistance and federal intervention, slightly more than 100 of the 100,000 school-age black children were integrated into the 422 school districts. Three years later the situation had not shown measurable improvement. Furthermore, no school integration had commenced in five Deep South states: Alabama, Georgia, Louisiana, Mississippi, and South Carolina. In four states—Arkansas, Florida, Virginia, and North Carolina—mere token integration had occurred—only 500 out of 800,000 black pupils. In 1960 only West Virginia and the District of Columbia could rightly claim that they had achieved integration. Reasonable success occurred in the border states of Oklahoma, Missouri, Maryland, Delaware, and Kentucky. By 1960 only 6 percent of the black children in the South were attending desegregated schools. It was apparent that the doctrine of gradualism that had emanated from the with-all-deliberate-speed principle was a major impediment to change. This is probably why there were approximately 60 cases protesting continuing school segregation pending court resolution at the end of the 1960 school year.

The pendulum began to swing toward increasing desegregation late in 1960. Several factors combined to account for a shift of sentiment: (1) There was national sympathy toward the student sit-in movement and Dr. Martin Luther King's passive-resistance strategies. (2) The nation literally convulsed at the sight of white Southern brutality and raw violence directed at the CORE-sponsored Freedom Riders throughout the South, particularly in Alabama. (3) A sense of moral outrage arose against the ugly faces of bigotry expressed by Southern whites with each effort to desegregate a school. (4) In Washington, D. C., there was a growing concern with the nation's image abroad, especially in the newly independent African states and in Europe. (5) Finally, the election of President John F. Kennedy, whose liberalism or sympathy was taken for granted, created a high degree of optimism among blacks and their supporters. These factors accelerated the pace of the civil rights movement, which began, in turn, a continuing process of profound social change.

The U. S. Commission on Civil Rights, established in 1957, compiled massive data on school desegregation, school by school, city by city, district by district, and state by state. The work of the commission, the accelerated pressure of the civil rights movement, a Justice Department oriented toward the enforcement of federal laws, and the death of President Kennedy created an atmosphere in which Congress seemed to have no choice but to enact the strong Civil Rights Act in 1964. This act, along with the Elementary and Secondary Schools Act of 1965, began to undermine the segregation forces and to erode resistance to compliance with the law. Congress had empowered the Office of Education of the Department of Health, Education, and Welfare to cut off funds from any school that refused to comply with desegregation regulations. Several school districts, faced with the dilemma of choosing between desegregation or reduced funds for segregated school programs opted for the former. Thus by 1968 there was substantial movement toward compliance with desegregation mandates. Still, more than two-thirds (68 percent) of black children were attending all-black schools in 11 Deep South states, and 12.3 percent of the black children (57.7 percent) were attending schools that were 80 percent or more black. Politicians who did not seem to favor desegregation would assert in 1970, however, that 97 percent of the *school districts* were desegregated. This was a misleading statement based on a curious fact: For a school district to be classified as desegregated, only one black student need be enrolled. Therefore, statistics on district desegregation are relatively meaningless when they do not tell us the proportion of black pupils and white pupils who are regularly attending school with each other. Nevertheless, one cannot deny that considerable school desegregation resulted in the 1960s, particularly in the South. By the same token, the South was the region in which hardened resistance to school desegregation was widespread. For instance, a common strategy employed by staunch segregationists was the establishment of "Christian schools" or academies for whites only. Approximately 3,500 segregated academies were established in the South between the 1954 *Brown* decision and 1976. Although many parents of children enrolled in the segregated Christian schools were fundamentalists who believed that the public school systems were "hostile to their religious beliefs," the majority were established to circumvent school desegregation.[8] The number of such schools as well as other private schools mushroomed during the post-1954 period. By 1980 the National Center for Education Statistics reported that there were 16,792 private elementary schools and 5,678 private high schools throughout the United States. Not all these institutions were established as a direct response to school desegregation; however, it is reasonable to assume that the majority of the religious or church schools established in certain sections of the country and in cities under serious court orders to desegregate public schools were spawned by desegregation mandates.[9]

In fact, the growth of fundamentalist Christian schools since 1954 has been phenomenal. For example, in the decade between 1970 and 1980, the Middle Atlantic and southern states had a 313.5 percent growth in non-Catholic religious schools. In the West, the increase was by 99 percent; in the North-Central–Midwest region, by 49.1 percent, and in the Northeast, these schools increased by 47.2 percent during the decade 1970–1980.[10] Pupil enrollment in religious schools was substantially greater in certain states than in others. For instance, in Florida, the number of pupils enrolled in such schools increased from 22,157 in 1970 to 130,720 in 1980. In Mississippi, the number rose from 10,903 in 1970 to 38,774; in Georgia, from 3,763 in 1970 to 69,208 in 1980; and in North Carolina, from 4,378 in 1970 to 48,755 in 1980. Religious school enrollments in non-Catholic schools more than doubled in Pennsylvania during the same period, rising from 21,569 in 1970 to 47,713 in 1980. In California the number of pupils climbed dramatically from 59,993 in 1970 to 106,830 in 1980. A similar trend was noted in Michigan where the number of pupils rose from 39,590 to 65,590 between 1970 and 1980.[11]

As a result of the continued resistance to school desegregation and the process of resegregation that had already begun in several communities, in 1972, many black students were still attending essentially segregated schools throughout the United States. For example, in 1972, the U.S. Commission on Civil Rights data showed that black pupils comprised 15.2 percent of all school children in continental United States. Of the 6.8 million black pupils, 36.3 percent were in schools that were from 0–49.9 percent minority, 18.5 percent were in schools that were 50–79.9 percent minority, and almost half (45.2 percent) were in schools that were 80–100 percent minority. By that date, most of the desegregation had occurred, in fact, in 11 southern states. In those states, for instance, 29.9 percent of all black pupils were in schools that were from 80–100 percent minority, compared to 55.9 percent in the North and West, and 59.8 percent of black pupils enrolled in schools with that composition in the six border states and the District of Columbia. Slightly less than one-half (46.3 percent) of black students in the South were enrolled in schools that were from 0–49.9 percent minority.[12]

By the mid-1960s the battle over public school integration and desegregation began to shift to the northern and western states as did the civil rights movement in general. The U.S. Supreme Court had already decided on a number of cases that would establish a legal framework for implementing court-ordered desegregation and which struck down several unconstitutional measures designed to circumvent or delay the process of desegregation. In *U.S.* v. *Jefferson County Board of Education,* 372, F. 2d 836, 847 5th Cir. (1966), the Court stated that "the only school desegregation plan that meets constitutional standards is one that works."[13] So-called "freedom-of-choice" plans, still favored by such groups as the National Association of Neighborhood Schools and some black parents in Boston, were rejected by the U.S. Supreme Court in *Green* v. *County School Board,* 391 US. 430 (1968). In that decision, the Court articulated the principle of "an affirmative duty to desegregate public schools" and that the school board should take whatever steps necessary to eliminate racial discrimination. In 1969, in *Alexander* v. *Holmes County Board of Education,* 396 U. D. (1969), the U.S. Supreme Court reminded the nation that the "with all deliberate speed" mandate enunciated in 1955 was no longer "constitutionally permissible"; therefore, school districts had an obligation to eliminate dual school systems at once.[14]

Busing as a tool for the elimination of all "vestiges of State-imposed segregation" from the public schools was sanctioned by the U.S. Supreme Court in *Swann* v. *Charlotte-Mecklenburg Board of Education,* 402 U. S. 1 (1971). The decision also supported the use of "mathematical ratios as starting points in shaping remedies" and in determining pupil assignments by race to public schools.[15] Because of the structure of the public school system in the Charlotte-Mecklenburg district (North Carolina), cross-district busing (metropolitanism) was necessary to accomplish school desegregation.

Armed with such legal precedents, many black parents outside the South, whose children confronted public school segregation, pressured northern and western school boards to terminate discriminatory practices. As the pressures mounted in the North and West, a pattern of resistance not indistinguishable from that observed in the South of the 1960s was frequent. Racial unrest and urban riots sometimes accompanied these efforts as whites in the North and West resisted school desegregation. Black parents and their supporters, many from white communities, understood that de jure segregation was illegal but little had been done in nonsouthern areas to attack the massive problems of de facto segregated schools found in the nonsouthern areas.

The major condition that fostered de facto segregation in the North and West was in the housing distribution of these areas. Housing in the North and West was considerably more segregated than generally thought by residents of other regions of the nation. As a result of a long tradition of establishing neighborhood areas according to race and ethnicity, almost all of the larger cities outside the South had clearly defined black and white areas. Many of these areas were "off-limits" to other races. The migration and concentration of blacks in the inner cities of the United States and accelerated flight of the white population to the suburban rings around the cities had created enormous problems of racial separateness in these communities. Investigations into the conditions of inner city schools point to the similarities between southern-style de jure segregation and northern-style de facto segregation—black and white pupils were still separate and unequal. These conditions also reveal the extent to which resegregation has occurred, as well as an explanation for the steady resistance to school desegregation evidenced in many northern communities in the 1970s and 1980s—three decades after the *Brown* decision.

DYSFUNCTIONAL CONSEQUENCES OF DESEGREGATION

Resegregation

One of the major dysfunctions of desegregation and of the failure to eradicate the original patterns of segregation is that of school resegregation; that is, segregation in schools or districts following their desegregation. Although the immigration and outmigration patterns in urban communities account for much resegregation, they are not totally responsible. But the inescapable conclusion is that the larger urban communities of the United States are becoming increasingly black and poor. That school systems, in many school districts, have achieved a black majority may be illustrated by the following examples: (1) In 1958 Atlanta, Georgia, operated a segregated school system in which 70 percent of the school children were white and 30 percent were black. By 1978 Atlanta had some 74,300 school children, 89 percent of whom were black and only 10 percent were white. (2) In Baltimore, Maryland, in 1970, about two-thirds (67 percent) of public school children were nonwhite and 33 percent were white. By 1978 the proportion of nonwhite pupils had climbed to 76 percent while white student enrollment declined to 24 percent of the 153,263 city pupils. (3) In 1970, of the 577,679 pupils enrolled in public schools in Chicago, 54.8 percent were black, 34.7 percent were white, and 8.9 percent were Hispanics. By 1983 blacks composed 60.1 percent, Hispanics, 20.4 percent, and whites 17 percent of the city's public schools. However, in Chicago in 1983, about 350 of the city's 597 schools had an enrollment that was 70 percent minority or greater and many schools were either all minority or all white. (4) Other large city school systems that had a majority of black pupils by 1983 included Cleveland (about 60 percent black); St. Louis (80 percent black); Detroit (about 83 percent black); Philadelphia (about 64 percent black); and many others.[16] As a general rule, the nearby suburban schools are overwhelmingly white student bodies.

Often where schools have desegregated, a pattern of *within school resegregation* was especially observed during the 1960s and 1970s. For example, some schools employed the technique of ability grouping of students, resulting in the separation of white students from black students. Portable classrooms were also used to segregate students; some students were segregated in libraries, on playgrounds, and in cafeterias. Segregation may still be assured by feeder patterns and controlled transfer policies. In the case of feeder patterns, movement from grade schools to junior high schools is devised so that white students enter certain schools that will remain predominantly white and black students enter schools destined to remain exclusively black.

Several cities that have a black majority student body also have black chief administrators of the school systems. Of the approximately 17,500 public school districts in the nation, about 50 of them are headed by black superintendents. Fifteen of the black superintendents in 1983 were women. Black women headed such school systems as those in Chicago (Ruth Love),* Philadelphia (Constance Clayton), Washington, D.C. (Floretta McKenzie), and Plainfield, New Jersey (Greta Shepard).[17] School systems headed by blacks are diverse in size and student body composition.

Displacements

In many instances displacements, demotions, and loss of jobs by black teachers occurred as a consequence of desegregation. In June 1973 the National Urban League, the National Education Association, the Southern Regional Council, and the Southern Center for Studies in Public Policy sent representatives to Atlanta for a special conference on employment displacement that resulted from school desegregation. They reported that, in the 17 southern and border states, approximately 6,000 black teachers and principals lost their jobs as a result of school mergers. Several thousand more were demoted, and the administrators in these states either hired or transferred approximately 25,000 white educators for positions that blacks should have filled. This represented a loss of about a quarter of a billion dollars in salaries for the black community.[18]

The major educational associations of the United States have also reported from time to time cases of demotion of black school principals to assistant principals—and of their being replaced by less competent white persons at desegregated schools. In some instances of demotion, black principals were given heavy teaching assignments, janitorial duties, and no administrative responsibilities. Early in the desegregation period, especially in the late 1950s and early 1960s, the firing of black teachers and the failure of schools to renew their contracts were common. Funds for compensatory educational programs for black children were diverted to activities other than the original purposes for which the funds were intended.

Unfair discriminatory practices in teacher assignments are still prevalent in many areas of the North. Urban black schools still have a disproportionately high number of less well prepared and less experienced teachers. A frequent pattern is to assign the more experienced and often better prepared white and black teachers to the more prestigious and predominantly white schools. The less well-prepared white teachers are sent to the inner cities, often under the inducement of receiving "combat pay"—that is, extra money incentives—for teaching in ghetto schools. In many inner-city schools, many teachers do not live in the neighborhood and thus have little or no appreciation of the types of problems encountered by students whose major preoccupations are with day-to-day survival. Many are insensitive to cultural differences in their students based upon social class struc-

---

*Ruth Love was subsequently replaced by a black male.

ture and different opportunity patterns. This insensitivity is usually reflected in their belief systems concerning the educability of the students.
Many, for instance, communicate to their students, especially to black
students, negative perceptions of the students' ability to learn, and these
students, sensing this, respond by not demonstrating evidence of having
learned.[19] This kind of teacher insensitivity is not confined to the inner-
city schools. It is also found among other types of authority figures, including some police officers and social workers. Given the already deeply
ingrained problems of identity crisis resulting from inequalities, we cannot fail to note how the negative attitudes that some teachers communicate to some of their students accelerate the psychological damages suffered by so many inner-city students.

During 1973 and 1974, several cities made serious efforts to alter the
distribution pattern of teachers in their public school systems so as to
create more realistic ratios of black and white teachers in the schools.
Among them is New Orleans, a city that a decade earlier had achieved a
national reputation because of its resistance to desegregating the McDo-
nough 19 and William Frantz schools. On July 10, 1972, the New Orleans
school board adopted a policy of assigning teachers in such a way that each
school in the district is 50 percent black and 50 percent white, with a 10
percent variance at the elementary level and a 5 percent tolerance at the
high school level. The order became effective as of that date, and principals and other administrators were to proceed to implement the new
policy in time for that fall's classes.[20]

In the New Orleans system 63 percent of the elementary school teachers and 51 percent of the high school teachers were black when the
"50–50" policy was promulgated. That is, 37 percent of the elementary
school teachers and 49 percent of the high school teachers were white. In
order to implement the 50–50 policy, 831 teachers (501 black and 330
white) were transferred. There were no mass resignations. In fact, of the
49 teachers who resigned subsequent to the mandate, only a handful did
so to avoid faculty desegregation. One should not infer from this that the
50–50 policy and the transfer of more than 800 teachers was greeted with
uniform enthusiasm. Some teachers complained about having to ride
across the Mississippi River to Algiers; others wanted to remain in the most
prestigious and progressive schools. Others had trepidations about working under the supervision of black principals because of their reputation
for "being harder on teachers," and some feared attending school functions in certain high-crime areas after school hours.[21] Nevertheless, the
plan went into effect as ordered and without major or serious consequences during its first year of operation. And it was carried out by a firm
school board that had already warned teachers either to accept assignments or leave the system.

Cities still vary considerably with respect to which black teachers and
administrators are employed in the school system. For instance, according
to the most recent report from the U.S. Commission on Civil Rights on this

subject, approximately 75 percent of the 1450 teachers in the Atlanta school system were black and 25 percent white. Twenty-five of 35 administrative positions were held by blacks and 10 by whites. Between 1970 and 1978, the composition of the school board changed from a 7–3 white majority to a 5–4 black majority. In Baltimore, 63 percent of the teaching staff and 63 percent of the school-based administrative staff were nonwhite, and whites had a 5–4 majority on the school board.[22]

Department of Implementation 1975 data from the Boston school system showed that in that year only 620 (12 percent) of the system's 5443 public school teachers were black and 86 percent were white. As white pupils fled the public school system either to all-white academies, parochial schools, or nearby suburban schools, and as the demand for more minorities in the teaching force increased, the racial composition of the teaching force changed. By 1989, the percentage of white teachers dropped to 66 (2,904 out of 4,385) while the percentage of blacks doubled to 24 and the percentage of "other minorities" in the teaching force rose from two (2) to 10 between 1975 and 1989.[23] During that period, blacks served, at varying times, as superintendent of schools and as chair of the Boston School Committee—significant changes in a city that was gripped by racial turmoil following court-ordered school desegregation during the mid-1970s. The total teaching force was reduced substantially by cutbacks resulting from the enactment of Proposition 2½ in 1981. Because of court rulings, black teachers, the last hired, were not required to bear most of the burden of teacher layoffs resulting from the tax relief measure.[24]

Although blacks and Hispanics comprise over 80 percent of all pupils enrolled in Chicago's public schools, about 61.5 percent of the administrators and 52 percent of the city's teachers are white. About 35 percent of the administrators and 42 percent of the teachers are black. Further, Chicago now has employed a black as school superintendent. By contrast, a majority of the public school teachers and a majority of the 13 members of the central board of education in Detroit are black. In Little Rock, Arkansas, the scene of one of the most widely publicized efforts to block school desegregation during the 1950s, slightly less than one-fourth (23 percent) of the administrative staff of the school system and 31 percent of its teachers are black. However, in Dade County (Miami) Florida, where blacks and Hispanics comprise 60 percent of pupil enrollment, whites hold about 64 percent of the teaching jobs and 77.7 percent of the administrative positions.[25] Although these city-wide statistics do not reveal the overall impact of desegregation on blacks, they do show that even in cities in which black pupils constitute the majority of enrollees, the white population, often suburban residents, still control a significant proportion, if not always a majority, of the teaching and administrative positions in these systems. Throughout the South and border states, many blacks did, in fact, lose positions as a result of the dismantling of the dual system of education.

It is estimated that black pupils represent approximately 16 percent of all public school enrollees; that black and other minority pupils will constitute more than half of all public school pupils by the year 2000. At precisely the moment that the racial composition of the nation's public school system is rapidly changing from white to black, Hispanic, and Asian, the proportion of teachers from minority groups is declining sharply. Less than 10 percent of the public school teaching force is represented by minority groups (i.e., blacks, 6.9 percent; others about 3 percent). By the year 2000, unless a major turnabout is made in the recruitment of more minorities into the teaching profession and a reduction in the proportion who are unsuccessful in passing teaching competency examinations as well as a reduction in the number who voluntarily leave the profession because of low salaries, problems of discipline, and disillusionment with the profession itself, that percent will drop precipitously to less than five percent.[26]

Drop-outs and Suspensions

A major allegation against school administrators in desegregated schools is that the suspension rate (sometimes referred to as "push outs") among blacks is considerably higher than for white pupils. The presumption is that a disproportionate number of these students are victims of discrimination by white administrators or by blacks who bend too far to accommodate white pupils and teachers. Although it is difficult to obtain conclusive national data on this subject, two reports are illuminating. First, a report by the U. S. Commission on Civil Rights does suggest that, in many cities across the nation, black pupils do account for a disproportionate share of school suspensions. For instance, black students accounted for 57.5 percent of all suspensions in Baton Rouge, Louisiana; 85 percent in Little Rock, Arkansas; 53.1 percent in Kansas City, Kansas; more than 50 percent in Dade County (Miami), Florida; 43.9 percent in Los Angeles (where Hispanics represented another 32.1 percent of all suspensions); and 78 percent in Pittsburgh.[27] A second and more recent study was conducted by the National Coalition of Advocates for Students and issued in 1988. This study sampled some 3,378 of the nation's 16,000 school districts. It revealed that black pupils are more than twice as likely as white pupils to be suspended. While white pupils compose 70 percent of the school enrollment nationwide, they account for 59 percent of the suspensions. By contrast, black pupils constitute 16 percent of the nation's public school enrollment but make up 30 percent of all suspensions.[28]

The problems generated by school suspensions are continuous and seem to follow suspended students, more often than not regarded as "troublemakers," into junior and senior high schools. For example, students suspended in elementary school are five to thirteen times more likely to be either suspended again, to fail, or to be absent from school. If the suspension occurs during a middle or junior high school year, that student is two or three times more likely to be suspended again, has more than a 50 percent chance of failing, and a 29 percent chance of actual expulsion.

This study reported inordinate discrepancies in suspension rates between black and white pupils in Ohio, Minnesota, Pennsylvania, Missouri, Wisconsin, Nebraska, Kansas, California, Iowa, and Mississippi.[29]

A related problem is the finding that nationwide black pupils are twice as likely to be physically punished or disciplined by school authorities and labeled mentally retarded and far less likely to be placed in classes for the gifted. With respect to corporal punishment, 5.2 percent of black students, compared to 2.28 percent of white students and 2.05 percent of Hispanic pupils, received corporal punishment. While less than 1 percent (0.87%) of all white pupils and less than 1 percent (0.56%) of Hispanic students were placed in "educable mentally retarded" classes, 2.3 percent of all black students receive that placement. On the other hand, 5.5 percent of white students but only 2.44 percent of black students and 2.41 percent of Hispanic students are placed in classes for the gifted. Blacks are significantly more likely to be placed in classes labeled "educably mentally retarded" in schools located in Alabama, Arkansas, South Carolina, North Carolina, Mississippi, Oklahoma, Michigan, Indiana, Nebrasks, and Iowa.[30]

The National Coalition of Advocates for Students argues that teachers seem unable to "handle students who are different in . . . any way," and that there is a tendency to overreact to black students, especially black males. This inability is reflected in the fact that four-fifths (80 percent) of all disciplinary actions resulting in corporal punishment and seven of every ten (70 percent) of all suspensions are meted out to male pupils.[31] Inability to handle black and other minority students or to create a successful and stimulating learning environment will continue to generate high drop-out rates, lack of preparation for college, and lack of training for a workforce that demands higher and higher order skills for normal functioning. As the Coalition suggests, school problems and the profound difficulty encountered in job attainment loom large in the escalating crime rate among black males. These problems can be remedied in part through stronger early intervention programs such as Head Start, attacking the problems in school systems that generate discrepancies between blacks, Hispanics, and whites in suspensions and class placements, and eliminating economic disabilities encountered by the families of "at risk" students.[32] It also seems evident that there is a compelling urgency to come to terms with attitudinal problems of some teachers and administrators that render them less likely to resolve behavioral problems that some pupils bring into the school as well as attitudinal constructs that make them more inclined to label minority students as "troublemakers" or educably mentally retarded or in need of "special education."

School Environment and Self-Esteem

The school environment is not always a rewarding experience for black pupils. There is a growing body of evidence reported in research by Epps,[33] Hare,[34] and others[35] to show that the high sense of self-esteem that black pupils bring from their homes to the schools is often lowered dramatically by negative within-school experiences. Unsatisfactory conditions in the schools are ultimately reflected in performance on tests and in the decision of blacks to even remain to complete a high school education. Although many teachers assigned to inner-city schools are indeed highly skilled and make gallant attempts, often quite successfully, to motivate black students, others do not.

Epps maintains that teachers "perceive minority students differently than they perceive white students."[36] Frequently, black and other minority students, irrespective of family background and income level, may be perceived as "problem" children with "educational deficits" and are, therefore, less educable than white students. Hare[37] and Lavin[38] raise the possibility of a connection between the grading practices of some teachers that result in lower course grades for black and other minority students, and the perceived social characteristics of pupils (e.g., sex and social class). Assessments of their performance, therefore, are not objective. In 1940, black students were still more likely to be assigned to "vocational and commercial tracks" as well as to slower academic tracks while middle- and upper-class youngsters, especially white pupils, are placed in college preparatory curricula and the faster academic tracks.[39] As a result of what Hare calls "structured educational failure," and an uncaring school environment, the relatively high sense of esteem brought from the home often collapses within the school itself. Consequently, all too many black students develop self-doubts about their capacity to perform at high educational levels. Parents, concerned teachers, and other role models sometimes find it difficult to undo the damage done to students with high potential by a discouraging school situation.

POSITIVE ASPECTS OF INTEGRATION

In order to understand the goals of integration we must make a critical distinction between terms, especially since the concepts integration and desegregation are often used interchangeably. Actually, the two terms are not synonymous. *Desegregation* is the removal from the social structure of legal and social barriers based upon racial and ethnic discrimination against a group. Implicit in desegregation is the conscious and systematic elimination of segregation in the society and the simultaneous realization of constitutional entitlements of citizenship.[40] This is basically a structural process and may or may not be accompanied by changes in the subjective perceptions or attitudes of individuals. *Integration* is, on the other hand, according to Clark, subjective and refers to attitudinal change in the hearts and minds of men and women.[41] It suggests the elimination of the sociopsychological barriers of interracial contact such as stereotypes, fears, and prejudices.

Desegregation, it was believed, would eradicate institutionalized segregation. The concern was not with changing the hearts and minds of segregationists; rather, it was an effort to respect the constitutional prerogatives of dispossessed people and assure them legal protection and the preservation of their rights. An even broader extension of the implications of desegregation was the optimistic belief in the possibility that children of different racial and ethnic characteristics would, at a more personal and subjective level, rise above the prejudices of their parents and forebears.

Advocates of integration maintain, however, that it is only through an integrated society that people can learn to respect one another's differences and appreciate the vitality of diversity. Through integration as a process, they believe, people come to share understandings and learn firsthand of cultural variation without denigrating or disparaging these differences. Integration, then, would involve the systematic elimination of racial animosity and ethnic prejudice as individuals come to understand how stereotypes and false assumptions about each other are truly inapplicable. Thus the path toward cultural, structural, civic, and other dimensions of assimilation would be more easily traversed if desired. In a word, this is the orthodox American goal—the merging of all parts into an integrated whole that is by definition better than the sum of its parts. As we will see in Chapter 13, this view has come under serious challenge by those who question the very legitimacy of the goal, let alone the improbability of achieving an integrated society. Nevertheless, the quest for integration has persisted as the major underpinning of the black struggle in America, which also stresses cultural pluralism and separatism as alternatives to assimilation. These are predictable responses to a process that has always been one way—from black to white.

But, more recently, integration has even broader implications. At issue is not only the question of equality of opportunity but also the actual realization of that opportunity. Why? Blacks and whites of liberal persuasion have come to realize that minority group individuals can share the same opportunity as whites to education and that some who may be much better prepared for jobs than others are *never* hired; they may not be promoted, and they may not be retained once they are hired. In a truly integrated society, the promise of opportunity is expanded into the achievement of results. There would be minority group members in high administrative positions of the school system—school superintendents, heads of boards of education, school principals of desegregated schools, or holders of other positions that involve invaluable contributions to the decision-making process. Presidents, chancellors, deans, and departmental chairpersons of desegregated institutions of higher learning would be black or of other racial or ethnic origins. As a result, black schoolchildren would be able to see them as role models and white schoolchildren would be able to begin the process of destroying false images and negative stereotypes of minority group members. The psychological impairments created by inferior status and the problems of limited achievement motivation could be gradually ameliorated. It is assumed, of course, that the system would treat minorities *and* majorities on the basis of objective opportunities for equal training and the achievement of job experience.

What, then, have been the accomplishments since the major efforts toward desegregation were initiated? With 1965 as a benchmark, a year after the Civil Rights Act, which used the promise of cutting off funds as a lever to promote compliance, we can point to a number of significant though not always dramatic changes and achievements. There have been noticeable improvements in the number of black adults enrolled in school. The number of black children between the ages of 3 and 4 attending nursery and kindergarten schools more than tripled between 1965 and 1981 as it rose from 11.8 percent in 1965 to 36.7 in 1981. The rate of black pupils between the ages of 5 and 17 rose throughout a 21-year period, 1960–1981. More than 95 percent of all black students in these age cohorts, with the exception of ages 16 and 17 in which 91 percent were in school, were matriculated in 1981. In fact, among 16- and 17-year-olds, the proportion of black pupils within that age cohort actually enrolled was slightly higher than that for whites in the same age group. In every age cohort employed by the Bureau of the Census, the proportion of blacks enrolled in school increased between 1960 and 1981.[42]

By 1986, the last year for which national data are available, 38.2 percent of black 3- to 4-year-olds, compared to 39.1 percent of white 3- to 4-year-olds were enrolled in nursery school. White and black 5- and 6-year-olds as well as those in the 7–13 age cohort approximated each other in the percentages enrolled in school. For instance, 95.2 percent of black and 95.3 percent of white 5- to 6-year-olds were enrolled in school. Similarly, 99.4 percent of black and 99.2 percent of white 7- to 13-year-olds were enrolled in schools. However, in the late teen years, racial discrepancies in school enrollment become significant and reflect racial differences in school drop-out and push-out rates. Among 16- to 17-year-olds, 93.2 percent of black pupils, compared to 92 percent of white pupils, are in school. However, in the 18–19 age cohort, 54.8 percent of white teenagers, compared to 49.4 percent of black teenagers, were still in school.[43] Even with these disparities, the proportions of both racial groups remaining in school represent significant improvements over their 1970 levels.

Despite the successes in enrollment, however, black children have an enormously high drop-out rate from high school. In some cities, it is estimated that almost half of all black youngsters drop out before completion of their senior high school years. Nationally, as shown in Table 6.1, the drop-out rate continued to decline for black and white students between 1970 and 1986. However, the 4.7 percent drop-out rate for black 16- and 17-year-olds is significantly higher than the 6.5 percent rate reported for white persons in the same age cohort. The gap between whites and blacks widens in the 18–21 and 22–24 age cohorts. As a result, at any level shown in Table 6.1, it is evident that black youngsters leave high school at a

Table 6.1 HIGH SCHOOL DROP-OUTS 14 TO 24 YEARS OLD, BY AGE AND RACE: 1970–1986

Age and race	Number of drop-outs (1,000)								Percent of population				
	1970	1975	1980	1982	1983	1984	1985	1986	1970	1980	1985	1986
Total drop-outs[a, b]	4,670	4,974	5,212	5,160	5,060	4,784	4,456	4,318	12.2	12.0	10.6	10.5
16–17 years	617	715	709	556	494	485	505	455	8.0	8.8	7.0	6.1
18–21 years	2,138	2,557	2,578	2,646	2,419	2,297	2,095	1,961	16.4	15.8	14.1	13.6
22–24 years	1,770	1,553	1,798	1,854	1,991	1,845	1,724	1,726	18.7	15.2	14.1	14.3
White[b]	3,577	3,861	4,169	4,080	3,950	3,831	3,583	3,497	10.8	11.3	10.3	10.3
16–17 years	485	594	619	478	424	421	424	394	7.3	9.2	7.1	6.5
18–21 years	1,618	1,980	2,032	2,056	1,897	1,852	1,678	1,566	14.3	14.7	13.6	13.1
22–24 years	1,356	1,169	1,416	1,467	1,531	1,429	1,372	1,408	16.3	14.0	13.3	13.9
Black[b]	1,047	1,024	934	937	913	789	748	707	22.2	16.0	12.6	12.0
16–17 years	125	115	80	66	62	55	70	52	12.8	6.9	6.5	4.7
18–21 years	500	540	486	519	436	373	376	345	30.5	23.0	17.5	16.5
22–24 years	397	337	346	332	396	339	279	272	37.8	24.0	17.8	17.3

[a]Includes other race groups not shown separately.

[b]Includes persons 14–15 years, not shown separately.

Source: U.S. Bureau of the Census, *Current Population Reports,* series P-20 No. 409 and earlier reports and unpublished data. (As of October; see headnote, table 243, for definition of drop-outs)

higher rate than white pupils. As pointed out in Chapter 2, dropping out of high school has untoward effects on black youth, especially in terms of their ability to obtain gainful employment. Until recently, a substantial portion of high school drop-outs could enlist in the military. That option is no longer available to them since the military sets as a minimum educational requirement for enlistment the completion of a high school education.

Black student performance on the Scholastic Aptitude Test (SAT) took a significant upswing in the late 1970s and 1980s. For a sixteen-year period, dating from the mid-1960s, SAT scores for the nation's college-bound seniors, irrespective of race, declined. A panel of experts, assembled by the College Entrance Examination Board, attributed test score declines to such factors as a reduction in the quality of schooling in the nation's schools, a lack of homework, too much time spent watching television, grade inflation, and home factors. Beginning in 1982, when the College Board made available test score data that identified racial groupings and their performance, SAT scores began a slow but steady increase. At that time, all the increases, verbal and on the math component, were attributable to the rise in scores registered by black and other minorities.[44]

Willie took a different view about the decline in SAT scores. He attributed this downturn largely to an increase in the number of students taking the tests. He argued that more students with extreme variations in the quality of schooling would tend to depress overall performance on such standardized tests as the SAT.[45] This improvement in test performance among blacks and other minorities may reflect exposure to a better quality of schooling. It may also suggest that they have become much more familiar with the method of taking standardized tests; in effect, they have become more "test-wise" and their "test-readiness" has improved. Nevertheless, attention must be given to the fact that, regardless of racial considerations, performance on the SAT is highly correlated with income levels. Generally, the higher the income, the higher the mean SAT score. Even though some pupils from low-income families do outscore some pupils from higher income levels, advantages of income are more often reflected in higher test scores. When tests are primary determinants of admission, educational opportunities for low-income students may be seriously curtailed. But, if tests are used diagnostically and poor scorers are given an opportunity to demonstrate strengths not revealed by tests, many such students perform well in college. Opponents to testing maintain that disregard for such facts further hardens class distinctions and politicizes testing.

Without question, the level of educational attainment among black Americans has steadily increased since the push for school desegregation accelerated. The median years of educational attainment for blacks 25 years or older rose from 9.8 in 1970 to 12.4 in 1987. During the same period, the median years of schooling among whites increased from 12.1 to 12.7 years.[46] Another measure of educational attainment is the degree to which the proportion of the population has completed less than five years of schooling. As shown in Table 6.2, the percent of blacks who had received only five years of schooling or less dropped dramatically from 14.6 percent in 1970 to 5.0 percent in 1987. The decline for the white population was from 4.5 percent in 1970 to 2.0 percent in 1987 while that for Hispanics fell from 19.5 percent in 1970 to 11.9 percent in 1987. By 1987, blacks almost approximated whites in the percentages with less than five years of schooling for individuals between the ages of 25–34 and 35–44. It is only among the elderly population (persons age 65 and older) that blacks are about five times more likely to have received only five years of schooling or less (Table 6.2).

Similar observations may be made with respect to high school completion rates. The American Council on Education's examination of a decade of data on high school completion by race revealed that the high school graduation gap between blacks and whites is closing. However, whites continue to be more successful in completing high school than either blacks or Hispanics. Between 1976 and 1986, for instance, the completion rate for black 18- to 24-year-olds rose from 67.5 percent to 76.4 percent. By contrast, the high school completion rates for white 18- to 24-year-olds rose from 79.8 in 1976 to 83.1 percent in 1986 while that for same-age Hispanics rose only from 55.6 percent to 59.9 percent.[47]

Different age cohorts vary dramatically with respect to the degree to which a high school education is completed (Table 6.3). Among 18- to 19-year-olds, the percent of blacks who had completed high school rose from 55.8 in 1974 to 64.9; for white persons of the same age, the increase was only modest or from 76.2 percent in 1974 to 76.6 percent in 1986. The gain for Hispanics was from 48.9 percent to 54.7 percent over the same period and for the same age group. It is only in the 20- to 24-year-old group that blacks show a significant narrowing of the gap between themselves and white persons in high school completion rates. In 1974, the gap was by 13.1 percentage points between whites (85.6 percent completion rate) and blacks (72.5 percent completion rate). Hispanic 20- to 24-year-olds lagged significantly behind both black and whites of the same age. Only 59 percent had completed high school in 1974 and the rise to 61.6 percent by 1986 was less than dramatic (Table 6.4).

ILLITERACY: BLACK AND WHITE

One of the overall consequences of the advances in formal schooling achieved by black Americans since the *Brown* decision has been a decline in the rate of illiteracy. Between 1959 and 1979, the rate of illiteracy among blacks between the ages of 14 and 24 dropped from 1.2 percent to 0.2 percent. The decline for the white population was from 0.5 percent in 1959 to 0.2 percent in 1979. In the 25–44 age group, the illiteracy rate for blacks in 1959 was 5.1 percent compared to 0.8 percent for whites. In

Table 6.2 PERCENT OF POPULATION WITH LESS THAN 5 YEARS OF SCHOOL AND WITH 4 YEARS OF HIGH SCHOOL OR MORE, BY AGE, RACE, AND HISPANIC ORIGIN: 1970–1987

(Persons 25 years old and over, as of April 1970 and 1980, and March 1975 and 1987)

Race and Hispanic origin	Less than 5 years of school								4 years of high school or more							
					1987								1987			
	1970	1975	1980	Total	25-34 yr	35-44 yr	45-64 yr	65 yr and over	1970	1975	1980	Total	25-34 yr	35-44 yr	45-64 yr	65 yr and over
All races[a]	5.5	4.2	3.6	2.4	.9	1.1	2.6	6.1	52.3	62.5	66.5	75.6	86.5	85.9	72.8	51.2
White	4.5	3.3	2.6	2.0	.9	1.1	2.1	4.6	54.5	64.6	68.8	77.0	87.2	87.1	75.1	53.7
Black	14.6	12.3	8.2	5.0	.6	.8	5.9	19.6	31.4	42.5	51.2	63.4	81.7	76.2	52.4	24.7
Hispanic[b]	19.5	18.5	15.5	11.9	5.6	8.9	17.0	31.2	32.1	37.9	44.0	50.9	60.3	57.4	41.9	20.8
Mexican	28.5	24.6	20.1	15.4	7.7	12.1	21.7	42.4	24.2	31.0	37.6	44.8	54.0	51.2	33.9	15.4
Puerto Rican	20.5	17.4	14.1	10.3	2.2	5.6	22.5	29.5	23.4	28.7	40.1	53.8	68.4	58.8	36.1	19.4
Cuban	8.2	7.3	7.3	6.1	1.2	1.6	8.6	12.2	43.9	51.7	55.3	61.6	83.1	68.1	56.5	36.9
Other[c]	8.8	7.6	8.3	5.7	2.3	4.8	7.0	17.5	44.9	58.0	57.4	61.5	68.8	69.2	56.8	25.6

[a] Includes races not shown separately.

[b] Hispanic persons may be of any race.

[c] Includes Central or South American and other Hispanic origin.

Source: U.S. Bureau of the Census. Census of Population. 1970 vols. I and II. 1980 Census of Population. Vol. I. Chapter C. Current Population Reports. series P-20. NO. 416, and unpublished data.

Table 6.3   HIGH SCHOOL COMPLETION OF PERSONS AGED 18–19 AND 20–24, BY RACE AND HISPANIC ORIGIN: 1974–1986

Year	Age 18 to 19				Age 20 to 24			
	Total	White	Black	Hispanic[a]	Total	White	Black	Hispanic[a]
	Percent of age group							
1974	73.4	76.2	55.8	48.9	83.9	85.6	72.5	59.0
1975	73.7	77.0	52.8	50.0	83.9	85.9	70.5	61.3
1976	73.1	75.4	58.2	50.9	83.7	85.4	71.9	58.0
1977	72.9	75.7	54.9	50.7	83.7	85.1	73.4	56.6
1978	73.5	76.3	54.9	48.9	83.7	85.2	73.5	58.7
1979	72.8	75.3	56.4	53.7	83.2	84.9	71.8	55.8
1980	73.7	76.1	59.3	46.1	83.8	85.1	74.3	57.1
1981	72.5	74.8	59.6	47.2	83.7	85.0	75.7	59.3
1982	72.0	74.5	58.2	51.7	84.1	85.4	76.2	60.2
1983	72.7	75.6	59.1	50.3	83.3	84.6	75.8	56.6
1984	73.3	75.5	63.0	58.3	84.6	85.7	79.3	60.7
1985	74.6	76.7	62.8	49.8	85.3	86.0	80.8	67.4
1986	74.6	76.6	64.9	54.7	84.8	85.4	81.0	61.6

[a]Most of the year-to-year differences in completion rates for Hispanics are not statistically significant due to the small size of the Hispanic sample. Hispanics may be of any race.

Note: Separate analyses were not done for Asians because they are not identifiable from the October Current Population Survey data tapes.

Source: U.S. Department of Commerce, Bureau of the Census, "School Enrollment—Social and Economic Characteristics of Students, October [various years]," Current Population Reports, Series P-20; and unpublished tabulations. See Also: National Center for Educational Statistics, The Condition of Education: Elementary and Secondary 1988. Vol.1., P. 90.

1979, illiteracy among persons within this age range fell to 0.5 percent for blacks and 0.2 percent for whites. Even more dramatic downturns were registered for blacks in older age groups. For instance, among blacks between the ages of 45 and 64, the rate of illiteracy dropped sharply from 11.3 percent in 1959 to 2.6 percent in 1979 while a sharp decline was also noted among those blacks above the age of 65. Illiteracy in this group fell from about one-fourth (25.5 percent) to approximately one-sixteenth (6.8 percent) between 1959 and 1979. Although the rates for the white population in each of these age groups also declined, they were already much lower than were illiteracy rates for blacks. In 1959 white 45- to 64-year-olds had an illiteracy rate of 1.8 compared to 0.5 in 1979. Whites over age 65 experienced a decline in illiteracy from 5.1 to 0.8 percent in 1959 and 1969, respectively.[48]

Nevertheless, illiteracy remains a nationwide problem that affects all races. It is estimated that 27 million adult Americans are unable to read above the fourth grade level and are defined as *functionally illiterate*.

Table 6.4 YEARS OF SCHOOL COMPLETED, BY AGE AND RACE: 1940–1987

	All persons					Black persons				
	Percent not high school graduates		Percent with 4 years of high school or more		Median school years completed	Percent not high school graduates		Percent with 4 years of high school or more		Median school years completed
Age and year	Total	With less than 5 yr. of school	Total	College, 4 yr. or more		Total	With less than 5 yr. of school	Total	College, 4 yr. or more	
25 years and over:										
1940	75.5	13.7	24.5	4.6	8.6	92.7	42.0	7.3	1.3	5.7
1950	65.7	11.1	34.3	6.2	9.3	87.1	32.9	12.9	2.1	6.8
1960	58.9	8.3	41.1	7.7	10.6	79.9	23.8	20.1	3.1	8.0
1970	47.7	5.5	52.3	10.7	12.1	68.6	14.6	31.4	4.4	9.8
1980	33.5	3.6	66.5	16.2	12.5	48.8	8.2	51.2	8.4	12.0
1985	26.1	2.7	73.9	19.4	12.6	40.2	6.2	59.8	11.1	12.3
1986	25.3	2.7	74.7	19.4	12.6	37.7	5.4	62.3	10.9	12.3
1987	24.4	2.4	75.6	19.9	12.7	36.6	5.0	63.4	10.7	12.4
25–29 years:										
1940	61.9	5.9	38.1	5.9	10.3	88.4	27.7	11.6	1.6	7.0
1950	49.5	4.7	52.8	7.7	12.0	80.4	16.8	22.2	2.7	8.6
1960	39.3	2.8	60.7	11.1	12.3	62.3	7.0	37.7	4.8	9.9
1970	26.2	1.7	73.8	16.3	12.6	44.6	3.2	55.4	6.0	12.1
1980	15.5	1.1	84.5	22.1	12.9	24.8	1.1	75.2	11.4	12.6
1985	13.9	.7	86.1	22.2	12.9	19.4	.4	80.6	11.5	12.7
1986	13.9	.9	86.1	22.4	12.9	16.7	.5	83.4	11.8	12.7
1987	14.0	.9	86.0	22.0	12.8	16.7	.4	83.3	11.4	12.7

Source: U.S. Bureau of the Census, U.S. Census of Population, 1940, 1950, 1960, 1970, and 1980, vol. I; and Current Population Reports, series P-20, No. 415 and forthcoming reports. [Through 1980, as of April 1; beginning 1985 as of March. Excludes Armed Forces, except members living off post or with families on post. Beginning 1980, excludes inmates of institutions. 1940 based on complete count; 1950 based on 20-percent sample; 1960 on 25-percent sample; 1970 on 20-percent sample; and 1980 on 17-percent sample; beginning 1985 based on Current Population Survey; see text, section 1. For definition of median, see Guide to Tabular Presentation]

These people are without the skills required for effective societal functioning (e.g., calculating change, filling out a job application, reading directions). They are distinguished from the 1.5 million who are *fundamentally illiterate*—people who cannot read or write. Beverly Cole points out that the number of adults who could be classified as illiterate rises to 45 million when the standard is raised to test the ability to read the text of a newspaper or magazine articles—a standard expected of persons who have an eighth grade reading level. The number escalates to 72 million when the standard is raised to reading at the high school level; that is, "the ability to read technical manuals in industry," for example.[49] Although reading comprehension problems are apparent in all groups of Americans, they are significantly more pronounced among blacks and Hispanics. This situation is a serious indictment on school systems that have socially promoted young people into senior high schools and graduated so many of them without helping them develop the kinds of skills needed for effective functioning in an increasingly technological society. It is equally a serious indictment on their parents who have not provided the kind of supervision and attention required by some young people merely to persuade them to learn and understand the importance of academic pursuits. Pupils themselves also share some of the blame for their educational deficits because so many disregard parental guidance that is given; they ignore counseling advice offered by teachers and are hindered by their contempt and disdain for learning, discipline, and school authority. This situation can be remedied by correcting in-school problems; stronger parenting and parental supervision; establishment of a larger number of service programs for illiterates and through motivational programs that stimulate learning for the sake of learning.

CONTEMPORARY ISSUES IN PUBLIC SCHOOL EDUCATION

In recent years, three issues have dominated discussions of school desegregation and access to equal educational opportunity: (1) busing, (2) tax exemptions to private schools, and (3) tuition tax credits.

Busing

By far the most volatile and politically divisive issue in public school education throughout the 1970s and into the 1980s is that of busing. The three U.S. presidents from the Republican Party from 1968 to 1988—Nixon, Ford, and Reagan—as well as hundreds of other aspirants for elective political office, attempted to persuade voters of their merit by calling attention to their opposition to court-ordered busing. In 1974 former President Richard Nixon called for antibusing legislation in a nationwide radio address on March 21. Perhaps less volatile, President Gerald Ford was not supportive of busing as a tool for school desegregation but did comparatively little to interfere with the judicial processes in support of this tool. On the other hand, President Ronald Reagan and his chief law enforcement officers, William French Smith, and especially Edwin Meese, the Attorney General of the United States, and William Bradford Reynolds, the Assistant Attorney General in charge of the U.S. Department of Justice, were far more adamant in their public opposition to busing. In fact, as will be stressed here, they took a number of steps deliberately designed to undermine the legitimacy of busing as remedial action against racially separate public schools.

The entire issue of public school education in urban areas involves several harsh but complicated realities. As cities become blacker and poorer, they correspondingly lose a viable tax base. Traditionally, taxes have supported public schools; but when the owners of property and revenue-producing businesses move to suburbia, and when major corporations and large holders of real estate within cities either pay no taxes or inordinately low taxes, the funding sources steadily decline. Concomitantly, residential property taxes in cities steadily climb, thereby draining resources of propertied persons who do remain. The refusal of most state legislators to relieve the situation reflects their characteristically antiurban stance and minimizes the probability of equal education. Thus suspicion is heightened that whites who control the power resources are not inclined to provide quality education to an all-black school system whether it is administered by blacks or whites.

Nevertheless, the U.S. Supreme Court has been more or less consistent since *Swann* v. *Charlotte-Mecklenburg* in upholding the constitutionality of busing as a tool to protect and safeguard the fundamental rights of black children to desegregated education in an essentially unitary school system. In addition to cases cited earlier on, busing was upheld by the U.S. Supreme Court in *Keyes* v. *School District No. 1*, 413 U.S. 189 (1973) which arose in Denver, Colorado. Importantly, the Court also enunciated in the *Keyes* case the principle that "a systemwide remedy is appropriate" when it is shown that an intentionally segregative policy is followed in any part of the school system.[50] One strategy that the Reagan administration employed to undermine busing was to attempt to overturn the essential presumption of systemwide racial discrimination when found in any part of the system as mandated in the *Keyes* case.[51] As of 1988, the Reagan administration had not been successful in joining a case that persuaded even a highly conservative Supreme Court to overturn the *Keyes* decision.

Yet the U.S. Supreme Court has been steadfast in the development of its "intent requirement." That is, the burden of proof is increasingly placed on the shoulders of the plaintiffs to prove that segregation found within a system was *intentionally* constructed. This means that just because discrimination exists, it cannot be presumed to have been by design. Consequently, desegregation advocates are compelled to spend enormous sums and endure lengthy litigation to *prove* "intentional discrimination."

The Reagan Administration, unlike the Carter Administration, which acted on the fact of the existence of segregation and discrimination as sufficient grounds for federal intervention, steadfastly refused to assist blacks and other minorities through their adherence to a requirement of "proof of intent" to discriminate.

The U.S. Supreme Court developed its philosophy of the sanctity of the intent requirement through a number of cases including *Washington* v. *Davis* (1976); *Village of Arlington Heights* v. *Metropolitan Housing Development Corporation* (1977); *Austin Independent School District* v. *U.S.* (1976); *U.S.* v. *Board of Commissioners of the City of Indianapolis, Indiana, No. 75-1730* (1978); *U.S.* v. *School District of Omaha,* 565 F 2d 127, 8th Cir. (1977), and *Dayton Board of Education* v. *Brinkman,* 433 U.S. 406 (1977). Even with these decisions that demonstrated how public housing patterns, for example, could have been designed to intentionally segregate school systems, or how intentional segregation occurred in some parts of the system and the system was required to eliminate that segregation caused by intentional acts, the U.S. Supreme Court has not abrogated the position it took in the *Keyes* case. Consequently, busing continues to be regarded by the Court as a constitutionally sound measure to eliminate intentional segregation within school systems.[52]

The issue of cross-district busing or metropolitanism was originally addressed by the U.S. Supreme Court in *Swann* v. *Charlotte-Mecklenburg.* Since that time, metropolitanism as a busing tool was raised in such cases as *Bradley* v. *School Board,* 412 U.S. 92 (1974), *Milliken* v. *Bradley,* 418 U.S. 717 (1974), and *Hills* v. *Gautreaux,* 425 U.S. 248 (1976). In *Bradley* v. *School Board,* the Court, evenly divided with Justice Powell abstaining, permitted to stand a district court's order that reversed a metropolitan desegregation order in Richmond, Virginia. In the *Milliken* case, the Supreme Court also reversed a decision in Detroit that had been affirmed by lower courts to employ metropolitanism which involved the city of Detroit and 53 suburban communities. The 5–4 decision pointed out that the state had not provided "sufficient grounds" for claiming intentional discrimination by the suburban schools. However, in the *Hills* case, the Court stated that under certain conditions, such as deliberate housing discrimination, metropolitan remedies may be permissible.[53]

Finally, extensive busing was approved by the courts in Nashville, Tennessee, in 1983 even after the Reagan administration had entered the case in support of antibusing advocates. In *Metropolitan County Board* v. *Kelly,* No. 82-702 (1983) and only after 27 years of litigation, the Appeals Court in the Sixth District ordered busing from kindergarten through high school as a means of eliminating "from the public schools all vestiges of State-imposed segregation."[54] Finally, under a court order to terminate school segregation in both the city of St. Louis and in 22 districts in St. Louis County, Missouri, an agreement was reached in 1983 between the relevant school boards to use cross-district busing to accomplish this purpose.

On what basis can busing be justified? Proponents claim that it is a viable and necessary technique to achieve the mandate of the affirmative duty to terminate discrimination in public schools. They argue that because of systemized patterns of circumvention by the various boards of education, as in Boston and Los Angeles, and white flight to escape desegregation, the goal of a nationwide desegregated school system cannot be achieved without some form of busing. They also observe that mistaken information has been communicated through the media and by antibusing politicians or community leaders about the degree of public support for busing. In so doing, reference is made to a March 1981 Harris poll which found that 54 percent of all parents whose children had been bused for school desegregation called busing a very satisfactory experience and 33 percent categorized busing as partially satisfactory. Only 11 percent of such families that had actually had busing experience regarded it as unsatisfactory.[55]

Proponents of busing also claim that another misperception is that the majority of students bused to school each day in the United States are bused for the purpose of achieving school desegregation. That assumption is absolutely false. The U.S. Commission on Civil Rights points out that about 55 percent of all pupils who attend public schools are bused daily to and from their schools. Of all those pupils, only 4 percent are actually bused for the purpose of racial desegregation.[56] It appears to some researchers that more pupils are transported each day to public, private, parochial, and non-Catholic Christian academies that are racially segregated than to schools for purposes of racial desegregation. Much of this transportation is paid with public funds.[57]

Advocates of busing claim that it facilitates the ultimate goals of an integrated society by encouraging individuals to learn about themselves and others through formal and informal patterns of social interaction; providing a better quality of education since in a school system where whites are present in large numbers, such quality will be protected, especially if they are from middle- and upper-class homes; and fostering the intermixture of pupils across racial, ethnic, and social class lines which is likely to improve the academic performance and heighten achievement motivation in all students in segregated schools. As a further consequence, they expect that reading scores and the whole range of academic skills will improve through provisions for better facilities and for competent teachers interested in every facet of the learning and teaching process.

Such views are articulated in data analyses and empirical research conducted by a large array of social scientists including Garibaldi,[58] Schneider,[59] Orr and Ianni,[60] Norbit and Collins,[61] and Scherer and Slawski.[62] In addition, using detailed studies and path analysis techniques on the National Longitudinal Study (NLS) of the high school class of 1972, McPhartland,[63] Thomas,[64] and Braddock[65] have identified other benefits of school desegregation. In their comparisons of black children in desegregated schools with those in segregated schools, they found that black children in desegregated schools tend to have a higher level of aspiration and of educational attainment, feel more optimistic about career opportunities, and are more likely to pursue academic programs or careers not "traditionally" found among black students. However, the latter finding may be partially explained by the tendency of black high school graduates from desegregated schools to attend predominantly white colleges that offer more diversified curricula and expanded program choices. Most black colleges are attended more often by black high school graduates from largely segregated schools. Further, black graduates of desegregated high schools tend to have a greater sense of political efficacy than those who graduate from segregated high schools. There is also a considerable body of evidence showing that the academic performance of black students in desegregated institutions, particularly on standardized tests, improved and that performance by white students "kept pace with presegregation levels."[66]

Social science research has provided findings that may be used either to support busing or to oppose it. For example, Coleman's 1967 study was the initial basis of significant support for busing as a tool for school desegregation.[67] In 1974, he published another study in which he reversed his original position and rejected busing as a viable tool for school desegregation.[68] After attacks against the methodology employed in his investigations and other criticisms against his research analysis made by sociologists during the annual meeting of the American Sociological Association, he toned down his claim but still insisted that busing is counterproductive primarily because of so much "white flight" and public opposition to it. However, other social scientists such as Reynolds Farley have shown through empirical research that the white flight phenomenon actually began on a large scale immediately following the end of World War II.[69] It was aided by federally financed programs that benefited the white middle class, such as access to FHA mortgages and other programs. Further, as stated in Chapter 2, manufacturing jobs began to shift from the central city to the suburb, sometimes out of reach for blacks in the central cities. Segregation patterns in housing rigidified segregation in schooling, and the suburbs became white retreats from the multiracial living arrangements found in several American cities. Farley also stated that the falling birth rate among whites helped to inflate the proportion of blacks and other minorities in central city schools even though birth rates among blacks were also falling but not at the same rate as that of whites.[70]

Coleman's 1967 study concluded that achievement was superior in integrated schools and that the background of a pupil's classmates was a major variable that affected success in school.[71] Achievement is also highly related to the availability and utilization of certain types of facilities and supplies such as chemistry and physics laboratories, language laboratories, textbooks, libraries, and computers. Not infrequently, severe shortages of achievement related facilities exist in ghetto schools.[72] These findings also explain why some black parents encourage busing to suburban schools where these facilities and equipment are more plentiful. One of the most successful efforts toward this end is the program being carried out by the Metropolitan Council for Educational Opportunities (METCO) in Boston. Under this program, which started in 1966 with 220 black children bused to seven suburban schools, by 1982, some 3,271 pupils from Boston were bused to 34 suburban communities. In effect, these parents did not oppose busing as long as they believed that the end result was quality education for their children. Even with the success of METCO and a similar but earlier program, called Operation Exodus, Boston was forced by the federal courts to desegregate its schools by busing if necessary in 1974.

Opposition

The range of opposition to school busing encompasses a curious mixture of true bigots and those parents who are genuinely concerned about their children's welfare and the quality of education they are likely to receive if busing occurs. The opposition also includes those persons who are committed to the concept of neighborhoods, "defended neighborhoods"[73] as it were, and community control over education. Some are white; some are black neoconservatives; some are blacks who are generally liberal on other issues. Other opponents are politicians who are not genuinely committed to anything but whatever seems likely to return them to elective office.

Opponents to busing also include "fair-weather liberal" social scientists who mask their opposition behind thinly veiled racist interpretations of highly suspect research, self-serving academic opportunists seeking national publicity, and those so-called militants or radicals, black and white, who are committed to educational separatism. The true bigots resist busing because of their commitment to segregation and the maintenance of white privilege and black subordination. Like their predecessors in Clinton, Tennessee, and Little Rock, Arkansas, many of the more extreme opponents are inclined to use violence to prevent busing for desegregation purposes. This finding was implicit in allegations against the KKK members for burning buses in Pontiac, Michigan, in 1971, and in the hatred on the faces of many protesters, adults and children alike, in Boston during the period between 1974 and 1977.[74]

Opponents to busing form various antibusing groups such as the Concerned Citizens of Canarsie, the Canarsie Chapter of the Italian-American Civil Rights League, and Restore Our Alienated Rights (ROAR). Unlike the behavior of voters and political leaders in Charlotte-Mecklenburg who decided to obey busing orders and voted out of office school board members who frustrated desegregation efforts, a different tactic was employed in other cities. For example, in Los Angeles, Dayton, and New York City, school board members who favored school desegregation or provided support to uphold the legality of busing as a tool for that purpose were either forced to resign or defeated at the polls. Boston was, until 1980, a classical example of how a school board hostile to busing could frustrate desegregation efforts. School board intransigence, coupled with inertia by the elected leadership and a general antipathy often expressed in the City Council, fueled emotions and probably created the environment within which the racial turmoil that characterized desegregation efforts between 1974 and 1980 exploded.[75] By 1983, however, Boston had elected two blacks to the School Committee for the first time in its history in addition to white members who were more reasonable, if not always entirely supportive, on the issue of court-ordered busing.

Unmistakably, there are many persons who do not support busing although they are strong advocates of improved race relations and equal educational opportunities for all citizens. Several persons in this camp believe in the importance of neighborhood schools, of having immediate access to their children in case of an emergency, and in the greater opportunities for their children to participate in extracurricular activities in schools closer to their place of residence than by having them in schools located several miles away.

There are also those parents who fear school violence and that their children will be attacked by belligerent blacks. Curiously, white antibusing proponents seem to feel that blacks have no justification to fear physical abuse and attacks when they are bused into predominantly white schools and neighborhoods. Evidence does not support this view of nonviolence. Even in the 1980s, there was ample media coverage of white violence against blacks as well as black violence against whites. In some schools, white students in northern communities, for example, have dressed in KKK robes and hoods for school functions or listed KKK affiliations in the school yearbook. Black students have been physically assaulted and white students have been physically and verbally abused by black pupils. The pressing issue is how to control such racial hatred and make the school environment a more positive situation for all students, regardless of racial differences.

Some black Americans oppose busing because they reject any notion that black children can only learn in the presence of white children since such views are patently racist and false. Others claim that the important issue is quality education, which can be obtained just as effectively in all-black schools if the appropriate financial resources, teachers, and learning environments were available. Still others resent the fact that black children have had to bear the burden of busing, getting up at ungodly hours in the morning to catch a bus to a school in which their children are often subjected to racial hostility and uncaring, if not prejudiced, teachers. Furthermore, some middle-class blacks, who reside in essentially predominantly black neighborhoods in which the largely black public schools are superior to those in poorer white neighborhoods, do not want their children to be bused to inferior white schools. Their fear is that their children will be subjected to lower academic standards and that their pace of learning will be slowed.

The salience of segregated housing for facilitating desegregated schooling has been demonstrated in the research of Pearce[76] and others.

Pearce, for instance, found in a 1980 study that interdistrict busing led to housing desegregation and that there was a close and positive relationship between housing desegregation and school desegregation. Moreover, where that occurred, busing was not required as would be otherwise. A similar observation was made by Saltman who asserted that just as segregated housing creates segregated schools, the latter may "reinforce and perpetuate segregated neighborhoods."[77] Thus the open housing movement may provide the best support to efforts to eliminate both school segregation and busing for that purpose.

The successes in school busing have not deterred its antagonists from pursuing their steadfast efforts to abolish it. During earlier national administrations, the belief prevailed that districts not complying with the mandates to desegregate would have federal funds terminated as provided under the Elementary and Secondary Education Act of 1965. In the 1980s Reagan years, however, that fear was less pronounced. One reason for the relative absence of trepidations among recalcitrant districts was the belief that the Reagan Administration was not likely to enforce such policies. This belief was predicated on public pronouncements by President Reagan that he was opposed to busing and favored voluntary plans. Furthermore, the chief law enforcement agents and agencies did not appear to be either enthusiastic or aggressive about enforcing antidiscriminatory legislation whether in schools or in employment.

President Reagan's behavior contradicted public pronouncements with regard to support for "voluntary desegregation programs." For instance, he and his administration *opposed* a voluntary desegregation plan devised by the school districts of Seattle, Pasco, and Tacoma, Washington, as well as in Nashville, Tennessee. In the Washington cases, *Seattle School District* v. *State of Washington,* the Reagan Administration reversed previous positions taken by the U.S. Department of Justice in other administrations, including those of Presidents Nixon, Ford, and Carter, by asking the U.S. Supreme Court to overturn a *voluntarily* agreed upon public school desegregation program. A mandatory busing plan had been voluntarily instituted by the school boards in Seattle, Pasco, and Tacoma but Washington voters in 1978 approved a referendum that would overturn the busing order. The three school districts sued for the restoration of their order.[78] In 1983 the U.S. Supreme Court agreed with the three school districts and reinstated the voluntary program. In effect, presidential actions seemed to be designed to circumvent the implementation of even a voluntary busing plan, although President Reagan continued to state his support for voluntary programs.

According to the U.S. Commission on Civil Rights, among school systems that have demonstrated the positive effects of school desegregation in terms of enabling pupils to understand how to live in a pluralistic society are those in Charlotte-Mecklenburg, Denver, Providence, Rhode Island, Tampa, Florida, and Tacoma, Washington.[79] In addition, the citizens in Louisville, Kentucky, have also demonstrated how compliance to a court order to utilize busing for school desegregation can be accomplished if the leadership structure is firm in its commitment to uphold the law and when the citizens are cooperative. Examples of communities in which obstructionist tactics were employed to prevent or slow the pace of school desegregation include Boston, Cleveland, Indianapolis, Los Angeles, and New Castle County (Wilmington), Delaware. In addition, because of the persistence of these obstructionist strategies the Commission claims that less than meaningful public school desegregation has occurred in such cities as New York City, Buffalo, and Pittsburgh.[80]

In every administration since busing was sanctioned by the U.S. Supreme Court, antibusing legislation has been introduced in Congress. In the waning days of his administration, President Carter vetoed such legislation. However, in the first few weeks of the Reagan administration, antibusing legislation was introduced in the U.S. Senate by Senators Orrin Hatch (R-Utah), J. Bennett Johnston (D-La.), and Jesse Helms (R-NC). The Johnston-Helms measure would restrict busing by limiting the time taken to move a child from home to school to no more than 15 minutes.[81] The future of such legislation is always unclear because of divided opinion among the various members of the U.S. Senate and House of Representatives about the efficacy of busing in the face of the necessity to uphold the law.

Controlled Choice

In recent years, some educators and planners have advocated a new policy device for school desegregation called "controlled choice." Its aim is to achieve a kind of balance between what Robert Dentler calls the "principle of wholly equal treatment and equalized opportunity." In his view, this compromise must be achieved in ways that make the "more advantaged and upwardly mobile subgroups" within the school district more amenable to racial desegregation.[82] Dentler also argues that controlled choice has the advantage of preserving and advancing the "value of choice" of schools by parents (consistent with the traditional view that many Americans have about freedom of choice) and eliminates so much of the rigidity that seems to characterize public school educational policy. It is also claimed that parents will send their children to schools outside their immediate neighborhoods when it is evident to them that quality education is at the end of the bus ride.[83] Controlled choice programs operate in 20 states and several individual school districts and in such cities as Boston, Chicago, New York, Philadelphia, and Little Rock.

Critics of controlled choice claim that it is tantamount to resegregation along racial and class lines. It is also argued that this policy favors the middle-class and high-achieving students, irrespective of race, and increases the probability that students at risk will remain at risk. In other words, "the poor and uneducated parents may lose out" in the contest for better schools because of their lack of information.[84] Some individuals will be forced to send their children to inferior schools within the system since all schools within the system are by no means equal in quality by any measure employed to test quality—whether in terms of programs, facilities, equipment, or personnel. It is also difficult to implement controlled choice in a manner that assures the attainment of its intended purposes.

Tax Exemptions to Private Schools

Prior to 1970, private schools that racially discriminated could obtain a tax-exempt status under existing policy of the federal Internal Revenue Service (IRS). These institutions could meet IRS qualifications for tax exemptions by not receiving aid either from a state or "one of its political subdivisions" when its operations violated the "Constitution or Federal Law."[85] In 1969 blacks in Mississippi filed a class action suit in which this tax-exempt status was protested because the identified Mississippi schools refused to admit black students. In the case of *Green* v. *Connally*, 330 F Supp. 1150 (D.D.C. 1971) and *Green* v. *Kennedy*, 309 F. Supp. 1127, 1129–30 (D.D.C. 1970), plaintiffs sought two responses. First, they sought to prevent the Secretary of the Treasury and the Commissioner of the IRS from approving applications for tax-exempt status from private schools that discriminated on the basis of race. Second, they wanted the Court to order the Treasury Secretary and the IRS Commissioner to rescind any status of tax exemption heretofore granted to such institutions. In 1970 the injunctive relief sought by the plaintiffs was granted by the Federal District Court for the District of Columbia. Thereafter, the IRS policy was to deny a tax-exempt status to schools that discriminated against students on the basis of race or color.[86]

This policy was subsequently upheld in other cases, such as *Wright* v. *Miller*, 480 Supp. 790 (D.D.C. 1979) and *Green* v. *Miller*, Civ. Action No. 69-1355 (D.D.C. May 5, 1980). However, in 1982, President Reagan ordered the IRS to discontinue this policy that had been in existence for approximately 11 years. Responding to widespread public indignation and bitterly worded allegations that the administration actually sanctioned the use of public funds to support racial discrimination and bigotry, the President and his administration decided to seek clarification of the legality of the IRS policy through an interpretation from the U.S. Supreme Court. The issue reached the Supreme Court in the cases of *Bob Jones University* v. *United States* and *Goldsboro Christian Schools, Inc.* v. *United States*. Bob Jones University in Greenville, South Carolina, which once denied admission to black students, had admitted blacks by 1982 but prohibited interracial dating and interracial marriage. Goldsboro Christian Schools in Goldsboro, North Carolina, denied admission to black students. Both institutions had sought tax-exempt status on religious grounds and President Reagan had supported their claim in January 1982 until the public outcry persuaded him to seek clarification from the Courts. In May 1983, the U.S. Supreme Court rendered a decision stating that such institutions that discriminate on the basis of race or color were not entitled to tax exemptions. The 8–1 decision (with Justice William Rehnquist casting the only negative vote) noted that such racially discriminatory policies violated the "fundamental public policy" against racial discrimination in education.[87]

Two important questions for the IRS to answer are how to monitor the 20,000 private schools in the United States, 85 percent of which are religiously affiliated, and how to ascertain when they are, in fact, engaging in racial discrimination. Critics of existing practices assert that there is a need for stronger federal guidelines to determine actual discrimination. Under existing guidelines, private schools need only claim that they do not racially discriminate; there is no strong monitoring mechanism that will enable a determination of the veracity of such statements.

Tuition Tax Credits

The issue of tuition tax credit or permission to deduct federal taxes by parents who send their children to private or parochial schools has been debated for years. A central argument in this debate is whether or not granting such deductions violates the constitutional mandate of separation of church and state. Another equally compelling argument centers on the impact of tuition tax credits on the public school system of the United States. Opponents to tax credits insist that such credits will ultimately undermine the public schools and that a two-tiered system of privileged, largely white schools versus poor, largely minority schools will result. Proponents, such as former President Reagan, claim that tuition tax credits will offer more freedom of choice for parents and enable them to obtain a high quality of education for their children. Besides, these advocates reason, it is only fair to those parents who also pay taxes that help support public education to receive federal deductions for private school tuition.

This issue was rejected by voters in Washington, D.C., by an overwhelming majority of about 9–1 in November 1981. However, a test case was filed in Minnesota that supported the perceived rights of parents to receive such credits. On June 20, 1983, the U.S. Supreme Court agreed that parents who send their children to private schools were entitled to such tax credits in the case of *Mueller* v. *Allen, No. 82–195* and that they did not violate the constitutional mandate of separation of church and state.

BLACKS IN HIGHER EDUCATION

Black Colleges in Transition

Much of what has been said earlier concerning the legal mandates for desegregation at the elementary and secondary school levels is also germane for experiences at the college and university levels. However, the desegregation efforts pertaining to graduate and professional schools began much sooner. Black colleges had come into existence during the mid-nineteenth century as a response to segregation and discrimination. The first to be founded were Wilberforce University in Ohio and Lincoln University in Pennsylvania before the end of the Civil War. Both were established to "Christianize" and educate blacks in a liberal education, and both had integrated faculties from their inception.

Most of the 123 black colleges and universities founded since then are located in the South, and they served an almost exclusively black student body. At the beginning the majority offered the equivalent of a good secondary school education. Subsequently, they evolved along the classical model of white liberal arts colleges. Originally serving a variety of purposes, some catered to an elitist social class while others attempted to democratize higher education. Some were better financed and better staffed, and offered a more rigorous curriculum that exacted higher standards. Others, on the other hand, did not uphold such rigorous and high academic standards. Because of serious problems (which will be described presently) that beset them from the outset, it is a tribute to their tenacity that they have continued for more than a century. Those philanthropic organizations that were instrumental in developing primary and secondary education for blacks played a major role in ensuring the survival of black colleges.

Functions

Black colleges provided opportunities for higher education throughout the period of de jure segregation; they served a clientele that could not be admitted to institutions serving whites, though those same institutions were supported by taxes paid by blacks; they offered blacks a chance for achievement when no one else would; they trained more than 80 percent of all black college graduates and in the process were responsible for the development of significant leadership forces in the black community. Furthermore, they came to be the source of considerable community pride, symbols of racial advancements, and part and parcel of the social mobility structure within the black community. Their very existence served as a continuing reminder of the intellectual acumen among black people and their teachers were visible role models worthy of emulation.

Problems

Yet, from the beginning, black colleges were plagued with essentially two types of problems—affective and organizational. Organizational problems were a function of management and the administrative structure of the institutions. Affective problems included those that emanated from social control and interpersonal relationships.

Organizational problems were also expressions of the role or self-perceptions that the college or university presidents had. They had inherited a model of administration from white predecessors, but in the process of emulating them tended to exaggerate their behavior. This development, combined with his/her suspicions of underlings, led inevitably to a type of "vest-pocket administration" characterized by presidential autonomy, secrecy, and the inability to delegate authority or decentralize the decision-making structure. In many cases his/her limited knowledge of finance exacerbated financial problems endemic in black colleges. These institutions were almost always in financial straits, struggling to survive, not knowing whether they would close before the year was over or even if teachers could be paid from month to month. Financial problems placed numerous constraints on the acquisition of educational resources and the ability to hire competent staff, which inevitably affected accreditation. Construction of new buildings was always in doubt and often delayed. The curriculum varied from one institution to another, but not infrequently teachers were required to be experts in several different fields and teach as many as fifteen to twenty semester hours. Although the heavy teaching loads were prevalent at several institutions, they did not occur at all of them. Nevertheless, this environment could hardly generate a high rate of scholarly productivity. Thus we must conclude that prior to World War II high scholarly productivity may have been neither encouraged nor adequately rewarded except at then noted centers of scholarly activity such as Howard University, Fisk University, and Atlanta University.

Affective problems covered a wide range of activities regulated by a deeply entrenched but highly exaggerated Puritan ethic. A rigid conceptualization of morality, which also prevailed at small sectarian white colleges, encompassed all aspects of social life in many black colleges. This included proscriptions against face-to-face dancing between the sexes, restrictions against unsupervised dating, regulations against card playing and various recreational games, smoking in public, drinking alcoholic beverages, and faculty-student social relations. A morbid fear of premarital pregnancy prevailed and, when it occurred, both the father and expectant mother were expelled. Similarly, a paternalistic orientation governed behavior between faculty and administrators.

This host of problems in no way denies the good fortune that the black colleges have had in attracting a cadre of dedicated, diligent, and persevering teachers and a few excellent administrators. They still do attract such lights. These are men and women who have devoted themselves to teaching and research under the most difficult educational conditions. Their work and the successes of their students substantiate the claim that less well-known institutions can train outstanding students and successful adults just as the more prestigious ones can. Both outstanding and poor students graduate from black colleges just as outstanding and poor students graduate from predominantly white institutions. That four-fifths of all black college graduates and holders of professional degrees received their undergraduate training at predominantly black colleges and universities is more than sufficient evidence of the value of these institutions. Moreover, black college graduates, natives of the South, now provide most of the professional black men and women who hold positions of importance both in and outside the South. They are the physicians and surgeons, the attorneys, the social scientists, the heads of academic departments in white universities, the successful business people, the accountants, and the engineers.

The proportion of successful and educated blacks who are of southern origin is far greater than those of northern birth. One explanation for this development lies in the high motivation of southern blacks to use education as a vehicle for upward mobility and survival in a highly segregated society. Southern blacks were also exposed to a larger array of educated role models than were northern urban blacks, who, because of social class barriers and institutionalized discrimination, were isolated from successful and achieving blacks. A further explanation is that southern black colleges were more accessible to college-age blacks and would admit them without regard for a quota system. In other words, despite the deprivations of income and allegedly inferior schools, black college students in the South were better able to seize educational opportunities and they did so in greater numbers. Perhaps, of even greater importance, they had black teachers who encouraged them to maximize their potential, pursue a college education, and achieve high goals commensurate with their abilities. Black urban youths in the North rarely experienced such concern from their high school teachers.

But discrimination and segregation set boundaries or limits on what black students could achieve in professional education and graduate training, particularly in the South and border states. This situation was also true in the North, where admission quotas were enacted. Blacks seeking postcollegiate training found it necessary to "go North" if they could afford the financial burden. Few ever received monetary support from northern and western institutions, which, again, served as an impediment to educational attainment.

To combat discrimination in higher education the NAACP embarked upon a plan to alter the structure of university admission patterns. The basic goal was to open the doors of graduate and professional schools in the southern and border states to black college graduates. One of the first successful test cases came in 1938 when the U.S. Supreme Court decided in *Missouri ex rel. Gaines* v. *Canada* that the University of Missouri must admit Lloyd Gaines to its school of law. A black student was ordered admitted to the University of Maryland Law School in 1935 in the case of *Maryland* v. *Murray.* This was a milestone achievement, since many states had required blacks to accept out-of-state tuition grants to finance postcollegiate education rather than admit them to their all-white universities. Gaines was not required to accept this type of grant. Another major breakthrough occurred in 1946 when Ada Lois Sipuel applied for admission to the school of law at the University of Oklahoma. The state of

Oklahoma was not inclined to establish separate law schools for black students, as had several southern states. Rather, despite the ruling in the Gaines case, the state attempted to force her to accept an out-of-state tuition grant. She refused, and, finally, in 1948, the University of Oklahoma was required to admit Ada Sipuel.

Two other cases pertaining to graduate education were significant in this earlier period: the *Sweatt* case in Texas and the *McLauren* case in Oklahoma. In the Texas case Herman M. Sweatt, a mail carrier, had applied for admission to the University of Texas Law School. Texas quickly established a makeshift law school for blacks in four basement offices as a pretense at separate-but-equal facilities. However, this facility did not contain adequate libraries, moot courts, faculty, and other educational resources available at the University of Texas. The U.S. Supreme Court ordered Sweatt's admission to the University of Texas in 1950 on the grounds that the black law school did not approximate equality with the university's law school. The *McLauren* case in Oklahoma dealt with the issue of segregation within schools that had already been desegregated. The Graduate School of Education at the University of Oklahoma had admitted G. W. McLauren but segregated him from his classmates. He was placed in an anteroom that adjoined the main classroom and was segregated in the dining room. Finally, he was admitted to class but segregated by a rope barrier. In 1950 the Supreme Court ruled that "substantial equality" was not provided by these arrangements and, therefore, McLauren had to be integrated in all facilities of the university. These five decisions also paved the way for the U.S. Supreme Court's favorable ruling in the 1954 *Brown* case.

Decisions reached by the U.S. Supreme Court regarding elementary and secondary education and the Civil Rights Act of 1964 have also had an impact on changes in higher education. In addition, during the 1970s, the most important Court decisions with respect to the efforts of blacks to gain access to higher education were those rendered in the original *Adams* v. *Richardson* case (presently referred to as *Adams* v. *Cavazos*) in 1973, and *The Board of Regents of the University of California* v. *Allan Bakke*. The *Adams* case was filed because the plaintiff sought relief from the effects of a continuing dual system of public education. This class action suit filed in 1969 resulted in a 1973 order issued by the U.S. District Court of Appeals in the District of Columbia that required the Department of Health, Education and Welfare to discontinue funds to institutions in violation of the Civil Rights Act of 1964.

Initially HEW was told to enforce compliance in only 10 state-college systems, including the state of Pennsylvania, in addition to some 200 elementary and secondary schools. This mandate was extended under the Carter Administration to cover all 18 southern and border states that once had de jure dual systems of public higher education. The *Adams* decision has been in continuous litigation since 1973 largely because the various states have not fully satisfied the NAACP, the Legal Defense Fund, nor the

Office of Civil Rights that they have taken sufficient steps to dismantle dual systems of education. States under the *Adams* litigation are under court order to enhance the historically black colleges. Enhancement and quality mean substantial improvements in the curriculum and program offerings at publicly supported black colleges, increase in the size of the faculty and equalizing faculty and administrative salaries, the desegregation of student bodies at all publicly supported institutions, and equalizing facilities as well as financial aid programs in these institutions. On several occasions, the various states have been ordered to submit "systemwide" desegregation plans to the Department of Health, Education and Welfare/Department of Health and Human Services and, more recently, to the U.S. Department of Education. Frequently, these state plans failed to meet approval by the Legal Defense and Educational Fund, which represented the original plaintiff in the case, or the federal government. However, since the *Adams* case was filed, the states, as a whole, have taken some steps toward improving the overall quality of education offered at the publicly supported historically black colleges. Modest desegregation of public institutions has occurred; a few additional programs have been established at black colleges and additional capital outlays for purchasing of equipment and the construction of new buildings have been allocated. But very few white students have ever enrolled in historically black public institutions.

Several presidents of these historic black public institutions and the National Association for Equal Opportunity in Higher Education (NAFEO) have either been directly opposed to or taken a skeptical view of the dismantling process. For them, the eventual outcome of that process might be the total elimination of black institutions that have played such a vital role in the development and provision of higher education to the black community. There is a tremendous fear of mergers with nearby predominantly white institutions, some established long after the black colleges were founded. It is not merely the merger that is dreaded but the strong probability that the black college will be subordinated to a younger, previously segregated, predominantly white institution. Indeed, it was only following a protracted court battle that the historically black Tennessee State University in Nashville won the right to have the previously white University of Tennessee/Nashville become an administrative division of Tennessee State University. Before that decision, there was a considerable amount of fear in the black community that Tennessee State University would lose its identity by a forced merger under the aegis of the younger and previously all-white University of Tennessee at Nashville.

These fears are also strengthened by the changing racial composition of such historically black institutions as Lincoln University in Missouri, West Virginia State College, and Bluefield State College in West Virginia. These institutions have now become predominantly white in student body composition and, for many, carefully nurtured black traditions have been lost. Nevertheless, the Court and the Legal Defense Fund are steadfast in their pursuit of the goal to terminate every vestige of a dual or segregated system of higher education. However, they, too, wish to preserve and strengthen the historically black institutions in ways that make them more competitive and attractive to college students of all races.

The *Bakke* case was a test of the right of an institution to facilitate access of black students to graduate and professional schools by setting aside a predetermined number of seats for their admission. In this instance, the medical college of the University of California at Davis had set aside 16 of its 100 seats in its first-year classes exclusively for minority students. Bakke claimed that since these seats were not available to white students, the University was engaging in an unfair quota system for admission which was discriminatory against white students. A similar suit had been filed in 1973 in the case of *DeFunis* v. *Odegarrd* that involved the law school of the University of Washington. However, by the time the *DeFunis* case reached the U.S. Supreme Court, the Court stated that it was moot because DeFunis had already been admitted to the university's law school. In the case of Allan Bakke, who had already been denied admission to five other medical schools (some suspect because of his age), his claim was that he had higher admission scores than many of the minority students who were admitted under this special quota system. The California Supreme Court upheld his claim and ordered him admitted. The university appealed and the case ultimately reached the U.S. Supreme Court.

This case was regarded by civil rights advocates as well as those persons who objected to special admission practices and the presumed use of quota systems by colleges and universities as the most momentous case since *Brown.* Importantly, the case found many organizations that had been allies during the civil rights struggles of the 1950s and 1960s on opposing sides. Most organizations representing blacks and other minority groups opposed Bakke because they viewed a decision in his behalf as a retreat from the movement toward equal access to education, especially on the graduate and professional school level. Most Jewish organizations, which long opposed what they viewed as quota systems, supported Bakke's claim. As a result, the schism between blacks and Jews first observed during the late 1960s appeared to deepen with the arguments unfolded in the Bakke case.

In 1978 the U.S. Supreme Court handed down a two-part decision on the Bakke case. On the one hand, the Court agreed by a 5–4 vote with Bakke that the University of California at Davis was operating an unconstitutional admissions program and, therefore, banned quota systems of the type employed. On the other hand, by a 4–4 split, the Court affirmed the legitimacy of the race variable as a permissible determinant of admissions whenever it served a state's compelling interest or need. Although many universities offered considerable latitude in interpreting the *Bakke* decision, it appears that those institutions that wished to alter their admissions programs to conform to the *Bakke* decision and still be aggressive in the recruitment of minority students did so (e.g., Temple University and Rutgers Medical School). On the other hand, many institutions used the support for Bakke's claim as justification for abandoning their feeble efforts to recruit and admit promising minority students.[88]

The *Adams* and *Bakke* cases have had a profound impact on the efforts of black and other minority students to equalize access to higher education. Their importance is probably best reflected in the changed enrollment patterns and distribution of black students in higher education.

Enrollment Patterns

The *Adams* and *Bakke* cases have influenced enrollment patterns of black students, but so have a number of other important factors. For instance, increases in the participation rates of blacks in undergraduate education were facilitated greatly by favorable court decisions, a broad range of responses by predominantly white institutions following the assassination of Dr. Martin Luther King in April 1968, and pressures exerted by black students enrolled in predominantly white institutions to expand the enrollment of black students beyond token levels. These actions resulted in profound changes. In 1960, for instance, black colleges enrolled more than half of all black college students in the United States. By 1970, one-third of the 400,000 black college students were attending historically black institutions.[89] By 1972–1973, however, fully three-quarters of the 727,000 black college students were enrolled in nonblack institutions outside the South.

In 1981 the National Center for Educational Statistics reported that more than 1.1 million black students were enrolled in colleges in the United States. They represented 10.3 percent of total enrollment. It had been 6.4 percent in 1960. Somewhat more than one-half of these students attended college in the southern and border states. Slightly more than one-third of those black students in the southern and border states were matriculated in predominantly black institutions. Most were in the historically black institutions (HBCUs) originally founded to provide education for blacks when they were excluded by law from attending white state-supported colleges and universities. The remainder of that third were in predominantly black institutions (PBIs) that were founded largely between 1955 and 1980, and became largely black by virtue of demographics or residential patterns. Three-fourths of the PBIs are community colleges.[90]

Nationally, by 1981 only about 18 percent of all black students were enrolled in HBCUs; 43 percent were matriculated at community colleges, and 39 percent were enrolled in the traditionally white colleges and universities. In fact, in some states, most of the blacks in colleges were found in the community colleges and proprietary institutions. The *Adams* case seeks to restructure this maldistribution.

Between 1960 and 1981, the college attendance rate of black 18- to

24-year-olds climbed from 18.4 percent to 28.0 percent. Among whites, the rise was from 24.2 percent to 32.5 percent. Within that period black and white 18- to 24-year-olds had reached parity in their college-going rates in 1975 when their rates were 32.4 and 32.0 for whites and blacks respectively.[91] By 1985, the college-going rate for blacks declined to 26.1 percent whereas the rate for whites continued to climb to 34.1 percent. The most recent data from the American Council on Education shows that college enrollment of black high school graduates continues to fall while high school completion rates are increasing. In fact, among black and Hispanics dependent on their parents (18–24-year-olds cohorts), college enrollment declined by 12 percent among blacks, 3.6 percent among Hispanics but rose by 3.6 percent among whites between 1976 and 1988.[92]

College Completion Rates

The increases in the volume of black student college enrollment noted above have been accompanied by a similar upward trend in their college completion rates. Among blacks over the age of 25, only 1.3 percent had completed four or more years of college in 1940, compared to 4.6 percent of the white population. In 1960, when the civil rights movement was achieving significant momentum, 3.1 percent of all blacks 25 years and over—compared to 7.7 percent of whites in the same age group—had attained four or more years of college training. A full decade later, blacks registered only a modest increase, up to 4.5 percent, in college completion. However, by 1970, more than one-tenth (11 percent) of all whites in this age cohort had attained four or more years of college education. By 1981, a significant growth in the college completion rates of blacks was noted. In that year, 8.2 percent of blacks, compared to 17.1 percent of whites age 25 and older had completed four or more years of college. It is evident that whites are more than twice as likely to have completed college than blacks.[93]

An examination of the 25–29 age cohort with respect to college completion shows a more favorable profile for black Americans. For instance, in 1960, slightly less than 1 in 20 (4.8 percent) of all blacks, compared to slightly more than 1 in 10 (11.1 percent) of all whites had attained this level of formal education. By 1981 black Americans had barely reached the proportion of persons within the population with four or more years of college registered by whites in 1960. In fact, 11.5 percent of blacks between the ages of 25 and 29, compared to 21.3 percent of whites, had achieved this level of educational attainment.[94]

By 1987, the Bureau of the Census reported that 10.7 percent of all blacks age 25 and over had completed four or more years of college. The 19.9 percent college completion rate for whites in this group almost doubled the rate registered for blacks. A similar pattern was observed among persons in the 25–29 age cohort. In that group, in 1987, 11.4 percent of the black population in contrast to 22 percent of whites in the same age group had completed four or more years of college.[95] The American Council on Education defines college completion as the attainment of a baccalaureate degree within six years. Its examination of the *High School and Beyond Study* showed that only 44.9 percent of all persons who entered college in 1980 had completed college by 1986. Only 25.6 percent of black college enrollees, compared to 48 percent of white college enrollees had completed the baccalaureate degree within the six-year time span. This study also showed that 71 percent of black high school graduates in 1980, 66 percent of Hispanics; 65 percent of Native Americans, 55 percent of whites, and 47 percent of Asians who entered college by 1982 had dropped out by 1986 without a college degree.[96] As shown in a number of studies[97] college persistence is tied to a plethora of factors ranging from financial needs, academic problems, to an undesirable school/college environment. Amelioration of college drop-out problems or efforts to increase persistence through college graduation must necessarily address those factors.

Quality and Equity

Many black Americans have become troubled by the potential for even more serious inequities regarding access to higher education due to the implementation of competency examinations and the higher admission requirements of some state systems. By 1983 competency examinations were required in approximately 37 states. Perhaps, the most highly publicized examination is that required of high school students in the state of Florida. In 1983, two-thirds of all high school seniors who failed the Florida Literacy Test were black; these students were awarded a "certificate of completion" and not their regular high school diplomas. Without high school diplomas, their lives are gravely affected. For instance, their chances for admission into college, the military, or for obtaining certain jobs were jeopardized. The legitimacy of the Florida test has been upheld by a Federal District Court judge in Tampa.[98]

Similarly, at least eight states in 1983 had initiated teacher competency examinations as a means of improving the quality of teachers. Again a disproportionate number of black teachers have been unsuccessful in attaining satisfactory scores on these examinations. All such competency examinations have raised serious and important questions about the quality of schooling received by a significant proportion of blacks, differential teacher expectations, and attention to the instructional needs of many minority students, the nature of learning environment in some public schools, and the academic preparation of potential teachers.

Several state systems, including those of California and Massachusetts, have raised entrance requirements for students seeking to enroll in public four-year colleges and universities. Not infrequently, a major emphasis is placed on higher cutoff points on SATs. Such requirements, like Rule 48 of the National Collegiate Athletic Association (NCAA), stimulated further debates over the appropriate use of standardized tests. Under this rule (which took effect in 1986 and was proposed over the objection of attending representatives of black colleges at the January 1983 meeting of the Association), freshmen eligibility requirements for participation in intercollegiate sports are to be raised to a minimum combined SAT score of 700 or a 15 on the test administered by the American College Testing Program (ACT), in addition to a 2-point high-school grade average (on a 4-point scale) and a minimum 2-point average in each of 11 college preparatory courses.

Opponents to such requirements insist that these changes are unfair and will be disadvantageous for many students from minority and low-income groups because, among other things, many of the courses required are not taught in some of these schools, and those that are taught are not taught very well. Not only is the question of poor schooling a tremendous obstacle, opponents also claim that standardized tests do not measure what students may accomplish through academic support services and increased motivation even when they are admitted with lower test scores. These students would be severely penalized by rigid adherence to such requirements. The Educational Testing Service and the College Board oppose the use of the SAT as an instrument of exclusion of students. They have insisted that all students, irrespective of race, can perform well on such tests if they are exposed to schooling of good quality.

Proponents of higher admissions standards claim that not only is there a need to improve the quality of students admitted to college, but that such advanced requirements may pressure elementary and secondary schools to do a far more effective job of preparing young people for college and the world of work. Some also insist that resistance to raised standards ignores the fact that thousands of black students perform extremely well on standardized tests, have excelled academically in college, and have demonstrated their abilities to compete with students of all races.

Regardless of the pros and cons of this debate, there is a continuing need to assure equal educational opportunity and pursue excellence in education. This dual goal may be accomplished through more effective cooperation among schools, colleges, and industry in the preparation of youngsters for academic life and entry into the job market.

A crucial observation is that the majority of black college students come from low-income homes. Approximately three-fifths of all black college students come from families whose annual incomes are lower than $18,000, and 40 percent come from families whose incomes are lower than $12,000 per year. Thus most black college students require financial aid in order to remain in school once they are admitted. This failure to supply needed financial assistance beyond the sophomore year accounts for a substantial portion of the high drop-out rate among black college students in predominantly white institutions. Obviously, other explanations also account for the high rate, such as: (1) lack of preparation for a rigorous college program, (2) failure of institutions to provide assistance for tutorial programs and supportive services once blacks are admitted, (3) failure of some students to take seriously the requirements of college, (4) lack of self-discipline for academic study, (5) the racial prejudice of white instructors who are bent upon exacting higher standards for black students than they require of white students, and (6) a new form of academic paternalism that permits high grades for less-than-adequate performance. But limited income probably takes the most heavy toll, since worry over how to pay tuition, room and board, and to purchase books interferes with the normal process of academic training.

BLACK STUDENTS IN WHITE COLLEGES

The problems just listed confront black students in general and are somewhat more acute for those blacks who are enrolled in predominantly white colleges. They are exacerbated by the belief that white institutions only mirror the prejudices and discrimination of the larger society. Many black students, for example, resent the prevailing tokenism in the recruitment of black students and black faculty in white institutions. They are still demanding a precise recruitment program that will result in a critical mass of black people at white institutions. Furthermore, in the late 1960s, a consistent complaint was the lack of sensitivity to and the incorporation of the black experience in the overall university milieu and in the curriculum of most American institutions. This feeling precipitated the black studies movement and led to the establishment of programs in black studies or Afro-American studies having mixed success in several hundred colleges—black and white—throughout the country. Some blacks also established Afro-American cultural centers and black living quarters. Black students are involved in day-to-day confrontations with faculty who allegedly grade them lower than whites and do not provide them with opportunities for make-up work on the same basis as for white students. By the same token, some black students feel victimized by those excessively liberal white faculty members who with a kind of paternalism wish to protect them from injustices.

Participation in communal activities at black cultural centers and Afro houses and in the affairs of the black community in which the white college is located occasionally relieve the inadequacy of social life. Dating poses other problems and anxieties. This is especially true for black females who often feel abandoned by black brothers for white females. The pain of rejection is all the more acute when the black male is or has been outspoken on black liberation and black power and vociferous in his claim that "black is beautiful." When black college women see these men walk arms locked with a white female, many conclude that these men are hypocrites who espouse only rhetoric. Black men who date across racial lines make the case that their personal lives must be separated from their ideological postures. The two are not necessarily coterminous.[99] Others rationalize interracial dating in economic terms, claiming that white women are freer with their money, that is, more willing to share it with them than black females. Still others secretly explain that they are only establishing linkages whereby white male racism can be managed through their association with white women.

Not all the dissatisfaction has come from poverty-stricken or low-income black students. Thomas Sowell, a black economist, charges that many white colleges have overlooked the needs of the black middle class in their rush to enroll "authentic ghetto types" and have failed to reward the former group of deserving students for high academic achievement by not granting them the fellowships, scholarships, and financial aid they need. In admission policies regarding the authentic ghetto type, he maintains that such institutions have given greater weight to factors such as political disposition, ideological stance, and the degree of social alienation rather than to evidence of strong academic achievement. He also claims that one of the direct consequences of rejecting black middle-class students is a reinforcement of old stereotypes about black inferiority and about the lower possibilities of educating black students, especially when poorly trained students who should never have been admitted at all fail.[100]

The black middle-class student, whether enrolled in a predominantly black college or a traditionally white institution, is sometimes caught in a dilemma—an identity crisis. This problem stems from a sense of estrangement, arising on the one hand from alienation to the experiences of the black ghetto and, on the other hand, from the desire to be authenticated as truly and unequivocably black. To be black for many of them is to engage in behavior that is contradictory to all they learned in middle-class socialization. They have been taught and trained to behave according to mainstream normative structures. To be black also means rejecting an internalized value system that is at variance with the value system alleged to be more representative and authentically black (e.g., rejection of a commitment to punctuality, time; rejection of the ethic of work that assumes an inherent goodness of hard work; rejection of study skills as acceptable routes for academic success). Occasionally, these values defy articulation by some advocates of blackness, except that they do not wish to become slaves to the white man's world and to the acquisition of material wealth as their parents have in many cases. But their parents wish to encourage black identity and racial pride and simultaneously persuade them to train themselves for competitive positions in a desegregated and highly individualized social structure. Other students see no inconsistency in their rejection of white values, their commitment to a black identity, and their preparation for work in either the mainstream or the black community. For them being a member of the black middle class poses no major problems, and many fully expect to share in the future leadership of the black community.

Clearly, all black students merely by virtue of their enrollment in a predominantly white university or college do not experience the types of problems described here. A significant number of students who entered college through Upward Bound programs as well as those who are of middle-class origins have successfully completed college and graduate or professional training. The roster of honor students among them increases year by year, and the number who have successfully integrated into the mainstream of college life is also on the upswing. This is evidenced by the numerous black student-body presidents; editors of yearbooks, reviews, and school papers; campus journalists; participants in student government; members of departmental clubs and other honor societies. Black athletes, too, are coming to realize their participation in college athletics involves a quid pro quo or a situation of exchange by which they contribute their athletic ability in return for a quality education usable when they leave college, and sometimes convertible into lucrative professional contracts.

Nevertheless, as studies by Walter Allen[101] and others[102] demonstrate, black students enrolled in predominantly white institutions often encounter excessive amounts of hostility. During the 1980s, black and other minority students encountered a brand of racism reminiscent of the bigotry experienced by black students who pioneered in college desegregation in the South during the 1950s and early 1960s. More than 250 colleges had incidents of campus racism documented in a two-year span during the last two years of the Reagan Administration. These incidents ranged from verbal abuse and the hurling of racial epithets or slurs to physical and sexual assaults against black students. This ethno-violence is attributed to such factors as the tone of indifference to racial justice as an American value that was set by former President Reagan and members of his cabinet; the hostility of former President Reagan to affirmative action and the tendency of many whites to project their failures on blacks and other minorities whom they claim to be a privileged group with respect to enrollment opportunities and selection for jobs; fear of contact with blacks and other minorities resulting from the socialization and internalization of negative stereotypes about these groups to an overall tolerance of bigotry and racial incidents as "isolated incidents" that did not result in the implementation of institutional policies designed to curb ethno-violence.[103] As the 1990s began, however, it was evident that on many college campuses, ranging from the University of Massachusetts/Amherst to the University of Michigan across the country to the University of California/Berkeley and Stanford University, corrective steps were in place to combat ethno-violence and establish some form of diversity program at predominantly white institutions.

GRADUATE AND PROFESSIONAL EDUCATION

Despite advances made during the 20-year period of 1960–1980 in the recruitment, enrollment, and graduation of blacks with doctorates and professional school degrees, there is an acute shortage of black professionals. In a study of enrollment and graduation trends of black students in graduate and professional schools during the decade of 1970–1980, Blackwell reported that the single most powerful predictor of success in these endeavors was the presence of black faculty. In other words, those institutions that have hired blacks in faculty positions are the same institutions that have done a better job of recruiting, enrolling, and graduating black students from professional schools. Yet, there is a critical shortage of black faculty; they constitute only 4 percent of all college and university faculty in the United States. In a field such as medicine, blacks represent a mere 1.8 percent of the total U.S. medical school faculty but 40 percent of those blacks are concentrated in the four historically black colleges of medicine: Howard University Medical School, Meharry Medical College, Charles Drew Medical Center, and Morehouse College School of Medicine. This shortage of black faculty underscores the importance of an aggressive Affirmative Action program for the recruitment and training of blacks for graduate and professional roles.[104]

One reason for that shortage of black faculty and other professionals is their underrepresentation in graduate and professional schools. In 1978, for instance, the 61,923 black students enrolled in all U.S. graduate schools represented a mere 6.2 percent of the total enrollment of 1.1 million graduate students. Whites comprised 88.9 percent; Hispanics, 2.5 percent; Asians, 2.1 percent; and American Indians, 0.4 percent. In 1980 the total enrollment of black students declined to 60,138 or 5.9 percent of total enrollment. By 1986, although the absolute number of black graduate students had increased, black representation among the total number of graduate students declined to 5 percent.[105]

Failure to recruit larger numbers of blacks for graduate studies is one of the explanatory factors that accounts for the rapid deterioration in the number of blacks who receive a doctoral degree each year. Between 1978 and 1988, blacks experienced a 14 percent decline in the number of them who received a doctoral degree. In 1988, black Americans received only 3.9 percent or 805 of the 22,789 doctoral degrees awarded American citizens. At no time between 1982 and 1988 did black Americans earn as many as 1,000 doctorates per year. The problem is especially acute among black males who in 1988 earned only 38 percent of the doctorates received by American blacks compared to the more than 60 percent of the total they received during the early 1970s.[106]

This failure of graduate schools to produce larger numbers of blacks with a Ph.D. or an Ed.D. degree means that fewer and fewer blacks are available for college and university teaching assignments. This shortage is one of the reasons why many prestigious organizations, such as the American Association for Higher Education and the American Association of University Professors, have thrown their weight behind the movement to increase the number of faculty from blacks and other minority groups.[107]

IMPACT OF REAGAN POLICIES ON BLACK EDUCATION

However, a gigantic effort must be mounted to undue the damage done by the Reagan Administration regarding reductions in federal monies to support graduate and professional education among blacks and other minority students. Cutbacks in funds for scholarships and loans had a seriously negative impact on black students who depended so heavily upon loans, compared to white students to support graduate/professional education. There is also evidence to show that black Americans are considerably less likely than are white and Asian students to be awarded teaching and research assistantships to support graduate studies. These factors, combined with a major assault against race-based economic disabilities and stronger recruitment programs mounted by institutions themselves, can help ameliorate the educational disparities at this level.[108]

NOTES

1. John Hope Franklin, *From Slavery to Freedom* (New York: Alfred A. Knopf, 1952), pp. 303–305.
2. Gunnar Myrdal, *An American Dilemma* (New York: Harper & Row, 1944), pp. 337–341.
3. *Report of the National Advisory Commission of Civil Disorders* (New York: Bantam Books, 1968), p. 434.
4. Robert R. Wheeler, "Public Schools, Public Policy, Public Problems: Some Observations and Suggestions," *Proceedings of the National Policy Conference on Education for Blacks* (Washington, D.C.: The Congressional Black Caucus, 1972), pp. 103–113.
5. Myrdal, *op. cit.,* p. 942.
6. The pattern of segregation in higher education had already been interrupted by virtue of a series of NAACP successes in gaining admission of black students into previously all-white graduate and professional schools in southern and border states.
7. *The Southern Manifesto* was a statement of defiance against the United States Supreme Court's 1954 school desegregation decision, signed by 19 senators and 77 representatives. It also was an effort to reinvoke the principle of states' rights in the field of education.
8. Charles F. Marden and Gladys Meyer, *Minorities in American Society,* 5th ed. (New York: D. Van Nostrand Co., 1978), p. 205.
9. Judith Cummings, "Non-Catholic Christian Schools Growing Fast," *The New York Times,* April 13, 1983, pp. 1, 23.
10. *Ibid.,* p. 22.
11. *Ibid.*
12. U. S. Commission on Civil Rights, *Twenty Years After Brown* (Washington, D. C.: U.S. Commission on Civil Rights, 1973), p. 49.
13. ———, *Desegregation of the Nation's Public Schools: A Status Report* (Washington, D. C.: U.S. Commission on Civil Rights, 1979), p. 1.
14. *Ibid.*
15. *Ibid.*
16. Cf. *Ibid.,* pp. 26–71 and Stuart Taylor, Jr., "Tax Exemption Ruling: An Old Question Still Lingers," *The New York Times,* June 14, 1983, p. B-16.
17. "Superwomen of Public Education," *Ebony* (June 1983): 88–92.
18. Reported in the *New York Times,* June 3, 1973, p. 26.

19. Among the scholars who have addressed this issue and reached similar conclusions are Kenneth B. Clark, *Dark Ghetto* (New York: Harper & Row, 1965), Chap. 6; Robert Rosenthal and Leonora Jacobsen, *Pygamalion in the Classroom: Teachers' Expectations and Pupils' Intellectual Development* (New York: Holt, Rinehart and Winston, 1968).

20. *New Orleans States Item,* August 31, 1972, p. 1.

21. *Ibid.*

22. *Desegregation of the Nation's Schools: A Status Report,* p. 28.

23. Data provided by Dr. Catherine A. Ellison, Sr. Implementation Officer; Boston Public Schools; March 6, 1990.

24. Cf. *op. cit.* and U. S. Commission on Civil Rights, *Teacher Layoffs, Seniority and Affirmative Action* (Washington, D. C.: U. S. Commission on Civil Rights, 1982).

25. *Ibid.*

26. Cf. Charles Whitaker, "The Disappearing Black Teacher," *Ebony* (January 1989):122–126; *Teacher Supply and Quality in the South: An Assessment of the State Role* (Atlanta: The Southern Education Foundation, 1989); Antoine Garibaldi, *The Revitalization of Teacher Education Programs at Historically Black Colleges: Four Case Studies* (Atlanta: The Southern Education Foundation, 1989); and David Rubin, "Shortage of *Minority* Teachers Is Reaching the Crisis Stage," *Boston Globe* (December 18, 1988), p. A22.

27. *Op. cit.,* passim.

28. Cf. "Study Finds Blacks Twice as Liable to School Penalties as Whites," *New York Times* (December 12, 1988), p. A16.; Muriel Cohen, "Study: U. S. Public Schools Suspend Blacks at Twice the Rate of Whites," *Boston Globe* (December 12, 1988), p. 56; and The National Coalition of Advocates for Students (Boston, December 1988).

29. *Ibid.*

30. *Ibid.*

31. *Ibid.*

32. *Ibid.*

33. Edgar Epps, "Impact of School Desegregation on Self-Evaluation and Achievement Orientation," *Law and Contemporary Problems* (1975): 300–313.

34. Bruce Hare, "Self-Perception and Academic Achievement Variations in a Desegregated Setting," *American Journal of Psychiatry,* 137 (1980): 683–689, and *The Rites of Passage: A Black Perspective* (New York: The National Urban League, 1982).

35. Cf. John McAdoo, "Father-Child Interaction Patterns and Self-Esteem in Black School Children," *Young Children,* 34 (1979): 46–53; Diane K. Lewis, "The Black Family: Socialization and Sex Roles," *Phylon* 36:3 (Fall 1975): 221–237; and R. D. Henderson, "Effects of Desegregation on Children," *The Urban Review* 13:5(1981): 201–227.

36. Epps, *op. cit.*

37. Hare, *op. cit.*

38. David E. Lavin, *The Predictions of Academic Performance* (New York: Russell Sage Foundation, 1965).

39. Hare, *op. cit.,* p. 14.

40. James W. Vander Zanden, *American Minority Relations* (New York: Ronald Press, 1966), pp. 9–10.

41. Kenneth B. Clark, "Desegregation: The Role of the Social Sciences," *Teachers' College Record,* 63 (1960): 16–171.

42. *Statistical Abstracts of the United States 1982–1983* (December 1983), p. 140.

43. *Statistical Abstracts of the United States 1989,* Table 201, p. 128.

44. The College Board, Press Release, April 6, 1983. Additional data provided by The College Board.

45. Cf. Charles V. Willie, *The Ivory and Ebony Towers: Race Relations in Higher Education* (Lexington, Mass.: D. C. Heath, 1981).

46. *Statistical Abstracts of the United States 1989,* Table 211, p. 130.

47. American Council on Education, *Minorities in Higher Education,* Seventh Annual Report (Washington, D. C.: American Council on Education, 1988), and Dennis Kelly, "Colleges Enroll Fewer Blacks and Hispanics," *USA Today* (January 15, 1990), p. D-1.

48. *Statistical Abstracts of the United States 1982–83,* p. 42.

49. Beverly P. Cole, "The Politics of Literacy," *Crisis* (May 1988): 8–9,20.

50. *Desegregation of the Nation's Schools: A Status Report,* p. 2.

51. James E. Blackwell and Philip Hart, *Cities, Suburbs and Blacks* (Bayside, N. Y.: General Hall, 1982), p. 202.

52. Blackwell and Hart, *op. cit.* pp. 2–4.

53. *Ibid.*

54. Linda Greenhouse, "High Court Bans Appeal on Busing by Nashville and Justice Department," *The New York Times,* January 25, 1983, p. 1.

55. Lee A. Daniels, "In Defense of Busing," *The New York Times Magazine,* April 17, 1983, pp. 34–98.

56. Cf. *Ibid* and U. S. Commission on Civil Rights, *Statement on Metropolitan School Desegregation* (Washington, D. C.: U. S. Commission on Civil Rights, 1977).

57. See Daniels, *op. cit.* p. 37.

58. Antoine M. Garabaldi, "The Effects of Desegregation: Is the Cup Half Empty or Half Full?" *The Urban Review* 13:4 (1981): 265–271.

59. Jeffrey M. Schneider, "Advantages of Desegregation to Whites: an Idea Seeking a Time—Next Time," *The Urban Review* 13:4 (1981): 261–263.

60. Margaret Terry Orr and Francis A. J. Ianni, "The Impact of Culture Contact and Desegregation on the Whites of an Urban High School," *The Urban Review* 13:4 (1981): 243–259.

61. George W. Norbit and Thomas W. Collins, "Cui Bono? White Students in a Desegregating High School," *The Urban Review* 13:4 (1981): 205–215.

62. Jacqueline Scherer and Edward Slawski, "Desegregation: Advantages to Whites," *The Urban Review* 13:4 (1981): 217–225.

63. James McPhartland and Jomills H. Braddock, "The Impact of Desegregation on Going to College and Getting a Good Job," in Willis D. Hawley (ed.), *Effective School Desegregation* (Beverly Hills, Calif.: Sage, 1981), pp. 141–154.

64. Gail Thomas, "Race and Sex Group Equity in Higher Education: Institutional and Major Field Enrollment Statuses," *American Educational Research Journal* 17:2 (1980): 171–181.

65. Jomils Braddock, Jr., "The Major Field Choices and Occupational Career Orientations of Black and White College Students," in Gail E. Thomas (ed.), *Black Students in Higher Education: Conditions Experiences in the 1970s* (Westport, Conn.: Greenwood Press), 1981), pp. 167–198.

66. Cf. Daniels, *op. cit.* and Gary Orfield, "School Desegregation and Housing

Policy: The Role of Local and Federal Governments in Neighborhood Segregation," *Integrated Education* 17 (May 1979): 48–53.

67. James S. Coleman, et al., *Equality of Educational Opportunity* (Washington, D. C.: U. S. Government, 1967).

68. James S. Coleman, et al., "Achievement and Segregation in Secondary Schools: A Further Look at Public and Private School Differences," *Sociology of Education* 55 (April/July 1982): 65–76, and James S. Coleman, *Power and the Structure of Society* (New York: Norton Publishing Co., 1974).

69. Reynolds Farley, "School Integration and White Flight," Unpublished Paper, Population Studies Center, The University of Michigan, Ann Arbor, 1975.

70. *Ibid.*

71. James Coleman, *op. cit.,* 1967.

72. Cf. Marden and Meyer, *op. cit.,* and Willie, *op. cit.*

73. Emmett H. Buell, Jr., "Busing and the Defended Neighborhood: South Boston, 1974–1977," *Urban Affairs Quarterly* 16 (1980): 161–168.

74. James E. Blackwell and Philip Hart, *Race Relations in Boston: Institutional Neglect; Turmoil and Change* (Boston: The Boston Committee, 1983).

75. Cf. Bert Useem, "The Boston Anti-Busing Movement," *American Sociological Review* 45 (1980): 355–369; Earl Smith, "Racism and the Boston School Crisis" *Black Scholar* 6 (1975): 37–41 and Laurie Dougherty, "Racism and Busing in Boston: Comments and Criticisms," *Radical America* 9 (1975): 65–92.

76. Diane Pearce, *Breaking Down Barriers: New Evidence on the Impact of Metropolitan School Desegregation on Housing Patterns* Washington, D. C.: Center for Policy Review, Catholic University School of Law, 1980).

77. Juliet Saltman, *Open Housing As A Social Movement* (Lexington, Mass.: D. C. Heath and Company, 1971).

78. Blackwell and Hart, *Cities, Suburbs and Blacks,* p. 202.

79. U. S. Commission on Civil Rights, *Desegregation of the Nation's Schools,* p. 72.

80. *Ibid.*

81. *Op. cit.,* p. 201.

82. Personal communication from Robert Dentler, February 16, 1990.

83. *Ibid.*

84. *Ibid.*

85. U. S. Commission on Civil Rights, *Discriminatory Religious Schools and Tax Exempt Status* (Washington, D. C.: U. S. Commission on Civil Rights, 1982), p.2.

86. *Ibid.*

87. Stuart Taylor, *op. cit.*

88. James E. Blackwell, *Mainstreaming Outsiders: The Production of Black Professionals,* 2nd ed. (Dix Hills, N. Y.: General Hall Publishing Co, 1987).

89. Fred E. Crossland, *Minority Access to College* (New York: Schoken Books, 1970).

90. National Center for Educational Statistics, *Bulletin* (September 1981), p. 1.

91. *Statistical Abstracts of the United States 1989,* p. 130.

92. American Council on Education, *op. cit.*

93. *Statistical Abstracts of the United States 1982–83,* p. 143.

94. *Ibid.*

95. *Statistical Abstracts of the United States 1989,* Table 211, p. 130.

96. American Council on Education, *op. cit.*

97. Blackwell, *op. cit.*

98. Fay S. Joyce, "Florida Literacy Test Snags Diplomas," *New York Times* (May 24, 1983), p. A-12.

99. Cf. Charles V. Willie and Arlene McCord, *Black Students at White Colleges* (Columbus, Ohio: Charles E. Merrill, 1970); Harry Edwards, *Black Students* (New York: The Free Press, 1970); Julia C. Elam (ed.), *Blacks on White Campuses* (Washington, D. C.: The National Association for Equal Opportunity in Higher Education, 1983); Walter R. Allen, "Black Student, White Campus: Structural, Interpersonal and Psychological Correlates of Success," *Journal of Negro Education,* 54 (2) (1985): 134–147; Walter R. Allen, "Race Consciousness and Collective Commitments Among Black Students on White Campuses," *Western Journal of Black Studies,* 8(3) (1984): 155–166.

100. Thomas Sowell, *Black Education: Myths and Tragedies* (New York: McKay Publishing Co., 1973).

101. Walter Allen, *op. cit.*

102. Blackwell, *op. cit.* and Gail Thomas (ed.), *U. S. Race Relations in the 1980s and 1990s: Challenges and Alternatives* (New York: Hemisphere Publishing Corporation, 1990).

103. James E. Blackwell, "Achieving Educational and Economic Equality in the Pursuit of Racial Harmony," Address Given at the Fourth Annual Joint Tulane-Xavier University Martin Luther King Week for Peace; Xavier University of Louisiana; January 16, 1990.

104. Blackwell, *op. cit.*

105. *Ibid.*

106. Delores H. Thurgood, Principal Investigator, *Summary Report 1988 Doctorate Recipients From United States Universities* (Washington, D. C.: National Academy Press, 1989).

107. The 1989 Annual Conference of the American Association of University Professors and the 1990 Annual Meeting of the American Association for Higher Education devoted major sections of their programs to this issue.

108. Blackwell, *Mainstreaming Outsiders, op. cit.*

Chapter
7

Housing: The Ghettoization of Blacks

*T*he issues of housing and residential segregation in the United States crystallize in microcosm the problems of segregation, discrimination, and injustice afflicting American life in general. Segregation in housing has far-reaching implications for behavior in a number of social institutions and daily behavior. It is reasonable to believe, for example, that school desegregation would be far more easily accomplished if housing were desegregated.[1] Historical evidence shows us, however, that this goal will continue to be difficult to attain. One of the most fundamental reasons for this difficulty is that housing patterns reflect the internal colonialism by which the powerful and privileged control the movements of the subordinate and less powerful. The reader is reminded that this concept is used to describe the control and manipulation of institutional life of a people by an external group.

INTERNAL COLONIALISM AND BLACK GHETTOIZATION

It can be argued that the present structure of housing patterns, which cordons off blacks from others in the larger community, is tantamount to an internal colony. Not only are blacks and whites physically separated from each other, but a white population that resides outside the territorial communities assigned to blacks owns, administers, and controls black resources, particularly land and property on which blacks reside, as well as many aspects of institutional life among the black population. Bankers and money lenders, mortgagers, captains of real estate, and the barons of federal and local governments own and control these properties. Housing has been the instrument for both separating the races physically and establishing the political supremacy of a dominant group. It both specifies and maintains racial territories as well as protects those boundaries deemed necessary for socioeconomic containment. Because the possession of housing is equated with the possession of power, there has been a persistent rapaciousness in acquiring it. The ownership of vast quantities of housing property has meant immense wealth, economic and political power, and social control.

One consequence is that through a historical process of migration and population shifts blacks became concentrated into identifiable geographical areas called ghettos. As we will see, ghettoization and domestic control by forces external to the black community occurred simultaneously through mutual facilitation. As noted previously, the majority of the black population were originally concentrated in rural areas of the South. Even though the races coexisted in close proximity to each other in the rural South immediately after emancipation, a pattern of racial separation followed on the heels of the decision rendered in the *Plessy* case. Territorial boundaries further separating the races, legitimating white control over land and related resources, soon followed. In general, whites controlled the land that blacks worked; few blacks ever achieved recognition as members of the landed aristocracy. White control over land and resources in the rural South placed limitations upon resource utilization by blacks and manipulated their movement from one area to another.

The subordinate status of blacks became even more apparent as they moved from isolated farms into urban communities because in the cities they were confined to specific geographical areas that even more sharply separated them from the white population. As blacks moved from farm to city and from southern city to northern urban communities, the emergent ecological pattern was one of increasing geographical concentration or racial clustering rather than dispersion. In most instances the teeming millions who moved from the South to the North between 1915 and 1970 ended up in the central zones of cities and have remained there. This situation contrasts with that of whites, who may have begun their urban experience in virtually the same geographical area but were able to redistribute themselves into the ever-widening periphery of the city and, finally, into resegregated suburban communities. This process of migration followed by concentration and aggressive confinement of blacks into more or less self-contained residential areas resulted in the establishment of black ghettos. The ghettos assumed a special ambience or character of their own. More important, for the moment, blacks did not have control over their ghettos, except in a most superficial way, although it may have appeared otherwise. The reason for this was because the land, buildings, and financial power were not in black hands to any appreciable degree. An almost invisible white power structure that sought to contain blacks by restricting their movement and limiting their access to scarce resources, on terms that they dictated, controlled the land, its use, and its dwellings. Exploitation undergirded by racism is thus a basic condition of containment in the ghetto. In Northern cities, as had happened in the South, blacks again found themselves ruled by an external group, the domestic colonizers.

Housing patterns assumed the characteristics of domestic colonialism: (1) when the white population realized that it could physically separate the blacks without violent resistance, and that this physical separation could form the essential elements of social boundaries between them; (2) when whites, as the dominant group, began to exploit their control over the housing market among blacks for their own financial and social purposes; (3) when they could deny access to better housing to those blacks who had sufficient income to purchase housing in white neighborhoods; (4) when whites established their control over the movement of blacks from one area to another; and (5) when they understood that they could translate their political dominance into administrative control over all other forms of institutional life among black people.

Although residential segregation supported boundaries already assumed to exist between the races, resulting invidious distinctions in the quality of housing had the added effect of establishing intragroup boundaries among blacks of different social classes or socioeconomic categories. As pointed out in Chapter 4, where one lives often defines how one is perceived by others and how one is viewed defines, in turn, social status in the community. Thus as whites vacated the "better areas" of the rising black ghetto, the more economically better-off and higher-status blacks invaded and succeeded them. This process accentuated differences among the various strata within the black social class system. Just as physical isolation of better-off whites was equivalent to social isolation of the white middle class from "poor white trash," a similar pattern of behavior emerged among blacks. The more economically and socially advantaged blacks anxiously established physical boundary lines between themselves and those considered beneath them in social status, and thereby restricted social contacts, except on their own terms. Thus Baldwin Hills of Los Angeles was socially distant from Watts; Shaker Heights in suburban Cleveland was spatially and socially separated from the Scoville-Central Avenue crowd; and the blacks in the far northwest of Washington, D.C., were far removed from those blacks residing in areas close to the Capitol. Although these boundaries are maintained and controlled by devices that originated in the external community, class conscious blacks often seek physical separation through housing as an instrument for reaffirming social distance between the haves and the have-nots. Thus housing discrimination provides further evidence of the interrelatedness of race and class in understanding the ramifications of both intragroup and intergroup behavior.

Although intragroup social boundary systems are of special interest in a study of the black community, the impact of racial separation through housing segregation has a far greater effect on the day-to-day life experiences of black people. Segregation in housing and the impregnable boundaries established through this process victimize blacks in education, in occupations and access to their jobs, in hospitals and medical facilities, and in other necessities of social life. The majority are forced to live under debilitating conditions within a social environment that, as persons outside the community observe, confirms stereotypes and negative perceptions attributed to the black population as a whole.

Nowhere is the housing crisis among blacks in the 1990s more evident than in the quality of housing offered to the black population. We should recall that the vision of the good life in America is supposed to be intertwined with the ownership of single-family homes. This view is considered a normal expectation, if not a God-given right of all Americans, irrespective of race, color or creed. An extension of it is the assumption that the single-family home or whatever housing the family has should be in a "decent" neighborhood. Although standards of decency vary from region to region and from class to class, an acceptable dwelling has certain attributes in common: (1) good physical condition, that is, the dwelling is not dilapidated; (2) the presence of hot running water and a private bath; and (3) adequate space, that is, there is no overcrowding.[2] A dwelling that does not meet these minimal conditions becomes suspect. Moreover, the dwelling should be in a neighborhood of adequately well-maintained housing that is relatively clean and free of litter.

HOME OWNERSHIP

According to the latest available census data, slightly more than two-fifths (42.8 percent) of all black Americans own their own homes in contrast to two-thirds (66.8 percent) of all white Americans. In 1980, 44.2 percent of blacks, compared to 67.8 percent of all white families, owned their homes. Thus while home ownership for white families, however slight, increased to its current level, it has dipped among black families. Largely because of the economic disparities between black and white family income, discrimination in the housing market, and the unavailability of affordable housing, blacks are considerably more likely than whites to be renters.

Regionally, a far greater proportion of southern blacks (47 percent) own their homes than blacks in any other part of the nation. Because of benign racism and ingrained self-sufficiency, the Northeast, which traditionally has enjoyed the reputation of liberalism, lags behind all other sections in black home ownership (29 percent). The West (40 percent) and the North-Central states (42 percent) approximate the national average of black home ownership. This description suggests that we need to know more about the quality of the houses owned by blacks and about the people who rent either privately owned apartments or public housing of one form or another, many of whom are at the mercy of rapacious landlords.

The relationship among employment, income, and housing is obvious in the disparities of home ownership among various segments of urban communities. In the central city where the unemployment rate and poverty level are the highest, and land space is limited, proportionately fewer people own their own homes and significantly more persons rent. In contrast, in areas outside the central cities, where not only more people are employed but also at higher salaries and in more prestigious occupations, home ownership is considerably more widespread and fewer people rent. Thus about one-third of all central-city blacks live in self-owned dwellings, whereas more than half of black suburbanites, or those living outside the central cities, own their homes. By contrast, almost two-thirds of central-city whites and approximately three-fourths of the white suburbanites own their homes. Disparities between the two groups in home ownership are inextricably intertwined with both race and economic conditions. If the black poor are unable to find suitable employment and compelled to work at poverty-level wages, they are neither likely to save sufficient money to pay for single-family dwellings nor to rent in the more desirable areas. In effect, the black poor are condemned to either substandard housing or to public housing, which in many cities is the epitome of economic and social degradation.

Plumbing

Owning a house does not necessarily mean that housing is adequate any more than renting means that the dwelling is automatically undesirable. In 1980 blacks occupied less than 10 percent of all occupied housing in the United States although they constituted almost 12 percent of the total population of the country. These black-occupied housing units constituted more than a quarter (27.6 percent) of all housing units in the United States having incomplete or substandard plumbing. This situation was a slight deterioration from the plumbing conditions existing a decade earlier. Then, as now, a disproportionately large number of black people were living in dwellings devoid of the basic plumbing facilities normally expected of American families irrespective of race or ethnicity, that is, a bathtub solely for occupants' use and a toilet that is functional (flushes). More than a million housing units occupied by blacks had plumbing inadequacies in 1980. Moreover, the higher the income, the more likely are persons to live in units in which the plumbing is complete. Similarly, housing units of greater financial values are more likely to contain complete plumbing units than houses of relatively low value.

Overcrowding

This is another characteristic of black-occupied housing units. According to Department of Health and Human Services standards, a unit is overcrowded when more than one person occupies a single room. By this measure approximately one-fifth of all black housing units are over-crowded in comparison to 7 percent of white housing units. Excessive crowding is particularly characteristic of rented dwellings, which contain sometimes double the number of persons per room than in owner-occupied dwellings. The stress on one person per room as the measure of overcrowding may somewhat obscure the problem, however, for it is a statistical average or a mean that in no way communicates the severe conditions of room density experienced by some poor black families in both rural and urban areas. It gives no indication, for instance, of the hundreds of thousands of families living in dwellings with three or more persons sleeping in one room.

Physical Conditions

The conditions of housing for the black population vary with socioeconomic class or more specifically with the amount of income. Fully two-thirds of all urban blacks are restricted to housing that does not meet required federal standards. The middle and upper classes have managed to overcome some limitations imposed by discrimination and racial isolation. Therefore, they are in a more favorable financial position for locating high-quality housing. If by chance they are behind the barriers of the ghetto wall, they live in the best housing available within the segregated black community. If they have managed to move into desegregated neighborhoods, their housing is equal to if not superior to that of their white neighbors, but they have been required, in all probability, to pay more for what they obtained than a white person would have had to pay for the same quality of housing.

By contrast, blacks at the lower end of the income and socioeconomic structure are not so fortunate. Houses range downward from a modest condition to a dilapidated one that defies belief—the last are usually houses worn by years of poor maintenance and progressive deterioration. The exteriors of these dwellings are commonly in a state of disrepair or in need of paint; roofing and windows beg replacement; siding, steps, and parts of front porches are often missing; the interiors violate most existing health and sanitation codes; peeling plaster, holes in ceilings, and broken floors may serve as points of entry for rats with voracious appetites, which, if unsatisfied, attack the human occupants of such dwellings. If plumbing is present, it may or may not be functioning properly. Sewage often backs up and overflows sometimes into the kitchen sink. Unscrupulous and rapacious landlords refuse to make necessary repairs because they feel repair costs will necessarily inflate rents in an already overpriced dwelling; they also realize that given the continuing pressure for housing generated by increasing immigration to the city, a seriously dilapidated unit will not remain vacant too long. Poverty-stricken home owners may not have sufficient money to pay for basic repairs, so many families attempt to repair facilities themselves or use the services of friends whenever possible. Of course, immense variations characterize the black community, so much so that even on a single street it is possible to move from the extreme of dilapidation to dwellings of superior quality.

Public Housing

The conditions under which blacks are forced to live, especially those at the lower echelons of the socioeconomic spectrum, are far worse in public housing. Fifty-two percent of public housing occupants in the United States are the poorer segments of the black population. This national average may be somewhat misleading, though, since in some cities the proportion of public housing occupied by blacks is considerably larger and approaches 100 percent. In others the proportion may be substantially less. Over the years, in contrast with its beginnings, public housing has become identified with the black poor. Whether black or white, standards and conditions are so far below the norm as to invite serious attention. But the conditions, across the country and city by city, are worse when these dwellings are occupied by blacks. A few illustrations may help to explicate the point.

Perhaps the classical case of public housing deprivation was the Pruitt-Igoe public housing development in St. Louis. Built more than three decades ago and winner of an architectural design award in 1958, the project deteriorated so rapidly and uncontrollably that a decision was made to destroy it entirely in 1973. This "monster," as it came to be known, consisted of about 33 buildings of 11 stories containing 2,567 units. At first the project was racially integrated. Poverty-stricken blacks, who moved up from the South, without jobs and with limited incomes, were finally forced onto public welfare and moved to Pruitt-Igoe. Simultaneously, whites steadily moved out. As this change was occurring, maintenance suffered, administration worsened, and security all but vanished. In time, Pruitt-Igoe became a symbol of public housing failure rife with crime, drug abuse, deviant behavior, physical attacks, sexual assaults in hallways, elevators and on project grounds, broken windows, serious plumbing and water problems, excrement in elevators, and a sense of fear, disaffection, and rejection by its inhabitants. Because of these and similar conditions in other public housing, a stigma became attached to public housing residents. This stigma is so powerful that once a person is identified as a project occupant he or she may very well be perceived as a drug user, a dope pusher, a rapist, an unwed mother on welfare, a good-for-nothing derelict, or a social and economic parasite.

The conditions of Pruitt-Igoe were not peculiar to that project alone. They are repeated again and again all across the country. They exist at the 1,206-unit Stella Wright Project in Newark, New Jersey, at the 3,600 unit Cabrini Green project in Chicago, and at several projects housing literally thousands of blacks and Puerto Ricans in New York City. Similar situations exist in Oakland, Cleveland, Atlanta, New Orleans, and Detroit. Too many people regard projects as urban jungles and concrete ghettos, and whether they are occupied by blacks or whites, the negative perceptions persist. However, the racist structure of the American society guarantees far more attention, better maintenance and repair systems, better security, more frequent garbage pickups, and improved conditions or facilities in public housing when a significant proportion of the occupants are white. Similarly, more systematic care is provided for the upkeep of any community where whites are in the majority in contrast to the types and range of services provided to predominantly minority, especially black and poor, areas. But the human tragedy perpetrated by these distinctions, invidious as they are, lies more poignantly in the distortions of the spirit and self-concept among people who devalue themselves because they have internalized demeaning negative perceptions projected upon them by others.

Facilities

Not only the types of dwellings people occupy but also the range of facilities contained in them reflect income inequities. Thus if the median income of blacks is nationally less than three-fifths that of the white population, then blacks would not likely have sufficient funds to match whites in their ability to purchase consumable goods and amenities. Almost three-quarters of all white American households contain a clothes washer and dryer. But only one-eighth of black households contain a clothes dryer and slightly more than one-half (51 percent) have any type of washing machine available. More than twice the number of white households possess some form of air conditioning, and four times as many of them contain central air conditioning systems.

The greater capacity of whites to purchase amenities extends further to their ability to own two or more houses—about 2 million Americans, most of them white, own a second home. This occurs at a time when one-sixth of the American population, disproportionately black, do not have decent houses to live in.[3]

TERRITORIALITY AND SENSE OF COMMUNITY

Despite the negative dimensions of racial isolation and the impediments of segregation and discrimination, blacks living among themselves have reaped a positive benefit—the development of a sense of community. Territorial confinement required adjustments and institutional arrangements to meet human needs. It also highlighted a need for mutual support and the sharing of limited resources as a means of survival. It fostered constructions of institutional arrangements for expressive and instrumental needs; it facilitated social participation, which in turn hastened intracommunity incorporation as well as a sense of corporate identity; it helped establish mechanisms for social control to assure general conformity to community expectations; and it created a segregated community that produced its own leadership structure with specific missions—the creation of ingroup solidarity or group cohesion, and the preparation of the black population to meet the requirements demanded by the larger society in order to gain equal access to shared values.

RESIDENTIAL MOBILITY

Thousands of black people change their place of residence one or more times during the course of the year. (See Chapter 1 for a discussion of push and pull factors.) Blacks in rural areas rarely move from one rural area to another. They are, however, frequently disposed toward abandoning the farm for the city. The most frequently observed pattern, until recently, showed rural southern blacks moving from the nearest southern city of some size, which was then used as a way-station prior to the final move away from the South altogether for points to the North and West. As shown in Chapter 1, the movement of blacks out of the South stabilized during the 1970s. As a result, 53 percent of all black Americans reside in the South. This return of larger and larger numbers of blacks to the South, in contrast to their steady outmigration up to 1970, can be attributed to a more positive racial climate in the South as well as to increasing job opportunities. In many ways, several northern communities seem as hostile to blacks as did the white South during the pre-1970 period. The movement of blacks to the South may also indicate a search for a better quality of housing, even though that region has far more substandard housing, much occupied by blacks. On the whole, the cost of housing is cheaper in the South than in other parts of the nation. In general, property taxes are also lower, even in many of the largest cities of the South.

INTRAURBAN PATTERNS

A study of blacks in Atlanta, Boston, Cleveland, Houston, and Los Angeles, conducted by Blackwell and Hart between 1978 and 1981, addressed, *inter alia,* their residential patterns. They reported that only 3.2 percent of the study participants had lived in their respective cities for less than one year. About 6 of every 10 (59.2 percent) had lived in their present cities for more than 16 years; 13.5 percent from 11 to 15 years; 13.8 percent from 6 to 10 years, and 19.4 percent had resided in the same city between one and five years.[4] Their findings also showed a considerable amount of "intracity stability." About 53 percent of the respondents had lived at the same address for five years or longer; however, 47 percent had moved within the year.[5]

Although the number of suburban blacks increased by more than one-third (34 percent) in the period between 1970 and 1977, for instance, blacks also participated in the "gentrification" movement. This term refers to a "back-to-the-city movement of the middle class." It appears that the majority of blacks involved in both suburbanization and gentrification are of a higher income and socioeconomic status than those blacks who remain in the cities.[6] Participants in suburbanization are in search of commodious housing of a high quality in close proximity to quality elementary and secondary schools, land space, and status symbols. On the other hand, participants in gentrification are likely to be comparatively younger persons who seek more immediate access to city services, perhaps to their jobs, and to the social and cultural life of the city without being encumbered with huge transportation costs. They often obtain abandoned housing at relatively low costs, restore these dwellings, and convert them to impeccable conditions. By contrast, poorer people who move within the city are often forced to move because of the destruction of their dwellings, eviction, or the takeover of their property through eminent domain.[7]

Although the absolute number of blacks who moved to suburbia increased dramatically during the 1970s, the physical integration of blacks did not mean that they were socially integrated in suburban communities. Thus residentially mobile blacks who move into predominantly white areas may or may not experience positive interaction with whites. In fact, they may not have any social interaction at all and may be residentially segregated in white communities. Racial considerations aside, most city dwellers see no "imperative obligation" to be sociable with one another. As a rule, they associate with persons either because they like each other or because there is some perceived mutual benefit derived from the association. Thus neighborliness in an urban context takes on a decidedly different meaning than in a small town or rural community where neighborhood friendship usually is so highly valued.

Advocates of contact theory in race relations assume that physical integration will eventually lead to social integration and, subsequently, to a reduction of prejudice. Whether or not housing integration per se substantiates this theory may be questionable. Reduction in prejudice may be a function of a number of important variables, some of which may be interconnected, including predispositions people bring to the newly integrated setting, the nature of the interaction (e.g., whether it is highly competitive or equal status involving some degree of cooperation to attain certain goals), and sustained social interaction through "within home" activities. As mentioned in Chapter 1, the Blackwell and Hart study showed that while blacks are likely to invite whites into their homes, whites do not tend to reciprocate and, if they do, it is only on a very superficial level. Further, many suburban blacks do not interact with each other and feel compelled to return to the city for most aspects of social life.[8] It may be ironic that, frequently, the most often "hand of welcome" is extended by white suburbanites than by black suburbanites to new black immigrants to suburbia.

Nevertheless, housing segregation continues to be a most serious problem throughout the United States. Using an index of segregation, based upon the number of blacks and nonblacks within a given block who would have to be moved to accomplish integration, several researchers have demonstrated the magnitude of the problem. For instance, Taeuber's 1983 study of 28 cities with the largest black population revealed that Chicago, Cleveland, and St. Louis are the most racially segregated cities in the United States. In each of these cities, with a segregation index above 90, more than 9 of every 10 blacks would have to be moved to reach an ideal segregation index. Of the 28 cities studied, the least amount of housing segregation was found in Oakland, Gary, and Detroit. Even at that, his data showed that more than one-half of all blacks in Oakland, for instance, would have to relocate to another area to achieve an acceptable level of housing integration.[9]

Farley's studies of attitudes and housing segregation showed that whites, much more so than blacks, do not want to live in desegregated housing. He found that only 12 percent of the blacks studied desired housing only in an all-black neighborhood; however, 85 percent preferred integrated housing. Farley's research also revealed that 27 percent of all whites studied would reject a neighborhood with even one black in it; 50 percent would reject a neighborhood containing about 20 percent of blacks, and 73 percent of the whites studied would not prefer a neighborhood that was two-thirds black. Further, about 41 percent of the whites studied said that they would move out if the neighborhood reached a black population of two-thirds.[10] Farley's research suggests that blacks are more likely to be hospitable and welcome whites as neighbors while whites are more likely to resent and disapprove of housing integration in the neighborhoods in which they live. However, there is some evidence which suggests that the higher the degree of cosmopolitanism among white neighbors the more tolerant they appear to be concerning social integration with blacks.[11] Cosmopolitanism is a multivariate concept, including such dimensions as high culture or aesthetic appreciation, liberal political beliefs, and a more universalistic perception of life—thinking is not constrained by community context.

TECHNIQUES OF HOUSING DISCRIMINATION

Discrimination in housing is a major social problem. It is deeply ingrained in American life and exacerbates already strained relations between the races. And it is the most basic manifestation of racial apartheid in the United States. Over time several techniques of discrimination that effectively barred blacks from having access to decent housing were institutionalized. These techniques will be discussed next.

Government Policy

Historically, the federal government has been the major perpetrator of housing discrimination. The historical antecedents for present-day conditions and inequities can be found in policy mandates promulgated by federal and local agencies, as well as in a policy of calculated inaction or "benign neglect." It should be noted that restrictive covenants, which will be discussed in greater detail shortly, preceded the Federal Housing Administration (FHA) by several years. But the government set the original standards that began and fostered residential segregation that effectively prevented blacks from having equal access with whites to decent housing. How did this situation become so pervasive in American communities? Beginning in the early 1930s, when this nation was deeply entrenched in a dehumanizing economic depression, the federal government embarked on a housing program designed to bring relief and improve the quality of housing mainly for white Americans. It embarked on a program predicated on the assumption that Americans had the right to own single-family dwellings. This was the theme that emerged from the President's Conference on Homebuilding and Home Ownership in 1932, which in turn, led to federal intervention in financing single-family homes by a number of new methods, among them: (1) the amortization of long-range mortgages, (2) provisions for federal insurances of home mortgages, and (3) assistance in securing housing credit needed over a relatively long period of time.[12]

The federal program led to the establishment of specific agencies that further stimulated the development of private dwellings, particularly for white Americans. Foremost among the agencies created during the New Deal period were: (1) the FHA, established as a requirement of the National Housing Act of 1934; (2) the Federal Home Loan Bank System, established in 1932; (3) the Home Owner's Loan Corporation; and (4) the Federal Farm Mortgage Corporation. The policies of the FHA were discriminatory from its inception. Beginning in 1935, for example, its handbooks dissuaded residential integration by discouraging the granting of mortgages for houses that were not in racially separate areas of the community. The FHA had redlined many neighborhoods, separating black and white residential areas from each other for the purpose of determining eligibility for FHA home mortgages. Banks, insurance companies, and private lenders were willing accomplices in the process of redlining and segregating residential areas, basing their refusal to invest in home mortgages for blacks on articulated FHA policies.[13] The policies of federal agencies not only perpetuated housing segregation with federal approbation but also encouraged the state and local levels to engage in practices that proved to be substantially more blatant and divisive. Thus the state and local agencies implemented legal restraints that, among other things, established residential zoning as a legitimate technique for maintaining and enforcing racial separation. Some enforced block-by-block segregation, while others vehemently and aggressively implemented restrictive covenants. The all-white National Association of Real Estate Boards, which throughout most of its 80 years of existence has barred black people, enthusiastically endorsed this approach.

The FHA policies during the 1930s and the 1940s did not completely satisfy its administrators, who seemed bent on creating and institutionalizing differences in the quality of housing for blacks and whites. Following the promulgation of the United States Housing Act of 1937, for example, the construction of public housing was to serve as a major instrument for combating the last stages of a lingering economic depression. Initially, housing units that were constructed housed the white population for the most part and admitted relatively few blacks. Public housing was, therefore, originally addressed to the needs of poor whites, but today it is assumed that public housing is mainly to house poor blacks. In some cities, as was previously stated, this is quite true.

There are approximately 1.2 million dwelling units located in 2,700 communities that form the core of the federal low-income public housing program. These units house approximately 3.4 million people. Of the 1.2 dwelling units, 59 percent are family-occupied and 41 percent are occupied by elderly persons. Almost two-thirds (63 percent) are occupied by minorities and 37 percent are whites. In 1952, the proportion of whites and minorities was reversed—a fact that accentuates the current identification of public housing with blacks and other minorities. Although blacks compose 52 percent of all low-income public housing units in the nation, they represent 66 percent of units occupied by the nonelderly population. As a result of housing authority practices with respect to the assignment of persons to public housing, racial segregation in them has solidified. In essence, few units are racially integrated. The majority are either all-white, all-black or overwhelmingly of one race or the other.[14]

Since the federal government has only constructed a little more than a million federally subsidized public housing units since 1937, and given the pressures for housing created by displacements and reduced purchasing power of the low income, the shortage of affordable housing continues to be critical. By contrast, in 1981 alone, the FHA support for middle- and upper-income family, largely white, housing was in excess of $5.4 billion.

Immediately after the end of World War II, even when the official policy of refusing to finance unsegregated housing was abrogated in 1949, the FHA continued to give preference to the financing of single-family dwellings in the growing white suburban ring. Not only did the FHA turn a deaf ear on housing for people whose earnings were below national median family incomes and for the elderly poor, but it did little to facilitate the construction of public houses for such groups. Even more amazingly, it encouraged the white exodus from the inner cities to the suburbs. One consequence of this is that not even 2 percent of all housing starts are in the area of public housing.

The policies of the various federal agencies helped to systematize many damaging stereotypes concerning the incorporation of the black population into residential neighborhoods, and to institutionalize all forms of racial segregation in housing. Myths were used to rationalize housing discrimination, and for a significant number of white homeowners and black middle-class social climbers, the myths assumed an aura of reality. One of these more widely held beliefs is that property value automatically depreciates once blacks move into a neighborhood. A series of sound and thoroughly systematic studies, beginning with the classical works of Luigi Laurenti[15] has failed to verify this assumption. Again, blacks who desegregate a white neighborhood are in the main economically much better off than their new white neighbors. They are not the equivalents of the European white ethnic immigrant family who buys a home. In the latter case, all members of the household—husband, wife, and children—participate to make the purchase of the new house a cooperative venture. In the case of blacks the purchasing of a house as well as its maintenance are a collaborative effort of only the husband and wife at best.

It is often assumed, particularly in the inner city, that black movement into a given dwelling is followed by housing deterioration. But this argument fails to take into consideration the already seriously deteriorating conditions of these dwellings when blacks inherited them from the white middle and working classes. Often, to make them salable these houses have been given cosmetic treatments that hide their basic dilapidation until the sale is completed. Thus the filtering process by which the more economically advantaged groups vacate homes in one area as they obtain newer ones in other areas does not necessarily mean that blacks obtain houses of substantially high quality. When people who have limited incomes for repair and maintenance purchase houses in filtered areas, the process of deterioration already begun will proceed, like a kind of self-fulfilling prophecy, to its predictable end.

The federal government further perpetuates housing discrimination by its failure to enforce fair housing legislation as well as in inequality of access to federally sponsored programs. In 1978 the Office of Voluntary Compliance of the Department of Housing and Urban Development (HUD) negotiated a "voluntary affirmative marketing agreement with the National Association of Realtors (NAR)."[16] The expressed purpose of this agreement was to facilitate fair housing in everyday practice. Although 439 local boards and 23 state associations signed the agreement that year, subsequent assessments of their performance show that these agencies do not follow HUD's fair housing regulations. For example, a study by the National Committee Against Discrimination in Housing (NCADH) showed that the majority of the implementation plans studied had "no declarations against redlining," had inadequate strategies for minority occupancy goals, did not provide for monitoring of their housing program by HUD, and had no adequate record keeping method for determining sales and rentals by race.[17] In effect, the voluntary agreements were relatively meaningless and HUD did not provide sufficient staff to mount an effective monitoring program of its own.

In addition, an analysis of the direct loan program operated by the Veterans Administration, conducted by the U. S. Commission on Civil Rights, showed immense discrepancies in the treatment of minorities and the white population. The Commission's findings revealed that blacks and other minorities constitute only 3.9 percent of all Veterans Administration (VA) borrowers, although 5.6 percent of all eligible persons for direct loans are minorities. When minorities are successful in obtaining loans, they are awarded smaller sums than whites. Further, minorities are invariably given a shorter period of time to repay the loans than white borrowers. This discrepancy is not a question of the inability of blacks and other minorities to meet the standard of eligibility. Quite the opposite, minority borrowers tend to have higher incomes and assets than whites which should assure eligibility. Yet whites receive 96.1 percent of all direct loans for housing through the VA while blacks receive 1.8 percent and Hispanics, 1 percent.[18] Again, as in all agencies that have a responsibility of enforcing laws and statutes governing housing, lack of enforcement is a major impediment to the actualization of fair housing.

The Real Estate System

The chicanery of the real estate institution has also prevented blacks from attaining equal access to decent housing. On a more formal level, real estate boards, which are controlled by whites, followed a code of segregation and racial separation during the 1930s, 1940s, and 1950s. There were no black realtors, or at least they were not in sufficient numbers, until the end of World War II. Even then, they were not members of the National Association of Real Estate Boards, which controlled and monopolized the housing market. Because of this few blacks were approved for showing and selling houses to black people; those who were approved could not use the registered term *realtor*, which was reserved for white entrepreneurs in real estate. Blacks then coined their own term to describe their activities in real estate, and black realtors became known as "realtists" when they formed the National Association of Real Estate Brokers in 1947.[19] Meanwhile, white realtors either refused to show houses to potential black buyers, or claimed that the house had just been purchased, or when finally forced to show a house to black buyers, would often inflate its price beyond the reach of the buyer, or they would handle the transaction in such a manner as to insult the intelligence of the buyer. These practices all too frequently forced blacks to withdraw from seeking housing in "all-white areas" and to make a painful retreat to the ghetto.

Not infrequently, real estate associations and some firms were in collusion with neighborhood associations, banks, mortgage firms, and lending agencies. Neighborhood associations entered into agreements with some real estate agencies guaranteeing them the prerogative of approving a potential buyer in their neighborhood before completing the final agreement to purchase. Some of these associations went so far as to assign a ranking system by which points were awarded potential buyers on the basis of color, education, income, occupation, and general desirability. These agreements effectively excluded blacks as well as other ethnic minorities considered "undesirables." Moreover, having been told that blacks were not acceptable to the members of the neighborhood association or, primarily, its leadership structure, blacks would occasionally be gently dissuaded from pursuing the issue any further on the pretext that "they would not be happy in such an incompatible area." Banks and mortgage and lending agencies refused to grant mortgages or to provide financial assistance needed to complete the deal if, indeed, blacks had managed to get that far in the transaction. Occasionally, they rationalized their refusals with claims of potential loss of white business—whites threatened to take their business elsewhere if blacks were permitted to obtain mortgages and to purchase houses. Appraisals were distorted, values inflated, and blacks were declared ineligible for loans.

Real estate agents also drew upon other discriminatory techniques designed to dissuade blacks from a course of residential desegregation or from the pursuit of adequate housing. Thus blacks were steered away from housing units situated in predominately white areas to areas that were largely black or already physically integrated. This was often done on the pretext of group compatibility. Others used the common practice of *block-busting*, which generated panic selling by white residents. Unscrupulous realtors would suggest to white homeowners that, following the entry of sometimes a single black family into one block, the entire block would be "going black." Fueled with the fears and myths of property depreciation, whites were admonished to "sell now" or later suffer a greater financial loss. Many chose to sell and often at low costs. Block by block, this process systematically accomplished white removal and replacement by blacks who purchased these houses at hugely inflated prices. Realtors thereby reaped excessive profits from expanding the black ghetto and driving a wedge between the races.

Zoning Laws

When these techniques failed in their effectiveness, and sometimes they were unsuccessful deterrents, state and local officials resorted to zoning for exclusionary purposes. Historically, zoning is an antecedent practice to a number of techniques presently in use to oppose neighborhood desegregation. It first came to the attention of the United States Supreme Court in the case of *Buchanan* v. *Worley* (1917). Louisville, Kentucky, had a statute that forbade incursion of members of one race into an area chiefly occupied by members of another race. The Supreme Court rejected this statute. Then, in 1927, New Orleans (in *Harmon* v. *Tyler*) attempted to exclude members of one race from an area chiefly occupied by members of another race without obtaining the latter's consent. In 1930 zoning was again tested in the case of the *City of Richmond* v. *Deans* because it had been used as a means of supporting the ban against interracial marriages. Under this mandate, a person could not buy in an area where the majority of the residents were persons he could not legally marry.[20] In both the *Harmon* and *Richmond* cases the U.S. Supreme Court reaffirmed and extended its decision reached in the *Buchanan* case.

Today, zoning laws are much subtler than those laws enacted prior to the advent of World War II. Zoning advocates attempt to circumvent racial considerations in their construction. But it is generally conceded that exclusions by race are the basic underpinnings of many zoning statutes or regulations regardless of how subtly they are hidden. Equally fundamental is the use of zoning ordinances in the basic struggle of control over land and its use. Zoning may be used for both exclusionary purposes and to determine how land may be best used for maximum benefit of the community. But when housing is the issue, zoning is used exclusively to restrict entry of certain groups of people into a community and to determine where they shall be contained. Some zoning ordinances impose restrictions on lot size, as in East Haddam, Connecticut, which in 1967 implemented a proposal establishing minimum lot sizes of one or two acres of land. In the prestigious North Plains area the minimum lot size was set at four acres. The United States Supreme Court, in 1964, had already ruled that the efforts of Sharon, Massachusetts, to rezone residential areas into four-acre lots were unconstitutional. Others establish acceptable footage requirements for new buildings and rigidly apply them to blacks but relax them for whites who wish to construct in the same area; or they bar apartments, public housing, multifamily dwellings, and cooperatives. Some set aside land for industrial use so as to restrict the amount of residential land that might be available for housing unwelcomed people. Similarly, municipalities have condemned land after learning that blacks would soon be occupying those areas.[21] The net effect of zoning regulations has been to continue denying blacks an opportunity to move into suburbia and, therefore, to confine them to restricted residential areas within the city boundaries.

Restrictive Covenants

At the same time that zoning laws were becoming institutionalized, another devious method of racial exclusion was applied to prevent residential desegregation. These were called "restrictive covenants," which are agreements in the purchase contract that a given piece of property will not be sold to certain categories of people. These contracts were to exist from 50 years to perpetuity and barred sale to such groups as blacks, Jews, Arabs, Armenians, Italians, Koreans, Asian-Americans, American Indians, Spanish-speaking Americans, Greeks, and others. Clearly, their intent was to exclude swarthy-complexioned Americans and, more forcefully, in some areas to extirpate blacks from certain residential areas. Many white Americans who shared similar sentiments knowingly and willingly endorsed this practice by including such clauses in their property contracts. In 1948, however, in the case of *Shelly* v. *Kraemer,* the U.S. Supreme Court stated that restrictive covenants were unenforceable. Subsequently, the so-called Van Sweringen covenant arose, which forbids the sale of property without consent of its original owner. Other variations of this covenant prevent the sale of property without consent of club members where neighborhood recreational facilities are involved, or the occupant may be expected to lease the land for 99 years without the possibility of transferring the property to another party.[22] When some real estate brokers began to disregard restrictive covenants following the decision reached in the *Shelly* case, persons adhering to the covenants sued them. Thus in the case of *Barrows* v. *Jackson* (1953)—which was sponsored, as were all the previously mentioned Supreme Court cases, by the Legal Defense and Education Fund of the NAACP—the Court concluded that damages could not be exacted from persons who had violated restrictive covenants. To award damages, the court concluded, would be tantamount to acknowledging their enforceability.

Violence

A further deterrent to the physical integration of blacks and whites is the penchant of whites to resort to numerous forms of violence against invading blacks. This violence occurs all across the nation—from Long Island to Boston to Cleveland to Miami to Los Angeles. It takes the form of firebombing, stonings, the breaking of windows, dumping of trash on lawns, burning of crosses on the black family's lawn, physical assaults against members of the black family, verbal abuse, insults, and racial slurs. This violence occurs in all types of neighborhoods, low-income, scatter site, or in affluent suburban communities. Sometimes, for fear of losing their lives and due to a lack of police protection, black families succumb to their fears and are, in fact, driven out of their new homes. In other instances, when adequate police protection is provided or when the attackers are arrested and convicted, either under city antidiscrimination ordinances or for violating the civil rights of the black dwellers, violence subsides and blacks remain in the new dwelling. Nevertheless, uncontrolled and unpunished violent persons too frequently prevent blacks and other minorities from living where they desire. Housing violence increased rapidly during the 1980s and is a major element in hate crimes.

URBAN RENEWAL

The U.S. Congress authorized a program of slum clearance in Title I of the Housing Act of 1949, which was again expanded in 1954. The original intent of this program was to clear slum land, redevelop it, and render it more habitable for former occupants. In time, because of the abysmal failure of the program and the disproportionate dislocations of urban blacks, urban renewal became synonymous with "black removal." Few public housing projects, for example, were constructed on land vacated by the largely nonwhite urban poor. The $1 billion appropriated for slum clearance and relocation of displaced families rarely aided blacks removed from their homes. Instead, blacks were shifted from one area to another. Even when new housing was constructed on land they had previously occupied, rents usually became too prohibitive to permit them to return to their original communities. In other instances high-rise governmental centers replaced houses previously occupied by black people. In some cases local agencies were unable to build anything because of a shortage of funds or because they had to scuttle poorly conceived redevelopment programs. Consequently, in several cities one can observe vacant block after vacant block in extremely expensive land areas and abandoned buildings condemned for urban renewal but never razed.

Black Resistance to Housing Desegregation

Another explanation for the failure of physical desegregation of housing lies in the unavailability of blacks willing to desegregate. Many blacks believe that residential relocation severs established community ties and fragments institutions; more and more black people have become increasingly inured to white resistance and discriminatory patterns of behavior and now question the value of the desegregation effort. Still other blacks feel an intense need for blacks to remain in identifiable neighborhoods set off by a clearly defined territorial demarcation within which the right of self-determination, community control, and the development of black institutions can be assured. They envision the racial ghetto as a promise of a strong power base for black people from which they can launch an all-out assault against a system that has perpetually denied them open admission as equals. Blacks in this group prefer to invest their time and energy in a continuing process of institution building and strengthening a black value system that can effectively impart a new sense of self-worth to black people. They reject the notion that blacks can only be free if they cavort with people of another race or if they are physically integrated with them. They do not believe that the myriad problems of the racial ghetto are insurmountable; they feel certain that with sufficient financial assistance black people have the talent and the technological know-how to solve these problems. Blacks who refuse to move from the black ghetto realize that the ghetto is a bitter and sometimes truculent place. It is diverse, excitingly viable, and it belongs to blacks who are determined to extricate its control from white bankers, mortgagers, realtors, and other members of the power structure who originally seized control of it and relegated blacks to a colonial status. The unanswered and difficult question is: To what degree can blacks succeed in this enterprise? Answering this question is perhaps why so many blacks relied so heavily upon federal legislation to assure access to better housing.

POST-1960 LEGISLATION AND COURT DECISIONS

Just as the federal government has traditionally been responsible for so deeply embedding residential segregation in American life, it has also been instrumental in effectuating changes in the quality of housing available to blacks.

The first major crack in the wall of housing segregation occurred when President Kennedy issued Executive Order 11063, which prohibited discrimination in federally assisted housing. By this time approximately 17 states and some 56 municipalities had enacted antidiscriminatory legislation in housing. However, this order was not all-inclusive and covered only 13 percent of housing not previously covered by existing local or state statutes, and only 23 percent of new housing starts.[23] Persons who violated the terms of the presidential order were subject to contract termination and to refusal of further governmental aid. By 1965, 20 states and the District of Columbia had enacted antidiscriminatory housing legislation covering some 80 million Americans.[24]

Although the Civil Rights Act of 1964 forbade segregation and discrimination in any program using federal funds, it had limited effectiveness because the act was not widely enforced. Pressure continued for a stronger law granting extensive enforcement authority. Some observers claimed that such a law was not approved by Congress in 1966 because of the direct action Dr. King and the Southern Christian Leadership Conference mounted through incursions into the white neighborhoods of metropolitan Chicago. If that is so, it is an ironical twist of history that his assassination may have been the prime mover in persuading Congress to enact a strong antidiscrimination bill in the Civil Rights Act of 1968, approved two weeks after his death. The crucial section pertaining specifically to housing was Title VIII of the Act, which became effective in 1970. Under its terms, prohibitions against discrimination covered approximately 80 percent of the nation's housing, excluding only the 20 percent that fell in the category of privately owned two-to-four dwelling units. Enforcement was theoretically assured by a tortuous, time-consuming process of complaint filing, investigation, persuasion for compliance, opportunities for relief, and the right of the U.S. Attorney General to intercede by taking court action to assure compliance and relief. Damages of up to $1000 could be collected once discrimination had been proved. If the complainant persisted and had the time to pursue this unwieldy process, and assuming that the person won the case, the house or the apartment could be sold or leased. Often, because the process is lengthy, persons in need of assistance give up in exasperation. Consequently, many violators go unpunished, and illegal practices continue to be widespread even in the 1990s.

Nevertheless, the Housing and Urban Development Act of 1968 (considered by President Johnson as a major breakthrough in meeting the problems of the poor) was a legal triumph for fair housing. It prohibited or made illegal a broad number of activities including: refusal to sell or rent on the basis of race, color, religion, sex or national origin; discrimination in the conditions or terms for the sale or rental of a dwelling; discrimination in advertising; blockbusting and "steering" misrepresentation or fraudulent statements relative to the unavailability of dwellings; denial of loans or setting unfair conditions as to the amount of loans available for purchasing, constructing, improving or repairing a dwelling.[25]

The 1968 Act, also referred to as the Omnibus Fair Housing Act, was followed by similar acts in 1969, 1970, the Housing and Community Development Act of 1974, the Equal Credit Opportunity Act of 1974, and the Urban Development Action Grant (UDAG) program in 1977. There have also been several attempts to strengthen the enforcement powers of both HUD and the Department of Justice to prevent violations of the mandates against discrimination under these measures. The 1968 Act and subsequent measures were designed to create or rehabilitate some 26 million housing units over a 10-year period. This included about 6 million federally subsidized dwellings as a response to the specific needs of the poorer elements in the Johnson Administration's Great Society. Included in this program were low-rent housing owned by the government, urban renewal, the development of wholly new cities, and the famous sections 235 and 236, which were essentially subsidy programs permitting the government to assume all interest costs in excess of 1 percent charged by the lender for home buyers and renters, respectively. The early effectiveness of this measure may be gleaned by the fact that within the first three years, 1968–1971, the number of subsidized units increased from 156,000 to 390,000; the majority were located in the central city.

Another federal program that has been of significant benefit to low-income persons is the Section 8 program of the U.S. Housing Act of 1937, "amended by Title I of the Housing and Community Development Act."[26] Under Section 8, HUD subsidizes the rents of low-income families not only to assist them in locating decent housing but also to promote "economically mixed housing." This goal is fostered by a rental supplement based upon the difference between the rent paid by the tenant and that charged by the renter. This amount is estimated to be from 15 to 25 percent of the tenant's income. Under most circumstances, a family may qualify for Section 8 assistance if its earning is less than "the current median income in the metropolitan area."[27] HUD permits rental subsidies in newly constructed buildings, in existing housing units, as well as in buildings that have undergone substantial rehabilitation. These arrangements were designed to expand housing opportunities for the low and moderately income families by helping some of them to move out of public housing projects.[28] In 1983, under Section 8, housing assistance was provided to more than 840,000 households in private rental housing. However, under a new "modified" Section 8 housing certificate program, about 61,000 existing units were scheduled to be transferred to this program. The modified Section 8 was phased in over a five-year period between 1983 and 1988.[29]

A basic objective of Title I of the Housing and Community Development Act of 1974 was to provide decent housing through the elimination of slums and urban blight, and by the involvement of private investment in community revitalization, especially in those areas that are experiencing a declining tax base. HUD made funds available for "demolition and restoration, temporary relocation assistance" and other activities designed to facilitate expanded access of low and moderate income families to better housing. The UDAG program was created in 1977 for the purpose of combating physical and economic deterioration. It specifically targeted those neighborhoods and "severely distressed and/or deteriorated cities" characterized by huge volumes of abandoned housing.[30] Between its inception and January 1983, HUD approved 1544 UDAG awards totaling $2.3 billion. Slightly more than 600 UDAG grants were awarded during the first two years of the Reagan administration. Only about eight percent of the UDAG grants to businesses for the purposes of restoration or rehabilitation have gone to minorities. Further, the Reagan administration continually curtailed the operating budget for the program. For instance, under the Carter administration, UDAG had an operating budget of $600 million but under Reagan, during FY '82, its budget was reduced by one-third to $400 million.[31]

Although these acts did permit a significant number of new housing starts, they also raised the level of expectations among literally thousands of urban blacks for new housing that never came their way. Further, it set the stage for victimization of blacks by money-hungry investors, bankers, mortgagers, and realtors. Unaccustomed to the intricacies of home purchasing, many unsophisticated inner-city blacks fell prey to unscrupulous speculators and incompetent FHA staff and inspectors who were easy marks for bribes. A typical devious practice was for speculators to purchase old homes and dress them up with superficial repairs in order to enhance their marketability. An FHA appraiser would assign them an inflated value, and unsuspecting buyers would be totally unaware of the hidden defects until later. The defective wiring, inadequate plumbing, and leaky roofs were so costly to repair that some recent home owners, who had invested comparatively little, simply decided to abandon the dwellings rather than assume the exorbitant repair costs. After these defaults, the abandoned property was returned to the federal government.[32] In the sale of rental property similar experiences were reported. The developers paid little attention to the needs and demands of tenants. As a result, many tenants walked away from their dwellings. It is estimated that HUD now owns more than 2.5 million vacant units, many of which have been abandoned or foreclosed. Yet, subsidies and UDAGs have worked. Ganier argues that the Section 8 program "produced a very good quality of housing." Although there were abuses in the program, such as permitting up to 20 percent of subsidized units in a program to be assigned to middle-income people, this is not justification for its phasing out by the Reagan Administration.[33]

FEDERAL GOVERNMENT AND THE HOUSING CRISIS

There is a major housing crisis in the United States. It is evident in (1) the failure of the federal government to provide leadership in the construction and maintenance of affordable housing; (2) the moral bankruptcy that characterized the Department of Housing and Urban Development (HUD) during the eight years of the Reagan Administration exemplified in the HUD scandal that erupted in 1989; (3) pervasive redlining by lending institutions throughout the United States that is so devastating that it robs blacks of a chance to purchase houses they can afford; and (4) the persistence of discriminatory practices by local government housing bureaus and a substantial number of white persons that denies blacks equal access to housing.

The Reagan Administration was not as supportive of subsidies and other housing assistance programs as were previous administrations. In fact, President Reagan forced HUD to bear the brunt of his assault on social programs designed to benefit poor whites, middle-income whites, minorities, and the homeless. During the eight years of the Reagan presidency, the HUD budget for federally assisted housing was slashed by 82 percent (a decline from $41.6 billion to $7.4 billion); in general, reductions in the agency's budget occurred every year. Under President Reagan, housing starts, for example, declined from 112,000 units in 1982 to only 72,000 in 1983; then to 45,000 in 1984, and the subsequent elimination of all new construction except 10,000 units for the elderly. Reagan's goal was the total extrication of the federal government from public housing construction. He and his successor, President George Bush, favored a controversial voucher system by which low-income families would be given vouchers for rental supplements marketed wherever they could locate housing. The Reagan Administration supported "housing stamps" on the premise that existing federal programs had become too costly, provided "too large a subsidy for too few people" without addressing the fundamental problem—that is, lack of adequate income among low-income people.[34] The Bush Administration also accepts the position that the housing crisis can, in part, be ameliorated through a voucher system. Critics of the voucher system claim that it will not work because: (1) the private sector has never been effective in providing housing for the poor, and very few private owners will even accept low and moderate-income individuals unless pressured—they often claim that it is virtually impossible to collect rent payments on a regular basis; (2) the voucher system will place low-and moderate-income individuals and families in direct competition with the middle class for "affordable decent housing," already in short supply; (3) as a result, housing discrimination will be accelerated, not diminished under a voucher system, especially against blacks, Hispanics, and other minorities;[35] and (4) in so many parts of the country people in need of housing are unable to use vouchers because of the acute housing shortage in those areas.

The dismantling of the HUD budget under the Reagan Administration had a devastating impact on the poor. It was tantamount to a federal retrenchment on practically all housing assistance programs under federal jurisdiction. It may also be viewed as a strategy to undermine a previously established federal commitment to fair and equal access to housing implicit in various housing orders, statutes, and national laws enacted during the 1960s and 1970s. In 1983, there were 3.4 million HUD-assisted housing units but with the demolition of a considerable number of units within that category, the total number of HUD-assisted housing units had declined substantially by the beginning of 1990. By 1982, two years after Ronald Reagan assumed the presidency, the HUD inventory consisted of 1.2 million public housing units; 844,000 Section 8 existing housing units; 475,000 units under Section 9's new construction and/or "substantial" rehabilitation: 342,000 Section 236 moderate rental units that did not receive operating assistance; 207,000 Section 236 units rental supplements; 235,000 Section 235 low-income home owners units; and 97,000 Section 202 housing for the elderly or handicapped.[36]

During the eight years of the Reagan presidency, not only was enforcement of anti-discriminatory statutes lax, a 1989 audit of HUD activities revealed major problems of mismanagement, influence peddling, theft of HUD funds, and favoritism in the award of HUD funds that exploded a major scandal in that agency. Many programs established to support the poor and underprivileged in their search for adequate housing were victimized by the greed of the well-to-do and the well-connected. Influential Republicans, including at least one former Reagan Cabinet member, benefited from lucrative "consulting" activities totaling millions of dollars simply by placing phone calls to HUD officials for the benefit of a client who sought a HUD grant. At least three congressional investigations into HUD activities during the Reagan years were initiated in 1989.[37]

By mid-1989, 28 of the 48 HUD programs were characterized as "problems" and three had been suspended: Co-Insurance, Title X, and Retirement Service Centers. The Section 8 Moderate Rehabilitation Program was suspended temporarily to strengthen operational procedures.[38] This program had been established as a lower-income assistance program under which developers were given subsidies and tax credits for rehabilitating low-income housing. Influence peddling by consultants with political connections allowed some contractors to obtain project approval in advance and without competitive bids.

As discussed in an earlier section of this chapter, UDAGs were created to generate development in "distressed cities" through such projects as restoration of blighted downtown or residential areas. Congressional investigations revealed enormous sums paid to consultants to arrange grants for friends or special clients. The Retirement Service Centers program was established by HUD Secretary Samuel Pierce. Its intended purpose was to provide housing as well as various support services for over age 70 low-income people and mortgage insurance to developers who initiated projects to assist the elderly. Congressional investigations showed that money from this program financed luxury projects for the well-to-do and that projects for the intended clients were too frequently unsupported.

Embezzlement was found among several HUD employees in various parts of the country. These were civil servants entrusted with responsibility of collecting/administering funds obtained through the sale of foreclosed properties. In toto, through mismanagement, influence peddling, and embezzlement, it is estimated that at least $2 billion was lost to HUD[39] and that a substantial proportion of that sum could have been used to support housing programs to help the poor and the homeless that were either underfunded or eliminated. This failure gives support to the thesis that the federal government is highly culpable in creating the housing crisis that is widespread in the United States and that it has not been aggressive in finding creative solutions to the problems of the poor and the homeless. Again, evidence to support this argument is found in the decline in federal housing assistance programs for the poor and middle-income groups during the Reagan years, decrease in federal subsidies, the slashing of budgets for the construction of new public housing, and the abuse of HUD programs that were designed to be of direct assistance to the needy.

Housing advocates, particularly minorities and the homeless in various parts of the nation, also challenged another practice of dynamiting or demolishing run-down public housing projects. During the 1980s, especially, housing authorities in such cities as Newark, N.J.; Bridgeport, Connecticut; Houston, Texas; Jacksonville, Florida; and Pittsburgh, Pennsylvania decided to demolish high-rise and low-level public housing structures that were in severe disrepair. However, these units were not replaced as required by a provision in the 1988 amendment to the United States Housing Act.[40] Under that amendment, demolished housing are to be replaced on a "one-for-one" basis. Although the federal government did approve some replacements, housing advocates suits against local housing authorities claimed that replacements were not in compliance with the 1988 amendments and that such failures worsened the problems of the low-income groups and the escalating homeless population.[41]

Another major impediment to the ability of blacks to purchase homes is the illegal but widespread practice of redlining (i.e., the refusal of banks to lend mortgage money for the purchase of housing in some areas due to race). Dedman reported findings from data analyzed by the *Atlanta*

Journal and Constitution that revealed a nationwide pattern of discrimination against blacks seeking mortgage money from savings and loans institutions. The researchers in this study analyzed the "records from 10 million applicants" from the nation's 3,100 savings and loans institutions covering the period between 1983 and 1988.[42]

This analysis showed that: (1) nationally, the rejection rate for home loans is 11.1 percent for whites followed by Asians with 12.2 percent; American Indians, 16.5 percent; Hispanics, 18.2 percent; and blacks with a national rejection rate of 23.7 percent; (2) blacks are therefore rejected for loans more than twice as often as whites; (3) high income blacks are rejected for home loans more often than low-income whites in 85 of the 100 largest metropolitan areas; (4) "race is a much better predictor" of success or failure in loan applications than gender or marital status; (5) the greatest disparities between blacks and whites in ability to obtain home mortgages was found in the Plains (30.9 percent rejection rate for blacks vs. 12.6 percent rate for whites) and Midwestern states (29.6 percent for blacks vs. 12.2 percent for whites), precisely the areas in which blacks have the highest incomes relative to that of whites; (6) blacks were rejected more than three times as often as whites in 30 of the 50 largest southern cities; yet the South has a lower rejection rate than the Plains and Midwestern States; (7) the highest rejection black-white disparity (9.25:1) was found in the Bridgeport-Milford area of Connecticut; and (8) the lowest regional black-white disparities in rejection rates were in the West (25 percent for blacks and 14.4 percent for whites) and the Northeast (13.4 percent for blacks vs. 9.1 percent for whites).[43]

Several large cities had a rejection rate that equalled or exceeded the national black-white rejection rate of 2.14:1. Among such cities were: New York (2.70:1); Philadelphia (2.40:1); Chicago (3.63:1); Cleveland (3.74:1); Pittsburgh (3.80:1); Milwaukee (3.90:1); Detroit (3.57:1); Baltimore (3.18:1); St. Louis (2.99:1); Boston (2.91:1); Birmingham (2.44:1); Atlanta (2.20:1), and Fort Worth-Arlington, Texas (2.24:1).[44]

Redlining has a number of deleterious consequences. For instance, credit discrimination may mean that individuals are unable to repair homes or purchase new ones. One consequence of that situation may be a deterioration of the physical quality of the neighborhood. Property values may decline. It may also perpetuate racial disparities in income and wealth and in the accumulation of wealth as well as negatively impact on the ability to borrow funds for education and other necessities.[45]

Findings from this study, as well as a similar study conducted in Boston[46] and by researchers at the University of Chicago[47], demonstrate a breakdown in the responsibilities of bank regulatory agencies. They also demonstrate failure of the U. S. Department of Justice to prosecute banks for failure to comply with the requirements of the Equal Credit Opportunity Act, failure of the federal government to enforce compliance to the 1977 Community Reinvestment Act which requires banks to serve the needs of the communities in which they operate or serve.[48] As Dedman points out, the Reagan Administration weakened the regulatory system that was constructed in the 1960s and 1970s to curb redlining. The number of attorneys and staff assigned to credit cases by the Justice Department was reduced. There was a 74 percent decline in the number of examiner hours "devoted to consumer regulations." HUD discontinued data collection on the location of FHA loans; enforcement of anti-discriminatory laws, in general declined as discrimination against blacks in lending agencies increased.[49]

That bias, racism, and discrimination were also evident during the 1980s in the resistance of communities like Yonkers, New York[50] to comply with federal court orders to construct low-income housing in parts of the city that would assure school desegregation; in the use of steering techniques and refusal of real estate agents in many parts of the country to show properties to blacks in predominantly white areas, thus creating and intensifying racial separation in cities and suburbs; the resistance of suburban communities to public subsidized housing; during years of giving preferences to whites in the assignments to public housing in such Boston communities as Charlestown and South Boston even when blacks had risen to the top of the list for housing;[51] and in the continued efforts of some cities to implement exclusionary zoning ordinances that would permit the construction of housing that would benefit low-income groups to one section of the community (e.g., Mount Laurel, N.J. and Huntington, L.I.).[52] Racism is evident also in continuing attacks against blacks and other minorities who seek housing in areas that have been traditionally all-white and in a significant amount of the "white flight" from cities. Throughout the country, the last decade has witnessed the movement of white persons from public housing in cities or into racially segregated public housing units. As a result of the exodus of whites, one sees a situation as in Chicago in which 95 percent of the city's 14,000 public housing residents are black.[53] During the 1980s, national leadership toward the elimination of racial bias in housing was silent; concrete ghettos escalated to the degree that many sections or communities were further manifestations of internally colonized communities.

PROTEST ORGANIZATIONS AND THE OPEN HOUSING MOVEMENT

Open housing was neither a spontaneous occurrence nor the work of a single racial group. The battle for open occupancy of apartments and single-family homes assumed the characteristics of a social movement as is well documented by Juliet Saltman in *Open Housing as a Social Movement.*[54] As such, it involved a huge cast of characters and organizations cutting across all racial and ethnic lines. The effort involved the combined work of the NCDH, the tireless, sustained, and largely legal efforts of the

NAACP, the "dwell-in movement"* sponsored by CORE during the early 1960s, and the Operation Equality Program sponsored by the National Urban League during the latter part of the 1960s and into the 1970s.

Collectively, these organizations attacked problems of unfairness in pricing, purchasing, and the previously discussed strategies and techniques used to circumvent open housing. They lobbied with both major political parties at local and state levels, and attempted to persuade governmental and political bodies to enact open-housing legislation. Systematically, they attacked racial quotas of the FHA and urged appointment of intergroup experts to deal with the problems related to physical integration of blacks into previously all-white residential communities. Suits were initiated to control the unjust dimensions of urban renewal, to stop serious dislocation and displacement of the poor, and to protect tenants' rights. (For example, the ruling in the 1969 case of *Thorpe* v. *Housing Authority of Durham, North Carolina,* prohibited landlords and other housing authorities from evicting occupants without fair notice or the possibility of arranging a hearing if warranted. Significantly, this decision affected millions of low-rent tenants in public housing at the time.) Conciliation, moral persuasion, and direct confrontation strategies were also employed to improve housing for blacks and other dispossessed groups.[55]

In addition to the aforementioned groups, it is important to note that throughout the past two decades, countless individuals and local fair housing organizations were instrumental in effecting change as part of a national movement against segregation in housing and for the opening up of decent housing to the black community.

BLACKS IN THE REAL ESTATE SYSTEM

Today, blacks control about 1 percent of the $350-billion housing market. Although this is a paltry sum of money in view of the numbers of blacks in the American population, it is, however, a significant improvement over the position blacks occupied in real estate prior to the 1960s. One explanation for this limited success lies in the formation and subsequent work of the 6,000-member National Association of Real Estate Brokers. This organization, organized in 1947, was the stimulus for the development of major black-owned mortgage firms and institutions such as United Mortgage Bankers of America, formed when the all-white Mortgage Bankers of America was inaccessible to blacks. The black association of real estate boards also established a series of auxiliary agencies necessary for real estate operation and management. Thus various specialists established themselves, including black developers, appraisers, brokers, and manag-

---

*"Dwell-ins" were a form of sit-in that involved prolonged occupation of a real estate sales office in order to prevent discrimination in the sale of houses or rentals.

ers. Today blacks are involved in property management, mortgage banking, and the buying and selling of real estate. No American city with a
fairly large black population is without black-owned mortgage banking
institutions. But blacks are still in the incipient stages of real estate activity.
Notwithstanding, they have begun to move aggressively in this field and
maximize their resources through cooperation, consolidation, and reciprocal relationships. Their position remains somewhat uncertain, however,
since so much of the business conducted by blacks, especially those con-
nected with community development corporations and UDAGs, is tied to
the federal government. Consequently, black realtors and developers continually fight against racism for a better distribution of wealth and income
among blacks, and for a more aggressive housing development program
under both federal and private sponsorship.[56]

Stimulated by the housing legislation of the 1960s, the federal government approved funds for the establishment of several new towns. Among
the first 10 approved was a $14-million loan (actually, the right to issue
government-backed bonds in that amount) to Floyd McKissick, former
National Director of CORE. McKissick's new town, called Soul City, North
Carolina, began in 1969 but was foreclosed by HUD in 1979 after the
federal, state, and local governments had contributed more than $27
million for its development.[57] The project never became sufficiently attractive to potential black and white residents, industry, and business to
become a viable enterprise.

One important development with respect to housing revitalization
efforts spearheaded by the private sector was the establishment of the
Local Initiatives Support Corporation, based in New York City and created by the Ford Foundation in 1980. Six banking institutions, insurance,
and industrial firms joined with the Ford Foundation (under the leadership of its president, Franklin A. Thomas, a black who had been president
of the Bedford-Stuyvesant Restoration Project and a member of the board
of directors of the New York Life Insurance Company) to assist in housing
development for low-income families, the construction of new office buildings, the transformation of downtown sections in need of rehabilitation,
and the construction of recreational facilities in various cities. The Local
Initiatives program is involved in more than 200 neighborhood projects
across the United States. This program demonstrated how the partnership
between private and public sectors for the revitalization of deteriorated
housing and other areas of the cities could be a successful venture. Perhaps, in the drive for a larger number of decent affordable housing units,
the revitalized open housing movement will seek greater ventures similar
to the Local Initiatives program as well as pressure the federal government to aggressively enforce its own legislation.

Finally, the black church is also involved in housing assistance pro-
grams. Although this involvement is nationwide, a few examples from
Atlanta are instructive on this point. In that city, such black churches as
Wheat Street Baptist, Friendship Baptist, Allen Temple, and the Central

United Methodist Church own more than 10,000 housing units. This housing includes facilities for low-income persons, housing and recreational facilities for the elderly, and for medium-income families.

POLICY COMMITMENTS

The Kerner Commission sponsored during President Johnson's Administration suggested a number of basic strategies for attacking the housing problem. Among its more salient imperatives was a demand for *enforcement* of all open-housing laws. The very fact that a housing crisis exists in the 1990s with respect to access of blacks and other minorities to decent and affordable housing is evidence of the failure of federal enforcement. (This is not to deny that all races suffer from the effects of the high cost of housing and high interest rates which make it virtually impossible for young families, especially, to purchase a house. However, this problem is compounded and severely increased when the factor of race is involved. Racial discrimination remains a powerful deterrent to fair housing.) There remains in the United States a lack of will to enforce housing laws. Housing is a victim of political expediency and reflects the magnitude of racism and the lack of commitment by public and private sectors in bringing relief to an appalling condition. In most local state elections in areas where such issues as the location of public housing or scatter-site dwellings are a matter of public debate, as in Yonkers New York in 1988, candidates are drilled about their positions on such issues. As a result, regardless of superior qualifications for the office, their electability may hinge in great measure upon the position taken with respect to public housing. There is in 1990 a great need for the articulation and implementation of a firm national housing policy that attacks head-on all impediments to the guarantees of equal access of American citizens to decent, affordable housing in the areas in which they choose to live. Without this mandate, even with the movement of a comparatively few blacks into suburban communities, housing will continue to reflect a situation that is tantamount to colonized black urban central city ghettos surrounded by largely white ruling elites in suburban communities.

NOTES

1. Meyer Weinberg, "Integrating Neighborhoods: An Examination of Housing and School Desegregation," *Journal of Housing* (December 1980): 630–636.
2. Cf. Nathan Glazer, "Housing Problems and Housing Policies," *The Public Interest* (Spring 1967): 21–51, and Joseph P. Fried, *Housing Crisis USA* (Baltimore: Penguin Books, 1971), p. 21.
3. Cf. U.S. Department of Commerce, *Provisional Estimates of Social, Economic and Housing Characteristics* (Washington, D.C.: Bureau of the Census, 1982), and *Summary of Housing Characteristics,* 1981.

4. James E. Blackwell and Philip Hart, *Cities, Suburbs and Blacks* (Bayside, N.Y.: General Hall, Inc.), p. 41.
5. *Ibid.*
6. Cf. Daphne Spain, John Reid, and Larry Long, *Housing Successions Among Blacks and Whites in Cities and Suburbs* (Washington, D.C.: U.S. Department of Commerce, Bureau of the Census, Special Studies Series P-23, No. 101, 1980), George Grier and Eunice Grier, *Black Suburbanization in the Mid-1970s* (Washington, D.C.: The Washington Center for Metropolitan Studies, 1978), and Wade Clark Roof and Daphne Spain, "A Research Note on City-Suburban Socioeconomic Differences Among Blacks," *Social Forces* 56 (September 1977): 15–20.
7. Ronald J. McAllister, et al., "Residential Mobility of Blacks and Whites: A National Longitudinal Study," *American Journal of Sociology* 77 (November 1971): 448–453.
8. Blackwell and Hart, *op. cit.*
9. Karl Taeuber, *Racial Residential Segregation 1980* (Madison: University of Wisconsin Press, 1983).
10. Cf. Reynolds Farley, et al., "Barriers to the Racial Integration of Neighborhoods: The Detroit Case," *The Annals of the American Academy of Political and Social Sciences* 441 (January 1979): 97–113, and "Chocolate City, Vanilla Suburbs: Will the Trend Toward Racially Separate Communities Continue?" *Social Science Research* 7 (1978): 319–344.
11. Cf. Carolyn R. Zeul and Craig R. Humphrey, "The Integration of Suburban Blacks in Suburban Neighborhoods: A Reexamination of the Contact Hypothesis," *Social Problems* 8 (Spring 1971): 462–474, and Blackwell and Hart, *op. cit.*, Chap. 6.
12. Glazer, *op. cit.*
13. Monroe W. Karmen, "Government Programs," *Black Enterprise*, 3 (August 1972): 22.
14. Wilhelmina A. Leogh and Mildred O. Mitchell, "Public Housing and the Black Community," *The Review of Black Political Economy* 11:2 (Fall 1980): 52–75.
15. Luigi Laurenti, *Property Values and Race* (Berkeley: University of California Press, 1960).
16. U.S. Commission on Civil Rights, *The Federal Fair Housing Enforcement Effort* (Washington, D.C.: U.S. Commission on Civil Rights, 1979), p. 59.
17. *Ibid.*
18. *Ibid.*, p. 120.
19. "Realty Era of the Specialist," *Black Enterprise* 3 (August 1972): 44.
20. Jack Greenberg, *Race Relations and the Law* (New York: Columbia University Press, 1959), p. 276.
21. Cf. *ibid,* and Herbert M. Franklin, "Zoning Laws," *Black Enterprise* 3 (August 1972): 25.
22. Greenberg, *op. cit.*
23. Charles Abrams, "The Housing Problem and the Negro" *Daedalus* (Winter 1966): 64–66.
24. George Grier and Eunice Grier, *Housing Segregation and the Goals of the Great Society* (Chicago: Quadrangle Books, 1966), p. 52.
25. The U.S. Commission on Civil Rights, *op. cit.*, p. 1.
26. *Ibid.*, p. 8
27. *Ibid.*
28. *Ibid.*

29. Mary K. Nenno, "The President's Budget: A Blueprint for the Future," *Journal of Housing* 39:2 (March/April 1982): 43–50.
30. Commission on Civil Rights, *op. cit.*
31. "UDAGs: Bright Spot in a Bleak Landscape, *Black Enterprise* (March 1983): 42.
32. *Thirty Years of Building American Justice* (New York: The NAACP Legal Defense and Educational Fund, 1970).
33. William Ganier, "Subsidized Housing Production: Profiting From Past Errors," *Journal of Housing* 40:3 (May 1983): 77–82.
34. Cf. Nenno, *op. cit.*, Robert A. Jordan, "The HUD Vanishing Act," *The Boston Globe* (March 17, 1983), p. 18, and *Black Enterprise* (March 1983), p. 43, and Julian Dixon, "Housing: Recognizing the Crisis, Taking Action," *Focus* (June 1989), pp. 3–4.
35. Jordan, *op. cit.*
36. Nenno, *op. cit.*
37. Cf. "The Nation: The Many Paths of the H.U.D. Investigation," *New York Times* (August 13, 1989), p. E-3; David Johnston, "There's Far to Go in Cleaning Up the H. U. D. Mess," *New York Times* (August 13, 1989), p. 4-1; Chris Apolar and Lynne Duke, "HUD Concedes Theft of Up to $20 Million," *The Washington Post* (June 17, 1989), p. 1, A7.
38. *Ibid.*
39. *Ibid.*
40. Anthony DePalma, "Newark Suit Would Keep High-Rises," *New York Times* (March 30, 1989), p. B-1.
41. *Ibid.*
42. Bill Dedham, "Racial Lending Gap Less In South Than Midwest," *The Atlanta Journal and Constitution* (January 22, 1989), p. 1; and "Blacks Turned Down for Home Loans From S&Ls Twice as Often as Whites," *The Atlanta Journal Constitution* (January 22, 1989), p. 1, A10.
43. *Ibid.*
44. *Ibid.*
45. *Ibid.*
46. Steven Marantz, "Study Said 4 Hub Banks Were Redlining in '80," *Boston Globe* (January 29, 1989), p. 25.
47. Cited in "Study: Blacks Segregated Despite Their Status," *Jet* (December 27, 1989): p. 27. Its findings show that Hispanics with four years or less of formal education encounter less segregation than blacks with a college degree.
48. Cf. Dedman, *op. cit.* and Alan Finder, "Bias Remains Persuasive in Region's Housing Market," *New York Times* (March 13, 1989), p. B-1; Steven Marantz, "Detroit: From Deepest Urban Blight, A Backlash," *Boston Globe* (March 5, 1989), p. 13; and Theresa Hanafin, "Atlanta: A Southern Attack on Skewed Lending," *Boston Globe* (March 5, 1989), p. 13.
49. *Ibid.*
50. James Feron, "How Yonkers Has Held Off on Housing," *New York Times* (January 19, 1990), p. E-1; Editorial, "Conscience and Law in Yonkers," *New York Times* (October 7, 1989), p. 22; Robert D. McFadden, "Stepping Back from Fiscal and Political Crisis: What Is Next for Yonkers?," *New York Times* (September 11, 1988), p. 36; and James Feron, "Yonkers Yields on Housing Plan to Avert Crisis: Revisions Sought," *New York Times* (September 11, 1988), p. 1.

51. Brian C. Mooney, "HUD Report: Policy Added to Segregation," *Boston Globe* (July 23, 1988), p. 1.
52. Alan Finder, *op. cit.,* and Eric Schmitt, "Zoning Is Only Bar to Cheaper Suburban Housing," *New York Times* (November 13, 1988), p. E-5.
53. William C. Schmidt, "Moving Out of Projects and Toward A Future," *New York Times* (February 3, 1989), p. A-32.
54. Cf. Juliet Saltman, *Open Housing as a Social Movement* (Lexington, Mass.: D. C. Heath-Lexington Books, 1971), pp. 53–59; and *A Fragile Movement: The Struggle for Neighborhood Stabilization* (Westport, Conn.: Greenwood Press, 1990).
55. Karmen, *op. cit.*
56. *Black Enterprise* (August 1972):44.
57. Harry A. Ploski and James Williams, *The Negro Almanac: A Reference on the Afro-American,* 4th ed. (New York: John Wiley & Sons, 1983), p. 83.

Chapter
8

Black Capitalism and Human Resources

*I*n recent years much has been said about black capitalism and the need for human resource development as instruments for eradicating economic poverty and underdevelopment in the black community. Of major concern are issues such as the present state of black businesses, their capacity to survive in a manner to serve needs of black people, their ability to become economically viable institutions within the American economic system, and the articulation of strategies or programs that will help to create a well-trained labor base among blacks. This chapter focuses on the structure of the contemporary black enterprise system and some of the factors that affect both its survival and viability as well as on problems of human capital development.

The structure of present-day black enterprises has its foundation in the construction of parallel institutions described in earlier chapters. Hence because of institutionalized segregation, blacks necessarily formed a business structure that catered almost exclusively to personal service functions (e.g., accommodations, barbering, cosmetics, burial establishments, small-scale retail establishments) not provided by the larger society.[1] Primarily because of their disadvantaged economic condition, particularly the paucity of capital, blacks have not generally been involved in producing, manufacturing, and large-scale manufacturing. Nor have they owned huge corporations or become mining industrialists, for example. Rather, black businesses were forced to become and remain relatively small scale, highly focused, and limited in their capacity to generate either capital or large-scale employment of black people.

This lack of capital formation, in addition to competition from white entrepreneurs operating within the black communities and the dependence of black businesses upon white suppliers, prevented blacks from becoming either "middle-man minorities"[2] or from developing the business interdependence characteristic of ethnic enclave entrepreneurship.[3]

CONTEMPORARY STRUCTURE OF THE BLACK ENTERPRISE SYSTEM

Studies of black businesses within the black community reveal that: (1) whites, and an increasingly larger number of Asians, not blacks, still own a significant majority of businesses in the black community; (2) white and other nonblack owners more often tend both to reside elsewhere and to hire persons from outside the black community, and (3) in general, non-black people continue to dominate the economic life of the black community. In this way, whites again play the role of domestic colonizers controlling the business life within the ghetto colony.[4] The 231,000 black-owned businesses represent only 1.98 percent of the total number of all business firms in the nation. The majority of these firms are concentrated in selected services (101,739 firms), retailing (55,428), transportation and public utilities (23,061), most of which are individually owned taxicabs, and in construction (21,101 firms). The underrepresentation of black ownership of various types of firms is indicated by their percentage of ownership in each category. For instance, blacks own only 0.2 percent of all construction firms; 0.1 percent of manufacturing firms; 5.5 percent of transportation and public utility firms; 0.2 percent of wholesale trade companies; 0.7 percent of all retail firms; 0.7 percent of the nation's financial, insurance, and real estate companies, and 2.8 percent of all companies classified as selected services (see Table 8.1).

The combined businesses owned by blacks receive about 1 percent of the total gross receipts of all businesses in the United States, despite the fact that the total revenues received by the largest 100 black-owned businesses were $6.75 billion in 1988.* Although the absolute number of black-owned businesses grew from 163,000 to 231,000 by 1977, which was accompanied by an overall growth in gross receipts, their proportion of total gross receipts actually declined during the 1970s and remained relatively constant during the 1980s. This disparity may be explained in part by the growth and expansion of white-owned businesses during that period which outstripped the growth of black enterprises. It may be further explained by the fact that a considerable portion of entrepreneurship expansion in the white community during the 1980s, for example, was in areas in which the representation of black entrepreneurship is minuscule (e.g., computer industries and related activities). Nevertheless, black-owned-businesses have undergone extensive diversification since the mid-

---

*See *Black Enterprise* magazine, June 1989 and June 1990

Table 8.1 NUMBER, GROSS RECEIPTS, AND EMPLOYEES FOR ALL BLACK-OWNED BUSINESSES BY INDUSTRY DIVISION[a]

Industry division	Total number of firms (× 1000)	Black-owned firms	Percentage of black firms	Gross receipts— all firms (in billions)	Gross receipts— black firms	Paid black employees
Construction	1,107	21,101	0.2	$ 72.6	$757,690,000	17,199
Manufacturing	207	4,243	0.1	38.5	613,665,000	15,790
Transportation and public utilities	419	23,061	5.5	22.8	509,443,000	7,624
Wholesale trade and retail	2,600	57,640	0.2	294.4	4,016,383,000	50,271
Finance, insurance, and real estate	1,404	9,805	0.7	66.6	641,372,000	15,361
Selected services	3,623	101,739	2.8	120.1	1,889,534,000	55,238
Other and not-classified industries	393	13,614	3.4	21.2	117,112,000	2,627
Total	9,833	231,203	2.3	$ 633.1	$8,645,200,000 (1.3% of total)	164,177

[a]These figures are based upon data collected in 1977. It is estimated in 1990 that the number of black-owned businesses has climbed to about 435,000.

Source: U.S. Department of Commerce, Minority Business Development Program, 1982.

1960s when the emphasis on black capitalism and strengthening black entrepreneurship was initiated.

Today, black-owned businesses are chiefly concentrated in the personal services as they have been in the past. Specifically, almost half of them are in this category of businesses. Personal services businesses include eating and drinking places, food stores, automobile dealers, service stations, barbershops, and the like.

Black-owned businesses tend to be small, self-owned, unevenly distributed in the country, and, characteristically, employ small numbers of individuals. Due to the enormous difficulties encountered by blacks in capital formation, and the high failure rate of small businesses during the first year, there is a growing trend toward partnerships for the establishment and maintenance of black-owned businesses. In 1980 the Bureau of Labor Statistics reported that 191,000 of the 231,000 black-owned businesses (87 percent) were so small as not to have paid employees.[5] In 1982 *Black Enterprise* magazine reported U.S. Department of Commerce data which showed that 50,000 black-owned businesses did not have paid employees.[6] Therefore, few black firms are in a position to provide significant employment opportunities for the black population. In fact, black-owned firms, as a whole, employ 164,177 persons—a ratio of less than one person per establishment. Among the types of businesses listed in Table 8.1 with paid employees, most blacks were employed in selected services that reported more than 55,000 employees. This category was followed in order by the retail industry, 45,737 employees; the construction industry, 17,197 employees; manufacturing, 15,790 employees; finance, insurance, and real estate, 15,361 employees; transportation and public utilities, 7,624 employees; and wholesale trade with 4,534 paid employees. Obviously, most black establishments are mainly operated by a number of unpaid family members.

CHARACTERISTICS OF THE TOP 100 BLACK BUSINESSES

The annual survey of black-owned businesses* (those enterprises in which at least 51 percent of control is in the hands of blacks) reported by *Black Enterprise* magazine divides them into two categories: (1) the top 100

---

*This section draws heavily from articles published in the June 1989 issue of *Black Enterprise Magazine*. However, Earl Graves, publisher of *Black Enterprise Magazine*, reported in the June 1990 edition that black-owned businesses were seriously damaged by the national economic slow-down, regional recessions and defense budget cuts of 1989. As a result, nineteen of the 1988 top 100 black businesses were in bankruptcy (three-fifths of them auto dealerships); distributors of petroleum products entirely disappeared, and several black-owned savings and loan companies failed in 1989. (See: Earl Graves, "Black Business at the Crossroads: the Publisher's Page," *Black Enterprise* (June 1990), p.11.

black-owned industrial/service companies and (2) the top 100 automobile
dealers. In addition, these enterprises are combined to produce a category
labeled the "Black Enterprise 100s."[7] The primary criterion for inclusion
in the top 100 is volume of sales during the rating period.

Table 8.2 lists the top 100 black businesses by industry. An examination of this table reveals that seven of ten of the top 100 companies are
in food or beverage and in the sale of automobiles. Slightly more than 5
percent each are construction and media enterprises. The remaining 19
percent of the top 100 companies are distributed unevenly among companies involved in computer information (4.6%); manufacturing (3.6%);
health care and beauty aids (2.8%); entertainment (2.5%); transportation
(1.9%); petroleum (0.6%); security/maintenance (0.4%), and miscella-
neous activities (2.0%).

The top 100 industrial service companies employ a total of 15,346
persons while the automobile dealers employ another 5,508. The total of
21,854 represents approximately 14 percent of all paid employees in
black-owned firms. The largest employer is TLC Beatrice International
Holdings Inc. which has a staff of 11,000. This company was acquired in
1987 through a leveraged buyout of Beatrice International Foods by a
black-owned Wall Street firm headed by Reginald F. Lewis, the new Chief
Executive Officer (CEO) of TLC. Beatrice International Foods is the cen-
terpiece of this multinational company and it has operations, involving
food processing and distribution, in Europe, Asia, and Latin America.[8] The
second largest employer is the Johnson Publishing Company, based in
Chicago, which publishes such well-known magazines as *Ebony* and *Jet.*
Only three other companies in the top 100 employ more than 1,000
persons: Trans Jones Inc. (a transportation company located in Monroe,

Table 8.2   DISTRIBUTION OF TOP 100 BLACK BUSINESSES, BY
INDUSTRY AND PERCENT OF TOTAL BUSINESS: 1989

Categories	Percent	Rank
Food/beverage	36.4	1
Automobile dealerships	34.3	2
Construction	5.7	3
Media	5.3	4
Computer information	4.6	5
Manufacturing	3.6	6
Health care/beauty aids	2.8	7
Entertainment	2.5	8
Miscellaneous	2.0	9
Transportation	1.9	10
Petroleum	0.6	11
Security/maintenance	0.4	12

Source: Adopted with permission from *Black Enterprise* (New York: Earl Graves
Publishing Co., Inc., June 1989): 190.

Michigan, with 1,332 employees); The Gourmet Companies of Atlanta (a food services and golf management company that has 1,437 employees); the Keys Group of Detroit (owners of fast-food operations employing 1,800 people); and The Maxima Corporation of Rockville, Maryland. The latter company is a systems engineering and computer management company that hires 1,000 persons. Twenty-three companies employed between 250 and 999 employees. However, 55 percent of the top 100 companies employed fewer than 100 persons each.[9]

Regionally, increasing diversification of black-owned businesses, coupled with the ability to acquire capital for the establishment of enterprises, resulted in a shift in the location of large entrepreneurs over the past decade. The South, in which more than half of the top 100 were located, accounts for 33 percent of these businesses. The Midwest is the location of 32 percent, followed by the Northeast (20 percent), and the Far West with 15 percent of the top 100 black-owned businesses.[10]

In terms of sales, the largest black-owned businesses reported in 1989 by *Black Enterprise* magazine were, in rank order: (1) TLC Beatrice International Holdings ($1.58 billion in sales); (2) Johnson Publishing Company ($216.5 million); (3) Philadelphia Coca-Cola Bottling Co., Inc. ($210 million); (4) H. J. Russell & Co., a construction, property management and food/beverage company located in Atlanta ($159.7 million); (5) Shack-Woods & Associates, a Ford dealership company based in Long Beach, California ($127 million); and (6) The Gordy Company (an entertainment company headquartered in Los Angeles with sales of $105 million).[11] The top 100 black-owned industrial/service companies and the top 100 auto dealers had a combined revenue of a $ 6.75 billion in 1988, a revenue increase of 10.7 percent over their 1987 earnings.[12]

Perhaps an indicator of the impact of financial support for the "minority enterprise" initiatives that began in the 1960s and early 1970s with federal government support is the period of time in which the top 100 companies were established. An examination of the top 100 industrial/service companies shows that 27 percent of them were established during the 1980s; 48 percent were founded during the 1970s; 9 percent were created during the 1960s; and 16 percent were in existence prior to 1959.[13] By contrast, automobile dealers are even more recent in origin. Eighty-one percent of the auto dealership companies were established between 1980 and 1989. Fourteen percent were established during the 1970s and only 5 percent were in existence prior to the 1970s.[14] The acquisition of dealerships by blacks from Ford Motor Company is illustrative of such changes. In 1967, Ford had granted dealerships to only two blacks. By 1989, there were 257 black dealers of Ford Motor Company, more than the combined total of blacks who had dealerships with Chrysler, General Motors, or Toyota (which had none).[15] As of 1990, blacks held 430 dealerships.

The recency of the acquisition of auto dealerships by black entrepreneurs reflects changing demographics of urban communities, the market situation in the automobile industry, pressures by black organizations on the automobile industry to actualize equal opportunity in the black community, and changing business interest among a significant portion of black entrepreneurs. Insensitivity and failure to make positive responses to these concerns, as well as problems discussed in Chapter 2, are a major reason why so many black grassroots leaders, especially, have called for a boycott of Japanese automobiles and other Japanese-made products.

A discussion of aggregates of business does not tell the whole story concerning the present state of black enterprises. A more definitive perspective regarding this matter can be gleaned from a descriptive analysis of specific categories of black enterprises. This kind of analysis, which follows next, also conveys more vividly major changes and, possibly, improvements in the efforts of blacks to become economically assimilated into American society.

BLACK BANKS

As early as 1888 blacks were directly engaged in banking. In that year, W. W. Browne, a minister in Richmond, Virginia, organized the first black-managed bank in the nation. Several banks were established particularly in the South, over the next several decades so that by the outbreak of World War I approximately 55 black-owned banking institutions existed in the United States. The majority of them had been organized in close association with black churches, fraternal organizations, and insurance firms. Their survival rate was relatively short, primarily because of inadequate capital, poor clientele, and problems associated with management philosophy (for instance, stress given to investments in low-yield securities, doubtful real-estate ventures, and loans generating small returns to black banks).

Between 1983 and 1989, the number of black-owned banks dropped from 44 to 35. The decrease in the number of black-owned banks reflects some of the problems experienced by the banking industry during the 1980s indicated by failures, mergers, or acquisitions. The overwhelming majority of black-owned banks are a phenomenon of the post-World War II era. Twenty-seven of the 35 banks in existence in 1989 were started since 1945. The remaining eight were established before 1950. Twenty-six (74 percent) of existing black-owned banks were formed between 1964 and 1989. After a period of decline following the Great Depression, the number of black-owned banks grew from 37 in 1974 to 48 in 1981 but this growth was followed by a precipitous numerical decline to 35 by 1989. At least four black-owned banks failed between 1985 and 1988. However, one of the failed black banks, Medical Center State Bank in Oklahoma City, was acquired by American State Bank of Tulsa. A second failed bank, Liberty National Bank in Seattle, was re-opened by black owners under the name of Emerald City Bank.[16] It should be noted that bank failures were almost commonplace during the 1980s. In 1987, some 201 banks across the United States failed. Troubles in the banking industry continued in 1988 when another 221 banks failed.

As reported in 1989, the combined assets of black-owned banks were $1.68 billion, which represented a 4.2 percent increase over their 1987 assets of $1.61 billion. Their combined assets represent approximately 1 percent of assets of all institutions in the banking industry. Five black-owned banks have assets in excess of $100 million: (1) Seaway National Bank of Chicago ($150 million); (2) Citizens Trust Bank of Atlanta ($121.2 million); (3) Freedom National Bank of New York City ($119.4 million*); (4) Independence Bank of Chicago (117.2 million); and (5) Industrial Bank of Washington, D. C. ($110.1 million).[17] In fact, however, the largest black bank holding company is Indecorps Inc. of Chicago whose assets total $230 million. Indecorp achieved this distinction by virtue of its purchase of Drexel National Bank, a previously white-owned bank in Chicago. The assets of Drexel National Bank combined with those of its second company, Independence Bank, account for the top ranking of Indecorp, Inc. By itself, Independence Bank ranks fourth among black-owned banks.[18] Eight banks have assets ranging from $55 million to $98.3 million. Ten banks have assets that range from $22 million to $48 million, and the assets of twelve banks range from a low of 8.2 million to $18.8 million.[19] Thus, despite the increase in assets of black-owned banks, these banks are relatively small. The significance of black banks, however, lies in both their present services as well as their potential for aiding in the rehabilitation and economic development of major segments of the black community.

All presently existing banks organized prior to World War II can be found in Washington, D. C. (1); North Carolina (2); South Carolina (1); Georgia (2); Virginia (2); and Tennessee (1). No black-owned banks were established in the North or border states until 1947 when the Douglas State Bank was organized in Kansas City. It was not until 1964 that the far West had its first black-controlled bank with the establishment of the Bank of Finance in Los Angeles, which is no longer in existence. The majority of black-controlled banks are located in Southern and border states (21), followed by the MidWest/North Central region (9) and the Northeast with four(4) banks.[20] The thirty-five banks combined have a total paid workforce of 1,657 persons. The range of paid employees is from a high of 142 (Seaway National Bank of Chicago) to a low of 11 (Victory Savings Bank of Columbia, South Carolina).

Traditionally, and in most recent times, black banks have been founded theoretically to serve the exclusive needs of black people. But the day-to-day realities of business transactions with banking institutions contradict the theory. One of these realities is the disinclination of the established banks to encourage loans for community development. They seem

---

*This bank failed in November 1990. Angered supporters expressed dismay at the U.S. government's failure to provide a bailout in view of the $500 billion cost of failed S & Ls.

to be much more conservative in their loan portfolios, less inclined to take risk applications, and much more oriented toward relatively safe, time-proved investments. By the same token, many of their loans have been at high risk, especially among those banks in which the management operated from a high level of social consciousness, granting loans based on social qualifications rather than on sound financial factors, and in those banks characterized by a shortage of managerical skills.

The 1980s brought additional problems to black-controlled banks. These difficulties included increased competition from larger financial service conglomerates, exhorbitant interest rates which lowered the margin of their profits, and the staggering rate of unemployment in the black community which affected both lending practices and deposit growth. Further, changes in federal policies with respect to banking laws concerning the amount of interest banks could pay to consumers set off tremendous competition between banks and thrift institutions for consumer savings and deposits.[21]

In contrast to the more established black-controlled banks, the higher failure rate of newer banks is undoubtedly attributable to their seemingly greater responsiveness to grant loans for black community development. They will invest more heavily in business loans, which do, in fact, have a much higher risk than either consumer or real-estate loans. Nevertheless, this more liberal orientation, in contrast to the more conservative philosophy of older institutions, reflects a commitment to help stimulate a more diversified business structure in the black community, which might, in turn, possibly broaden the base of the bank's wealth. But the problem of taking greater lending risks is minuscule when compared to the problem of undercapitalization, which is common to black-controlled banks. It is this perpetual undersupply of capital that forces some black bankers into a cautious and overprotective posture regarding loan portfolios. This situation also stimulated such agitation from community development advocates for greater assistance from white institutions doing business in the black community. It is one of the primary justifications, for insistence, by Reverend Jesse Jackson, the late Dr. Martin Luther King, and the NAACP's Fair Share Program, that whites who do business in black ghettos should help increase assets for black banks by depositing some of their profits in these black establishments. That the need for capital is serious is further shown by the load that black-controlled banks are expected to carry. As mentioned earlier, the total assets of black banks are a minute share of the assets of the banking industry in the United States. White-controlled banks, with less than 1 percent of their assets directed in this manner, actually provide a small fraction of loans, on a comparative basis, for blacks and other minorities during the course of the year. By contrast, black banks use approximately 10 percent of their assets for business loans. However, as a result of pressure from black organizations and individual black leaders, many large financial institutions and major corporations regularly make deposits in black-owned banks as a means of increasing the capital readily available to them. Corporations, such as General Motors,

Greyhound, Miller Brewing Company, Anheuser-Busch, and Sears, Roebuck are among the leaders in this endeavor to shore up black banking institutions through capital formation.

SAVINGS AND LOAN ASSOCIATIONS (S&LS)

Aside from the insider trading scandal that rocked Wall Street during the latter half of the 1980s, perhaps the most notorious episode in the financial industry in recent years has been the downfall of the savings and loan industry. Industry problems stemmed from fraudulent lending practices and widespread mismanagement of thrifts all across the nation. So many thrifts became insolvent that the federal government was forced to come to the rescue of that industry through an unprecedented bail-out program that was estimated in the late 1990s to cost as much as $500 billion, a classical example of what was referred to in Chapter 2 as "welfare for the rich." In 1989 alone 281 S&Ls went into government conservatorship.[22]

Within the black community, these financial institutions have smaller assets and about a third the number of employees as black-owned commercial banks. In 1988, the 33 black-controlled S&Ls had combined assets of $1,394,678,000. Their assets ranged from a high of $264.6 million (Independence Federal Savings Bank of Washington, D. C.) to a low of $5.78 million (Equity Federal Savings Bank of Denver, Colorado).[23] In general, assets in these institutions increased significantly between 1970 and 1990. For instance, in 1972, the largest of the 44 black-owned S&Ls then in existence had total assets of $60 million. The decline in the number of black S&Ls reflects the overall national problems suffered by the savings and loan associations consequent to a deteriorating economy, inflation, high interest rates, depression level unemployment, mismanagement, and poor decisions in lending practices. As a result of these practices, many federally insured savings and loan associations were merged with government assistance or swallowed up by larger, considerably more solvent, institutions. For the first time in the 95 year history of black S&Ls, their combined assets broke the $1 billion mark by the end of 1982. They have experienced almost yearly growth since that time.

Geographically, the associations are not well distributed since 20 of the 33 are located in the South; 5 in California; 4 in the Northeast; 3 in the North Central region; and 1 in the Midwest. Although all are located in urban communities, the absence of S&Ls in several cities having a large black population illustrates the relative inaccessibility of banking institutions purportedly established to serve the needs of black people, For example, no S&L controlled by blacks exists in such cities as Gary or Dallas-Fort Worth or Philadelphia and the United Federal Savings and Loan Association of New Orleans was in serious trouble at the beginning of 1990. Moreover, those that exist in cities with a particularly large black population, such as Detroit, Houston, St. Louis, and Baltimore, have assets

under $20 million each and many of the smaller S&Ls were either insol-
vent or marginally insolvent in terms of their net worth in 1988.[24] Essentially, savings and loan associations share the same shortcomings as the
banks and trust companies discussed in the preceding section.

LIFE INSURANCE COMPANIES

Until the emergence of relatively large companies in communications and
entertainment, energy-related industries, automobile sales, construction,
and publishing firms, the most successful and largest black enterprises
were insurance companies. Like all other parallel institutions within the
black community, they arose because of the discriminatory practices of a
segregated society. As with banking institutions, life insurance companies
originated in association with black churches, lodges, Freemasons, benev-
olent societies, and other voluntary associations. Also, they were not infrequently associated with funeral establishments. Throughout the South, for
example, where black undertaking establishments were among the more
successful enterprises, associated life insurance and burial companies
arose in conjunction with them and flourished.[25]

Three factors account for their continued success and prosperity as
economic enterprises: (1) prejudice, (2) discrimination, and (3) appeal to
the emotions of black people of all socioeconomic groups. This appeal was
addressed to a basic wish to see loved ones "put away" as stylishly as
possible. This desire often resulted, even now, in a form of economic
exploitation by the management of funeral or burial establishments,
which often persuaded blacks, irrespective of social class identification, to
provide the best arrangements for their deceased relatives. Expensive
capital outlays would be required for a coffin, limousines, a wake, and
other items. Thus the business of burying the deceased could become
unimaginably expensive. Burial insurance became an imperative; fortu-
nately, such insurance is usually inexpensive in terms of cost-benefit ratios
per family member.

As of 1988, only 31 of all insurance companies in the United States
were black controlled or black managed. Their combined premium value
declined by 7.83 percent between 1987 and 1988 or from $233.6 million
to $215.3 million. Their assets declined from $806.6 million to $806.2
million during the same period. Their combined number of employees fell
from 5,833 to 5,088 between 1987 and 1988. Again, their assets represent
about one-half of one percent of the total assets of the insurance industry.[26]

The most successful and second oldest bank is the North Carolina
Mutual Life Insurance Company, headquartered in Durham, North Carolina. Its total assets in 1988, 92 years after its founding, were $217.4
million.[27] The founders of this company also established the Mechanics
and Farmers Bank and the Mutual Savings and Loan Association of Dur-

ham, North Carolina, thus making this city one of the centers of black capitalism in America. The success of the North Carolina Mutual Life Insurance Company can be attributed to its ability to exploit a segregated market and, equally important, to sound management and fiscal responsibility by those persons who controlled the organization throughout its life. Astute men such as John Merrick, Asa T. Spaulding, Joseph W. Goodloe, and William Kennedy brought to Durham an acumen for high quality banking and insurance that assured a successful operation.

The second most successful insurance company is the Atlanta Life Insurance Company. Although it is six years younger than the North Carolina company and has smaller assets ($133.8 million), the assets controlled by Atlanta Life Insurance Company exceed those of the North Carolina company. This situation results from the recent tendency of Atlanta Life to grow by route of acquisition of other smaller companies. For example, in 1985 Atlanta Life bought Mammoth Life Insurance of Louisville, Kentucky, which ranks eighth on the list of black-owned insurance companies and which has assets of $29 million. In 1990, Atlanta Life acquired the ninth-ranking black-owned insurance company, Pilgrim Health and Life Insurance Company of Augusta, Georgia. Pilgrim Life Insurance company has assets of $15.8 million and represents the fourth acquisition of insurance companies by the Atlanta Life Insurance Company since 1984. This company is also noted for shrewdness of fiscal management, excellence of service to its customers, and for having had as its chief executive officer N. B. Herndon (who was one of the richest black men in the United States) and the business acumen of Jesse Hill, Jr, his successor and president. Under Hill's leadership, the Atlanta Life Insurance Company now has coverage in at least 15 southeastern states.[28]

Black insurance firms are also unevenly distributed throughout the nation. Thirty-five of the 50 states are not represented by black-owned insurance companies. One-third (11) of the 31 insurance companies are located in Louisiana alone. Alabama is the headquarters of four companies; Georgia (2); Mississippi (2); Illinois (2); Tennessee (2); and one each in North Carolina, California, Kentucky, New York, Colorado, Michigan, and Arizona.[29] The concentration of insurance companies in Louisiana is explained in part by its somewhat liberal laws that permit the establishment of insurance companies. However, Louisiana's black-owned insurance companies tend to be relatively small and in 1988, none had assets of $10 million or more. The recessions of the mid-1970s and early 1980s, high unemployment that forces many blacks to discontinue insurance coverage, the increasing number of blacks who became insured with larger white-owned insurance companies, plus low profits derived largely from premium income—all have slowed the overall growth of black insurance companies. Four companies folded between 1973 and 1980. Nevertheless, these companies experienced a 34-percent growth in ordinary policy sales between 1973 and 1983 and many have been strengthened by diversification and contracts from large white-owned corporations. For instance, the

North Carolina Mutual Insurance Company has subsidiaries in communications, including ownership of two cable television stations and AM and FM radio stations. This company won a $42-million employee life insurance contract in 1982 from Heublein, Inc., parent company of Kentucky Fried Chicken. Four black-owned insurance companies signed agreements in 1982 with R. J. Reynolds Industries "for $392 million in company-paid life insurance." These companies were North Carolina Mutual, Golden State Mutual (California), United Mutual (New York), and Supreme Life (Illinois).[30]

DIVERSIFICATION AND OTHER ENTREPRENEURIAL ACTIVITIES

In recent years there has been a strong movement away from the traditional "mom and pop" types of business that have repeatedly formed and disappeared in the black community. This has meant placing considerably less emphasis on neighborhood grocery stores, shoe repair shops, dry cleaning establishments, and barbershops, and greater stress on other enterprises such as automobile dealerships, advertising and public relations agencies, consulting firms, energy development, communications and publishing, the cosmetic industries, and filling the vacuum in the supermarket business left in the black ghetto following the white exodus of the 1960s and early 1970s. But two somewhat contradictory perspectives on black businesses were simultaneously in operation. One called for diversification at a time when money was tight and not particularly forthcoming for new business ventures. The other called for the establishment of small businesses, sometimes not indistinguishable from the traditional mom and pop type, designed to create a larger but relatively economically powerless capital class since funds were cut off, for instance, before they could be firmly established as viable enterprises.

However, because of the business acumen, imagination, and managerial skills of several blacks, coupled with their ability to obtain funding from the private sector and federal sponsorship, despite efforts of President Reagan to dismantle the entire minority business enterprise assistance programs, many blacks have moved into previously unchartered ventures among black Americans. For example, the *Black Enterprise* top 100 list for 1989 includes business ventures ranging from computer systems integration to engineering and technical support, radio and TV broadcasting cable operations, steel processing and distribution, petroleum products distribution, telecommunications, publishing, food products, aerospace manufacturing, construction and transportation. Black entrepreneurship in the 1990s also includes accounting firms and Wall Street trading firms that have achieved important attention. For example, the Mitchell/Titus accounting firm of Philadelphia and Washington, D. C., is one of the top 50 accounting firms in the United States. Clients of this firm include the NAACP, the employees' pension fund of Pepsico Inc., Time Warner Inc, Bristol-Myers and others.[31] Diversification is increasingly the chief characteristic of the larger and more successful black entrepreneurial activities.

Despite such changes, successes, and improvements in black entrepreneurship, these enterprises are still confronted with the persistent problem of finding the most efficacious method of reaching the $261 billion black consumer market. One method that appears to be effective is called Black Expo USA. This exposition of goods and services offered by black businesses travels to various regions populated by large segments of the black community and areas that will provide a great deal of exposure to black entrepreneurs. In 1990, Black Expo 90 traveled to four major cities: Atlanta, Philadelphia, Washington, D. C., and New York City. During the first Black Expo USA (1988), some 150 businesses participated.[32]

Radio and Television Stations

Primarily because substantial capitalization is required for organizing radio and television stations, blacks were slow to establish or buy controlling interests in them. In 1970 there were only 14 black-owned radio stations in the nation. By the end of 1989, blacks owned 170 radio stations and 13 television stations. Even with this apparent progress, blacks represent only 2 percent of the owners in the broadcast industry.[33] In 1982 the National Cable Television Association reported that 16 of the 4,690 cable systems in the United States that were then already established or under construction were largely black-owned. Further, blacks owned a tremendously successful satellite program network, Black Entertainment Television (BET).[34]

The major impetus for this growth in the participation of blacks within the broadcast industry was a change in policy by the Federal Communications Commission (FCC). In 1977 the FCC made a public commitment to minority participation and ownership in the broadcast industry. Consequent to a 1977 conference on minority ownership, the FCC initiated a "distress sale policy" that permits broadcasters in danger of losing their licenses to sell the license to a minority person or group which, in turn, permits the seller to obtain a tax certificate that assured "three years of tax deferment on . . . capital gains."[35] The FCC also established a Minority Enterprise Division for information dissemination concerning "available properties and changing technologies."[36] During the period 1977–1982, at least one black was a member of the FCC. The presence of a socially conscious commissioner who was black helped to persuade the FCC to embark on an aggressive policy toward expanding opportunities to minorities for the ownership of radio and television companies, and for exerting pressure on the broadcast industry to recruit and hire more minorities in general. Between 1977 and 1981 the number of blacks employed in the broadcast industry rose from 10,600 to approximately 13,900. In the same period, black officials and managers increased from 1,035 to 1,499.[37] One of the most successful achievements was concluded in 1982 when, after several years of "struggle," television station WNAC-TV, the CBS affiliate in Boston, was sold to the New England Television Corporation. Twenty-three blacks control 13 percent of the stock in the new company which operates Boston's Channel 7 (WNEV-TV), the sixth largest television market in the United States. The company elected as its president Bertram Lee, a black businessman.

The success in broadcasting opportunities experienced by blacks during the presidency of Jimmy Carter have been threatened under policies of the Reagan Administration. For instance, the Office of Management and Budget (OMB) recommended that the FCC discontinue an important practice which required broadcasters to file Form 395, an affirmative action report. Without this form, the commissioners were denied perhaps their most effective monitoring tool with respect to employment of and ownership by minorities. In the first year of the Reagan Administration, the number of radio stations acquired by minorities through the distress sale and tax certificate policy dropped dramatically from 31 in 1980 to 19 in 1981.[38]

In early 1990, the U. S. Supreme Court decided to review the FCC "distress policy" which had served as a major instrument for increasing access of blacks and other minorities to ownership of television and radio stations. This decision was the outcome of the Supreme Court's acceptance of cases about the constitutionality of the "distress policy," each claiming that the rights of white males were abrogated by the FCC rulings. Affirmative action proponents feared that the ultra-conservative Rehnquist Court would agree with white male challengers as it had done on several occasions in decisions rendered in 1989. If so, the probability of minorities purchasing increased numbers of telecommunications properties would be seriously impaired. But, in a surprise move, in June 1990, the U. S. Supreme Court reached a decision that was favorable to minorities. In the case of *Metro Broadcasting Inc.* v. *Federal Communications Commission,* the Court ruled that preferential treatment for minorities as a means of facilitating increased ownership of broadcast licenses and diversity in the broadcast industry is constitutional. As a result, the "distress policy" and related affirmative action tools remain intact.

With the acquisition or establishment of more black-owned radio and television stations, blacks have organized two strong, competitive black radio networks: (1) the National Black Network (NBN), the larger of the two, and (2) the Sheridan Broadcasting Company. Gupta reports that one of the most profitable companies in the Sheridan group is the Inner-City Broadcasting Company, headed by Percy Sutton, who served as president of the Manhattan Borough in the City of New York for a period of 10 years in the 1970s. The Inner-City Broadcasting company is, in many ways, a prototype of successful contemporary black enterprises. It has the advantage of sound leadership and management, strong capitalization, plus the ability to participate in joint ventures for purposes of diversification and continued development. For instance, in its early development, it attracted as stockholders such persons as Roberta Flack, an internationally known singer; Billy Taylor, jazz pianist; Betty Shabazz, the widow of Malcolm X; and the financial support of influential New York bankers. These persons helped to make the initial purchase of radio station WLIB-AM and subsequently established a second station, WBLS-FM, now one of the leading stations in New York City. The company now owns seven radio stations located in such communities as New York, Los Angeles, Berkeley, California, and Mt. Clemens, Michigan. Inner-City Broadcasting Company also purchased the famous Apollo Theater in Harlem and modernized it. The company also acquired Amistad Electronics in Grand Prairie, Texas, by virtue of a foreclosure on a loan. It owns Inner-City Management and Consulting, and is in a joint venture with Data Black Opinion Poll, Inner Unity Cable TV, and the Sheridan Broadcasting Network.[39]

Franchising

During the 1970s many black entrepreneurs turned to the acquisition of franchises of established businesses. Until that time, franchising was largely a business activity common only to the white community. Even though some white corporations had outlets in the black community, blacks did not own them. Organizations such as Reverend Jesse Jackson's Operation PUSH and the NAACP exerted pressure on these companies to provide business opportunities for blacks since purchases by blacks accounted for huge proportions of their profits. Because parent companies also wished to strengthen or expand business in a lucrative market area, they agreed to sell franchises to blacks. In 1975 less than 1 percent of all franchises in the United States were owned by blacks. By 1982, blacks owned approximately 5,500 franchises, representing about 1.5 percent of the approximately 450,000 franchises in the nation. Of the franchises owned by blacks, however, it is estimated that 2,300 are service stations.[40]

These franchises cover an immense array of business activities, ranging from fast-food industries—McDonald's, in which blacks own 457 franchises, IHS Gold card, 7-Eleven, Hardee Food Systems, Inc., Taco Bell, West Coast Video, Burger King, Kentucky Fried Chicken, Popeye Chicken outlets, and Chicken George—to franchises in the Goodyear Tire Company and auto rentals. Franchises are low-risk ventures with a first year success rate of 95 percent compared to 85 percent failure rate for other types of small businesses.[41] They are effective largely because of their structure. For instance, the parent company awards a license to a "franchise" to sell a given product or service as it prescribes. The franchise agrees to pay the parent company, or "franchisor," a specified percentage of gross sales and to adhere to regulatory norms established by the franchisor. The franchisee is also provided intensive management training and consultation by the franchisor and sometimes is assisted with purchasing and the establishment of a line of credit with suppliers—all activities that promote success.

Distributorships

Similarly, many blacks who began their forays into the business world as distributors of products from large white organizations have become enormously successful through their abilities to expand these opportunities into other business ventures. One of the more successful persons who began in this manner is Willie Davis, owner of Willie Davis Distributing, headquartered in Los Angeles. After graduating from Grambling College, Willie Davis played professional football with the Cleveland Browns and the Green Bay Packers. While playing for Green Bay, he enrolled in the MBA degree program at the University of Chicago. In 1964 he was turned down for an off-season job by the Joseph Schlitz Brewing Company; however, in 1970 he purchased a distributorship from that company for $500,000 which he amassed through $150,000 in personal savings as a professional athlete for 12 years, a bank loan, and securities from his property holdings. By 1972, Willie Davis was on the board of directors of the Joseph Schlitz Brewing Company and later became a member of the Board of Trustees of the University of Chicago from which he had earned the MBA degree. Between 1970 and 1982, Davis was able to parlay the profits from his beer distributing company into other lucrative investments that included the ownership of four of the five black-oriented radio stations in Los Angeles; chief operating officer of All-Pro Broadcasting; controlling interest in radio stations in Houston (KYOK-AM), Milwaukee (WAWA-AM), and complete ownership of station KQIN-AM in Seattle. In addition, his company now owns a trucking subsidiary, a significant interest in an office supply company in Appleton, Wisconsin, and he is the major stockholder in Alliance Bank, located in Culver City, California.[42]

Similarly, a number of blacks have become successful entrepreneurs because of that rare combination of ability, business acumen, managerial skills, and success in obtaining initial capital—all displayed by Willie Davis. For instance, Pettis Norman, a former professional football player for the Dallas Cowboys and San Diego Chargers, operates his own investment company which has Burger King franchises and real-estate investments. George Johnson, founder and president of Johnson Products Company began his company at the age of 26 in 1954 with a $250 loan from a finance company that was obtained ostensibly to take a vacation. His company is one of the most successful cosmetics and hair products manufacturers in the nation. Wally Amos, founder of Famous Amos Chocolate Cookies Company, began his company in 1975 with a $25,000 investment obtained from friends and celebrities.[43] He is now one of the approximately 200 black millionaires in the United States. Finally, Robert Maynard, who in 1979 became the first black person to serve as editor and publisher of a major metropolitan newspaper, purchased the controlling interest in that newspaper, *The Oakland Tribune,* in 1983.

ROLE OF THE FEDERAL GOVERNMENT AND THE EXTERNAL CORPORATE STRUCTURE IN BLACK CAPITALISM

Six interrelated factors account for the growth and expansion of black-owned enterprises since the latter half of the 1960s: (1) a shift in emphasis of the civil rights movement; (2) the death of Dr. Martin Luther King, Jr.; (3) increasing aggressiveness of blacks in business; (4) the overall response of the federal government to black economic ventures; (5) the growing assistance of major white corporations to underwrite capitalization of black businesses, an action stimulated in part by the work of Operation PUSH and the NAACP; and (6) the emergence of blacks to leadership positions in big city politics, especially black mayors who insisted that blacks obtain a fair share of city contracts. In brief, after the successes of the early 1960s the civil rights movement had begun to redirect its emphasis from strictly civil rights issues toward the problems of urban poverty, unemployment, and "getting a piece of the action" for minority businesses. This new direction coincided with pressures exerted by leading black businessmen and with complaints from blacks on the periphery of the business world that they were not receiving their share of direct benefits from government largess. The enactment of the Small Business Act during the Johnson administration did stimulate the development of business enterprises among members of minority groups. Funds were relatively slow in coming, however, and a significant proportion of fund applicants soon became disenchanted with bureaucratic red tape and other impediments to immediate capitalization and startups. Shocked, undoubtedly, by the assassination of Dr. King and stirred by the violent eruptions triggered by his death, the federal government began to take concrete steps that at once appeared to be more responsive to the needs of urban minorities.

The Small Business Administration

The Small Business Act established the Small Business Administration (SBA), which was empowered to stimulate, through loans and loan development programs, enterprises in the minority ghettos. Furthermore, through its Section 8(a), or the "set-aside" program initiated in 1968, the federal government was to give priority to minority group businesspeople in the awarding of federal contracts. By making low-interest loans available to blacks and other minorities and by giving them access to federal contracts, the SBA sought to increase the number of black capitalists.

However, it was not until the late 1960s that the SBA began to assist minorities to any appreciable degree. Community business development organizations, local structures established to promote black capitalism, were not even conceived until 1966, and they also expanded slowly.

As a result of the Section 8(a) program, the establishment of the Minority Business Development Program (MBDA), and the enforcement of Public Law 95-507 which mandated affirmative action within the SBA with respect to the negotiation and awarding of federal contracts and by prime contractors with the federal government, many small businesses initiated by blacks survived and prospered. With federal support, these small businesses were able to obtain much needed credit, management training, and develop a business track record. The viability of minority businesses was also fostered by the establishment of 100 national centers by the SBA which "provide management and technical assistance" to black and other minority-owned firms. In recent years, however, the Section 8(a) program and the SBA, in general, have been criticized by minority businesses and some members of the Congressional Black Caucus for changes in the definition of "small" and shifts in policies that "graduate" black businesses from assistance too quickly. Under the terms of the size and standards regulations of the SBA, a company may no longer be considered small if its annual earnings and gross receipts amount to $4 million or more. If that is the case, a company may be legally cut off or graduated from the program. Under 1981 Section 8(a) regulations, participating companies must leave the program after five years irrespective of their needs or growth patterns. The new rules do permit a possible one-year extension under highly restrictive circumstances. The Reagan administration was sharply criticized for its 1981 budgetary cutbacks which resulted in a significant drop in loans to black and other minority businesses.[44] In other words, despite former President Reagan's public promises to shore up opportunities for minority businesses, the reality is that the Administration drastically reduced the loan development program for minority businesses which undermined the important process of capital formation, instituted limitations on the Section 8(a) minority procurement program, and failed to move aggressively toward persuading the corporate structure to accelerate and expand their support of minority business enterprises.

In 1981, for the first time since 1975, the absolute dollar value of federal loans to minority businesses declined. In addition, in the first year of the Reagan Administration, the number of minority-owned businesses receiving loans from the federal government (5,200) plummeted to its lowest number since 1970.

The federal government also established the Office of Minority Business Enterprise (OMBE) by an executive order issued by President Nixon in April 1969. This order was highly suspect from the beginning because President Nixon was not regarded as a supporter of causes that the black community deemed important. It was also believed that the Nixon Administration was not especially eager to promote black capitalism, even though on an earlier occasion, the President had used the rhetoric of black militants and promised black businessmen "a piece of the action." When the OMBE began operations with an initial budget of approximately $3 million under a white director, those suspicions were confirmed. Moreover, for approximately two years the office floundered without specific directions and without a clear mandate other than that of coordinating agencies already in existence within the federal government whose functions were, in part or entirely, to increase the development of black enterprises. The office was intended to coordinate and conduct public relations, to function as an information clearinghouse that might direct interested minorities to specific sources of funding. Its power was limited since it could not release funds, force existing agencies to capitalize new business ventures, or guarantee support for proposed business startups.

Pressure from the National Advisory Council on Minority Business and various other sources finally persuaded President Nixon to issue another executive order that strengthened the OMBE and made it a more effective agency for stimulating enterprise capitalization. Housed in the Department of Commerce, the new order enabled the OMBE to appropriate funds directly to technical and managerial organizations, help locate technical assistance for minority enterprises, and develop business resource centers throughout the country. Since the creation of OMBE through Executive Order 11628, every president has signed the reaffirmation of the order, including President Reagan. During the first two years of the Reagan administration, OMBE received federal funding that facilitated the organization's ability to operate its four main programs: (1) the operation of 100 business development centers; (2) the support of technology and communications centers; (3) the operation of 18 export-import organizations designed to assist minority firms to participate in the international business market; and (4) the acquisition program designed to advance business development.

MESBICS

In 1969 the Minority Enterprise Small Business Investment Company (MESBICS) was created as another mechanism of venture capitalization.[45] By 1983, the estimated 135 active MESBICS provided services to about 3,200 portfolios which had an average of 15 employees. Between 1969 and 1983, some 4,000 small companies were financially assisted by the MESBICS including more than 70 percent of the companies listed in the Black Enterprise Top 100, from 70 to 80 percent of all black-owned franchises, and about 90 percent of black-owned communications firms. The MESBICS operated with $120 million in private capital investments plus $130 million in SBA money in 1983. In 1984, the Reagan Administration allocated $45 million for MESBICS. Thereafter, money for MESBICS was victimized by Gramm-Rudman mandates. As a result of these constraints, appropriations were reduced to the 1990 level of $36 million. During the same period, 1985–1990, private-sector support for MESBICS almost totally disappeared.[46] Support funds declined even as it was demonstrated that MESBICS-financed companies earned more than $1 billion in 1988, for example, and employed in excess of 17,000 persons.[47] New legislation, HR2971, was introduced in Congress in 1990 that was designed to increase funds for MESBICS.

In 1982, former Representative Parren Mitchell (D-Md.) successfully maneuvered acceptance of an amendment to the Surface Transportation Act of 1982 which was signed into law by President Reagan in 1983. The primary purpose of the law was to raise highway construction and repair revenues through the levying of a five-cent gasoline tax. The Mitchell Amendment states that 10 percent of the money collected under STA must be spent with minority vendors. The MBDA serves as an information clearinghouse to assure that potential minority vendors with skills in some aspect of highway and bridge construction and repair are informed about this opportunity. In 1982, minority businesses received $415 million or 5 percent of the $8 billion spent by the Department of Transportation.[48] Since then, a major problem developed regarding eligibility of such funds. This problem centered on the classification of white women as "minorities," and many racial minorities (blacks, Hispanics, Asians, and Native Americans) do not accept this classification. They also fear that classifying white women as minorities perpetuates racial discrimination and substantially reduces chances of racial minorities from actually attaining equal access to such funds. In their view, if a choice is to be made by a white male between a black-owned firm and a white female-owned firm, inevitably the white male will select the white female-owned company. This position is essentially the stance taken by the National Association of Minority Contractors (NAMC). Its executive director has argued that the inclusion of white women in the eligibility list for such set-asides subverts the original intention and expressed purposes of set-asides and hinders the economic empowerment of blacks and other disadvantaged minorities.[49] Evidence of his claims may be found in the fact that white female-owned firms received awards three times as large as those received by black-owned firms in the Dan Ryan Expressway Repair Project in Illinois in 1988.[50]

White private corporations have also supplemented and augmented the work of the federal government, especially since the 1960s. The American Bankers Association, for instance, established Minbancs, capital corporations that permit minority institutions to use expanding deposits for loans. This activity provides an additional source for operational capital, development funding, and expansion. The National Alliance of Businessmen, with Henry Ford II as chairman, was established to create more jobs for the hard-core unemployed, and the National Urban Coalition was established to improve business technology among black entrepreneurs. Other banking institutions, such as the Bank of America, and such manufacturing organizations and huge companies as IBM, Xerox, and General Motors, also provided technical assistance programs and some startup or promotional resources.

These accomplishments are unmistakably impressive, but the other side of the business coin is not so positive. It may be as Andrew Brimmer once commented, "a cruel hoax" to perpetrate upon black people the hope of black capitalism as a major method of escaping the depths of poverty and economic deprivation under present conditions.[51] Certainly the SBA finds itself perpetuating a paradoxical situation that calls for the end of mom and pop businesses while at the same time its loans go essentially to sole proprietors or individually managed small establishments. In addition, the failure rate of black business in this period has been six times as high as normally expected. This failure stems primarily from the lack of experience and business training, lack of management skills, and the inability of many new ventures to attract competently trained staffs for management and day-to-day operations. They also fail because of racial exploitation of many black businesses. The inexorability of undercapitalization, despite government and white corporate intervention, continues to plague black business ventures and leads directly to their demise. All too often, the government seems to expect swift and miraculous achievements within the first or second year, and if these are not forthcoming, funds and loan support subside. Significantly, the majority of black business failures occur during the first year because they lack adequate capital. Once they have been initiated or started up, the expectation appears to be that they should be able to function independently. Obviously, with such a high failure rate, support is withdrawn all too soon.

In the 1980s, bankruptcies and business failures were a major problem for American businesses in general. These problems were induced by a prolonged recession from which it was particularly difficult for some businesses to recover. Between 1978 and 1981, the number of business failures skyrocketed from 6,669 to 17,043, and in 1981 alone, some 47,000 businesses filed for bankruptcy.[52] In the first eight months of 1982, some 16,845 businesses had already failed, compared to 11,385 over the same period in 1981. Black businesses failed at a rate of 70 per 10,000 businesses or 103 during the first six months of 1982.[53]

The social milieu and economic condition of the ghetto, which is the locus of the majority of new business ventures, raise serious questions about the ability of black communities to support both small businesses and huge corporate structures despite the multi-billion consumer market located there. The market is not concentrated but is widely dispersed among hundreds of pocket areas where blacks are located. Success and failure are related to income disparities, unemployment and low occupational status, limited financial assets among blacks and their relatively high family debts, low-saving capacities, and unwise spending patterns.

With stronger capitalization and sound management, larger numbers of black businesses can prosper, and the gains for the entire black community can be substantially more than the psychological satisfaction derived from the knowledge that a few black brothers and sisters are "making it" in areas once monopolized or controlled by whites in the black community and in the nation as a whole.

SELF-HELP ORGANIZATIONS: ADAPTIVE RESPONSES

To ameliorate the conditions of poverty, undercapitalization, inadequately trained management, personnel, and operations, and to stimulate broader participation by blacks in finding solutions to such problems, a number of adaptive responses evolved in the form of self-help organizations. The diversity of these responses is reflected in the broad range of activities they have encompassed within a relatively short period. Although attention is focused here on Operation PUSH and the NAACP, the omission of other programs does not diminish their significance. More attention could be directed to efforts such as the Black Panther Food Program which operated so successfully during the 1960s and 1970s; the Operation Industrialization Centers which have trained 640,000 people since 1967 for an immense variety of jobs; the Urban League's manpower training programs; the National Association for the Southern Poor (NASP) which helps low-income farmers obtain loans; and the hundreds of black cooperatives organized to sustain and retain the black farm population and to promote agricultural diversification as well as to make blacks self-sufficient in food production.

The Covenants of PUSH

This organization, Operation PUSH: People United to Serve Humanity, was an outgrowth of the leadership and ideological conflicts that emerged full-blown after the assassination of Dr. King. Established in 1971, it is essentially an extension of the work commenced by the Chicago chapter of Operation Breadbasket which was started in the late 1960s by the Southern Christian Leadership Conference. Under the leadership of Reverend Jesse Jackson, who subsequently emerged as perhaps the most charismatic and highly publicized civil rights figure of the 1970s and 1980s, the focus of attention was shifted from the utilization of moral suasion to dynamic activism as an instrument of social change. The Reverend Jackson started to employ such pressure resources as boycotts, picketing, and generalized demonstrations. He used the power of the boycott, fortified by skillful market research on the volume of money spent by blacks on a given product, as a major weapon to persuade large corporations to assist in the economic development and empowerment of blacks.

The first notable success along these lines was the "covenant" reached with General Foods, signed on September 21, 1972. Under this agreement, a model was established that would be followed in exacting covenants from several other white corporations during the 1970s and 1980s. In the General Foods Covenant, the agreement consisted of ten items that covered provisions for jobs to black people, the continuation of a black college recruitment program, contracting black entrepreneurs for special services, the use of black lawyers, physicians, and dentists by the company, investment in and utilization of black-owned banks, insurance firms, advertising agencies, and black public relations companies.[54] Subsequently, PUSH negotiated agreements with such companies as the Joseph Schlitz Brewing Company, the Seven-Up Company, the Burger King Corporation, Heublein, Inc., and the Coca-Cola Company. It was not successful in its efforts to establish a similar agreement with the Anheuser-Busch Company because that company claimed that its record already demonstrated an outstanding commitment to minorities in all areas generally covered by the covenant. PUSH also created PUSH International Trade Bureau as the agency for monitoring and implementing the covenants reached between PUSH and the various corporations.

The Heublein Company owns such diverse enterprises as A-1 steak sauce, Harvey's Bristol Cream Sherry, Inglenook California Wine, Smirnoff Vodka, Black and White Scotch Whisky and, of course, Kentucky Fried Chicken (KFC). By 1982, it operated 780 Kentucky Fried Chicken outlets and nine of them were black franchises. Under the terms of the agreement reached in March 1982, Hublein promised to expand the number of black franchises to approximately 112 by 1987, which, in turn, should create an additional 1,500 jobs representing more than $430 million in wages. In order to achieve the goal of an increased number of black franchise owners, Heublein developed a capital formation program to finance the construction of Kentucky Fried Chicken units, and committed itself to arrange for $3.3 million in credit available for black franchise candidates. Other components of the covenant include: (1) increase the company's advertising with black-owned media and black-owned advertising agencies to multimillion-dollar levels; (2) a commitment to purchase more than 15 percent of its group term life insurance through black-owned insurance companies; (3) to continue to expand its deposits with 11 minority-owned banks, nine of which are black, to a level of $20 million, and to expand its "operational presence" in an even larger number of minority banks in such areas as store "depositories, investments and income tax deposits;" (4) to retain professional services of black lawyers and certified public accountants (CPAs); (5) to strengthen its affirmative action program so that the number of blacks in management and lower-level jobs will be increased from the 1982 level; (6) to continue its financial support to minority organizations such as the United Negro College Fund, the NUL, the NAACP and, possibly, provide matching grants to black institutions and organizations such as the Martin Luther King, Jr. Center for Social Change, as well as the establishment of an internship program for minority students to work at its companies in Hartford and Louisville; (7) to increase the dollar value of its purchasing through the five-year-old Minority Purchasing Program from the 1982 level of $9.8 million to $11.5 million in each year through 1987; and (8) to investigate the possibility of involving black distributors of its wine products.[55]

Operation PUSH discovered that black Americans account for approximately 15 percent of Burger King's annual volume, about 30 percent of the Coca-Cola Company's market, and about 15 percent of the Seven-Up Company's volume. As a result of negotiations, it was able to complete a covenant, similar to the covenant negotiated with Heublein, valued at $500 million with the Burger King Corporation, $34 million with Coca-Cola Company, and $25–$30 million with the Seven-Up Company.[56] It is estimated that about $1 billion in job and market opportunities were opened up to blacks by virtue of the agreements signed between Operation PUSH and these four companies.[57]

The NAACP Fair Share Program

This program was established in 1982 as an economic development endeavor for persuading the private sector to commit more resources for the hiring of blacks, the establishment of minority procurement programs, assistance of developmental and management programs for black businesses and individuals, and the appointment of more blacks to corporate boards. Within the first year of operation the NAACP signed nine pacts with trade associations and with such companies as the Georgia Power and the Mississippi Power.[58] During the 1983 Annual Convention of the NAACP in New Orleans, Robert D. Lund, vice-president of the General Motors Corporation (GM), stated GM's fair share program. GM embarked on a minority dealer program in 1967 with 21 minority dealers. In 1983, the number had grown to 159, and increased throughout the 1980s with anticipated improvements in the automobile industry. GM established a Dealer Development Academy to provide training, expertise, and assistance to potential dealers. It pledged to continue its MESBIC, Motor Enterprise, Inc., through which loans are made to 146 minority firms. In 1982 GM deposited approximately $523 million in minority-owned banks and pledged to continue that activity. Similarly, GM carries about $350 million in group life insurance for its employees through four minority-owned banks in addition to $10.5 billion in property damage insurance carried with minority-controlled banking institutions. It also pledged to continue its use of minority brokerage houses, advertising agencies, and suppliers in its Minority Supplier Program.[59] Also, during its 1983 annual convention, Benjamin Hooks, Executive Director of the NAACP, announced the signing of fair share agreements with the Kroeger Food Chain and the Brown and Williams Tobacco Company valued at more than $200 million.

Since 1981, Fair Share agreements have been signed with the NAACP, PUSH, the League of United Latin American Citizens (LULAC), and HACER. However, by the end of 1989, at least 62 Fair Share Agreements had been signed with the NAACP and PUSH had obtained Covenants from 12 corporations that were valued at $6 billion over five years. Under the Covenants signed with PUSH, the companies agreed to hire increasing numbers of blacks at all corporate levels, increase the number of service contracts with black entrepreneurs, and place blacks on corporate boards.[60] Although Fair Share Agreements and Covenants will, indeed, assist in the overall economic empowerment of blacks, it is the black ownership of capital, the establishment of a greater number of viable black businesses whose owners will provide jobs to black Americans that will move the efforts for economic empowerment further and at a swifter pace.

The Miller Brewing Company has focused on expanding employment opportunities for black Americans as well as minority business development. As the company expanded and its overall number of employees grew, there was also a significant increase in the absolute number and proportion of black employees in the company. For instance, in 1972, the 52 black employees represented a token percentage of 2.5 percent of the 2,034 employed persons in the company. In 1976 the company's workforce of 4,756 persons included 578 blacks or 12.1 percent of the total. In 1982, the 2,077 blacks working for the Miller Brewing Company constituted 15.7 percent of an entire workforce of 13,179. In addition, the company operates an aggressive program for minority business participation, utilizes the services of 450 minority vendors and several minority purchasing companies, advertising companies, banking institutions, contributes to black educational programs, and participates actively in the NUL's Black Executive Exchange Program (BEEP) which assists black college students to prepare for work in business and industry.[61]

Despite these efforts, as well as the work done by additional companies such as Allstate Insurance Company through its Minority Vendors program and Sears in its minority employment program, blacks have yet to make major employment gains with the large American corporations. They remain a rarity on the corporate boards or as managers and directors of the Fortune 500. Among the blacks who do manage to break the "corporate barrier," many feel the bitter sting of pernicious racism, rejection, isolation, and loneliness.[62]

PROBLEMS OF BLACK BUSINESSES

Aside from the already discussed problems, without a doubt the most serious issue revolves around crime in the urban ghetto. High ghetto crime rates have reached epidemic proportions. They raise insurance premiums to astronomical proportions and are the direct cause of many business failures in the black ghetto. One SBA survey revealed that small businesses account for about two-thirds of all losses from robberies, and that the armed robber of a commercial enterprise leaves one in five of his victims either fatally wounded or physically injured.[63]

Black businesses, like American businesses as a whole, are compelled to spend more for crime prevention—monies that could be reinvested in business activities. They primarily protect themselves from inordinate losses that are the result of employee theft, embezzlement, pilferage, and fraud. These criminal activities, in addition to those committed by people outside the company, result in extremely heavy financial losses and enormous social costs to black businesses and the black community each year. The decision to locate a business enterprise is often dictated by important quality of life issues such as the prevalence of crime within a community. Furthermore, perceptions of high rates of criminal activity may be a serious impediment to potential customers' desire to patronize a firm or for suppliers and distributors to provide much needed services to enterprises located in high crime areas. In recent years, black businesses and community citizens have combined their collective resources to initiate crime watch programs—a matter of special concern to black residents of high crime areas since they fully appreciate the negative impact of the loss of special and much needed services should many existing businesses shut down because of uncontrollable crime.[64]

One final aspect of black business deserves brief attention. Illegal business operates in the black community in much the same way that it does in the white community. It is believed that a huge share of black revenue comes from organized crime, gambling, drug trafficking, stolen property, prostitution, and other illegal activities. No one actually knows the extent of the holdings possessed by the lords of the underworld and by those who control the "shaded society." Moreover, even though exorbitant sums of money are generated in the black community, little remains there since these illegal business ventures tend to be controlled by forces external to the community itself.

HUMAN RESOURCE NEEDS

It may be assumed that, despite the retrenchment in the expansion of employment opportunities imposed by policies of the Reagan Administration, there remains an even more compelling need for highly skilled and professionally trained black Americans. Unfortunately, as demonstrated in Chapter 6, there are critical shortages of blacks in all professional fields. For instance, the various schools of business and management annually graduate about 57,000 persons with MBA degrees. Only about 5 percent or slightly more than 2,000 are black and many of them are hired by white-owned firms. Hence, high level managerial skills are in relatively short supply and great demand among black business. Training programs for middle-level managers and job training programs for individuals to meet the growing and changing demands of a high technology-oriented society have not been adequately financed nor have they been fully supported by the federal government.

Major efforts are imperative for training a greater supply of black Americans to meet the changing job opportunity structure and the needs of an expanding black business enterprise system. However, as mentioned in Chapter 2, unless new job opportunities are opened and the legitimacy of training and hiring blacks is taken seriously, major intergroup conflicts will result. Skilled training and professional expertise, reinforced by an actualized commitment to change, are a *sine qua non* for maintaining a viable black community.

NOTES

1. For a discussion of the history and development of black businesses, see Gunnar Myrdal, *An American Dilemma* (New York: Harper & Row, 1944), pp. 308–316; Theodore Cross, *Black Capitalism* (New York: Atheneum, 1969); the June 1982 and June 1983 issues of *Black Enterprise* (on which I have relied heavily for references in this chapter), and Wilson Butler, "Entrepreneurial Enclaves: An Exposition into the Afro-American Experience," *National Journal of Sociology,* 2:2 (Fall 1988): 127–166.
2. Butler, *ibid.*
3. *Ibid.*
4. Howard E. Aldrich, "Employment Opportunities for Blacks in the Ghetto: The Role of White-Owned Businesses," *American Journal of Sociology,* 78 (May 1973): 1403–1425.
5. U. S. Department of Labor, "Employment and Earnings" (Washington, D. C.: Bureau of Labor Statistics, 1980), p. 530.
6. Elliot D. Lee, "The Black Enterprise Board of Economists Looks at the Future," *Black Enterprise* (June 1982), p. 192.
7. Cf. "Building a New Tradition," *Black Enterprise* (June 1983): p. 70; "The Top 100 Black Businesses," *loc. cit,* pp. 79–87; and The Editors, "Tomorrow, The World: B. E. 100s Overview," *Black Enterprise* (June 1989): 187–192.
8. Cf. Alfred Edmond, Jr., "Dealing at the Speed of Light," *Black Enterprise* (June 1988): 150–162; and "Industrial/Service Companies," *Black Enterprise* (June 1989): 199–207.
9. *Ibid.*
10. The Editors, *op. cit.,* p. 196.
11. *Ibid.,* p. 199.
12. *Ibid.,* p. 187.
13. "Industrial Service Companies," *loc. cit.*
14. *Ibid.*
15. "Ford—Out Front With Minority Dealers," *Black Enterprise* (June 1988): 189; information provided by Archie Colander, Jr., Minority Business & Employment Administrator; NAACP; May 18, 1989.
16. Mark Fortune, "Vaulting Into New Ventures," *Black Enterprise* (June 1989): 245–252; and Alfred Edmond, "A 'Golden Opportunity' for Black Firms," *Black Enterprise* (April 1990): 33.

17. *Op. cit.*
18. *Op. cit.*, p. 246.
19. *Ibid.*
20. *Ibid.*
21. William D. Bradford, "In the Interest of Survival," *Black Enterprise* (June 1983): 103.
22. *Op. cit.*
23. Anne W. Kimbrough, "Feeling the Heat: Management of Majority Thrifts Has Reform-Minded Legislators Breathing Fire," *Black Enterprise,* (June 1989): 265–268.
24. "Savings and Loans," *Black Enterprise* (June 1989): 271–272.
25. "Banks," *Black Enterprise* (June 1983): 3–34.
26. The Editors, "Fortify or Die: Insurance Overview," *Black Enterprise* (June 1989): 285–288.
27. "Insurance," *Black Enterprise* (June 1990): 290–291.
28. William C. Hocker, "Atlanta Life Buys Pilgrim, Moves into South Carolina," *Black Enterprise* (February 1990): 24.
29. *Op. cit.*
30. "The Benefits of Innovation: Insurance Overview," *Black Enterprise* (June 1983): 137–138.
31. Pamela D. Sharif, "After Merger, Accounting Firm Targeting Expansion," *Black Enterprise* (April 1990): 22, and Richard D. Hylton, "Minority Firms Feel the Pinch," *New York Times* (April 16, 1989), p. F-4.
32. Mamadou Chinyelu, "Black Expo to Hit 4 Cities," *Black Enterprise* (April 1990): 26.
33. Udyan eq. Gupta, "Integrating the Airwaves," *Black Enterprise* (June 1982): 125–127.
34. Edmund Newton, "Countdown to Takeoff," *Black Enterprise* (June 1982): 128–132.
35. *Ibid,* p. 125.
36. *Ibid.*
37. *Ibid,* p. 126.
38. *Ibid.*
39. *Ibid,* p. 132.
40. Monte Trammer, "Franchising: The Low Risk American Dream," *Black Enterprise* (June 1982): 87–89.
41. Ibid., p. 88.
42. Ron Harris, "The House That Willie Built," *Black Enterprise* (June 1983); 90–96.
43. "Self-Made Millionaires," *Ebony* (May 1983): 53–58.
44. Cf. *Black Enterprise* (March 1982), *passim;* (June 1982), *passim;* and (June 1983), *passim.*
45. "Banks," *Black Enterprise* (June 1982), *passim.*
46. Cf. William C. Hocker, "New Debentures Bill Should Help MESBICS," *Black Enterprise* (February 1990): 43; and B. Wright O'Connor, "What's Next for the SBA?" *Black Enterprise* (June 1989): 137–138.
47. *Ibid.*
48. Bebe Moore Campbell, "Five Cents Gas Tax Promises Business Opportunities for Blacks," *Black Enterprise* (July 1983): 32.
49. Cf. Luther Brown, "Women vs. Minorities: The Debate Rages," *Black Enterprise* (June 1988): 65–66.

50. *Ibid.*
51. Andrew Brimmer, "Economic Integration and the Progress of the Negro Community," *Ebony,* 25 (August 1970): 119–121.
52. Cited in *Black Enterprise* (April 1982): 31.
53. *Ibid.*
54. See *Amsterdam News,* September 30, 1972, B-B, for text of this covenant.
55. Covenant: Operation PUSH-Heublein, Inc., March 16, 1982; made available by Reverend Jesse Jackson, President of Operation PUSH.
56. See: *A Covenant Between the Seven-Up Company and Operation PUSH,* July 17, 1982; *Covenant Among Operation PUSH, Inc., Burger King Corporation, and the Minority Franchise Association,* April 18, 1983, and *A Moral Covenant Agreed To by the Coca-Cola Company and Operation PUSH,* August 10, 1981. These documents were provided by Reverend Jesse Jackson.
57. *Newsletter, International Trade Association of Operation PUSH,* 2:2 (February–March 1983).
58. S. Lee Hilliard, "Demanding Fair Share," *Black Enterprise* (August 1983): 40–42.
59. Robert D. Lund, "Remarks," made in a paper presented during the NAACP Life Membership Luncheon, NAACP Annual Convention, New Orleans, La., July 13, 1983.
60. Communication from NAACP Economic Development Program (May 18, 1989). See also Alex Poinsett, "The New Civil Rights Movement: The Drive for Economic Equality," *Ebony* (August 1989): 76–78.
61. *The Miller Commitment* (Milwaukee, Wis.: The Miller Brewing Company), *passim.*
62. Cf. George Davis and Gregg Watson, *Black Life in Corporate America: Swimming in the Mainstream* (New York: Doubleday) 1982; Carlton E. Spitzer, *Raising the Bottom Line: Business Leadership in a Changing Society* (New York: Longman, 1982); Floyd Dickens and Jacqueline Dickens, *The Black Manager: Making It in the Corporate World* (New York: Amacon, 1982).
63. R.G. Collago, "Closing Down on Crime," *Black Enterprise* (April 1983): 39–46.
64. *Ibid.*

Chapter
9

Black Political Power

*T*he slogan "black power," first echoed during the summer of 1966, escalated fear and strained social relationships between the races and within the black community primarily because its meaning was so widely misunderstood. When rationality finally supplanted emotionalism, many black persons could agree that a major focus of black power was how to gain access to the political structure of American life and effect enduring economic and social changes. This consensus makes explicit the manifest significance of political leverage in transforming power relations between groups of unequal status.

This chapter examines a number of issues related to changing power relations among black and white participants in the political process. Among the issues raised are: the historic roles of the black populace in politics and the black struggles for political inclusion; strategies for increasing political participation; factors accelerating or impeding political involvement by black Americans; schisms in the civil rights movement; the emerging dominance of blacks in big-city politics; differential responses to blacks by the Carter, Reagan, and Bush Administrations; structures that facilitate power redistributions among societally determined unequals and the role of Jesse Jackson in the Democratic Party.

THE DEVELOPMENT OF A POLITICAL MASS

It is often argued that the acquisition of political power depends upon, among other things, the presence of numbers of people. Essentially, according to this thesis, distinct groups of people may achieve group power if they vote collectively and uniformly on the same issues over time and for one of their own group. In this sense group solidarity is manifested in a "consciousness of kind" as it relates to political behavior. If such groups persist in collective or bloc-voting behavior over time and if their numbers are large enough to affect voting outcomes, they may in time gain partial or complete control of the government, especially at local levels. This thesis is fundamentally a politics of numbers predicated upon the assumption that the participants are both sufficiently well organized and motivated to mobilize their resources, whether in terms of individual voters, financial support, or whatever else is needed, and that their activities will be oriented toward a common goal, the acquisition of power. It also assumes that people aspire for political participation mainly because the rewards and gratifications anticipated are worth the energy expended in the process. Thus if the anticipated rewards are inadequate and the probability for goal attainment is not high, then groups are less likely to be motivated to gain political power than if the situation were the reverse.[1] In other words, the acquisition of political power by a minority is a highly complex phenomenon involving numbers of people, the strength of their social organization, the effectiveness to which whatever resources they possess are mobilized for goal attainment, and the position assumed by the dominant group in this process.

Historical Trends

One of the basic problems that the black community has had to confront since emancipation is that of acquiring and maintaining a critical mass— that is, a sufficient number of people for influencing political outcomes or decisions in regard to collective black interests. This need was implicit in the equal rights conventions conducted by blacks during 1865 in such states as Virginia, South Carolina, North Carolina, Tennessee, and Mississippi. However, it was the Fifteenth Amendment to the Constitution (1870), which guaranteed the rights of black men to vote, that paved the way for large-scale participation of blacks in the political process. In general, the mood of the First, or Radical, Reconstruction was such that newly enfranchised blacks felt that their rights would be protected and that positive consequences would redound to them if they exercised political prerogatives. Hence blacks voted in such large numbers, particularly in the South, that black elected officials served in the U.S. Congress and Senate until 1901, interrupted only by a two-year period (from 1887 to 1889) when no blacks served in either branch of Congress. Although Hiram R. Revels and Blanche K. Bruce, who represented Mississippi as U.S. senators (between 1870 and 1881), are the most familiar names of national politicians during the period, some 20 black men served in the House of Representatives between 1869 and 1901. Most of these men came from the upper Southern states, particularly the Carolinas; however, others represented such Deep South states as Alabama, Georgia, Florida, Mississippi, and Louisiana.

During Reconstruction, in addition to national elective positions, blacks held innumerable state and local offices (e.g., state senators and representatives; mayors, judges, members of all state courts, education superintendents; and one, P. B. S. Pinchback, served as acting governor of Louisiana for a short time). Hence this form of political leverage, relative to the power and prestige of the positions held, enabled blacks to promote a number of political and educational reforms of far-reaching significance, namely, the democratization of state constitutions and educational systems during Reconstruction.

The political power achieved by blacks in the South was short-lived. By virtue of a series of events commencing with the Compromise of 1877, southern whites took systematic steps to disfranchise southern blacks and, subsequently, retard their political integration into American life. The Compromise of 1877 was essentially an agreement by the North to remove the federal troops, which had protected rights of black people, and to reestablish home rule in the South in exchange for southern support for Rutherford B. Hayes, whose election to the presidency was hanging in the balance. With federal troops removed, the white South was not only free to establish home rule but to revert to its previous position of complete dominance over the black population. Also, northern Republicans thereby abdicated responsibilities for the social, economic, and political development of black people by devolving it to white southerners. The result was that whatever external support blacks once counted on for the attainment of a just life was no longer available.

Methods of Disenfranchisement

The process of disfranchising blacks in the South assumed essentially eight forms: (1) Blacks were not permitted to vote in many places following changes in state constitutions. (2) The Enforcement Act of 1870 and the Civil Rights Act of 1875 were declared unconstitutional, both of which had protected the principle of universal suffrage. (3) A *grandfather's clause* was enforced whereby eligibility for voting was determined on the basis of having an acknowledged grandfather who had voted in federal elections prior to 1866. (4) *White primaries* were held that excluded all but members of the Democratic party from participating in an election, a strategy that made that party a private all-white club. (5) A *poll tax* was required of potential voters, which varied in sum from state to state and from jurisdiction to jurisdiction; but the enormity of the tax precluded most blacks and a sizable number of whites, when it was applied to them, from exercising the rapidly attenuating right of franchise. (6) *Literacy tests* demanded that potential voters be able to read and recite from memory previously unspecified sections of either a state or federal constitution, as was done under the Boswell Amendment of 1946 in Alabama. (7) *Gerrymandering* permitted a jurisdiction to redistrict voters in such a way as to neutralize black voters by reducing their proportion in the new district. (8) *Violence* was used, either through the Ku Klux Klan (KKK) or other more spontaneously organized groups or hostile individuals—all of which effectively deterred blacks from voting. Often, violence took the form of lynchings, physical assaults, and various reprisals against potential black voters. By the turn of the century the majority of black southerners were effectively eliminated from the polls, and their political power had been totally destroyed at local, state, and national levels. In the meantime, although northern black citizens continued to participate in the electoral process, the impact of their votes was inconsequential. Their political power was severely limited and would so remain until the advent of the mass black exodus from the South to the North during World War I.

Despite these impediments to political participation, blacks neither acquiesced to white dominance nor resigned themselves to a subordinate political status. For example, the racially integrated Niagara Movement gave rise to the NAACP, organized in 1909 to restore political rights to black Americans.

For more than 75 years the NAACP and, later, the Legal Defense Fund (LDF) have been a major force for regaining and maintaining political rights for black people. It may also be said that literally all of the contemporary minorities have benefited from legalistic battles won by the NAACP-LDF even though their plaintiffs have usually been black. The value of this organization as an instrument for social change can be gleaned from cases representative of its many victories: (1) the elimination of the grandfather's clause in the case of *Guinn* v. *the United States* (1915); (2) first, the reduction of the impact of white primaries as a restraining factor against black voters in *Nixon* v. *Herndon* (1927) and *Nixon* v. *Condon* (1932) and, then, the destruction of white primaries in *Smith* v. *Allright* (1944) followed by *Rice* v. *Elmore* (1947), in which the U.S. Supreme Court invalidated them as a violation of the Fifteenth Amendment; (3) attacks against obstructionist tactics involving abbreviated time periods for black registrants as in *Lane* v. *Wilson* (1939); (4) the abrogation of gerrymandering by the U.S. Supreme Court, which involved Tuskeegee in Macon County, Alabama, in the case of *Gomillion* v. *Lightfoot* (1969); and (5) the enactment of the Twenty-fourth Amendment to the U.S. Constitution, which abolished all poll taxes. Moreover, the association's sustained attack against lynchings and physical abuse substantially reduced or curtailed such occurrences to sporadic episodes.

The effectiveness of the NAACP and LDF in reenfranchising a fairly large number of blacks can be attributed to a highly organized internal structure and ability to mobilize numerous resources to attain their goals. They welcomed whites to their ranks and valued their financial support. The organizations have retained an interracial membership, despite adverse publicity in the late 1960s, and they continue to be oriented toward the goal of a racially integrated society in which black Americans would become full and equal participants. The primary tactic for attaining this goal has been and continues to be legalistic. Their financial support is based upon membership fees and voluntary contributions. However, their resources extend far beyond finance and a strong membership to include a large pool of talented personnel, most especially a core of legal tacticians and strategists.

Two immediate consequences resulted from the persistent efforts to enfranchise blacks: (1) blacks did begin to register in such a manner as to become an important political force; and (2) a shift in party affiliation occurred. Black importance as a political force was reflected in the degree to which the large political machines courted their votes in every region of the country. The shift from the Republican party to the Democratic party probably began as early as 1928 and was all but a *fait accompli* by 1940.

Party Machines

By virtue of the successes of the NAACP in enfranchising an increasingly larger number of black voters in the South, the number of black voters in 1932 was a substantial increase over the decimated residue existing in 1901. Southern machines courted black voters on the promise that their support would result in what Dahl calls both divisible and indivisible benefits to them.[2] Undoubtedly, the attainment of jobs was the more important divisible benefit for low-status blacks, whereas the acquisition of community needs, such as a playground, was among the more valued indivisible benefits. (Divisible benefits seem to be synonymous with Hubert Blacock's concept of competitive resources.)[3] Thus the Byrds of Virginia could promise blacks a denunciation of the KKK or sponsor anti-lynching legislation in exchange for black votes. William C. Hartsfield in Atlanta could promise a better economic life for blacks in his meetings with the boss of the black machine there, A. T. Walden, in return for black support at the polls.[4] But these were largely paternalistic overtures, and, as Banfield observes, people like Hartsfield, for example, never provided either divisible or indivisible benefits for black Atlantans.[5] Some machine bosses, such as Boss Crump in Memphis, abided by segregationist principles when the alternative was integration or segregation. In one instance, Crump refused to support Dr. T. E. Walker, his black counterpart in Memphis, in Walker's bid to ensure a desegregated seating arrangement for a Marian Anderson concert in 1940.

Machine politicians in the North relied more on political patronage as a means of attracting black voters. Through the patronage system blacks could be placed in low-level positions and be guaranteed dependable, although low-paying, employment. Occasionally, more influential black supporters would be rewarded with a relatively important judgeship, or some black person might be elected as an alderman or city councilman. These factors were crucial elements in the election of Republican Oscar DePriest of Chicago in 1929 as the first black congressman since 1901. He was succeeded by a black Democrat, Arthur W. Mitchell, who served from 1935 to 1943. He, in turn, was succeeded by William Dawson, who was joined by Adam Clayton Powell from New York in 1945. They, as well as other blacks who were to follow them to Congress, owed their political success to the conjoining of demographic/ecological factors with machine politics and a rising black consciousness.

Shifts to the Democratic Party

Historically, blacks have always been affiliated more predominantly with one political party than another. Primarily because of the historical association of President Lincoln with emancipation, blacks were loyal for a half-century or more to the Republican party. Black allegiance to the Republicans was fostered by solid evidence that the Democratic party was for three-quarters of a century, largely antiblack. However, in the period of reenfranchisement, beginning from about 1915 to the present time, the Democrats initiated programs and policies that successfully severed blacks from the Republican party and drew them within the orbit of Democratic politics. The Republicans themselves abetted this process by practices that favored privileged classes or appeared to be antiblack. Hence they excluded blacks from the inner circles of local Republican activities, isolated them at meetings, and treated them with disdain and contempt. Simultaneously, Democrats, especially from the 1928 presidential election on, overtly wooed black voters.

Following Roosevelt's victories in 1932 and 1936, he made two shrewdly conceived political moves that accelerated the shift of blacks toward the Democratic party. First, he established a black cabinet comprised of highly respected black leaders, who were advisers on black affairs, many of whom were prestigious educators like Mary McCloud Bethune, founder of Bethune-Cookman College in Florida. Dr. Bethune was the Director of the Division of Negro Affairs of the National Youth Administration (NYA) and was, for all practical purposes, the head of Roosevelt's black cabinet. President Roosevelt appointed more than 100 blacks to federal positions in the period between 1933 and 1940. Although subordinated to white directors of heads of agencies and without significant political authority, black appointees perceived themselves as participants in the decision-making process; they received high status and prestige in the black community and were regarded by whites as respectable black leaders who were a "credit to their race." In addition to specific appointments, Roosevelt initiated meetings in the White House with black leaders. Members of the established cabinet were encouraged to seek the advice of black leaders on matters of direct concern to them. In this manner disenchanted blacks were somewhat placated, since it appeared that the Roosevelt Administration was concerned with the plight of the poor and with including blacks in decision-making processes.

The second step was the inclusion of blacks in many New Deal program benefits. As expected, blacks, hard hit by the Great Depression, were in need of substantial relief. Many found employment through the various

Public Works Administration projects. Charges of discrimination in the Civilian Conservation Corps were duly investigated, and discrimination there somewhat abated. But discrimination was rampant in several federal agencies during FDR's Administration. Black farmers and sharecroppers were also adversely affected by New Deal agricultural policies (e.g., discriminatory soil conservation programs, unequal incomes between black and white farm workers, underrepresentation of black agricultural extension workers, and so on). Even so, a spirit of optimism prevailed when blacks were made aware of frequent public appearances of Eleanor Roosevelt with Mary McCloud Bethune despite criticisms in the white community. This apparent genuine concern by Eleanor Roosevelt accelerated black movement toward the Democratic party. This process, initiated in the 1928 election, was discernible in 1932, quite apparent in 1936, and complete by 1940. Blacks had abandoned the Republican party—and were safely ensconced in the Democratic stronghold and committed to the position that greater social, economic, and political benefits were to be derived from their support of the Democratic party.

Similarly, Democratic party bosses were quick to perceive the pivotal character of the black vote in closely contested elections at all levels. Largely because of this capacity to influence political outcomes, blacks have to some degree benefited from Democratic machine politics, patronage, and party support but not to the degree of success experienced by white ethnics in earlier times. For example, presidential decisions to expand black participation in the military (FDR) and to desegregate the armed forces (H. S Truman) were motivated in a large measure by the desire for support of black voters. White ethnics, on the other hand, were more successful in gaining control over entire systems and subsystems within municipal and state governments (e.g., teaching, public works, fire and police departments).

The pivotal nature of blacks in closely contested elections can be illustrated by several instances: (1) In 1940 black votes helped Roosevelt gain 190 electoral votes that proved to be the margin of victory over Wendell Willkie.[6] (2) Black voters undoubtedly provided much of the narrow margin of victory for Truman over Dewey, Strom Thurmond, and Henry Wallace in 1948 after Truman insisted upon a strong civil rights platform at the Democratic national convention. (3) The fact that blacks gave John F. Kennedy from 68 to 80 percent of their votes helped him win the 1960 election by a margin of 112,827 out of 68,770,294 votes cast. (Significantly, the 250,000 blacks who voted for Kennedy in Illinois helped him carry that state by 9,000 votes; the 95,000 who voted for him in Texas enabled him to defeat Nixon by 45,000 votes there; similarly, they provided margins in South Carolina and Michigan. Had Kennedy lost those states or even suffered slight shifts in black votes or if a significant number of blacks had stayed at home, as they did in 1968, Richard M. Nixon might have been President eight years sooner than he was.[7]) It is apparent that by 1960 blacks had begun to exert themselves in a "politics of participants."[8] They had begun to form a collective political conscience regarding the relationship of their votes to quid pro quos from the Democratic party. These events occurred in the context of the first of four divisions of the civil rights movement—a period of accommodation and agitation.*

THE CIVIL RIGHTS MOVEMENT AND CONFRONTATION POLITICS

Historical Conditions

As blacks shifted to the Democratic party, the achievement of political, economic, and social integration in American life was far from reality. Institutional racism, discrimination, and systemic segregation persisted throughout the American social system. Race riots had resulted in the deaths of several black persons during the 1940s; many were unjustly imprisoned attempting to desegregate public accommodations and buses while others were brutally murdered (as was Emmett Till in Mississippi in 1955 for "disrespecting a white lady"). When Mrs. Rosa Parks, a black seamstress in Montgomery, Alabama, refused to relinquish her bus seat to a white man and was arrested, the stage was set for the emergence of confrontation politics by black citizens. The impulsive act of a tired black woman who defied the tradition of blacks' vacating their seats for whites catapulted Dr. King to international prominence as the leader of the Montgomery Improvement Association, head of the Southern Christian Leadership Conference (SCLC), the personification of passive resistance, and the articulate spokesman of the civil rights movement. But Mrs. Parks' act was an experience with which the masses of southern blacks could immediately identify; her arrest aroused their indignation and anger and, as a result, provided the basis for the group cohesion so vital in social movements. The decision by blacks in Montgomery to boycott buses stimulated blacks in other cities such as Tallahassee, Florida, to undertake similar acts of protest. School systems erupted in violence in several Southern and border cities; President Eisenhower mobilized federal troops in Little Rock;[9] Dr. King's home was bombed and so was that of his aide, Reverend Fred Suttlesworth, in Birmingham. The more violent white Americans became, the more determined black Americans seemed to protest racial injustice and inequality in American life.

In this context an understandable rationale was provided for disavowing total dependence on legalistic forms of social protest, which created

---

*I divided the civil rights movement in the United States into four somewhat overlapping periods: (1) 1920–1954: accommodation and agitation; (2) 1954–1969: protest, confrontation, and concessions; (3) 1970–1980: stagnation, and (4) 1980– : retrogression and attempted revitalization (see my article: "Persistence and Change in Intergroup Relations: The Crisis Upon Us," *Social Problems* 29:4 [April 1982]: 325–346).

gradual social change, and for their replacement by more direct forms of political activism. Undoubtedly, the most significant single event that mobilized political activism among blacks and redirected strategies of protest was the sit-in movement. The most highly publicized episode was that initiated by four black college students from North Carolina A&T College in Greensboro in a dime store (Woolworth's) in February 1960. However, this tactic had been successfully employed by the NAACP Youth Council in Oklahoma City in 1958 in which they protested institutionalized segregation and racial discrimination in lunchrooms, soda fountains and department stores. The sit-ins staged by the NAACP Youth Council in Oklahoma City led to the desegregation of more than 100 facilities and places of public accommodation by 1960.

The events in Oklahoma did not receive as much national attention as the sit-ins in Greensboro. National network television coverage of the sit-ins in Greensboro drew immediate attention to the immense potential of sit-ins as a potent weapon against segregation and discrimination. Thus they became an effective use of pressure resources (that is, those that draw upon such practices as sit-ins, boycotts, picketing, and so on) as a means of changing power relations. Just as the bus boycotts had forged interracial coalitions among intergroup organizations, the sit-in movement captured the attention of black students throughout the South, of liberal and radical white students in other parts of the country, and accelerated the drive to break down the barriers of racial apartheid. This movement had the psychological impact of transforming a seemingly passive, amorphous population into a highly activist and cohesive group.

Escalation of Conflict

The white South responded to the sit-in movement by massive arrests of college students, expulsions, and physical violence. Student supporters of the movement met at Shaw University and formed the Student Nonviolent Coordinating Committee (SNCC) later in 1960. The committee (often called SNICK) first followed Dr. King's philosophy of passive resistance but subsequently disavowed that strategy for CORE's tactics of direct action. The "in-movement" encompassed a broad range of activities that attacked segregation in public accommodations—all single tactic, direct action, and goal specific. Hence sit-ins were followed by "wade-ins," "kneel-ins," "dwell-ins," and "jail-ins." CORE joined the movement, providing attacks against structured segregation on several flanks. The most notable of the forays were the freedom rides through the South, particularly Alabama, in 1961. Freedom riders were viciously assaulted in Birmingham, Alabama, and McComb, Mississippi, and their bus was upended and burned in Anniston, Alabama, in May 1961. An increasing number of blacks and whites joined the freedom riders and the movement, and while white violence escalated, resistance stiffened.

Mass direct action, such as freedom rides, was accompanied by public demonstrations, boycotts, and picketing. Although techniques seemed somewhat diffuse, each tactic was goal specific—desegregate a certain facility or open up jobs for blacks and other minorities. Constraint goals were employed to attain competitive rewards. Black protest organizations, including the NAACP, CORE, SNCC, SCLC, coalesced to form informal coordinating councils of human rights to reconcile differences and maintain a cohesive structure. Yet each organization remained relatively specialized in its approach to identical goals. Dr. King's SCLC, for instance touched the nation's conscience through passive resistance and nonviolence; the NAACP provided legal services and bail money for freedom riders and other protesters and joined with CORE and SNCC in massive demonstrations against institutions such as five-and-ten-cent stores and Sears Roebuck. Throughout all the demonstrations, boycotting, and picketing, blacks were unerringly peaceful. They withstood without aggressive retaliation to the German shepherds unleashed by Bull Conners in Birmingham, physical assaults in Anniston, firehoses in Orangeburg, electric cattle prods in Plaquemines Parish, Louisiana, and police brutality in several places. As "law-and-order" men abused them, blacks responded with "We shall overcome." But, this continuous violence climaxed when NAACP leader Medgar Evers was assassinated in Mississippi in 1963.

In terms of national unity, coordination of civil rights organizations, and concerted efforts to achieve the goal of integration, perhaps the finest hour came on August 27, 1963, when more than 250,000 peaceful demonstrators of all races, religious creeds, and ethnic origins joined to protest racial discrimination and segregation in a massive march on Washington. Those who assembled there had heard the NAACP's futile slogan, "Free by '63," and they had heard President Kennedy's televised broadcast telling the nation in June 1963 that "discrimination was morally wrong"; they also knew that blacks had neither attained occupational and income parity nor ended discrimination in all public accommodations through freedom rides. Leaders like Roy Wilkins, Bayard Rustin, James Farmer, and John Lewis addressed these issues and the frustrations of the masses. But it was Dr. King's ringing indictment of ubiquitous racial apartheid, political injustice, and inequalities of opportunities in American society in his "I Have a Dream" peroration that electrified the nation and raised the level of the consciousness of guilt on that fateful day in August—the same day that the tireless militant, great black intellectual W. E. B. DuBois died in Accra, Ghana. But the nation all but returned to business as usual shortly afterwards.

Within a matter of weeks bombs killed four black school girls who were attending Sunday school in Birmingham, Alabama. Within a matter of months in Dallas an assassin's bullets felled the one president whom blacks uniformly perceived as their friend. But had it not been for these two events, cruel as they were, many doubt whether or not Congress would ever have passed the Civil Rights Bill of 1964.

This measure, which many believe was enacted as a final gesture to the liberalism of John F. Kennedy, was of immense importance. It was designed to end all forms of discrimination and segregation in public accommodations, as well as in employment in which agencies received any form of federal support, and to further limit the evasions of the 1960 civil rights voting bill.

The 1960 act had made violations of court orders in voting a federal crime. It also authorized the appointment of referees to assure the registration of properly qualified blacks. The Civil Rights Bill of 1965 strengthened the earlier voting bill by demanding uniform standards for registering voters in federal elections; it made a sixth-grade education proof of literacy unless otherwise proved by election officials in court; and it guaranteed rights of appeal against denials of voter registration through the articulation of an appeals procedure involving legally constituted panels, the U. S. Attorney General, and, if necessary, a direct appeal to the Supreme Court. The immediate impact of this measure was that blacks began to register to vote in unparalleled numbers.

Although voter registration projects in Mississippi and other Deep South states were effective in increasing the number of black registered voters, white resistance remained. Black workers were intimidated by the use of economic reprisals or sanctions against them by their employers as well as by both threatened and actual violence. Registrars attempted to curtail the number of black registrants by such devices as slowing down the registration process, closing the office earlier than scheduled, or by simply hiding when blacks came to register.[10]

Much to the astonishment of many blacks, President Lyndon Johnson seemed serious in his public pronouncements about creating a just and Great Society for all people irrespective of race, religion, or ethnic origin. Thus his political acumen, coupled with the increasing pressure from civil rights groups, accounted for the passage of the Civil Rights Act of 1965.

The 1965 act suspended literacy tests as a requirement for voting, authorized the use of federal examiners in the South to protect the rights of potential black voters, and extended several provisions of the 1964 Act to cover state and local, as well as federal, elections. Thus the way was paved for even more significant increases in the proportion of eligible black voters. Organizations such as SNCC, the Voter Registration Project, individuals such as Julian Bond and John Lewis, and an enormous army of volunteers from all parts of the country cooperated in voter registration drives throughout the South.

Again, a crisis precipitated, to some degree, both the passage of the voting rights bill and the outpouring of manpower, assistance from various parts of the country. During the summer of 1964,* three young civil rights workers—James Chaney (black) and Michael Schwerner and Andrew

*The 1964 Mississippi Summer Project was a major effort by blacks, joined by northern white youth, against widespread resistance to desegregation by the white population in Mississippi.

Goodman (both white and, perhaps, representative of the large number of Jewish activists involved in the movement at this stage)— were murdered in Mississippi; a series of urban disruptions that imperiled national peace shocked the country. In early 1965, prior to the enactment of the new voting rights law, Malcolm X was assassinated; federal intervention was necessary in the confrontation of civil rights marchers at the Selma, Alabama, bridge so that a peaceful march to Montgomery could proceed. During that march, three white Unitarian ministers were mercilessly assaulted, and one, Reverend James Reeb, subsequently died. Mrs. Viola Liuzzo, a white civil rights worker who had joined the Selma–Montgomery marchers from Detroit, also met death as a result of gunshot wounds inflicted upon her by white terrorists in an ambush on Highway 80. Aside from the responses of a conscience-pricked white northern public, the federal government was increasingly worried about its international image, since every act of violence in the United States, directed against civil rights groups or individuals, was front-page news in the world press. The international reputation of the United States as a multiracial society structured on high principles of justice, freedom, and equality was becoming severely tarnished. As a result, the government began to respond more quickly and more forcefully to the demands of protesters and to protect their rights.

However, a combination of circumstances further explains the favorable response of the federal government to the demands advanced by various civil rights groups. First, the civil rights movement until the mid-1960s had directed its major thrust toward a specific goal, the elimination of discrimination and segregation in such areas as public accommodations, libraries, schools, and voting. Second, these demands neither contradicted nor countervailed the basic principles of freedom and equality implicit in the American Constitution, especially in the Fourteenth Amendment. Third, the larger white society did not perceive assenting to the demands made by civil rights groups as a major threat to its welfare, since, for one thing, the white society continued to improve its status by moving into higher-paying, more prestigious positions. Thus blacks tended to fill positions vacated by whites rather than to move into highly competitive situations with them. Fourth, the federal government, as well as several local jurisdictions, recognized the growing political strength of black voters gained by virtue of well-orchestrated voter registration drives—also evidence of the movement of blacks toward a kind of participation politics.

Yet, the responses through legislation addressed to specific demands by civil rights groups primarily benefited the black middle and upper classes. Enacted legislation had the unintended function of raising the level of aspirations and expectations among black lower classes, who would soon cry for "a piece of the action." In time, for instance, they would seek to seize control of the antipoverty programs and an array of community-oriented programs stimulated by Johnson's Great Society legislation as their exclusive domain. However, federal and local government responses were both conciliatory and restricted to rather narrow parameters. But aspirations remained high. It is the disjunction between heightened aspirations or expectations and limited observable gratifications for the masses of people that paved the way for violent confrontations in urban centers.[11] This was particularly true for urban blacks in the North who felt excluded from civil rights gains.

Urban Rebellions

Although the conditions of urban blacks in the North were in a sense objectively better than those of southern blacks, deprivation is relative. Blacks in the North and West are not inclined to measure their objective condition by standards under which blacks in the South are believed to live. They measure their economic, social, and political advancement by the norms and standards prevailing in their local communities in the North and West. It makes little difference to a black man in Watts, California, that his median income may be $2,000 more than the median income of a black man of equal education, training, and experience in Alabama when his own median income is $4,000 less than that of his white counterpart in West Los Angeles. Blacks in Cleveland or Detroit care far less that their housing conditions may be superior to housing provided rural blacks in Mississippi than that their own situation is decidedly substandard in comparison to housing available to white citizens in Cleveland and Detroit. Thus the conditions encountered depict the relativity of deprivation and point to the fundamental basis for differential expectations and reward systems. When conditions of deprivation converge with conditions of police brutality, ghetto exploitation by unscrupulous landlords, dishonest, merchants, pressures of overcrowded dwellings, and fear of crime, the essential ingredients for rebellion prevail.

Beginning with the "riots" of the summer of 1964, urban unrest escalated in severity and proportion in each year through 1968. It began in New York's Harlem in July 1964 and spread to the Bedford-Stuyvesant section of Brooklyn. Then incipient revolutions of black masses shook other communities, including Rochester, New York, Patterson and Elizabeth, New Jersey, Chicago, and Philadelphia. In the summer of 1965 the six-day uprising in the Watts section of Los Angeles nearly immobilized parts of Los Angeles in what became known as the Watts insurrection. The human toll included 34 dead and more than 1,000 injured. Almost 4,000 people were arrested in this rebellion, and property damages totalled approximately $40 million. What triggered the uprising was the allegedly unwarranted arrest of a black person who was subjected to police brutality, but actually the underlying causes went much deeper—they were the culmination of all the deprivations and denied opportunities blacks perceived in relation to white privilege and advantage. And more uprisings were forthcoming. In 1966 they occurred from Omaha to Lansing, Michigan, and from Chicago to Atlanta. The summer of 1967 witnessed a carnage probably never previously duplicated except in times of open warfare in the United States. Destruction, disaster, and hopelessness gripped this nation, which seemed unable to determine appropriate remedies. In Detroit alone in the events of the summer of 1967 about 42 people died, 386 were injured, 5,567 were arrested, and scores of buildings were burned and looted, with property damages in excess of $45 million. Newark was the scene of devastating destruction of human life and personal property. In all, during the first nine months of 1967, racial disturbances ripped apart approximately 164 American communities,[12] and during the summer months alone rebellions occurred in approximately 35 cities.[13]

Then came that fateful day of April 4, 1968, when an assassin felled the most revered civil rights leader of modern times, Dr. Martin Luther King, Jr. His death precipitated immediate and retaliatory responses by black people of all ideological dispositions and social classes. The United States was quickly engulfed in a national crisis in which rioting, rebellion, insurrections, carnage, looting, and burning were at the epicenter. Major rebellions occurred in Washington, D.C., Chicago, and more than 100 other cities, resulting in at least 46 persons killed, thousands injured, and millions of dollars of personal property lost. More than 50,000 federal troops and National Guardsmen were summoned to quell the disturbances throughout the United States. Later that summer, 11 persons were killed in a shootout in Cleveland, and the National Guard was mobilized for action during a riot in Miami while the Republican national convention was in session. When the insurrections were spent, blacks realized more than ever that the nation had moved into a more repressive state, taking on many attributes of a police state in which reactionary law-and-order forces had gained control of all levels of government. Indeed, some feared the possibility of incarceration in World War II concentration camps reportedly being reactivated for just that purpose.

The riots, rebellions, and insurrections were more directed to retail stores than to public institutions primarily because the retail establishments symbolized institutionalized exploitation of blacks in their day-to-day lives. As it became clear that white-owned establishments in black ghettos were under attack, black owners of businesses hastily scribbled signs on doors and windows, such as "Soul Brother" and "Black Owner," as a means of protecting themselves from total destruction. In many instances white merchants admired for their support of black people in employment and in achieving other goals were also spared. However, many innocent victims of black despair were not so fortunate.

Perhaps an unintended consequence of the urban rebellions was that they left the civil rights movement in shambles. The traditional black leadership seemed incapable of containing the century of controlled frustration that exploded on the urban scene. The loss of Dr. King was a crushing blow to black and white people alike, even though his leadership was being subjected to serious attack by militant blacks particularly and by those who disagreed with his apparent alignment with the Students for a Democratic Society antiwar activists. It has often been said that blacks lost their most effective leader and whites lost their closest friend and ally with King's assassination. With his death new forms and new approaches already in the offing two years earlier began to gain strength as a political force among black people.

Black Power and Black Liberation Strategies

No one knew what Stokely Carmichael meant in 1966 when he pronounced his intention to claim black power for American blacks, not even the American press. In what has been described as "press-orchestrated hysteria,"[14] however, black power immediately became a divisive, extremely feared, and much maligned concept. A great part of the fear sprang from the use of the expression by a person who had encouraged blacks to take up arms in self-defense against white oppressors. With leadership changes, SNCC had long since abandoned nonviolent advocacy and supplanted it with a freedom-by-whatever-means-necessary posture. Many Americans, white and black, interpreted the speeches and addresses given by Carmichael and H. Rap Brown as inflammatory and racially divisive. Moreover, the fragile coalition between black and white student members of SNCC disintegrated under the increasing militance assumed by the black leadership of SNCC. Thus when Carmichael shouted "black power," bored newspapermen covering the civil rights march through Mississippi had a story tailored for national attention.

White people in America interpreted black power as antiwhite, a demand for shared values at their expense, as blacks "getting something for nothing," as an infringement on their prerogatives, or as an impending physical assault on white people in general.

Black militant advocates of black power sensed that the American white public was perturbed but probably reluctant to escalate violent attacks against black Americans for fear of adverse publicity. The strategy, however, called for a rhetoric of militance and revolution as a new instrument for effectuating change. They explained, also, that black power meant the development of self-determination, a rekindled sense of personal worth, pride in one's blackness, a glorification of black culture, and a need for utilizing the black experience as a unifying force in the black community. For many of this group the only authentic black experience, however, resulted from socialization and social nurturing in a lower-class black ghetto. Middle-class blacks were highly suspect; integrationists became "toms" and "aunt saras" or "oreos." This group demanded avowed blackness as defined by ghetto experience and adherence to much of the philosophy articulated by the late Malcolm X. Indeed, a new cult of personality emerged in Malcolm X, who achieved status as a national hero and who was somewhat beatified in death largely because of his strong emphasis on black self-acceptance, black self-awareness, and the positive dimensions of black identity.

If the concept raised questions and doubts in the minds of white

Americans, it aroused mixed reactions in the black community. Some blacks thought at first that black power smacked of racism in reverse; others viewed it as a highly separatist philosophy; others appreciated its more nationalistic fervor and its efficacy for severing the umbilical cord between white liberals and predominantly black organizations. In this category were those persons who questioned the sincerity of those white liberals in the movement who showed a penchant for eschewing conflict situations and who seemed to have relied instead on the critical element of their financial support to dictate to blacks how to behave and what strategies to call upon in specific situations. Black power was an opportunity for blacks to assert their independence and move rapidly toward self-determination. CORE opted for this movement and almost immediately lost much of its financial support, which led to internal problems. The NAACP and the National Urban League slowly accepted a revised conceptualization of the slogan "black power," attributing to it, and rightly so as it turned out, a renewed thrust for economic, political, and social advancement by black people for black people. But the Black Panther Party, founded in 1966, claimed that the only possibility for revolutionary change was through a coalition between blacks and white socialist radicals, uncompromisingly committed to revolutionary nationalism.

The black power movement spawned a new type of militance in the black urban community, captivating rhetoric, ideological schisms, and a demand for black studies programs as well as innumerable disruptions when these demands were not readily met. Most important of all, the black power movement spawned black liberation, which came to address itself as a movement for the unification of blacks of all ideological perspectives, social classes, and shades of color into a new single cohesive structure with the primary goal of reordering power relations within American society. As a result, the traditional black establishment structure diminished in power as a more amorphous leadership structure evolved at the grassroots level. But a quiet revolution beginning at the ballot box was to raise blacks to a new level from a politics of participation toward a politics of governance.[15] To move blacks toward that goal during the 1960s two major black power conventions were held: (1) Adam Clayton Powell convened the first major black power conference in Washington, D.C., on September 3, 1966. This conference attracted about 169 representatives from approximately 64 organizations and 18 states. (2) The National Conference on Black Power was convened at Newark immediately following the insurrection there in July 1967. Among the more salient conference demands were those that called for an immediate tripling of the number of blacks in Congress, the election of black mayors, more city and state elected officials, and the appointment of a greater number of blacks to high federal positions.

In effect, blacks were calling for an end to what Chuck Stone described as "the revolving-door Negro" in federal appointments. This term refers to a long-established pattern of appointing a few blacks to breakthrough positions in the federal government without appointing black replacements when they later vacate such positions. As a result, the number of blacks in high-level governmental positions is restricted to a few individuals who are shifted from one position to another, and the net gain for blacks remains minimal.[16] Significantly, these demands were addressed to "getting into the system" rather than destroying the system per se. Blackness, too, meant using the power of the ballot, as ethnic immigrants had done before them, for the election of black officials and in the appointment of other black individuals to responsible leadership roles. Thus black power achieved a new level of respectability in the black community.[17]

Schisms in the Movement

The 1960s had been a period of unparalleled social change induced by protests, urban confrontations, and passive resistance throughout the United States. The civil rights movement pricked the conscience of America and called world attention to the injustices experienced by blacks and other outsider groups in the United States. It had attracted participants from all races, all classes, and persons with divergent ideological orientations and philosophies who collectively forged strategies to transform and move toward a genuine revolution in race relations and power redistribution. For instance, the Black Panther Party (BPP), under the leadership of Huey Newton, Eldridge Cleaver, and Bobby Seale encouraged what Newton called "revolutionary nationalism."[18] A part of that philosophy called for seizing power "by any means necessary." Black power militants, many of whom had been extremely active in SNCC insisted upon a far more aggressive action-oriented strategy than the passive resistance advocated by Reverend Martin Luther King. Hence, the militance they embraced was moved from rhetoric to action. The rhetoric of violence was not eschewed in speeches given by Stokeley Carmichael.[19] Nor did such book titles as H. Rap Brown's *Die, Nigger, Die* and Julius Lester's *Look Out Whitey, Black Power Is Gonna Get Your Momma*, reduce the fears that the advocacy of black power had inflamed.

These differences in strategy for effective social change, based upon divergent philosophical underpinnings, accelerated a growing schism in the civil rights movement. The emerging problems were both inter- and intraorganizational in nature. For instance, dissension in the BPP illustrates intraorganizational difficulties. Stokley Carmichael abandoned the Black Panther party over "what was essentially a race versus class debate."[20]

He went into a self-imposed exile and traveled to Africa, China, Cuba, and Puerto Rico in 1969. In 1970 Carmichael was "drilled" by the U. S. Senate Internal Security Subcommittee about his travels. This action was strongly protested by several groups who charged that Carmichael was subjected to undue harassments.[21] In the meantime, Eldridge Cleaver, once the head of the Black Panther party, and other members of the party's leadership disagreed over policy with respect to revolutionary strategies. Cleaver exiled himself to Algeria in 1968 to avoid imprisonment for parole violation.[22] The Black Panther party had always been, at best, on the periphery of the traditional organizational structure of the civil rights movement. Its orientation toward violent tactics moved it farther from mainstream civil rights organizations.

Similarly, the Congress of Racial Equality (CORE) and the Student Nonviolent Coordinating Committee (SNCC) also experienced widespread dissension and internal conflict by the beginning of the 1970s. CORE, once racially integrated when under the leadership of James Farmer, became an almost all-black organization under Floyd McKissick and Roy Innis. Its membership composition coincided with an emphasis on the "black power philosophy" and an increasingly militant strategy. One consequence of this change was a decimation of its membership and financial support. SNCC had been founded, too, as a multiracial organization on the heels of the Greensboro sit-ins in 1960. It had attracted young blacks, such as Julian Bond (who became a state senator in the Georgia legislature), Marion Barry (who became mayor of Washington, D.C.), and John Lewis (who became a member of the U.S. House of Representatives). It also included an influx of young middle-class whites sympathetic to its program. Stokley Carmichael, once-active leader of SNCC, left that organization to join the Panthers. In the late 1960s, SNCC moved to the North, and by so doing lost a great part of its constituency. H. Rap Brown changed the name of the organization in 1969 to the Student National Coordinating Committee—a change that signaled determination to employ retaliatory violence if necessary.[23] As a result of the philosophical shift coupled with a more aggressive organizational posture and the loss of many of its members to full-time study, participation in antipoverty programs, anti-Vietnam war activities and other endeavors, SNCC lost its influence in the civil rights movement.[24]

By contrast, differences that emerged over the role of white liberals in the civil rights movement cut across all organizations and had already surfaced by 1970. They appeared first over strategy and policy issues coincident to the escalation of confrontation politics. Many white liberals wished to avoid strategies that seemingly led to violent confrontations. Some felt that, by virtue of their substantial financial contributions, they should play a more prominent role in policy-making decisions. Both views were soundly rejected by many blacks in the movement. Undoubtedly, some white liberals, consciously or subconsciously, found it difficult to accommodate themselves to black leadership.[25]

Perhaps the most serious interorganizational split occurred between blacks and Jews who had stood together for years in the struggle for equal opportunity and to end racial segregation and discrimination. These differences surfaced early in the 1970s during the community control debates in the Ocean-Hill and Brownsville school districts of New York City which divided blacks and Jews. It was evident in the "Black Agenda" fashioned at the 1972 Black Agenda Conference in Gary, Indiana, especially with regard to items that dealt with American foreign policy toward Israel and the Palestinians. Ultimately, blacks and Jews found themselves in strong disagreement over such issues as affirmative action involving "quotas," timetables and "goals," busing for school desegregation, special admissions programs for graduate and professional schools, foreign policy in the Middle East, Israeli relations with South Africa, and the relationship of some black leaders with Yasser Arafat, leader of the Palestinian Liberation Organization (PLO).

Specifically, most prominent Jewish organizations opposed governmental policy on affirmative action in hiring, and supported the plaintiffs in the DeFunis, Bakke, and Weber cases that involved what they believed to be the use of quotas and "reverse discrimination" that favored blacks for admission to professional schools and provided access to jobs and promotions. In general, black organizations view busing as an absolutely necessary tool to facilitate school desegregation. Some Jewish groups characterized it as counterproductive and as a stimulant to white flight. Jewish organizations were angered by the public appearances and presumed relationships of cordialty and support between Reverend Jesse Jackson, president of Operation PUSH, Reverend Joseph Lowery, head of the Southern Christian Leadership Conference, and Yasser Arafat, head of the PLO. On the other hand, 200 black leaders, representing the most diverse and divergent black organizations in terms of philosophical orientations and strategy tactics, met in New York City in August 1977 to protest what they believed to have been pressure from Jewish groups which led to the resignation of Andrew Young as the U.S. Ambassador to the United Nations because of his secret meeting with PLO representatives.

An earlier meeting had been convened by the Black Leadership Forum, initiated by Vernon Jordan (then president of the National Urban League) that also expressed serious concern over the same issue. Many blacks felt that not only had Israeli leaders and members of the Jewish community pressured President Carter to ask for Ambassador Young's resignation,* but that the entire American foreign policy in the Middle East was too one-sided and imbalanced in its favor of Israel with a denial of legitimate Palestinian rights. Other blacks believed that Israel sold arms to South Africa which were used to further oppress the majority black population, and that the U. S. government had not exerted the same kind of pressure on Israel to discontinue such trading of arms for money nor to effect a more humane policy toward Palestinian Arabs and Palestinian Jews living in Israel.[26]

In more recent years, many blacks opposed Israel's invasion of Leba-

---

*Wanda K. Fishman amplifies the black-Jewish rift over this issue in a most insightful article; cf. Note 26.

non and the subsequent destruction that followed in the summer of 1982. The fact that many prominent American Jews also opposed this Israeli action is clear evidence that the American Jewish community is not a monolithic enterprise, and that many Jews in the United States remain supportive of black Americans on all issues discussed here. Yet blacks and Jews found that the tension existing between them was further exacerbated in 1983 over the position taken by their respective groups with regard to the removal of three commissioners of the U.S. Commission on Civil Rights by President Reagan, and his success in replacing them with persons whose philosophy was more compatible with his on such issues as affirmative action, busing, and enforcement of federal policies. Prominent Jewish organizations, such as the American Jewish Committee, supported President Reagan on his action while prominent, largely black organizations, such as the NAACP vehemently opposed what they regarded as an unprecedented effort to tamper with the integrity and independence of the Commission.

Despite these areas of disagreement between black and Jewish organizations over the types of issues discussed so far, leaders of these groups and others have attempted reconciliation, and some claim that these differences have been grossly exaggerated. For instance, Bayard Rustin, former executive director of the A. Phillip Randolph Institute, was a central force in the effort to mend embittered relationships between blacks and Jews. Vernon Jordan not only chastized Reverend Jackson and Reverend Lowery for their meeting with Yasser Arafat but has continued to advocate cooperation between these groups. Benjamin Hooks, executive director of the NAACP, has also suggested concerted action toward the same goal.

The Kivie Kaplan Institute conducts seminars on methods of healing wounds between blacks and Jews.[27] These meetings, held alternatively in the headquarters of the NAACP and the United Hebrew Congregation in New York, have emphasized areas of mutual concern and issues of special importance to both blacks and Jews. Topics covered range from voting rights, budget cuts, capital punishment, legal aid to the poor, the defense budget to dangers from the far right. Nevertheless, conference participants have not avoided the more divisive issues of affirmative action, American policies toward the Middle East and United States' relations with Third-World nations, in general. By attacking these issues in concert, participants in the Kivie Kaplan Institute are convinced that mutual trust and intergroup confidence can be rebuilt.[28] Another effort at reconciliation was a National Conference on Blacks and Jews held at Savannah State College, Georgia in 1983. The resulting resolutions were similar to concerns expressed at the Kivie Kaplan Institute. However, the emergence of Reverend Jesse Jackson as a determined presidential candidate during the primaries of 1984 and 1988—and the opposition to him expressed among many members of the Jewish community—underscored the fragility of such efforts. Jewish opposition to Reverend Jackson was based upon his strong relationship to anti-Israeli leaders in the Arab world, such as

Yasser Arafat; his advocacy of a Palestinian homeland in the Middle East; his endorsement of quotas in the implementation of affirmative action; his close association with Minister Louis Farrakhan, leader of the Nation of Islam; and Reverend Jackson's use of the pejorative terms *hymie* and *hymietown* in reference to Jews and New York City, which has a large Jewish population. Although Reverend Jackson belatedly apologized for his use of these "ethnophaulisms," he was unsuccessful in mobilizing significant Jewish support for his candidacy. Nevertheless, other leaders of the black community and 95 trustees of the Union of American and Hebrew Congregations continued their efforts to strengthen black-Jewish relationships and rebuild traditional alliances in the civil rights movement, despite allegations of Jewish racism directed primarily against Jewish demonstrators opposed to Reverend Jesse Jackson.*

As inferred earlier, the election of Ronald Reagan as President of the United States and the realization of the havoc inflicted on the black community by his policies helped mobilize black organizations toward a greater sense of unity and cooperation. This theme of rebuilding traditional alliances between the various civil rights organizations, the labor movement, and other former allies was sounded at various conventions, seminars, and conferences in the 1980s. A central element in this new spirit of interorganizational cooperation was the determination to contain Reagan's assault on civil rights.

RACIAL CONFLICT SINCE 1970

The racial conflict and turmoil that characterized the 1960s subsided after 1969. Explanations for the decline in urban rebellions are varied: (1) fear of federal intervention that might result in the internment of blacks in "concentration camps" created from the internment facilities used for Japanese-Americans and prisoners of war during World War II; (2) decimation of the leadership structure of many militant organizations through arrest and imprisonment, and character assassination; (3) use of destabilizing tactics by the FBI such as infiltration, agents, provocateurs, and informers; (4) cooptation of militants by their employment in highly lucrative jobs at city, state, and federal levels; (5) a false belief that the progress actually achieved in the 1960s toward improving the status of blacks was self-perpetuating; and (6) the growing awareness that urban conflicts were somewhat counterproductive since they tended to result in greater human and physical costs to blacks, and because they were believed to have been a major factor in the loss of substantial financial support from whites for the civil rights movement.

Nevertheless, violence against blacks continued throughout the 1970s and 1980s, and some manifestations of urban unrest were evident in several cities across the nation. For instance, violence against blacks occurred

---

*See subsequent section on Jesse Jackson.

in connection with resistance to court-ordered busing for school desegregation in such places as Lamar, South Carolina; Pontiac, Michigan; Newark, Boston, Louisville, and Denver. Violence against individual blacks occurred in several places ranging from KKK attacks in Alabama, California, Georgia, and Florida, to snipers felling blacks in Salt Lake City, Buffalo, and the rifle shooting of Vernon Jordan while on a business trip in Indiana. Blacks were also killed, assaulted, and maimed by whites in such places as Brooklyn and Staten Island in New York, and Boston in the 1970s and 1980s.

Urban violence occurred in Circero, Illinois, Augusta, Georgia, and Melbourne, Florida. But the most serious urban uprising of blacks since 1969 was in Miami, Florida in 1980. This violence, like other subsequent episodes in 1981 and 1982 followed allegations of police brutality or of the killing of a black person by a police officer. Violence in Miami's Liberty City and Overtown districts underscores the continued frustration and alienation felt by thousands of urban blacks who feel the depths of economic and social deprivation, and that the improvements in the condition of other Americans, and advances made by recent immigrants to the United States, such as the Cubans in Dade County, Florida, have locked them out and deeply enmeshed them in a condition of worsening poverty, housing, education, and brutalization by the police.[29] Overtown and Liberty City may be only the tip of a powderkeg waiting to explode in many other cities across the United States where urban blacks are more and more victimized by high unemployment, inadequate housing and what many regard as a federal administration hostile to black Americans.

Resurgence of Racism and Anti-Black Violence in the 1980s

During the latter part of the 1980s, violence against blacks and hate crimes against blacks and other minorities escalated. Once again, in Miami's Liberty City and Overtown, largely black sections, riots erupted in January 1989 following the shooting of a black civilian by an Hispanic police officer. The black male was being chased by police for violation of a traffic offense. However, a significant portion of the black community argued that this man's death was another indicator of the use of unnecessary force by police officers.[30] A similar charge was made in Teaneck, New Jersey, in April 1990 when a black teenager was shot in the back by a white police officer. That incident triggered more violence as blacks protested what they viewed as police brutality against blacks. Also, during the 1980s, several communities in the New York area became national synonyms for violence by whites against blacks. Among them were New York City, Brooklyn, Bensonhurst, and Howard Beach. In addition, in 1989, an NAACP official in Savannah, Georgia, and a white Alabama federal judge who had decided civil rights cases were killed by letter bombs sent to them. All across the country, blacks were subjected to what many people have referred to as "a resurgence of racism"—on college campuses, police attacks against black college students celebrating Black Greekfest and other black citizens.

White supremacist groups became more vitriolic and violent in their hatred than any group since the pre-1965 Ku Klux Klan sprang up in various parts of the nation. These groups included Posse Comitatus, White Aryan Resistance (WAR), The Order, White Aryan Resistance Youth (consisting of the White Student Union/Aryan Youth Movement), and other neo-Nazi groups. In the view of the Southern Poverty Law Center of Montgomery, Alabama, and the Anti-Defamation League of B'nai B'rith, a new group called the Skinheads was the most dangerous of all.[31]

The primary organizer of the Skinheads is believed to be the White Aryan Resistance who regard the Skinheads as "frontline warriors" in the movement against the victims of their hate: blacks, Jews, Hispanics, Asians, liberals, gays. Skinheads are usually young persons from blue-collar classes, who are noted for their violence and their attire. Their name is derived from the fact that they shave their heads, wear Nazi and satanic emblems, leather boots, and black leather jackets. Although a more extensive discussion of their crimes can be found in Chapter 12, suffice it to say at this juncture that Skinheads were charged with a number of racial assaults against blacks and other minorities during the 1980s.[32] The Klan was also once again prominent during the 1980s, especially with attacks by Klan members against civil rights marchers celebrating Martin Luther King's birthday in Forsyth County, Georgia, in 1988.

THE POWER OF THE BLACK VOTE

Compared to the proportion of white registered and actual voters, black voting behavior has until recently left a great deal to be desired. The black vote has always been smaller than normally expected in terms of the size of the black population for reasons explained earlier in this chapter. In addition, voting among blacks has been traditionally much more pronounced among the smaller middle and upper classes and among the better educated than among the lower classes, which possess a higher proportion of the voting-age black population. The basic goal of participation was to reduce apathy and increase motivation for expanded political involvement. However, with the enactment of the previously described voting rights legislation, combined with favorable decisions by the U.S. Supreme Court and voter registration drives mounted in the 1960s, 1970s, and 1980s, the increased proportion of registered black voters has made them a political force of substantial political power.

Blacks sought to maintain and expand that potential political power in their 1982 successful drive to influence the U.S. Congress to renew the 1965 Voting Rights Act. Although finally signed by President Reagan, he was originally opposed to its extension in its present form, as he had opposed the 1964 Civil Rights Act. The Voting Rights Bill was extended for 25 years, that is, from 1982 to the year 2007. Of special importance were amendments that strengthened Sections 2 and 5 of the Act. Under new guidelines, the Act made it possible to establish a fact of voting rights discrimination using the "results test" or the actual existence of discriminatory practices as opposed to the "intent test," previously sanctioned by the U. S. Supreme Court in the case of *Mobile* v. *Bolden.* Under the intent test, plaintiffs were required to prove actual intent to discriminate even though discrimination resulted from long-standing practices (e.g., at large elections that prevented blacks from holding elective offices even in districts in which they constituted a majority).

The new amendments forbid any election practice that denies access of blacks and other minorities to the political process. Section 5 covers the controversial "preclearance" requirement. This section requires nine states (Alabama, Florida, Georgia, Louisiana, Mississippi, North Carolina, South Carolina, Texas, and Virginia) and parts of 13 other states to obtain prior federal approval before any changes can be made in their election procedures. The rationale for this requirement was that when the Voting Rights Act was first approved in 1965 these states and jurisdictions had deliberately constructed impediments that prevented blacks and others from voting. In 1982 the U. S. Congress still felt compelled by circumstances that existed in those areas to retain and strengthen the preclearance provision. In several states, black voter registrations and ability to vote were restricted by such practices as changing polling places without ample notices, limiting hours for registration to times when blacks were not likely to be able to travel to the registrars' offices, intimidation, and violence. In 1983 Reverend Jesse Jackson finally persuaded Assistant Attorney General William Bradford Reynolds, the Chief of the Civil Rights Division of the Department of Justice to travel to Mississippi for an on-site investigation of voting rights violations. As a result of that visit, 300 federal officers were dispatched to Mississippi to insure that blacks would be able to register to vote.

Blacks also began to closely monitor reapportioning and redistricting practices in several states. Under the one-person-one-vote principle, the size of the population dictates the number of representatives a given district or jurisdiction may elect. Therefore, numerical representation in the House of Representatives, for instance, is a function of the size of the population and not the number of registered voters. Monitoring the redistricting process became a critical issue when blacks observed that districts were being reconstructed in several states so as to gerrymander blacks out of political power. Consequently, blacks and other minorities persuaded the Justice Department to review redistricting plans in several districts in such states as New York, Georgia, South Carolina, Texas, and Mississippi.

Voter Registration Programs

The importance of the Voting Rights Act of 1965 and its extension, in addition to a redistricting process that protects the rights of black voters, can be gleaned from a brief examination of the following information: In 1952 the estimated number of black voters in the South was about 1,008,614 and they exercised limited influence on the outcome of the national elections. The 2,174,200 Southern registered black voters in 1964 more than doubled the 1952 figure. By 1966, a year after the passage of the Voting Rights Act of 1965, the number of registered black voters in the South almost tripled as it climbed to 5,684,000. During the 1968 election year, 72 percent of all blacks in the North and West had registered and were in a position to influence elections in many areas of the nation. By 1980 the estimated number of black registered voters had reached 11 million. Nevertheless, over a third of the 17 million blacks of voting age had not registered. In the 1980 national elections, only two-fifths (40 percent) of all blacks of voting age voted and 61.3 percent of registered black voters actually voted.[33] Even though blacks gave about 90 percent of their votes to Carter, if a larger share of blacks had actually voted in several key states, they would have provided the difference needed in total electoral votes to reelect President Carter in 1980. NAACP data also showed that blacks comprised "10 percent of the voting age population in 18 states, 20 percent of the voting age population in 64 congressional districts, and . . . 50 percent or more of the voting age population in 103 counties," most of which were located in the South.[34]

"Operation Big Vote" and subsequent voter registration drives from 1980 onward focused on both registering increased numbers of blacks and on influencing blacks to actually vote in local, statewide, and national elections. The success of these efforts is evident by the impact that black voters made on the outcome of the mid-term elections in 1982. Not only were their votes instrumental in electing blacks to political office (see following section), they also helped elect a number of white officials sympathetic to the concerns of the black population. For instance, they helped to elect an old nemesis and former segregationist, George Wallace, to another term as Governor of Alabama. Their votes helped elect Mark White to the governorship of Texas, Mario Coumo to the governorship of New York, and William Clinton to recapture the governorship of Arkansas. Their votes were instrumental in the defeat of several Republicans who had been aligned with President Reagan's programs of Reagonomics that had such a devastating impact on social programs which aided the working class among minority and white populations. However, blacks in California did not vote in sufficient numbers to help Mayor Thomas Bradley of Los Angeles win the gubernatorial election in 1982 or in 1986. But blacks were quite successful in other 1986 and 1988 local and state elections and increasing their numbers in Congress.

Impact on Local and National Elections

As a result of voting registration drives and campaigns to stimulate voting by blacks, such as "Come Alive on October 5" and "Punch 10" in Chicago, as well as the efforts of Operation PUSH, the NAACP, and the SCLC, blacks scored enormous successes in 1982. In the most celebrated and hotly contested election of the year, their votes helped Harold Washington, then a U. S. Representative, capture the mayoralty of Chicago. Twenty-one blacks, including four new persons, were also elected to the U. S. House of Representatives, and scores of blacks won local and state offices.

The contest in Chicago was a racially divisive and bitter episode. Representative Washington, benefiting from a massive grassroots effort in the black community that was aided by an effective radio campaign mounted through four black-oriented radio stations, surprised incumbent Mayor Jane Byrne and heir apparent Richard Daley, son of the late and powerful Daley machine founder, by winning the Democratic primary. Ordinarily, the winner of the Democratic primary would have been guaranteed victory in the final election since no Republican had been elected Mayor of Chicago in 56 years. However, many white ethnics, blue-collar workers, and the Chicago Federation of Labor could not or would not support Washington either because he was black or because of his previous conviction for income tax evasion. The contest was made even more racially divisive by the campaign slogan used by his Republican opponent, Bernard Epton, which stated "Epton, Before It's Too Late." Many persons interpreted the slogan to be racist in nature and a direct appeal to those whites who feared the election of a black male to the highest political office in the city.[35] Nevertheless, Washington emerged as the victor, supported by 99 percent of the black vote, 18 percent of the white vote, and about 50 percent of the Hispanic vote. Epton lost with 81 percent of the white vote and approximately 50 percent of the Hispanic vote. Washington's victory in the nation's third largest city created enormous excitement among black voters throughout the United States. Black voters were instantly galvanized by Chicago's demonstration of the potential power of cohesion, concerted efforts by groups such as the Rainbow Coalition, and solidification of the black voters behind a candidate of their choice.

It also stirred anew speculations about the possibilities of a black candidate for the presidency of the United States. Speculations were transformed into reality when Jesse Jackson announced his candidacy and ran against Vice President Mondale and Senator John Glenn for the Democratic Party's candidate in the 1984 national elections. As discussed in a subsequent section, though Jesse Jackson lost his bid against Mondale, he became a major force in national politics. He demonstrated to black voters, as well as to his nonblack followers, the ultimate power of the ballot and the salience of political participation. Reverend Jesse Jackson paved the way for others to follow.

The importance of Jackson's consciousness-raising regarding exercising the right to vote and thereby "make the difference" was clearly evident in the various municipal and state-wide elections of 1989. In New York City, for example, for years many blacks had been disillusioned and unhappy with Mayor Koch largely because of what they believed to have been his antiblack sentiments and actions. However, because of political factions and the lack of a black candidate whose appeal transcended his blackness, Mayor Koch appeared to have been unbeatable. During the 1988 presidential race Mayor Koch directed a number of highly inflammatory statements against Reverend Jesse Jackson which resulted in a more determined effort by blacks and other displeased and embarrassed groups to the defeat three-term mayor. Their opportunity arose when David N. Dinkins, Manhattan's Borough President, defeated Koch for the Democratic Party's nomination and subsequently defeated a very popular Republican opponent, District Attorney Robert Giulani in the citywide election for New York's mayor.

In winning the mayoralty, Dinkins became the first black to head the nation's largest city. That success meant that in 1989 blacks were serving as mayors of the largest American cities (New York, Los Angeles, Philadelphia) except Chicago where a black incumbent had earlier been defeated by in-fighting among blacks themselves. Dinkins ran a successful campaign as "the healer of racial antagonisms." He received 92 percent of the black vote, 65 percent of the Hispanics', 35 percent of the Jewish, and 27 percent of the white votes.[36] However, the margin of victory was quite slim over his Republican challenger as polls had predicted much wider margins. Analysts reluctantly concluded that many white voters lied to pollsters and convinced them that they intended to vote for Dinkins but once in the privacy of the voting booth could not permit themselves to vote for a black candidate.

A second beneficiary of Jackson's campaign to register blacks as voters was the election of Lt. Governor L. Douglas Wilder to the governorship of Virginia. As in New York, Wilder's election was a political milestone. He is the first black in the history of the United States to be *elected* as a state governor. (He is not the first black to serve as governor; that honor belongs to P. B. S. Pinchback who briefly served as Louisiana's governor during the Reconstruction period). Not only did the massive turnout by black voters help provide the razor-thin victory for Wilder, so did the substantial crossover vote he received from white female Republicans who embraced his pro-choice stand on abortion. Nevertheless, the elections of Dinkins and Wilder may also signal a new turn of events in American politics with respect to the type of black candidate who is able to successfully attract white voters.

In 1989, there were 7,226 black elected officials, representing approximately 1.4 percent of all elected officials in the United States. Of these 24 were in the U. S. House of Representatives,* the largest number since Reconstruction. The state of New Jersey had elected a black to the U. S.

---

*As a result of the 1990 elections, two more blacks (one from Louisiana, the other from Connecticut) won seats to the House. William Jefferson (D., La.) became the first black elected to the House from Louisiana in 100 years.

House of Representatives for the first time and a black was also elected to replace Representative Mickey Leland who was killed in a plane crash while on a trip to investigate the problem of hunger in Ethiopia. No blacks have served in the U. S. Senate since Edward Brooke of Massachusetts left office in 1978. Of all black elected officials in 1989, 424 were in state legislatures; 793 were county officials; 3,595 held municipal positions; 760 held elective judicial/law enforcement offices; and there were 299 black mayors,* 26 of whom headed governments of cities with populations of 50,000 or more.[37] Blacks were mayors of 19 cities with a population in excess of 100,000. Their black population ranged from a low of 17 percent of total population to a high of 70 percent (Gary, Indiana, and Washington, D. C.). Other large cities with black mayors included: Detroit, Baltimore, Cleveland, New Orleans, Oakland, Newark, Birmingham, Seattle, Atlanta, Newport News, Hartford, Roanoke, Inglewood, California, and Dayton, Ohio. In 1989, the mayoralty election was historic in that for the first time blacks were elected as mayors in Seattle, Washington; Durham, N. C.; and New Haven, Connecticut.

In toto, the number of black elected officials increased by almost 500 percent between 1970 and 1989. In an absolute sense, the number of black elected officials climbed from 1,469 in 1970 to 7,226 in 1989. The number of blacks in state elective positions rose from 169 in 1970 to 424 in 1989 while the number of county officials jumped from 92 in 1970 to 793 in 1989. During the same period, blacks elected to municipal positions increased from only 623 in 1970 to 3,595 in 1989 (Table 9.1). Redistricting is of special importance since it is evident that most blacks elected for national offices and in some local situations come primarily from areas in which blacks have either a majority or a substantial portion (40 percent or more) of the population. However, in some areas, such as in the case of Tom Bradley as Mayor of Los Angeles or Norman Rice as Mayor of Seattle or Chester Jenkins as Mayor of New Haven or of Alan Wheat to the U. S. House of Representatives from Kansas, or Representative Dellums from California, coalitions between blacks, whites, and others were the primary reasons for their success.

Profound differences exist among the states in terms of the number of blacks who hold elective offices. As shown in Table 9.2, it is evident that the largest numbers of blacks holding state elective positions are in states with a substantial black population and in which redistricting reflected the concentration of blacks in certain geographic areas. The majority of elected blacks are found in Alabama, Mississippi, Louisiana, South Carolina, Georgia, Illinois, North Carolina, Tennessee, Arkansas, Michigan, California, New York, and the District of Columbia.

Increasing numbers of black women hold elective offices. Between 1975 and 1989, the number of black women holding elective offices almost

---

*The number of black mayors climbed to 316 in 1990.

Table 9.1. CHANGE IN NUMBER OF BLACK ELECTED OFFICIALS BY CATEGORY OF OFFICE: 1970–1989

Year	Total BEOS		Federal		State		Substate regional		County		Municipal		Judicial/law enforcement		Education	
	N	% Change	N	% Change	N	% Change	N	% Change	N	% Change	N	% Change	N	% Change	N	% Change
1970	1,469	—	10	—	169	—	—	—	92	—	623	—	213	—	362	—
1971	1,860	26.6	14	40.0	202	19.5	—	—	120	30.4	785	26.0	274	28.6	465	28.5
1972	2,264	21.7	14	0.0	210	4.0	—	—	176	46.7	932	18.7	263	−4.0	669	43.9
1973	2,621	15.8	16	14.3	240	14.3	—	—	211	19.9	1,053	13.0	334	27.0	767	14.6
1974	2,991	14.1	17	6.3	239	−0.4	—	—	242	14.7	1,360	29.2	340	1.8	793	3.4
1975	3,503	17.1	18	5.9	281	17.6	—	—	305	26.0	1,573	15.7	387	13.8	939	18.4
1976	3,979	13.6	18	0.0	281	0.0	30	—	355	16.4	1,889	20.1	412	6.5	994	5.9
1977	4,311	8.3	17	−5.6	299	6.4	33	10.0	381	7.3	2,083	10.3	447	8.5	1,051	5.7
1978	4,503	4.5	17	0.0	299	0.0	26	−21.2	410	7.6	2,159	3.6	454	1.6	1,138	8.3
1979	4,607	2.3	17	0.0	313	4.7	25	−3.8	398	−2.9	2,224	3.0	486	7.0	1,144	0.5
1980	4,912	6.6	17	0.0	323	3.2	25	0.0	451	13.3	2,356	5.9	526	8.2	1,214	6.1
1981	5,038	2.6	18	5.9	341	5.6	30	20.0	449	−0.4	2,384	1.2	549	4.4	1,267	4.4
1982	5,160	2.4	18	0.0	336	−1.5	35	16.7	465	3.6	2,477	3.9	563	2.6	1,266	−0.1
1983	5,606	8.6	21	16.7	379	12.8	29	−17.1	496	6.7	2,697	10.0	607	7.8	1,377	8.8
1984[a]	5,700	1.7	21	0.0	389	2.6	30	3.4	518	4.4	2,735	1.4	636	4.8	1,371	−0.4
1985	6,056	6.2	20	−4.8	396	1.8	32	6.7	611	18.0	2,898	6.0	661	4.0	1,438	4.9
1986	6,424	6.1	20	0.0	400	1.0	31	−3.2	681	11.4	3,112	7.4	676	2.3	1,504	4.6
1987	6,681	4.0	23	15.0	417	4.3	23	−25.8	724	6.3	3,219	3.4	728	7.7	1,547	2.9
1988	6,829	2.2	23	0.0	413	−1.0	22	−4.3	742	2.5	3,341	3.8	738	1.4	1,550	0.2
1989	7,226	5.8	24	4.2	424	2.7	18	−18.2	793	6.9	3,595	7.6	760	2.9	1,612	4.0

[a]The 1984 figures reflect blacks who took office during the seven-month period between July 1, 1983 and January 30, 1984.

Source: Joint Center for Political and Economic Studies, A National Roster of Black Elected Officials 1989, p. 10. Reprinted by permission.

tripled; that is an increase from 530 to 1,814. The male to female ratio of black elected officials declined from 5.71 to 2.98 (Table 9.3). Black women occupy 98 seats (1.3 percent of total) in state legislatures; 110 positions in county governing bodies (13.9 percent of positions held by blacks); and 65 or 21.7 percent of all the black mayors. They also hold more than a fourth (26.5 percent) of the 3,296 municipal council seats occupied by blacks in 1989. Black women are also represented among elective positions in education. For example, in 1990, seven black women were members of state education agencies; 19 were members of university and college boards, and 505 were members of local school boards. In sum, black women held 532 of the 1,612 (33 percent) of all positions in education to which blacks were elected.[38]

Such advances by blacks in elective offices have created a strong appreciation of how much political power they can garner either on their own or by forging coalitions with other groups—Hispanics, Native Americans, and that core of the white population supportive of efforts to include increasingly larger numbers of blacks in the political process. Holding elective positions, however, can have little more than a symbolic value unless black officials are able to facilitate economic empowerment, improve educational opportunities, or advance the overall standard of living and assure a better quality of life for blacks in deteriorating urban communities. Political empowerment must be translated into economic and social benefits for the outsiders in American society.

Political empowerment depends upon active participation in the political process. National and local leaders in the black community are still mindful of the huge numbers of unregistered blacks in states that are central to national elections. One reason the Voter Registration Project, based in Atlanta, Georgia, the Reverend Jesse Jackson, and more and more voluntary organizations in the black community continue to mount voter registration campaigns is to build greater political clout among black elected officials. Without that political clout, combined with their own demonstrated extraordinary competence and talent, it would probably have been more difficult for Representative William Gray to become House Budget Committee Chairman and then to be elevated to Democratic Whip or for Attorney Ronald Brown to be elected Chairman of the Democratic National Committee.

JESSE JACKSON AND THE DEMOCRATIC PARTY

Unmistakably, the emergence of Jesse Jackson as a national political figure has had a profound impact on the Democratic Party and on the American electorate. Rising from an aide to the late Reverend Martin Luther King, to the founder of Operation Breadbasket and of People United to Save Humanity (PUSH) to a legitimate contender for the presidency of the United States, Jackson has changed America's political landscape. The

Table 9.2   BLACK ELECTED OFFICIALS AS A PERCENTAGE OF ALL ELECTED
OFFICIALS, BY STATE: JANUARY 1989

State	Blacks as a percent of voting-age population	Elected officials		
		Total	Black	% Black
Alabama	22.0	4,315	694	16.1
Alaska	3.8	1,865	4	*
Arizona	2.4	3,191	12	*
Arkansas	12.0	8,331	318	3.8
California	6.0	19,279	275	1.4
Colorado	4.0	8,035	14	*
Connecticut	4.0	9,929	63	0.6
Delaware	13.8	1,227	23	1.9
District of Columbia	65.9	325	242	74.5
Florida	13.0	5,368	179	3.3
Georgia	31.0	6,556	483	7.4
Hawaii	2.2	160	1	0.6
Idaho	*	4,678	0	*
Illinois	16.0	38,936	444	1.1
Indiana	9.0	11,355	68	0.6
Iowa	1.2	17,043	9	*
Kansas	5.0	16,410	23	*
Kentucky	5.0	7,481	68	0.9
Louisiana	27.0	4,985	521	10.5
Maine	*	7,147	3	*
Maryland	24.0	2,032	118	5.8
Massachusetts	4.0	13,888	38	*
Michigan	13.0	19,292	306	1.6
Minnesota	1.2	19,013	12	*
Mississippi	33.0	4,950	646	13.1
Missouri	10.0	17,115	163	1.0
Montana	*	5,646	0	*
Nebraska	2.7	15,064	4	*
Nevada	4.8	1,174	10	0.9
New Hampshire	*	6,883	3	*
New Jersey	12.0	9,345	199	2.1
New Mexico	1.6	2,096	6	*
New York	13.0	26,343	252	1.0
North Carolina	21.0	5,554	449	8.1
North Dakota	*	15,141	0	*
Ohio	9.0	19,750	216	1.1
Oklahoma	6.0	9,290	115	1.2
Oregon	1.2	8,366	9	*
Pennsylvania	8.0	33,242	139	*
Rhode Island	2.5	1,120	10	0.9
South Carolina	26.0	3,692	373	10.1
South Dakota	*	9,249	3	*
Tennessee	15.0	6,841	146	2.1

Table 9.2 (*Continued*)

State	Blacks as a percent of voting-age population	Elected officials		
		Total	Black	% Black
Texas	11.0	26,987	312	1.2
Utah	*	2,588	1	*
Vermont	*	8,021	2	*
Virginia	18.0	3,118	144	4.6
Washington	2.4	8,032	20	*
West Virginia	3.1	2,838	24	0.8
Wisconsin	5.0	18,238	24	*
Wyoming	*	2,338	2	*
Total	11.1	503,862	7,191	1.4

*Less than 0.5 percent.

Note: The 35 BEOs in the Virgin Islands are not included in this table, because the Virgin Islands are not included in the 1987 Census of Governments.

Source: Joint Center for Political and Economic Studies, *A National Roster of Black Elected Officials 1989,* p. 11. Reprinted by permission.

Table 9.3 TOTAL NUMBERS OF MALE AND FEMALE BLACK ELECTED OFFICIALS SINCE 1975

Year	Male BEOs	Female BEOs	Male BEO/ female BEO ratio
1975	2,973	530	5.71
1976	3,295	684	4.81
1977	3,529	782	4.51
1978	3,660	843	4.34
1979	3,725	882	4.22
1980	3,936	976	4.03
1981	4,017	1,021	3.93
1982	4,079	1,081	3.77
1983	4,383	1,223	3.58
1984*	4,441	1,259	3.52
1985	4,697	1,359	3.45
1986	4,942	1,482	3.33
1987	5,117	1,564	3.27
1988	5,204	1,625	3.20
1989	5,412	1,814	2.98

*The 1984 figures reflect the number of blacks who took office during the seven-month period between July 1, 1983, and January 30, 1984.

Source: Joint Center for Political and Economic Studies, *A National Roster of Black Elected Officials 1989,* p. 19. Reprinted by permission.

national election of 1984, when Jackson's Rainbow Coalition achieved national prominence, was only suggestive of the role that Jackson would play in the 1988 election. A charismatic leader, extraordinarily powerful speaker and commanding presence, Jackson's appeal rested largely on his message to people who felt outside the mainstream of American society. His populist stance embraced positions that the progressive wing of the Democratic Party espoused: social justice for poor whites and oppressed racial minorities; better housing; quality education and access to schools through the enforcement of federal regulations; preservation of the environment; the rights of labor unions; child care; taxes on the well-to-do; social justice across racial lines; and equality of opportunity to all citizens. To black Americans, Jesse Jackson was champion par excellence of the right "to be included" in the political decision-making processes and no longer considered token bystanders without influence.

Jesse Jackson was a formidable contender in the 1988 contest for the Democratic Party's nominee for the presidency. On "Super Tuesday" (March 8, 1988), Jackson won five Deep South states: Alabama, Georgia, Louisiana, Mississippi, and Virginia. He ran second in eight states: Florida, Maryland, Massachusetts, Missouri, North Carolina, Rhode Island, Tennessee, and Texas. He polled more of the popular vote than either one of the remaining Democratic contenders: Michael Dukakis, Albert Gore, Richard Gephardt, and Paul Simon. His most outstanding victory during the campaign was in South Carolina, his birthplace, where he won 54 percent of the votes cast by caucus members.[39] In total, Jesse Jackson ultimately came in either first or second in 46 of 54 contested elections for the Democratic nominee. Jackson entered the Democratic Convention with approximately 1,000 delegates or about 30 percent of the total number. Not one "super" delegate went to Jesse Jackson; one State Chairman (Ed Cole of Mississippi) and one U.S. Senator (Hollings of South Carolina) but no governors cast their votes for Jesse Jackson. Clearly, the Democratic "establishment" did not support Jesse Jackson. In terms of age, Jackson's supporters were primarily in the 18–45 age group while Dukakis won voters over the age of 45. Jackson was unable to garner sufficient support from white blue-collar workers, farmers, and labor union members to propel him into the nomination for his Party's standard-bearer. Significantly, wherever he spoke, there were massive turnouts of whites in the farm belt, in industrial communities, and among members of the white working class. Yet, as poll data would later show, about a fifth of all white voters said they would not vote for a black candidate no matter how qualified he or she was for the presidency.[40]

Even with his massive popular appeal, and despite the fact that he ran second in delegates to Michael Dukakis, the Democratic Party was extremely reluctant to reward Jesse Jackson in the traditional manner of placing him on the ballot as its nominee for the Vice Presidency. The failure of Michael Dukakis, the ultimate nominee who suffered a humiliating loss to George Bush and the Republican Party, to select Jackson as his choice for the Vice Presidential spot angered a large segment of the black population and other Jackson supporters. Fearing the high probability of a low black turnout during the national elections and massive disaffection of blacks with the Party itself as a protest to the Democratic establishment's treatment of Jackson, insiders in the Democratic Party assured Jesse Jackson that he would play a prominent role at the national convention in Atlanta. In fact, Jesse Jackson dominated the Democratic National Convention, and the Democratic Party made a number of concessions to him.

Among Jackson's victories were the following: (1) a commitment for the "creation of a new Vice-Chair of the Democratic National Committee"; (2) 15 additional black members of the Democratic National Committee; (3) support for expanded participation of blacks in the party through the election of additional "state party chairs, vice- chairs and other officers"; (4) commitment to fund Jackson's expanded voter registration program; (5) a commitment that Jackson's staff would play a significant policy role in the federal government should Governor Dukakis win the presidency; (6) greater "democratization" of Party rules as indicated by a reduction in the number of "super-delegates" and "the elimination of the winner-take-all" system for subsequent national elections; (7) such changes on the Democratic platform as the declaration of South Africa as a "terrorist state" and the imposition of tougher sanctions against South Africa as well as affirmative action based upon goals and timetables, and statehood for the District of Columbia.[41] The majority of the delegates would not endorse Jackson's support for Palestinian rights nor his higher taxes for the well-to-do nor his "no first use of nuclear weapons" proposal.[42]

Lucius Barker[43] and Ronald Walters,[44] both authorities on the Jackson campaign, add to this list of victories for Jesse Jackson the fact that he provided the possibility of a legitimate black candidate for the presidency of the United States; he demonstrated a capacity to mobilize black voters as a major political resource; and he showed that black political success depends upon the success of blacks in such additional areas as the media and the mobilization of financial resources. Importantly, Jesse Jackson's efforts paved the way for others who, in fact, are succeeding in the one area where he has not been successful: winning an elective office.

Some claim that Jackson missed his opportunity to demonstrate his electibility when he declined to run for Mayor of Washington, D. C., after Mayor Barry was arrested on drug abuse charges. Others claim that Jesse Jackson's ego is so powerful that he must continue to be in the limelight as, for example, during his highly publicized trip to South Africa on the eve of Nelson Mandela's release from prison and his alleged efforts to share the spotlight with Mandela. Some political columnists have raised the question of whether or not Jesse Jackson's political era is ending.[45] From that perspective, such questions take on a special salience in view of the fact that the high-profile black winners in the November 1989 elections distanced themselves from Jesse Jackson during their campaigns in order to be assured of greater support from white voters. Supporters of this claim argue that many white voters might be far more willing to accept a person like David Dinkins, L. Douglas Wilder, or Norman Rice than they would a person who is as feared by such a large segment of the white population and as so widely distrusted among Jewish voters as Reverend Jesse Jackson, Notwithstanding, it may be quite premature to ignore Jackson's power in the Democratic Party—a position of influence that cannot be denied, at least as the 1990s begin.

Jackson's high profile status is evident in his decision to become a candidate for the "shadow senatorship" of the District of Columbia (a non-voting lobbying position aimed at obtaining statehood for the District of Columbia)*; his decision to host his own televised talk show (the Jesse Jackson Show); and his immense success in helping to gain the release of 47 hostages held by Iraq after that nation's invasion of Kuwait in August 1990.

RELATIONSHIP BETWEEN BLACKS AND PRESIDENTS CARTER, REAGAN, AND BUSH

Blacks almost unanimously supported candidate Jimmy Carter in the presidential election of 1976, and continued to back President Carter in his reelection bid of 1980. In each case, they gave him approximately 90 percent of their vote. Carter responded by naming blacks to highly visible and important positions in a broad range of federal and international functions. As stated earlier, his appointments of blacks to Cabinet positions, of Andrew Young as Ambassador to the United Nations, of the largest number of blacks appointed to federal judgeships in the history of the nation, and of 16 blacks as ambassadors to foreign nations were welcomed by the black community. These actions coupled with President Carter's support of affirmative action, his endorsement of busing for school desegregation, his use of persuasion on the United States Office of Civil Rights, the Justice Department, and the Attorney General to be vigorous in their enforcement of federal antidiscrimination statutes and regulations made blacks feel that, once again, they had a friend in the White House. They were willing to overlook some of his blunders and apparent timidity as the 1980 election neared for fear that the election of an unfriendly Republican president would retard their progress toward economic, social, and political empowerment.

When President Carter lost the 1980 election to Ronald Reagan, the black population was gripped with trepidations about the future. Eight years of the Reagan era confirmed their harshest suspicions since Reagan

---

*Jesse Jackson was elected to this position in November 1990.

set back civil rights gains and race relations by such a large measure that recovery is not likely in some areas in the foreseeable future. It became just how apparent his ideological positions were when he brought Nixon's "southern strategy" to a new level during the campaign of 1984. In Mississippi, Reagan shouted "The South Shall Rise Again"—a slogan that represented a clarion call for white supremacy. That southern strategy, by means of which the Republican Party would woo and win over white Democrats who resented civil rights gains made by blacks under Democratic presidential leadership, has worked. Indeed, the defection of white Democrats, particularly in the South, is a constant phenomenon so much so that many in some regions of the nation view the Republican Party as the party of white Americans and the Democratic Party as the party that supports the aspirations of blacks and other minorities.

Former President Reagan was in no way sympathetic to the aspirations of blacks for economic, social, and educational opportunities. He steadfastly opposed affirmative action, busing for school desegregation, and job opportunity programs. He slashed budgets for social programs that were of direct benefit to oppressed minorities and poor whites. He also repeatedly annihilated budgets to support civil rights enforcement and he reduced the credibility of the U. S. Commission on Civil Rights to such a degree that many people reached the conclusion that it would be better to abolish the Commission than to have one that was viewed as the President's idealogue. His support for tuition tax credits to private schools and tax exemptions for schools that discriminate against blacks and other minorities were viewed as efforts to undermine school desegregation and support white parents who had opted to send their children to all-white "Christian academies" and private schools rather than have them attend desegregated schools with blacks, Hispanics, Asians, and Native Americans.

Mr. Reagan's influence on the judicial system will be of profound importance for years into the twenty-first century. These judges make decisions regarding equal employment opportunity, civil rights, and other issues that affect the well-being of American citizens. During his eight years as president, Ronald Reagan appointed more than half (385 of 757) the judges; this number was more than any president in American history had appointed to lifetime positions. The overwhelming majority of his appointments were white males who passed the litmus test of being ideologically right. Of his 385 judicial appointments, only seven (1.8 percent) went to blacks (six to district courts and one to a court of appeals). By contrast, President Carter appointed 38 blacks out of 265 judicial appointments or 14.3 percent of total appointments. In addition, Mr. Reagan was successful in appointing a conservative majority to the U. S. Supreme Court.[46] The impact of that majority has already been observed in the decisions rendered by the Rehnquist Court discussed in Chapter 2 which are viewed by many as an erosion of equal employment opportunity.

The presidential campaign of George Bush had a number of racist overtones, particularly as represented in the ads about Willie Horton. This black male had been released on a prison furlough and while on furlough raped a white woman. To critics of this ad, the implication was that a vote for Dukakis was a vote for black male rapists of white women. Mr. Bush denied racism and pointed out that he was a long-time supporter and fund-raiser for black organizations and that he was firmly committed to racial justice in American society. Once elected President, Mr. Bush made the kinds of overtures to black leaders that were never made by his predecessor. For example, he met with members of the Congressional Black Caucus and representatives of major civil rights organizations. He addressed black groups such as the Joint Center for Political and Economic Studies. During his first year, 8 percent of his 568 federal appointments went to blacks. Among these appointees are the Secretary of Health and Human Services, Dr. Louis Sullivan; the Chairman of the Joint Chiefs of Staff, General Colin Powell; the Director of the Office of Personnel Management, Constance Newman; the Chief of the Social Security Administration, Gwendolyn King. In addition, he made several statements attacking racial violence and bigotry during the first year of his presidency and did not appear to be as staunchly antiblack as Ronald Reagan seemed. In that sense, it is not surprising that in four consecutive NY Times/CBS News polls the majority of blacks gave a favorable rating to Bush for his job performance.[47]

A favorable rating of President Bush by black Americans must be viewed as tentative or as merely a reflection of the fact that Bush has been for many blacks a welcome relief from the antiblack sentiments attributed to Ronald Reagan. However, black Americans may not realize that Bush appears to be following Reagan's footsteps with regard to judicial appointments. He vetoed federal legislation designed to undue the damages to equal employment opportunity inflicted by Reagan appointees to the Supreme Court in anti-affirmative action decisions rendered during the first half of 1989. Of the 47 vacant judgeships during his first year of presidency, Bush nominated only one black person to fill a vacancy. President Bush announced that he was "the education president" but he slashed the education budget that is of special benefit to blacks and other minorities. Some critics claim that he may well be following the same ideological line of his predecessor but in a less offensive way.[48]

Black Conservatives

A major exception to the above observation about President Reagan comes from the positions taken by black conservatives. This relatively small band of black businessmen and women, Republican politicians, and some educators support many of the Reagan positions. However, they are not a monolithic group. Lee Daniels draws a distinction between (1) black conservative politicians and (2) black philosophical conservatives. The former group is committed to the encouragement of blacks to participate in a two-party system and break the 50-year alliance between blacks and the Democratic Party. They believe that greater benefits may be gained by blacks through membership and active participation in both Democratic and Republican politics and that the Republican Party has the potential strength to provide even greater benefits to black Americans. By contrast, the philosophical black conservatives are aligned with the most right-wing notions espoused by President Reagan and his supporters. This view is essentially one that is antiaffirmative action, antipublic welfare, antibusing for school desegregation, and many proponents have come to believe that race is no longer a major determinant of one's status and opportunity in American society.[49]

Manning Marable divides "black Reaganites" into four groups: (1) conservative black politicians; (2) black philosophical conservatives; (3) black corporate executives and business managers; and (4) former black power activists.[50] His first two categories are indistinguishable from Daniel's classification. His third category consists of corporate blacks and Reagan administrative appointees who, in his view, had neither "ideological commitment to civil rights" nor a strong defense of traditional institutions" which characterize the black community.[51] The fourth group includes those Marable labels as former "would-be-militants" who have become "disenchanted with liberalism and protest politics." He views these people as "black Reaganite accommodationists."[52]

In December 1980, one month after the election of Ronald Reagan as President, a group of black conservatives met in San Francisco to form a New Coalition for Economic and Social Change. This group rejected as outmoded the programs and approaches to civil rights advocated by traditional black civil rights groups. They failed to develop a "conservative black agenda," and found themselves unable to effectively challenge the traditional leadership. However, they held a second conference in 1982 which was cosponsored by the Conservative Heritage Foundation. Their president, Clarence Pendleton, became chairman of the U.S. Commission on Civil Rights. Although this group has yet to evidence influence on the black masses, it is financially supported by such wealthy, conservative and predominantly white companies as the Coors Beer Company and Getty Oil.[53]

OTHER STRATEGY CONFERENCES AND GROUPS

Since the 1972 Black Agenda Conference was held at Gary, Indiana, several additional efforts have attempted to capitalize on the theme of that conference—"unity without uniformity." Special efforts have been made to maximize the strengths found in the divergent perspectives prevalent within the black community while still pursuing a common goal of restructuring power arrangements in American society.

On August 30, 1980, during the fourth convention of the National

Black Political Assembly, held in New Orleans, the idea of a National Black Independent Political Party (NBIPP) was accepted. The founding convention of NBIPP was held in Philadelphia, November 21–23, 1980, and the party's first Congress was held in Chicago during August 1981. This party accepts neither the Democratic nor the Republican parties as organizations that can adequately promote the best interests of blacks. They argue, employing a separatist philosophy, that revolutionary changes in the political system can best occur through actions of blacks themselves for themselves.[54]

Other groups are more interested in building and revitalizing coalitions between blacks and civic, political and labor organizations. Included among these are the Black Leadership Forum, founded in 1977, the Lawyers' Committee for Civil Rights under Law, the Black United Front, established in 1980, and the Leadership Conference on Civil Rights, established in 1950. These groups vary in size and sometimes have overlapping membership. For example, the Leadership Conference on Civil Rights consists of approximately 157 organizations, including black fraternal groups, the NAACP, the NUL, Organization of Chinese Americans, the Mexican American Legal Defense Fund and the Anti-Defamation League of B'nai B'rith. Members of the Black Leadership Forum include the NAACP, NUL, Operation PUSH, SCLC, the Congressional Black Caucus, the Martin Luther King Center for Social Change, the National Council of Negro Women, and many other organizations.

Many members of these bodies joined in the Solidarity March held in Washington, D. C. on September 19, 1981, to protest and publicly oppose programs initiated by the Reagan Administration that were detrimental to the cause of civil rights and to American working-class people of all races. In addition to such areas of cooperation, black elected officials have organized themselves into a variety of organizations that hold periodic meetings for the promotion of their own efforts to include more blacks in the political process and assure broader political participation. Among these groups are the National Black Conference of Local Elected Officials, the National Conference of Black State Legislators, the National Conference of Black Mayors, and some are members of the National Black Coalition for 1984.

Although the 1972 Black Agenda Conference may have attracted great attention and served as the precursor to similar conventions in subsequent years, it was not the first of its type among black Americans. Unquestionably, it was not their first attempt to form political parties. Indeed, blacks historically have formed political parties at either the state or national level for approximately 100 years. However, in more recent times state-level political parties included the Mississippi Freedom Democratic Party, which challenged the seating of white Democrats at the 1964 Democratic convention in Atlantic City, the Black Panther Party in Lowndes, Alabama, and the Democratic Party of Alabama, which spearheaded the rise in the number of black elected officials in that state from

1967 onward. At the national level, blacks formed the National Independent Political League (1912), the National Labor Congress (1924), the National Negro Congress (1936), the Afro-American Party (1960), the Freedom Now Party (1964), and the Freedom and Peace Party (1968). Each of these parties was short-lived as was the attempt at Gary. At this point, there is no way to measure with confidence how successful NBIPP will be.

In April 1989, 1,000 blacks, headed by prominent leaders of the civil rights movement, assembled in New Orleans for the African-American Summit 1989. This meeting was referred to by some as the most important black unity meeting since the Gary Summit of 1972. The purpose of the Summit was to set a "black agenda" for the 1990s and into the twenty-first century. The emphasis was on unity among blacks; economic empowerment as the next phase of the civil rights movement; strengthening the black family; investment of $8 billion of public pension funds to rebuild decaying inner cities heavily populated by the black underclass, and reparations for "the descendants of slaves." Although participants included Reverend Jesse Jackson, Correta Scott King, and Ronald Brown, many well-known leaders did not attend. Among these were Benjamin Hooks, head of the NAACP; Mayor Andrew Young, and Rep. William Gray, Louis Farrakhan attended and addressed the delegates. While he was not embraced by all delegates, in the "spirit of unity," Louis Farrakhan was permitted to address the delegates and received an enthusiastic response.[55]

Later in 1989, unity was dealt a major blow by the publication of *And The Walls Came Tumbling Down,* an autobiography by Dr. Martin Luther King's staunchest ally during the heyday of the civil rights movement, Reverend Ralph Abernathy. In that volume, Abernathy supported previous FBI claims of infidelity by the late Dr. King, an allegation that was denounced by the overwhelming majority of the nation's civil rights leaders. Reverend Abernathy continued to defend the authenticity of his claims until his death in April 1990. Again, his death also signalled the dawning of a new political leadership in the black community.

NOTES

1. For an extensive discussion of power and related theories, see Hubert M. Blalock, Jr. *Toward A General Theory of Minority Group Relations* (New York: John Wiley & Sons, 1967); Robert Bierstedt, "An Analysis of Social Power," *American Sociological Review,* 15 (December 1950): 730–738; James E. Blackwell, "The Power Basis of Ethnic Conflict in American Society," in *The Uses of Controversy in Sociology,* Lewis Coser and Otto Larsen (eds.) (New York: The Free Press, 1976), pp. 179–196; and James C. Davies, "The J-Curve of Rising and Declining Satisfaction as a Cause of Some Great Revolutions and a Contained Rebellion," in *Violence in America: Historical and Comparative*

Perspectives, Hugh Davis Graham and Robert Gurr (eds.) (New York: Bantam Books, 1969).

2. Robert Dahl, *Who Governs?* (New Haven, Conn.: Yale University Press, 1961), p. 21.
3. Blalock, *op. cit.*
4. Hanes Walton, *Black Politics* (New York: J. P. Lippincott, 1972), pp. 58–69.
5. Edward Banfield, *Big City Politics* (New York: Random House, 1965), p. 301.
6. Henry Lee Moon, *Balance of Power: The Negro Vote* (Garden City, N.Y.: Doubleday, 1948), p. 198.
7. For a discussion of both fluctuations in and influences of black voter participation cf.: Chuck Stone, *Black Political Power in America* (New York: Dell Publishing Co., Inc., 1948); Thomas Pettigrew, "White-Negro Confrontations," in Eli Ginsbert (ed.), *The Negro Challenge to the Business Community* (New York: McGraw-Hill, 1964), pp. 39–55; Theodore White, *The Making of the President 1960* (New York: Atheneum, 1961), p. 323; John Dean, *The Making of a Black Mayor* (Washington, D.C.: The Joint Center for Political Studies, 1973); and Daniel P. Moynihan, "Political Perspectives," in Eli Ginsbert (ed.), *The Negro Challenge to the Business Community* (New York: McGraw-Hill, 1964), pp. 71–80.
8. For a discussion of the politics of participation and the politics of governance cf. Charles V. Hamilton, "Racial, Ethnic and Social Class Politics and Administration," *Public Administration Review,* 32 (October 1972): 638–648.
9. Wilson Record and Jane Cassels Record, *Little Rock, U.S.A.* (San Francisco: Chandler Publishing Company, 1960), pp. 35–119.
10. Clarence Mitchell, "The Civil Rights Scene," *The Crisis* 87:9 (September 1980): 349–357.
11. Cf. Charles V. Hamilton and Stokely Carmichael, *Black Power: The Politics of Liberation in America,* for a discussion of the restraints posed upon blacks in Lowndes County, Alabama, during the mid-1960s and for an elaboration of efforts to curtail black political participation in the South. It should be stressed, however, that with successful voter registration in that county blacks in 1973 controlled major sections of the decision-making structure, including the county sheriff position.
12. This discussion is essentially in agreement with positions taken by several writers such as Pettigrew, *op. cit.,* and William Gamson, *Power and Discontent* (Homewood, Ill.: Dorsey Press, 1968).
13. *Report of the National Advisory Commission on Civil Disorders* (New York: Bantam Books, 1968), pp. 112–115.
14. Stone, *op. cit.,* p. 24.
15. *Ibid.,* p. 16.
16. Hamilton, *op. cit.,* refers to the politics of participation and the use of the electoral process as a means of involvement in local and national politics, whereas governance is the result of sustained bloc-voting which creates political leadership roles by blacks to the degree that they control the instruments of government at one level or another.
17. *Op. cit.,* p. 75.
18. Huey P. Newton, *Revolutionary Suicide* (New York: Harcourt, Brace, 1975).
19. Carmichael *op. cit.,* p. 18.
20. Cf. Manning Marable, "Beyond the Race-Class Dilemma," *The Nation* (April

11, 1981): 417–436, and James E. Blackwell, "Persistence and Change in Intergroup Relations: The Crisis Upon Us," *Social Problems,* 29:4 (April 1982): 325–346.

21. Harry A. Ploski and James Williams (eds.), *The Negro Almanac: A Reference Work on the Afro-American,* 4th ed. (New York: John Wiley, 1983), p. 62.
22. *Ibid.*
23. *Ibid.,* p. 259.
24. *Ibid.*
25. Blackwell, *op. cit.,* p. 333.
26. Cf. *op. cit.,* pp. 240–242; *Time,* October 29, 1979, p. 6; Wanda K. Fishman, "Reinterpreting the Andrew Young Affair: An Analysis of Black-Jewish Distortions in the Changing U.S.-Mideast Policy of 1979–1980," *The Western Journal of Black Studies* 5:2 (Summer 1982): 129–138.
27. "Kivie Kaplan Institute Brings Blacks, Jews Together," *The Crisis,* 88:7 (August/September 1981): 364–365.
28. *Ibid.*
29. The U. S. Commission on Civil Rights, *Confronting Racial Isolation in Miami* (Washington, D. C.: U. S. Commission on Civil Rights, 1982), *passim.*
30. Jeffrey Schmalz, "Miami Tensions Simmering Three Months After Violence," *New York Times,* April 10, 1989.
31. Cf. *Klanwatch: Intelligence Report* (Montgomery, Al.: The Southern Poverty Law Center, February 1989, No. 42); David S. Wilson, "Old and New Racist Groups Are Reported Joining," *New York Times* (October 27, 1988), p. 9: Peter Applebome, "New Report Warns of Alliance of Racist Groups," *New York Times* (February 6, 1989); Wayne King, "Violent Racism Attracts New Breed: Skinheads," *New York Times* (January 1, 1989), p. 35; Associated Press, "Group Claims It Sent Mail Bombs," *Times-Picayune* (December 29, 1989), p. A-3; *New York Times,* "Threatening Letters Linked to Bombings," *Times-Picayune* (December 30, 1989), p. A-4; and Ronald Smothers, "Agents Await Clues in Rash of Bombings," *Times-Picayune* (January 7, 1990), p. A-17.
32. *Ibid.*
33. Ploski and Williams, *op. cit.,* p. 30.
34. "The NAACP Voter Education Project," *The Crisis,* 86:8 (October 1979): 354.
35. Cf. Tom Brune, "Race Becomes Issue in Chicago Mayoral Vote," *Boston Globe* (April 3, 1983), p. 2; Andrew H. Malcolm, "Chicago," *New York Times Magazine* (April 10, 1983), pp. 24–72; Nathaniel Sheppard, Jr., "Victor's Backers See Shift in Power," *New York Times* (April 14, 1983), p. B-15; and Howell Raines, "Effects of Chicago Race," *New York Times* (April 14, 1983), p. B15.
36. Earl Graves, "A New Decade of Political Power," *Black Enterprise* (January 1990): 9; Alfred Edmond, Jr., "Black Officials Face Challenges of the '90s," *Black Enterprise* (January 1990): 15.
37. *Black Elected Officials: A National Roster* (Washington, D. C.: Joint Center for Political and Economic Studies, 1989), pp. x–7.
38. *Ibid.,* p. 2.
39. "Political Trend Letter," *Focus* (March 1988): 5 and "Political Trend Letter," *Focus* (July 1989): p. 5.
40. Excerpted from Interview with Jesse Jackson on *The Today Show* (July 20, 1988).
41. *Op. cit.*

42. *Ibid.*
43. Lucius Barker, *Our Time Has Come: A Delegate's Diary* (Urbana: University of Illinois Press, 1987).
44. Ronald Walters, *Black Presidential Politics in America: A Strategic Approach* (Stony Brook: State University of New York Press, 1987).
45. Cf. Robert Jordan, "Is The Jackson Political Era Ending?," *Boston Globe* (December 3, 1989), p. A-5; The Associated Press, "Jackson Rules Out Race for Washington Mayor," *Times-Picayune* (February 27, 1990), p. A-4; The Associated Press, "Jackson Visits Black Leader, Squatters' Hut in Soweto," *Times-Picayune* (February 9, 1990), p. A-18; and Cox News Service, "Black Unity, Coalition with Whites Urged by Jackson," *Times-Picayune* (February 8, 1990), p. A-16.
46. "Political Trend Letter: Bush's Bad Start on Appointing Black Judges," *Focus* (June 1989): 6.
47. Tom Wicker, "Bush and Blacks," *New York Times* (April 17, 1990), p. B-7; *USA Today* (April 16, 1990), p. 3.
48. Wicker, *op. cit.*
49. Cf. Lee Daniels, "The New Black Conservative," *The New York Times* (October 4, 1981), p. 20., and James E. Blackwell and Philip Hart, *Cities, Suburbs and Blacks* (Bayside, N.Y.: General Hall, Inc. 1982), pp. 183–196.
50. Manning Marable, "Reaganism, Racism and Reaction: Black Political Realignment in the 1980s," *The Black Scholar* (Fall 1982): 2–15.
51. *Ibid.,* pp. 8–9.
52. *Ibid.*
53. Ploski and Williams, *op. cit.*
54. Marable, *op. cit.,* pp. 12–14.
55. Tyler Bridges, "Blacks Roused by Calls for Unity," *Times-Picayune* (April 24, 1989), pp.1, A-8. See also: Aldon Morris, *The Origins of the Civil Rights Movement* (New York: The Free Press, 1984); and Hanes Walton, Jr., *When The Marching Stopped* (Albany, N.Y.: State University of New York Press, 1988), and *Invisible Politics: Black Political Behavior* (Albany: State University of New York Press, 1985).

Chapter
10

The Military and Black Life

Although blacks have always served in the armed forces of the United States, their roles have depended upon government policy. The government has followed a pattern that progressed from official segregation and discrimination to a policy of integration, which has in recent times permitted "voluntary separatism," which will be explained shortly. This shift in governmental policy occurred not always because of a more liberal governmental philosophy but often as an appropriate response to pressures or conditions that threatened the cohesion of the American military system. Changes within the military system have historically and characteristically transpired slowly, grudgingly, and cautiously. During the past century the increasing aggressiveness and militancy of the American black community has played a profound role in moving the American military toward change.

HISTORICAL THEMES

Four themes seem to emerge regarding black experiences in the armed services, namely, (1) blacks have been moving, although with resistance and interruptions, toward assimilation into the military; (2) a high correlation exists between racial identity and the experiences of people in the military system and as ex-servicemen or women; (3) the black community has never displayed organized opposition toward military service per se (rather, its protests have tended to be directed against its systematic patterns of discrimination, racism, segregation, and exclusion); and (4) racial conflict within the military community is not a recent phenomenon and, further, may reveal racial animosities or prejudices only temporarily allayed by needs for protection in combat situations.

This chapter examines the historical roles performed by blacks in relation to governmental policies and their consequences for contemporary black experiences in military life. Primary attention is devoted to blacks in the military during and since American involvement in the Vietnam War.[1]

GOVERNMENTAL POLICY AND HISTORICAL ROLES OF BLACKS

For more than 150 years U.S. government policies of exclusion and segregation prevented blacks from gaining full participation within the military system whenever they were permitted entry. This observation may be illustrated by brief examples from wars in which the United States has participated.

First, with the courage displayed by blacks such as Crispus Attucks, the first American to die in the cause of the Revolution, many blacks sought to volunteer for service with the Revolutionary army. General George Washington expressed his opposition to their inclusion in four orders issued through the Council of General Officers of the Continental Congress. It was only after the threat posed by Lord Dunmore's proclamation (issued November 7, 1777) guaranteeing unconditional freedom to male slaves who volunteered to serve with the British that Washington recommended the enlistment of blacks. The 5,000 blacks who served in the segregated army and the 1,500 or more who served in the navy were not only involved in combat but performed innumerable service roles. They worked as cooks, construction laborers, servants, and in other support capacities. But when the new nation's freedom had been won, Congress prohibited blacks from serving in any branch of the armed services, including state militias, the navy, and the marines.[2] A similar pattern of threats followed by exclusion occurred during the War of 1812 but on a much smaller scale.

Second, during the Civil War, decisions relative to the incorporation of blacks in either the Confederate army or the Union army were complicated by the issues of slavery, manumission, and fugitive slaves. No consistent governmental policy existed regarding either those issues or the conscription of blacks. Inconsistencies reflected regional policy distinctions as well as different perceptions of the importance of black people in achieving either the goal of national unity or of regional secession. Policy changes occurred solely because of changing definitions of the situation as couched in terms like "acts of military necessity." Therefore, the Confederacy, motivated by the need to combat external threats to internal security, initially responded by impressing blacks into support services (e.g., construction of military installations, work as railroad repairmen, cooks, mechanics, hospital aides, and so on). Thousands of able-bodied slaves escaped rather than submit to this new form of tyranny with no promise of manumission. General Robert E. Lee reluctantly approved an order to permit the enlistment of 2,000 blacks into the Confederate army, with freedom being exchanged for loyalty, only after his army had encountered serious military setbacks. Thus official inclusion was made an act of military necessity.

Early in the Civil War Northern blacks were permitted to enlist in the Union army but on a segregated basis, whether in combat or in service roles. Initially, however, a primary concern regarded appropriate dispositions to be made of fugitive and captured slaves. The problem was resolved by the Confiscation Act of 1861, which authorized Union troops to free captured slaves. President Lincoln's Emancipation Proclamation (which he called an "act of military necessity" and which became effective on January 1, 1863) undoubtedly helped swell the ranks of the U.S. Coloured Troops. Although incorporated into the Union army structure, blacks still did not enjoy equal status. Inequities were observed in the paucity of blacks certified as commissioned officers (a total of 100 throughout the war), in the inequality of pay (the salary of whites ranged from $13 to $100 whereas that of the 178,975 black soldiers was established at $7 per month), in the inferior supplies assigned to blacks, and the health conditions under which blacks labored, resulting in a mortality rate among blacks believed to be 40 percent higher than that of whites. Indeed, 38,000 black soldiers lost their lives, and thousands more were seriously wounded.[3] It is interesting to note, however, that during the Civil War in contrast to World Wars I and II when the nation was presumably considerably more enlightened, 16 black soldiers and five black sailors were awarded the Congressional Medal of Honor. None was so honored in either of the world wars.

Third, the roles of blacks in the Indian wars illustrate how blacks, a subordinate group themselves, were forced to subordinate another group attempting to protect itself from territorial encroachments and violations of its sovereignty. Simultaneously, the migrant superordinates white settlers, whose authority over the subordinated blacks had already been established in other territories and states, used that subordinate group for protection against native Indians who resisted their encroachments. Specifically, the four black units that remained after the Civil War (there had been as many as 150 during the war) were added to the regular army in 1866, sent initially to protect carpetbaggers in the South, and later transferred to the rapidly expanding Western frontier to protect white settlers against "hostile" Indians. Reaction of white settlers to a black military were both peculiar and expected as defined by the nature of the social and territorial situations.

The white people of the Western domain, for example, treated blacks of the 9th Cavalry with open hostility as they arrived in Wyoming in 1885.

Their internalization of stereotypes and prejudices against blacks is reflected in their love for watching "coon dances," a major recreation in that locale in that period. According to substantial evidence, nevertheless, attitudes were far less hostile and considerably more accommodating the closer the communities were to the Indian reservations. In those instances, under the threat of hostile Indian tribes, blacks and whites learned to subordinate racial animosities and become more tolerant of each other.[4] Thus by the time that the 24th Cavalry of blacks and the 10th Cavalry of blacks arrived in Cheyenne to eliminate cattle wars, interracial hostility had somewhat abated at least on a superficial level. It was, however, the white citizens of Wyoming who called blacks "buffalo soldiers" because they believed that a similarity existed between the hair of blacks and that of the buffalo who roamed the Western territory. Unmistakably, hostility was only temporarily suppressed, since blacks were lynched in Wyoming in 1913 and that state early enacted laws prohibiting interracial marriage and integrated schools.

As the war with Spain broke out, the army ordered the four black regiments stationed in the Western states and territories to assist in the conquest of Cuba and Spanish territories in the West Indies. In addition 16 regiments of black volunteers also distinguished themselves in battle. Their primary motive for joining the military was economic betterment in the face of mounting discrimination associated with the return of white supremacy and agricultural displacements resulting from an economic recession, the spread of the boll weevil, and changing demographic patterns.

Fourth, the Brownsville incident illustrates the unwillingness of dominant group members to accept authority roles of low-status minorities over them, and also illustrates how accusations against black men of sexual abuse of white women may be used to heighten animosities and lead to brutalities against the innocent. Briefly, the 25th Infantry Regiment, composed of black soldiers and white officers, was stationed at Fort Brown near Brownsville, Texas, in 1906. Widespread resentment over their assignment to that area soon escalated into physical abuse, racial and discriminatory acts. One night in August, during an alleged raid on Brownsville, Mrs. Evans, a white woman, claimed to have been "almost raped" by a black man believed to have been from the infantry. However, the allegations were never substantiated during a jury trial. President Roosevelt, undoubtedly motivated by political considerations because of the forthcoming elections, sent General G. A. Garlington to Brownsville to initiate further investigations of the matter. Despite General Garlington's persistent questioning, none of the blacks spoke up. Nonplused by what he called "a conspiracy of silence," Garlington recommended that all 167 black members of the regiment be punished. President Roosevelt thereupon dishonorably discharged them—the first and only incident of mass punishment in American military history.[5] Sixty-six years later in 1972, under the leadership of Congressman Augustus Hawkins, Army Secretary Froelkhe revoked the dismissal order and exonerated all 167 men. Only two of the men were living at the time. They subsequently received a paltry sum in back pay—a small recompense for the years of hardship and intolerable conditions they and their compatriots had endured for a lifetime.

Fifth, an organized protest movement among dispossessed blacks who sought assimilation or integration into American life arose on the heels of the Brownsville incident. It originated with the formation of such organizations as the NAACP and the Urban League, whose causes were advanced by militant leaders such as W. E. B. Du Bois, A. Philip Randolph, and Elijah Muhammad—the latter two men refusing to serve in a segregated military during World War I. The stated goal of blacks was still full assimilation, not exclusion, into a military that had denied them entry except under extreme pressure and on a segregated basis. These organizations and individuals joined with several others to force abrogation of exclusionary policies and guarantee equal rights to men who served in the military. As a result of the Selective Service Act of 1917, about a third of the 2,290,525 blacks who registered were summoned for service during World War I. Further, the enactment and implementation of the Selective Service Act of 1940 was required to assure that blacks would be called into active duty during World War II because the policy of exclusion had been reimposed between the two wars. Thus 800,000 blacks went into the army, 165,000 into the navy, 17,000 into the marines (which had barred blacks in World War I), 24,000 into the merchant marine, 3,000 into the Coast Guard, 1,000 into the air force (trained primarily at a segregated base in Tuskeegee, Alabama), and 4,000 women each into the WACS and WAVES.[6]

In both world wars blacks encountered barriers of segregation and discrimination both on and off base at home and abroad. The units were segregated; training was initially segregated (and would remain so until limited integration occurred in World War II); proportionately fewer blacks were commissioned as officers, never reaching even 1 percent of the total officer force; discrimination occurred in housing both on and off base (barracks, clubs, mess halls, and recreational facilities were segregated and unequal, and black soldiers were often pushed to extremes to locate off-base housing in hostile communities); transportation services were not readily available to blacks; and separate USOs reflected traditional barriers to social integration. Moreover, the pattern of assigning blacks to low-status occupational roles in the military, which was so evident as early as the Revolutionary War, still persists even now. For example, important and distinguished combat units such as the 92nd and 93rd army divisions (both world wars), the 369th, 371st, and 372nd regiments (World War I), and the 99th Pursuit Squadron (World War II), made outstanding contributions in foreign battle zones. Collectively, they won hundreds of symbols of recognition for outstanding military performances— the Croix de Guerre, Distinguished Flying Cross, the Navy Cross, the Purple Heart—but not one Congressional Medal of Honor. Often the 92nd army division was maligned and falsely accused of cowardice. During World War II, blacks constituted 9 percent of all enlisted men, 2.8 percent of all ground combat troops, but almost half (45 percent) of the Quartermaster Corps. Almost four-fifths (78.1 percent) of all black army males were assigned to service branches. And in the navy they were largely radiomen, yeomen, shipfitters, quartermasters, stewards, carpenters, gunner's mates, and stockkeepers.[7]

American prejudice and institutionalized dominance were transported by the military to foreign shores. As a consequence, various myths and stereotypes regarding black Americans were employed to prevent the establishment of equal status relationships between American blacks and Europeans. For example, a letter from General Pershing's headquarters to the French military under the title "Secret Information Concerning the Black American Troops" suggested to the French that they should not become too socially compatible with blacks and under no circumstances should they "spoil the negroes." The "secret information" warned the French against violating American social etiquette governing black-white relations. Taboos included shaking hands, eating together, and other forms of socializing.[8] The French were told that blacks were apelike, prone to sexual violence, and they were also told of accentuated notions of black male virility as measured by presumed excessive genital size. Such statements were designed to create effective barriers between blacks and the French, to reduce competition for French women, and to reinforce stateside notions of white supremacy. However, there is no evidence that such statements were effective restraints against social relationships across color lines in Europe. Similar ideas during World War II were frequently the basis of violent interracial confrontations, riots, and maltreatment of black military personnel. Numerous confrontations occurred and seemed to have subsided only when troops were involved in prolonged combat situations necessitating harmonious relationships for mutual survival. It is this type of imposed social situation that has in many instances led to a reduction of prejudice.[9] This thesis is under serious attack, however, by virtue of the exigencies of black involvement in the Vietnam War.

Although the marines desegregated in 1942, other branches of the military did not. Protest organizations stepped up the attack against segregation and discrimination in the military and began to exploit the power implicit in the pivotal character of the black political position. Their work coupled with the influential publication *To Secure These Rights* (1947), authored by the newly created U.S. Civil Rights Commission, helped to persuade President Harry S Truman to issue Executive Order 9981 on July 26, 1948, which banned discrimination in the armed forces on the basis of race, religion, color, or national origin. On July 27, 1948, General Omar Bradley avowed his intention to resist this policy and continue military segregation.[10] Despite his opposition, desegregation occurred and was complete six years later, but discrimination remained in the military. In the larger society, in the meantime, civil rights organizations and human relations associations continued their attack against off-base discrimination in housing, transportation, and educational facilities. Discrimination was attacked both as a constitutional violation and as a violation of morality explicit in the spirit of the American Creed. How could one be demanded to defend democracy abroad when segregation and discrimination ravaged people at home? It was this type of inconsistency that weighed so predominantly in the disillusionment of returning black soldiers who participated in the Red Summer of 1919 and the riots of the 1940s. It was the recognition of injustice involved in job discrimination at military installations and in war-related industries during and following the wars that provided the rationale for many fair employment practices statutes. As a consequence of protestations and legal actions against discrimination, many barriers to desegregation began to disintegrate. Directives were issued promoting desegregation in housing for military families, both on and off base, and by 1963 the USOs that occupied federal buildings were also integrated. School desegregation on military bases became more widespread. American blacks' experiences in the Vietnam War, however, particularly at its height during the late 1960s, reflected in microcosm the fundamental character of black-white relations at home, where confrontation politics escalated to alter power relations between blacks and whites.

THE VIETNAM PERIOD

Black Americans did not express discernible opposition to American involvement in the Vietnam War until the mid-1960s. Failure to oppose the war may have been due to the fact that many black persons worked in military installations and service-related industries. For them the primary factor was economic security. But as these facilities were closed or as cutbacks in them resulted in widespread unemployment, the concerns of blacks heightened. The opposition to the war stemmed from the continuing reports on (1) the disproportionate number of blacks being shipped to Vietnam and (2) the disproportionate number of blacks being killed during the war. Perhaps the opposition of blacks was based to a lesser degree upon an identity with the darker-skinned "enemies" with whom some blacks may have felt a kindred relationship based upon color. They raised serious questions as to why one low-status people of color should be fighting another people of color in order to maintain the dominance of essentially white superordinates over both groups. Other blacks may have felt more constrained to die in the struggle for black liberation at home than to die fighting in another man's war 10,000 miles away. This may have been especially the case among those who realized that blacks sustained an estimated death rate as high as one-fourth of the American total and accounted for about one-sixth of the total number of casualties during a 1965–1966 period. Blacks were outraged by these mortality and casualty rates. A deeply rooted pattern of inequities that placed a disproportionate number of blacks in front-line combat conditions was also a source of focal concern.[11]

This situation—involvement in Vietnam—revealed multiple patterns of discontinuities, strains, and polarization within all branches of the military, which not only reflected conditions external to the military system itself but also deeply ingrained internal problems. Further, it was apparent that many of the highly publicized pronouncements of planned changes and improvements in social conditions within the military were at best superficial, having no direct impact on the fundamental issues of equality of opportunity and military justice. This situation may be illustrated in a number of ways.

Structure of Black Participation

Let us examine the structure of black participation at various levels of the Vietnam War. During the first five years of the 1960s, blacks composed about 15 percent of all persons drafted into the military even though their proportion in the total population never exceeded 11 percent during the same time. Their proportion in the army, where the majority of blacks went, approached 15 percent by 1965, and roughly the same proportion of blacks acted as combat troops in Vietnam from that point to 1970, the period of heaviest fighting there. Blacks constituted 20 percent of *all* combat troops in Vietnam at that time. During the five-year period 1965–1970, however, only 7.1 percent of white troops were assigned to Vietnam and, proportionately, were underrepresented in both casualties and deaths.[12] Simultaneously, the proportion of black officers in the army, for example, showed a steady decline from 3.6 percent of the total number of army officers in 1966 to 3.2 percent in 1969, and rose only to 3.4 percent in 1970. This pattern existed despite the promulgation by the army of policy AR0600-21, which stipulated equal opportunity and equal treatment—clearly illustrating a contradiction between policy and behavior. In each of the other branches of the military the proportion of black officers was less than 1 percent of the total. Therefore, a disproportionately higher percentage of blacks were drafted, sent into combat in Vietnam, and died or suffered wounds, while they were underrepresented in the higher echelons of the command and overrepresented at the bottom layers of the system.

Structure of the Selection Process

The structure of participation is inextricably linked with the structure of the selection process and subsequent assignments in the military following formal induction. The failure of blacks to qualify for skilled training as measured by tests administered during the selection process may partially explain the preponderance of those assigned to combat duty. Racial and cultural biases are suspected of being so severe in the Armed Forces Qualification Tests (AFQT) as to reduce substantially the number of blacks, already victims of inadequate educational preparation in many school systems throughout the country, who can be assigned to technical and skilled jobs. The armed forces provide an array of approximately 237 occupational fields in almost 300 specialty and technical training schools. Despite these apparent opportunities, blacks are still overrepresented in low-skilled positions and combat branches. Even in 1971, which presumably showed improvements over the 1966–1970 Vietnam period, blacks performed 16.3 percent of low-skilled combat services and 19.6 percent of service and supply specialties, even though they constituted slightly more than 12 percent of all enlisted personnel. At the same time, they were underrepresented in the higher-skilled technical fields, constituting 7 percent of communications and intelligence specialists and 4.9 percent of the electronics equipment specialists.[13]

The overwhelming majority of black officers were similarly assigned to the supply-and-procurement sections, which in itself raises serious questions of the meaning of "professionalization of the military" as the concept applies to blacks. On the other hand, some evidence suggests that some blacks who qualify for special training do not wish to undergo it for a variety of reasons ranging from the time commitment to a desire to remain with friends in other nonspecialty low-skilled areas. Since this group seems to be in the minority, there is inadequate support for the rationalization that blacks do not want specialty training to account for inequities in job assignments within the military.

Structure of Promotions

The promotion system within the military has not permitted substantial upward mobility of blacks, although some blacks have used the military to enhance their opportunities for upward mobility in the larger society. Blacks seem to be locked into a promotion system that white military officials control. Black servicemen and officers often complain that they have been discriminated against in the promotion process, especially when it is apparent to them that less qualified whites are advancing to higher grades with undue rapidity. During the Vietnam period blacks were disproportionately clustered around the lower pay grades as well as the lower-status grades in all armed services. In 1970, for example, blacks constituted only 2.2 percent of all officers in the armed services, which was only slightly more than double the proportion they held during World War II. The change is significant only in the sense that the proportion was abysmally inadequate in the first instance. But even at the levels of E-2* and E-3 blacks state that they have often waited a year or more to move, for instance, from E-2 to E-3, whereas a white enlisted man often received an immediate promotion upon his arrival in Vietnam.

One consequence of discrimination in the military is the profoundly

---

*E-2 refers to the rank of private while E-3 is the rank of private first class.

negative impact on attitudes among blacks regarding the military. In a detailed study[14] conducted in Vietnam, Wallace Terry surveyed 833 white and black servicemen, 392 enlisted men, 175 black officers, 181 white enlisted men, and 85 white officers. He found few distinctions in attitudes among blacks regarding military service, namely, that black enlisted men consistently agreed that the military was a poor place for blacks to be. This response was found among enlisted men in the army (75 percent), the air force (77 percent), the marines (73 percent), and the navy (64 percent). Black officers tended to support the view expressed by enlisted men when asked about difference of treatment between the races, but not to the same degree. Almost three-quarters (72 percent) of black enlisted men and slightly less than half (48 percent) of black officers believe that the military treats whites better than blacks. They were closer in agreement regarding opportunities for promotion inasmuch as almost two-thirds (64 percent) of black enlisted men and slightly less than half (45 percent) of black officers claimed that whites were being promoted at a faster rate. Further, about 50 percent of the enlisted men and nearly 30 percent of the black officers maintained that blacks were given more dangerous assignments. Terry also noted that a significant majority of blacks preferred to eat and live with other blacks, thereby pointing to racial polarization in Vietnam.[15]

White officers and enlisted men did not uniformly share these perceptions. For example, only about 2 percent maintained that blacks were given more dangerous assignments; 5 percent of white officers in contrast to 41 percent of the black officers believed that whites were being awarded more medals than blacks. Other data indicated that white enlisted men and officers felt that conditions in Vietnam were worsening, but they seemed to deny changes in racial problems.[16] Apparently, then, perceptual discontinuities exist between blacks and whites regarding conditions in the military system. Moreover, it is undoubtedly true that divergences in viewpoints tend to widen with increases in experiences with the military since socialization patterns among blacks and whites in the military may vary markedly and thereby influence differences in attitudes toward the military.

Structure of Grievance

Divergent attitudes regarding privilege and prerogatives are often reflected in the structure of grievance. Aside from the areas already identified, grievances during the Vietnam period can be categorized into six overlapping areas, namely: (1) social relations, (2) violence and physical confrontations, (3) sensitivity to identity needs, (4) housing and medical services, (5) access to the command structure, and (6) injustices in the military justice system. It is the failure to make appropriate responses to one or more of these intertwining systems of grievances that led to outbreaks of violence that have further had an untoward effect on veterans discharged into civilian life.

Social Relations   On a social level blacks complained that whites were more favored in the dispensation of leave privileges. But whites complained that blacks could avoid punishment for such minor infractions as not wearing a hat, taking more food than allowed on the first serving, or not queuing up properly. Though these were extremely minor complaints, they were important, nonetheless, within the given social context we are discussing. Moreover, then, as now, they have a way of expanding, and under prolonged tensions or unrelieved anxieties only one relatively minor incident, such as a person cutting a line, may trigger violent confrontations.

Both on and off base, many other observers, including the writer, have substantiated the polarization observed by Terry. Cleavages are often indicative of estrangement and alienation between the races rooted in patterns of social relationships observed almost immediately upon induction. Whereas blacks and whites may appear to be totally devoid of prejudice and bigotry under fire and when it is to their mutual advantage to each other, this camaraderie is not necessarily transferred back to the base or to social activities in surrounding communities. In fact, frequently, manifestations of racial intolerance appear in various forms on and off military installations, for example, in the KKK-style cross burnings at Camranh Bay in 1968 on the heels of the death of Martin Luther King as well as at a navy base called Bien Bah Bay. Some whites also wore simulated KKK costumes at Que Viet in South Vietnam as a way of celebrating the death of Dr. King, and they raised Confederate flags on tanks, jeeps, and trucks at Da Nang. At first, aware of the stateside black power movement, blacks responded by making makeshift flags that predictably espoused black power. Then with the formation of black organizations such as the Ju Jus, the Mau Maus, and others that remained nameless, they began to use complicated and intricate handshakes involving the use of the thumb, the palms of hands, and the slapping of fists. These greetings, referred to variously as the "power," the "dap," and the "pound," often angered whites who could not appreciate their symbolic value. Some sought to force discontinuation of black pride greetings. Whenever the opportunity arose, blacks dressed in specific identifying uniforms (e.g., black shirts and gloves), which often symbolized both pride and self-determination.

Violence and Physical Confrontations   Blacks probably had their share of the 550 reported cases of "fraggings" in Vietnam.[17] (Fraggings consist of throwing a hand grenade at a superior officer or a hostile individual. The concept may also refer to almost any other form of attack except face-to-face encounters.) Physical confrontations occurred off base in Saigon, on other bases, in communities in Vietnam as well as Hong Kong, where many service people vacationed on "rest and recuperation," and on several navy ships. The precipitating incident may have been an invasion of blacks into a white club or recreational area or competition for local women or a racial slur or physical attack on either a white person or a black serviceman. Whatever the overt triggering incident was, it was only a superficial manifestation of more deeply rooted conflict. Thus, the violence at Long Binh stockade, where blacks constituted 50 percent of the prison population, may have had its origins in injustices of the military justice system. A riot there resulted in the death of one white person and the destruction of most of the installation. Lives were lost in confrontations at Tenshaw and Piang Tri in Vietnam.

Not only in Vietnam but also in West Germany and in the United States, as we have seen, racial conflicts occurred. There were street brawls in Stuttgart and racial confrontations near Munich, Frankfurt, and elsewhere. But it was during the summer of 1969 that the nation was literally gripped in cataclysmic episodes of racial explosions and violent confrontations at numerous stateside bases. They shook Forts Dix, Lee, Sheridan, Carson, Gordon, Hood, Jackson, Belvoir, Knox, Still, and Bragg.

In the early 1970s, most notable episodes of racial conflict occurred on the U.S.S. *Kitty Hawk,* the U.S.S. *Constellation,* the *Hassayama,* the *Sumter* during 1972, and at Midway Island as well as at the naval correctional facility at Norfolk, Virginia. As a result of a 15-hour brawl on the *Kitty Hawk,* 46 persons were injured, and, at first, all 25 men charged with rioting were black. One white sailor, accused of assaulting a black petty officer, was added to the list approximately ten days after the trial commenced. The navy found it difficult to establish a riot charge by its own definition of the term; consequently, it gave most blacks lesser charges or cleared them altogether. The white sailor was freed after 23 minutes of deliberation by an all-white panel. In the *Constellation* case, perhaps the next most celebrated case, 130 sailors, including 123 blacks, staged a sit-in to protest inequities in the discharge pattern and job assignments on the ship. Essentially, these incidents were triggered by what appeared to be a relatively innocuous event such as stepping on someone's toe or requesting a sailor to take one sandwich at a time. However, they were only symptoms of much more fundamental problems. As a result, the navy has directed the implementation of major reforms.

Identity Needs During the Vietnam period, blacks have often complained, especially since the new thrust toward black identity and black pride, that the military was not responsive to its needs. Specifically, the food in the dining hall was not satisfactory, the post exchanges (PXs) did not carry black literature or "rakes" for Afro hair and cosmetic supplies, or the barbers did not know how to style the hair of black people. All branches of the armed services, at home and abroad, made substantial efforts to meet the demands for such supplies and facilities. They added soul music to juke boxes; menus included soul food; PXs stocked black magazines such as *Ebony, Jet,* and *Tan,* Afro hair products and cosmetics used by blacks, and wearing apparel such as dashikis and jewelry, including bracelets and black crosses. The Army and Air Force Exchange Service (AAFES) sent barbers to innumerable installations in Europe and Asia, particularly to teach local barbers how to style the hair of blacks in military service. In this manner many apparent sources of unrest were confronted.

Housing and Medical Services   It has been somewhat more difficult to control the responses of local citizens to blacks in the military, especially in the area of housing. In West Germany blacks seem to have experienced the greatest difficulties in finding suitable housing accommodations off base. This is attributed to the breakdown of those existing directives and regulations concerning listings of discriminating renters and owners. Housing discrimination persists in some instances because the command structure fails to follow through on registered complaints. And in other instances officials acquiesce to local practices that effectively discriminate against blacks in housing.[18] Perhaps to avoid problems the American government allegedly acquiesced to demands by the government of Iceland against sending blacks to NATO bases in that country.[19]

Insensitivity to the medical needs of blacks still persists to some degree. Except for the air force, the military has shown no consistent interest in research on sickle-cell anemia, which affects blacks almost exclusively. Nor has it uniformly recognized that pseudofolliculitis, exaggerated shaving bumps cured only by wearing a beard, affects a substantial proportion of black men. The military (except the air force) refuses to accept, for medical reasons, not shaving long enough to cure the condition.[20]

The Command Structure

The military power structure is largely pyramidal and is characterized by a command structure that is so rigidly stratified that its subordinates are able to subvert and sabotage the mandates of those at its top. As a consequence, military personnel, in general, black and white, do not feel that they have access to the decision-making apparatus. Many grievances go unheeded, and many directives such as the highly publicized Z-grams issued by the former chief officer of the navy, Admiral Elmo R. Zumwalt, Jr., reportedly fall short of implementation. As a result, planned improvements in the status and conditions of personnel are not made as rapidly as anticipated, if they are made at all. Moreover, all branches of the service now have an Equal Opportunity (EO) officer of some kind, but even these officers do not have direct access to those having ultimate responsibility for decision making. At the level of the Pentagon, for example, the EO officer is often no higher than a deputy assistant secretary rather than an assistant secretary, which means that the stratification system denies direct access to the Secretary of Defense. He must always transmit ideas, programs, and strategies for change through an intermediary. The system, therefore, makes lower-level servicemen even farther removed from the important functionaries in the chain of command. Therefore, many come to feel that no one in the system cares. The presence of black officers does not necessarily alleviate tensions created by strains between the enlistees and officials in the chain of command. Perceptions play a major role in determining the effectiveness of black officers with black enlistees as well as influencing the latter's assessments of black officers. These perceptions may be selectively influenced by age grades, the degree to which the officer is self-conscious of his status difference and his ability to maximize the advantages of status, his sense of objectivity, and, in sum, how he is regarded by the black enlistees (that is, is he an "oreo," a "tom," "a committed black," or "strictly a military man").

The Military Justice System

It is in the structure of the military justice system, however, that we find the preponderance of problems confronting blacks, both those at present in the military and those who are veterans. It is estimated that of the nearly 500,000 Vietnam veterans who returned to the United States with less than honorable discharges about 200,000 were black. "Less than honorable discharges" is a composite term for all persons discharged from the armed forces with a classification of one of three types of discharges: (1) undesirable, (2) bad conduct, and (3) dishonorable. Bad conduct and dishonorable discharges are issued as a consequence of sentences of Special and General Court-martial.[21] The fourth and fifth types of discharges issued by the armed forces are "honorable" and "general" discharges. These types are granted through administrative action, most frequently by a commanding officer. As a result of this tremendous latitude given to commanding officers to render administrative military discharges, opportunities for bias to dictate decisions with respect to the type of discharge granted are immense.

Although it cannot be claimed that bias is always the dominant factor in the types of military discharges received by blacks, it is evident that blacks are overrepresented in the number of recipients of less than honorable discharges. For instance, in 1972 near the end of the Vietnam War, black veterans received about one-third (32.6 percent) of the dishonorable discharges, one-fifth (20.7 percent) of the bad conduct discharges, and approximately one-sixth (16.1 percent) of the general discharges. Yet, blacks comprised only 12.6 percent of the military.[22]

The problem of military justice is even broader for it embraces the entire fabric of the justice system, including who has the likelihood of being charged with an offense, the nature of behavior classified as offensive, and the whole process of administering justice. Under Article 15 of the military code, officers may arbitrarily exact nonjudicial punishments, and service personnel may also accept these punishments without appearing for a court-martial. Unfortunately, many servicemen and servicewomen do not realize that an accumulation of such nonjudicial punishments may result in dismissal from service on the grounds of unsuitability for continued service. Further, it may be only after they are discharged that they came to realize that the type of discharge a person possesses is of inestimable significance for adjustment as a veteran, whether in terms of access to employment or in terms of the public's perception of the veteran. Even then, they may not realize how difficult it is to remove the stigma of a bad discharge.

During the Vietnam period, a disproportionate number of blacks received Article 15 punishments. For example, by June 30, 1972, blacks had received more than a quarter (25.5 percent) of all nonjudicial punishments meted out in the armed forces. Moreover, in terms of specific Article 15 punishments, almost three-fourths of blacks (71.7 percent) in comparison to almost two-thirds (63.1 percent) of all whites who were AWOL received Article 15 punishments during the reporting period.[23]

Similar conditions existed regarding pretrial confinements. The proportion of blacks placed in pretrial confinement was greater (21.2 percent) than their percentage in the total armed services (13.1 percent). Discrepancies varied markedly from service to service. Blacks were also more likely to remain in pretrial confinement five days longer on the average than white enlisted men throughout the service, and white military personnel were much more likely to have their pretrial confinement terminated without any form of judicial or disciplinary action.[24] In many cases in Vietnam and West Germany blacks were held in pretrial confinement for up to 30 days on such trivial charges as having their hair too long or without ever having formal charges made against them.[25]

It is the accumulation of Article 15 offenses resulting in nonhonorable or less than honorable discharges that is plaguing Vietnam veterans today. Across the board, from service to service, blacks receive a far greater share of such discharges than their proportions in each branch of the service would normally suggest. In contrast to white servicemen, the proportion varies from roughly five times the rate for white servicemen in the air force (10.3 percent blacks vs. 2.8 percent whites) to almost twice as many blacks than whites in the army (11.3 percent vs. 6.2 percent white), the navy (17.5 percent black vs. 9.8 percent white), and the marines (22.4 percent black vs. 13.4 percent white). However, it is in the marines that one observes that almost one-quarter (or 22.4 percent) of all blacks were discharged nonhonorably in the 1971–1972 period.[26] Many of them are the same men whose AFQT scores were so low as to place them in low-level jobs in the military, and they are less prepared to find jobs upon reentry into civilian life. The stigma of a bad discharge compounds the problem, since it inevitably means that they are the last to be hired and the first to be fired during periods of economic strain. Thus men who went into the service to obtain a marketable skill that would give them a modicum of upward mobility in civilian life now sense a deep frustration due to unfulfilled expectations. All too frequently, they come to feel that they have risked their lives and endured harassment or discrimination by superior officers for unfulfilled expectations in both the military life and the civilian life.

PROBLEMS OF VIETNAM VETERANS

The problems experienced by Vietnam veterans irrespective of race or ethnicity were enormous. However, racial barriers to equal opportunity have had a profound impact on black veterans of the Vietnam War. They found themselves trapped in a multitude of adjustment problems encompassing a broad range of social and psychological conditions. Aside from the difficulties imposed by an inordinate number of less than honorable discharges, they faced a staggering unemployment rate and inadequate access to higher education.

Unemployment

During the 1970s, unemployment among black Vietnam veterans reached a crisis proportion. The problem was especially acute for those veterans in the 20 to 24 age cohort, those with limited education and few marketable skills, as well as those who carried nonhonorable discharges. For instance, among minority veterans between the ages of 20 and 24, most of whom were black, the unemployment rate in the final quarter of 1973 was 23.2 percent. By comparison, the unemployment rate for their nonveteran counterparts was 14.1 percent at that time.[27] Further, data from the Bureau of Labor Statistics showed that the proportion of black unemployed veterans was generally twice as high as that for white Vietnam veterans. This condition conformed to the profile of the regular nonveteran population.

Undoubtedly, the unemployment situation helps to explain why blacks have tended to reenlist in higher ratios than has been the case of whites since 1970.[28] The reenlistment rate among blacks in all branches of the military is about 36 percent compared to 25 percent for white military personnel in all branches of the armed forces.[29] First-term reenlistments for all races tend to increase during periods of economic decline (e.g., periods of recession when civilian unemployment is high), and to be higher among members of the army than among those in other branches of the military.[30] In 1973 the first-term reenlistment rate reported by the Department of Defense (DoD) for all branches of the military was 24 percent and 38 percent for the army (it was only 13 percent for the Marine Corps). During the recession of 1975, DoD overall reenlistment rose to 37 percent while that for the army increased only slightly to 39 percent, but reenlistment in the Marine Corps rose sharply to 20 percent. In 1981 when the unemployment rate was 7.8 percent for whites and 17.1 percent for blacks, reenlistments for DoD overall was 43 percent while in the army the rate was 55 percent. The Marines had a 27 percent rate.[31]

Although reenlistments helped to alleviate the unemployment problem among some black veterans, severe economic disabilities and prolonged hardships were often the plight of those veterans who, during much of the 1970s and into the 1980s, either did not or could not, because of less than honorable discharges, opt for that possibility. Countless numbers of black veterans, those with or without honorable discharges, joined the swelling ranks of the black discouraged workers, dismayed by protracted failure to find work. They were disillusioned by assaults on their sense of well-being, precipitated by what many regarded as an impregnable barrier of a society hostile to those stigmatized by service in Vietnam—a society which tended to categorize Vietnam veterans as social misfits, drug addicts, somewhat mentally suspect, and possibly as traitors to the philosophical position that Americans had neither right nor responsibility to intrude into the internal affairs of another country. These situations added substantially to the general malaise and alienation pervasive among Vietnam veterans.

Education

With respect to training and education, the Vietnam experience was a singular disappointment to many black Americans. This problem was especially found among those persons who had expected to leave the military with marketable skills and those who thought they would be able to obtain military benefits sufficient to achieve more formal education. The claim is often made that "veterans' benefits and assistance are grossly inadequate" to facilitate the kind of upward mobility that the black veteran imagined possible during actual service.[32] As a consequence of the general lack of training programs, many blacks were forced into semi-skilled and unskilled jobs, or were unemployed while continuing to hope that work would become available.[33] Perhaps they would be in more propitious circumstances if they had received marketable skills while in the service instead of being relegated disproportionately to combat and service divisions, and if so many employers in the private sector did not perceive Vietnam veterans as incurable "junkies."

The Concerned Veterans from Vietnam was organized in 1968 to assist black veterans in obtaining jobs and housing; however, because a large proportion of them have received less than honorable discharges and are, therefore, unable to locate suitable jobs, the Concerned Veterans are now directing their primary attention toward changes in military justice. The Veterans Administration operates the OUTREACH program, which is designed to assist veterans in, among other things, finding employment. The National Urban League mounted a multimillion dollar program for supporting on-the-job training programs involving veterans in 32 cities, and the Opportunities Industrialization Centers also include veterans in their programs. With their collective assistance thousands of jobs have been located for veterans.

It is extremely difficult for the Vietnam veteran who is a college aspirant to pursue a college education unless he has saved a substantial part of his military pay or is able to obtain some form of outside aid, whether from family or public or private financial resources. The GI benefits provided the current veterans clearly are not as adequate as those provided the veterans of World War II, for example. GIs today receive benefits of $4,004 if they have no dependents, $5,568 with one dependent, and up to $5,805 with two dependents. Nevertheless, by 1974, a million and a half educationally disadvantaged veterans—that is, high school drop-outs— had received precollege training under the GI bill then in force. Others do have the financial resources available and have completed college and professional training.

Aside from widespread unemployment and educational needs, many Vietnam veterans often experience mental, physical, emotional, and morale problems. (The next chapter also deals with this.) The Vietnam War was highly controversial almost from its inception, becoming an issue that divided the nation politically and emotionally as American involvement escalated. Except for the prisoners of war, veterans of this war, unlike veterans of any previous war, did not return to this country honored by ticker-tape parades on Fifth Avenue, Wall Street, or down Main Street, U.S.A. An uncompassionate federal government has done little or nothing to compensate the average GI for services rendered in a hated war. Many of them are ashamed of their participation and often attempt to disappear into the masses for fear of suffering the fate of the socially and politically outcast. Many suffered anxieties brought on by various forms of reentry crisis—whether mental, physical, emotional, or moral. In recent years, attention has been focused on the prevalence of a condition called posttraumatic stress disorder which has affected Vietnam veterans. Yet, a significant number of veterans were able to make a suitable adjustment upon returning to the United States.

In fact, in recent years, a larger body of research has shown that posttraumatic stress syndrome is far more widespread among Vietnam veterans than previously assumed. One example is a 1988 study by Steven D. Stellman sponsored by the American Legion. This longitudinal five-year study of 6,810 Legionnaires focused on combat veterans of the Vietnam War. Stellman's study revealed that there was a strong association between heavy combat duty and the occurrence of psychological and other health disorders. These problems were found among two-thirds of all veterans who had experienced heavy combat duty. Earlier studies of 3 million veterans indicated that only 15 percent of the Vietnam veterans suffered from this disorder or from what people in earlier wars had labeled "combat fatigue." Stellman's data showed that the problem is far more severe and widespread and that the disorder lasts substantially longer than previously projected. In addition, Stellman's research substantiated previous research which showed that Vietnam veterans who experienced heavy combat duty are at greater risk for personal alienation, divorce, and sexual problems. With respect to blacks specifically, the *Report of the Working Group on Black Vietnam Veterans* suggests that since a higher proportion of blacks than whites received heavy combat duty, the problems of posttraumatic stress and related health and social problems are significantly greater among black Vietnam veterans.[34]

THE POST-VIETNAM PERIOD

The All-Volunteer Forces and Blacks

The All-Volunteer Forces (AVF) was created in 1973 with the abolition of mandatory military conscription. In that year, the active United States forces consisted of 2,241,200 men and women. Thereafter, the total number of persons in the new AVF declined steadily until 1980 when a slight increase in participants in the military services was reported by the DoD. More specifically, between 1974 and 1979, the number of persons in the military declined from 2,150,600 to 2,013,200. In 1980, hwever, as the unemployment situation worsened in the United States, the number of persons in the AVF rose to 2,036,700. By March 1982, the total number of men and women on active duty in the military reached 2,106,925. Blacks composed approximately one-fifth (19.8 percent) of all persons on active duty in the United States military.[35]

In the same period, the total number of black enlistees increased steadily throughout the 1970s and paralleled closely the growing unemployment crisis experienced by young blacks in the United States. In absolute numbers, there were 236,000 in 1974, a slight decline in 1975, and an increase in 1977 to 278,900 as a mild recovery from the recession occurred. The enlistment of blacks made a sharp upturn in 1977 when the total number of blacks in the military stood at 291,800, and by 1980, there were 347,000 blacks enlisted in the four major branches of the military. In 1981, when the unemployment rate among blacks was in excess of 17 percent and that of black teenagers approximated 50 percent, 352,348 (or 21.6 percent of the total) black men and 45,056 (or 27.7 percent of the total) black women were enlisted in the U.S. military.[36] By March 1983, the total number of blacks in the military had climbed to an apparent peacetime high of 419,778 which undoubtedly reflected the worsening and precarious situation of black Americans in the civilian economy. The overwhelming majority of blacks continue to select and be selected by the army which is followed in order by the air force, the navy, and then the Marine Corps. In short, there is a close correlation between economic downturns for blacks in the general population and increases in enlistments among thousands of young black men and women who volunteer for the military service. They perceive military service as a reasonable alternative to civilian unemployment and to the social and economic disabilities that unemployment entails.

As of March 1989, the active duty military force consisted of 2,115,773. Of that number 400,094 (22.2 percent) were black enlisted men and women and 20,421 (6.7 percent) were black officers.[37]

Blacks are unequally distributed among the four branches of the military. (The following figures do not include blacks in the Coast Guard since it is under the administration of the Department of Transportation.) In

1983, blacks composed 33.2 percent of the Army; however, by March 1989, that proportion had fallen to 30.7 percent. Nevertheless, blacks, who compose roughly 12 percent of the U. S. population, are significantly overrepresented in the U. S. Army. In 1989, 200,912 black men and women were serving in the Army. In contrast to 1983, when they represented 22 percent of the Marines, by 1989, blacks constituted 20.5 percent (36,565) of the Marines. However, in an absolute sense, blacks are more likely to serve in either the Navy or the Air Force than they are to serve in the Marines. In 1989, 81,633 blacks were serving in the Air Force, constituting 17.4 percent of the total number of enlistees in that branch of military service. In the Navy, 80,984 (16 percent) of its members were black in 1989.[38] As previously stated, a major reason for the overrepresentation of blacks in the military, aside from high unemployment in the civilian population, is the fact that blacks reenlist at higher rates than whites.[39]

The navy has been the most resistant of all military branches to the inclusion of blacks, despite their qualifications and ability to perform well on standardized tests. The problem was so severe that in 1979 both the NAACP and the American Civil Liberties Union charged the navy with racial discrimination and operating a policy of white preference.[40]

Even more recently, the problem of bias in the navy was the subject of a major internal investigation by the navy itself. This report found evidence of widespread, though often subtle, bias directed against blacks, Hispanics, and other minorities. This bias took one or more of several forms: (1) lower marks on their evaluations and fitness reports against sailors and officers—a most serious matter since such reports become a part of their permanent record and are carefully appraised with respect to promotions; (2) avoidance of minority areas or minority publications for recruitment advertisements as a method of reducing the number of minority volunteers for the navy; (3) failure to incorporate racial and ethnic equality in training and to provide equality of access to technical fields once in the navy; (4) failure to provide equal opportunity training for officers so as to enhance their chances for promotion; (5) failure to provide opportunities for minority officers to attain prestigious positions in the navy; (6) failure to inform blacks and Hispanics of how to succeed in the military; (7) perpetuating a nearly all-white aviation and submarine duty force by excluding them from the training required to qualify for such duties; (8) a slower pace of promotion of blacks and Hispanics; (9) racial slurs and jokes directed at blacks and Hispanic sailors and officers; and (10) a general hostile atmosphere in the navy that is experienced by blacks and other minorities.[41]

It was also reported that, as a result of exclusion from the technical fields, blacks are ghettoized in some areas such as storekeepers, 33 percent of whom are black. By contrast, only 4.4 percent of the electronic technicians are black. Blacks and Hispanics are also far less likely than whites to be assigned to the Navy headquarters or as aides to admirals. As a result of this report, prepared by 24 navy men and women, Admiral Carlisle A. H. Trost accepted the 75 proposed changes for amelioration of the racial bias problem in the navy.[42]

Inequality in the distribution of blacks in the various branches of the military is matched by their maldistribution by occupational specialization. Specifically, blacks are "heavily represented in the combat specialties" and inadequately represented in other areas, especially in some of the technical specialties. In fact, 40 percent of all soldiers on "front-line duty" in the Second Division in Korea were black in 1982.[43] For instance, Butler reported in 1982 that 19.6 percent of all black enlisted men were employed in the infantry, gun crews, and as seaman specialists. Only 13.9 percent of white enlistees were so employed. About one-fifth (20.5 percent) of all white male enlistees were employed in "functional support and administration." Approximately 12 percent of black male enlistees and 8.2 percent of white male enlistees were employed as service and supply handlers. On the other hand, 11.1 percent of white male enlistees, compared to only 4.4 percent of black male enlistees were employed as electric equipment repairmen, 22.9 percent of white and 17.1 percent of black male enlistees had as their principal occupation the position of electrical/mechanical equipment repairmen. White male enlistees were more frequently found in other technical and allied specialists occupations as craftsmen and in "non-occupational training" than were black enlistees.[44]

This maldistribution of blacks in occupational categories has been attributed to: (1) racial discrimination in the selection process, as was the case during the Vietnam period; (2) lower test scores achieved by blacks on the Armed Forces Qualification Test (AFQT); (3) what Alvin Schenixer labels the "macho factor," which refers to the penchant for many blacks to volunteer for such "elite" combat units as the Airborne and Ranger whose reputation for danger and impressive uniforms seem appealing to their members, and (4) the financial rewards associated with "high-risk units."[45]

Black Officers in the Military System

Although blacks compose 22.2 percent of the military, they represent only 6.7 percent of its officers. However, this percentage is a modest gain over the 4.9 percent black officers observed in 1981. In 1989, they comprised 10.5 percent (11,192) of Army officers; 5.4 percent (5,670) of Air Force officers; 4.9 percent (983) of Marine officers; and 3.6 percent (2,576) of all officers in the U. S. Navy.[46] Although President Bush elevated General Colin Powell to the highest ranking position in the American military, chairman of the Joint Chiefs of Staff, it is difficult to determine the degree to which his presence in that position will force military personnel to promote more deserving blacks or if the status quo will remain. Improvements in the proportion of blacks among the officer ranks may occur if the military promotes more blacks from the noncommissioned ranks, and if more blacks are commissioned as officers in ROTC programs at black and white colleges, and if current blacks below the rank of brigadier general are promoted in all branches of the military.[47]

CURRENT RACIAL ISSUES IN THE MILITARY

In the 1980s, perhaps the most critical issues in the military with implications for race relations focused on three primary areas: (1) the racial composition of the military, especially the army, and what this supposedly portends for combat readiness; (2) the quality of the military; and (3) attitudes of the allied nations, especially members of the NATO alliance, toward the racial composition of the American military. Each of these factors has special implications for race relations in the military. All were addressed in a recent study by the Brookings Institution, and during a 1982 symposium on "Blacks in the Military" sponsored by the Washington, D.C.-based Joint Center for Political Studies.[48]

Racial Composition

The All-Volunteer Force (AVF) has been criticized for being "too black." This charge is levied particularly at the army since about one-third of its members are black. In addition, with the exception of the navy, blacks are overrepresented in all other branches of the U.S. military. Critics of the racial composition of the AVF raise doubts about the degree to which black Americans, many of whom have been direct victims of racism, prejudice, and discrimination in the United States, can be counted on to defend the country in times of military conflict. Others cast their criticisms in terms which sometimes mask covert racism when they question the capacity of blacks to perform important leadership roles in combat situations. Still others have expressed serious concern about the racial makeup of the military because of the undue burden placed upon minority youth to defend the nation and the concomitant underrepresentation of the white middle class, particularly, in the military. These observers envision a repetition of the Vietnam era in which the white middle class was especially underrepresented in combat units in Vietnam while blacks, other racial minorities, and poor whites tended to be overrepresented in front-line units. In their view, the most effective remedy for this imbalanced situation is to require some form of universal national service for all young Americans.[49]

Given the current racial composition of the military, the Brookings Institution 1982 study estimated that in the event of a war involving ground conflict, blacks would, indeed, sustain from 30 to 50 percent of all casualties initially inflicted upon the United States. That ratio would be, therefore, significantly higher than the casualty rate experienced by blacks at the height of the Vietnam War. Not only would that situation pose major problems within the military itself, it would probably have tragic consequences among civilians.[50]

Quality of the Military

The issue of racial composition is often used as a euphemism for arguments relative to quality within the military. Persons who raise this concern often point to the tendency of blacks to score lower on various tests such as the AFQT, the high school drop-out and completion rates, and other black-white discrepancies in objective measures of academic achievement. While blacks as a group do score lower than whites as a group on most objective tests, Schenixer's data revealed that the average black enlistee has a "higher educational attainment level" than do average white enlistees. He showed, for instance, that of all blacks recruited for the army in 1981, 90.6 percent of them, compared to 76.3 percent of white enlistees, had successfully completed high school. Ten years earlier, in 1971, among persons in the military, whites had achieved a higher level of educational attainment than blacks.[51] In 1983 about 78 percent of all black and 65 percent of all white officers had completed college.[52] As a result of such findings, the Pentagon vehemently denies allegations that the military enlistees are poorly qualified; rather, it maintains that the men and women of the military compare quite favorably with their counterparts in the civilian population with respect to high school completion rates and performance on standardized tests.

Attitudes of NATO Allies Toward Blacks

Opposition and negativism raised about the racial composition of the military are not confined to the United States. Some allied nations, especially those in continental Europe such as West Germany, have "grave concern" about the growing black presence in the American military forces sent to their countries. Gilliam reported that the West Germans have complained about "cultural conflicts" between themselves and blacks as well as the ability of the U.S. Army, composed of a 33 percent black population, to defend Germany and other nations in Western Europe in times of conflict.[53] Given the fact of intense racial hostility directed against blacks by many citizens of West Germany and the reported difficulties that blacks have had in finding off-base housing there, as well as the problematic social relations encountered by many blacks throughout West Germany, it is not unreasonable to conclude that much of the concern with the so-called quality issue actually masks a resurgence of notions of racial superiority prevalent among many Europeans toward black Americans. Since the defense of Western Europe in times of impending and actual conflict depends so heavily upon anAmerican military presence, it is imperative for the United States to stand firm on a policy of nondiscrimination—a policy that does not accommodate any form of

racial prejudice or bigotry. Even though they also employ equal employment opportunity (EEOC) officers, in 1982 blacks in Germany were angered by the KKK philosophy expressed by the military's EEOC officer of
the U.S. Army Engineer Division.[54]

Other Issues

With the growing awareness of problems relative to prejudice, discrimination, and the opportunity structure, all branches of the military are apparently attempting to effect significant internal change. They have undertaken massive recruitment drives, through advertisements in the black
press, for example, which point to the military as an employment alternative to the problems of civilian life. These advertisements in the print and
electronic media and recruiters at important meetings of predominantly
black organizations describe in detail the available opportunities for specialty training in the military.

In addition, the various service academies are making special efforts
to increase the number of black male and female cadets who, once accepted, are entitled to four years of free education. However, the success
of recruitment programs, such as that of the U.S. Coast Guard Academy,
was threatened by cutbacks in appropriations by the Reagan Administration. In that academy, the position of Minority Recruitment Officer was a
major casualty of the cutbacks imposed by the Reagan budget in 1982. In
1983 the 16 blacks made up only 1 percent of the 889 cadets at the Coast
Guard Academy, compared to about 2.5 percent in 1978. A major problem
here is that blacks tend to have an unusually high dropout rate from the
Coast Guard Academy. The number of blacks in other academies improved between 1968 and 1985. In 1968 only 10 black cadets were in the
graduating class of the U.S. Military Academy at West Point, 4 at the Naval
Academy, and 5 at the Air Force Academy. By 1980, the graduating classes
consisted of 29, 48, and 37 blacks from the Military, Naval, and Air Force
academies, respectively. The 1985 class consisted of 75 black men and
women at the Military Academy, 49 black men and women at the Naval
Academy, and 115 black men and women at the U.S. Air Force Academy.[55]

The air force and the navy have become considerably more aggressive
in the recruitment of blacks. They have initiated attractive scholarship
programs in order to induce more blacks to enlist in these services. The
army initiated many activities of this sort in the late 1970s when Clifford
Alexander, Jr., a black American, served as Secretary of the Army.

To improve race relations and reduce interracial conflict the Department of Defense and all branches of the services have established special
programs, such as leadership training, race relations seminars, and encounter groups dealing with intergroup tensions, throughout the United
States and in some overseas posts. The power structure of the military is
undergoing modest changes, as represented by the proportion of black

officers in the various branches of the military in 1989, compared to the situation a decade earlier. However, blacks remain grossly underrepresented in the leadership structure. And, further, it will perhaps require far more radical alterations of greater substance to create a more democratic structure in the American military system than exists at the present time. However, unwavering commitment and implementation of governmental policies in the military that help to eliminate barriers to equal participation may have positive carry-over consequences for creating a more just civilian social system.

NOTES

1. Among the more extensive studies of blacks in the military are Bernard C. Nalty and Morris J. McGregor (eds.), *Blacks in the Military: Essential Documents* (Wilmington, Del: Scholarly Resources, Inc., 1981); Harry A. Ploski and James Williams (eds.), *The Negro Almanac: Reference Work on The Afro-American,* 4th ed. (New York: John Wiley and Sons, 1982); Ronald W. Perry, *Racial Discrimination and Military Justice* (New York: Frederick A. Praeger, 1976); Richard Stillman, *Integration of the Negro in the U.S. Armed Forces* (New York: Frederick A. Praeger, 1968); Lerone Bennett, *Before the Mayflower,* 4th ed. (Chicago: Johnson Publishing Company, 1969), Benjamin Quarles, *The Black American* (Glenview, Ill.: Scott Foresman & Co., 1967), and Jay David and Elaine Crane (eds.), *The Black Soldier From the American Revolution to Vietnam* (New York: William Morrow and Company, 1971). I have relied heavily upon their data.
2. Cf. Stillman, *op. cit.,* p. 8, and John Hope Franklin, *From Slavery to Freedom* (New York: Alfred A. Knopf, 1952), p. 290.
3. Franklin, *ibid.*
4. Frank N. Schubert, "Black Soldiers and the White Frontier: Some Factors Influencing Race Relations," *Phylon: The Journal of Race Relations,* 32 (Winter 1971): 410–416.
5. Lewis N. Wynne, "Brownsville: The Reaction of the Negro Press," *Phylon: The Journal of Race Relations* 32 (Summer 1972): 153–160.
6. For an excellent discussion of these issues and the following cf. Ploski and Williams, *op. cit.,* pp. 789–903; Peter G. Nordie, et al., *Improving Race Relations in the Army* (McLean, Va: Human Sciences Research Center, Inc., 1972), p. 68; and Franklin, *op. cit.,* p. 467.
7. *Ibid.,* and see Bennett, *op. cit.*
8. Franklin, *op. cit.,* pp. 465–467.
9. Samuel Stouffer's classic study of the American soldier illustrates this point with highly significant data. Cf. Samuel Stouffer, *The American Soldier: Adjustments During Army Life,* Vol. 1 (Princeton, N.J.: Princeton University Press, 1949).
10. Nordie, *op. cit.,* p. 73
11. Cf. Charles Moskos, Jr., "Deliberate Change: Race Relations in the Armed Forces," in Russell Endo and William Strawbridge (eds.), *Perspectives on Black America* (Englewood Cliffs, N.J.: Prentice-Hall, 1973), p. 62, and Charles Mos-

kos, Jr., "Racial Integration in the Armed Forces," *American Journal of Sociology,* 72 (September 1966): 133–148.

12. Lewis C. Olive, Jr., "Duty, Honor, Country But No Reward," *The Urban League News,* 3 (April 1973):31.

13. These are Department of Defense figures cited in the hearings sponsored by the Congressional Black Caucus. See "Racism in the Military," *Congressional Record,* Vol. 118, No. 166, Part II (Washington, D.C.: U.S. Congress), October 14, 1972.

14. Wallace Terry, *The Bloods: The Black Soldier in Vietnam* (New York: Viking Press, 1973).

15. *Ibid.*

16. *Ibid.*

17. *Congressional Record, op. cit.*

18. *Ibid.*

19. *Ibid.*

20. *Ibid.*

21. Robert L. Hill, "Minority Vets at a Deadend," *Focus* 3:2 (December 1974): 4–5.

22. Cf. *Ibid,* and Perry, *op. cit., passim.*

23. Gilbert Ware, "The Spider Web and Racism in the Armed Forces," *The Urban League News,* 3 (April 1972): 5.

24. *Ibid.*

25. *Ibid.*

26. These figures were provided by the National Urban League Research Department and are based upon data in the "Administrative Discharges Study," *Task Force on the Administration of Military Justice in the Armed Forces,* October 13, 1972.

27. Hill, *op. cit.,* p. 4.

28. *Ibid.*

29. Data provided by the Defense Manpower Data Center of the Pentagon.

30. *Defense 82, Special Almanac Issue* (Arlington, Va: American Forces Information Service, 1982), p. 30.

31. *Ibid.*

32. Hill, *op. cit.*

33. These studies were prepared by the Urban League Research Department and from data in the U.S. Department of Defense Report, *The Negro in the Armed Forces: A Statistical Factbook,* 1971.

34. Stallman's research is quoted in Ben A. Franklin, "Study Finds Vietnam Combat Affecting Veteran's Health," *New York Times* (November 12, 1988), p. 7. See also Readjustment Counseling Service, *Report of the Working Group on Black Vietnam Veterans* (Washington, D. C.: Readjustment Counseling Service, Undated, circa 1987).

35. Cf. *Defense 82,* pp. 24,30, and Joint Center for Political Studies, "Blacks and The Military," *Focus* (August 1982): 1–4.

36. Cf. *ibid.* and *Black Enterprise* (October 1982), p. 36.

37. The Department of Defense, *Defense 89: Almanac* (Washington, D. C.: U. S. Department of Defense, 1989), pp. 24,30 and Marc DeFrancis, "Who Defends America? Race, Sex and Class in the Armed Forces," *Focus* (March 1989):7.

38. *Defense 89,* p. 30.

39. Cf. *Defense 82* and *Black Enterprise* (October 1982), p. 36.

40. Ploski and Williams, *op. cit.,* p. 316.

41. Richard Halloran, "Wide Bias Against Minorities in Navy," *New York Times* (December 20, 1988), p. A20.
42. *Ibid.*
43. Joint Center for Political Studies, *op. cit.,* p. 4.
44. Cited in *ibid.,* pp. 3–4.
45. *Ibid.*
46. *Defense 89,* p. 30.
47. *Op. cit.,* p. 4.
48. Cf. Martin Binkin, Alvin Schenixer et al., *Blacks and the Military* (Washington, D.C.: Brookings Institution, 1982), and Joint Center for Political Studies, *op. cit.*
49. Joint Center for Political Studies, *ibid.*
50. Binkin, et al., *op. cit.*
51. Binkin, et al. *op. cit.,* p. 3.
52. Data provided by the Defense Manpower Data Center of the Pentagon.
53. Dorothy Gillman, "Blacks in the Army: A Matter of Necessity," *Black Enterprise,* (October 1982): 31.
54. Ploski and Williams, *op. cit.,* p. 856.
55. *Ibid.,* pp. 876–886.

Chapter
11

The Health of Black Americans

*I*n a society that is stratified along race and class lines, health status is a function of one's position in the social structure. This observation is consistent with the position taken by Wilkinson who argues that structural positions regarding such matters as health status reflect invidious ranking along racial lines.[1] Inasmuch as blacks rank lower than whites in the American stratification system, while morally unacceptable, it is a reality that health problems among blacks are much more severe than they are within the white population. In other words, as Reed and associates point out, blacks suffer an enormous disadvantage in health status, compared to whites in the United States.[2] Blacks are at greater risk throughout their life span. They do not live as long as whites; because of this inequality in life expectancy, 59,000 more deaths occur in the black population than would occur if the races were equal in life expectancy.[3] This observation holds regardless of the measure employed to determine mortality rates.[4]

Despite significant improvements in the health conditions of Americans as a whole, most researchers, policy-makers, and ordinary citizens seem to agree that America is suffering from a major health crisis. That crisis is evident not only in the prevalence of certain diseases, like the widening spread of Acquired Immune Deficiency Syndrome (AIDS), but in the limited access of millions of Americans to adequate health care, maldistribution of health-care providers, the 37 million Americans without health insurance, and inability to pay for health care that is available in nearby areas. These problems are particularly exacerbated for blacks because of the untoward conditions experienced by an inordinate proportion of the black population as discussed in earlier chapters. Among these conditions are extremes of unemployment and poverty, lower annual incomes for individuals and families compared to the wages received by whites, poorer housing and discrimination in housing that takes its toll on the mental health of its victims, undercapitalization of black businesses that makes it difficult for those enterprises to provide job opportunities for large numbers of blacks, and daily encounters with prejudice and discrimination which reinforce the alienation and disenchantment that many minorities feel in a society dominated by white persons.

In this chapter, the focus is on the health conditions of black Americans and some factors that help explain differentials in health status. Racial differences, as discussed below, occur in every aspect of health; that is, from infant mortality to life expectancy to death. The widening gap between blacks and whites is observed in all indices of health.

INFANT MORTALITY

Although the infant mortality rate within the United States has declined rapidly over the past decades, the United States still ranks 22nd in the world in the survival rate of children. Despite improvements in the infant mortality rates for all Americans and in the infant mortality rates of blacks, a black child is twice as likely to die before reaching the end of the first year of life as a white child in the United States. Between 1960 and 1988, the infant mortality rate among white infants fell from 22.9/1,000 live births to 8.9/1,000 live births. Over the same period, black infant mortality dropped from 44.3 to 18/1,000 live births. The rate for whites and blacks declined rapidly between 1960 and 1980 when the decline was from 22.9 to 11.0 for whites and from 44.3 to 21.4 for blacks.[5] During the 1980s, when programs to protect the lives and welfare of women, infants, and children were mercilessly slashed by the Reagan Administration, the declines in infant mortality were slowed. In some cities, such as Washington, D. C., and Detroit, the infant mortality rate of black babies is higher than that found in some Central American developing nations. Reed's examination of racial differentials in infant mortality led him to conclude that, if black and white rates were the same, at least some 6,000 additional black babies would survive each year.[6]

The eight leading causes of death among infants are, in order: (1) birth defects (20.5%); (2) low birth weight/prematurity/respiratory stress syndrome (17.7%); (3) sudden infant death syndrome or SIDS (13.6%); (4) maternal complications including premature labor (3.7%); (5) oxygen shortage at birth (2.5%); infections excluding pneumonia/influenza and sexually transmitted diseases or STDs (2.4%); (6) falls, poisoning, and other unintentional injuries (2.3%); (7) placenta complications (2.1%); and (8) pneumonia/influenza (1.7%).[7] Although birth defects are the leading cause of infant deaths, developmental disabilities (low birth weights) seem to more greatly differentiate along racial lines. More than 250,000 babies are born at a low weight of 5 ½ pounds or less, and black infants are twice as likely as white infants to be low-weight babies.[8] This racial disparity in birth weights and in infant mortality, in general, may be explained by poverty, low income, poor prenatal care, lack of information about health care during pregnancy, and poor nutrition.[9] A common explanation for racial differences in the occurrence of low-weight births is the higher rate of teenage pregnancy among blacks and that teens are more likely to give birth to low-weight babies. However, that conclusion is disputed by data which show that in 69 percent of black infant deaths, the mothers are 20 years of age or older, and by the fact that black mothers between the ages of 20 and 34 have an infant mortality rate that is twice that of white mothers in the same age cohort.[10] Therefore, age of mother is not a fully explanatory variable; rather, other socioeconomic factors, class inequality, structural conditions, and access to information are substantially more important in understanding racial differences in infant mortality rates.[11]

LIFE EXPECTANCY

The National Center for Health Statistics reported in 1989 that for the previous three consecutive years, the life expectancy rate of blacks declined and that the gap between blacks and whites in expected years to live was widening. This trend is disturbing especially in view of the fact that for several years, the racial gap had been narrowing. In 1960, white Americans could expect to live 69.1 years while the life expectancy rate for "black and other races" was 8.3 years less or 60.8 years. In 1970, the white population had a life expectancy rate of 71.7 years while a "black" person born that year could expect to live 64.1 years or a racial gap of minus 7.6 years.[12] As life expectancy for both races increased to 1984, the racial gap had fallen to 5.6 years. Since that time, through 1987, the racial gap in life expectancy increased to 6.2 years.[13] In the meantime, life expectancy for whites continued to rise and reached 75.6 years while that for blacks was only 69.4 years.[14] Particularly troublesome is the high death rate among black males. As of 1988, the life expectancy rate of black males was approximately eight years less than that of black females. A study reported in *The New England Journal of Medicine* in 1990 stated that a male in Bangladesh, one of the poorest nations in the world, has a better chance of reaching the age of 65 than a black male living in the Harlem community of New York City.[15]

Among the factors offered to explain the reduced life expectancy rate among blacks are rising death rates attributed to drugs, homicides, disproportionately higher death rates among blacks from diabetes, kidney diseases, and cirrhosis of the liver caused by alcoholism, AIDS, and infant mortality.[16] If, indeed, a decline in life expectancy among blacks can be explained solely by those factors, it can be reasonably concluded that these are behavioral explanations and significant changes in social behavior can improve life expectancy rates. However, that is not the entire picture.

For example, a 13-year study of 8,806 black and white adults conducted by the Federal Centers for Disease Control in Atlanta (CDC) concluded that only about one-third of the difference in black/white death rates can be explained by "preventable risk factors" (e.g., alcohol consumption, diabetes, cholesterol level, smoking, high blood pressure). Income differences, clearly a structural factor with which race is highly associated, account for 38 of the remaining 69 percent difference between blacks and whites. This study also showed that the mortality rates for blacks were substantially higher in some age cohorts than that among whites. As an example, in the 35 to 54-year-old group, the death rate among blacks was 149 percent higher than that for whites in the same age bracket. Differences in income as an explanatory factor reveal racial disparities in access to health care, and those aspects of personal behavior that are correlated with one's position in the social structure.[17] Findings from this study are born out also by data from Massachusetts that reveal a strong relationship between income inequities and higher death rates among blacks.[18]

LEADING CAUSES OF DEATH

Irrespective of race, the leading causes of death in the United States are: (1) diseases of the heart; (2) malignant neoplasms; (3) accidents and adverse effects; (4) cerebrovascular diseases; (5) chronic obstructive pulmonary diseases; (6) pneumonia; (7) suicide; (8) diabetes; and (9) chronic liver disease, cirrhosis.[19]

AIDS ranks 15th in overall cause of deaths but is the 10th leading cause of deaths among blacks. In an absolute sense, of the 13,130 deaths attributed to AIDS in 1987, white males accounted for 65 percent while black males accounted for 25 percent of the deaths.[20]

Among blacks, heart disease and stroke account for approximately 40 percent of all excess deaths for persons less than 70 years of age ("excess" deaths refer to the difference between the actual death and the number of deaths that would have occurred had blacks had the same death rates as whites for each age cohort and both sexes).[21] Over a 25-year span, 1960–1986, deaths attributed to strokes were reduced by 61 percent in the United States. In the 16-year period, 1970–1986, stroke deaths declined by 53 percent. However, that dramatic improvement has not been experienced by all groups nor in all regions of the country. For example, Edward Roccella reported at the 1990 meeting of the American Association for the Advancement of Science that the death rate among blacks in the Southeastern part of the United States attributed to strokes is substantially higher than that of whites or of blacks living in other parts of the nation. This disparity is especially true between blacks in that region compared to blacks living in other regions. Black males in the Southeastern United States have a stroke death that is 44 percent higher than black males living in other parts of the country. Black females have a stroke rate 27 percent higher in the Southeastern region compared to black women elsewhere.[22]

A contributing factor to strokes is diastolic blood pressure over 115 or high blood pressure. Roccella's research showed that black men in the Southeastern region are three times more likely to have high blood pressure than black men in other parts of the country. He also found that black women with high blood pressure are significantly more likely to be overweight (almost three-fourths of them) than black women who reside in other regions (about half of them).[23]

The second leading cause of death in the United States is cancer. At one period, during the decades of the 1950s and 1960s, the cancer death rate among blacks was increasing at a rate double that among whites. Thereafter, the rate among whites began to outrace those cancer deaths among blacks. During the 1980s, particularly, racial and gender disparities became more noticeable. As of 1990, reports from the CDC indicate a higher prevalence among blacks than whites for cancer of the esophagus, larynx, lung, stomach, cervix, pancreas, and breasts. In general, white women are more likely to have cancer than are black women but black men are more likely to have cancer than are white men.[24] However, black female cancer patients are 20 percent less likely to survive cancer than are white females and black males are 30 percent less likely than white males to survive cancer.[25] The Centers for Disease Control reported in 1990 that black women are two times as likely as white women to die from cervical cancer even though deaths from cervical cancer declined by 11 percent between 1980 and 1987. Yet black women are more likely than white women to obtain a PAP test. However, they do not obtain the same kind of follow-up treatment or care.

As Friend[26] and Reed[27] point out, many cancers are associated with certain occupations and one race may be more frequently employed in these occupations than members of another race. For example, blue-collar occupations occur in workplace environments that often expose employees to carcinogenic substances (e.g., blacks in the steel industry and whites in printing, rubber, and leather industries). Although white women have a higher rate of breast cancer than black women, that rate may be explained by differences in education and age at which a woman has her first child. Breast cancer is more prevalent among the affluent and white women are older than black women when their first child is born. Differentials across racial lines once again may reflect an information deficit about early detection, racial differences in medical care, difference in knowledge about warning signs about cancer, and different belief systems regarding the salience of early detection.[28]

OTHER DISEASES

It is estimated that more than 3 million people in the United States have noncorrectable vision problems. About 890,000 people in this group are blind in both eyes. A study reported in 1990 by Tielsch and Sommer indicated that the rate of blindness and visual impairment among blacks is almost twice that found in whites. They also reported that racial differentials increase to the disadvantage of blacks with increasing age. Between the ages of 40 and 79, the rate of visual impairment among blacks is higher than among whites. Thereafter, blindness was slightly higher (8 percent) than it was for whites (7.23 percent). However, a significant amount of the visually impaired persons could probably have their problems corrected merely through an eye examination and a new pair of glasses.[29]

Increasingly significant research is being reported on the relationship between race, class, and lead poisoning. Earlier on, lead poisoning was referred to as encephalopathy. It was associated almost exclusively with the ingestion of lead paint. With increasing research, it has been found that lead poisoning can occur not only by direct ingestion of lead paint but through lead-contaminated soil and dust.[30] Nationally, roughly 16 percent of children in the United States suffer from lead poisoning but at least 55 percent of all black children have been so contaminated by lead that it will cause neurological damage.[31]

The effects of lead poisoning during infancy can show up throughout childhood and early adulthood. A study reported in the *New England Journal of Medicine* (January 1990) revealed that these effects include higher drop-out rates from school, higher incidence of reading disabilities, higher absenteeism from school and lower rank in high school class.[32] Earlier, Reed reported that high levels of lead poisoning impair motor coordination and neurological functioning and are also associated with problems of behavior control.[33] His study of 16 census tracts in Boston showed that blacks in those areas are at a higher risk for lead poisoning than are residents of other parts of the city. Lead poisoning, too, is a preventable disease but strong public intervention is still required to enable children to live in a lead-free environment.

New epidemiological research also shows that the rate of kidney failure among blacks is significantly higher than previously believed. Stacy C. Fitzimmons analyzed ten years of data for the National Institutes of Health. Her analysis covered such areas as dialysis and kidney transplants as related to race and age adjusted for sex. According to the findings of this study, in 1986, whites accounted for 66.4 percent (20,600 cases of renal disease or kidney failure) but blacks, while composing only 12 percent of the total American population, accounted for 26.8 percent or 8,302 cases.[34]

These data also show that black men afflicted with hypertension or diabetes have inordinately high rates of kidney failure, especially in some age categories. For example, the kidney failure rate among black men between the ages of 25 and 44 who also suffer from hypertension is twenty times that of white men in the same age cohort. In general, 33 percent of kidney failure incidence among blacks can be attributed to hypertension, whereas only 5 to 10 percent of that incidence is found within the black population. This research also points out that hypertension damages small blood vessels in the kidney and impairs the filtering and blood purification process.[35]

Approximately 100,000 people are in dialysis but about one-third of those individuals are black. On the other hand, as Leary reported, white males are about twice as likely as blacks to receive kidney transplants.[36] All of these are problems necessitating appropriate intervention at crucial stages in a person's life. Such interventions refer to special attention to people at risk; elimination of economic disparities that influence access to health care; reduction of cultural barriers against organ donations; and more aggressive action to find suitable matches between donors and recipients.[37]

ACQUIRED IMMUNE DEFICIENCY SYNDROME (AIDS)

AIDS first received national attention in 1981. Initially, AIDS was regarded as a "gay disease," found exclusively among white male homosexuals. At that time and throughout most of the 1980s, the black community, as well as the Hispanic community, gave little public acknowledgment of the prevalence of the disease among blacks. This pattern of denial can be attributed to the strong cultural taboo against homosexuality in both the black and Hispanic communities. However, as the disease spread with alarming speed and proportions and was found among intravenous drug users in the homosexual, bisexual, and heterosexual populations as well as among innocent children, blacks began to acknowledge the existence of this disease in that population as well as in all others.

The World Health Organization (WHO) reported in 1990 that worldwide the number of reported cases of AIDS climbed to 203,599 by the end of 1989. This number represented an increase of 36,942 over the number of cases reported in 1988. In 1989, the United States accounted for 56 percent (113,211 cases) of all AIDS cases reported from all parts of the world.[38] By June 30, 1990, the total number of AIDS cases in the United States had risen to 139,765. Of that number, at least 85,000 had died.

In the United States, AIDS accounts for 65 percent of the deaths among white males and 25 percent of the deaths among black males. Although AIDS remains a disease that is more widespread among homosexual and bisexual men (66 percent), it is rapidly becoming a disease that is prevalent among the poor, black, and Hispanic heterosexual intravenous drug users, and children of drug users, particularly addicted women who sell sex for drugs. The Centers for Disease Control reports that blacks are twice as likely as whites to contract AIDS; more than 50 percent of all women afflicted with the disease are black; approximately 70 percent of babies born with the AIDS virus are black and about 24 percent of all males with AIDS are black.[39] Researchers generally agree that the high incidence of AIDS within the black and Hispanic communities is the direct result of the higher incidence of intravenous drug use in which dirty needles are exchanged by users often resulting in contamination in which carriers of the virus who are also drug users have sexual relations often transmitting the disease to the newborn.

Edward O. Laumann, a researcher at the National Opinion Research Center of the University of Chicago, claims that the incidence of AIDS in the United States has been distorted. In his view, the occurrence of AIDS is much higher than is reported by the Centers for Disease Control. This distortion is due to the fact that the CDC uses estimates based upon cases reported to official agencies but white Americans are more likely to "be treated discreetly" and less likely to come to the attention of reporting agencies. At the time his study was reported, the CDC indicated that whites account for 60 percent of the cases, blacks 26 percent, and Hispanics 14 percent (March 1989). Laumann claims the white proportion is actually about 72 percent of all AIDS cases.[40] CDC data also indicate that AIDS is the 9th leading cause of death among children between the ages of 1 and 4 and 7th among young people between the ages of 15 and 24. Children are vulnerable to their parents' disregard for safe sex. Young people are often convinced of their invincibility and do not use contraceptives when engaging in sexual relations. The spread of AIDS explodes!

DRUG ABUSE AND THE BLACK COMMUNITY

The American public has become increasingly conscious of the prevalence of drugs and the reported higher incidence of drug abuse in the United States in the past two decades. Many would argue that comparatively little attention was paid to this problem of illegal drug use until the drug crisis victimized the sons and daughters of the white middle class. According to this argument, frequently heard among street people, there was no concerted effort to study the causes of drug addiction and no organized program to legalize either stimulants or narcotic drugs as long as drug abuse was believed to be a problem of black ghetto dwellers and white musicians. While this argument has merit, it should be pointed out that during the 1950s Alfred Lindesmith[41] and others argued unsuccessfully that the basic problem of drugs in America is the law itself and not the people who use them. Society establishes definitions of legality and illegality as it chooses. Thus the associative problems of drug addiction, such as organized crime and other forms of deviant behavior, did not arise when the use of drugs was not societally defined as deviant behavior. Nevertheless, today, the use of certain types of drugs is considered illegal in the American society and is, therefore, in violation of the normative social order.

The 1990s drug argot include "rock," "rock candy," or "white cloud" for *crack;* "snow," "girl," or "white girl," for *cocaine;* "horse," "boy," "H," or "smack" for *heroin;* "angel dust," "boat," "dust," and "loveboat" for *PCP;* and "Mary Jane," "smoke," and "fire" for *marijuana.* There is also a newer and more powerful drug found less frequently in the black community called *ice.* The alarming rapidity with which crack spread during the latter half of the 1980s and the knowledge of its immediate addictive powers, coupled with the realization that other forms of deviant behavior were associated with the desire to obtain crack, heightened the nation's awareness of the drug problem.

For several years prior to the presidential campaign of 1988, Reverend Jesse Jackson had assailed the federal government for its callous indifference to the drug problem in the United States and attacked the Reagan Administration for budget cuts of programs designed to combat the problem. During the election primaries, he raised the nation's awareness about the magnitude of the problem, its pervasiveness from Wall Street to inner city ghettos to suburbia and farmlands, and made a "war against drugs" one of his campaign platforms. As the nation's attention was aroused, other presidential candidates embraced an anti-drug message as one of their commitments. The ultimate presidential victor, George Bush, appointed a high level official to have exclusive responsibility to develop a strategy for combating the drug menace to American society.

All the major television networks included hours of prime time to heighten public awareness. Often, unfortunately, these programs were so biased as to leave the impression that the only users are blacks and Hispanics and that the drug problem has somehow escaped the white community. It is widely believed that a disproportionate number of the estimated 500,000 crack users are minorities. However, the proportion of white users of crack and other drugs may be undercounted due to the tendency of middle-class white addicts to seek out private sources for treatment and care. There is also the high probability that white addicts who may be more concerned about concealing their identity from the public are less willing than poor black or Hispanic intravenous drug users to be photographed during an interview for prime-time television. Thus, distortion and selective perception reinforce the stereotypes of black and Hispanic drug addicts. Yet, there is evidence to show that drug use is as much a problem among young whites as it is among young blacks and that white high school seniors are more likely to use drugs than are black high school seniors.[42]

Nonetheless, the black community is plagued by a devastating drug problem. This community stands to lose a major segment of its young black males to the drug culture, gang violence associated with drugs, school drop-outs, and a grave reduction in the overall quality of life because of deviant behavior induced by the drug problem (see Chapter 12). Illicit drug trafficking is big business in the United States. Its estimated payoff is approximately $150 billion. In the black community, the drug economy is believed to range from $16 to $29 billion dollars annually. Some high level suppliers of cocaine make as much as $100,000 per week while their "entry-level" teenage pushers may also earn into the thousands of dollars per week.[43]

It is the personal wastage of young lives, infants, and families, the destruction of traditional values about the meaning and efficacy of education and work and respect for human life and property that threaten to tear the social fabric of the black community. Throughout the black community there is a deep concern about the social and mental health of all too many of its children who see people murdered in gang wars over drug issues, and about young people who will sell drugs or serve as look-outs in order to earn quick money for designer clothing, jewelry, beautiful automobiles, or high fashion sneakers. Rationales for this deviant behavior range from addiction to attainment of material status symbols by any means necessary, peer pressure and differential association, to drugs as an escape from the ravages and brutalities of poverty.

Statistics on drug behavior, like statistics on deviant behavior in general, tend to be contradictory and misleading. The illegality of drug use makes drug-abuse statistics all the more unreliable, since violators of drug laws tend to function as furtively as police forces will permit. There is evidence, however, that the use of illegal drugs, especially crack cocaine in recent years, has steadily increased since the decades of the 1960s. Then, it was estimated that the number of drug addicts in the United States varied from 20,000 to 60,000. By the end of the 1960s, with the rise of the drug culture in mecca cities such as San Francisco and the return of Vietnam veterans reportedly exposed to widespread drug abuse, law enforcement agents raised the alarm of a rapidly expanding drug crisis. Some estimates ran as high as 600,000 in the early 1980s.[44] That was before the discovery of crack, whose users are estimated to approximate at least 500,000. One major problem with substance abusers is the difficulty in pinpointing accurate numbers by virtue of the fact that some individuals regularly abuse multiple drugs.

The best available evidence indicates that drug addicts in the United States. tend to be concentrated in large cities such as New York, Chicago, Boston, Los Angeles, San Francisco, Detroit, and Philadelphia. They also congregate in smaller cities, towns, and hamlets. In Caplovitz's 1976 study of heroin addicts in New York, a central demographic finding was that the heroin addict was likely to be male, unmarried, minority, and under age 25 with less than a high school education. He also concluded that blacks and Puerto Ricans constituted approximately 75 percent of all addicts in New York City; however, they composed about 50 percent of the city's population.[45] As measured by 1982 data from the more than 30,000 treatment centers in America, 43.6 percent of all addicts are black; 35.7 percent are white; 19.8 percent are Hispanics, and 0.9 percent are "other."

The patterns of drug use vary with age, race, and type of drug. For instance, it is estimated that 30.9 percent of all persons between the age of 12 and 17 in the United States have tried marijuana and that 16.7 percent are current users. Among persons age 18 to 25, approximately 68 percent have smoked marijuana at least once and 35.4 percent are current users. In the age category of 26 years and above, 19.6 percent have smoked marijuana and 6 percent are current users. In 1979, 17 percent of nonwhite and 15 percent of white 12- to 17-year-olds used marijuana; 36 percent of the white and 34 percent of blacks between the ages of 18 and 25, and 6 percent white and 8 percent blacks aged 26 and older were current users of marijuana. Cocaine use was concentrated in the 18–25 age cohort. In this group, 27.5 percent of all persons had tried it and 9.3 percent were current users. This age group also had the highest concentration of "ever used" and current users of all other substances including heroin, hallucinogens, inhalants, amphetamines, stimulants, and sedatives.[46]

Although drug abuse is primarily a phenomenon of urban communities, it extends beyond the downtrodden neighborhoods of the inner city to suburban communities. In effect, substance abuse cuts across all social class lines and pervades the entire occupational fabric. For instance, there are several programs in the United States that cater to professionals (e.g., physicians, dentists, lawyers, architects, actors, entertainers, and athletes) to help them overcome drug addiction. Within cities both drug addiction and illicit drug use appear to be located in areas characterized by low income, poor housing, and high rates of crime and delinquency. These neighborhoods also contain a greater proportion of broken homes, high rates of unemployed men, working women, and relatively low educational attainment levels.[47] Whether the focus is on illicit use or on dependent drug addiction, statistics on the locations of drug abuse must be interpreted with care because of the transient nature of users. This is especially the case within the black community, to which a fairly substantial transient white population flocks because of a higher degree of anonymity such communities provide them.[48] However, frequent media accounts of drug busts in various parts of the nation reveal that the "barons" who actually control the flow of illicit drugs into the United States are white and that many of them reside in well-to-do suburban communities. Such accounts also reveal the degree to which the drug abuse problem has, in fact, extended to all parts of the metropolitan community.

The federal government has finally recognized that drug abuse is not confined to the black ghettos. Consequently, increasing sums of money are allocated to public and private universities and agencies to research the all-encompassing dimensions of the drug abuse problem and to develop programs for rehabilitation. Such programs are funded by the National Institute of Mental Health, the Veterans Administration, the Department of Defense, and the Department of Housing and Urban Development. The Reagan Administration stepped up its initiatives in 1983 to control the entry and distribution of drugs into the United States. Such efforts underscore the enormity of the control problem since America has about 96,000 miles of border. Mrs. Nancy Reagan also continued her primary project of drug abuse education as a means of preventing drug use among young people in the United States.

But the black community, impatient with the slow process of research, and wearied from being the subjects of too much research, has declared war on drugs. It is distressed by the presumed disproportionate number of blacks who are hooked and immobilized by their dependence on narcotizing drugs. Pitiful and poignant cases of black babies born as addicts because of the addiction of their mothers and the knowledge that, in some treatment centers, one in eight narcotic addicts is aged 15 and under have elicited demands for immediate ameliorative action within the black communities of urban cities. In response to this situation programs such as "Report a Pusher," organizations such as Mothers Against Dope, Black Citizens Patrol, and Vietnam Veterans Against Drugs and Crime, as well as an untold number of drug education programs have been developed throughout the nation. These voluntary associations are oriented toward eliminating the suppliers, pushers, and corrupt police known to be involved in drug trafficking as well as those who seem unconcerned with the self-destruction of blacks because drug trafficking is such a highly lucrative business enterprise.

Treatment and rehabilitation programs operate in hospitals and special clinics. Those hospitals that have historically attempted to rehabilitate the addicted, located in Lexington, Kentucky, and Forth Worth, Texas, have not enjoyed notable success in controlling the spread of addiction. Methadone maintenance centers, which sponsor a program that fosters the substitution of the drug methadone for heroin as a means of reducing heroin dependency, are under attack for their apparent inability to produce total withdrawal from drugs. Many addicts also claim that this program is merely the substitution of one type of dependency for another except that methadone makes them more lethargic and generally apathetic. Rehabilitation, treatment, and maintenance programs will be absolutely useless unless we are willing to confront head-on those conditions in the social structure that create in some individuals the need to escape through the use of narcotic drugs. These structural conditions involve economic deprivation, limited access to employment or to the opportunity system in general, and oppressive racism. For those who are already hooked on drugs, the first step is to create an environment that will encourage them to seek assistance in coming to terms with those situations that fostered drug dependency as an adaptive response.

ALCOHOLISM AND EXCESSIVE DRINKING

Although millions of dollars have been expended in support of research pertaining to alcoholism and heavy drinking, our knowledge of this subject remains limited and incomplete. Contradictions and uncertainties prevail in terms of what actually constitutes alcoholism, its etiology, its relative incidence, and the effects of alcohol upon the physiology of the drinker. These shortcomings are due largely to serious methodological weaknesses inherent in much of the research. In recent years, however, more sophisticated research has broadened our understanding of the nature of alcoholic addiction and heavy drinkers. There is still a strong tendency, nevertheless, to treat heavy drinking and alcoholism as if they were conceptually interchangeable.

Heavy drinking is excessive drinking that may over the long run, often as long as 15 or 20 years, lead to alcohol addiction. By alcoholic addiction, or alcoholism, we mean dependency upon alcohol as a means of retreat or escape from the daily responsibilities and demands of life. This dependency is so pronounced that the individual feels unable to enjoy life or to establish satisfying social relationships without relying upon alcohol.

It is estimated that a total of 120 million drinkers of alcoholic beverages in the United States consume an average of 2.83 gallons of absolute alcohol annually. Of all drinkers, approximately 13.7 million are classified as "problem drinkers"; that is, their drinking is of such a severe nature that it interferes with their normal functioning but they are not classified as alcohol addicts.[49] It is also estimated that the absolute number of confirmed alcoholics in the United States is somewhere between 6 and 9 million persons. These numbers are considerably larger than even the very best estimates of the number of drug addicts in the United States. Social scientists know less about alcoholism, excessive drinking, or social drinking among American blacks than perhaps any other racial or ethnic group in America.[50] Research conducted during the 1960s, though, provided illuminating data regarding drinking among black Americans. It was then estimated that about 69 percent of the white population and 62 percent of the black population were drinkers but that slightly more black drinkers (23 percent) than whites (17 percent) were classified as heavy drinkers.[51]

Although evidence regarding racial differences in rates of alcoholism is contradictory, most studies seem to indicate that both rates of heavy or excessive drinking and alcoholism are higher among blacks than among whites.[52] Many findings are highly suspect relative to comparative rates reported and, not infrequently, serve to perpetuate the mythical "black pathology syndrome." But more scientifically sound investigations lend tentative support to the hypothesis that alcoholism is increasingly a social problem in the black community. For example, a 1965 Manhattan borough study reported that the rate of alcoholism among blacks was 28 per 1,000 persons while that for whites was 16. However, dramatic reversals occur in rates when measured against amounts of education. That is, when whites and blacks with ten or more years of education were tested the rate for whites was 20 alcoholics per 1,000 persons but only 12 for blacks.[53] This finding suggests that more highly educated whites are more likely to become alcoholics than more highly educated blacks. Conversely, one may also assume that alcoholism is more widespread among the less educated blacks than among those having more years of schooling. High educational attainment is a deterrent to alcoholism among blacks but does not appear to have the same effect on whites.

Although alcoholism is largely a male phenomenon, it is by no means peculiar to men. The high visibility of male alcoholics may actually inflate their disproportionality as related to the low visibility of women alcoholics and heavy drinkers in American culture. Most studies of sex differences in drinking behavior tend to agree that black women are more likely to be abstainers than white women, for example. Less than one-half (49 percent) of black women are drinkers in comparison to 61 percent of white women. It is interesting to note, however, that although fewer black women drink, the proportion of heavy drinkers among them is about three times the proportion of drinking white females classified as heavy-escape drinkers. The actual percentages were 11 and 4 for black and white females, respectively.[54] The sex ratio for alcoholism appears to be greater among whites than among blacks. For instance, among whites there is only 1 female alcoholic to every 6.2 male alcoholics, but among black alcoholics there is 1 female to every 1.9 male alcoholics.[55] More recent observations about skid-row women who are heavy drinkers illuminate this subject further. Gerald Garrett and Howard Bahr found evidence among New Yorkers that shows, contrary to expectations, that black men are not overrepresented on skid row. The proportion of black men on skid row in the Bowery is approximately the same as the proportion of black men in New York. One of every four New Yorkers is a black male; and, proportionately, one of every four skid-row inhabitants is a black male. But black women are overrepresented there, constituting approximately 40 percent of the skid row female population. The researchers also found evidence to support previous investigations that both black men and women drinkers have a higher proportion of the heavy drinkers among skid rowers. It should be stressed that Garrett and Bahr did not conclude that black men and women on skid row are disproportionately found among the alcoholics there.[56] The comparatively lower proportion of drinking black women is explained by several factors. It is hypothesized, for example, that the greater degree of religiosity among black women, coupled with cultural expectations of the female role, restrains them from indulging in drinking. Another assumption is that black women have a greater responsibility thrust upon them by adverse economic factors that are not only conducive to abstinence but only allows heavy drinking rather than alcoholism among those black women who do drink.[57]

As has been suggested, one must be cautious in interpreting comparative data about rates of both alcoholism and heavy drinking among blacks and whites. Higher rates of drinking behavior among blacks may be more of a reflection of high visibility among black consumers than would normally be the case if they had the same opportunity to receive private care as do many white alcoholics, male and female. Furthermore, the measures of heavy drinking as opposed to socially acceptable drinking are not clearly delineated from one study to another. Societal toleration of excessive drinking among the white population may be so flexible as to deflate the proportion of whites who are defined as either heavy drinkers or as confirmed alcoholics.

According to deprivation and congruence theories, alcoholism among blacks may be an adaptive response to frustrations that have their roots in racial oppression and exploitation. It may also represent escape or withdrawal (retreatism) from the exigencies of a social world that shuts them out or makes life itself somewhat intolerable. We know that many alcoholics experience status inconsistency and that others attempt to endure downward mobility. Alcoholism may once again be an adaptive response to both situations. Because of economic deprivations, lower incomes, and low-status occupational pursuits, black alcoholics seeking treatment more frequently become wards of the state or public treatment centers. Thus their visibility in statistics is heightened.

MENTAL HEALTH

Our knowledge of the prevalence and distribution of emotional health problems within the black population is seriously limited. This problem stems largely from inconsistencies in interpretations of what behavior actually constitutes psychotic and psychoneurotic behavior. It is embedded in our confused understandings of the relationship between socioeconomic status and social behavior. Furthermore, rates of some forms of mental disorders among blacks often result from overdiagnosis (labeling a disease more severe than it actually is), particularly by white psychiatrists. The tendency among white psychiatrists to overdiagnose psychoses among blacks is a manifestation of one way in which cultural bias impedes objective perceptions. It also shows the inability of white psychiatrists to understand the various nuances of black culture and the persons socialized in the American black culture.[58] If there were more than the 175 known black psychiatrists in the United States and if they, by virtue of their being black, could comprehend the nuances of black culture, perhaps prevalence and incidence data relative to the types of emotional health problems among blacks would be more reliable.

Most studies on mental illness have established a linkage between social class, or socioeconomic position, and both the incidence and the prevalence of certain types of mental illness. In general, the highest rates of mental disorders are found among the lowest socioeconomic and occupational groups, and, conversely, the lowest rates are among the more economically advantaged. From the early studies conducted by Robert E. L. Faris and H. W. Dunham, who followed an ecological approach to this problem in determining prevalence distribution, to more recent investigations, this theoretical position appears to be substantiated. For instance, R. E. Clark claimed that the higher the occupational level, the lower the rates of schizophrenia and, conversely, schizophrenic rates are highest among persons with low-status occupations.[59] Confirmations on this finding appeared in a plethora of studies including research conducted by August B. Hollingshead and F. C. Redlich in New Haven,[60] the widely known Midtown Manhattan Study conducted by Leo Srole and his associates,[61] and in the more recent investigations undertaken by Dunham[62] and W. A. Rushing.[63] One could therefore draw the inference that since blacks are concentrated in low-status occupations as well as residentially confined to the central city, rates of mental disorders would be high among them.

Although evidence strongly endorses the linkage between social class and mental illness, there are other serious ramifications of the association. First, the prohibitive cost of psychotherapy or psychiatric care is often beyond the capacity of all but comparatively few black Americans to afford. Consequently, only those persons whose aberrant behavior is sufficiently serious, in terms of personal injury to others, or who are personally destructive so as to require societal intervention are likely to obtain psychiatric care. Evidence indicates that these individuals tend more often to be institutionalized and are less likely to receive private psychiatric treatment. Second, since a disproportionately large number of blacks who suffer from mental health problems are institutionalized, they have a greater probability of being disproportionately represented in most categories of mental disorder and of being overdiagnosed as psychotics rather than psychoneurotics. Thus one would expect the rates of nonwhite or black mental illness to be higher than rates for whites when data from state hospitals are analyzed. Conversely, though, as Benjamin Pasamanick has observed, in 1962, rates of mental illness, both psychotic disorders and psychoneurotic behavior, are highest for whites in private institutions and Veterans Administration (VA) hospitals. White admissions for psychoneuroses in private and VA hospitals were at the rate of 62.29 per 1,000, while the rate for blacks was 27.35 per 1,000, but the overall rates of admission of psychoses for whites and blacks were 9.46 and 7.04, respectively. However, the most remarkable disparity occurred in the analysis of noninstitutional data. Here, Pasamanick observed that the rate of serious mental illness among whites at 5.20 per 1,000 is ten times greater than that of blacks at 0.5 per 1,000.[64] Third, if one holds the social class variable constant, prevalence by types as related to racial identification appears more distinctive. Benjamin Malzberg, in holding social class constant, observed higher rates of schizophrenia, general paresis, and alcoholic psychoses among blacks. He also observed higher rates of old-age psychoses, involutional psychoses, senile psychoses, and manic-depressive behavior among whites.[65] Thus different types of psychoses are found within each group. Undoubtedly, these responses are a functiion of different cultural experiences.

Melvin Kohn and John A. Clausen raised the question as to whether or not rates of mental illness in various occupational groups and in different parts of the city more accurately reflect *concentration* of cases in the lowest socioeconomic strata. Examining data on schizophrenia in Hagerstown, Maryland (with a population of 36,000), and several studies regarding area characteristics and rates of schizophrenia, they concluded that there was a much stronger correlation between social class and schizophrenia in large urban communities than in smaller communities. Thus the larger the city, the greater will be the probability of a strong association between the prevalence of schizophrenia and lower-status groups.[66] It is also suggested by this finding that stresses and strains brought to bear on individuals who are concentrated in poverty-stricken, low-income, and highly congested areas of the cities result in various forms of mental illness. However, the evidence is as yet too inconclusive to draw definitive generalizations regarding either incidence or prevalence of specific types of mental health problems among various groups. More reliable conclusions await extensive national research.

Another problem with mental health statistics is that, as in Russia, a diagnosis of mental illness can be used by law enforcement agencies as a powerful form of social control. A study by the Institute for Southern Studies and Southern Exposure reported in 1989 that black people in the South are three times more likely than southern whites to be committed to mental institutions. It also reported that blacks are much more often than whites misdiagnosed for serious mental illnesses. Approximately 37 percent of all persons involuntarily admitted to the 72 state mental hospitals from which data were gathered were black. The hospitals covered in this study were located in Florida, Texas, North Carolina, South Carolina, Tennessee, Virginia, Georgia, Mississippi, and Louisiana. This study confirms reports from the National Institute of Mental Health that psychiatrists often overdiagnose blacks. Earlier, Blackwell, Hart, and Sharpley had also called attention to this problem.[67]

SUICIDE

In recent years, the black community has experienced an unparalleled rise in the rate of suicide among its members. Between 1950 and 1977, for instance, the suicide rate for black males increased from 6.8 to 11.4 per 100,000 resident population. During the same period, the black female rate rose from 1.6 per 100,000 to 3.5 per 100,000 resident population.[68] Within the black population, suicide is a frequent occurrence among late teens and young adults. However, there is some evidence that the rate actually increases among blacks up to the age of 34 and drops off sharply. For instance, Davis found that 47 percent of all suicides among blacks occurred among persons between the ages of 20 and 34 and that, within this age group, black males who committed suicide accounted for 36 percent of the total number while females represented only 11 percent of all suicides recorded in the black population.[69] Davis also revealed that within the age range of 25–29, the suicide rate among black males is higher than that of white males in the same age cohort.[70] This view of the rapidly rising rate of suicide in the black community is also supported by research conducted by Miles. His research shows that the suicide rate among black males increased 80 percent over the fifty year period, 1929–

1979, and that the rising rates are especially noticeable among young blacks in Northern urban communities.[71]

Most research on urban blacks tends to agree that the rate of suicide among blacks between the ages of 20 and 35 is approximately twice that of whites in the same age cohort. However, suicide rates among elderly white persons is substantially higher than that for elderly blacks.[72] Steele's 1977 study showed that blacks and whites do not differ significantly with respect to the frequency of suicide attempts. However, this observation appears to be contradicted by Gibbs' 1981 finding that white females tend to be more afflicted with depression, a measure of pre-suicidal tendency, than either young black or Hispanic females.[73]

The most recent report from the National Center for Health Statistics (1988) shows that suicide is the eighth leading cause of death in the American population. It is the third leading cause of death among persons in the age group 15–24 and it is twice as high among whites as among blacks.

To explain the essentially reverse trends in the rate of suicide between blacks and whites, Richard Seiden offers what he calls a "survivor hypothesis." In his view, only the strongest blacks survive the various adversities endured by black people in a hostile, discriminatory society. By the time those blacks reach senior citizen years, they have developed such a repertoire of coping strategies and have so many support mechanisms in an extended family network that suicide is not considered. On the other hand, young blacks are so often in a condition of anger and rage over their untoward conditions, the lack of opportunity within the social structure, their sense of futility and hopelessness about the possibilities of ever achieving whatever goals they dream of, that many never quite develop effective strategies for managing their problems. For them, the only alternative is suicide. By contrast, young whites may be beset with other types of personal problems but not the sort experienced by youthful blacks. The white elderly are more prone to serious adjustment problems and loneliness which stem from isolation from family members and loss of status in retirement.[74] As a result, they have a suicide rate that is three times that of elderly blacks.

HEALTH CARE AND HEALTH-CARE SYSTEMS

It is evident that far too little attention has been given to the delivery of health care to the black population. This has been a low priority in America. Thousands of black people die needlessly because of grossly inadequate health-care systems, while others are allowed to suffer unnecessarily because of discrimination and segregation in health care.

The inadequacy of health care reveals, among other things, extreme shortages of health-care workers as well as malfunctions in the distribution of health-care systems. The increasing numbers of black physicians and dentists, limited as the rise is, have been accompanied by increasing specialization and the urbanization of the black population. This, in turn, has not only helped to inflate the cost of medical and dental care but has also meant the shifting of black medical and dental services to urban areas. As a consequence of this movement, many rural areas in the United States are without a physician or a dentist. Residents of these areas must often travel several miles for any form of medical or dental care.

Blacks see physicians and dentists less often than whites, and when they do come in contact with them, it is more likely to be in hospital clinics, neighborhood clinics, and emergency rooms. In general, as is the case for the white population, the higher the annual income the more likely is the person to visit a physician's office for medical care. Among blacks, for instance, about half (50.5 percent) of persons from families with incomes under $5,000 per year, compared to slightly more than three-fifths (62.5 percent) of those with incomes in excess of $10,000 visit a physician's office. About 32 percent of blacks in the lowest income category (under $5,000), compared to 18.9 percent of those with incomes over $10,000 see physicians in emergency rooms. Among whites in the lowest income group, 54.2 percent visit the physician's office while 69.9 percent of those with incomes in excess of $10,000 make such visits for medical care. Only 12.5 percent of whites in the lowest income group and 11 percent of those in the higher, above $10,000 per year category see physicians in an emergency room situation.[75] Other studies show that blacks tend to use medical services less frequently and more episodically than other ethnic groups. This tendency may be accounted for by different degrees of cosmopolitanism and parochial group structures or greater folk orientation toward medical care among blacks than among whites,[76] or the higher degree of skepticism among blacks about both the availability of medical services and the quality of services given to them.[77] Importantly, there is a serious gap in information flow between the knowledge that blacks do not have about available services and the quantity of medical services actually available to them even in their residential areas.[78]

The problem of inadequacy in health-care delivery is evident in other areas such as health insurance and available hospital services. Blacks and other minorities do not have the benefits of participation in health insurance programs as the white population. Further, the continuing upward spiral in unemployment among blacks during the 1980s resulted in the loss of insurance coverage for thousands of previously insured blacks. In 1982 the U. S. Commission on Civil Rights reported that about 90 percent of health insurance is obtained through one's place of employment.[79] The loss of jobs makes it extremely difficult, if not impossible, for most working-class people, blacks and whites alike, to maintain even a reasonable level of health insurance coverage because of enormously high premiums. Most Americans under the age of 65 are covered by some form of health insurance. In 1976, for instance, about 88 percent of all Americans under the age of 65 were covered by public or private health insurance plans. About 92 percent of all whites, compared to 80 percent of all blacks, between the ages of 14 and 64 were covered by some form of health insurance program. Among unemployed men, the Civil Rights Commission reported in 1982 that 67 percent of white males, 54 percent of black males, 42 percent of Hispanic males, and 28 percent of American Indian males were covered by health insurance programs.[80] Blacks who worked in highly unionized industries, such as in communication, transportation, and public utilities were far more likely to remain adequately covered during a period of unemployment than blacks who worked in other occupations. The same was true for the white population.[81]

Of the 50 black hospitals established when medical care was more segregated by race than by income, no more than 30 remain, and these are fighting merely to survive. In 1983, Flint-Goodrich Hospital in New Orleans, which was once the only place where black physicians from several parts of the South could hospitalize their patients, was sold to a white company. Black physicians in New Orleans could not raise sufficient capital to purchase it from Dillard University, the historically black college that owned the facility. Flint-Goodrich was closed because it had become too expensive for the university to operate and that was due primarily to a distorted patient/medical-cost ratio. Other historically black hospitals are also in extreme difficulty primarily because of diminishing financial resources, accessibility of integrated facilities to blacks, and their abandonment by black physicians who have flourishing private practices and affiliations with larger, often better equipped, predominantly white hospitals. Nevertheless, many black physicians continue to maintain a strong commitment to improving health care and health-care institutions within the black community. Also, many black communities are attempting to gain their share of benefits granted under a series of federal acts designed to improve the quality of community health care. For instance, they are taking advantage of research opportunities provided under the National Sickle Cell Anemia Control Act in order to contain a disease whose two types, sickle-cell trait and incurable sickle-cell anemia disease, are said to disproportionately affect the black population. It is estimated that the sickle cells are found in about one in 12 blacks while the active sickle-cell disease is found in blacks at a rate of one in 600 which is twice the 1 in 1200 rate observed in the white population.[82]

Also, black community members, including health professionals and practitioners, have taken advantage of laws that provided for the establishment of comprehensive health-planning agencies, community health services, consumer education and training programs, neighborhood health centers, community mental health centers, and health maintenance organizations. These groups attempt to involve both consumers and providers of health care in a cooperative enterprise in which both share in decisions regarding community health needs and how to meet them. Intelligent responses to such needs may occasionally require community lay individuals to be trained to participate on health boards or in hospital management and administration or devise implementable strategies for effective disease prevention and control. They must also learn ways of motivating community members to be less episodic in taking advantage of available health-care services and of reducing the degree of skepticism regarding these services. Health-care personnel have also established on-site community services in which they work for specified periods of time in neighborhood centers, whether in housing projects or in storefronts or local clinics. Greater use is also being made of outpatient services for those persons who cannot afford to lose valuable work time for prolonged periods of hospitalization. Still greater use should be made of psychiatric services to combat rising rates of suicide among black Americans with emphasis on the development of prevention programs.

On another level blacks have begun to attack the problem of discrimination in the employment of medical personnel in health-care systems and to increase their representation among higher-level professional and administrative positions in the health-care field. Blacks are also attempting to prevent further occurrences of the exploitation of subjects in medical research as in the case of the U.S. Public Health Services Study of syphilitics in Tuskegee, Alabama, and in alleged illegal sterilization of mentally retarded black girls in Montgomery, Alabama.[83] However, improvements in health care of the black population will require a steady infusion of funds for health maintenance, for research to combat debilitating diseases, a stepped-up pace of training health professionals and practitioners, a better distribution of services throughout the nation and within cities, and effective programs that result in wider use of available health-care services by the black population closer to their places of residence. Accomplishing that goal was one reason for the founding in 1988 of the Black Health Research Foundation.

NOTES

1. Doris Wilkinson and Gary King, "Conceptual and Methodological Issues in the Use of Race as a Variable: Policy Implications," *The Milbank Quarterly* 65:1 (1987): 56–71.
2. Wornie L. Reed and Carolyn W. Arnold, "Health and Medical Care," in Wornie L. Reed (ed.), *Summary Assessment of the Status of African-Americans, Vol. 1* (Boston: William Monroe Trotter Institute of the University of Massachusetts/Boston, 1989), p. 1.
3. *Ibid.*
4. *Ibid.*
5. *Statistical Abstracts of the United States 1989,* Table 106, p. 76.
6. *Op. cit.*
7. Gina Kolata, "Defects Top Cause of Infant Deaths," *New York Times* (September 22, 1989), p. A-18.
8. Cf. Bruce Alpert, "Infant Death Rate Deplored," *Times-Picayune* (February 8, 1990), p. A-7, and "Infant Mortality Rate May Be Rising, Panel Says," *Times-Picayune* (March 1, 1990), p. A-10.

9. Wornie L. Reed, "Racism and Health: The Case of Black Infant Mortality," in Peter Conrad and R. Kern (eds.), *The Sociology of Health Illness: Critical Perspectives,* 3rd ed. (New York: St. Martin's Press, 1990).

10. *Ibid.*

11. *Ibid.*

12. Philip J. Hilts, "Growing Gap in Life Expectancies of Blacks and Whites Is Emerging," *New York Times* (October 9, 1989), p. A-8, and *Statistical Abstracts of the United States 1989,* Table 106, p. 71.

13. *Ibid.*

14. Cf. Tim Friend, "USA's Health Report: Disparity 'Cries Out for Attention'," *USA Today* (March 16, 1990), p. 1; "Black and White Death Rates Continue to Differ, Study Says" *New York Times* (September 27, 1989), p. 1; and Dan Sperling, "Health Gap Widening for Minorities," *USA Today* (September 27, 1989), p. 1.

15. *Op. cit.*

16. *Ibid.*

17. See "Income, Lifestyle Among Factors in Black Death Rate," *Times-Picayune* (February 9, 1990), p. A-11; and "The Gap Continues to Grow," *Los Angeles Times* (February 17, 1990), p. B-6.

18. Dolores Kong, "Social, Economic Factors Seen in Black Deaths," *Boston Globe* (December 9, 1989), p. 1.

19. *Statistical Abstracts of the United States 1989,* Table 119, p. 80.

20. Tim Friend, *op. cit.,* p. 2.

21. Reed, *op. cit.,* 1989, pp. 1–2.

22. Marilyn Elias, "Southeastern Blacks' Stroke Rate Is Still High," *USA Today* (February 16, 1990), p. D-1.

23. *Ibid.*

24. Reed, *op. cit.*

25. Friend, *op. cit.*

26. *Op. cit.*

27. *Op. cit.*

28. *Op. cit.,* p. 6.

29. "Blacks More Prone to Blindness, Study Finds," *Times-Picayune* (February 8, 1990), p. A-8.

30. *Op. cit.,* p. 7

31. Friend, *op. cit.* and Tim Friend, "Lead Exposure May Cause Kids Lifelong Harm," *USA Today* (January 1, 1990), p. D-1.

32. *Ibid.*

33. *Op. cit.*

34. Warren E. Leary, "Some Black Groups Are Found at High Risk of Kidney Failure," *New York Times* (April 6, 1989), p. B-15.

35. *Ibid.*

36. *Ibid.*

37. *Ibid.*

38. "Reported AIDS Cases Topped 200,000 in 1989," *Times-Picayune* (January 4, 1990), p. A-3.

39. Cf. Robert A. Jordan, "Blacks Waking Up to AIDS Threat," *Boston Globe* (April 30, 1989), p. 77; Walter Goodman, "Other Faces of AIDS: A Frank Investigation," *New York Times* (September 12, 1989), p. C-20.

40. "Chicago Study Says AIDS Cases in U. S. Are Underestimated," *New York Times* (June 9, 1989), p. A-8.
41. Alfred Lindesmith, *The Addict and the Law* (New York: Random House, 1965), pp. 93–134.
42. Cf. "Drugs a White Problem, Too," *Times-Picayune* (January 9, 1990), p. B-6, and "Drug Economy in Black America Is Between $16 Billion and $20 Billion," *Ebony* (August 1989): 109.
43. "Study Cites Racism in Mental Diagnosis," *Boston Herald* (October 16, 1989), p. 1.
44. Note that there are problems with such statistics, for they are based largely upon reports of individuals who come to the attention of the law, persons who are hospitalized in public institutions, and projections based upon such data. They do not take into consideration the relatively higher proportion of whites who receive treatment in private institutions or from private physicians. Thus it is possible that these statistics are highly distorted.
45. David Caplovitz, *The Working Addict* (New York: City University Graduate School and University Center, Metropolitan Drugs and Industry Project, 1976).
46. *Statistical Abstracts of the United States 1980,* p. 129.
47. Cf. *Task Force Report: Narcotics and Drug Abuse,* The President's Commission on Law Enforcement and Administration of Justice (Washington, D. C.: Government Printing Office, 1967), pp. 3, 48–49; I. Chein et al., *The Road to H* (New York: Basic Books, 1964); I. Chein and E. Rosenfeld, "Juvenile Narcotic Use," *Law and Contemporary Problems,* 22 (1957): 52–68; and Harold Finestone, "Kats, Kicks and Color," in M. Stein et al., *Identity and Anxiety* (Glencoe, Ill.: The Free Press, 1960).
48. R. E. Clark, "The Relationship of Schizophrenia in Occupational Income and Occupational Prestige," *American Sociological Review* 13 (1948): 325–330.
49. Joseph Julian and William Kornblum, *Social Problems* (Englewood Cliffs, N. J.: Prentice-Hall, Inc. 1983), p 217.
50. Harrison M. Trice, *Alcoholism in America* (New York: McGraw-Hill, 1966), p. 22.
51. Don Callahan, *Problem Drinkers* (San Francisco: Jossey-Bass, 1970), p. 139.
52. Julian Roebuck and R. G. Kessler, *The Etiology of Alcoholism: Constitutional, Psychological and Sociological Approaches* (Springfield, Ill.: Charles C. Thomas, 1972).
53. *Ibid.,* p. 203.
54. Cf. Don Callahan, Ira H. Casin, and Helen M. Crossley, *American Drinking Practices* (New Brunswick, N.J.: Rutgers Center of Alcohol Studies, 1969), pp. 48, 142, and Rommel Benjamin and Mary Benjamin, "Sociocultural Correlates of Black Drinking: Implications for Research and Treatment," *Journal of Studies on Alcohol,* 9 (1981): 241–247.
55. Margaret Bailey, Paul Halberman, and Harold Alksne, "The Epidemiology of Alcoholism in an Urban Residential Area," *Quarterly Journal of Studies on Alcohol,* 26 (1965): 19–40.
56. Cf. Howard Bahr and Gerald Garrett, *Disaffiliation Among Urban Women* (New York: Bureau of Applied Research, 1971), and Gerald R. Garrett and Howard Bahr, "Women on Skid Row," *Quarterly Journal of Studies on Alcohol,* 34 (December 1973):1228–1243.
57. Roebuch and Kessler, *op. cit.*

58. Benjamin Pasamanick, "A Survey of Mental Illness in an Urban Population," *The American Journal of Psychiatry,* 119 (1962): 299–305, and Alex Wesson, "The Black Man's Burden: The White Clinician," *The Black Scholar* (July/ August 1975): 13–18.

59. Clark, *op. cit.*

60. August B. Hollingshead and F. C. Redlich, *Social Class and Mental Illness: A Community Study* (New York: John Wiley and Sons, 1958).

61. Leo Srole et al., *Mental Health in the Metropolis: The Midtown Manhattan Study* (New York: McGraw-Hill, 1962).

62. H. W. Dunham, *Community and Schizophrenia: An Experimental Analysis* (Detroit: Wayne State University Press, 1965).

63. W. A. Rushing, "Two Patterns in the Relationship Between Social Class and Mental Hospitalization," *American Sociological Review,* 34 (1969): 533–541.

64. Pasamanick, *op. cit.*

65. Benjamin Malzberg, *Statistical Data for the Study of Mental Diseases Among Negroes in New York State* (Albany, N.Y.: Research Foundation for Mental Hygiene, 1964).

66. Cf. Melvin Kohn, "Social Class and Schizophrenia: A Critical Review and a Reformulation," *Schizophrenia Bulletin* (Winter 1969): 60–79, and John A. Clausen and Melvin L. Kohn, "The Ecological Approach to Social Psychiatry," *American Sociological Review,* 60 (1954): 140–151.

67. James E. Blackwell, Robert Sharpley, and Philip Hart, *Health Needs of Urban Blacks* (Boston: The Solomon Fuller Institute, 1977).

68. Harry A. Ploski and James Williams, *The Negro Almanac: A Reference Work on the Afro-American* (New York: John Wiley and Sons, 1983).

69. Robert Davis, "Suicide Among Young Blacks: Trends and Perspectives," *Phylon* 43:4 (December 1982): 307–314.

70. *Ibid.*

71. Dwight E. Miles, "The Growth of Suicide Among Black Americans," *The Crisis,* 86:10 (December 1979): 430–433.

72. Robert E. Steele, "Clinical Comparison of Black and White Suicide Attempters," *Journal of Consulting and Clinical Psychology,* 45:6 (1977): 982–985.

73. Jewelle Taylor Gibbs, "Depression and Suicidal Behavior Among Delinquent Females," *Journal of Youth and Adolescence* 10:2 (1981): 159–167.

74. Richard Seiden, "Mellowing With Age: Factors Influencing the Non-White Suicide Rate," *International Journal of Aging and Human Development* (January 1982), pp. 265–284.

75. *Statistical Abstracts of the United States 1980,* p. 112.

76. Cf. Edward Suchman, "Socio-medical Variations Among Ethnic Groups," *American Journal of Sociology,* 70 (November 1964): 319–331, and Edward Suchman, "Social Factors in Medical Deprivation," *American Journal of Public Health,* 55 (November 1965): 1725–1733.

77. Herman James, "Health Orientations, Health Opportunities and the Use of Medical Services: Toward a Clarification of the Relationships," an unpublished manuscript based upon a study of black and white subjects in Pittsburgh, 1967–1970.

78. Blackwell and Hart, op. cit., *passim.*

79. U. S. Commission on Civil Rights, *Health Insurance: Coverage and Employment for Minorities and Women* (Washington, D. C.: U. S. Commission on Civil Rights, 1982), p. 6.

80. *Ibid.*, pp. 15–19.

81. *Ibid.*

82. Ploski and Williams, *op. cit.*, p. 487.

83. The Tuskegee syphilis study was brought to national attention in 1972 when it was discovered that 431 black men had been denied treatment for syphilis over a 40-year period between 1932 and 1972. The purpose of the study was to determine the long-range effects of syphilis on the human body. However, as a result of this study, at least 28 of the participants died, but the number of possible deaths resulting from participation and lack of treatment could approximate 100 if further investigations were undertaken. In addition, a charge of illegal sterilization was brought against an OEO-funded family-planning clinic in Montgomery, Alabama, in 1973. The allegation was that two teenage black girls, one of whom was mentally retarded, were sterilized without the consent of their illiterate parents. This case focused on what was believed to be a much wider practice of sterilizing mentally retarded girls, and the use of sterilization as a requirement for continued support through public assistance for women on welfare.

Chapter
12

Blacks and the Criminal Justice System

One of the external images of the black community is that it exists in perpetually uncontrollable social pathology. Such images are reinforced by mass media accounts of alleged deviant behavior of black persons while nonblack individuals also involved in nonconformist behavior are not identified. These images are sustained by a selective perception that attributes generalized deviancy to the entire black population on the basis of violations of the normative order committed by a relatively small number of black individuals. Images of black pathology are also created by conditions in the social structure that generate deviancy as the most efficacious adaptive mechanism for survival in a hostile society.

In regard to behavioral norms, Americans as a whole are not perceptibly distinguishable from other groups. The overwhelming majority of black people in America, like the majority of Americans in general, conform to normative expectations in their social behavior. They are *normal.* They are *law-abiding citizens* engaged in the daily business of improving their social and economic status in American society. Others, due to a wide spectrum of reasons, deviate from societal norms in one or more of several different ways.

In this chapter we focus on criminal behavior—that form of social deviation that represents violations of the rules of normative order beyond the limit of social toleration. Both definitions of deviancy and dispositions made of deviants, such as persons defined as criminals, are a function of power. Until recently, blacks have been powerless—a fact that may help to explain deviancy among them. Crime is chosen for discussion in this chapter because of the black community's national concern over the problems and consequences of crime as a social problem and because of the ubiquitous fear of crime in the American society. This chapter also devotes specific attention to race differentials in the criminal justice system in the United States and to a range of interventions designed to combat the spread of crime.

CRIMINAL BEHAVIOR

Numerous problems are associated with interpretations of data on crime and delinquency. One of the more universal problems is the inaccuracy of statistics relative to crime incidence. Generally, the sources of this problem reflect serious defects in the varied components of the criminal justice system itself. For example, one fundamental source of inaccuracy is the heavy volume of unreported crime. Criminal statistics are by no means uniform from one jurisdiction to another. There is no uniformity in the degree of record-keeping efficiency or even in the data collection process that is so fundamental to the reliability of incidence statistics. Inaccuracy in statistical data on crime and criminals may further depend on individual perceptions of behavioral patterns, which, in turn, lead law enforcement agents to render selective judgments of what does and does not constitute criminal behavior.

It is precisely this possibility of racial bias at the time an initial judgment regarding alleged criminality is made that makes criminal statistics pertaining to black Americans so highly suspect. Even so, we have come to accept the fact that the instrumentation of the law is the function of an interrelated network of decision makers who comprise a power structure including the police, prosecutors, judges, and jurors—all of whose judgments determine who is labeled a criminal. Objectivity is not always achieved in ascriptions of criminality since subjective bias may consciously or subconsciously influence decisions. Subjective evaluations interfere with objectiveness and may help to explain why black Americans particularly are overrepresented in many forms of criminal behavior; this may also explain why blacks are more frequently suspected of an offense, apprehended, and booked. The very fact that blacks are more frequently brought to trial and sentenced, often without respect for rules of evidence and due process, reflects both their limited power and lack of influence on adjudication. The implications are broad and extend to other areas since blacks are less often paroled but more likely to become recidivists. But blacks, as a group, are not more prone to criminal behavior. They are more often exposed to conditions in the social structure that may lead to their disproportionate representation in criminal statistics. Further, as stated in Chapter 1, the black population is considerably younger than the white population. Consequently, more blacks show up in high crime age cohorts which, in turn, may reflect higher crime rates for the black population as a whole.

Arrest Data on Violent Crimes by Race

Arrest data over the past generations reveal that blacks on an average are arrested four times as frequently as whites. This generalization holds true when age and sex variables are considered. Rates also vary with the offense committed and the area of the city within which violations of the law allegedly occurred. Moreover, the arrest rates for whites are significantly lower for crimes against blacks than arrest rates for blacks who commit crimes against white persons. Further, racial disparity in arrest rates between areas within a metropolitan area may be explained by a number of observations: (1) The tolerance level among whites for nonconformity among blacks is considerably lower in those communities where blacks are in the minority than is the case in communities where blacks are in the majority. Thus deviance is not only likely to be more noticeable, but is also more likely to come to the attention of the police and lead to arrests. (2) Subjective definitions of deviance influence the initial decision that determines who is to be arrested for delinquent or criminal behavior. For instance, research by Chambliss, Piliavian, and Brier showed that a police officer's decision to arrest is often influenced by such extralegal offender characteristics as demeanor, appearance, and race.[1] The salience of extralegal factors not only with respect to the decision to arrest, but in terms of other stages in the criminal justice system, has been addressed by other researchers such as Lizotte[2] and Black[3] who also demonstrate that these kinds of factors do enter into the decision-making process in ways that are deterimental to black Americans. (3) Higher arrest rates for blacks appear to be highly and positively correlated with high amounts of police discretion; that is, the vagueness and ambiguity of certain situations might permit a greater degree of flexibility in the selection of alternatives available to police officers and police bias has a greater likelihood of entering into the decision to arrest. Similarly, discretionary authority might also allow bias to influence other dimensions of the criminal justice process. (4) Racial disparity in arrest rates may also reflect "demographic bias," and the intensity or frequency with which specific residential communities are patroled by police officers.[4] In other words, police officers may be more likely to patrol those ecological areas of a community that are characterized by a high rate of crime, and if police officers enter those areas with a high expectation of discovering criminal activity, then they are more likely to find criminal behavior in actions they might be more inclined to dismiss if observed in other areas of the metropolitan community. Blacks complain, justifiably so, that they are subjected to unwarranted stopping, questioning, searching, and arresting when there is no evidence that a crime has been committed.

Sometimes the arrests of blacks are merely an effort on the part of the police to "save face." In 1983, the United States Supreme Court ruled unconstitutional a California vagrancy law after a black plaintiff, Edward

Lawson, successfully argued that he had been unduly harassed by police officers because he refused to identify himself as he walked through a white residential area in San Diego. Lawson was arrested 15 times and finally took his case to the U.S. Supreme Court where in a 7–2 decision (*Kollender* v. *Lawson,* No. 81-1320), the Supreme Court stated that the California law violated the prohibition against "unreasonable search and seizure" that is guaranteed in the Fourth Amendment to the Constitution.

Similar violations against blacks that also demonstrated how the discretionary authority of police officers may result in unwarranted harassment, and allegations of discrimination against police, occurred in the case of the "Zebra" killings in San Francisco in the early to mid-1970s. In that instance, the police department with mayoral encouragement ordered a stop and search of *all black males* who supposedly fit the description of the Zebra killers. (All the victims were white and their alleged killers were black.) There was an outcry of indignation over this practice since there was no evidence that mass numbers of whites suspected of killing blacks would have been similarly treated, and, further, the practice was a violation of the rights of the almost 600 black men stopped under this directive. Most blacks who were stopped were given passes indicating that they had cleared police inspection—reminiscent of the pass system under apartheid in South Africa. Moreover, civil rights and civil liberties groups asserted that no similar procedures had been implemented in San Francisco against white men who may have fit the description of the "Zodiac" killer who began his terror earlier on. Essentially, a double standard operates when the victims are white and the accused are black. Again, police bias influences the initial determination to suspect and arrest blacks.

This bias and the unrestrained employment of police power coalesce to inflate arrest rates of black Americans. These factors may be only a *partial* explanation for the enormous disproportionality of arrests of blacks which show that, even though blacks represent slightly less than 12 percent of the national population, they comprise 29.6 percent of all persons arrested for criminal behavior in the United States. Therefore, the acknowledged high volume of crime in the black community must be understood within the framework of the foregoing observations. Nevertheless, the volume of crime within the black community itself, especially in the poorer sections but also against the more affluent blacks, has created pervasive fear of crime that influences citizen behavior and, unfortunately, reinforces demeaning stereotypes concerning black criminality.

VIOLENT OR AGGRESSIVE CRIMES BY RACE

The Uniform Crime Reports (UCR) of violent crimes include offenses of murder, forcible rape, robbery, and aggravated assault. These may also be referred to as aggressive offenses, since they do violence to persons. The ratio between the proportion of blacks in the total population and their arrest rates for violent crime is excessive.[5] Whites have a total violent crime index of 51.7 percent while blacks have a violent crime index of 46.8 percent. This index represents the proportion of all crimes in the category accounted for by specific arrest rates of the particular group. The crime index total for whites is 62.4 percent while that of blacks is 35.6 percent. The total index is a combination of the violent crime index and the property crime index. The latter index is 65.3 percent for whites and 32.6 percent for blacks. In 1988, white persons accounted for 68.6 percent of all persons arrested for crimes while blacks accounted for 29.6 percent of arrested individuals.

The severity of crime in the black community and the vulnerability of the black population to crime can be gleaned from data released in 1990 by the Department of Justice. Its National Crime Survey of crime between 1979 and 1986 revealed that (1) blacks were approximately six times more likely to be murdered than whites; (2) blacks were twice as likely as whites to be victimized by rapes; (3) twice as likely to be robbed than whites; (4) much more likely than whites to be victimized by aggravated assault, physically attacked or threatened with violence, or to be attacked with such weapons as guns or knives; and (5) more likely than whites to be injured during robberies.[6] The findings from this seven-year study are consistent with 1988 data that will be analyzed below.

The 1988 data showed that blacks account for more than half (53.5 percent) of all persons arrested in the United States for murder and nonnegligent manslaughter. White persons accounted for 45.0 percent (Table 12.1). Previously, when this offense was disaggregated into felony murder and manslaughter by negligence, the data showed that whites accounted for almost 8 of every 10 persons arrested for manslaughter by negligence while blacks represented one-fifth of such arrests. Among persons aged 18 years and older, 53 percent of all persons arrested for murder and nonnegligent manslaughter are black while 45.5 percent are white. In the age category of under age 18, almost six of every ten (57.1 percent) of persons arrested for this offense are black while more than four of every ten (45.5 percent) are white. It is apparent that blacks are grossly overrepresented in arrest data for murder and nonnegligent manslaughter.[7]

Murder

Differences between black and white populations in rates of murder and negligent manslaughter may be partially explained by social and economic advantages of whites when appearing in a court of law. Because whites are generally able to hire more competent lawyers and have greater success at plea bargaining, killings by white people are more likely to be defined as negligent homicides rather than as felonious murders. On the other hand, poor blacks are often not informed of evidentiary rules or not apprised of due process. They are often unable to afford competent lawyers or secure legal aid from persons who have a vested interest in

Table 12.1 TOTAL ARRESTS, DISTRIBUTION BY RACE: 1988
(9,933 Agencies; 1988 Estimated Population 187,818,000)

Offense charged	Total arrests					Percent distribution[a]				
	Total	White	Black	American Indian or Alaskan Native	Asian or Pacific Islander	Total	White	Black	American Indian or Alaskan Native	Asian or Pacific Islander
Total	10,067,447	6,903,070	2,977,266	105,050	82,061	100.0	68.6	29.6	1.0	.8
Murder and nonnegligent manslaughter	16,090	7,243	8,603	99	145	100.0	45.0	53.5	.6	.9
Forcible rape	28,036	14,775	12,853	218	190	100.0	52.7	45.8	.8	.7
Robbery	110,427	40,072	69,130	481	744	100.0	36.3	62.6	.4	.7
Aggravated assault	302,311	174,177	123,058	2,843	2,233	100.0	57.6	40.7	.9	.7
Burglary	329,812	220,998	103,249	2,673	2,892	100.0	67.0	31.3	.8	.9
Larceny—theft	1,157,150	758,752	372,574	12,221	13,603	100.0	65.6	32.2	1.1	1.2
Motor vehicle theft	151,719	89,115	59,984	883	1,737	100.0	58.7	39.5	.6	1.1
Arson	14,374	10,559	3,591	124	100	100.0	73.5	25.0	.9	.7
Violent crime[b]	456,864	236,267	213,644	3,641	3,312	100.0	51.7	46.8	.8	.7
Property crime[c]	1,653,055	1,079,424	539,398	15,901	18,332	100.0	65.3	32.6	1.0	1.1
Crime Index total[d]	2,109,919	1,315,691	753,042	19,542	21,644	100.0	62.4	35.7	.9	1.0
Other assaults	683,182	423,697	247,839	6,580	5,066	100.0	62.0	36.3	1.0	.7
Forgery and counterfeiting	72,860	47,156	24,902	398	404	100.0	64.7	34.2	.5	.6
Fraud	260,376	170,228	87,873	1,031	1,244	100.0	65.4	33.7	.4	.5
Embezzlement	11,467	7,388	3,926	54	99	100.0	64.4	34.2	.5	.9
Stolen property; buying, receiving, possessing	123,853	70,839	51,568	709	737	100.0	57.2	41.6	.6	.6
Vandalism	224,275	166,540	53,812	2,064	1,859	100.0	74.3	24.0	.9	.8
Weapons; carrying, possessing, etc.	162,365	95,092	64,937	813	1,523	100.0	58.6	40.0	.5	.9
Prostitution and commercialized vice	78,346	45,163	31,968	404	811	100.0	57.6	40.8	.5	1.0

Table 12.1 (Continued)

Offense charged	Total arrests					Percent distribution[a]				
	Total	White	Black	American Indian or Alaskan Native	Asian or Pacific Islander	Total	White	Black	American Indian or Alaskan Native	Asian or Pacific Islander
Sex offenses (except forcible rape and prostitution)	77,870	59,856	16,626	823	565	100.0	76.9	21.4	1.1	.7
Drug abuse violations	844,300	503,125	334,015	3,224	3,936	100.0	59.6	39.6	.4	.5
Gambling	17,613	8,221	8,373	27	992	100.0	46.7	47.5	.2	5.6
Offenses against family and children	49,643	31,572	16,444	542	1,085	100.0	63.6	33.1	1.1	2.2
Driving under the influence	1,279,121	1,125,107	130,375	14,187	9,452	100.0	88.0	10.2	1.1	.7
Liquor laws	488,993	429,309	46,737	10,109	2,838	100.0	87.8	9.6	2.1	.6
Drunkenness	599,295	478,479	104,459	14,867	1,490	100.0	79.8	17.4	2.5	.2
Disorderly conduct	569,475	358,840	200,717	7,087	2,831	100.0	63.0	35.2	1.2	.5
Vagrancy	27,969	16,351	10,882	632	104	100.0	58.5	38.9	2.3	.4
All other offenses (except traffic)	2,197,185	1,399,855	755,704	19,788	21,838	100.0	63.7	34.4	.9	1.0
Suspicion	10,973	4,686	6,140	44	103	100.0	42.7	56.0	.4	.9
Curfew and loitering law violations	54,847	44,219	8,766	557	1,305	100.0	80.6	16.0	1.0	2.4
Runaways	123,520	101,656	18,161	1,568	2,135	100.0	82.3	14.7	1.3	1.7

[a]Due to rounding, percentage may not total 100.

[b]Violent crimes are: murder, forcible rape, robbery, and aggravated assault.

[c]Property crimes are: burglary, larceny-theft, motor vehicle theft, and arson.

[d]Includes arson.

Source: Uniform Crime Report: Crime in the United States (Washington, D. C.: U. S. Department of Justice, Federal Bureau of Investigation, 1989), 186.

their welfare. As a result, blacks are not as successful in plea bargaining or in having felonious murder crimes reduced to ones that are considered less serious or less socially injurious. Further, they may also be more frequently victimized by the right of lawyers to exercise peremptory challenges in jury selection on essentially racially discriminatory grounds. Biases of attorneys in the utilization of peremptory challenges, granted by the U.S. Supreme Court in *Swain* v. *Alabama* (1965), may be especially detrimental to blacks since a jury that is biased in its demographic composition may be biased in its decision.

Felonious murders, those murders resulting from robberies, sex motives, and premeditation, and from other felonious acts—and crime in general—have reached such staggering proportions in the black community that they constitute a major social problem. Indeed, murder is the leading cause of death among blacks between the ages of 20 and 29, and the fourth overall leading cause of deaths among black males. It is peculiarly ironic that at this moment in history, when a vast array of black Americans express apprehension about whites practicing systematic genocide against American blacks and when everyone is exhorted to "get things together," black Americans are criminally victimizing each other. This victimization is in criminal homicides, felonious murders, physical assaults, maimings, rapes, and crimes against property owned by black people. For instance, the homicide victimization rate among blacks continues to climb to unprecedented levels each year. As shown in Table 12.2 the number of black male homicide victims more than doubled between 1960 and 1979. In absolute numbers, black male homicide victims spiralled upward from 3,345 per 100,000 resident population in 1960 to 7,938 per 100,000 in 1979. The overall black male homicide rate almost doubled as it rose from 36.7 percent to 64.6 percent in 1960 and 1979, respectively. The black female homicide rate climbed from 1,013 in 1960 to 1,874 per 100,000 resident population in 1979. The actual homicide rates were 10.4 in 1960 and 13.8 in 1979 for black females. During the same period the absolute number of white male homicide victims almost quadrupled while their homicide rate jumped from 3.6 to 10.1. The white female homicide victimization rate and their absolute numbers more than doubled between 1960 and 1979. Nevertheless, blacks are about six times more likely to become homicide victims than are whites in the general population.

Homicide continues to be a leading cause of death among urban blacks, particularly among black males. McAllister reported that while white men have a 1 in 80 chance of dying from murder, black men have a 1 in 10 chance of being killed in their lifetime. Homicide is the leading cause of death among the 5.1 million black males between the ages of 15 and 24. In the 20–24 age group, one in three black males die of homicide.[8] The National Crime Survey data released by the Department of Justice in 1990 showed that the murder rate among blacks was 31.2 per 100,000. By contrast, the murder rate among whites was 5.4 per 100,000.

The highest murder rate in the United States in 1989 was in Washing-

Table 12.2 HOMICIDE VICTIMS BY RACE AND SEX: 1950–1979*

| Year | Homicide victims | | | | | Homicide rate[b] | | | | |
| | Total[a] | White | | Black | | Total[a] | White | | Black | |
		Male	Female	Male	Female		Male	Female	Male	Female
1950	7,942	2,586	952	3,450	890	5.3	3.9	1.4	(NA)	(NA)
1955	7,418	2,439	922	3,126	846	4.5	3.4	1.2	(NA)	(NA)
1960	8,464	2,832	1,154	3,345	1,013	4.7	3.6	1.4	36.7	10.4
1965	10,712	3,660	1,379	4,376	1,147	6.5	4.4	1.6	43.4	10.5
1968	14,686	5,106	1,700	6,283	1,418	7.4	6.0	1.9	60.0	12.3
1969	15,477	5,215	1,801	6,770	1,463	7.7	6.1	2.0	63.8	12.5
1970	16,848	5,865	1,938	7,265	1,569	8.3	6.8	2.1	67.6	13.3
1971	18,787	6,455	2,106	8,157	1,807	9.1	7.3	2.3	74.2	14.9
1972[c]	19,638	6,820	2,156	8,594	1,768	9.4	7.7	2.3	76.8	14.4
1973	20,465	7,411	2,575	8,216	1,965	9.8	8.3	2.8	72.5	15.8
1974	21,465	7,992	2,656	8,480	1,978	10.2	8.9	2.8	73.8	15.7
1975	21,310	8,222	2,751	8,092	1,929	10.0	9.1	2.9	69.6	15.1
1976	19,554	7,568	2,547	7,327	1,767	9.1	8.3	2.7	62.2	13.6
1977	19,968	7,951	2,787	7,135	1,734	9.2	8.7	2.9	59.7	13.2
1978	20,432	8,429	2,771	7,118	1,739	9.4	9.2	2.9	58.7	13.0
1979	22,550	9,392	2,942	7,938	1,874	10.2	10.1	3.0	64.6	13.8

*Rates per 100,000 resident population in specified group. Beginning 1970, excludes deaths to nonresidents of U.S. Deaths for 1979 classified according to the ninth revision of the International Classification of diseases; for earlier years, classified according to the revision in use at the time, see text, p. 57. See also *Historical Statistics, Colonial Times to 1970,* series H 971–978.

NA: Not available.

[a]Includes races not shown separately.

[b]Rate based on enumerated population figures as of April 1 for 1950, 1960, and 1970; July 1 estimates for others.

[c]Based on a 50-percent sample of deaths.

Source: U.S. National Center for Health Statistics, *Vital Statistics of the United States,* Annual 1980, p. 178.

ton, D. C., where a record 434 people were killed.[9] It is estimated that black males accounted for almost 80 percent of those deaths. Similarly, black males accounted for approximately two-thirds of the murder victims in other cities that set 1989 records for murder: New Orleans; Philadelphia; Kansas City, Missouri; Milwaukee; and Columbus, Ohio. Other cities also experience a high murder rate; for example, Los Angeles, Detroit, Chicago, Baltimore, and Memphis. Nationally, about 49.3 percent of murder victims are white and 48.1 percent are black.

Experts in law enforcement and social scientists, as well as the average citizen in metropolitan communities, are convinced that the major factor in the rising murder rates is the drug war. Competition for trafficking turf; arguments over payments for distribution or sales, jealousies over distribution successes and huge payoffs as well as personal vendettas lead to an escalation of drug-related deaths. In some cities, victims are assassinated, found with hands tied behind their backs and/or shot from the rear of an automobile. Persons are gunned down in restaurants or by passerbys as they stand on a street corner. Without question, the drug problem is a major factor in violence not only in the black community but in American society in general.

In violent crimes, such as homicides, offenders and victims are likely to know each other, and in about 90 percent of the cases, the offender and the victim are of the same race. Family violence research shows that violent deaths within families caused by family members are also increasing. Women are more likely to be killed by their husbands or ex-husbands than they are to kill them. But victims also include children and grandparents or other relatives.[10]

As inferred earlier, arrest rates for murder vary according to geographic characteristics such as location in the metropolitan community. In cities, many of which are now heavily populated by blacks, blacks account for 61.6 percent of all persons arrested for murder and whites represent 37 percent of murder arrests (Table 12.3). Close approximations of this distribution hold even when the data are analyzed by race and age. Blacks, therefore, are much more likely than whites to be arrested for murder in cities.[11]

In the suburbs, on the other hand, places in which the black population is a mere one-sixteenth of the total population, whites account for two-thirds (66.5 percent) and blacks almost one-third (32.3 percent) of persons arrested for murder (Table 12.4). Nevertheless, the black arrest rate for murder in suburban communities is approximately six times greater than their proportion of the suburban population in the United States would suggest. Again, whether in cities or suburbs, murder, like violent crime in general, is substantially more likely to be intraracial rather than interracial.[12] Further, there is some evidence that the majority of blacks arrested for murder are either unemployed or employed in menial types of occupations.[13] *This occupational profile supports the theoretical position that intrarace murders originate in frustrations related to economic deprivations or stem from the devastating consequences of poverty and the resulting social alienation.* Aggressive responses to frustrations originating in conditions within the social structure obviously are not always directed toward the sources of the frustration; rather, such frustrations are intrapunitive and turned inward toward members of one's own group.[14] These behavioral patterns may also have their roots in a socialization process in which studied manifestations of *machismo* or masculinity are highly prized. They typify subconscious internalization of negative self-value and images attributed to blacks by the dominant group as well as a deeply ingrained belief system that leads the offender to believe that his offense against a member of his own group will not be as severely punished as one perpetrated against a member of the majority population.

Fratricide

Intragroup murders, or fratricide, reflect an inner turmoil of societally induced rage that ultimately reduces many young black men into walking time bombs ready to explode in violent behavior at what appears to be the most insignificant incident, such as an argument over a dime or the use of racial epithets. Also, unresolved love triangles and suspicions of infidelity may precipitate a sudden release of rage resulting in murder.[15]

The general findings reported in studies in New York and other localized studies in such cities as New Orleans and Detroit support the overall observation that a significant majority of homicides are fratricidal or intragroup in nature. A significant proportion of fratricidal violence occurs among young people in the teen years. Often, this form of black-on-black crime involves killings of young males who refuse to hand over a pair of sneakers or jewelry to the attacker(s). It may stem from a simple argument that may, in earlier times, have been resolved either through a handshake or a fistfight that would have been forgotten within hours, or even from being embarrassed by losing a game of cards. Some teenagers have been killed by other teenagers because they refused to try crack or smoke marijuana and some have been the victims of hold-ups at fast food restaurants or by random shootings. Although a very small proportion of the black male teenage population participates in such acts, that number is sufficient to heighten the fears and suspicions many people have about black male teenagers.

Aggravated Assaults

These are unlawful attacks upon a person for the purpose of inflicting severe bodily injury. As a rule, the attack is accompanied by the use of a weapon capable of producing serious bodily injury or even death. Most persons arrested for this offense in 1988 were white males, over the age of 18, who live in cities and in suburbs. In terms of total arrests, almost three-fifths (57.6 percent) of all persons arrested for this offense were

Table 12.3 CITY ARRESTS, DISTRIBUTION BY RACE: 1988
(6,891 Agencies; 1988 Estimated Population 128,522,000)

Offense charged	Total arrests					Percent distribution[a]				
	Total	White	Black	American Indian or Alaskan Native	Asian or Pacific Islander	Total	White	Black	American Indian or Alaskan Native	Asian or Pacific Islander
Total	7,869,070	5,137,436	2,583,330	79,663	68,641	100.0	65.3	32.8	1.0	.9
Murder and nonnegligent manslaughter	12,356	4,567	7,610	64	115	100.0	37.0	61.6	.5	.9
Forcible rape	21,518	10,099	11,121	138	160	100.0	46.9	51.7	.6	.7
Robbery	98,535	33,877	63,564	406	688	100.0	34.4	64.5	.4	.7
Aggravated assault	238,178	127,545	106,859	1,858	1,916	100.0	53.6	44.9	.8	.8
Burglary	249,773	157,410	88,254	1,757	2,352	100.0	63.0	35.3	.7	.9
Larceny-theft	994,206	639,381	331,700	10,995	12,130	100.0	64.3	33.4	1.1	1.2
Motor vehicle theft	123,733	67,941	53,742	607	1,443	100.0	54.9	43.4	.5	1.2
Arson	10,749	7,456	3,117	89	87	100.0	69.4	29.0	.8	.8
Violent crime[b]	370,587	176,088	189,154	2,466	2,879	100.0	47.5	51.0	.7	.8
Property crime[c]	1,378,461	872,188	476,813	13,448	16,012	100.0	63.3	34.6	1.0	1.2
Crime Index total[d]	1,749,048	1,048,276	665,967	15,914	18,891	100.0	59.9	38.1	.9	1.1
Other assaults	546,463	318,695	218,640	4,808	4,320	100.0	58.3	40.0	.9	.8
Forgery and counterfeiting	54,230	33,995	19,594	288	353	100.0	62.7	36.1	.5	.7
Fraud	140,589	87,810	51,248	474	1,057	100.0	62.5	36.5	.3	.8
Embezzlement	7,599	4,787	2,713	27	72	100.0	63.0	35.7	.4	.9
Stolen property; buying, receiving, possessing	99,563	53,495	44,919	514	635	100.0	53.7	45.1	.5	.6
Vandalism	181,886	129,837	48,908	1,541	1,600	100.0	71.4	26.9	.8	.9
Weapons; carrying, possessing, etc.	132,474	72,161	58,406	589	1,318	100.0	54.5	44.1	.4	1.0
Prostitution and commercialized vice	75,156	42,983	31,024	376	773	100.0	57.2	41.3	.5	1.0

Table 12.3 (Continued)

Offense charged	Total arrests					Percent distribution[a]				
	Total	White	Black	American Indian or Alaskan Native	Asian or Pacific Islander	Total	White	Black	American Indian or Alaskan Native	Asian or Pacific Islander
Sex offenses (except forcible rape and prostitution)	59,221	43,313	14,802	618	488	100.0	73.1	25.0	1.0	.8
Drug abuse violations	681,504	377,547	298,600	2,084	3,273	100.0	55.4	43.8	.3	.5
Gambling	15,020	6,301	7,825	21	873	100.0	42.0	52.1	.1	5.8
Offenses against family and children	26,270	16,293	8,639	351	987	100.0	62.0	32.9	1.3	3.8
Driving under the influence	799,238	694,863	89,450	8,673	6,252	100.0	86.9	11.2	1.1	.8
Liquor laws	380,916	330,442	39,647	8,618	2,209	100.0	86.7	10.4	2.3	.6
Drunkenness	494,825	386,270	94,864	12,443	1,248	100.0	78.1	19.2	2.5	.3
Disorderly conduct	509,352	310,447	190,735	5,538	2,632	100.0	60.9	37.4	1.1	.5
Vagrancy	25,896	14,689	10,507	619	81	100.0	56.7	40.6	2.4	.3
All other offenses (except traffic)	1,731,714	1,041,862	656,094	14,733	19,025	100.0	60.2	37.9	.9	1.1
Suspicion	9,921	3,845	5,958	21	97	100.0	38.8	60.1	.2	1.0
Curfew and loitering law violations	51,956	42,091	8,633	419	813	100.0	81.0	16.6	.8	1.6
Runaways	96,229	77,434	16,157	994	1,644	100.0	80.5	16.8	1.0	1.7

[a]Due to rounding, percentages may not total 100.

[b]Violent crimes are: murder, forcible rape, robbery, and aggravated assault.

[c]Property crimes are: burglary, larceny-theft, motor vehicle theft, and arson.

[d]Includes arson.

Source: Uniform Crime Report: Crime in the United States (Washington, D. C.: U. S. Department of Justice, Federal Bureau of Investigation, 1989), 195.

Table 12.4 SUBURBAN AREA[a] ARRESTS, DISTRIBUTION BY RACE: 1988
(4,641 Agencies; 1988 Estimated Population 75,424,000)

Offense charged	Total arrests					Percent distribution[b]				
	Total	White	Black	American Indian or Alaskan Native	Asian or Pacific Islander	Total	White	Black	American Indian or Alaskan Native	Asian or Pacific Islander
Total	3,272,163	2,626,180	619,483	13,815	12,685	100.0	80.3	18.9	.4	.4
Murder and nonnegligent manslaughter	3,461	2,303	1,117	13	28	100.0	66.5	32.3	.4	.8
Forcible rape	8,257	5,749	2,438	34	36	100.0	69.6	29.5	.4	.4
Robbery	21,052	10,513	10,391	87	61	100.0	49.9	49.4	.4	.3
Aggravated assault	86,570	62,006	23,651	507	406	100.0	71.6	27.3	.6	.5
Burglary	105,720	82,255	22,606	428	431	100.0	77.8	21.4	.4	.4
Larceny-theft	374,275	270,592	99,145	1,760	2,778	100.0	72.3	26.5	.5	.7
Motor vehicle theft	39,515	28,839	10,262	153	261	100.0	73.0	26.0	.4	.7
Arson	5,138	4,329	764	23	22	100.0	84.3	14.9	.4	.4
Violent crime[c]	119,340	80,571	37,597	641	531	100.0	67.5	31.5	.5	.4
Property crime[d]	524,648	386,015	132,777	2,364	3,492	100.0	73.6	25.3	.5	.7
Crime Index total[e]	643,988	466,586	170,374	3,005	4,023	100.0	72.5	26.5	.5	.6
Other assaults	211,349	160,278	49,225	972	874	100.0	75.8	23.3	.5	.4
Forgery and counterfeiting	25,258	17,941	7,140	99	78	100.0	71.0	28.3	.4	.3
Fraud	111,240	77,877	32,851	173	339	100.0	70.0	29.5	.2	.3
Embezzlement	4,106	2,808	1,268	19	11	100.0	68.4	30.9	.5	.3
Stolen property; buying, receiving, possessing	42,873	28,895	13,589	172	217	100.0	67.4	31.7	.4	.5
Vandalism	80,263	68,549	11,182	262	270	100.0	85.4	13.9	.3	.3
Weapons; carrying, possessing, etc.	46,138	34,229	11,545	129	235	100.0	74.2	25.0	.3	.5
Prostitution and commercialized vice	6,028	4,127	1,789	34	78	100.0	68.5	29.7	.6	1.3

Table 12.4 (Continued)

Offense charged	Total arrests					Percent distribution[b]				
	Total	White	Black	American Indian or Alaskan Native	Asian or Pacific Islander	Total	White	Black	American Indian or Alaskan Native	Asian or Pacific Islander
Sex offenses (except forcible rape and prostitution)	24,568	21,375	2,979	92	122	100.0	87.0	12.1	.4	.5
Drug abuse violations	229,993	172,723	56,179	591	500	100.0	75.1	24.4	.3	.2
Gambling	2,773	1,875	857	3	38	100.0	67.6	30.9	.1	1.4
Offenses against family and children	23,940	16,120	7,673	76	71	100.0	67.3	32.1	.3	.3
Driving under the influence	556,756	515,204	37,558	1,898	2,096	100.0	92.5	6.7	.3	.4
Liquor laws	174,595	164,197	9,276	735	387	100.0	94.0	5.3	.4	.2
Drunkenness	196,399	171,346	22,292	2,225	536	100.0	87.2	11.4	1.1	.3
Disorderly conduct	165,725	132,816	31,964	557	388	100.0	80.1	19.3	.3	.2
Vagrancy	4,903	3,833	1,002	54	14	100.0	78.2	20.4	1.1	.3
All other offenses (except traffic)	654,604	506,222	143,839	2,388	2,155	100.0	77.3	22.0	.4	.3
Suspicion	2,783	2,310	448	10	15	100.0	83.0	16.1	.4	.5
Curfew and loitering law violations	18,625	16,796	1,706	55	68	100.0	90.2	9.2	.3	.4
Runaways	45,256	40,073	4,747	266	170	100.0	88.5	10.5	.6	.4

[a]This excludes central cities but includes suburban city and county law enforcement agencies within metropolitan areas.

[b]Due to rounding, figures may not add to total.

[c]Violent crimes are murder, forcible rape, robbery, and aggravated assault.

[d]Property crimes are burglary, larceny-theft, motor vehicle theft, and arson.

[e]Includes arson.

Source: Uniform Crime Report: Crime in the United States (Washington, D. C.: U. S. Department of Justice, Federal Bureau of Investigation, 1989), 222.

white and two-fifths (40.7 percent) were black. In cities, whites accounted for 53.6 percent and blacks represented 44.9 percent of persons arrested for aggravated assault. In suburbs, whites accounted for 71.6 percent and blacks 27.3 percent of persons arrested for this offense (Tables 12.1, 12.3, and 12.4).

In 1989, 48 percent of the victims of aggravated assault were black and 41 percent were white. However, there were 14 aggravated assaults for every 1,000 blacks and 9 for every 1,000 whites. Of the 456,864 persons arrested for violent crimes in the United States in 1988, almost two-thirds (66.1 percent) were arrested for aggravated assault.

Like criminal homicides, in most cases the offender and the victim in aggravated assaults are known to each other—either as members of the family unit, neighbors, or acquaintances. This situation creates a problem in arrest clearance since it is difficult to persuade a victim to testify against the alleged offender. Further, the victim often fears recrimination by the offender or friends of the offender once the victim testifies against an alleged offender. It is undoubtedly for this reason that less than 40 percent of adults prosecuted for aggravated assault are convicted. Others may be convicted on a lesser charge as a consequence of plea bargaining or because of the refusal of the victim to press charges against the offender.

Forcible Rape and Attempted Rape

This type of offense refers to the employment of force or the threat of force in order to have carnal knowledge, usually of a female. It is to be distinguished from *statutory rape,* which refers to having carnal knowledge of an underage person with consent and without force.

Research on forcible rape shows that: (1) the actual number of persons arrested for rapes has increased in recent years (e.g., an increase of 5.5 percent between 1979 and 1980); (2) variations in rates among cities of different population sizes are not negligible (for instance, the arrest rate is 71 per 100,000 persons in the population for cities with a population of 250,000 or more and only 18 per 100,000 in small towns with a population between 10,000 and 24,999); (3) racial distinctions exist in victimization— the victim is likely to be a black female; (4) intraracial cases of sexual assaults are treated less severely than interracial rape cases, especially if the accused and convicted is a black male; and (5) the incidence of rape within the white population is increasing.

In 1988, 52.7 percent of all persons arrested for rape in the United States were white while blacks accounted for 45.8 percent of total arrests for this offense. The percentages for persons age 18 and over arrested for rape were quite similar to the national totals: 53.4 percent white and 45.2 percent black. Among persons under the age of 18 arrested for rapes, blacks account for 50 percent of the total and whites 48 percent.[16] In cities, slightly more than half (51.7 percent) of those arrested for rape are black while 46.9 percent are white. In suburbs, however, almost seven of every ten (69.6 percent) of persons arrested are white compared to the 29.5 percent attributed to black persons (Tables 12.1 and 12.3). Although the majority of the 28,036 persons arrested for rape are white, blacks are overrepresented in these arrests data as illustrated by both the national percentages and the proportion of blacks who live in suburbia.

It is known that black women have a much higher victimization rate than white women. The United States Department of Justice's 1979 study of rape victimization in 26 American cities demonstrated that blacks and other minorities have a rape victimization rate that is 1.7 times higher than that of white females. In this study, the rape victimization rate for blacks and other minorities was 115 compared to 67 per 100,000 for white women.[17] Blacks and other minority women, therefore, had an attempted rape victimization rate 1.4 times that of white women. Their attempted rape victimization incidents occurred at the rate of 213/100,000 for blacks and other minority women and 154/100,000 for white women.[18] However, when the analysis focused on race and age as the predictor variables with respect to rape victimization, the data revealed that young white women, ages 12 to 19, were at greater risk for rape victimization than black and other minority women. Rapes occurred at the rate of 356/ 100,000 for white and 270/100,000 black and other women in that age cohort. The vulnerability of black and other minority women to rape victimization and attempted rape victimization increased dramatically, however, in the age cohort of 20 to 34. In that age range, while white women were victimized by forcible rape at the rate of 139/100,000, black and other minority women experienced a rate of 292/100,000 in the population. With respect to attempted rape victimization, black and other minority women were victimized at a rate of 355/100,000 while white women were victimized at the rate of 196/100,000.[19]

Rape and attempted rape are also related to other demographic factors such as income and race of the victim. Among white and black or nonwhite women, the risks of both rape and attempted rape victimization decrease with increasing family income. In other words, white women from higher incomes are less likely to be victimized than are white women from families with lower incomes. Specifically, the rape victimization rate for white women from families with incomes of less than $7,500 per year is five times greater than that for white women whose family income is in excess of $15,000 per year. Rape victimization rates were 119 and 23 per 100,000, respectively, for these two income groups. A similar pattern was observed with respect to attempted rape victimization among white women in which the rates were 242/100,000 among those with incomes of less than $7,500 per year and 117 for white women from families with annual incomes in excess of $15,000. Among black and other minority women from the below $7,500 range, the rape victimization rate was 127/100,000; it was only 22 for those nonwhite women from families with annual incomes in excess of $15,000. The attempted rape victimization rates for the two income categories were 237/100,000 and 185/100,000 for the income groups of under $7,500 and over $15,000, respectively. In this regard, the two racial groups were more or less indistinguishable at the extreme income levels. However, within the middle range of annual incomes of $7,500 to $14,999, a major difference emerged. Black and other minority women were almost three times more likely than white women to be a rape victim. White women had a rape victimization at the rate of 45/100,000 while nonwhite women experienced rape victimization at the rate of 129/100,000. Nonwhite women also had a substantially higher attempted rape victimization rate (189/100,000) than did white women (129/100,000).[20]

With respect to race, rape, and attempted rape victimization, the study by the United States Department of Justice confirms earlier studies by several researchers which showed that rape is usually an intraracial offense. Whenever a lone offender was the perpetrator, in 9 of 10 cases of rapes of nonwhite women the offense was committed by a nonwhite offender. The same pattern was observed when the victim was white, and the offender was also white. Regarding attempted rapes, in 95 percent of the cases in which nonwhite women were the victim, a minority male was the offender. In 94 percent of the cases in which a white woman was the victim, the lone offender was a white male. Further, white males who are multiple offenders are more likely to victimize white females (i.e., in 9 of 10 cases) than they are to victimize minority women. Similarly, multiple offenders who are nonwhite males attack minority women three-fourths of the time. But with respect to attempted rape by mixed race multiple offenders, the white female is victimized in 74 percent of the cases, and is also the victim in 87 percent of the cases of actual rape.[21]

The 1988 Justice Department National Crime Survey data shows that the rape victimization rate is 1.5 per 1,000 black women compared to 0.8/1,000 white women.[22] Black women, not indistinguishable from white women along this dimension, are more likely to be raped by a stranger than by someone they know. Again, national data shows that rape by a stranger is twice as likely to occur than rape from an acquaintance.[23] However, during the 1980s, "acquaintance rape," and "date rape" seemed to have increased dramatically, especially in the white population. Whether or not the increase was real or merely reflected a greater propensity for women to report this form of rape awaits more systematic study. Previously, women seemed reluctant to report acquaintance and date rape. Explanations for underreporting such rapes range from feelings of guilt that their own behavior may have induced the sexual transgression, embarrassment, fear that they might not be believed, and reluctance to cause possible imprisonment for a person they know.

Rapes are intraracial crimes; that is, white men are far more likely to rape white women than are black men and a black woman is much more likely to be raped by a black man than she is by a white man. Nevertheless, beliefs in racially charged myths and stereotypes about the black male rapists bent on sexual gratifications with a white female persists in the United States. Such belief patterns are transmitted through socialization as a boundary-maintenance device to socially separate the races. Thus it becomes relatively commonplace for persons who have internalized such prejudices to readily believe accusations such as those in the famous 1989 Boston case in which a white man falsely accused a black man of attacking him and killing his pregnant wife.

In any analysis of interracial rape cases, one must be extremely cautious about the statistical data uncovered in police and court records, for instance. This caution stems largely from the historical fact that the credibility of white females accusing black men as rapists has seldom been challenged. But the black female's veracity is suspect whether she points the accusing finger at a black or white male.[24] In the case of both white and nonwhite women, due primarily to the persistence of a "macho" image of male perogatives as well as to notions that the new emphasis on sexual freedom in American society has lessened morality among women, too, women often have an inordinately difficult time *proving* rape. Many women do not wish to subject themselves to unsympathetic police officers who frequently behave in ways that actually blame the victims. As a result, many victims never come forward to report either the actual incidence of rape or an attempted rape. Hence, the incidence of rape reported in police and other statistics is probably higher than reported.

ACQUISITIVE CRIME

Robbery

Defined as a "vicious type of crime" occurring in the victim's presence, robbery is committed to obtain valued property by the use of force or the threat of force. Robberies, including assault to commit robbery as well as attempted robberies, constitute one-fourth of all violent crimes. When assault to commit robbery and attempted robbery are included, robberies constitute about a third of all violent crimes. But robbery is also acquisitive since its primary motive is the acquisition of money or property through illegal means. Of the 110,427 persons arrested for robbery in the United States in 1988, 69,130 or 62.5 percent were black and 36.3 percent or 40,072 were white (Table 12.1). The representation of blacks in robbery arrests has increased significantly since 1981 when they accounted for 56.9 percent of the arrests while the proportion of whites declined from 41.0 percent. This change may reflect, among other things, the rapidly deteriorating economic status of the black male in the United States. During the thirteen-year period between 1976 and 1986, the nation experienced at least two back-to-back recessions that impacted heavily on black men. In that interim, the percentage of full-time employed black men dropped from 44 percent to 35 percent. In other words, almost two-thirds of all black males are not employed full-time—a fact that may be reflected in robbery and other acquisitive crimes and which may contribute to other violent behavior.

The degree to which location is a factor in racial arrests for robbery is reflected in other data displayed in Tables 12.1 and 12.3. An examination of those data sets reveals that: (1) 64.5 percent of persons arrested in cities are black while 34.4 percent are white; and (2) blacks and whites are almost equal in the proportion of persons arrested for this offense in suburbs. There whites account for 49.9 percent and blacks 49.4 percent of all persons arrested for robbery. In 1988, 2.0 percent of the households headed by a black person, compared to 0.8 percent of those headed by a white person were victimized by robbery. Whether in cities or suburbs, blacks are almost three times as likely as whites to be victimized by robbery. In 1989, for every 1,000 blacks in the population there were 13 robberies but only five robberies for every 1,000 white persons. It is most reasonable to conclude that, since most violent crimes are intraracial, black suburbanites who experience robbery are more likely to be victimized by black offenders than by white offenders, and white victims are more likely to be victimized by white offenders.[25]

During 1988, 5 percent of all American households were victims of at least one burglary and 17 percent were victimized by at least one completed or attempted theft. Most vulnerable households were those with higher incomes, those in urban areas, and households occupied by black persons. Over a fourth (27 percent) of all households with incomes of $27,000 or more annually were victimized by crime. Almost three of every ten (29 percent) and three of every ten (30 percent) of all urban households were touched by crime. But the most vulnerable households are those headed by Hispanics. All told, in 1988, some 23 million households in the United States "experienced a theft or burglary or had a member who was raped, robbed or assaulted."[26]

Black households were more likely than white households to be victimized by a serious violent crime in 1988. Sixteen percent of the black households touched by crime in 1988 had a member who was either raped, robbed, or victimized by aggravated assault, compared to 9 percent of the white households that had a similar experience.[27]

Property crimes (burglary, larceny-theft, motor vehicle theft, and arson)—acquisitive crimes—account for 78 percent of all crimes for which persons were arrested in 1988. The property crime index for blacks is 32.6 percent while that index for whites is 65.3 percent. Again, although the overwhelming majority of individuals arrested for property crimes are white, blacks are overrepresented among persons arrested because blacks compose only 12 percent of the nation's population. One example of property crimes will illustrate racial and locational differences in arrest rates.[28]

Burglary

This occurs when there is an unlawful entry into a structure, not involving force, to commit a felony or theft. Between 1981 and 1988, the percentage of households touched by this offense steadily declined from 7.4 percent (1981) to 5.4 percent (1988). That decline is reflected in the number of persons arrested for this offense. Arrests for burglary dropped from 490,000 in 1981 to 329,812 in 1988. Yet, burglaries are frequently occurring property crimes and rank second only to larceny-theft in the number of persons arrested for property crimes.[29]

In cities and in suburbs, most persons arrested for burglary are white (Table 12.1 and 12.3). White persons account for more than half of persons arrested in cities (53.6 percent) and more than three-fourths (77.8 percent) of the burglary arrests in suburbs. By contrast, blacks constitute 44.9 percent and 21.4 percent in cities and suburbs, respectively. Of all persons who are under the age of 18 arrested for burglary, 70 percent are white and 27 percent are black.

OTHER OFFENSES

White collar crimes listed in Tables 12.1 and 12.3 include such offenses as forgery, fraud, and embezzlement. In each of these categories, whites account for roughly two-thirds (65 percent) of all persons arrested. These crimes provide further illustrations of race-class distinctions in crime since these crimes are usually committed by middle- and upper-income whites during the course of their daily occupations. These are not physically violent crimes; they are crimes committed by "respectable" persons who are usually regarded as upstanding citizens. The degree of social injury resulting from white-collar crime is considered less harmful than that resulting from violent crimes. Yet the amount of money lost through white-collar crimes, as in insider trading, stock frauds, and anti-trust violations, approaches $300 billion. However, society has a high level of toleration for such offenses and offenders, and is less inclined to stereotype the white middle-class and white upper-classes as criminals, as is often done in the case of the black population, especially in the lower and underclass. One need only recall the all-white cast of offenders in Watergate and the Wall Street insider trading cases to realize the magnitude of white-collar crime even in high places. Even when these persons are convicted and sentenced, they are more likely to be incarcerated in institutions in which they have special privileges—access to tennis courts and other facilities ordinarily unavailable, if not denied, convicts from lower classes.

Even though a banker in Chicago or Los Angeles or a Wall Street stockbroker may be convicted of a white-collar crime involving several million dollars, that person is often granted a much lighter sentence than a young black or a poor white convicted of burglary or robbery. In the former case, that person may never serve a day in jail but is offered a chance to work off the sentence through "community service" and a fine in lieu of imprisonment.

This inequity in the administration of justice has profound impact on poor blacks and whites, whose observations of such blatant disparities lead to the inevitable conclusion that the law is made to benefit the rich and powerful—the privileged and well-to-do—and to constrain the less fortunate.

Sex crimes include prostitution and commercialized vice and other offenses except forcible rape and prostitution. White persons account for 76.9 percent of sex offenses that do not include forcible rape and prostitution and 57.6 percent of all persons arrested for prostitution. White persons also account for almost three-fifths (59.6 percent) of all persons arrested for drug abuse violations. Blacks account for almost 40 percent of such arrests.

As previously stated, it should not be surprising that, since the majority of people in the United States are white, they would account for the majority of persons arrested for crime. That fact is further illustrated in other arrests in which whites constitute the majority: vandalism (74.3 percent); violation of liquor laws (87.8 percent); drunkenness (79.8 percent); offenses against family and children (63.6 percent); and driving while under the influence (of alcohol or drugs; white persons account for 88 percent of all persons arrested). It is also important to note that white persons account for 82 percent of the runaways but over half (56 percent) of all persons arrested for "suspicion" are black (Table 12.1).

The various rates for both aggressive and acquisitive crimes reveal an immense disproportionality within the black population between their arrest rates and the rate that should ordinarily be expected in terms of the size of the black population. Blumstein's most insightful analysis of prison data along the dimension of the race variable and Clayton's study of blacks in the Georgia penal system demonstrate the magnitude of the problem of disproportionality. Blumstein, for instance, showed that a disproportionate number of black males, especially those in their twenties, are incarcerated in the prisons of the United States. He cites a 1979 Bureau of the Census study that was conducted for the U.S. Bureau of Justice Statistics which revealed that in 1979, 74,150 of the 2,384,000 black males in their twenties were in prison. That number represented an incarceration rate for this age and race cohort of 3,068 per 100,000. This incarceration rate is approximately 25 times that of the population. In other words about 1 black male out of every 33 in his twenties is in prison on any given day.[30] The incarceration rate for this particular age group of young blacks has a disproportionality rate of approximately 7 to 1 in relation to the rate for white males of the same age.[31]

In toto, about 47 percent of all prison inmates are black. This shockingly high rate of disproportionality may be attributed not to a greater proclivity of blacks to commit criminal offenses but, in a very large measure, to racial bias throughout the criminal justice system. This argument is found in the research of a number of social scientists including Dunbaugh,[32] Christianson[33], and Lizotte[34].

When Clayton examined data on Georgia prisoners, he discovered that blacks with a "prior juvenile record" received harsher punishment than white persons with the same type of offense and whose background was similar to that of blacks in prison.[35] Although Hagan acknowledged the evidence of disparity in sentencing rates between the races, he concluded that extralegal inmate characteristics such as race do not heighten the predictability of judicial decisions.[36] Nevertheless, when one examines variables that have a strong relationship with socioeconomic position and race including such extralegal factors as employment, occupation, and dispositions on cases in which immense judicial discretion prevails, the evidence seems overwhelming that racial bias is a contributing factor of enormous magnitude to the overrepresentation of blacks in prisons.[37]

The number of persons in the nation's prisons increased by 7.4 percent between 1987 and 1988 or a growth by 43,967 for a total of 627,402 in 1988. The estimated total number of persons incarcerated in the nation's prisons in 1989 was 701,000. While the incarceration rate increased by 75 percent between 1980 and the end of 1988, that is, from 139/100,000 to 244/100,000, there is no evidence that Americans actually feel any safer.[38] The total number of prisoners has doubled in at least 15 states and more than tripled in another four. The inmate population in prisons has also about doubled since 1980.

This growth is attributed to the "law and order" commitments of the Reagan administration by which law enforcement officers were urged to make more arrests and "get criminals off the streets," increasing arrests for drug violations such as trafficking in drugs or distributing them as well as a demand for tougher sanctions against persons convicted of crimes and the rapidly increasing intolerance of the public for criminal behavior. The crime issue has also become more and more politicized so much so that few politicians will run the risk of being labeled "soft on crime." They, too, demand more prisons and their cries appear to become louder in cases of black-on white crime as opposed to black-on-black crime or white-on-black crime. Thus the prison industry has reached the level of $13 billion per year.[39]

Hate Crimes

During the 1980s an old and terrifying type of crime resurfaced. This type of crime is called "hate crimes" because the victims are singled out for physical attacks, beatings, or murder solely because of their race, ethnicity, religion, or sexual preference. Individuals may be singled out also for intimidating haunts, harassment, slurs or epithets which always accompany physical injuries inflicted on them. Hate crimes are especially directed against blacks, Jews, and gays.[40]

These crimes have been monitored since their reemergence by the Southern Poverty Law Center and by the Anti-Defamation League of

B'nai B'rith. Both organizations claim that the major perpetrators of hate crimes are neo-Nazi groups, particularly the Skinheads. Members in this group are white, young, and drawn largely from blue-collar families. Yet, some documented offenders, as are many who paint swastika signs on churches and synagogues, come from the white middle- and upper-classes. There is some evidence that Skinheads have become increasingly organized and that they have strong alliances with other hate groups such as the Ku Klux Klan and White Aryan Resistance (WAR). They are motivated by their ideology of white supremacy and by hatred, raw bigotry, and a commitment to use violence against those who would reject that ideology. Violence is the chief instrument by which they feel white supremacy can be maintained.[41]

Although the actual size of the Skinhead organization is unknown, a 1988 study by the Anti-Defamation League (ADL) reported that at least 2,000 members were operating in 21 states. A 1990 report by the Southern Poverty Law Center indicated that active membership in the Skinheads grew to 3,000 in 1989. Skinheads are an extremely violent organization. Its members attack unsuspecting victims with knives, baseball bats, their own heavy steel-toed boots, and other lethal weapons. They were implicated in four murders during 1988. In Portland, Oregon, alone in 1988, Skinheads were implicated in 30 assaults, some involving a gang of 20 or more that attacked one person.[42]

Because of their violence and the numerous deaths and injuries resulting from it as well as their role in deepening racial animosities which some states wish to combat, several states enacted anti-hate crime legislation. In 1981, Maryland became the first state to pass legislation by which hate crimes can be monitored and in 1987 some 445 hate crimes were reported to police forces in that state. Forty-three states and the District of Columbia have statutes designed to combat harassment, intimidation, and vandalism based upon race, color, religion, or sexual preference. However, 12 states strengthened existing legislation to make it easier to monitor hate crimes and bring offenders to justice. These states are: Maryland, Florida, Idaho, Washington, Oregon, Nevada, Montana, Texas, Michigan, Minnesota, Massachusetts, and Rhode Island.[43]

In 1990, the Congress of the United States passed the Hate Crimes Statistics Act which was subsequently signed into law by President Bush. Under this legislation, the U. S. Attorney General is required to compile data on hate crimes. This information would become part of the annual Uniform Crime Reports that are compiled from law enforcement data submitted from jurisdictions throughout the United States. This is the first time in the nation's history that such a requirement has been signed into law that provides a solid statistical measure of the volume and extent of racially motivate offenses.[44] Importantly, not only can hate crimes be monitored by law enforcement agencies but these agencies and community groups can more effectively collaborate in developing strategies by which hate crimes can be combatted.

CRIMES AGAINST BLACKS BY BLACKS

Throughout the United States residents of black communities perceive black-on-black crime as a major social problem. Increasingly, they realize their high vulnerability to crimes of murder, robbery, rape, assault, and generalized burglary. This heightened sense of awareness has produced an immeasurable amount of fear of crime within the black community. Black women fear being raped even when unaware of their much higher chances of being victimized. Men and women, young and old, fear physical assaults and muggings whether they reside in the upper middle-class Baldwin Hills district of Los Angeles, the upper-class Shaker Heights district of metropolitan Cleveland, or in the working-class areas of Harlem.

We have already shown in Chapter 8 how vulnerable black businesses are to crime victimization, especially those that operate in the poorer black ghettos across the nation. Robberies, burglaries, shoplifting, and other felonies place a heavy financial toll on businesses in the ghettos and central cities of America.[45] Hence such crimes have serious consequences for the overall economy of the black community—businesses are forced to relocate and to pay higher insurance rates and higher prices for poorer services.

In a study of blacks in five metropolitan communities (Atlanta, Boston, Cleveland, Houston, and Atlanta), Blackwell and Hart revealed that the fear of crime pervades the entire black community structure. No social class and no residential community can transcend this fear of crime.[46] Residents have often followed the pattern of ghetto businesses by placing guard bars over doors and windows of their dwellings. Some houses and businesses install two or three heavy padlocks on doors as deterrents to burglars and robbers. Business people who can afford to do so construct expensive security systems. Many "mom and pop" grocery storeowners carry handguns or keep them readily available in case of attack. Occasionally, when an elderly man in distress is forced to use his weapon in self-defense, the result is the loss of life or serious bodily injury. Gas stations, record shops, package liquor stores, cleaning establishments, and drug stores are constant targets. The homes of many black community residents, the poor and the economically privileged alike, stand a good chance of being victimized by thievery of some kind during the course of any year. And with each occurrence the quality of life in the city deteriorates a little bit more.

One explanation for the increase of crimes by blacks against blacks and other groups in the black community is the lack of enforcement of laws by the police. The problem is seriously exacerbated by the limited amount of security and by the paucity of police assigned to the black community. A prevalent attitude among black community residents is that the police force is composed of unconcerned whites who may, themselves, be partially responsible for the innumerable ripoffs occurring within the black community on a daily basis. The distrust of policemen is ubiquitous, and it also extends to black policemen who seem unsympathetic to the exigencies and vagaries of ghetto life.

Throughout the country, from city to city, the proportion of blacks on police forces is considerably lower than their proportion in the urban population. This observation is borne out by data presented in Table 12.5 which provides, inter alia, the officer-to-population index for 25 largest cities in the United States. The closer the index approximates the number 1.0 the greater parity between the number of officers and the population of blacks, Hispanics, or females. For this analysis, the focus of attention is on black police officers.

Only 11 percent of New York's 27,478 police officers are black; thus the officer-to-population is .44, meaning that blacks are grossly underrepresented on the police. Similarly, of the 12,378 police officers in Chicago, 22.4 percent are black and the officer-to-population index is .67, substantially higher than that found in New York City. Detroit has an officer-to-population index of .76 and 48 percent of its 5,132 member police force is black. Other cities whose officer-to-population index is .70 or above are Washington, D. C. (.78); Boston (.71); San Diego (.74); San Antonio (.77); Atlanta (.78); Pittsburgh (.78); and Phoenix (.90). Some cities in which blacks constitute a majority of the population have a particularly low officer-to-population index. An example of this disparity is New Orleans in which blacks compose only 29.9 percent of its 1,330 member police force and an officer-to-population index of .54 (Table 12.5). The black population of New Orleans represents 60 percent of the total city population. At the federal level, particularly regarding the Federal Bureau of Investigation (FBI), blacks and Hispanics are also abysmally underrepresented and some minority members of the FBI report harassment and prejudice from their colleagues. In 1989, of the 9,586 FBI agents, only 419 or 4.3 percent were black, and 453 or 4.7 percent were Hispanics.[47]

Given these statistical realities, it is relatively easy for blacks to conclude that they are indeed administered, manipulated, and controlled by a while occupation force. It provides evidence for the theoretical claim that the black urban ghetto is a colony policed largely by white mercenaries. This theme is even more strongly reinforced by the relative paucity of black officers who hold the rank of police sergeant, lieutenant, captain, or chief. Black police chiefs in cities such as Atlanta, Detroit, Houston, New York, New Orleans, Washington, D. C., and Charleston, South Carolina, are exceptions to the general rule. Even in those cities, it should be noted, parity does not exist in terms of the black officer-to-population index. And the concern that blacks express over the issue of police brutality is grave in several cities.

There is a widespread belief within the black community that most acquisitive crimes—robberies, burglaries, muggings—murders, and felonious assaults are associated with the problem of drug abuse. This view was expressed by a significant portion of the participants in the Blackwell and Hart study, and it is cited among blacks as one of the most urgent concerns within the metropolitan communities of the five cities investigated. Blacks *believe* that habitual drug abusers, without adequate means of support, will engage in criminal behavior to support a drug habit that may cost users as much as $500 per day. Some addicts, in desperate need for funds have been known to sell their children and some prostitute themselves in order to obtain money for drugs.

This relationship between drugs and sex is an issue of major concern to health-care providers in the 1990s. Reports are extensive of young mothers trading sex for drugs in crack houses and weaning their children on crack smoke.[48] Crack plays a major role in the upsurge of AIDS in the black and Hispanic heterosexual communities. Men who may have contracted AIDS through needle sharing and have access to crack as well sometimes exchange crack with addicted women for sexual pleasures thereby transmit the disease.

Michael Marriott[49] claims that crack plays a major role in the "soaring homicide rates" of such cities as New York City and that it has more than tripled the number of cocaine addicts in New York alone since 1986. His examination of New York State statistics showed that the number of "regular cocaine users" exploded from 182,000 in 1986 to 600,000 in 1988. In addition, crack is associated with an increase in the number of neglected and abused children from parents abusing drugs. Seventy-three percent of the deaths attributed to abuse and neglect in 1987 in New York were from parents who abused drugs.

Drugs are heavily implicated in the escalating gang violence in such cities as Los Angeles and New Orleans. Drugs, especially crack, also account for the rapidly growing prison population throughout the country. As a result, civilian jails are unacceptably overcrowded which, in turn, exacerbates already tense situations in the prisoner community. Local governments cannot construct prison facilities rapidly enough to alleviate the problem of overcrowdedness. The problem remains and is likely to worsen without an adequate drug control policy.

Gang-Related Crimes

These kinds of crimes are also on the increase in the black community. During the 1970s, several major cities of the United States, including Los Angeles, New York, Chicago, Philadelphia, Detroit, and San Francisco experienced a resurgence of gang activity. In recent years, hundreds of deaths, homicides, and manslaughters have been attributed to juvenile and young adult gang activities. Gangs have committed a major portion of the violent crimes for which young blacks have been arrested. The gangs, also called "posses" in the East, of the 1990s are somewhat different from those of the 1950s in the sense that the more recent gangs are better equipped with more sophisticated weaponry and are often expert in professional killings. Police have confiscated such weapons as zip guns, rifles, automatic pistols, and, in some instances, submachine guns from huge

Table 12.5 FEMALE AND MINORITY REPRESENTATION AMONG FULL-TIME SWORN OFFICERS IN THE 25 LARGEST MUNICIPAL POLICE DEPARTMENTS IN THE UNITED STATES: 1987

City	Full-time sworn officers	Females		Blacks		Hispanics	
		Percent of sworn officers	Officer-to-population index	Percent of sworn officers	Officer-to-population index	Percent of sworn officers	Officer-to-population index
New York City	27,478	10.7%	.24	11.0%	.44	10.5%	.53
Chicago	12,478	10.6	.24	22.4	.56	5.1	.36
Los Angeles	7,032	8.8	.20	11.3	.67	16.0	.59
Philadelphia	6,809	10.3	.23	19.2	.51	1.9	.50
Detroit	5,132	18.9	.42	48.0	.76	1.1	.46
Houston	4,506	9.2	.22	13.5	.49	10.9	.62
Washington, D.C.	3,878	14.0	.27	54.8	.78	2.3	.82
Baltimore	2,919	9.4	.20	21.8	.40	.4	.40
Dallas	2,280	11.8	.26	11.5	.39	5.7	.46
Milwaukee	1,941	8.6	.19	11.2	.48	3.6	.88
Boston	1,939	7.0	.15	15.9	.71	2.7	.42
San Francisco	1,870	10.2	.23	8.5	.67	9.9	.80
Phoenix	1,850	7.5	.18	4.3	.90	10.4	.70
Cleveland	1,700	10.5	.24	21.7	.50	2.4	.77
San Diego	1,612	12.2	.27	6.6	.74	10.2	.68

Table 12.5 (*Continued*)

City	Full-time sworn officers	Females		Blacks		Hispanics	
		Percent of sworn officers	Officer-to-population index	Percent of sworn officers	Officer-to-population index	Percent of sworn officers	Officer-to-population index
St. Louis	1,573	5.3	.11	22.1	.48	0	(N/A)
San Antonio	1,374	5.6	.13	5.6	.77	38.2	.71
Denver	1,335	8.6	.19	5.5	.46	15.1	.80
New Orleans	1,330	9.0	.20	29.9	.54	1.8	.53
Atlanta	1,317	13.4	.28	51.7	.78	.9	.64
Columbus, Ohio	1,245	11.4	.25	13.3	.60	0	(N/A)
Seattle	1,117	9.5	.21	5.6	.59	1.9	.73
Kansas City, Mo.	1,085	9.2	.20	12.9	.47	2.2	.67
Newark	1,056	1.0	.02	25.4	.44	5.3	.28
Pittsburgh	1,055	15.4	.34	18.8	.78	0	(N/A)

Note: The officer-to-population index is computed by dividing the percentage of sworn officers who belong to a given group by the percentage of the general population for blacks and Hispanics and by the percentage of the civilian labor force for females, as reported in the 1980 census. For example, if Hispanics comprised 12% of all sworn officers and 24% of the city's residents, the officer-to-population index number would be .50 (12 divided by 24). Black percentage figures do not include Hispanics.

Source: Bureau of Justice Statistics Special Report, *Police Departments in Large Cities, 1987* (Washington, D. C.: U. S. Department of Justice, 1987), 6.

arsenals of weapons owned by gang members. The gangs of the 1990s are also reported by police to provide protection for drug users and guard service for drop-off stations. Some members have become sophisticated in hustling, whether it is defined as pimping for prostitutes or simply making an easy living as a human parasite or "con artist."

The new gangs persist because they are a source of personal belonging or affiliation for homeless, nomadic, jobless youths who at an early age have already become alienated from the social system. They persist because the need to be accepted by a group and to have one's masculinity fulfilled through courage, "heart," and sexual prowess is fundamental to the subculture in which they live. These are not Albert Cohen's nonutilitarian gangs out on a lark.[50] They are purposeful and goal oriented as evidenced in their determination to protect their members or to rob and burglarize in order to survive in what for many of them is an extremely cruel and rejecting social milieu. They also persist because the conditions of deprivation in the social structure sustained through prolonged abject poverty and limited access to legitimate means for achieving culturally defined success goals have nurtured them. But the devastating brutalities of gang life dramatize with chilling force the degree of anomie, normlessness, and alienation that engulfs black youths at an early age.

Los Angeles is considered the gang capital of the United States. It is estimated that at least 80,000 persons belong to approximately 600 organized gangs in Los Angeles. These gangs are noted for their violence and ethnic identification with such groups as Mexicans, blacks, Samoans, Armenians, and Fijians. By far, the largest and most well-known gangs are tied to the black and Mexican populations. The most widely noted gangs include the West Side 90 Gangsters; the West Side N-Hood gang; the Tray Gangsters, The Crips (regarded as the most powerful federation of black gangs), the East Coast Crips; the Five Deuce Crips; the Bounty Hunters; and the Bloods.[51]

The violence attributed to Los Angeles gangs is evident by the number of violent crimes committed by them. In 1987, some 30,000 gang crimes in Los Angeles were reported to the police. In 1988, it was estimated that gangs committed more than 5,100 violent crimes; 2,500 people were injured in gang-related actions, and about 380 deaths were gang-related in Los Angeles.[52] It is likely that gang-related crimes, which range from murder, assaults, shootings, stabbings, and rapes to verbal intimidations are underreported because of the extreme fear law-abiding citizens have of violent gangs.

People are terrified of the weapons used by gang: Uzis, AK-47s, revolvers, pistons, shotguns, automatics—357 magnums, Intertecs, also known as Tech-9 or "Baby Uzi"—a semiautomatic handgun containing a 20-round magazine, and others. They fear gangs because they know that all persons injured by gangs are not gang members. Some are innocent persons, including children, walking on a street, sitting in their automobiles, or standing waiting for a bus.[53] Because of the widespread fear of loss of safety and the deteriorating quality of life in cities, many communities have mounted special programs to combat drug trafficking, crack houses, and other forms of crime. Los Angeles, for example, has made available a cadre of 1,000 police officers to "take back the streets" through periodic "sweeps" in gang-populated areas. Los Angeles also has a special squad of police officers who are part of an intervention called "Operation Safe Streets."[54] In New Orleans, the Third Shiloh Missionary Baptist Church, located in close distance to one of the worst housing projects in the city, the Desire Housing Project, went into the real estate business in order to reduce the influx of crack in the neighborhood. Specifically, the church purchased two crack houses and plans to buy additional dwellings known to be crack houses or places in which drug dealing is known.[55] (Other programs are described later in this chapter.)

A great deal of the violence ascribed to gangs in Los Angeles, Boston, New York, Chicago, and Philadelphia is associated with the rise in crack trade and turf wars triggered by the desire to control lucrative drug markets. Again, these gangs have changed dramatically from the innocence portrayed by Albert Cohen and other sociologists in the 1950s.

Organized Crime

Since the post-World War I period, organized crime has existed within the black community. Information on this subject is understandably scanty and fragmented. Historically, it has always been assumed that organized crime in the black community was controlled through black front men by white mobsters who lived outside the community. They controlled prostitution and gambling rings, loan sharking, the numbers game, narcotics trafficking, organized burglary gangs, bookmaking, and other forms of organized criminal behavior. All of these activities continue to be highly lucrative enterprises in the black neighborhood—so much so that some police officials now claim that black mobsters are attempting to seize control over organized crime in the black community.

Organized crime cannot operate without some form of police corruption. Whenever it exists, whether in black or white communities, whether controlled by blacks or whites, it is reasonable to assume that law enforcement agents at one level or another are being paid for protective services. Accordingly, prostitution rings, burglary rings, drug trafficking, and the numbers game, for example, are permitted to flourish because corrupt police officials give tacit if not formal approval in exchange for regular, lucrative payoffs.

Perhaps of all the forms of crime alleged to be controlled by organized crime forces now institutionalized within the black community, "playing the numbers" is the most common. It is estimated that in New York City alone 40 percent or more of black and Puerto Rican community members play the "policy game" or make parimutuel bets. The numbers system is functionally organized into three components: *runners, controllers,* and *bankers.* Runners, who compose the largest segment of this structure and who rank at the bottom in social standing, are collectors of bets and money. They, in turn, report their funds to controllers, the second largest component. After coding bets, controllers turn them over to the bankers whose major responsibility is covering bets and record keeping. Bankers are believed to have the most direct association with organized criminal elements. Functional differentiation extends to responsibilities for paying off different levels of law enforcement agents for protection. Thus the local patrolmen are paid by runners; uniformed police officers and detectives are paid by controllers; and bankers distribute payoffs to city and police officials at high levels. In essence, the numbers game is big business involving about $3 billion in annual receipts obtained from thousands of bets ranging from a nickel or a dime up to hundreds of dollars. Despite its possible connections with organized crime, the numbers game flourishes also because people like it. Many of its participants do not perceive it as illegal behavior; or they find it indistinguishable from church bingo games or race track betting—both of which are legal in most states. They do not believe that society is in any way socially injured by their betting on numbers. Many hope that the numbers game will provide a big "hit" that will give them a ticket out of the ghetto plus a new lease on a much better life.[56]

RACISM IN THE ADMINISTRATION OF CRIMINAL JUSTICE

Discriminatory practices and prejudice in the administration of justice remain a serious problem. Evidence suggests that approximately 75 percent of white police officers assigned to predominantly black precincts expressed some form of prejudice or antipathy toward black people. About 10 percent of black officers assigned to predominantly black precincts harbor extreme antiblack attitudes. Given these antiblack sentiments, the chances of blacks coming to the attention of the law are excessive even under the most ordinary circumstances. Once confronted by the police, blacks frequently claim to be subjected to status degradation, physical and verbal abuse, and to be referred to in terms of racial epithets.[57] Even black police officers are sometimes confronted by racial bigotry and insensitivity from fellow white officers. Some white officers have been either reprimanded or released from their city's police force for such behavior, including dressing up in the attire of the Ku Klux Klan.

Discrimination is pervasive in the criminal justice system. Blacks are more often victimized by deadly force and police practices such as choke holds. The problem of excessively high rates of deadly force and bias against blacks prompted several investigations by the U.S. Commission on

Civil Rights during the 1970s and persuaded the Commission to raise the question, "Who is guarding the guardians?" in their publication by the same title.[58] Such allegations have also triggered congressional hearings such as the 1983 session in New York City, chaired by Congressman John Conyers (D-Mich.). Blackwell and Hart cited several instances of known and suspected unwarranted use of deadly force by police officers in such cities as Los Angeles and Houston. They reported that U. S. Department of Justice data revealed in 1981 that 45 percent of all police homicides in the United States are committed against the black population, and that complaints of excessive force by police officers in 1980 represented a 92 percent increase over the number of complaints registered in 1979. In Los Angeles where blacks compose 18 percent of the population, over half of the persons shot and exactly half of all persons killed by the police in a four-year period (1974–1978) were black, but blacks represented only 36 percent of all persons arrested at that time. More than a quarter (28 percent) of all blacks fired on by the Los Angeles police were unarmed. A similar pattern of police firing on unarmed blacks was also observed in Houston.[59] Unwarranted beatings of black civilians precipitated uprising, riots, and urban unrest in many communities during the early 1980s, including the Algiers section of New Orleans and the Overtown and Liberty City sections of Miami. A major problem regarding the penchant of some police officers to shoot fleeing suspects is that in some states, such as Florida, state laws do not prohibit police officers from "shooting to kill." Most frequently, the victims are blacks, other racial minorities, and poor whites. Irrespective of the identity of the victims, the U.S. Commission on Civil Rights has reminded the American society that unbridled use of deadly force is a treacherous problem that must be curtailed.[60]

Discrimination against blacks in the criminal justice system also occurs in the infrequency with which blacks are granted probation; in the comparatively higher bails required of blacks for relatively minor offenses; in longer sentences given to blacks than to whites, averaging 20 months longer for blacks than whites in some offenses such as drug abuse; and in the tendency for a greater proportion of blacks to be imprisoned and to serve out most of their terms than whites. It is estimated that, nationally, slightly less than half of all inmates in the nation's prisons are blacks. Even in prisons, until recently, racial segregation was the norm. It is still practiced in some prisons. Black inmates are continually demeaned and brutalized by the prison system and, once again, by its power forces comprised predominantly of authoritarian white guards and administrators. As at Attica, Sante Fe, Lorton in Washington, D.C., Joliet in Illinois, or Reidville in Georgia, black prison inmates often claim physical attacks by guards, racism among administrators, a differential privilege and work assignment system based upon race, and a low probability of attaining parole. They are not unlike white prisoners who also suffer from the consequences of a prison system that has become overcrowded to alarming proportions. If they happen to be incarcerated in some states such as Texas (37,000),

California (35,000), New York (30,018) and Florida (27,000), they know how insufferable the ripple effects of overcrowding can be extended to other serious problems. Others fear victimization by psychosurgery related to behavioral modification programs. Many become highly political, defining themselves as political prisoners victimized by a capitalist, racist society. Not only is white racism magnified, but interethnic conflicts exacerbate deeply rooted prejudices. Thus racism is associated with the criminal justice system at all levels—from officers to trial judges to parole boards and probation officers.

The death penalty is more often used against blacks than against whites. In 1990, the General Accounting Office, which is an agency of the U. S. Congress, issued a report entitled *Death Penalty Sentencing.* Its analysis of some 28 studies on the death penalty revealed a pattern of racial discrimination in the use of the death penalty in the United States. Race made a difference in 82 percent of the cases in whether or not the defendant was given the death penalty. Specifically, persons who murdered whites are much more likely to be sentenced to die than persons who kill blacks. This study is supportive of conclusions previously reached by Amnesty International and such social scientists as Michael Radelet.[61] Yet, some 38 states have reinstituted the death penalty since 1976 when the U. S. Supreme Court mandated stricter guidelines for its use.[62] However, the U. S. Supreme Court seems unimpressed by the voluminous statistical data that reveals a systematic pattern of racial discrimination in the use of the death penalty.

As of June 1989, the NAACP Legal Defense and Educational Fund reported that there were 2,160 persons on death row in the U. S. prisons.[63] Of that number, 40 percent are black, 52 percent are white, 6 percent are Hispanic, and 2 percent are American Indian. Of all prisoners executed since 1976, 39 percent were black and 56 percent were white.[64] However, whites are significantly more likely to have their sentences commuted and blacks, once sentenced to die, are more likely to die.

PSYCHOSOCIAL THEORIES OF CRIMINAL BEHAVIOR

How, then, can criminal behavior among blacks be explained? Explanations of human behavior are invariably fraught with problems, and no single theory can completely account for either conformity or deviance from the normative order.

Aggressive offenses, such as crimes of murder and aggravated assault, may indeed be the result of deeply embedded frustrations that originate in social deprivations and interpersonal conflicts induced by the social structure. Proponents of a *deprivation theory* argue that frustration induced by abhorrent forms of economic and social discrimination may lead to aggressive acts against a victim who at a critical moment in time is defined as weak.[65] Similar to *learning and reinforcement theory,*[66] deviance is viewed as a response to environmental pressures. Certain types of stimuli call for specific types of responses. In this case, the response is defined as deviant behavior.

Another claim is that criminal behavior, aggressive or acquisitive, is learned behavior. It is learned in association with other criminals, and it is assumed that the socializing experiences of individuals who become criminals have permitted them to internalize an excess of definitions favorable to violations of the law over those definitions that are unfavorable to illegal behavior. This is a major theme in *differential association theory*. [67] Essentially, most offenders have had contact with other offenders, who socialize them into deviancy, and they, in turn, become socializers for others. This is the basis for both the cause and the cycle of recidivism among offenders. Accordingly, criminal behavior among blacks may be related to social and economic conditions in the social structure that force blacks to live in communities where the frequency and intensity of deviant behavior induce a socialization pattern that is at variance with the normative order. Furthermore, whereas certain traditions common to a given locale may be in conflict with the morality of criminal law, they are not defined as criminal by local norms. But criminal behavior is also a function of *differential opportunity,* since all persons and groups do not have equal access to attain culturally prescribed goals or rewards through legitimate means.[68]

Both differential opportunity and goals-means theory are forms of *congruence theory,* which regards social systems as highly integrated and as having priority over individuals. However, individuals may experience personal strains in cases of ambiguity in the norms of the group or when the norms seem contradictory or logically incongruous. Presumably, certain goals are culturally prescribed as normative, and the routes prescribed for their attainment are legitimated by the social system. Even in the face of disjunctions between the end—a socially accepted goal—and the means—an illegal method of achieving means—individuals are presumed to possess cognitive orientations. Individuals have alternatives. They may conform to societal expectations; they may innovate; they may engage in ritualistic behavior irrespective of consequences (retreatism); or they may rebel by rejecting the goals and the means. Persons who are poor, limited in money, economically deprived, and who, in general, do not have the means to achieve culturally defined success and who endorse success as an acceptable goal select alternative routes such as criminal behavior for goal attainment. In this sense, acquisitive crime—burglary, robbery, thievery—among blacks may be partially explained. But these are precisely the people who are the victims of repressive measures for the most minute forms of deviant behavior. Repeated acts of repression may have a reinforcing effect in the sense that once *labeled* a criminal, the individual may come to believe that he is indeed a criminal and, consequently, reorder his behavioral system in such a way as to conform to that deviant expectation.[69]

An important point should be reiterated here. Although the primary focus of this section has been on crime among blacks, it should never be assumed that the sole argument is that blacks are *more* criminal than whites or that crime is a peculiarity of the black community. A discussion of this kind is inescapable, though nonetheless painful, in an examination of diversity in the black community. Clearly, the overwhelming majority of black Americans are law-abiding citizens and will remain so even in the face of relentless economic deprivations and ravaging racial discrimination. Historical experiences demonstrate beyond a shadow of a doubt that blacks have an infinite capacity for adaptation and have employed a variety of adaptive responses to racial prejudice and subordination. Criminal behavior itself may in fact be one mode of adaptation to the myriad stresses and strains of living in a racist society that still denies blacks equal access to socially defined shared values.

GHETTO CONTROL PROGRAMS

Black Americans are undoubtedly more greatly disturbed by the disproportionate volume and rate of crimes attributed to blacks in the black communities than are any other groups of American people. The very presence of high rates of both aggressive and acquisitive crimes as compared to high rates of white-collar crimes and burglaries by whites in the white communities is no valid justification for the pervasive stereotypes about blacks and criminality. Yet these stereotypes persist because of their convenience or because of racist thinking that allows individuals to accept them as unequivocal truths.

In recent years in an effort to combat increasing rates of both aggressive and acquisitive types of criminal offenses black community residents organized a number of preventive programs. In response to inadequate protection by police to black community residents, blacks organized citizens' task forces in many cities throughout the nation. Such groups attempt to improve police surveillance and to ensure prompt action by law enforcement agencies when criminal behavior is suspected. They also organized radio patrols as crime alert systems. Organized largely as a response to the urban revolts of the 1960s, youth patrols function primarily in many cities as a buffer between the black community and the police, protecting property, disseminating information, and "monitoring police activities." In few places have youth patrols found it easy to maintain an effective balance between themselves and the police mainly because police have limited control over them.[70] Vietnam veterans organized groups called Vietnam Veterans Against Crime and many joined De Mau Mau for the purpose of combating or controlling drug trafficking and crimes against the black poor and elderly. Radio programs, such as "Buzz the Fuzz," broadcast over an all-black Chicago radio station, tend to foster attitudinal changes of blacks toward police and to promote responsibility among black community residents to report suspected criminal offenses to the police. Concerned Citizens Organizations and Friends of the Police stress the acquisition of better street lighting and improvements in the social justice system as well as in the social structure as first steps in eliminating the conditions that give rise to criminal behavior. Programs such as the Philadelphia Citywide Development Corporation (PCDC) stress security, self-help and crime-watch activities. They emphasize the importance of cooperation between local neighborhood groups and businesses to pool their efforts for combating the crime that plagues all of them. Block-watch programs, as in Philadelphia, are found in many black communities from coast to coast and in some communities, such as Los Angeles where there are 128 youth gangs, community activists have persuaded some of the youth gangs to join in the fight against crime. Few of the 128 gangs are black.[71]

Despite the upswing in community participation in crime prevention programs, urban communities must come to terms with the problem of mistrust of the police that is so prevalent in the black community. It is a mistrust that stems largely from allegations of police bias, police bigotry, and police violence which many blacks believe is entirely too ubiquitous in big city police departments.

This tendency toward violence and unwarranted employment of force against black suspects raises serious questions about the credibility of many police as law enforcement officers, strengthens perceptions of racial prejudice among police officers, and escalates allegations of police brutality. Indeed, disharmonious relationships between the black community and law enforcement officers originate most fundamentally in charges of police brutality. Vociferous blacks claim that police are "trigger happy" when confronted with black people and that their ingrained hatred or fears of black people stimulate more brutalizing responses when encountering blacks suspected of criminal offenses. This situation—combined with alleged corruption and disregard for the welfare of black people—has prompted proponents of community control to focus attention on the police as an important institution requiring direct accountability to local community people. It is mainly by virtue of these persistent efforts that personnel changes in the police force assigned to black communities have occurred and city-wide programs designed to alter radically the negative images of police officers are being formed.

NOTES

1. Cf. William Chambliss, and R. H. Nagasawa, "On the Validity of Official Statistics: A Comparative Study of White, Black and Japanese High School Boys, *Journal of Research on Crime and Delinquency*, 6 (1969): 71–77.
2. A.J. Lizotte, "Extra-Legal Factors in Chicago's Criminal Courts: Testing the Conflict Model of Criminal Justice." *Social Problems*, 25 (1978): 564–580.

3. D. Black, "The Social Organization of Arrest," *Stanford Law Review,* 23 (1976): 1087–1111.

4. Cf. Alfred Blumstein, "On the Racial Disproportionality of U.S. Prison Populations," *Journal of Criminal Law and Criminology* 73:3 (1982): 1259–1281, and Obie Clayton, "A Reconsideration of the Effects of Race in Criminal Sentencing," *Criminal Justice Review,* 8:2 (1983): 15–20.

5. The following discussion is based largely upon data presented in the Federal Bureau of Investigation, *Sourcebook of Criminal Justice Statistics 1989* and *Bureau of Justice Statistics Bulletins.*

6. Reported in Bill Nichols, "Study Crime Hits Blacks Hardest," *USA Today* (April 23, 1990), p. 3. and in "Blacks More Likely Victims of Violence," *Times-Picayune* (April 23, 1990), p. 3.

7. See *Sourcebook of Criminal Justice Statistics 1989,* Table 38, p. 187.

8. Bill McAllister, "The Plight of Young Black Men in America," *The St. Louis American* (March 8–14, 1990), p. 1.

9. Andrea Stone, "Homicides Break Record in 8 Cities," *USA Today* (December 29, 1989), p. 1.

10. Cf. Patsy A. Klaus and Michael R. Rand, *Family Violence: Special Report* (Rockville, Md.: National Criminal Justice Reference Service, 1984), and Murray Strauss, Richard Gelles, and Suzanne Steinmetz, *Behind Closed Doors: Violence in the American Family* (Garden City, N. Y.: Doubleday, 1980).

11. *Sourcebook, op. cit.,* Table 44, pp. 196–197.

12. James E. Blackwell and Philip Hart, *Cities, Suburbs and Blacks* (Bayside, N. Y.: General Hall, Inc. 1982).

13. David Burnham, "Black Murder Victims in the City Outnumber White Victims 8 to 1," *The New York Times* (August 5, 1973), p. 1. This study was based upon a computer analysis of police records for 1971.

14. Cf. Alvin Pouissant, *Why Blacks Kill Blacks* (New York: Emerson Hall Publishers, 1972); Kenneth Clark; *Dark Ghetto* (New York: Harper & Row, 1965), Chap. 5; and Gresham Sykes, *Crime and Society* (New York: Random House, 1956).

15. Marvin Wolfgang, *Crime and Race* (New York: Institute of Human Relations, 1970): *op. cit.,* pp. 43–45.

16. *Sourcebook, op. cit.*

17. M. Joan McDermott, *Rape Victimization in 20 American Cities* (Washington, D. C.: U. S. Department of Justice, 1979), p. 6.

18. *Ibid.*

19. *Ibid.,* p. 7.

20. *Ibid.,* p. 11.

21. *Ibid.,* p. 16.

22. Nichols, *op. cit.* and Times-Picayune, *op. cit.*

23. McDermott, *op. cit.*

24. Joseph C. Howard, Sr., "The Administration of Rape Cases in the City of Baltimore and the State of Maryland," a paper prepared for the Monumental Bar Association, Baltimore, August 1967.

25. Bureau of Justice Statistics, *Households Touched by Crime 1988* (Rockville, Md., Justice Statistics Clearinghouse, June 1989), p. 3.

26. *Ibid.*

27. *Ibid.*

28. *Sourcebook, op. cit.*

29. *Op. Cit.*
30. Blumstein, *op. cit.*
31. *Ibid.*
32. J. D. Dumbaugh, "Racially Disproportionate Rates of Incarceration in the United States," *Prison Law Monitor* 1(1979): 205–206.
33. Scott Christianson, "Our Black Prisons," *Crime and Delinquency* 1 (1981):364.
34. Lizotte, *op. cit.*
35. Clayton, *op. cit.*
36. J. L. Hagan, "Social and Legal Construction of Criminal Justice: A Study of the Pre-Sentencing Process," *Social Problems* 22 (1975): 620–637.
37. Blumstein, *op. cit.*
38. Cf. Andrew Malcolm, "More and More, Prison is Answer to Crime," *The New York Times* (November 26, 1989), p. 4-1; Sam Meddis, "Drugs Fuel 35% Rise in Crime Rate," *USA Today* (April 9, 1990), p. 1; and David Nyhan, "An Imprisoned Nation," *Boston Globe* (April 25, 1989), p. 11.
39. Malcolm, *op. cit.*
40. Cf. "Skinheads Blamed for Year's Worst Attacks," *Klanwatch: Feb. 1989.* (Montgomery, Alabama: Southern Poverty Law Center 1989), p. 1; *Law Report (March 1990)* (Montgomery, Alabama: The Southern Poverty Law Center), p. 3; *Young and Violent: Growing Menace of America's Neo-Nazi Skinheads* (New York: The Anti-Defamation League of B'Nai B'rith 1988); David Wilson, "Old and New Racist Groups are Reported Joining," *The New York Times* (October 25, 1988), p. 9.
41. *Ibid.*
42. *Klanwatch,* p. 5.
43. *Ibid.*
44. Cf. Wilson, *op. cit.;* and "Senate OKs Tracing Hate Crimes," *Times-Picayune* (February 9, 1990), p. 4.
45. R. G. Gallazo, "Closing Down on Crime," *Black Enterprise* (April 1983), pp. 39–40.
46. Blackwell and Hart, *op. cit.,* passim.
47. Lloyd Shearer, "FBI Making Progress, Except," *Parade Magazine* (April 23, 1989), p. 16.
48. Andrea Stone, "First Wave of Crack Kids Hits Schools," *USA Today* (March 9, 1990), p. 1.
49. Michael Marriott, "After 3 Years, Crack Plague in New York City Gets Worse," The *New York Times*, February 20, 1989, p.1.
50. Albert Cohen, *Delinquent Boys: The Culture of the Gang* (Glencoe, Illinois: Free Press, 1955).
51. Sonia L. Newsier, "How a Deputy Stresses Brains Over Brawn in Battling Gangs," *The Wall Street Journal* (December 29, 1988), p. 1; Pamela Reynolds, "Violence is a Way of Life in L. A. Gangs," *Boston Globe* (July 24, 1988), p. 69.
52. *Ibid.*
53. *Op. cit.*
54. *Ibid.*
55. Frances Frank Marcus, "Project on Piety Street: Reclaim Crack Houses," *The New York Times* (May 12, 1989), p. 12.
56. "Crime and Black Business," *Black Enterprise* 3 (April 1973), pp. 41–44.
57. The topics discussed in this section are amplified in references such as William

A. Bonger, *Race and Crime* (New York: Columbia University Press, 1973); Wolfgang, *op. cit.;* and *The U. S. Commission on Civil Rights Reports, 1961* (Washington, D. C.: U. S. Government Printing Office, 1962).

58. The U. S. Commission on Civil Rights, *Who Is Guarding the Guardians?* (Washington, D. C.: Government Printing Office, 1981), Chap. 2.

59. Blackwell and Hart, *op. cit.*

60. *Ibid.*

61. General Accounting Office, *Death Penalty Sentencing* (Washington, D. C.: Government Printing Office, 1990).

62. Andrew H. Malcolm, "Society's Conflict on Death Penalty Stalls Procession of the Condemned," *The New York Times* (June 19, 1989), p. B-10.

63. *Ibid.*

64. *Ibid.*

65. Cf. Gordon Waldo and Simon Dinitz, "Personality Attributes of the Criminal: An Analysis of Research Studies, 1950–1965," *Journal of Research in Crime and Delinquency* 4 (1967): 185–202.

66. Irvin G. Sarason, "Verbal Learning, Modeling and Juvenile Delinquency," *American Psychologists,* 23 (1968): 254–266.

67. Cf. Sutherland and Cressey, *Criminology* (Santa Barbara: University of California Press, 1970), p. 142.

68. For a discussion of differential opportunity theory and goals-means theory cf. Richard Cloward and Lloyd Ohlin, *Delinquency and Opportunity* (Glencoe, Ill.:The Free Press, 1960), and Robert K. Merton, *Social Theory and Social Structure* (Glencoe, Ill.: The Free Press, 1957).

69. For an elaboration of major themes previously presented, cf. Clarence Schrag, *Crime and Justice: American Style* (Rockville, Md.: (National Institute of Mental Health, 1971).

70. Ann Knopf, *Youth Patrol* (Waltham, Mass.:Brandeis, 1969).

71. R. G. Gallazo, *op. cit.,* p. 44.

Chapter 13

The Black Community in the American Society of the 1990s and Beyond

*I*n various ways throughout this book, we have attempted to address the nine essential questions posed in the preface. We defined the black community, showed how it was formed and held together, and demonstrated the immense diversity within a community united by both the external threats and impositions of white racism and its inner resources. Each preceding chapter demonstrated the inapplicability of singular theoretical models to the analysis of the black community. But it was clear that in some instances one theory more so than another—whether social systems theory, internal colonialism theory, or parallel institutions theory—may have been more useful. Other theoretical referents were employed in the analysis of crime in the black community.

REVIEW OF CENTRAL ISSUES IN THE BLACK COMMUNITY

In addition to reviewing some of the basic ideas posed in previous chapters, we will now focus primarily on the process of radicalization of the black community in America.

It was argued that the black community in America is a product of white oppression, racism, and patterned repression. Black people have been systematically excluded from equal participation in the life and culture of American society as an assimilated minority because of the imposition and subsequent institutionalization of sociolegalistic policies never before directed against other minority groups. These policies involved, at varying stages of time, chattel slavery, manumission with gradual or ortho-dox assimilation, segregation, integration, neglect, and retreat. The alter-natives open to black Americans at once were reduced to a form of accom-modation that necessitated the formation of separate, parallel institutional arrangements as functional requirements for meeting their basic and fun-damental needs.

A boundary-maintenance system was established between blacks and whites in the United States, not by black people, but it was imposed upon them by whites in control of the American power structure. This system was predicated on one factor alone—*race.* A close scrutiny of black-white relations in the United States reveals the high salience of the race factor It is the factor of race that historically divided the American republic. It is race that gave rise to and nurtured theories of group supremacy and group inferiority. It is race, with its derivative of "color purity," that forged distinctions within a nascent black community through the im-primatur of an aristocracy of color among black people. This latter distinc-tion originated the first antagonistic class lines among black people which so disunified blacks that the formation of a true community built upon group solidarity was delayed. It was race that permitted white Americans and social science theoreticians either deliberately or subconsciously to come to regard black people as a monolithic undifferentiated mass (and for others to change their positions with the acquisition of more scientific knowledge). Hence race and racism provided the impetus for the develop-ment and enforcement of a segregated social structure sustained by legal-ized discriminatory social policies without due regard for intragroup dis-tinctions.

Two kinds of forces have always been at work in the black community: (1) *centripetal forces*—elements that draw members of a minority group toward their own group, and (2) *centrifugal forces*—those elements that magnetize minority group members in the direction of the dominant group's cultural values, societal norms, and institutional arrangements. Centripetal forces facilitated black community formation; embodied the commonality of experiences of black people with white racism and racial oppression; included a desire to escape the debilitating psychological con-sequences of day-to-day contact with repressive conditions, as well as a need to belong to an accepting and status-rewarding group, and a wish to participate in the process of institution building and cultural revitaliza-tion. These forces were abetted by proscriptive norms such as sanctions by the white community against exogamous marriages, which, of course, almost always minimized social interaction.

Hence, black Americans were posed with the dilemma articulated by Du Bois more than eight decades ago—the dilemma of "twoness." Blacks, according to Du Bois, are *within* America but not *of* America; they have the soul of an American by virtue of limited acculturation that contain-ment on American soil has necessitated and encouraged. Yet cognitively, their blackness is inescapable. They recognize what blackness portends in a society in which privilege is a function of color differentiation. For many, there is an obvious contradiction implicit in the utilization of race as the basis for categorical treatment, patterned segregation and discrimination, and condemnation to exile from the opportunity structure when theoretically the United States is touted as an open society. Because of this contradiction, Du Bois' view that the problems of the color line would be the most significant domestic issue facing the American populace in the twentieth century has been vindicated by the events of the century's first 90 years.

Early on, beginning with the differentiation between house and field slaves and continuing through emancipation/Reconstruction, blacks embarked upon a course that tacitly recognized this duality. On the one hand, blacks responded to the policies of exclusion by constructing institutional arrangements that *included* blacks. Out of these arrangements emerged a viable black community—segregated, isolated, and contained as a unique colony within the larger white society. This community is primarily composed of: (1) the family, a social structure predicated upon a system of social stratification and intragroup inequality; (2) economic organizations and occupational pursuits; (3) educational institutions; (4) organized religion; and (5) political behavior. It has also developed systems for maintenance through housing, health care, recreation, and participation in those suprasocietal institutions oriented toward mutual protection and the control of deviance. The institutional arrangements of the black community are designed to serve both expressive and instrumental function related to the fulfillment of human needs of black people as a people. However, we should stress again that there is no single black community and that communities over time have come to be differentiated in terms of social class variables, color, size (e.g., small rural, large urban, and intermediate types), as well as a sense of identity and ideological perspectives.

Black Americans, however, have never been totally satisfied with policies and practices of exclusion, since throughout their history in America the majority of them have embraced the belief that they are indeed Americans entitled to all the advantages and responsibilities entailed in American citizenship. Since the First Reconstruction the overwhelming majority have acceded to the orthodox view that they, like white ethnic immigrants, are to become assimilated into whatever is defined as mainstream America. This meant to the rank-and-file black person access to what sociologists call shared values and scarce resources. More specifically, it meant structural and civic assimilation into a society relatively free from the restraints of prejudice and discrimination plus the right to make the free choice to engage in courtship, cohabitation, and marriage across racial and ethnic lines as desired. In the long and protracted history of this struggle to become an American, integration was substituted for assimilation primarily because the goal was to *become a part of the society* rather than to *become engulfed by the society.*

The black American's systematic struggle against virtually implacable racism has highlighted the goal of integration of black people as part of the larger American society. This struggle spawned protest movements and protest organizations, which were, at the initial stages of their formation, united in that common purpose. Resistance to integration and desegregation also resulted in violence and social strains. At the outset the NAACP, CORE, the National Urban League, the Southern Christian Leadership Conference, and the Student Non-Violent Coordinating Committee were committed to the goal of an integrated society. As we will see once more, it was the failure of this objective or its perceived unattainability that inevitably led to a politicization and radicalization of the protest movement among black people in the United States.

The evidence that an integrated American society has not been achieved is irrefutable. This fact was demonstrated in a variety of ways.

1. Barriers to employment opportunities, which lead as expected to income inequity, have not disappeared. Proof of this assertion is found in the excessive rates of unemployment, subemployment, and underemployment among black adults, teenagers, male and female. It is also found in the disproportionate number of blacks still mired below the low-income levels despite the important income gains made by some blacks since the 1960s.

2. Although significant improvements have been made in the educational structure of the South, now, four decades after the 1954 Supreme Court desegregation decision, white flight to the suburbs and Northern resistance to school desegregation have created a dual school system almost as severe as any that operated in the South prior to 1954, and resegregation has occurred in many desegregated systems.

3. Despite the enactment of remedial housing legislation, housing in the urban ghetto is abysmally bad, and the increase of blacks in suburbia is minuscule. Urban renewal has been a disaster frequently accentuating urban blight through abandonment and unalterable decay. This physical environment also has an affective impact on the human condition and human spirit, for no person can live in such a social and physical milieu every day without experiencing some form of alienation and discontent.

4. Black capitalism, which had an auspicious beginning, and significant growth, has not been as productive as its architects anticipated. It has not generated the predicted economic viability in spite of hundreds of new venture start-ups, many of which have failed due to undercapitalization, lack of community support, crime, and governmental impatience. Black capitalism generated a number of successful ventures, but their direct dividends for the masses of black community residents are open to serious question. Finally, whether we speak of problems and successes (and there are many) in all of these areas or in the military and the political arena, one fact is indisputable—a major portion of the black population

did not achieve measurable benefits from the civil rights movement of the 1960s.

THE RADICALIZATION OF BLACK AMERICA

It is precisely because of the persistence of the types of problems just
reviewed and the failure of the black masses to feel included that an
increasing number of black Americans of all social classes now look
askance at integration. For those persons who see an interchange of integration with assimilation the orthodox view of the inevitability of assimilation is now seriously challenged. The new goal substituted for integration/
assimilation is *liberation.* In this view integration is nothing more than a
strategy that may be called upon to achieve a liberated status *within* the
United States.

Integretion versus Liberation

Liberation means the complete freedom of black Americans and entails
an "equal distribution of decision-making power."[1] Liberated blacks are
more concerned about freedom as individuals and of blacks as a group of
people than they are about physical proximity to white people. They are
especially concerned about their capacity to obliterate white oppression
as well as their ability to challenge cherished American values that are
inconsistent with the black experience in white America. They are committed to the unity of blacks as a people living in a nation that is as much
theirs as it is that of any other group of people inhabiting it. But implicit
in the liberated person's demands for the right of self-determination is the
willingness to take a stand for that cause on American soil.

    The liberationists have come to adopt this position because they feel
that the integrationist philosophy or strategy has not achieved its ultimate
goal of an open society in which people compete as equals and are in fact
judged on the basis of merit. They have come to this position because they
can observe that even more than a century after emancipation black
Americans remain a *subordinate* group ranking near the bottom of the
social scale. Even the black stratification system is a subordinate, essentially proletarian system. Here we are speaking of the position of a group
rather than individual achievements. The exceptions to the rule are
merely that and nothing more! The goal is to achieve a just and free society
in which people have an equal chance to obtain equal results—in which
people can indeed achieve to the best of their abilities. But the exclusionary practices of the past remain with us. The promises of a Great Society
have not been fulfilled for the masses of black people. The failures in
employment, income maintenance, housing, and opportunities to provide
for the instrumental needs of the family, combined with limited opportunities in the business world, inadequacies in the political system, the
administration of justice, and provisions for decent health care—all have

forced black Americans to take another look at integration. We cannot conclude, however, that integration is no longer an appropriate strategy. Nor can it be claimed with any degree of certitude that the majority of black Americans are disenchanted with integration. The evidence suggests that from three-quarters to nine-tenths of all blacks remain committed to integration. But this is not the entire picture.

The civil rights movement achieved its greatest success in breaking down the barriers of institutionalized segregation in the Deep South, particularly in the areas of public accommodations, personal services, school desegregation, and in broadening the scale of job opportunities. It failed, however, to recognize the impact of limited gains on the rising expectations of the masses of blacks. It failed to anticipate either the gravity or the magnitude of the frustrations that followed the awareness of Northern urban ghetto blacks that somehow they had been left behind in the process of the second emancipation of southern blacks. They were still the victims of social injustice in every aspect of life—mired in poverty and crime-infested ghettos. The movement had little meaning for them. Rising rates of unemployment, perpetually low incomes, the inability to hold jobs, and the lack of resources to escape an ever-widening ghetto with all of its problems exacerbated the fundamental problems of second-class citizenship, and magnified the tensions and anxieties that characterized blacks' daily existence. The few black members of Congress in Washington prior to 1965, such as Adam Clayton Powell and William Dawson, were more symbolic to the rank-and-file Northern black than directly beneficial. Governmental patronage is unknown to the masses of blacks—few jobs ever came their way because of the election of a black member of Congress. The net effect of this pattern of denial predictably exploded in the previously described urban unrest, violent deaths of the 1960s, and systematic repression of the 1970s. With that explosion came a new turn of events in black protest: Black Power was the clarion cry.

The fears provoked by the emergence of black power as a slogan and as a philosophy must be placed in the context of the institutionalized fear that has historically characterized the lives of countless of thousands of black people both prior and subsequent to the civil rights movement of the 1960s. Those fears stemmed unalterably from the abuses of white power, which were manifested, for example, in physical assaults, lynchings, maiming, raping of black women, and castrating black men. These are the conditions that spawned such radical groups as the Deacons of Defense, De Mau Maus, Afro-Sets, and black paramilitary groups in general. While whites were predictably puzzled by black power, black Americans used the slogan as a basis for nationalistic revitalization.

Forms of Black Nationalism

This phenomenon is a direct outgrowth of the interminable struggle of black Americans for inclusion in the American mainstream. It is the consequence of the failure to deal effectively with urgent problems in the black community. It represents failures of structural assimilation and the perceived unattainability of an integrated society. As an ideology, its major theme is the right to cultural, economic, social, and political self-determination and the control of black destinies by black people. The three major forms of black nationalism are: (1) separatism, (2) cultural nationalism, and (3) revolutionary nationalism. Like integration, each may be viewed as a strategy for the achievement of the ultimate goal of the liberation of American blacks.

Advocates of a *separatist philosophy* assert that it is not synonymous with segregation as is claimed by integrationists. The distinction between the two concepts is that segregation is an imposed condition, whereas people choose to be separated in order to be included within a group rather than to be excluded from another. The most fundamental aspect of separatist ideology is the right of self-determination, which embraces the freedom of black people to exercise control over their own destinies and welfare. Historically, separatist nationalism can be traced to the founding of the American Colonialization Society in 1816. This was an incipient back-to-Africa movement that managed to survive for almost half a century. The success of the movement can be gleaned from its relatively large expenditures of $205 million to accomplish the return of 12,000 blacks to Africa. A sizable proportion of those who returned to Africa were slaves whose manumission was contingent upon their departure from the United States.[2] In this century the most successful effort toward the formulation of a separatist ideology was led by Marcus Garvey in his "Back to Africa" movement. Between 1914 and until the virtual collapse of Garveyism in 1923 he launched the most successful black nationalist movement ever organized in the United States. Whereas the Harlem Renaissance* had a wide appeal among the black intelligentsia, mainly in the black middle class, as an aggressive response to the conditions of blacks during and immediately following World War I, Garvey made his strongest appeal to the black lower class. He convinced black people that black is beautiful a half century before Malcolm X, Stokely Carmichael, H. Rap Brown, or James Brown came into national prominence. Garvey instilled self-acceptance through an elaborate system of titles, honors, and social rewards. He glorified everything black and created a sense of self-worth among a lower-class black population that was so victimized by the brutalities of racial hatred, segregation, and discrimination. An inspirational and spellbinding orator, his speeches enthralled the audience so convincingly that many believed that the realization of their dreams of freedom and liberation was imminent. He was, indeed,

---

*The Harlem Renaissance, occurring during the 1920s, was a period of unparalleled achievements by blacks in music, literature, and the arts. It was a kind of revival of learning among blacks in which cultural and intellectual attainments were viewed as the special mission of American blacks.

their black Moses! Anywhere from 3 to 6 million blacks followed him until he was convicted for mail fraud and later deported. The collapse of Garveyism, forced by the federal government, which feared the mass organization of black people as a clear and present danger, deepened the sense of pessimism and disillusionment among the nation's impoverished blacks. It undoubtedly affected middle-class black Americans, too, even though they had been in the forefront of the opposition to Garveyism, denouncing him as a demagogue. The protest literature of the period, primarily that produced during the Harlem Renaissance is, in fact, a vindication of Garvey's observations of the inhumane conditions inflicted upon black people in white America. The radicalization process, however, was undoubtedly kept alive by protest literature such as in the writings of Claude McKay, Sterling Brown, Langston Hughes, Richard Wright, and, three decades later, in the eloquence of James Baldwin's *The Fire Next Time* and *Nobody Knows My Name.* Although these writers did not espouse a separatist social thought, they were instrumental in focusing attention on the pernicious forms of social injustice and racism that prevailed throughout the United States.

Garveyism was an expression of *physical separation,* which stressed the goal of the establishment of a territorial base, a kind of national homeland, within which the right of self-determination could be assured. Physical separation may take one of at least three different forms. First, it may involve a "Back to Africa" movement once advocated by Stokely Carmichael. But this is not likely to happen, since a significant majority of black Americans have cast their lot in America and are not inclined to engage in a mass emigration to Africa as the motherland. Furthermore, the major key to internal unity within African states is tribal identity, not national identity. Without the ability to establish prerogatives of tribal affiliation and with the improbability that American blacks will be received as a "long-lost tribe," notions of a mass return of American blacks to Africa are illusory.

Second, physical separation may also connote the creation of a separate black nation out of five or six Deep South states in the continental United States. This position was advocated by the Republic of New Africa and by the Nation of Islam—the Black Muslims. Within this proposed homeland, created by partitioning the United States, blacks would be free to rebuild their own institutions, develop a separate culture, and simultaneously emancipate themselves from their mental enslavement to white America. Their desire to establish a homeland through partitioning the United States was an admission of the futility of mounting an effort to persuade American blacks to engage in a new "Back to Africa" movement, which, of course, placed this group in conflict with those who espoused the return of blacks to the African motherland. It may also be construed as acquiescence to white racism—a signal that blacks have tired of the struggle to claim their social, economic, and political entitlements as American citizens.

The Black Muslims, in more recent times, were the first black nationalist group to advocate the creation of a separate black nation through partitioning the United States. (However, the Communist party has intermittently suggested this goal since about 1920.) Undoubtedly, the southern states were selected because of their higher proportion of blacks from other areas who would return to the South as the new black nation. In the late 1950s and during the early 1960s, national attention was called to the Muslim philosophy primarily through the fiery, exciting, and captivating oratory of Malcolm X. To the black proletariat working class and to the thousands of black prisoners throughout the nation's jails and prisons who were already in despair of American justice, the Muslims carried their message of black pride, positive self-images, and the necessity to free oneself from mental enslavement by "white devils." They offered an opportunity for blacks to rediscover themselves as a people through understanding the greatness of their African heritage. Their religion was enshrouded with a mysticism overlaid by a philosophical justification for relegating white society to the status of the devil. In their view, as articulated by Malcolm X in the early 1960s, the white man should be avoided and hated for evils visited upon Afro-Asian people, and it was incumbent upon black people to be prepared to fight white people if necessary in self-defense.

The philosophy provoked a widespread fear among white Americans that was translated into systematic harassment by local, national, and federal officials of Muslims and their followers. Internal friction was manifested by the movement of Malcolm X away from many of the views espoused by Hon. Elijah Muhammad, by the allegations of betrayal that followed his assassination in 1965, and by the defection of thousands of members from the traditional philosophy following the death of Elijah Muhammad in 1975. In the interim between the deaths of Malcolm X and Elijah Muhammad, the actual membership of the Muslim population in the United States fluctuated so much that it is still extremely difficult to determine the precise number of members. Nevertheless, it is estimated that there are about 137 sites in which Mosques of the American Muslim Mission are located. This group is headed by Iman Wareet Deen Muhammad, the son of the late Elijah Muhammad, who disavowed many of the traditional teachings of his father and welcomed whites into the movement. As stated in Chapter 5, Minister Louis Farrakhan broke with Iman Wareet Deen Muhammad in 1977 and reestablished the Nation of Islam which espouses the orthodoxy of the Muslims under Elijah Muhammad's leadership.

During the presidential primaries of 1984, Minister Farrakhan received considerable national attention in the American press. Several events contributed to this publicity. For instance, he took the unprecedented step of urging Muslims to register to vote and declared his support for the candidacy of Reverend Jesse Jackson. In fact, when it was revealed that threats had been made against Reverend Jackson's life, Minister Farrakhan supplied bodyguards for Reverend Jackson from the Fruit of Islam security forces of the Nation of Islam. Another contributing factor for Minister Farrakhan's media attention was his condemnation of a *Washington Post* reporter, Milton Coleman, himself a black man, for revealing the derogatory statements about Jews made by candidate Reverend Jesse Jackson, and for what many interpreted as threats against Milton Coleman, as well as against Jews, should any physical harm be inflicted upon Rev. Jackson. During several subsequent public addresses and television appearances, Farrakhan denied allegations of anti-Semitism and of "black racism." One of his arguments was that each time that a strong black leader emerges on the American scene, there is a systematically orchestrated media effort to discredit him. He cited examples of what he believed to be media attempts to discredit Reverend Jackson in 1984 and earlier efforts of character assassination, harassment, and/or intimidation of such black leaders as Reverend Martin Luther King, Medgar Evers, Elijah Muhammad, Malcolm X, Fred Hampton (leader of the Black Panthers in Chicago who was killed, allegedly by policemen), H. Rap Brown, and Stokely Carmichael (early leaders in the SNCC movement), as well as against earlier black leaders such as Marcus Garvey and Paul Robeson. Minister Farrakhan's position with respect to the role of the media in discrediting strong black male leaders is shared by many rank-and-file members of the black community. Finally, his addresses before such non-Muslim organizations as the National Conference of Black Mayors and his appearance for interviews on national television (e.g., CBS Morning News, May 14, 1984, and College Lectures) have created a new public awareness of orthodox Muslim views on a number of issues with respect to politics, racial inequality, poverty, crime, and intergroup relations. Nonetheless, his fiery, apocalyptic oratory, and statements interpreted by many Americans as at least reminiscent of the black militancy of the 1960s rekindled anxieties and fears among many within the white community.

The third aspect of physical separatism is that encompassed by the concept of community control. This may take the form of black control of entire cities or parts as in the Mandella movement in Boston, or counties through capturing the majority of powerful elective positions (for instance, as mayors, councilmen, commissioners, and county sheriffs) and appointed positions (such as police chiefs) via the established political process, or it may mean the establishment of autonomous black communities within the geographical boundaries of a city controlled by a white power structure. In the latter type, advocated by CORE, the emphasis is on the ability of blacks to control the decision-making aspects of institutional life within the black community. Thus, as was pointed out in Chapter 6, community-control advocates would support separate all-black schools under the aegis of all-black administrators and staff. In essence, in this regard they would demand that an equitable share of city revenue be granted to black community leaders for the internal management of black institutional affairs. Simultaneously, they would seek to establish a separate black economic system and a political structure within the black community directly responsive to its crucial needs. Opponents of this position maintain that instead of liberating blacks from white society, community control would invariably force the dependency of blacks on the largesse of the white power structure. Instead of decolonizing blacks, community control would create even more highly visible black colonies within the boundaries of the larger political structure. Thus the goal of black self-determination and liberation would not be indistinct from that which exists after working hours every day in contemporary American society. There is, of course, nothing inherently objectionable about either community control or other efforts of blacks to force Americans to redistribute power and resources more equitably. It is also true that separatists provide a compelling argument that recognizes how separate all Americans now are and always have been in this country. Whereas community control might accomplish quasi-autonomy, there is no guarantee that those blacks in control of the economic system, for example, would be any less exploitative of other blacks than those whites in control of the present system. In this view black capitalism under community control is synonymous to capitalism in the larger society. Only the color is different!

A second major theme in nationalism is that of *cultural nationalism.* This term is often used interchangeably with cultural pluralism and Afrocentricity. Proponents of this position assert the need to revive the black cultural heritage. They envision a cultural liberation of black Americans by first persuading blacks to accept their own identity as black persons as well as through the establishment of cultural linkages with Africa, the mother continent. The ideology of cultural nationalists is in a sense a vindication of the Herskovits thesis of African survivals in the United States and, in part, a repudiation of the Frazier argument that blacks are uniquely Americans without significant traces of Africanism. Cultural nationalists celebrate the distinctiveness of black people as it is manifested, for instance, in soul music, hair styles of men and women, a black value system, black literature, black theater, Afro-American studies, and various patterns of life in black America that identify and distinguish black people from others.

They seek neither integration nor physical separation; rather, they seek to practice black cultural forms while coexisting with other groups of people in the United States. However, their emphasis on the need to build a black culture is in a sense an admission that notable defects in the cultural organization of black American life stem largely from the disparate forces of isolation of one class from another, the diversity of the experiences of black people in America regarding confrontations with segregation, and rebuffs to attempted integration. It is similarly an acknowledgment of the presence of the essential elements of a culture that have not been fully structured or unified into an integral system.

During the 1960s, 1970s, and late 1980s, many individuals attempted to communicate Afrocentricity and their identity as cultural nationalists by giving high visibility to their blackness through such external symbols as Afro hair styles: corn rollers, fades and dreadlocks; the wearing of dashikis and other African-style attire, and various forms of greetings and salutations. (Ultimately, the real value of many of these external symbols was diluted as they were imitated, copied or reintroduced as new cultural innovations by the white population. For instance, black actress Cicely Tyson wore her hair in a corn-roll style years before white actress Bo Derek reintroduced and popularized it in the motion picture *10.*) Others who also advocate cultural nationalism claim that external symbols possess primarily a psychological importance. For this group there is no inherent connection between identification through attachments to external symbols and the actualization of commitment to the ability to be of value to black people. This fact was underscored during the 1970s when many blacks discovered that some of the people who wore the most dashing dashikis and the biggest Afro hair styles were "hustling" or exploiting other blacks in ways that were as detrimental to blacks as the victimization they experienced at the hands of white racists. In the 1980s, many of those external symbols disappeared as blacks focused more intently on cultural development, and expanded their second renassiance of art, music, literature, history, and religion.

Afrocentricity   This revival of interest in African heritage and culture is captured in what is called Afrocentricity. This perspective argues that numerous components of African culture have been adopted by black Americans and are spreading throughout American culture. Such elements include musical styles; fashion and dress styles (e.g., Kenfe, bandanna headbands, Kufi hats, harem pants, African beads); hair styles (e.g., braids, dreadlocks, fades, tribal symbols cut into the hair, Afros), life-styles, and various foods. It is also maintained by proponents of Afrocentricity that the degree to which African culture is an increasingly widespread element in American culture is not only inadequately treated in American education but should be incorporated in elementary and secondary education curricula.[3] However, it may also be argued that what is viewed as Afrocentricity is already captured in cultural nationalism.

Notwithstanding, cultural nationalism is a movement toward black solidarity not too dissimilar from other forms of cultural revitalization. It is imperative as a process of reclaiming a past too long condemned and denied. This stress on cultural revival among black people finds expression in the philosophical articulations of such writers as Harold Cruse and among the leading advocates of the more than 1,200 college black studies programs and Afro-American cultural centers throughout the United States. The struggle to establish the legitimacy of black studies calls attention to the monumental problems cultural nationalists faced in the 1970s.

Finally, *revolutionary nationalism* is the third major theme of black nationalism. Proponents of this form of nationalism are equally committed to the goal of black liberation, but their strategy is a radical departure from those strategies advanced by either integrationists, separatists, or cultural nationalists. Revolutionary nationalists are convinced that the only effective strategy for black liberation is the complete overthrow of the present American political and social system and its subsequent replacement by what they perceive as a new and more just political and social form. On a most pragmatic level, revolutionary nationalists accept the fact that this process of overthrow and replacement will necessarily involve a protracted and bitter struggle, since its success depends upon the ability to destroy totally the social organization of the current social system. By the same token, a true revolution has as its necessary preconditions the ability of its potential organizers to dramatize the dysfunctions of the current systems; to demonstrate the abuses of power and authority by those who have political and economic power within the social system; to attack systematically that power structure in such a manner as to communicate to others that power is eroding and authority is disintegrating and that the best interests of the masses can be served by the overthrow of the incumbents. These conditions must, in turn, generate a mass following—a significant group of adherents who are willing to escalate the incipient struggle into violent activity to accomplish the downfall of those in power.

Assuming, then, that these factors are necessary preconditions to a true revolution, it should be apparent that the episodic urban conflagrations of the 1960s were not revolutionary. They were revolts, riots, or perhaps insurrections. But depending upon the degree of social organization developed by their leaders and the resources mobilized by such groups over time, the riots and revolts may be classified as precursors to an insipient revolution. The early history of the Black Panther organization and, perhaps, of SNCC under the leadership of H. Rap Brown, suggests that they should be called revolutionary nationalists. But their movement, important as it was for transforming the pace, strategy, and diversity of the quest for structural change in American society, never moved beyond the insipient prerevolutionary stage. Further, the ideological schism that had developed among Black Panthers by 1970 hastened the downfall of the organization itself. Eldridge Cleaver went into exile in Algeria; finally, negotiated his return to the United States and announced that he is a born-again Christian. In the early 1980s, Cleaver lectured extensively on his new religion—lectures and public pronouncements which often suggested that he had become a proponent of the new conservative philosophy. The entry of Bobby Seale in the 1973 mayoralty campaign of Berkeley, California, in which he finished second in a field of eight candidates, marked a radical departure from the Seale revolutionary posture vividly communicated during the trial of the Chicago Seven,*

---

*The Chicago Seven were anti-Vietnam war activists who staged massive demonstrations during the 1968 Democratic National Convention. They were arrested and tried on a number of charges.

when he was gagged to prevent violent outbursts in the courtroom. He is no longer active in the Black Panther party; he lectures throughout the country and wrote his autobiography, *A Lonely Rage,* which was published in 1979. Huey Newton, after years of police and governmental harassment, imprisonment, and threat of imprisonment, went to graduate school and, in 1980, received a Ph.D. degree from the University of California, but was gunned down in Oakland in 1989. H. Rap Brown, after numerous encounters with the law, as he fought for revolutionary justice, became an active Muslim, changed his name to Mamile Abdullah Al-Amin, and is the spiritual leader of the Muslims in Atlanta where he also operates a grocery store.

Other revolutionary nationalists are localized groups that modeled themselves after the Panthers in stressing self-defense. Numerous organizations of this type, once extremely active and troublesome to local and federal law enforcement agencies, have almost disintegrated. The Black Liberation Army, which viewed the police as the enemy—the brutal enforcers of the system's social and political injustices against black people—was forced deeper into the underground by the agencies it defined as the enemy. The Symbionese Liberation Army was literally destroyed following police attacks and shootouts which emanated from the kidnapping of newspaper heiress Patty Hearst. Other self-defense organizations occasionally effect a militantly nationalistic posture with their affinity for inflammatory rhetoric and highly sophisticated weaponry. In fact, some of these underground groups could be called paramilitary organizations.

To what extent is the liberation of black people through revolution now possible in the United States? This approach seems doomed to failure for a number of reasons. First, its theoreticians have tied themselves ideologically to the cause of all Third World peoples both in continental United States and in other parts of the world. Although there is great merit in this association, given the collective experiences of blacks in the Western white world, it is absolutely foolhardy to assume that other Third World nations will, at least in the foreseeable future, intercede directly in the internal affairs of the United States in behalf of the black cause. The history of the relationships between the United States and other nations does not suggest this possibility as an acceptable alternative despite the evidence that the United States has been repeatedly guilty of doing precisely that—interfering in the internal affairs of another nation. But this is a question of the use of not only power but force at the expense of expendable and relatively powerless groups. Moreover, many Third World groups will in all probability find it more expedient in promoting self-interest to pay only lip service or give a sympathetic ear or offer political asylum to blacks in their struggle rather than mount a direct intervention strategy.

Second, the success of a revolution depends upon effective mobilization of major resources such as military power, modern war instruments, mechanized warfare, and financial support. Even though the estimated monetary value of the black economy in the United States is about $264 billion, it is naïve to conclude that blacks are unified or in agreement on revolution as the most efficacious strategy for black liberation. Probably no more than 5 percent of the black population—and the majority of these are among the economically downtrodden who invariably are attracted to revolutionary causes but are devoid of the economic capability to support a revolution of major proportions—have become dedicated revolutionaries. Thus in open warfare the military might of the United States would be too powerful against revolutionary blacks.

Third, the repressive forces of the federal government and its ability to destroy militant groups through infiltration and the use of agents provocateurs have already been demonstrated in a number of ways. Leaders are usually jailed on "trumped-up charges" and removed from direct action for substantial periods of time. Unanticipated police raids have resulted in the deaths of leaders, while others have died of mysterious causes. Infiltrators, obviously paid informers, all too frequently have revealed plans, strategies, and programs of militant groups before they could be effectively implemented. To be successful, revolutionaries must be able to provide satisfactory solutions to such problems.*

What then is left for black revolutionaries to do? Two alternatives are open to them. They can either accept the inevitability of their failure or engage in protracted guerrilla warfare, which, if successful, can unnerve a community, a city, or a nation that believes itself to exist in a state of siege by a powerful enemy of revolutionary guerrillas. They may engage in political kidnapping, ambushing, and sniper attacks designed to frustrate and effect retaliatory harassment against the authority system. But this type of activity is not likely to gain support from the masses of people unless it proves effective in goal attainment. It is likely to alienate sympathizers to their cause among the black elite, the petite bourgeoisie, and the lumpen proletariat which envision the possibility of massive retaliation by the reactionary forces of the larger society, forces that feel threatened by this activity.

The rhetoric of unity has been replaced with unity without uniformity—a clear recognition of the extreme diversity prevalent in the black community of America—and with the right of black people to choose from a number of alternatives, be they adherence to integration, absorption through assimilation, or black nationalism with its components of separatism, Afrocentricity, cultural nationalism, and revolutionary nationalism. As things now stand, blacks seem to be more committed to both integration (that is, becoming a part of the American society as distinguished from assimilation, or being absorbed by the American society) and cultural nationalism than they are to other available alternatives. And they see themselves as black Americans!

---

*They may also need either the support or neutrality of white working classes, which are now the source of much antiblack sentiment.

CHANGING POWER RELATIONS

Whatever the choice, blacks in the 1990s are somewhat united around the commonality of their experiences in America. Further, blacks in the 1990s have an enlightened understanding of both accomplishments and failures of the civil rights movement. Initially, the movement's goals were too limited and narrowly focused on transformations in the legal structure. Although these changes were imperative, they were only a necessary precondition for more extensive alterations in power relations between the races. The elimination of de jure segregation and discrimination was only a first major barrier that had to be dismantled in order to address other patterns of systematic exclusion and deprivations structured on institutionalized racism and ubiquitous discrimination. After the momentous achievements of the 1950s and 1960s, the movement sputtered and stagnated in the 1970s. This situation can be explained by the tendency of many leaders of social movements to relax the pressures that assured their achievements whenever it appears that some definable goal is in sight or that the forces behind alterations in the social system will be self-sustaining. Many blacks, who moved into middle class during the 1960s and early 1970s, seemed convinced that pressure tactics were no longer necessary for systemic and enduring social change. They were lulled into believing that their newfound *access* to the opportunity structure was clear evidence that the conditions of the black masses would uniformly improve only if they acquired the requisites of middle-class status—proper schooling, standard English, and so-called "white dress." Hence, active participation in civil rights endeavors lost a great deal of its popularity. Membership in major organizations, such as the NAACP and CORE, declined and many well-educated middle-class young blacks never fully developed an appreciation of the price paid by previous generations of blacks for the opportunities they came to take for granted. The kind of enemy that was so easily identified during the struggles of previous decades was not as easily defined.

The movement also faltered because many of its leaders were slow to formulate new strategies for capitalizing upon changes in the legal structure. They found it difficult to translate legal gains into substantive improvements in the political and economic life of the black masses. In part, this situation was due to temporary losses in momentum when organizations experienced major leadership changes. For instance, the untimely death of Dr. Martin Luther King, Jr., in 1968 not only robbed the Southern Christian Leadership Conference of its primary leader, it meant the loss of the titular head of the entire civil rights movement. Neither Roy Wilkins of the NAACP, nor Vernon Jordan of the NUL, nor Floyd McKissick and Roy Innis of CORE had the kind of mass appeal and charismatic leadership possessed by Reverend King.

Organizational changes and some persons identified with leadership roles within the movement either left it entirely or died. For instance,

Floyd McKissick turned his attention to Soul City which ultimately failed as a new town. Roy Innis was caught up in a major struggle for control of CORE, accused of fraudulent activities and intimidation, and challenged in court by James Farmer and other former leaders within CORE for its control. Innis won his court battle in 1983 but CORE is no longer the highly respected organization it was in earlier times. James Farmer, a founding leader of CORE, became the Executive Director of the Coalition of American Public Employees and is no longer active in the movement. Vernon Jordan resigned his position with the NUL in 1981 and joined a private law firm in Washington, D.C. Roy Wilkins, who for several decades was the articulate powerful voice of the NAACP, retired in 1977 and died in 1981. Margaret Bush Wilson who had become NAACP President and Benjamin Hooks, who had succeeded Wilkins as Executive Director, were subsequently involved in a power struggle. This highly publicized conflict reached its zenith in 1983 when Mrs. Bush suspended Hooks who, in turn, was overwhelmingly supported by the NAACP National Board of Directors and reinstated. For an inordinate time the media focused on that internal struggle and conflict within the NAACP as well as difficulties between the NAACP and the NAACP-Legal Defense and Educational Fund rather than on their new initiatives designed to address the more immediate problems of blacks and the poor people of America.

Other activists shifted to different targets or strategies and new leaders emerged. For instance, Imamu Amiri Baraka (formerly Leroi Jones), an internationally known militant, and somewhat of a revolutionary leader of the 1960s, became a community organizer in Newark and, subsequently, head of Afro-American studies at SUNY/Stony Brook. Marian Wright Edleman, who established the NAACP-Legal Defense and Educational Fund in Mississippi and who braved gauntlets of hostile crowds in Mississippi to walk many young children to newly desegregated schools in the 1960s, went to Washington, D.C. As head of the Children's Defense Fund, an organization founded by the Southern Center for Public Policy, she is perhaps the most widely known public advocate of children's rights in the United States. Julian Bond, an early leader of SNCC and an architect of voter education and registration drives, was a member of the Georgia state legislature, lectures widely, and remains in the forefront of the civil rights movement in the 1990s. Coretta Scott King has dedicated herself to the development of the Martin Luther King, Jr. Center for Social Change in Atlanta, and campaigned successfully to make her husband's birthday, January 15, a national holiday. She remains an outspoken leader in the movement. Bayard Rustin headed the A. Philip Randolph Institute and remained an incisive social critic, writing and speaking against racial injustices until his death in 1988. New leaders include John Jacobs who succeeded Vernon Jordan at the Urban League, and Eddie Williams, President of the Joint Center for Political and Economic Studies in Washington, D.C. The Reverend Jesse Jackson emerged as the most charismatic black leader of the 1970s and 1980s.

Such changes are indicative of the degree to which thousands of blacks gained access to various aspects of the social, economic, and political systems in American society. However, gaining access also meant that other beneficiaries of the civil rights struggle were sometimes coopted by the dominant group power structure. That cooptation silenced them. They were no longer public champions of civil rights for the masses. Perhaps, too many black middle-class beneficiaries of the movement did little to counteract the new manifestations of racism that characterized the 1970s and 1980s. It was not the physical outrages of bigotry witnessed in Placquemines Parish, Louisiana; Selma, Anniston, and Birmingham, Alabama; nor at Orangeburg, South Carolina; nor Jackson, Mississippi. It was the racism with new code words such as "law and order themes," "qualified" blacks, "quotas," "reverse discrimination," "welfare chislers," and neoconservatism of the Nixon-Ford years; the rush to accept the ideas espoused by some black Americans that the nation has finally transcended the impediments of race if only blacks embraced the work-education ethic and pulled themselves up into the middle class where life chances were presumably more equal. This rhetoric took on a new dimension in 1980 with such themes as "getting big government off our backs," "new federalism," and new right philosophy, all of which reached full bloom under the Reagan administration.[4]

As housing deteriorated and as evidence mounted which showed that even the black middle class enountered enormous impediments to better housing, civil rights organizations turned increasing attention to that issue. As the black underclass grew to depression-level numbers and to include higher proportions of the total black population, a stark truth became shocking reality—a huge segment of the black population had never been touched by the economic and social progress of the 1960s. As politicians and bureaucrats attempted to gerrymander political districts and imposed new barriers to deliberately circumvent the Voting Rights Act of 1965, the greater was the realization that the struggle by blacks for enfranchisement was not entirely won merely by the enactment of enabling legislation when the federal government did little to enforce the law. And the more black leaders understood that organized boycotts could still be an effective weapon in their arsenal of strategies to persuade businesses that reaped gigantic profits from black customers, the greater was their proclivity to persuade such businesses to enter into covenants and fair share agreements by which some of these profits would be returned to the black community.

These situations occurred at precisely the same time that the nation was experiencing the most serious downturn in its economy since the depression of the 1930s. It was argued earlier on that a nation such as the United States is considerably more willing to share some semblance of power, as manifested in access to jobs, higher incomes, and public accommodations when a substantial proportion of the dominant group does not have a sense of status-threat by the gains of the minority. On the other hand, whenever they feel that their own position in the social structure is seriously jeopardized by the escalating demands of the relatively power-less minority, they regroup to challenge those demands in whatever way they deem fruitful.[5] Given the fact so much attention was given by the media to the few successes toward economic and political empowerment and expanded educational opportunity by blacks during the Carter years, and the Rip Van Winkle approach to civil rights by the black rank-and-file in the late 1970s, it should not have been surprising to discover that opponents to the modest achievements made by blacks would have re-grouped to halt those advances at a propitious time.

IMPACT OF THE REAGAN PRESIDENCY ON BLACK AMERICANS

Those opponents found their leader in Ronald Reagan whose campaign rhetoric revitalized the right wing, appeased the neoconservatives, and made many racists feel that, finally, there would be someone in the White House who would not be and could not be labeled a "friend of the black people." Even the phrase "President of all the people" was interpreted by many to mean "pro-white and antiblack." This theme was subsequently embraced by other white candidates for political office when their oppo-nents were either a black or a "liberal white person." The implication of the phrase, "of all the people" was that black, minority, or liberal white candidates would represent a *special interest* group to the detriment of the white population. After his election, despite public announcements to the contrary, many members of outsider groups quickly came to believe that Reagan's own actions and certainly the implementation of his policies confirmed that reality and that he would turn back the clock to pre-1954 days in the United States. Thus the White House and the Department of Justice, which for 30 years or more had been viewed as supportive of racial equality, then became a clearly defined enemy that civil rights organiza-tions could specify for their constituencies. A new momentum was possi-ble to mobilize popular support to hold on to those achievements or gains of the previous 30 years.

What caused the federal government to be defined as the enemy? In earlier chapters, several explanations were provided in terms of those policies of the Reagan administration which generally marked a calculated retreat from previously favorable governmental actions. We are reminded of the systematic assault on Affirmative Action by President Reagan, Attor-neys General Smith and Edwin Meese, Chief of the U.S. Justice Depart-ment Reynolds, and David Stockman. All publicly stated, on several occa-sions, their intense opposition to several affirmative action programs that were instrumental in propelling thousands of blacks, minorities, and white women into the economic mainstream. Their unwillingness to enforce

even existing laws slowed economic progress and stalled education desegregation at all levels—elementary, secondary, collegiate, graduate and
professional school. Despite the "pride" President Reagan spoke of in
signing the extension of the Voting Rights Law of 1965 in his August 1983
address before the American Bar Association in Atlanta, the indisputable
fact is that a large segment of the American population are fully cognizant
of his extreme hesitance and reluctance to sign that extension.

A large number of the 300 black mayors found it extremely difficult
to accept President Reagan's statements of the need to revitalize American cities when they know that American cities lost $70 billion in much
needed federal support during the first two years of the Reagan Administration. Black businesses were optimistic in December 1982 when President Reagan announced his commitment to a new support program
whereby the federal government would purchase $22 billion in goods and
services from minority businesses between 1983 and 1985, and that the
federal government would provide $1.5 billion in credit for the formation
of minority-owned businesses over a 10-year period. In the meantime,
they also recoiled from the fact that regulatory changes in the SBA, especially the Section 8(a) set-aside program, were simultaneously contributing
to the demise of several minority-owned businesses. At the same time that
the President and the Attorney General's office claimed that the "legal
rights of all Americans were going to be protected by the U.S. Government," the public became aware of the fact that a Reagan Administration-
imposed budget in 1981 had resulted in a 25-percent cutback in the
budget for the Legal Services Corporation which caused a 30-percent
reduction in its staff and the closing of more than 300 offices throughout
the United States from which legal aid to the poor had been administered.
Reagan appointees to the U.S. Supreme Court are slowly curtailing civil
rights gains and President Bush seems committed to many of Reagan's
policies.

At the precise moment that President Reagan was "communicating"
to the nation that his economic recovery program was working, the federal government itself released statistical data which showed that, in August 1983, some 15 percent of all Americans (34.2 million) were living in
poverty. These figures meant that 36 percent of all blacks were living in
poverty and that blacks, who made up slightly less than 12 percent of the
national population, accounted for 28 percent of *all* Americans below the
poverty level. Recovery for whom? Further, even after Assistant Attorney
General Reynolds accompanied Jesse Jackson on a voting rights tour of
Mississippi and 300 federal officers were dispatched to Mississippi to monitor the August 1983 statewide elections, *all* the voting machines broke
down in one county where blacks had registered in substantial numbers.
All ballots in that county had to be invalidated. In effect, blacks defined
the federal government as its enemy because their hard-won gains were
eroding daily under the Reagan Administration, and because of the widespread belief that the President himself had established a social milieu in

which it was no longer immoral or unfashionable to engage in racist behavior. Trepidations of how injurious to blacks four additional years under a Reagan Administration would be stimulated a revitalization in the civil rights movement.

Evidence of this revitalization first emerged during the mid-year elections of 1982 and 1986 when huge numbers of minorities and white women turned out to vote. It was accelerated by the efforts to elect Harold Washington as mayor of Chicago and Wilson Goode to be successful in his bid to become mayor of Philadelphia. It was apparent in the nationwide voter registration drives initiated by all major civil rights organizations in the early 1980s, and the accompanying programs for the political socialization of blacks and other minorities. Not only were efforts advanced to reestablish old coalitions, especially between civil rights groups and labor organizations, but special attention was given to a new imperative—the formation of what came to be known as the "rainbow coalition," or cooperation between blacks, Hispanics, Asians, and white women. The Reverend Jesse Jackson, for instance, attended the annual meeting of major Hispanic organizations and they, in turn, attended the annual meeting of Operation PUSH in 1983. Although the press often claimed that Jackson's rainbow coalition never materialized, that assertion is false. While it is evident that he was not successful in attracting a huge white following during the presidential primaries, the fact of equal significance is that he was able to attract many white persons because they believed that he was the only candidate to devote serious attention to the issues of racism, poverty, and inequality in addition to other issues of national and international interest. Further, he energized the black voters in ways that revealed a new understanding of political efficacy and black voting power. Civil rights advocates were also instrumental in blocking the confirmation of nominees to the Supreme Court whose views they believed to be hostile to the struggle of minorities and women for social, political, and economic justice.

Furthermore, the major civil rights organizations have now turned their attention to the needs of the poor, the underclass, and the downtrodden as well as toward protecting the gains achieved by those in the higher economic categories. They focus not exclusively on better jobs but on getting jobs for the masses, on improved housing and health conditions, on attacking the problems of the educationally disadvantaged. Some organizations finally addressed other compelling needs such as controlling crime and drug abuse in the black community, strengthening the black family, and reducing the problem of functional illiteracy among black youth. These are gargantuan problems in the black community, and they must be faced head-on first by blacks themselves. Although unemployment and poverty can undermine the family structure, they do not necessarily *destroy* family systems. The maintenance of strong family values can be a vital instrument and accompaniment to appropriate sex education programs that will curtail the upward spiral in illegitimacy and the ever-increasing numbers of poor single mothers in the black community. Governmental policies that assist in this process are important but a great deal of the responsibility for ameliorating this problem rests with the black community. Similarly, changes in educational policies, and systematic monitoring of teaching and teacher behavior in schools may help to curtail the growing problem of functional illiteracy. However, black parents have a prior responsibility to monitor and take an active role in the education of their own children, to know where they are, to see that they are in school and that they are not disciplinary problems while in school, to raise questions about schooling, homework, and relations with school authorities, and to create a positive learning environment within their own homes. Poverty must not be used as *the* excuse for inability to function in contemporary society. There are too many examples of persons within the black community who succeeded despite their origins in what appeared to have been a cycle of poverty. The black middle and upper classes, no matter where they are located residentially, can be a major instrument for change. Financial contributions should be accompanied by contributions of expertise, knowledge, and organizational skills to help rebuild, consolidate, and strengthen basic social, economic, and political institutions within the black community so that all black Americans can feel independent, proud, self-assured, and fully capable of standing firm in the challenges against bigotry and racial injustice.

THE SALIENCE OF RACE IN AMERICAN SOCIETY

Those challenges may be far more formidable than those who claim that race is no longer a powerful force in American society would conclude. The nation must come to terms in the 1990s with the emergence of violent hate groups throughout the U.S. and the resurgence or resurfacing of racism on as many as 250 college campuses. It is an absolute imperative to discontinue calling manifestations of racism and bigotry "isolated incidents" and combat the spread of racism either in its more subtle forms or in overt manifestations in colleges and universities as well as throughout the society—in workplaces, public accommodations, housing, and elsewhere. It is equally imperative for governmental leaders, the judicial system, and the American public itself to impose heavy sanctions on such groups that practice racial hatred in its most virulent forms like Skinheads, neo-Nazi organizations, and paramilitary groups. So-called "respectable bigotry" is just as intolerant and pernicious as blatant bigotry. It is often cloaked under the mantle of well-chosen code words that effectively communicate to the prejudiced person a message of racial superiority of the white population and intolerance of minorities. It has already allowed at least one ex-Klan member to be elected to a state legislature from which he almost advanced to the U. S. Senate.

The U. S. Supreme Court in 1990 has a conservative majority by virtue of Reagan's appointments. As pointed out in Chapter 9, there is evidence that President Bush, as indicated by his judicial appointments to lower courts, is continuing Reagan's practice of using ideology as the litmus test for judicial appointments. This situation does not bode well for blacks and other racial minorities. The U. S. Supreme Court also rendered decisions during the first six months of 1989 that either undermined such programs as minority set-asides or made it extremely difficult for such programs to meet the Court's strict scrutiny test of constitutionality. For that reason, civil rights organizations and their white supporters lobbied the U. S. Congress to enact corrective legislation, The Civil Rights Act of 1990. President Bush vetoed this legislation.

As we approach the twenty-first century, the nation must also deal with a society that is still racially divided and one in which blacks and whites differ in perspectives about racial progress. Polls indicate that the majority of the white population say they believe in racial integration. They also believe (however, erroneous that is) that the dream of a racially just society articulated by Dr. King in 1963 has been achieved. *Unfortunately, positive attitudes are not always translated into positive behavior.* Therein lies a major problem when an enormous discontinuity exists between attitudes and behavior. Blacks, on the other hand, admit some progress but insist that it has been modest at best and has not touched a growing underclass. Blacks are also committed to federal, state, and local governmental interventions for enforcement of civil rights laws, equal employment opportunity, and fair housing statutes constructed to end discriminatory and unjust practices.

Throughout this book, we have indicated that blacks are greatly concerned about conditions that threaten to undermine the community's internal institutional structure and the impact of external conditions on individual members of the black community. As a result of the retrenchment of support during eight years of a hostile Reagan Administration, bombardment of the self-centered impulses unleashed over that period, and breakdown in the power and control of traditional institutions on its individual members, problems within the black community mounted. Realizing the magnitude of these conditions during the 1980s, black leaders, churches, and voluntary associations began to address these internal problems. It may take years, however, to resocialize the alienated and reestablish that vital commitment to the traditional values of family, respect for self, the elderly and others, reciprocity, and belief in one's own capacity to succeed through hard work and by legitimate means when so many young blacks *believe* they are pariahs in a white-dominated society. Thus the task in the 1990s is indeed formidable but not insurmountable. We have provided evidence to show that efforts are already in progress designed to ameliorate such conditions.

We conclude as we began with the assertion that no single sociological theory or explanatory model is a sufficient tool for understanding the dynamic character of the black community and its relationship to the larger American society. Instead, we found considerable utility in drawing upon a variety of theoretical frameworks for explanatory purposes. Thus, on either a microsociological or macrosociological level, a kind of synergism prevailed in our employment of theoretical constructs. Functionalism or systems theory and conflict theory tell us a great deal about the internal structure of the black community as well as its external relationship to the larger society, whether or not the black community is perceived as a subsystem with parallel institutions or as an internal colony. Furthermore, on a microsociological level, we used a variety of established theories and classification schemes, such as anomie, relative deprivation, differential association, and social learning, as instruments for understanding *behavior* as it relates to the social structure or macrosociological conditions.

Finally, it is the interaction among race, color, and class that has the most profound impact upon the internal structure of the black community, its social organization, its relationship to the larger society, and, ultimately, social interaction among individual members of both black and white communities. Race, color, and class establish and maintain relatively impregnable boundaries between the two social systems. Historically, color was employed as a fundamental principle of internal stratification and social differentiation. In that sense, color is no longer imperative but race remains a wall of division, a barrier to social and economic integration, and the principle impediment to equal educational opportunity, decent housing, and better health care. Without question, one's life chances are improved as one climbs the economic and social class ladders, but achieved upward mobility is no guarantee in and of itself that black Americans will no longer encounter racism. It may be less blatant and more subtle but it is nonetheless racism, and the recipient feels its terrible sting. The strategies that blacks employ to combat racism may vary along a number of dimensions. The leadership structure within the black community may become even more diffused but that should not be taken as evidence of a leaderless group. Approaches to changing power relations with the ultimate goal of racial equality may take different forms but there is unity in diversity. *Hence, it is once more evident that the black community is a highly diversified aggregate of people whose social organization and internal unity remain in many ways a collective response to the external social forces unleashed by white racism, oppression, and systematic repression in the United States.*

NOTES

1. Cf. Lerone Bennett, "Liberation," *Ebony* 25 (August 1970): p. 36, and Bob Blauner, *Black Lives, White Lives: Three Decades of Race Relations in America* (Berkeley: University of California Press, 1989).
2. Roy Wilkins, "Integration," *Ebony, op. cit.,* p. 54.
3. Asante, Molefi Kete, *The Afro-Centric Idea* (Philadelphia: Temple University Press, 1987).

4. Similar views are expressed by John Blassingame, "The Revolution That Never Was: The Civil Rights Movement, 1950–1980," *Perspectives: The Civil Rights Quarterly* 14:2 (Summer 1982): 3–15. I benefited from his insightful and penetrating analysis of this issue.
5. James E. Blackwell, "Persistence and Change in Intergroup Relations: The Crisis Upon Us," *Social Problems* 29:4(April 1981): pp. 325–346.

Bibliography

Abrams, Charles, "The Housing Problem of the Negro," *Daedalus* (Winter 1966): 64–66.

"Administrative Discharges Studies," *Task Force on the Administration of Military Justice in the Armed Forces* (October 13, 1972).

Adolescent and Young Adult Fathers: Problems and Solutions. (Washington, D.C.: Children's Defense Fund, 1988).

Aldrich, Howard E. "Employment Opportunities for Blacks in the Ghetto: The Role of White-Owned Businesses," *American Journal of Sociology* 78 (May 1973): 1403–1425.

Alexander, B. "The Black Church and Community Empowerment," pp. 45–69 in R. L. Woodson (ed), *On the Road to Economic Freedom* (Washington, D. C.: Regenry Gateway, 1987).

Allen, Joyce, E., "The Forgotten Poor: Blacks in Rural Areas," *Focus* (July 1988): 5–6.

Allen, Walter R., "Black Student, White Campus: Structural, Interpersonal and Psychological Correlates of Success," *Journal of Negro Education* 54(2) (1985): 134–147.

———, "Race Consciousness and Collective Commitments Among Black Students on White Campuses," *Western Journal of Black Studies* 8:3 (1984): 155–166.

Alpert, Bruce, "Infant Death Rate Deplored," *Times-Picayune* (February 8, 1990), p. A-7.

———, "Infant Mortality Rate May be Rising, Panel Says," *Times-Picayune* (March 1, 1990), p. A-10.

American Council on Education, *Minorities in Higher Education* (Seventh Annual Report) (Washington, D. C.: American Council on Education, 1988).

Amsterdam News (September 30, 1972), p. B-B.

Anderson, Bernard (p. 192) in Elliot D. Lee (ed.), "The Black Enterprise Board of Economics Look into the Future," *Black Enterprise* (June 1982).

Anderson, Jack, "Who Owns America?" *Parade Magazine* (April 16, 1989), pp. 4–6.

Apolar, Chris, and Lynne Duke, "HUD Concedes Theft of Up to $20 Million," *The Washington Post* (June 17, 1989), pp. 1, A-7.

Applebome, Peter, "New Report Warns of Alliance of Racist Groups," *The New York Times* (February 6, 1989), p. 1.

Asante, Molefi Kete, *The Afro-Centric Idea* (Philadelphia: Temple University Press, 1987).

Ashe, Authur, *A Hard Road to Glory: A History of the African-American Athlete, Vol. One: 1619–1919* (New York: An Amistad Book—Warner Books, 1988).

Ashkin, Steve, "Turmoil in the Ranks," *Black Enterprise* (September 1982): 59–64.

Associated Press, "Group Claims It Sent Mail-Bombs," *Times-Picayune* (December 29, 1989), p. A-3.

"Backstage," *Ebony* (May 1989): 2.

Bahr, Howard, and Gerald R. Garrett, *Disaffiliation Among Urban Women* (New York: Bureau of Applied Research, 1971).

Bailey, Margaret, Paul Halberman, and Harold Alksne, "The Epidemiology of Alcoholism in an Urban Residential Area," *Quarterly Journal of Studies on Alcohol* 26(1965): 19–40.

Banfield, Edward, *Big City Politics* (New York: Random House, 1965).

"Banks," *Black Enterprise* (June 1989): 3–34.

Barker, Lucius, *Our Time Has Come: A Delegate's Diary* (Champaign-Urbana: University of Illinois Press, 1987).

Barringer, Felicity, "Number of Nations' Poor Remains at 32 Million for a Second Year," *The New York Times* (October 19, 1989), p. A-24.

Bendix, Reinhard, and Seymour Lipset (eds.) *Class, Status and Power* (New York: Free Press, 1966).

Benjamin, Rommel, and Mary Benjamin, "Sociological Correlates of Black Drinking: Implications for Research and Treatment," *Journal of Studies on Alcohol* 9(1981): 241–247.

Bennett, Lerone, *Before the Mayflower,* 4th ed. (Chicago: Johnson Publishing Company, 1969).

———, "Liberation," *Ebony* 25 (August 1970): 36.

———, "The Making of Black America: The Black Worker, Part X," *Ebony* (December 1972): 73–79.

Bernard, Jessie, *American Community Behavior* (New York: Holt, Rinehart and Winston, 1949).

Berry, Mary F., and John Blassingame, *Long Memory: The Black Experience in America* (New York: Oxford University Press, 1982).

Bierstedt, Robert, " An Analysis of Social Power," *American Sociological Review* 15 (December 1950): 730–738.

Billingsley, Andrew, *Black Families in White America (Englewood Cliffs, N. J.: Prentice-Hall, 1968).*

Binkin, Martin, and Alex Schenixer et al., *Blacks in the Military* (Washington, D. C.: Brookings Institution, 1982).

Black, D. "The Social Organization of Arrest," *Stanford Law Review* 23(1976): 1087–1111.

Black Elected Officials: A National Roster 1989 (Washington, D. C.: Joint Center for Political Studies, 1989).

Black Enterprise (August 1972), p. 44.

—— (March 1982).

—— (April 1982).

—— (June 1982).

—— (October 1982).

—— (June 1983).

—— (February 1988).

"Blacks in Hollywood: What Roles Do They Play,'" *West 57th, CBS Program* (May 27, 1989).

"Blacks More Likely Victims of Violence," *Times-Picayune* (April 23, 1990), p. 3.

"Blacks More Prone to Blindness, Study Says," *Times-Picayune* (February 8, 1990), p. A-8.

Blackwell, James E. "Achieving Educational and Economic Equality in the Pursuit of Racial Harmony (Address given at Fourth Annual Joint Tulane-Xavier University Martin Luther King Week for Peace; Xavier University of Louisiana; January 16, 1990).

——, *Mainstreaming Outsiders: The Production of Black Professionals,* 2nd ed. (Dix Hills, N. Y.: General Hall Publishing Co., 1987).

——, "Persistence and Change in Intergroup Relations; The Crisis Upon Us," *Social Problems* 29:4 (April 1981): 325–346.

——, "The Power Basis of Ethnic Conflict in American Society," pp. 179–196 in Lewis Coser and Otto Larsen (eds.), *The Uses of Controversy in Sociology* (New York: Free Press, 1976).

——, "Social and Legal Dimensions of Interracial Liaisons," pp. 219–243 in Doris Y. Wilkinson and Ronald Taylor (eds.), *The Black Male in America* (Chicago: Nelson-Hall, 1977).

——, *Youth and Jobs* (Boston: William Monroe Trotter Institute of the University of Massachusetts/Boston, 1987).

——, *Youth Unemployment and Unemployment in Massachusetts: Outreach Initiatives* (Boston: William Monroe Trotter Institute of the University of Massachusetts/Boston, 1987).

——, and Philip Hart, *Cities, Suburbs and Blacks* (Bayside, N.Y.: General Hall, Inc., 1982).

——, *Race Relations in Boston: Institutional Neglect, Turmoil and Change* (Boston: The Boston Committee, 1983).

————, and Marie Haug, "Relations Between Black Bosses and Black Workers," *The Black Scholar* 4 (January 1973): 36–43.

————, Robert Sharpley, and Philip Hart, *Health Needs of Urban Blacks* (Boston: The Solomon Fuller Institute, 1977).

Blalock, Hubert M., Jr., "A Power Analysis of Racial Discrimination," *Social Forces* 39 (1969): 53–69.

————, *Toward a General Theory of Minority Group Relations* (New York: John Wiley & Sons, 1967).

Blassingame, John W. "Status and Social Structure in the Slave Community," pp. 109–122 in Randall M. Miller (ed.), *The Afro-American Slaves: Community or Chaos* (Malabar, Fla.: Robert E. Krieger Publishing Co., 1981).

————, "The Revolution That Never Was: The Civil Rights Movement, 1950–1980," *Perspectives: The Civil Rights Quarterly* 14:2 (Summer 1982): 3–15.

Blauner, Robert, "Black Culture: Myth or Reality," Chap. 19 in Norman Whitten and John Swed (eds.), *Afro-American Anthropology* (New York: Doubleday 1970).

Blauner, Bob, *Black Lives, White Lives: Three Decades of Race Relations in America* (Berkeley: University of California Press, 1989).

Blauner, Robert, "Internal Colonialism and Ghetto Revolt," *Social Problems* 16 (Spring 1969): 393–408.

Bluestone, Barry, and Bennett Harrison, "The Grim Truth About the Job Miracle, *The New York Times* (February 1, 1987), p. B-14.

Blumberg, Paul, *Inequality in the Age of Decline* (New York: Oxford University Press, 1980).

Blumstein, Alfred, "On the Racial Disproportionality of U. S. Prison Populations," *Journal of Criminal Law and Criminology* 73:3 (1982): 1259–1281.

Bonacich, Edna, "A Theory of Ethnic Antagonisms: The Split Labor Market," *American Sociological Review* (October 1972): 547–559.

Bonger, William, *Race and Crime* (New York: Columbia University Press, 1973).

Bookbinder, Hyman, "Did The War on Poverty Fail?" *The New York Times* (August 20, 1989), p. E-3.

Boyd, Frederick V., "Black Enterprise Board of Directors Report: Unemployment," *Black Enterprise* (March 1983): 63–66.

Braddock, Jomills, Jr., "The Major Field Choices and Occupational Career Orientations of Black and White College Students," pp. 167–198 in Gail E. Thomas (ed.), *Black Students in Higher Education: Conditions and Experiences in the 1970s* (Westport, Conn.: Greenwood Press, 1981).

Bradford, William D., "In the Interest of Survival," *Black Enterprise* (June 1983): 103.

Bridges, Tyler, "Blacks Roused by Calls of Unity," *Times-Picayune* (April 24, 1989), pp. 1, A-8.

Brimmer, Andrew, "Economic Integration and the Progress of The Negro Community," *Ebony* 25 (August 1970): 119–121.

————, "Foreign Employment and Economic Welfare," *Black Enterprise* (April 1982): 82.

Broderick, Carfred B., "Marital Stability," *Marriage and the Family*, 2nd ed. (Englewood Cliffs, N. J.: Prentice-Hall 1984), Chap. 1.

Brooks, Joseph F., "The Decline of Black Landownership," *Focus* 11:5 (May 1983): 6.

Brown, D. R., and Ronald Walters, *Exploring the Role of the Black Church in the Community* (Washington, D. C.: Institute for Urban Affairs of Howard University, 1979).

Brown, Luther, "Women Vs. Minorities: The Debate Rages," *Black Enterprise* (June 1988): 65–66.

Brown, Tony, "Economics: The Final Stage of the Civil Rights Movement (an address given before the Commonwealth Club of California, February 20, 1987).

Brune, Tom, "Race Becomes Issue in Chicago Mayoral Vote," *Boston Globe* (April 3, 1983), p. 3.

Buckley, Walter, *Sociology and Modern Systems Theory* (Englewood Cliffs, N. J.: Prentice-Hall, 1967).

Buell, Emmett H. Jr., "Busing and the Defended Neighborhood: South Boston, 1974–1977," *Urban Affairs Quarterly* 16 (1980): 161–168.

"Building a New Tradition," *Black Enterprise* (June 1983): 70.

Bureau of the Census, *Characteristics of the Population Below the Poverty Level: 1981*, Current Population Reports, Series P-60, No. 138 (Washington, D. C.: U. S. Department of Commerce, March 1983).

Bureau of Justice Statistics, *Households Touched by Crime 1988* (Rockville, Md.: Justice Statistics Clearinghouse, June 1980).

Bureau of Labor Statistics, *Projections 2000* (Washington, D. C.: U. S. Government Printing Office, 1989).

Burnham, David, "Black Murder Victims in the City Outnumber White Victims 8 to 1," *The New York Times* (August 5, 1973), p. 1.

Butler, Wilson, "Entrepreneurial Enclaves: An Exposition Into the Afro-American Experience, *National Journal of Sociology* 2:2 (Fall 1988): 127–166.

Caldwell, Earl, "The Rising Status of Commitment," *Black Enterprise* (December 1978): 38–42.

Callahan, Don, *Problem Drinkers* (San Francisco: Jossey-Bass, 1970).

Callahan, Don, et al., *American Drinking Practices* (New Brunswick, N. J.: Rutgers Center for Alcohol Studies, 1969).

Campbell, Bebe Moore, "Five Cents Gas Tax Promises Business Opportunities for Blacks," *Black Enterprise* (July 1983): 22.

Caplowitz, David, *The Working Addict* (New York: City University Graduate School and University Center, Metropolitan Drugs and Industry Project, 1976).

"Careers and Opportunities in 1989," *Black Enterprise* (February 1989): 67–70.

Carson, Emmett D., "Despite Long History, Black Philanthropy Gets Little Credit as 'Self-Help' Tool," *Focus* (June 1987): 3.

Cayton, Horace, and St. Clair Drake, *Black Metropolis: A Study of Negro Life in a Northern City* (New York: Harper and Row, 1945).

Chambliss, William, and Nagasawa, R. H., "On the Validity of Official Statistics: A Comparative Study of White, Black and Japanese High School Boys," *Journal of Research on Crime and Delinquency* 6 (1969): 71–77.

Chass, Murray, "Baseball Salaries Are Reaching the Upper Deck," *The New York Times* (December 13, 1988), p. B-9.

———, "Highest-Paid Player, It's Your Pick," *The New York Times* (February 12, 1989), Section 8, p. 3.

Chein, I., et al., *The Road to H* (New York: Basic Books, 1964).

———, and E. Rosenfeld, "Juvenile Narcotic Use," *Law and Contemporary Problems* 22 (1957): 52–68.

"Chicago Study Says AIDS Cases in U. S. Are Underestimated," *The New York Times* (June 9, 1989), p. A-8.

"Children Having Children," *Time* (December 9, 1985), pp. 78–90.

Chinyelu, Mamadou, "Black Expo to Hit 4 Cities," *Black Enterprise* (April 1990): 26.

Christianson, Scott, "Our Black Prisons," *Crime and Delinquency* 1 (1981): 364.

Clark, Kenneth, *Dark Ghetto* (New York: Harper and Row, 1965).

———, "Desegregation: The Role of the Social Sciences," *Teachers' College Record* 63 (1960): 16–171.

Clark, R. E., "The Relationship of Schizophrenia in Occupational Income and Occupational Prestige," *American Sociological Review* 13 (1948): 325–330.

Clausen, John A., and Melvin L. Kohn, "The Ecological Approach to Social Psychiatry," *American Sociological Review* 60 (1954): 140–151.

Clayton, Obie, "A Reconsideration of the Effects of Race in Criminal Justice Sentencing," *Criminal Justice Review* 8:2 (1983): 15–20.

Cleage, Albert B., Jr., *The Black Messiah* (New York: Sheed and Ward, 1968).

Cloward, Richard, and Lloyd Ohlin, *Delinquency and Opportunity* (Glencoe, Ill.: The Free Press, 1960).

Clymer, Adam, "Joblessness Causes Stress and Gloom About Nation," *The New York Times* (February 2, 1983), p. A-19.

Cohen, Muriel, "Study: U. S. Public Schools Suspend Blacks at Twice the Rate of Whites," *Boston Globe* (December 12, 1988), p. 56.

Cohen, O. Jack (tr.), *Pre-Capitalistic Economic Formations,* Karl Marx; Eric Hobsbawn (ed.) (New York: International Publishers, 1921).

Colander, Archie, Jr., *Minority Business and Employment Administrator*, NAACP (Discussions with on May 18, 1989).

Cole, Beverly P., "The Politics of Literacy," *Crisis* (May 1988): 8–9.

Coleman, James S., *Power and the Structure of Society* (New York: Norton Publishing Co., 1974).

———, et al., "Achievement and Segregation in Secondary Schools: A Further Look at Public and Private School Differences," *Sociology of Education* 55 (April/July 1982): 65–76.

———, *Equality of Educational Opportunity* (Washington, D. C.: U. S. Government Printing Office, 1967).

Collago, R. G., "Closing Down on Crime," *Black Enterprise* (April 1983): 39–46.

Collins, Sharon M. "The Making of the Black Middle Class," *Social Problems* 30:4 (April 1983): 369–382.

Cone, James H., *A Black Theory of Liberation* (Philadelphia: J. B. Lippincott, 1970).

——, *Black Theology and Black Power* (New York: Seabury Press, 1969).

——, *For My People: Black Theology and the Black Church* (Maryknoll, N.Y.: Orbis Books, 1988).

"Conscience and Law in Yonkers," *The New York Times* (October 7, 1989), p. 22.

Conyers, James Y., "Negro Passing: To Pass or Not to Pass," *Phylon* 24 (1963), pp. 215–224.

Coombs, Ordie, "Still Without the Substance of Power," *Black Enterprise* (December 1978): 28–33.

Covenant: Operation PUSH—Heublein, Inc. March 16, 1982. Made Available by Reverend Jesse Jackson, President of PUSH.

Cox News Service, "Black Unity, Coalition with Whites Urged by Jackson," *Times-Picayune* (February 8, 1990), p. A-16.

Cross, Theodore, *Black Capitalism* (New York: Antheneum, 1969).

Crossland, Fred E., *Minority Access to College* (New York: Schocken Books, 1970).

Cummings, Judith, "Non-Catholic Christian Schools Growing Fast," *The New York Times* (April 13, 1983), pp. 1, 23.

Cutright, Philips, and Herbert L. Smith, "Intermediate Determinants of Racial Differences in 1980 U. S. Normal Fertility Rates," *Family Planning Perspectives* 20:2 (May/June 1988): 119–123.

Dahl, Robert, *Who Governs?* (New Haven, Conn.: Yale University Press, 1961).

Dahrendorf, Ralf, *Class and Class Conflict in Industrial Society* (Palo Alto, Calif.: Stanford University Press, 1959).

Daniels, Lee A., "In Defense of Busing," *The New York Times* (April 17, 1983), pp. 34, 98.

——, "The New Black Conservative," *The New York Times* (October 4, 1981), p. 20.

David, Jay, and Elaine Crane (eds.), *The Black Soldier from the American Revolution to Vietnam* (New York: William Morrow, 1971).

Davies, James E., "The J-Curve of Rising and Declining Satisfaction as a Cause of Some Revolutions and a Contained Rebellion," in Graham, Hugh David, and Robert Gurr (eds.), *Violence in America: Historical and Comparative Perspectives* (New York: Bantam Books, 1969).

Davis, George, and Gregg Watson, *Black Life in Corporate America: Swimming in the Mainstream* (New York: Doubleday, 1982).

Davis, Kingsley, and Wilbert E. Moore, "Some Principles of Stratification," *American Sociological Review* 10 (1945): 242–249.

Davis, Robert, "Suicide Among Young Blacks: Trends and Perspectives," *Phylon* 43:4 (December 1982): 307–314.

Dean, John, *The Making of a Black Mayor* (Washington, D. C.: Joint Center for Political Studies, 1973).

Dedham Bill, "Blacks Turned Down for Home Loans from S & Ls Twice as Often as Whites," *The Atlanta Journal and Constitution* (January 22, 1989), p. 1, A-10.

————, "Racial Lending Gap Less in South than Midwest," *The Atlanta Journal and Constitution* (January 22, 1989), p. 1.

Defense 82, Special Almanac Issue (Arlington, Va.: American Forces Information Service, 1982), p. 30.

Defense 89, Special Almanac Issue (Arlington, Va.: American Forces Information Service, 1989), p. 30.

DeFrancis, Marc, "Who Defends America? Race, Sex and Class in the Armed Forces," *Focus* (March 1989): 7.

Dentler, Robert A., Personal Communication, February 16, 1990.

DePalma, Anthony, "Catholic Churches Move to Embrace Blacks," *The New York Times* (January 24, 1989), p. B-1.

————, "Newark Suit Would Keep High-Rises," *The New York Times* (March 30, 1989), p. B-1.

Desegregation of the Nation's Public Schools: A Status Report (Washington, D. C.: U. S. Commission on Civil Rights, 1979).

Dickins, Floyd, and Jacqueline Dickins, *The Black Manager: Making It in the Corporate World* (New York: Amacon, 1982).

Dionne, E. J., "Poor Paying More for Their Shelter," *The New York Times* (April 18, 1989), p. A-18.

Dixon, Rep. Julian, "Housing: Recognizing the Crisis, Taking Action," *Focus* (June 1989), pp. 3–4.

"Don't Ignore Impact of Ethnic Market in U. S. Economy: NAMD Prexy," *Jet* (June 26, 1989): 23.

Doten, Patti, "Beyond Corporations' Glass Ceiling," *Boston Globe* (August 31, 1989), p. 77.

Dougherty, Laurie, "Racism and Busing in Boston: Comments and Criticisms," *Radical America* 9 (1975): 65–92.

"Drugs A White Problem, Too," *Times-Picauyune* (January 9, 1990), p. B-6.

"Drug Economy in Black America Is Between $16 Billion and $20 Billion," *Ebony* (August 1989): 109.

Duberman, Lucille, *Social Inequality: Class and Caste in America* (Philadelphia: Lippincott, 1976).

Dumbaugh, J. D., "Racially Disproportionate Rates of Incarceration in the United States," *Prison Law Monitor* 1(1979): 205–206.

Dunham, H. W., *Community and Schizophrenia: An Experimental Analysis* (Detroit: Wayne State University Press, 1965).

"Editorial," *The New York Times* (January 7, 1983).

Edmond, Alfred, Jr. "Black Officials Face Challenges of the '90s' " *Black Enterprise* (January 1990), p. 15.

———, "Dealing at the Speed of Light," *Black Enterprise* (June 1988): 150–162.

———, "A 'Golden Opportunity' for Black Firms," *Black Enterprise* (April 1990).

Edwards, Harry, *Black Students* (New York: The Free Press, 1970).

———, telephone discussion, April 5, 1983.

Elam, Julia C. (ed.), *Blacks on White Campuses* (Washington, D. C.: The National Association for Equal Opportunity in Higher Education, 1983).

Elias, Marilyn, "Southeastern Blacks' Stroke Rate Is Still High," *USA Today* (February 16, 1990), p. D-1.

Elkins, Stanley, *Slavery* (Chicago: University of Chicago Press, 1959).

Ellison, Catherine A., Sr. Implementation Officer; Boston Public Schools; Correspondence dated March 6, 1990.

Elwood, David T., *Poverty in the American Family* (New York: Basic Books, 1988).

Emblen, Roger G., *Society Today,* 2nd ed. (Del Mar, Calif.: CRM Books, 1973).

Epps, Edgar, "Impact of School Desegregation on Self-Evaluation and Achievement Orientation," *Law and Contemporary Problems* (1975): 300–313.

Farley, Reynolds, et al., "Barriers to the Racial Integration of Neighborhoods: The Detroit Case," *The Annals of the American Academy of Political and Social Sciences* 441 (January 1979): 97–113.

———, "Chocolate City, Vanilla Suburbs: Will the Trend Toward Racially Separate Communities Continue?" *Social Science Research* 7 (1978): 319–344.

Farley, Reynolds, "School Integration and White Flight" (Unpublished paper, Population Studies Center, The University of Michigan, Ann Arbor, 1975.

———, and Walter R. Allen, *The Color Line and the Quality of Life in America* (New York: Russell Sage Foundation, 1987).

Federal Bureau of Investigation, *Bureau of Justice Statistics* Bulletins, 1987, 1988, 1989.

Federal Bureau of Investigation, *Sourcebook of Criminal Justice Statistics 1989* (Washington, D. C.: U. S. Government Printing Office, 1990).

Feron, James, "How Yonkers Has Held Off on Housing," *The New York Times* (January 19, 1990), p. E-1.

———, "Yonkers Yields on Housing Plan to Avert Crisis: Revisions Sought," *The New York Times* (September 11, 1988), p. 1.

Finder, Alan, "Bias Remains Persuasive in Region's Housing Market," *The New York Times* (March 13, 1989), p. B-1.

Finestone, Harold, "Kats, Kicks and Color," in Stein, M., et al., *Identity and Anxiety* (Glencoe, Ill.: The Free Press, 1960).

Fisher, Sethard, *Power and the Black Community* (New York: Random House, 1970).

Fishman, Wanda K., "Reinterpreting the Andrew Young Affair: An Analysis of Black Jewish Distortions in the Changing U. S.-Mideast Policy of 1979–1980," *The Western Journal of Black Studies* 5:2 (Summer 1982): 129–138.

"Ford-Out Front with Minority Dealers," *Black Enterprise* (June 1988): 189.

"Fortify or Die: Insurance Overview," *Black Enterprise* (June 1989): 285–288.

Fortune, Mark, "Vaulting into New Ventures," *Black Enterprise* (June 1989): 245 to 252.

Franklin, Ben A., "Study Finds Vietnam Combat Affecting Veteran's Health," *The New York Times* (November 12, 1988), p. 7.

Franklin, Herbert M., "Zoning Laws," *Black Enterprise* (August 1972): 25.

Franklin, John Hope, *From Slavery to Freedom* (New York: Alfred A. Knopf, 1952).

Frazier, E. Franklin, *Black Bourgeoise* (New York: The Free Press of Glencoe, 1957).

———, *The Negro Family in the United States* (Chicago: University of Chicago Press, 1939).

———, *The Negro in the United States* (New York: The Macmillan Co., 1949).

Freeman, Richard, *The Black Elite* (New York: McGraw-Hill, 1976).

Fried, Joseph P., *Housing Crisis USA* (Baltimore: Penguin Books, 1971).

Friend, Tim, "Black and White Death Rates Continue to Differ, Study Says," *USA Today* (September 27, 1989), p. 1.

———, "Lead Exposure May Cause Kids Lifelong Harm," *USA Today* (January 1, 1990), p. D-1.

———, "USA's Health Report: Disparity Cries Out for Attention," *USA Today* (March 16, 1990), p. 1.

Gallazzo, R. G., "Closing Down On Crime," *Black Enterprise* (April 1983), pp. 39–40.

Gamson, William, *Power and Discontent* (Homewood, Ill.: Dorsey Press, 1968).

Ganier, William, "Subsidized Housing Production: Profiting from Past Errors," *Journal of Housing* 40:3 (May 1983): 77–82.

Garibaldi, Antoine, "The Effects of Desegregation: Is the Cup Half Empty or Half Full," *The Urban Review* 13:4 (1981): 265–271.

———, *The Revitalization of Teacher Education Programs at Historically Black Colleges: Four Case Studies* (Atlanta: The Southern Education Foundation, 1989).

Garrett, Gerald R., and Howard Bahr, "Women on Skid Row," *Quarterly Journal of Studies on Alcohol* 34:4 (December 1973): 1228–1243.

General Accounting Office, *Death Penalty Sentencing* (Washington, D. C.: Government Printing Office, 1990).

George, Nelson, "The New Bidding Game in Sports," *Black Enterprise* (January 1983): 28–32.

Gersham, Carl, "A Matter of Class," *The New York Times Magazine* (October 5, 1980).

———, "The Black Plight, Race or Class," *The New York Times Magazine* (June 27, 1980).

Gibbs, Jewelle Taylor, "Depression and Suicidal Behavior Among Delinquent Females," *Journal of Youth and Adolescence* 10:2 (1981): 159–167.

Gillman, Dorothy, "Blacks in the Army: A Matter of Necessity," *Black Enterprise* (October 1982): 31.

Glasgow, Douglas, *The Black Underclass* (San Francisco: Jossey-Bass Publishers, 1980).

Glazer, Nathan, "Housing Problems and Housing Policies," *The Public Interest* (Spring 1967): 21–51.

———, and Daniel Patrick Moynihan, *Beyond the Melting Pot* (Cambridge, Mass.: The M.I.T. Press, 1963).

Goldman, Sheldon, "Reagan's Judicial Appointments," *Focus* (March 1985): 4.

Goodman, Walter, "Other Faces of AIDS, A Frank Investigation," *The New York Times* (September 12, 1989), P. C-20.

Gordon, Milton, *Assimilation in American Life* (New York: Oxford University Press, 1964).

Graves, Earl, Address to the 78th Annual National Urban League Convention, (Detroit, Michigan, August 2, 1988), unpublished.

———, "Black Business at the Crossroads." (Publisher's Page), *Black Enterprise* (June 1990), p. 11.

———, "A New Decade of Political Power," *Black Enterprise* (January 1990): 9.

Greenberg, Jack, *Race Relations and the Law* (New York: Columbia University Press, 1959).

Greenhouse, Linda, "Court Bars a Plan Set Up To Provide Jobs for Minorities," *The New York Times* (January 24, 1989), p. 1.

———, "High Court Bans Appeal on Busing by Nashville and Justice Department," *The New York Times* (January 25, 1983), p. 1.

———, "New Limit Is Placed on Scope of 1866 Civil Rights Law," *The New York Times* (June 23, 1989), p. A-8.

Grier, George, and Eunice Grier, *Black Suburbanization in the Mid-1970s* (Washington, D. C.: The Washington Center for Metropolitan Studies, 1978).

———, *Housing Segregation and the Goals of the Great Society* (Chicago: Quadrangle Books, 1966).

Griffin, Noah W., "Broadcasting," *Crisis* (June/July 1989): 28–32, 66.

Gupta, Udyan, "Integrating the Airwaves," *Black Enterprise* (June 1982): 125–127.

Guttmacher, Alan, *Teenage Pregnancy: The Problem That Won't Go Away* (New York: Alan Guttmacher Institute, March 1981).

Hagan, J. L., "Social and Legal Construction of Criminal Justice: A Study of the Pre-Sentencing Process," *Social Problems* 22 (1975): 620–637.

Haines, Herbert H., *Black Radicals and the Civil Rights Mainstream, 1954–1970* (Knoxville: University of Tennessee Press, 1988).

Halberstram, David. "Champions We Never Knew," *The New York Times* (December 4, 1988), p. 11.

Halloran, Richard, "Wide Bias Against Minorities in Navy," *The New York Times* (September 20, 1988), p. A-20.

Hamilton, Charles V. "Racial, Ethnic and Social Class Politics and Administration," *Public Administration Review* 32 (October 1972): 638–648.

———, and Stokely Carmichael, *Black Power: The Politics of Liberation in America* (New York: Random House, 1967).

Hanafin, Theresa, "Atlanta: A Southern Attack on Skewed Lending," *Boston Globe* (March 5, 1989), p. 13.

Hare, Bruce, "Self Perception and Academic Achievement Variations in a Desegregated Setting," *American Journal of Psychiatry* 137(1980): 683–689.

Hare, Nathan, *Bringing the Black Boy to Manhood* (San Francisco: Black Scholar Press, 1986).

———, *The Black Anglo-Saxons* (New York: Macmillan, 1970).

———, and Julia Hare, *The Endangered Black Family* (San Francisco: The Black Scholar Press, 1987).

Harris, Ron, "The House That Willie Built," *Black Enterprise* (June 1983): 90–96.

Hatchett, David, "Blacks and the Mass Media," *Crisis* (June/July 1989): 18–26, 68.

Henderson, A. M., and Talcott Parsons (trs.), *The Theory of Social and Economic Organization,* Max Weber (Glencoe, Ill.: The Free Press, 1947).

Henderson, R. D., "The Effects of Desegregation on Children," *The Urban Society* 13:5 (1981): 201–227.

Henshaw, Stanley K., and Jenifer Van Fort, "Teenage Abortion, Birth and Pregnancy Statistics," *Family Planning Perspectives* 21:2 (April 1989): 85–89.

Herbers, John, "Census Data Reveal 70s Legacy, Poorer Cities and Richer Suburbs," *The New York Times* (February 27, 1983), p. 1.

Higginbotham, A. Leon, Jr., *In the Matter of Color: Race and the Legal Process* (New York: Oxford University Press, 1978).

Hill, Robert, *Economic Policies and Black Progress: Myths and Realities* (Washington, D. C.: National Urban League Research Department, 1981).

Hill, Robert L., "Minority Vets at a Deadend," *Focus* (December 1974): 4–5.

Hill, Robert B., et al., *Research on the African-American Family: A Holistic Approach* (Boston: William Monroe Trotter Institute of the University of Massachusetts/Boston, 1989).

———*The Strengths of Black Families* (New York: Emerson Hall Publishers, 1972).

———, telephone interview, June 15, 1983.

Hilliard, S. Lee, "Demanding Fair Share," *Black Enterprise* (August 1983): 40–42.

Hilts, Philip J., "Growing Gap in Life Expectancies of Blacks and Whites Is Emerging," *The New York Times* (October 9, 1989), p. A-8.

Hocker, William C., "Atlanta Life Buys Pilgrim, Moves into South Carolina," *Black Enterprise* (February 1990), p. 24.

———, "New Debentures Bill Should Help MESBICS," *Black Enterprise* (February 1990): p. 43.

Hollingshead, August B., and F. C. Redlich, *Social Class and Mental Illness: A Community Study* (New York: John Wiley and Sons, 1958).

Hooks, Benjamin L., "Publishers Foreword," *Crisis* (May/June 1989): 4.

Howard, Joseph C., "The Administration of Rape Cases in the City of Baltimore and the State of Maryland," A paper prepared for the Monumental Bar Association, Baltimore: August 1967.

Hylton, Richard D., "Minority Firms Feel the Pinch," *The New York Times* (April 16, 1989), p. F-4.

"Income, Lifestyle Among Factors in Black Death Rate," *Times-Picayune* (February 9, 1990), p. A-11.

"Industrial Service Companies," *Black Enterprise* (June 1989): 199–207.

"Insurance," *Black Enterprise* (June 1989): 290–291.

"Interview with Nathan Hare," *Crisis* (March 1986): 30–35.

Jackson, Derreck Z., "An Urgent Role for Black Church," *Boston Globe* (February 19, 1989), p. A-26.

Jackson, Jesse, comments made in interview on the *NBC Today Show* (July 20, 1988).

Jacobs, Patricia, President, AMESBICS, telephone interview (July 27, 1983).

James, Herman, "Health Orientations, Health Opportunities and the Use of Medical Services: Toward A Clarification of the Relationships," an unpublished paper based upon a study of black and white subjects in Pittsburgh, Pa., 1967–1970.

"Japanese Racial Insensitivity—Again," *Focus* (July 1988): 2.

"Japanese Slurs on Blacks Causing Rifts Between Them," *Jet* (October 31, 1988): 12.

Jet (July 5, 1989): 25.

Johnson, Julie, "High Court Called Threat to Blacks," *The New York Times* (July 10, 1990), p. A-14.

Johnston, David, "There's Far to Go in Cleaning up the H. U. D. Mess," *The New York Times* (August 13, 1989), p. 4-1.

Joint Center for Political Studies, "Blacks and the Military," *Focus* 1(August 1982): 1–4.

———, "Immigration and Black America," *Focus* (February 1983): 1–4.

Jones, Elise F., et al., "Teenage Pregnancy in Developed Countries: Determinants and Policy Implications," *Family Planning Perspectives* 17:2 (March/April 1985): 53–63.

Jones, Kenneth M., "The Black Male in Jeopardy," *Crisis* (March 1986): 17–21.

Jones, Terri, "Japan's Hiring Policies Blasted," *Boston Globe* (January 1, 1989), p. 17.

Jordan Robert A., "Blacks Waking Up to AIDS Threat," *Boston Globe* (April 30, 1989), p. 77.

———, "The HUD Vanishing Act," *Boston Globe* (March 17, 1983), p. 18.

———, "Is the Jackson Political Era Ending?," *Boston Globe* (December 3, 1989), p. A-5.

Joyce, Fay S., "Florida Literacy Test Snags Diplomas," *The New York Times* (May 24, 1983), p. A-12.

Julian, Joseph, and William Korbblum, *Social Problems,* 4th ed. (Englewood Cliffs, N. J.: Prentice-Hall, 1983).

Karmen, Monroe, W., "Government Programs," *Black Enterprise* (August 1972): 22.

Kelly, Dennis, "Colleges Enroll Fewer Blacks and Hispanics," *USA Today* (January 15, 1990), p. D-1.

Kelly, James E., "Numbers Versus Moral Realism and Teenage Pregnancies," *America* (February 14, 1987), pp. 131–136.

Kimbrough, Anne W., "Feeling the Heat: Management of Majority Thrifts Has Reform-minded Legislators Breathing Fire," *Black Enterprise* (June 1989): 265–268.

King, Martin Luther, Jr., *Stride Toward Freedom* (New York: Ballentine Books, 1960).

King, Wayne, "Violent Racism Attracts New Breed: Skinheads," *The New York Times* (January 1, 1989), p. 1.

"Kivie Kaplan Institute Brings Blacks, Jews Together," *Crisis* 88:7 (August/September 1981): 364–365.

Klanwatch: Intelligence Report (Montgomery, Alabama: The Southern Poverty Law Center, February 1989, No. 42).

Klaus, Patsy A., and Michael R. Rand, *Family Violence: Special Report* (Rockville, Md.: National Criminal Justice Reference Service, 1984).

Knopf, Ann, *Youth Patrol: An Experiment in Community Participation* (Waltham, Mass.: Brandeis University, 1969).

Kohn, Melvin, "Social Class and Schizophrenia: A Critical Review and a Reformulation," *Schizophrenia Bulletin* (Winter 1969): 60–79.

Kolata, Gina, "Defects Top Cause of Infant Deaths," *The New York Times* (September 22, 1989), p. A-18.

Kong, Dolores, "Social, Economic Factors Seen in Black Deaths," *Boston Globe* (December 9, 1989), p. 1.

Kornblum, William, "Lumping the Poor: What Is the 'Underclass'," *Dissent* (Summer 1984): 295–302.

Kristol, Irving, "The Negro of Today Is the Immigrant of Yesterday," *The New York Times Sunday Magazine* (September 11, 1966), p. 50.

Kronus, Sidney, "Some Neglected Areas of Negro Class Comparisons," pp. 236–249 in Edgar Epps (ed.), *Race Relations* (Cambridge, Mass.: Winthrop Publishers, 1973).

Landry, Bart, "Growth of the Black Middle Class in the 1960s," *Urban League Review* 3:2 (Winter 1978): 3.

———, and Margaret P. Jendrek, "Employment of Wives in Middle-Class Black America," *Journal of Marriage and the Family* 40 (November 1978): 787–797.

Lardner, James, "Rich, Richer; Poor, Poorer," *The New York Times* (April 19, 1989), p. A-27.

Lauer, Robert H., *Social Problems and the Quality of Life,* 4th ed. (Dubuque, Iowa: William C. Brown Publishers, 1989).

Laurenti, Luigi, *Property Values and Race* (Berkeley: University of California Press, 1960).

Lavin, David E., *The Predictions of Academic Performance* (New York: Russell Sage Foundation, 1965).

Law Report (March 1990) (Montgomery, Alabama: Southern Poverty Law Center, 1990).

Leary, Warren E., "Some Black Groups Are Found at High Risk of Kidney Failure," *The New York Times* (April 6, 1989), P. B-15.

Lee, Elliot, D., "The Black Enterprise Board of Economists Looks at the Future," *Black Enterprise* (June 1982), p. 192.

Lenski, Gehard, *Power and Privilege: A Theory of Stratification* (New York: McGraw-Hill, 1966).

Leogh, Wilhelmina, and Mildred O. Mitchell, "Public Housing and the Black Community," *The Review of Black Political Economy* 11:2 (Fall 1980): 52–75.

Levitan, Sar A., et al., *Still a Dream: The Changing Status of Blacks Since 1860* (Cambridge, Mass.: Harvard University Press, 1975).

Lewis, Diane K. "The Black Family: Socialization and Sex Roles," *Phylon* 36:3 (Fall 1975): 221–237.

Lewis, Sir Arthur, "Black Americans and the Changing World Economy," *Black Enterprise* (March 1983), p. 36.

Lieberson, Stanley, "A Societal Theory of Race and Ethnic Relations," *American Sociological Review* 26 (December 1961): 902–910.

Liebow, Elliot, *Talley's Corner: A Study of Negro Street Corner Men* (Boston: Little Brown, 1966).

Lindesmith, Alfred, *The Addict and the Law* (New York: Random House, 1965).

Lizotte, A. J., "Extra-Legal Factors in Chicago's Criminal Courts: Testing the Conflict Model of Criminal Justice," *Social Problems* 25 (1978): 564–580.

Lund, Robert D., Remarks made in a paper presented during the NAACP Life Membership Luncheon, NAACP Annual Convention, New Orleans, La., July 13, 1983.

Lyons, Douglas, C., "Black Labor Leaders," *Ebony* (June 1989): 42–47.

Magnet, Myron, "America's Underclass: What to Do?," *Fortune* (May 11, 1987): 131–150.

Malcolm, Andrew H., "Chicago," *The New York Times Magazine* (April 10, 1983), pp. 24, 72.

———, "More and More, Prison Is the Answer to Crime," *The New York Times* (November 26, 1989), p. A-1.

———, "Society's Conflict in Death Penalty Stalls Procession of the Condemned," *The New York Times* (June 19, 1989), p. B-10.

Malzberg, Benjamin, *Statistical Data for the Study of Mental Diseases Among Negroes in New York State* (Albany, N. Y.: Research Foundation for Mental Hygiene, 1964).

Marable, Manning, "Beyond the Race-Class Dilemma," *The Nation* (April 11, 1981): 417–436.

———, "Open Season on Blacks—Again," *Los Angeles Sentinel* (January 8, 1987), p. A-7.

———, "Reaganism, Racism and Reaction: Black Political Realignment in the 1980s," *The Black Scholar* (Fall 1982): 2–15.

Marantz, Steven "Detroit: From the Deepest Urban Blight, A Backlash," *Boston Globe* (March 5, 1989), p. 13.

———, "Study Said 4 Hub Banks Were Redlining in '80." *Boston Globe* (January 29, 1989), p. 25.

Marcus, Frances Park, "Project on Piety Street: Reclaim Crack Houses," *The New York Times* (May 12, 1989), p. 12.

Marden, Charles F., and Gladys Meyer, *Minorities in American Society*, 5th ed. (New York: D. Van Nostrand Co., 1978).

Marriott, Michael, "After 3 Years, Crack Plague in New York City Gets Worse," *The New York Times* (February 20, 1989), p. 1.

Marx, Karl, *Das Capital;* Max Eastman (ed.) (New York: Modern Library, 1968).

———, *Pre-Capitalist Economic Formations,* Eric Hobsbawn (ed.), Jack O. Cohen (tr.) (New York: International Publishers, 1921).

———, *The Communist Manifesto* (Chicago: Regnery, 1969).

McAdoo, Harriett, *Black Families* (Beverly Hills, Calif.: Sage Publications, 1981).

———, "Black Kinship," *Psychology Today* (May 1979): 67–79, 110.

McAdoo, John, "Father-Child Interaction Patterns and Self-Esteem in Black School Children," *Young Children* 34 (1979): 46–53.

McAllister, Bill, "The Plight of Young Black Men in America," *The St. Louis American* (March 8–14, 1990), p. 1.

McAllister, Ronald J., et al., "Residential Mobility of Blacks and Whites: A National Longitudinal Study," *American Journal of Sociology* 77 (November 1971): 448–453.

McDermont, M. Joan, *"Rape Victimization in 20 American Cities* (Washington, D. C.: U. S. Department of Justice, 1979).

McFadden, Robert D., "Stepping Back from Fiscal and Political Crisis: What Is Next for Yonkers?," *The New York Times* (September 11, 1988), p. 36.

McFate, Katherine, "Defining the Underclass," *Focus* (June 1987), 8–9, 11.

McGhee, James, *Running the Gauntlet: Black Men in America* (New York: The National Urban League, 1985).

McPhartland, James, and Jomills Braddock, Jr., "The Impact of Desegregation on Going to College and Getting a Good Job," pp. 141–154 in Willis D. Hawley (ed.), *Effective School Desegregation* (Beverly Hills, Calif.: Sage Publishing Co., 1981).

Meddis, Sam, "Drugs Fuel 35% Rise in Crime Rate," *USA Today* (April 9, 1990), p. 1.

Merton, Robert K., "Insiders and Outsiders: A Chapter in the Sociology of Knowledge," *American Journal of Sociology* 78 (July 1972): 9–47.

———, *Social Theory and Social Structure* (Glencoe, Ill.: The Free Press, 1975).

Metzger, Paul L., "American Sociology and Black Assimilation: Conflicting Perspectives," *American Journal of Sociology* 76 (January 1971): 627–647.

Miles, Dwight E., "The Growth of Suicide Among Black Americans," *Crisis* 86:10 (December 1979): 430–433.

The Miller Commitment. (Milwaukee, Wisc.: The Miller Brewing Company, 1984).

"Ministers Mobilize Against 'the Death of a Race,' " *Ebony* (August 1969): 160–164.

"Minorities in Newsrooms Are Now at a Crisis Stage," *Jet* (July 31, 1989): 18.

"The Missing Father Myth," *Time* (December 9, 1985), p. 9.

Mitchell, Clarence, "The Civil Rights Scene," *Crisis* (September 1980): 349–357.

Moon, Henry Lee, *Balance of Power: The Negro Vote* (Garden City, N.Y.: Doubleday, 1948).

Mooney, Brian C., "HUD Report: Policy Added to Segregation," *Boston Globe* (July 23, 1988), p. 1.

Morris, Aldon, *The Origins of the Civil Rights Movement* (New York: The Free Press, 1984).

Moskos, Charles Jr., "Deliberate Change: Race Relations in the Armed Forces," p. 62 in Russell Endo and William Strabbridge (eds.) *Perspectives on Black America* (Englewood Cliffs, N. J.: Prentice-Hall, 1973).

———, "Racial Integration in the Armed Forces," *American Journal of Sociology* 72 (September 1966): 133–148.

Moss, James A., "Brashier's Black Middle-Class: A Rebuttal," *Crisis* (August/September 1979): 307–310.

"Mothers Raising Mothers," *U. S. News and World Report* (March 17, 1986): 48.

Moyers, Bill, Report on the Black Family on CBS and similar reports on PBS.

Moynihan, Daniel P., *The Negro Family: The Case for National Action* (Washington, D. C.: U. S. Department of Labor, 1965).

———, "Political Perspectives," pp. 71–80 in Eli Ginsbbert (ed.), *The Negro Challenge to the Business Community* (New York: McGraw-Hill, 1984).

Myrdal, Gunnar, *An American Dilemma* (New York: Harper and Row, 1944).

NAACP Economic Development Program Brochure (May 18, 1989).

"NAACP Voter Registration Project," *Crisis* (October 1979): 354.

Nalty, Bernard C., and Morris McGregor (eds.), *Blacks in the Military: Essential Documents* (Wilmington, Del.: Scholarly Resources, Inc., 1981).

Napper, George, *Blacker Than Thou: The Struggle for Campus Unity* (Grand Rapids, Mich.: William B. Erdmans Publishing Co., 1973).

National Center for Educational Statistics, *Bulletin* (September 1981).

NBC Nightly News (June 17, 1983).

———, "Special Report" (July 10, 1989).

"Negro, Black and African-Americans," *The New York Times* (December 22, 1988), p. A-22.

Nenno, Mary K., "The President's Budget: A Blueprint for the Future," *Journal of Housing* 39:2 (March/April 1982): 43–50.

———, *New Orleans States Item* (August 31, 1972), p. 1.

Newsletter, International Trade Association of Operation PUSH 2:2 (February/March, 1983).

Newsier, Sonia L., "How a Deputy Stresses Brain Over Brawn in Battling Gangs," *The Wall Street Journal* (December 29, 1988), p. 1.

"Newspapers: Minority Hiring Weak," *USA Today* (August 25, 1988), p. 28.

Newton, E., and U. Gupta, "Blacks and the Mass Media," *Crisis* (June/July 1989): p. 7ff.

————, "Fighting Back in Hollywood," *Black Enterprise* (September 1982): 35–39.

Newton, Edmund, "Countdown to Takeoff," *Black Enterprise* (June 1982): 128–132.

Newton, Huey P., *Revolutionary Suicide* (New York: Harcourt Brace, 1975).

New York Times, June 3, 1973, p. 26.; June 15. 1989, p. A-26; August 20, 1989, p. F-3.

Nichols, Bill, "Study: Crime Hits Blacks Hardest," *USA Today* (April 23, 1990), p. 3.

"Nissan to Pay $605,600 to Settle Race and Bias Case," *The New York Times* (February 4, 1989), p. 8.

Norbit, George W., and Thomas W. Collins, "Cui Bono? White Students in a Desegregating High School," *The Urban Review* 13:4 (1981): 205–215.

Nordie, Peter G., *Improving Race Relations in the Army* (McLean, Va.: Human Sciences Research Center, Inc., 1972).

Nyhan, David, "An Imprisoned Nation," *Boston Globe* (April 25, 1989), p. 11.

O'Connor, B. Wright, "What's Next for the SBA?," *Black Enterprise* (June 1989): 137–138.

Olive, Lewis C., Jr., "Duty, Honor, Country, But No Reward," *The Urban League News,* 3 (April 1973): 31.

Orfield, Gary, "School Desegregation and Housing Policy: The Role of Local and Federal Governments in Neighborhood Segregation," *Integrated Education* 17 (May 1979): 48–53.

Orr, Margaret Terry and Francis A. J. Ianni, "The Impact of Culture Contact and Desegregation on the Whites of an Urban High School," *The Urban Review* 13:4 (1981): 243–259.

Parker, Frank R. "The Supreme Court: Which Way on Civil Rights," *Focus* (October 1988), p. 6

Parsons, Talcott (tr.), *The Protestant Ethic and the Spirit of Capitalism,* Max Weber (New York: Scribner, 1930).

————, *The Social System* (New York: The Free Press, 1951).

Pasamanick, Benjaminm "A Survey of Mental Illness in an Urban Population," *The American Journal of Psychiatry* 119 (1962): 229–305.

Passell, Peter, "Forces in Society and Reaganism Helped Dig Deeper Hole for Poor," *The New York Times* (July 16, 1989), p. 1.

Pear, Robert, "Broad Recovery Essential for Job Creation," *The New York Times* (November 28, 1982), p. 28.

————, "Reagan Asks Wide Cuts in Programs to Aid Poor," *The New York Times* (January 29, 1983), p. 6.

———, "U. S. Pensions Found to Lift Many of Poor," *The New York Times* (December 20, 1988), p. 1.

Pearce, Diane, *Breaking Down Barriers: New Evidence on the Impact of Metropolitan School Desegregation on Housing Patterns* (Washington, D. C.: Center for Policy Review, Catholic University School of Law, 1980).

Perry, Ronald W., *Racial Discrimination and Military Justice* (New York: Frederick A. Praeger, 1976).

Petroni, Fran A., "Interracial Dating: The Price Is So High," in Irving Stuart and Lawrence Abt (eds.), *Interracial Marriage* (New York: Grossman Publishers, 1973).

Pettigrew, Thomas, "White-Negro Confrontations," pp. 39–55 in Eli Ginsberg (ed.), *The Negro Challenge to the Business Community* (New York, McGraw-Hill, 1964).

Philips, Ulrich B., *Life and Labor in the Old South* (Boston: Little, Brown, 1929).

Pinkney, Alphonso, *Black Americans* (Englewood Cliffs, N. J.: Prentice-Hall, 1969).

Pivin, Frances Fox, and Richard Cloward, *Regulating the Poor* (New York: Vintage Books, 1971).

Ploski, Harry, and James Williams, *The Negro Almanac: A Reference Work on the Afro-American* (New York: John Wiley & Sons, 1983).

"Political Trend Letter: Bush's Bad Start on Appointing Black Judges," *Focus* (June 1989): 6.

"Political Trend Letter," *Focus* (March 1987): 7–8.

"Political Trend Letter," *Focus* (March 1988): 5.

"Political Trend Letter," *Focus* (July 1989): 5.

Poole, Isiah, "The Disappearing Civil Servant," *Black Enterprise* (February 1983): 91–94.

Porterfield, Ernest, *Black and White Mixed Marriage* (Chicago: Nelson Hall, 1978).

Poussaint, Alvin F., "Black Men Must Organize," *Black Scholar* (May/June 1987): 12–15.

———, *Why Blacks Kill Blacks* (New York: Emerson Hall, 1972).

"Poverty: Who Are the Poor," *USA Today* (September 1, 1988), p. 8A.

Quarles, Benjamin, *The Black American* (Glenview, Ill.: Scott Foresman & Co., 1967).

"Racism in the Military," *Congressional Record* 118:166, Part II (Washington, D. C.: U. S. Congress, 1972).

Raines, Howell, "Effects of Chicago Race," *The New York Times* (April 14, 1983), p. B-15.

Ramjug, Peter, "Minority Women Management Jobs Rising at Banks," *Boston Globe* (August 28, 1989), p. 10.

Readjustment Counseling Service, *Report of the Working Group on Black Vietnam Veterans* (Washington, D. C.: Readjustment Counseling Service, 1987).

"Realty Era of the Specialist," *Black Enterprise* (August 1972): 44.

Record, Wilson, and Jane Cassels Record, *Little Rock, U. S. A.* (San Francisco: Chandler Publishing Co, 1960).

Reed, Wornie L., "Racism and Health: The Case of Black Infant Mortality," in Peter Conrad and R. Kern (eds.), *The Sociology of Health Illness: Critical Perspectives,* 3rd ed. (New York: St. Martin's Press, 1990).

Reed, Wornie, and Carolyn W. Arnold, "Health and Medical Care, in Wornie L. Reed (ed.), *Summary Assessment of the Status of African-Americans, Vol. 1* (Boston: William Monroe Trotter Institute of the University of Massachusetts/ Boston, 1989).

"Reported AIDS Cases Topped 200,000 in 1989," *Times-Picayune* (January 4, 1990), p. A-3.

"Report Finds Poverty Among Children Up," *The New York Times* (February 2, 1989), p. C-13.

Report of the National Advisory Commission on Civil Disorders (New York: Bantam Books, 1968).

Reynolds, Pamela, "Violence as a Way of Life in L. A. Gangs," *Boston Globe* (July 24, 1988), p. 69.

Rinder, Irwin, "Minority Orientations: An Approach to Intergroup Relations Theory" *Phylon* 26 (Spring 1965): 5–17.

Robinson, Frank, *Extra Innings: My Life in Baseball* (New York: McGraw-Hill, 1988).

Rodgers-Rose, La Frances (ed.), *The Black Woman* (Beverly Hills, Calif.: Sage Publications, 1980).

Roebuck, Julian, and R. G. Kessler, *The Etiology of Alcoholism: Constitutional, Psychological and Sociological Approaches* (Springfield, Ill.: Charles C Thomas, 1972).

Roof, Wade Clark, and Daphne Spain, "A Research Note on City-Suburban Socioeconomic Differences Among Blacks," *Social Forces* 56 (September 1977): 15–20.

Rosenthal, Robert, and Lenora Jacobsen, *Pgymalion in the Classroom: Teachers' Expectations and Pupils' Intellectual Development* (New York: Holt, Rinehart and Winston, 1968).

Rubin, David, "Shortage of Minority Teachers Is Reaching Crisis Stage," *Boston Globe* (December 18, 1988), p. A-22.

Rushing, W. A., "Two Patterns in the Relationship Between Social Class and Mental Hospitalization," *American Sociological Review* 34(1969): 533–541.

Rustin, Bayard, "What's in a Name?" *The New York Times* (February 1, 1989), p. A-25.

Saltman, Juliet, *Open Housing as a Social Movement* (Lexington, Mass.: D. C. Heath & Co., 1971).

————, *A Fragile Movement: The Struggle for Neighborhood Stabilization* (New York: Greenwood Press, 1990).

Sampson, William A., and Vera Milam, "Interracial Attitudes of the Black Middle Class: Have They Changed?," *Social Problems* 23 (December 1975): 53–65.

Sampson, William A., "New Insights on Black Middle Class Mobility," *Urban League Review* 5:1 (Summer 1980): 21–24.

Sarason, Irvin G., "Verbal Learning, Modeling and Juvenile Delinquency," *American Psychologist* 23 (1968): 354–366.

Sargent, Edward, "Unwed, Absent Fathers," *Sisters* (Fall 1988): 28–31.

"Savings and Loans," *Black Enterprise* (June 1989): 271–272.

Schaefer, Richard T., *Racial and Ethnic Groups,* 2nd ed. (Boston: Little, Brown & Co., 1984).

Sherer, Jacqueline, and Edward Slawski, "Desegregation: Advantages to Whites," *The Urban Review* 13:3 (1981): 217–225.

Schermerhorn, Richard A., *Comparative Ethnic Relations: A Framework for Theory and Research* (New York: Random House, 1970).

Schmalz, Jeffrey, "Miami Tensions Simmering Three Months After Violence," *The New York Times* (April 10, 1989), p. A-25.

Schmidt, Peggy, "Women and Minorities: Is the Industry Ready?," *The New York Times* (October 16, 1988), p. F-5.

Schmidt, William E., "Moving Out of Projects and Toward a Future," *The New York Times* (February 3, 1989), p. A-32.

Schmitt, Eric, "Zoning Is Only Bar to Cheaper Suburban Housing," *The New York Times* (November 13, 1988), p. E-5.

Schneider, Jeffery M., "Advantages of Desegregation to Whites: An Idea Seeking a Time—Next Time," *The Urban Review* 13:4 (1981): 261–263.

Scholtz, John K., "Reforming the Tax Structure," *Focus* (April 1983): 5.

Schrag, Clarence, *Crime and Justice: American Style* (Rockville, Md.: National Institutes of Mental Health, 1971).

Schubert, Frank N., "Black Soldiers and the White Frontier: Some Factors Influencing Race Relations," *Phylon* 32 (Winter 1971): 410–416.

Schulz, David A., "The Role of Boyfriend," pp. 136–144 in *Coming Up Black: Patterns of Ghetto Socialization* (Englewood Cliffs, N. J. Prentice-Hall, 1969).

Sege, Irene, "Growing Gap Shown Between Rich, Poor," *Boston Globe* (May 15, 1989), p. 17.

———, "Poverty's Grip on Children Widens," *Boston Globe* (March 12, 1989), p. 1.

"Self-Made Millionaires," *Ebony* (May 1983): 53–58.

Seiden, Richard, "Mellowing with Age: Factors Influencing the Non-White Suicide Rate," *International Journal of Aging and Human Development* (January 1982): 265–284.

"Senate OKs Tracing Hate Crimes," *Times-Picayune* (February 9, 1990), p. 4.

Sharif, Pamela D., "After Merger, Accounting Firm Targeting Expansion," *Black Enterprise* (April 1990): 22.

Shearer, Lloyd, "FBI Making Progress, Excerpt," *Parade Magazine* (April 23, 1989), p. 16.

Shelling, Thomas C., *The Strategy of Conflict* (Cambridge, Mass.: Harvard University Press, 1960).

Sheppard, Nathaniel, Jr., "Victor's Backers See Shift in Power," *The New York Times* (April 14, 1983), p. B-15.

Shibutani, T., and L. M. Kwan, *Ethnic Stratification: A Comparative Approach* (New York: The Macmillan Co., 1972).

Silk, Leonard, "Economic Scene: Reasons to Fear a Recession," *The New York Times* (August 25, 1989), p. D-2.

Simms, Margaret C., "Black Youth Face Uncertain Jobs Future," *Focus* (April 1988), p. 6.

"Skinheads Blamed for Year's Worst Attacks," *Klanwatch* (Montgomery, Ala.: Southern Poverty Law Center, February 1989), p. 1.

Smith, Earl, "Racism and the Boston School Crisis," *Black Scholar* 6 (1975): 37–41.

Smothers, Ronald, "Affirmative Action Booms in Atlanta," *The New York Times* (January 27, 1989), p. A-10.

———, "Agents Await Clues in Rash of Bombings," *Times-Picayune* (Special from the *New York Times*), (January 7, 1990), p. A-17.

———, "Atlanta's Minority Plan Is Struck Down," *The New York Times* (March 3, 1989), p. A-14.

Sowell, Thomas, *Black Education: Myths and Tragedies* (New York: McKay Publishing Co., 1973).

Spain, Dafhne, et al., *Housing Successions Among Blacks and Whites in Cities and Suburbs* (Washington, D. C.: U. S. Department of Commerce, Bureau of the Census, Special Studies Series P-23, No. 101, 1980).

Sperling, Dan, "Health Gap Widening for Minorities," *USA Today* (September 27, 1989), p. 1.

Spitzer, Carleton E., *Raising the Bottom Line: Business Leadership in a Changing Society* (New York: Longman, 1982).

Srole, Leo, et al., *Mental Health in the Metropolis: The Midtown Manhattan Study* (New York: McGraw-Hill, 1962).

Stack, Carol, *All Our Kin: Strategies for Survival in a Black Community* (New York: Harper & Row, 1978).

Stampp, Kenneth, *The Peculiar Institution* (New York: Alfred A. Knopf, 1956).

Staples, Robert, *The Black Family: Essays and Studies,* 2nd ed. (Belmont, Calif.: Wadsworth Publishing Co., 1978).

———, "Black Male Genocide," *Black Scholar* (May/June 1987): 2–9.

———, *Black Masculinity: The Black Male's Role in American Society* (San Francisco: The Black Scholar Press, 1982).

Statistical Abstracts of the United States 1980.

Statistical Abstracts of the United States 1982.

Statistical Abstracts of the United States 1982–1983.

Statistical Abstracts of the United States 1989.

Steele, Robert E., "Clinical Comparisons of Black and White Suicide Attempters," *Journal of Consulting and Clinical Psychology* 45:6 (1977): 982–985.

Stember, Charles, *Sexual Racism* (New York: Elsevier Publishers, 1976).

Stillman, Richard, *Integration of the Negro in the U. S. Armed Forces* (New York: Frederick A. Praeger, 1968).

Stone, Andrea, "First Wave of Crack Kids Hits Schools," *USA Today* (March 9, 1990), p. 1.

———, "Homicides Break Record in 8 Cities," *USA Today* (December 29, 1989), p. 1.

Stone, Chuck, *Black Political Power in America* (New York: Dell Publishing Co, Inc., 1968).

Stouffer, Samuel, *The American Soldier: Adjustments During Army Life, Vol. 1* (Princeton, N. J.: Princeton University Press, 1949).

Strauss, Murray, et al., *Behind Closed Doors: Violence in the American Family* (Garden City, N. Y.: Doubleday, 1980).

Stuart, Taylor Jr., "Tax Exemptions Ruling: An Old Question Still Lingers," *The New York Times* (June 14, 1983), p. B-16.

"Study: Blacks Segregated Despite Their Status," *Jet* (December 27, 1989): 27.

"Study Cites Racism in Mental Diagnosis," *Boston Herald* (October 16, 1989), p. 1.

"Study Finds Blacks Twice as Liable to School Penalties as Whites," *The New York Times* (December 12, 1988), p. A-16.

Suchman, Edward, "Social Factors in Medical Deprivation," *American Journal of Public Health*, 55 (November 1965): 1725–1733.

Summary of Housing Characteristics 1981 (Washington, D. C.: U. S. Government Printing Office, 1981).

Sutherland, Edward, and Donald Cressey, *Criminology* (Santa Barbara, Calif.: University of California Press, 1970).

"Superwomen of Public Education," *Ebony* (June 1983): 88–92.

Sykes, Gresham, *Crime and Society* (New York: Random House, 1956).

Taeuber, Karl, *Racial Residential Segregation 1980* (Madison: University of Wisconsin Press, 1983).

Task Force Report: Narcotics and Drug Abuse. The President's Commission on Law Enforcement and Administration of Justice (Washington, D. C.: U. S. Government Printing Office, 1967).

Taylor, R. J., "Correlates of Religious Non-Involvement Among Black People," *Review of Religious Research* 30:2 (1988): 126–139.

———, et al., "Black Americans' Perceptions of the Socio-Historical Role of the Black Church," *Journal of Black Studies* 18:2 (1987): 123–137.

Terry, Wallace, *The Bloods: The Black Soldier in Vietnam* (New York: Viking Press, 1973).

The Associated Press, "Jackson Rules Out Race for Washington Mayor," *Times-Picayune* (February 27, 1990), p. A-4.

———, "Jackson Visits Black Leader, Squatters' Hut in Soweto," *Times-Picayune* (February 9, 1990), p. A-18.

"The Benefits of Innovation: Insurance Overview," *Black Enterprise* (June 1983): 137–138.

The College Board, Press Release, April 6, 1983.

The Department of Defense, *Defense 89: Almanac* (Washington, D. C.: U. S. Department of Defense, 1989).

"The Gap Continues to Grow," *Los Angeles Times* (February 17, 1990), p. B-6.

"The Nation: The Many Paths of the H. U. D. Investigation," *The New York Times* (August 13, 1989), p. E-3.

The National Coalition of Advocates for Students, *Special Report on Suspensions* (Boston, Mass.: December 1988).

The National Urban League, *The Black Pulse Survey Report* (Washington, D. C.: Research Department of the National Urban League, 1980).

"The New Civil Rights Movement: The Drive for Economic Equality," *Ebony* (August 1989): 76–78.

The Rites of Passage: A Black Perspective (New York: The National Urban League, 1982).

Thirty Years of Building American Justice (New York: The NAACP Legal Defense and Educational Fund, 1970).

Thomas, Gail E., "Race and Sex Group Equity in Higher Education: Institutions and Major Field Enrollment Statuses," *American Educational Research Journal* 17:2 (1980): 171–181.

———, *U. S. Race Relations in the 1980s and 1990s: Challenges and Alternatives* (New York: Hemisphere Publishing Corporation, 1990).

"Threatening Letters Linked to Bombings," *Times-Picayune* (Quoted from *The New York Times*), (December 30, 1989), p. A-4.

Thurgood, Delores H., Principal Investigator, *Summary Report 1988 Doctorate Recipients from United States Universities* (Washington, D. C.: National Academy Press, 1989).

Time, (December 9, 1985).

Time (October 29, 1979), p. 6.

Tolchin, Martin, "Officials in Cities and States Vow to Continue Minority Contractor Programs:" *The New York Times* (January 25, 1989), p. A-18.

"Tomorrow, the World: B. E. 100s Overview," *Black Enterprise* (June 1989), Editors' pages 187–192.

"The Top 100 Black Businesses," *Black Enterprise* (June 1983): 79–87.

Trammer, Monte, "Franchising: The Low Risk American Dream," *Black Enterprise* (June 1982): 87–89.

Trice, Harrison M. *Alcoholism in America* (New York: McGraw-Hill, 1966).

"UDAGS: Bright Spot in a Bleak Landscape," *Black Enterprise* (March 1983): 42.

Unchitelle, Louis, "As Jobs Increase, So Does Insecurity," *The New York Times* (May 1, 1988), p. F-25.

USA Today (April 16, 1990), p. 3.

U. S. Blacks: A Minority in Major League Baseball," *Jet* (June 26, 1989), p. 50.

Useem, Bert, "The Boston Anti-busing Movement," *American Sociological Review* 45 (1980): 335–369.

U. S. Commission on Civil Rights, *Confronting Racial Isolation in Miami* (Washington, D. C.: U. S. Commission on Civil Rights, 1982).

———, *Desegregation of the Nation's Public Schools* (Washington, D. C.: U. S. Commission on Civil Rights, 1979).

———, *Discriminatory Religious Schools and Tax Exempt Status* (Washington, D. C.: U. S. Commission on Civil Rights, 1982).

———, *Health Insurance: Coverage and Employment for Minorities, and Women* (Washington, D. C.: U. S. Commission on Civil Rights, 1982).

———, *The Federal Fair Housing Enforcement Effort* (Washington, D. C.: U. S. Commission on Civil Rights, 1979).

The U. S. Commission on Civil Rights Reports, 1961 (Washington, D. C.: Government Printing Office, 1962).

U. S. Commission on Civil Rights, *Statement on Metropolitan School Desegregation* (Washington, D. C.: U. S. Commission on Civil Rights, 1977).

———, *Teacher Layoffs, Seniority and Affirmative Action* (Washington, D. C.: U. S. Commission on Civil Rights, 1982).

———, *Twenty Years After Brown* (Washington, D. C.: U. S. Commission on Civil Rights, 1973).

———, *Who Is Guarding the Guardians?* (Washington, D. C.: Government Printing Office, 1981).

U. S. Bureau of the Census, *The Social and Economic Status of the Black Population in the United States, 1971* (Washington, D. C.: Government Printing Office, 1972).

U. S. Department of Commerce, *The Black Population in the United States 1985* (Bureau of the Census, Current Population Reports, Series P-20, No. 442, November, 1989).

———, *Household and Family Characteristics, March 1980* (Washington, D. C.: Government Printing Office 1980).

———, *Marital Status and Living Arrangements, March 1981* (Washington, D. C.: Bureau of the Census, Current Population Reports, Series P-20, No. 372, June 1982).

———, *Provisional Estimates of Social, Economic and Housing Characteristics* (Washington, D. C.: Government Printing Office, 1982).

U. S. Department of Defense Report, *The Negro in the Armed Forces: A Statistical Factbook, 1971.*

U. S. Department of Justice, FBI, *Sourcebook of Criminal Justice Statistics 1989* (Washington, D. C.: Government Printing Office, 1990).

U. S. Department of Labor, "Employment and Earnings," (Washington, D. C.: Bureau of Labor Statistics, 1990).

Valentine, Charles A., *A Culture of Poverty* (Chicago: University of Chicago Press, 1968).

Vander Zanden, James, W., *American Minority Relations* (New York: Ronald Press, 1966).

Van Woodward, C., *The Strange Career of Jim Crow* (New York: Oxford University Press, 1957).

Ventura, Stephanie, "Trends and Differentials in Births to Unmarried Women in the United States, 1970–1976," (Hagerstown, Md.: National Center for Health Statistics, 1980, November 1981).

Waldo, Gordon, and Simin Dinitz, "Personality Attributes of the Criminal: An Analysis of Research Studies, 1950–1965," *Journal of Research in Crime and Delinquency* 4 (1967): 185–202.

Walters, Ronald, *Black Presidential Politics in America: A Strategic Approach* (Stony Brook: SUNY Press, 1981).

Walton, Hanes, *Invisible Politics: Black Political Behavior Power and Mass Behavior* (Albany: State University of New York Press, 1985).

———, *Black Politics* (New York: J. P. Lippincott, 1972).

———, *When the Marching Stopped* (Albany: State University of New York Press, 1988).

Ware, Gilbert, "The Spider Web and Racism in the Armed Forces," *The Urban League News* 3 (April 1972): 5.

Warren, Roland, *The Community in America* (Chicago: University of Chicago Press, 1972), p. 9.

Washington, Erwin, "Why? and What Can Be Done?" *Crisis* (June/July 1989): 34–40, 66.

Washington, Joseph, *Black Religion* (Boston: Beacon Press, 1964).

Weber, Max, *The Protestant Ethic and the Spirit of Capitalism,* Talcott Parsons, (tr.) (New York: Scribner, 1930).

———, *The Theory of Social and Economic Organization,* A. M. Henderson and Talcott Parsons (trs.) (Glencoe, Ill.: The Free Press, 1947).

Weinberg, Meyer, "Integrating Neighborhoods: An Examination of Housing and School Desegregation," *Journal of Housing* (December 1980): 630–636.

Wesson, Alex, "The Black Man's Burden: The White Clinician," *The Black Scholar* (July/August 1975): 13–18.

Wheeler, Robert R. "Public School, Public Policy, Public Problems: Some Observations and Suggestions," *Proceedings of the National Policy Conference of Education for Blacks* (Washington, D. C.: The Congressional Black Caucus, 1972), pp. 103–113.

Whitaker, Charles, "The Disappearing Black Teacher," *Ebony* (January 1989): 122–126.

White, Theodore, *The Making of the President 1960* (New York: Atheneum, 1961).

Whiteside, Larry, "Fading Dreams: Minority Development More Mirage Than Reality," *Boston Globe* (November 15, 1988), p. 77.

"Why Black Men Have the Highest Cancer Rate," *Ebony* (March 1983): 69–73.

Wicker, Tom, "Bush and Blacks," *The New York Times* (April 17, 1990), p. B-7.

Wilensky, Harold, and Charles Lebeaux, *Industrial Society and Social Welfare* (New York: Russell Sage Foundation, 1958).

Wilkerson, Isabel, "Many Who Are Black Favor New Term for Who They Are," *The New York Times* (January 31, 1989), p. 1.

Wilkins, Roy, "Integration," *Ebony* (August 1970): 54.

Wilkinson, Doris Y., "The Stigmatization Process: The Politics of the Black Male's Identity," pp. 145–158 in Doris Y. Wilkinson and Ronald Taylor (eds.), *The Black Male in America* (Chicago: Nelson Hall, 1977).

———, *Black Male/White Female* (Cambridge, Mass.: Schenkman, 1974).

———, and Gary King, "Conceptual and Methodological Issues in the Use of Race as a Variable: Policy Implications," *The Milbank Quarterly* 65:1 (1987): 56–71.

Williams, Christopher C., "Advising the New Administration," *Black Enterprise* (January 1989): 49–53.

Willie, Charles V., *A New Look at Black Families* (Bayside, N. Y.: General Hall, Inc., 1981).

———, *The Class and Caste Controversy* (Bayside, N. Y.: General Hall, Inc., 1979).

———, *The Ivory and Ebony Towers: Race Relations in Higher Education* (Lexington, Mass.: D. C. Heath, 1981).

———, and Arlene McCord, *Black Students at White Colleges* (Columbus, Ohio: Charles E. Merrill, 1970).

Wilmore, Gayraud S., *Black Religion and Black Radicalism* (New York: Doubleday Anchor Books, 1973).

Wilson, David S., "Old and New Racist Groups Are Reported Joining," *The New York Times* (October 27, 1988), p. 9.

Wirth, Louis, "The Problems of Minority Groups," pp. 347–372 in Ralph Linton (ed.), *The Science of Man in the World of Crisis* (New York: Columbia University Press, 1945).

Wolfgang, Marvin, *Crime and Race* (New York: Institute of Human Relations, 1979).

Work, John W., *Race, Economics and Corporate America* (Wilmington, Delaware: Scholarly Resources, Inc., 1984).

Wynne, Lewis N., "Brownsville: The Reaction of the Negro Press," *Phylon* 32 (Summer 1972): 153–160.

Young and Violent: The Growing Menace of America's Neo-Nazi Skinheads (New York: The Anti-Defamation League of B'nai B'rith, 1988).

"Youth, School and Family in Transition," *Urban Education* 16 (October 1981): 261–277.

Zeul, Carolyn R., and Craig R. Humphrey, "The Integration of Suburban Blacks in Suburban Neighborhoods: A Reexamination of the Contact Hypothesis," *Social Problems* 8 (Spring 1971): 462–474.

Author Index

Subject Index